WE SHALL BE HEARD:

An Index to Speeches
By American Women,
1978 to 1985

by
BEVERLEY MANNING

The Scarecrow Press, Inc.
Metuchen, N.J., & London
1988

Also by Beverley Manning:
  Index to American Women Speakers,
  1828-1978 (1980).

British Library Cataloguing-in-Publication data available.

Library of Congress Cataloging-in-Publication Data

Manning, Beverley, 1942-
    We shall be heard : an index to speeches by American
women, 1978 to 1985 / by Beverley Manning.
        p.   cm.
    Updates: Index to American women speakers, 1828-1978.
    ISBN 0-8108-2122-2
    1. Speeches, addresses, etc., American--Women authors--
Indexes.
    2. Women--United States--History--20th century--Sources--
Indexes.
    3. Women orators--United States--Indexes. I. Manning,
Beverley, 1942- Index to American women speakers, 1828-1978.
II. Title.
Z1231.07M37 1988
[PS408]
016.815'54'08092--dc19   88-6644

CONTENTS

iii

INTRODUCTION

This volume updates my Index to American Women Speakers, which covered the period from 1828 to 1978, with coverage from 1978 to 1985. The lively debate on women's issues has continued in the decade since the first volume was researched. The Equal Rights Amendment is a closed issue for now, but many issues are still being debated, such as sex discrimination in employment, affirmative action, women in business enterprises, comparable worth, equity in pension and insurance, education opportunities, women and poverty, abortion, safe birth control, the role of women in the military, the status of minority women, women in politics and political office, rights of older women including social security, violence against women, pornography and rape; and feminist views on women in literature, religion, history, the arts, and theatre. I have tried to provide balanced coverage of conservative and liberal viewpoints on these contemporary issues. Important women from this period include Helen Caldicott, Rosalynn Carter, Geraldine Ferraro, Paula Hawkins, Carter Heyward, Nancy Kassebaum, Audre Lorde, Barbara Mikulski, and Patricia Schroeder.

For historical coverage, newly published collections on such figures as Jane Addams, Susan B. Anthony, Crystal Eastman, Mother Jones, Lucretia Mott, Kate Richards O'Hare, and Elizabeth Stanton are included. I have also located earlier resources on Emily Balch, Louise De Koven Bowen, Mary Richmond, and Eleanor Roosevelt.

The index is intended to assist college and high school students in locating printed sources for speeches by women. These speeches can be difficult to locate if you don't move beyond periodical and newspaper indexes, or speech anthologies. Conference and symposium papers are excellent entry into women's issues. Documentary histories, collections of lectures, anthologies in women's studies, and sermons are all useful. Government documents are a fine resource. The issues covered in congressional hearings reflect the most immediate concerns of women: family, education, and employment. Every senator and congresswoman who served in Congress from 1978 to 1985 has been included.

All bibliographic information was verified on the OCLC computer system. Computer access has permitted the expansion of the

Subject Index. Many speeches have been entered under more than one subject heading to bring out all facets of the speech. Subject headings were selected from the <u>Library of Congress Subject Headings</u> (9th Edition and Supplements). The Subject and Title Indexes both refer to the Author Index.

The Author Index is the primary index of this work. Each citation in the Author Index refers to an entry in the Bibliography and includes author, title of the speech, author and/or title of the source, and page numbers. Many entries in the bibliographic section are listed by title when multiple authors are featured. A standard periodical citation is used: author, title, title of periodical, volume, date, pagination. Government documents were cited in two ways. When the entire document is indexed, it is listed in the Bibliography and cited in the same format as books. When only one speech is cited from a document, the document is cited in full under the author entry like a periodical, and not listed in the Bibliography.

I wish to express my gratitude for support and assistance to Elisa Taylor, Teresa Naranjo, Sue Marsh, and Grace Derrick for technical assistance in using the word-processing system of the University of Connecticut Computer System; and to Lois Fletcher and Marilyn Noronha for providing their Interlibrary Loan Services to obtain the hundreds of volumes I needed to examine for my research.

Beverley Manning
University of Connecticut at Hartford
Harleigh B. Trecker Library
West Hartford, Connecticut

BIBLIOGRAPHY

AAAS Seminar on Women in Development (1975: Mexico). Women and World Development, edited by Irene Tinker, Michele Bramson, and Mayra Buvinic. New York: Praeger, 1976.

Addams, Jane. Jane Addams on Education, edited by Ellen Condliffe Langemann. New York: Teachers College Press, 1985.

_____. Peace and Bread in Time of War, and Patriotism and Pacifists in War Time, with an introductory essay by John Dewey. Edited by Blanche Weisen Cook. Silver Spring, MD: National Association of Social Workers, 1983.

Alcoholism and Alcohol Abuse Among Women, Research Issues: proceedings of a workshop, April 2-5, 1978, Jekyll Island, Georgia. Rockville, MD: Department of Health, Education and Welfare, Public Health Service, Alcohol, Drug Abuse, and Mental Health Administration, National Institute on Alcohol Abuse and Alcoholism. Washington: U.S.G.P.O., 1980.

All the Women Are White, All the Blacks Are Men, But Some of Us Are Brave: Black Women's Studies, edited by Gloria T. Hull, Patricia Bell Scott and Barbara Smith. Old Westbury, NY: The Feminist Press, 1982.

American Birth Control Conference (1st: 1921: New York). Birth Control: What It Is, How It Works, What It Will Do; the Proceedings of the first American Birth Control Conference held at the Hotel Plaza, New York, November 11, 12, 1921. New York: Birth Control Review, 1921?

The American Jewish Woman: A Documentary History, edited by Jacob Rader Marcus. New York: KTAV Publishing House; Cincinnati: American Jewish Archives, 1981.

Aptheker, Bettina. Woman's Legacy: Essays on Race, Sex, and Class in American History. Amherst: University of Massachusetts Press, 1982.

Balch, Emily Greene. Beyond Nationalism: The Social Thought of Emily Green Balch, edited by Mercedes M. Randall. New York: Twayne, 1972.

1

Berkshire Conference on the History of Women (5th: 1982: Vassar College). Women and the Structure of Society, edited by Joann K. McNamara and Barbara J. Harris. Durham, NC: Duke University Press, 1984.

Beyond Androcentrism: New Essays on Women and Religion, edited by Rita M. Gross. Missoula, MT: Scholars Press for the American Academy of Religion, 1977.

Beyond Domination: New Perspectives on Women and Philosophy, edited by Carol C. Gould. Totowa, NJ: Rowman & Allanheld, 1984.

Beyond Their Sex: Learned Women of the European Past, edited by Patricia H. Labalme. New York: New York University Press, 1980.

Biopolitics and Gender, edited by Meredith W. Watts. New York: Haworth Press, 1984.

Birth Control and Controlling Birth: Women-Centered Perspectives, edited by Helen B. Holmes, Betty B. Hoskins, and Michael Gross. Clifton, NJ: Humana Press, 1980.

Block, Jeanne Humphrey. Sex Role Identity and Ego Development. San Francisco: Jossey-Bass, 1984.

Blueprints for Living: Perspectives for Latter-Day Saint Women, edited by Maren M. Mouritsen. Provo, UT: Brigham Young University Press, 1980. 2 vols.

Bowen, Louise Hadduck (de Koven). Speeches, Addresses, and Letters of Louise de Koven Bowen, Reflecting Social Movements in Chicago. Ann Arbor, MI: Edwards Brothers, Inc., 1937. 2 vols.

Breaking the Sequence: Women, Literature, and the Future, edited by Vicki Mistaccio, assisted by Mei-Mei Ellerman, Margaret E. Ward. Wellesley, MA: Wellesley College, Center for Research on Women, 1981.

Brown, Olympia. Suffrage and Religious Principle: Speeches and Writings of Olympia Brown, edited by Dana Greene. Metuchen, NJ: Scarecrow Press, 1983.

Brown, Rita Mae. A Plain Brown Rapper. Oakland, CA: Diana Press, 1976.

Building Feminist Theory: Essays from Quest, A Feminist Quarterly, edited by Quest Staff. New York: Longman, 1981.

California. Legislature. Joint Committee on Legal Equality. Women in the Justice System: transcript of hearing of the Joint Committee on Legal Equality; Los Angeles, California, February 22, 1974. Sacramento, CA: The Committee, 1974.

The Challenge of Change: Perspectives on Family, Work, and Education, edited by Matina Horner, Carol C. Nadelson and Malkah T. Notman. New York: Plenum Press, 1983.

A Challenge to Social Security: The Changing Roles of Women and Men in American Society, edited by Richard V. Burkhauser, Karen C. Holden. New York: Academic Press, 1982.

The Challenge to Women, edited by Seymour Farber and Roger H. L. Wilson. New York: Basic, 1966.

The Changing Composition of the Workforce: Implications for Future Research and Its Application, edited by Albert S. Glickman. New York: Plenum Press, 1982.

The Changing Risk of Disease in Women: An Epidemiologic Approach: a symposium held at the Johns Hopkins University, Baltimore, Maryland, October 22-23, 1981, edited by Ellen B. Bold. Lexington, MA: D. C. Heath, 1984.

Changing Roles of Women in Industrial Societies: a Bellagio Conference, March 1976. New York: The Rockefeller Foundation, 1977.

Charlotte Towle Memorial Symposium on Comparative Theoretical Approaches to Casework Practice (1969: University of Chicago). Theories of Social Casework, edited by Robert W. Roberts and Robert H. Nee. Chicago: University of Chicago Press, 1970.

Class, Race, and Sex: The Dynamics of Control, edited by Mary S. Hartman and Lois W. Banner. New York: Harper & Row, 1974.

Coming to Light: American Women Poets in the Twentieth Century, edited by Diane Wood Middlebrook and Marilyn Yalom; prepared under the auspices of the Center for Research on Women, Stanford University. Ann Arbor: University of Michigan Press, 1985.

Comparable Worth: Issue for the 80's: A Consultation of the U.S. Commission on Civil Rights. Washington: U.S. Commission on Civil Rights, 1985. 2 vols.

Comparable Worth: New Directions for Research, edited by Heidi I. Hartmann. Washington: National Academy Press, 1985.

Conference on Non-Sexist Early Childhood Education (1976: Arden House). Perspectives On Non-Sexist Early Childhood Education, edited by Barbara Sprung. New York: Teachers College Press, 1978.

Conference on "Scholars and Women" (1981: University of Maryland). Women's Studies and the Curriculum, edited by Marianne Triplette. Winston-Salem, NC: Salem College, 1983.

Conference on the Educational and Occupational Needs of American Indian Women (1976: Albuquerque, NM). Conference on the Educational and Occupational Needs of American Indian Women, October 12 and 13, 1976. Washington: U.S. Department of Education, Office of Educational Research and Improvement, National Institute of Education, 1980.

Conference on the Educational and Occupational Needs of Asian-Pacific-American Women (1976: San Francisco, CA). Conference on the Educational and Occupational Needs of Asia-Pacific-American Women, August 24 and 25, 1976. Washington: U.S. Department of Education, Office of Educational Research and Improvement, National Institute of Education, 1980.

Conference on the Educational and Occupational Needs of Black Women (1975: Washington, DC). Conference on the Educational and Occupational Needs of Black Women, December 16 and 17, 1975: compendium. Washington: U.S. Department of Education, Office of Educational Research and Improvement, National Institute of Education, 1980. 2 vols.

Conference on the Educational and Occupational Needs of Hispanic Women (1976: Denver, CO and Washington, DC). Conference on the Educational and Occupational Needs of Hispanic Women, June 28 and 30, 1976, December 10 and 12, 1976. Washington: U.S. Department of Education, Office of Educational Research and Improvement, National Institute of Education, 1980.

Conference on the Educational and Occupational Needs of White Ethnic Women (1978: Boston, MA). Conference on the Educational Needs of White Ethnic Women, October 10 and 13, 1978. Washington: U.S. Department of Education, Office of Educational Research and Improvement, National Institute of Education, 1980.

Conference on the History of Women (1977: St. Paul, MN). Woman's Being, Woman's Place: Female Identity and Vocation in American History papers, edited by Mary Kelley. Boston: G. K. Hall, 1979.

Conference on the National Longitudinal Surveys of Mature Women (1978: United States Department of Labor). Women's Changing Roles at Home and On the Job: proceedings of a Conference on the National Longitudinal Surveys of Mature Women, sponsored by the National Commission for Manpower Policy in cooperation with the Employment and Training Administration, Department of Labor. Washington: The Commission, 1978.

Conference on the Sociology of the Languages of American Women (1976: New Mexico State University). Proceedings of the Conference on the Sociology of the Languages of American Women, edited by Betty Lou Dubois and Isabel Crouch. San Antonio, TX: Trinity University, 1978.

Conference on Women and Lay Ministry (1976: St. Michel's Church, Milton, MA). Women and Lay Ministry: Our Experiences and Theology: panel presentations and theology papers from the Conference on Women and Lay Ministry, held May 8, 1976, at St. Michel's Church, Milton, Mass. sponsored by the Episcopal Women's Action and the Commission on Women and Ministry, Diocese of Massachusetts. West Newton, MA: EWA, 1977.

Conference on Women and the Workplace (1976: Washington, DC). Conference on Women and the Workplace, June 17-19, 1976, Washington, DC: proceedings, editor, Eula Bingham; sponsors, Society for Occupational and Environmental Health, National Institute for Occupational Safety and Health, National Foundation --March of Dimes; cosponsors, Coalition of Labor Union Women. Washington: The Society, 1977.

Conference on Women in the Labor Market (1977: Barnard College). Women in the Labor Market, edited by Cynthia B. Lloyd, Emily S. Andrews, and Curtis L. Gilroy. New York: Columbia University Press, 1979.

Conference on Women's Health Issues (1984: Chicago, IL). The U.S. Public Health Service, Region V, Department of Health and Human Services Conference on Women's Health Issues, January 25, 1984. Chicago: The Dept., 1984.

Conference on Women's History (1976: Washington, DC). Clio Was a Woman: Studies in the History of American Women, edited by Mabel E. Deutrich and Virginia C. Purdy. Washington: Howard University Press, 1980.

Conference on Women's Studies and the Humanities (1983: University of North Carolina at Greensboro). Equity and Excellence: A Conference on Women's Studies and the Humanities: a conference report, edited by Sandra Morgen, Judith White. Durham, NC: Duke-UNC Women's Studies Research Center, 1983.

Conference on Work in the Lives of Married Women (1957: Columbia University). Work in the Lives of Married Women: proceeding of a Conference on Womanpower held October 20-25, 1957 at Arden House, Harriman Campus of Columbia University. New York: Columbia University Press, 1958.

Cooper Union for the Advancement of Science and Art. Women, Society and Sex, edited by Johnson E. Fairchild. New York: Sheridan House, 1952.

Cornell Conference on Women (1969: Cornell University). Proceedings, edited by Sheila Tobias, Ella Kusnitz and Deborah Spitz. Pittsburgh, PA: KNOW, Inc., 1969.

Covert Discrimination and Women in the Sciences, edited by Judith A. Ramaley. Boulder, CO: Published by Westview Press for the American Association for the Advancement of Science, 1978.

The Custom-Made Child?: Women-Centered Perspectives, edited by Helen B. Holmes, Betty B. Hoskins, and Michael Gross. Clifton, NJ: Humana Press, 1981.

Dixon, Marlene. The Future of Women. San Francisco: Synthesis Publications, 1983.

Douglass, Jane Dempsey. Women, Freedom, and Calvin. Philadelphia: The Westminster Press, 1985.

Eastman, Crystal. Crystal Eastman on Women & Revolution, edited by Blanche Wiesen Cook. New York: Oxford University Press, 1978.

The Education of Women for Social and Political Leadership; a symposium at Southern Methodist University, in honor of its semicentennial year, 1915-1965. Dallas: Southern Methodist University, 1967.

Eisenstein, Sarah. Give Us Bread, But Give Us Roses: Working Women's Consciousness in the United States, 1890 to the First World War. London; Boston: Routledge & Kegan Paul, 1983.

Equal Employment Policy for Women; Strategies for Implementation in the United States, Canada, and Western Europe, edited by Ronnie Steinberg Ratner. Philadelphia: Temple University Press, 1980.

Ethical Issues in Sex Therapy and Research: Reproductive Biology Research Foundation Conference, edited by William H. Masters, Virginia E. Johnson, Robert C. Kolody. Boston: Little, Brown, 1977-1980. 2 vols.

The Evolving Female: Women in Psychosocial Context, edited by Carol Landau Heckerman. New York: Human Sciences Press, 1980.

Expanding the Role of Women in the Sciences: proceedings, edited by Anne M. Briscoe and Sheila M. Pfafflin. New York: New York Academy of Sciences, 1979.

Female Soldiers--Combatants or Noncombatants? Historical and Contemporary Perspectives, edited by Nancy Loring Goldman. Westport, CT: Greenwood Press, 1982.

Feminism and Art History: Questioning the Litany, edited by Norma Broude and Mary D. Garrard. New York: Harper & Row, 1982.

Feminism and Process Thought: The Harvard Divinity School / Claremont Center For Process Studies symposium papers, edited by Sheila Greene Devaney. New York: E. Mellen Press, 1981.

Feminist Frontiers: Rethinking Sex, Gender, and Society, edited by Laurel Richardson and Verta Taylor. Reading, MA: Addison-Wesley, 1983.

Feminist Visions: Towards a Transformation of the Liberal Arts Curriculum, edited by Diane L. Fowlkes and Charlotte S. McClure. University: University of Alabama Press, 1984.

Forensic Science Symposium on the Analysis of Sexual Assault Evidence (1983: Quantico, VA). Proceeding of a Forensic Science Symposium on the Analysis of Sexual Assault Evidence, July 6-8, 1983, co-host Federal Bureau of Investigation, co-host Metro-Dade Police Department, Miami, Florida; Forensic Science Research and Training Center, Laboratory Division, FBI Academy. Quantico, VA: The Center, 1983.

Freedom, Feminism, and the State: an Overview of Individualistic Feminism, edited by Wendy McElroy. Washington: Cato Institute, 1982.

Frye, Marilyn. The Politics of Reality: Essays in Feminist Theory. Trumansburg, NY: Crossing Press, 1983.

The Future of Difference, edited by Hester Eisenstein and Alice Jardine. New York: Barnard College Women's Center; Boston: G. K. Hall, 1980.

Gendered Subjects: The Dynamics of Feminist Teaching, edited by Margo Culley and Catherine Portuges. Boston: Routledge & Kegan Paul, 1985.

German Feminism: Readings in Politics and Literature, edited by Edith Hoshino Altbach, Jeanne Clausen, Dagmar Schultz, Naomi Stephan. Albany: State University of New York Press, 1984.

Gilbert, Sandra M. The Norton Anthology of Literature by Women: the Tradition in English, edited by Sandra M. Gilbert and Susan Guber. New York: Norton, 1985.

GLCA Women's Studies Conference (4th: 1978: Rochester, Indiana). The Structure of Knowledge: A Feminist Perspective: Proceedings of the Fourth Annual GLCA Women's Studies Conference, November 10-12, 1978, edited by Beth Reed. Ann Arbor, MI: GLCA Women's Studies Program, 1979.

GLCA Women's Studies Conference (5th: 1979). Toward A Feminist Transformation of the Academy: Proceedings of the Fifth Annual GLCA Women's Studies Conference, November 2-4, 1979, edited by Beth Reed. Ann Arbor, MI: GLCA Women's Studies Program, 1980.

GLCA Women's Studies Conference (6th: 1980). Toward a Feminist Transformation of the Academy, II: Proceedings of the Sixth Annual GLCA Women's Studies Conference, November 7-9, 1980, edited by Beth Reed. Ann Arbor, MI: GLCA Women's Studies Program, 1982.

GLCA Women's Studies Conference (7th: 1981). Toward a Feminist Transformation of the Academy, III: Proceedings of the Seventh Annual GLCA Women's Studies Conference, November 6-8, 1981, edited by Beth Reed. Ann Arbor, MI: GLCA Women's Studies Program, 1982.

Hamilton, Edith. The Ever-Present Past. Prologue by Doris Fielding Reid. New York: Norton, 1964.

Handbook of Feminist Therapy: Women's Issues in Psychotherapy, edited by Carol S. Robb. Boston: Beacon Press, 1985.

Harrison, Beverly Wildung. Making the Connections: Essays in Feminist Social Ethics, edited by Carol S. Robb. Boston: Beacon Press, 1985.

Health Needs of the World's Poor Women, edited by Patricia W. Blair: based on the proceedings of the International Symposium on Women and Their Health, sponsored by Equity Policy Center and held June 8-11, 1980 in Port Deposit Maryland. Washington: EPOC, 1981.

Hellwig, Monika K. Christian Women in a Troubled World. New York: Paulist Press, 1985.

Her Immaculate Hand: Selected Works By and About the Women Humanists of Quattrocento Italy, edited by Margaret L. King and Albert Rabil, Jr. Binghamton, N.Y.: Center for Medieval and Early Renaissance Studies, 1983.

Heyward, Carter. Our Passion for Justice: Images of Power, Sexuality, and Liberation. New York: Pilgrim Press, 1984.

Historic Documents. Washington: Congressional Quarterly, 1980-84.

Hormonal Contraceptives, Estrogens, and Human Welfare, edited by Marian Cleeves Diamond and Carol Cleaves Korenbrot. New York: Academic Press, 1978.

Howe, Florence. Myths of Coeducation: Selected Essays, 1964-
1983. Bloomington: Indiana University Press, 1984.

Humphreys, Sarah C. The Family, Women, and Death: Comparative Studies. London, Boston: Routledge & Kegan Paul, 1983.

Hyman Blumberg Symposium on Research in Early Childhood Education (8th: 1976: Johns Hopkins University). Women and the
Mathematical Mystique; Proceedings of the Eighth Annual Hyman
Blumberg Symposium on Research in Early Childhood Education,
edited by Lynn H. Fox, Linda Brody, and Dianne Bobin. Baltimore: Johns Hopkins University Press, 1980.

"I Am Honored to Be Here Today...": Commencement Speeches by
Notable Personalities, comp. by Donald Grunewald. New York:
Oceana Publications, 1985.

Images of Women in American Popular Culture, Angela G. Dorenkamp
et al. San Diego: Harcourt Brace Jovanovich, 1985.

Images of Women in Antiquity, edited by Averil Cameron and Amelie
Kuhrt. Detroit: Wayne State University Press, 1983.

Immaculate & Powerful: The Female in Sacred Image and Social
Reality, edited by Clarissa W. Atkinson, Constance H. Buchanan,
and Margaret R. Miles. Boston: Beacon Press, 1985.

Immigrants and Refugees in a Changing Nation: Research and
Training: proceedings of a conference held at the Catholic University of America, Washington, D.C., May 12-14, 1982, edited
by Lucy M. Cohen, Mary Ann Grossnickle. Washington: Catholic University of America, Department of Anthropology, 1983.

International Birth Control Conference (6th: 1926: New York).
Reports and Papers, edited by Margaret Sanger. New York:
The American Birth Control League, 1925-1926. 4 vols.

International Birth Control Conference (7th: 1930: Zurich). The
Practice of Contraception: An International Symposium and Survey, edited by Margaret Sanger and Hannah M. Stone; with a
foreword by Robert L. Dickinson; from the Proceedings of the
Seventh International Birth Control Conference, Zurich, Switzer-
land, September, 1930. Baltimore: Williams & Wilkins, 1931.

International Conference on Women and Food (1978: University of
Arizona). A Conference on the Role of Women in Meeting Basic
Food and Water Needs in Developing Countries; Focusing on the
United Nations World Food Conference Resolution on Women and
Food, proceeding; editor Ann Bunzel Cowan. Washington: Con-
sortium for International Development: Distributed by Office of
Women in Development, Agency for International Development,
International Cooperation Agency, 1978. 3 vols.

International Women's Year Conference on Women in Public Life
(1975: Lyndon Baines Johnson Library). Women in Public Life:
Report of a conference cosponsored by the Lyndon Baines Johnson Library and the Lyndon Baines Johnson School of Public Affairs, November 9-11, 1975, edited by Beryl A. Radin and Hoyt
H. Purvis. Austin: The School, 1976.

International Working Party of Family Policy (1977: Arden House).
Family Policy: Government and Families in Fourteen Countries,
edited by Sheila B. Kamerman and Alfred J. Kahn. New York:
Columbia University Press, 1978.

Jones, (Mother) Mary Harris. Mother Jones Speaks: Collected
Writings and Speeches, edited by Philip S. Foner. New York:
Monan Press; Distributed by Pathfinder Press, 1983.

Kelly, Joan. Women, History, and Theory: The Essays of Joan
Kelly. Chicago: University of Chicago Press, 1984.

Kennedy, Florynce. Color Me Flo: My Hard Life and Good Times.
New York: Prentice-Hall, 1976.

Kirkpatrick, Jeane J. The Reagan Pheonomenon, and Other Speeches
on Foreign Policy. Washington: American Enterprise Institute
For Public Policy Research, 1983.

Learning Our Way: Essay in Feminist Education, edited by Charlotte Bunch and Sandra Pollack. Trumansburg, NY: Crossing
Press, 1983.

Lerner, Gerda. The Majority Finds Its Past: Placing Women in
History. New York: Oxford University Press, 1979.

Liberal Education and the New Scholarship on Women; Issues and
Constraints in Institutional Change. A Report of the Wingspread
Conference, Wingspread Conference Center, Racine, Wisconsin,
October 22-24, 1981. Washington: Association of American Con-
ference, 1981.

Lloyd-Jones Symposium (1979: University of Georgia Continuing
Education Center). Rethinking College Responsibilities for
Values, Mary Louise McBee, guest editor. San Francisco:
Jossey-Bass, 1980.

Lorde, Audre. Sister Outsider: Essays and Speeches. Trumansburg, NY: Crossing Press, 1984.

Margaret Sanger Centennial Conference (1979: Northampton, MA).
The Margaret Sanger Centennial Conference, November 13 and
14, 1979, Anne Harper, commentator; Dorothy Green and Mary-
Elizabeth Murock, editors. Northampton, MA: Sophia Smith Collection, Smith College, 1982.

Miniconsultation on the Mental and Physical Health Problems of Black Women (1974: Washington, DC). Miniconsultation on the Mental and Physical Health Problems of Black Women, March 29-30, 1974: proceedings. Sponsored by the Black Women's Community Development Foundation in collaboration with Black Women Organized for Action (San Francisco) (et al.); supported by John Hay Whitney Foundation (et al.). Washington: The Foundation, 1975.

Mitchell, Juliet. Women, the Longest Revolution. New York: Pantheon, 1984.

Morgan, Robin. Going Too Far: The Personal Chronicles of a Feminist. New York: Random House, 1977.

Mott, Lucretia. Lucretia Mott, Her Complete Speeches and Sermons, edited by Dana Greene. New York: E. Mellen Press, 1980.

My Country Is the Whole World; An Anthology of Women's Work on Peace and War, comp. by Cambridge Women's Peace Collective. London, Boston: Pandora Press, 1984.

My Troubles Are Going to Have Trouble with Me; Everyday Trials and Triumphs of Women Workers, edited by Karen Brodkin Sacks and Dorothy Remy. New Brunswick, NJ: Rutgers University Press, 1984.

NASW Conference on Social Work Practice With Women (1st: 1980: Washington, DC). Women, Power and Change: selected papers from Social Work Practice in Sexist Society: First NASW Conference on Social Work Practice With Women, September 14-16, 1980, Washington, DC; Anne Weick and Susan T. Vandiver, ed. Washington: National Association of Social Workers, 1982.

Nin, Anaïs. A Woman Speaks: The Lectures, Seminars, and Interviews of Anaïs Nin, edited by Evelyn J. Henz. Chicago: Swallow Press, 1975.

O'Connor, Ellen M. Myrtilla Miner; A Memoir. New York: Arno Press, 1969.

O'Hare, Kate Richards. Kate Richards O'Hare; Selected Writings and Speeches, edited, with an introduction and notes by Philip S. Foner and Sally M. Miller. Baton Rouge: Louisiana State University Press, 1982.

Older Women in the City, sponsored by Department for the Aging, City of New York. New York: Arno Press, 1970.

Outspoken Women; Speeches by American Women Reformers, 1635-1935, edited by Judith Anderson. Dubuque, IA: Kendall/Hunt, 1984.

A Panel Discussion from The Scholar and the Feminist V: Creating Feminist Works; with Elizabeth K. Minich (et al.): a conference sponsored by The Barnard College Women's Center. New York: Barnard Women's Center, 1978.

Perspectives on Power: Women in Africa, Asia and Latin America, edited by Jean F. O'Barr. Durham, NC: Duke University, Center for International Studies, 1982.

Pleasure and Danger: Exploring Female Sexuality, edited by Carole S. Vance. Boston: Routledge & Kegan Paul, 1984.

The Politics of Women's Spirituality: Essays on the Rise of Spiritual Power Within the Feminist Movement, edited by Charlene Spretnak. Garden City, NY: Anchor Press, 1982.

The Prism of Sex: Essays in the Sociology of Knowledge: proceedings of a symposium; sponsored by WRI of Wisconsin, Inc., edited by Julia A. Sherman and Evelyn Torton Beck. Madison: University of Wisconsin Press, 1979.

Psychology and Women: In Transition, edited by Jeanne E. Gullahorn. Washington: V. H. Winston & Sons; New York: Distributed by Halstead Press, 1979.

The Psychology of Women: Future Directions in Research, edited by Julia A. Sherman and Florence L. Denmark. New York: Psychological Dimensions, Inc., 1978.

Public Forum on Women's Rights and Responsibilities (1978: Las Vegas, NV). Public Forum on Women's Rights and Responsibilities: proceedings of a public forum sponsored by the Nevada Advisory Committee of the United States Commission on Civil Rights, prepared by Gloria A. Lopez and Sally E. James. Washington: The Commission, 1979.

Reed, Evelyn. Problems of Women's Liberation; a Marxist Approach. 5th ed. New York: Pathfinder Press, 1971.

Report of the YWCA National Consultation for Programs on Domestic Violence: Battered Women, December 10-12, 1980, prepared by Program United National Board, YWCA. New York: Communications, National Boards, YWCA, 1981.

The Representation of Women in Fiction, edited by Carolyn G. Heilbrun and Margaret R. Higonnet. Baltimore: Johns Hopkins University Press, 1983.

Rethinking the Family: Some Feminist Questions, edited by Barrie Thorne with Marilyn Yalom; prepared under the auspices of The

Center for Research on Women, Stanford University. New York: Longman, 1982.

Reweaving the Web of Life: Feminism and Nonviolence, edited by Pam McAllister. Philadelphia: New Society Publishers, 1982.

Reynolds Conference (2nd: 1975: University of South Carolina). South Carolina Women Writers: proceedings of the Reynolds Conference, University of South Carolina, October 24-25, 1975, edited by James B. Meriwether. Spartanburg, SC: Published for the Southern Studies Program, University of South Carolina by Reprint Co., 1979.

Richmond, Mary Ellen. The Long View; Papers and Addresses by Mary E. Richmond, edited by Joanna Colcord and Ruth Z. S. Mann. New York: Russell Sage Foundation, 1930.

The Role and Status of Women in the Soviet Union, edited by Donald R. Brown. New York: Teachers College Press, 1968.

The Role of Women in Conflict and Peace, edited by Dorothy G. McGuigan. Ann Arbor: University of Michigan, Center for Continuing Education of Women, 1977.

The Role of Women in Librarianship: 1876-1976: The Entry, Advancement, and Struggle for Equalization in One Profession, edited by Kathleen Weibel and Kathleen M. Heim, with assistance from Diane J. Ellsworth. Phoenix, AZ: Oryx Press, 1979.

The Role of Women in the Middle Ages: papers of the sixth annual conference of the Center for Medieval and Early Renaissance Studies, State University of New York, Binghamton, 6-7 May 1972, edited by Rosemarie Thee Morwedge. Albany: State University of New York Press, 1975.

Scott, Anne Firor. Making the Invisible Woman Visible. Urbana and Chicago: University of Illinois Press, 1984.

Sex Differences in Behavior: A Conference, edited by Richard C. Friedman (et al.). New York: John Wiley, 1974.

Sex, Race, and the Role of Women in the South: essays, edited by Jean E. Friedman ... (et al.). Jackson: University Press of Mississippi, 1983.

Sex Segregation in the Workplace: Trends, Explanations, Remedies, Barbara F. Reskin, editor; Committee on Women's Employment and Related Social Issues, Commission on Behavioral and Social Sciences and Education, National Research Council. Washington: National Academy Press, 1984.

Sexism and Church Law: Equal Rights and Affirmative Action, edited by James A. Coriden. New York: Paulist Press, 1977.

Sexist Religion and Women in the Church; No More Silence! Edited by Alice L. Hageman, in collaboration with the Women's Caucus of Harvard Divinity School. New York: Association Press, 1974.

Sisterhood Surveyed: proceedings of the Mid-Atlantic Women's Studies Association 1982 Conference, edited by Anne Dzamba Sessa. West Chester, PA: West Chester University, 1983.

Social Justice and Preferential Treatment: Women and Racial Minorities in Education and Business, edited by William T. Blackstone and Robert D. Heslep. Athens: University of Georgia Press, 1977.

Spinning a Sacred Yarn: Women Speak from the Pulpit. New York: Pilgrim Press, 1982.

Split-Level Lives; American Nuns Speak on Race, edited by Sister Mary Peter Traxler. Techny, IL: Divine Work Pub., 1967.

Stanton, Elizabeth Cady. Elizabeth Cady Stanton, Susan B. Anthony: Correspondence, Writings, Speeches, edited and with a critical commentary by Ellen Carol DuBois; foreword by Gerda Lerner. New York: Schocken, 1981.

Stein, Gertrude. Lectures in America. New York: Vintage, 1975.

Take Back the Night: Women on Pornography, edited by Laura Lederer. New York: Morrow, 1980.

Taylor, Lily Ross. Party Politics in the Age of Caesar. Berkeley: University of California Press, 1949.

Taylor, Lily Ross. Roman Voting Assemblies from the Hannibalic War to the Dictatorship of Caesar. Ann Arbor: University of Michigan Press, 1966.

Theories of Women's Studies, edited by Gloria Bowles and Renate Duelli-Klein. Berkeley: Women's Studies, University of California, 1980.

Theories of Women's Studies II, edited by Gloria Bowles and Renate Duelli-Klein. Berkeley: Women's Studies, University of California, 1981.

Thompson, Clara. Psychoanalysis: Evolution and Development, by Clara Thompson, with the collaboration of Patrick Mullahy. New York: Grove Press, 1950.

Those Preachin' Women: Sermons by Black Women, edited by Ella Pearson Mitchell. Valley Forge, PA: Judson Press, 1985.

Today's Girls, Tomorrow's Women; a national seminar, June 13-15, 1978, Wingspread Conference Center, Racine, Wisconsin. New York: Girls Clubs of America, 1980.

Toward a Balanced Curriculum: A Sourcebook for Initiating Integration Projects; based on the Wheaton College Conference, edited by Bonnie Spanier, Alexander Bloom and Darlene Boroviak. Cambridge, MA: Schenkman Pub. Co., 1984.

Toward the Second Decade: The Impact of the Women's Movement on American Institutions, edited by Betty Justice and Renate Pore. Westport, CT: Greenwood Press, 1981.

Training Conference (1st: 1984: Washington, DC). Interagency Committee on Women in Federal Law Enforcement: first annual training conference, July 11, 1984: conference proceedings. Washington: The Committee, 1985.

The Undergraduate Woman: Issues in Educational Equity, edited by Pamela J. Perun. Lexington, MA: Lexington Books, 1982.

U.S. Commission on Civil Rights. Hearing Before the United States Commission on Civil Rights ... held in Chicago, Illinois. Washington: The Commission, 1974. 2 vols.

U.S. Commission on Civil Rights. Hearing Before the United States Commission on Civil Rights ... held in Denver, Colorado, February 17-19, 1976. Washington: U.S.G.P.O., 1977.

U.S. Congress. House. Committee on Armed Services. Military Personnel and Compensation Subcommittee. Benefits for Former Spouses of Military Members: hearing before the Military Personnel and Compensation Subcommittee of the Committee on Armed Services, House of Representatives, Ninety-seventh Congress, first session, November 5, 1981. Washington: U.S.G.P.O., 1983. 2 vols.

U.S. Congress. House. Committee on Armed Services. Subcommittee on Military Personnel. Hearings on H.R. 6569, Registration of Women, before the Military Personnel Subcommittee of the Committee on Armed Services, House of Representatives, Ninety-sixth Congress, second session, March 5 and 6, 1980. Washington: U.S.G.P.O., 1981.

U.S. Congress. House. Committee on Armed Services. Subcommittee on Military Personnel. Women in the Military: hearings before the Military Personnel Subcommittee of the Committee on Armed Services, House of Representatives, Ninety-sixth Congress,

first and second sessions, November 13, 14, 15, 16, 1979 and
February 11, 1980. Washington: U.S.G.P.O., 1981.

U.S. Congress. House. Committee on Education and Labor. Civil
Rights Act of 1984: joint hearings before the Committee on Education and Labor and the Subcommittee on Civil and Constitutional
Rights of the Committee on the Judiciary, House of Representatives, Ninety-eighth Congress, second session, on H.R. 5490 ...
hearings held in Washington, D.C., on May 9, 15-17, 21, 22,
1984. Washington: U.S.G.P.O., 1984.

U.S. Congress. House. Committee on Education and Labor. Subcommittee on Elementary, Secondary, and Vocational Education.
Hearing on Women's Educational Equity Act: hearing before the
Subcommittee on Elementary, Secondary, and Vocational Education of the Committee on Education and Labor, House of Representatives, Ninety-eighth Congress, second session, hearing held
in Washington, D.C., April 5, 1984. Washington: U.S.G.P.O.,
1984.

U.S. Congress. House. Committee on Education and Labor. Subcommittee on Employment Opportunities. Oversight Hearings on
Equal Employment Opportunity and Affirmative Action: hearings
before the Subcommittee on Employment Opportunities of the Committee on Education and Labor, House of Representatives, Ninety-
seventh Congress, first session. Washington: U.S.G.P.O.,
1982. 2 vols.

U.S. Congress. House. Committee on Education and Labor. Subcommittee on Employment Opportunities. Oversight Hearings on
the OFCCP's Proposed Affirmative Action Regulations: hearings
before the Subcommittee on Employment Opportunities of the
Committee on Education and Labor, House of Representatives,
Ninety-eighth Congress, first session, hearings held in Washington, D.C. on April 15 and 18; and June 8, 1983. Washington:
U.S.G.P.O., 1983.

U.S. Congress. House. Committee on Education and Labor. Subcommittee on Labor-Management Relations. Legislative Hearing
on Pension Equity For Women: hearing before the Subcommittee
on Labor-Management Relations of the Committee on Education
and Labor, House of Representatives, Ninety-eighth Congress,
first session on H.R. 2100 ... hearing held in Washington, D.C.,
on November 1, 1983. Washington: U.S.G.P.O., 1984.

U.S. Congress. House. Committee on Education and Labor. Subcommittee on Labor-Management Relations. Legislative Hearing
on Pension Issues; hearing before the Subcommittee on Labor-
Management Relations of the Committee on Education and Labor,
House of Representatives, Ninety-seventh Congress, second session, on H.R. 1641 ... H.R. 3632 ... H.R. 6462 ... hearing

held in San Francisco, California, on October 14, 1982. Washington: U.S.G.P.O., 1983.

U.S. Congress. House. Committee on Education and Labor. Subcommittee on Labor-Management Relations. Pension Equity For Women: hearing before the Subcommittee on Labor-Management Relations of the Committee on Education and Labor, House of Representatives, Ninety-eighth Congress, first session on H.R. 2100 ... hearing held in Washington, D.C., on September 29, 1983. Washington: U.S.G.P.O., 1984.

U.S. Congress. House. Committee on Education and Labor. Subcommittee on Select Education. Adolescent Pregnancy: hearings before the Subcommittee on Select Education of the Committee on Education and Labor, House of Representatives, Ninety-fifth Congress, second session, on H.R. 2146, July 24, 1978. Washington: U.S.G.P.O., 1978.

U.S. Congress. House. Committee on Education and Labor. Subcommittee on Select Education. Hearing on Domestic Violence: hearing before the Subcommittee on Select Education of the Committee on Education and Labor, House of Representatives, Ninety-eighth Congress, first session, hearing held in Washington, D.C., June 23, 1983. Washington: U.S.G.P.O., 1983.

U.S. Congress. House. Committee on Energy and Commerce. Subcommittee on Health and the Environment. Health and the Environment Miscellaneous: hearings before the Subcommittee on Health and the Environment of the Committee on Energy and Commerce, House of Representatives, Ninety-eighth Congress, first session. Washington: U.S.G.P.O., 1983-85. 7 vols.

U.S. Congress. House. Committee on Energy and Commerce. Subcommittee on Health and Environment. Health Budget Proposals: hearings before the Subcommittee on Health and the Environment of the Committee on Energy and Commerce, House of Representatives, Ninety-eighth Congress, first session, on Medicaid, Maternal and Child Health Initiatives, July 15, 1983; Medicare Cost Savings ... H.R. 1106, H.R. 3590, July 18, 1983. Washington: U.S.G.P.O., 1983.

U.S. Congress. House. Committee on Energy and Commerce. Subcommittee on Health and the Environment. Pregnancy-Related Health Services: hearings before the Subcommittee on Health and the Environment of the Committee on Energy and Commerce, House of Representatives, Ninety-ninth Congress, first session on Prevention of Low Birthweight, February 25, 1985 ... H.R. 927, March 21, 1985, Family Planning Reauthorization, March 27, 1985. Washington: U.S.G.P.O., 1985.

U.S. Congress. House. Committee on Foreign Affairs. American

Neutrality Policy. Hearings before the Committee on Foreign
Affairs, House of Representatives, Seventy-sixth Congress,
first session, on Present Neutrality Law (Public res. no. 27)
(75th Congress), proposed amendments thereto, and related
legislation affecting the Foreign Policy of the United States,
April 11, 12, 13, 17, 18, 19, 20, 21, 24, 25, 26, 27, 28, and
May 2, 1939. Washington: U.S.G.P.O., 1939.

U.S. Congress. House. Committee on Foreign Affairs. Subcommittee on Human Rights and International Organizations. U.S.
Contribution to the U.N. Decade for Women: hearing before
the Subcommittee on Human Rights and International Organizations of the Committee on Foreign Affairs, House of Representatives, Ninety-eighth Congress, second session, September 18,
1984. Washington: U.S.G.P.O., 1985.

U.S. Congress. House. Committee on Government Operations.
Intergovernmental Relations and Human Resources Subcommittee.
Barriers to Self-Sufficiency for Single Female Heads of Families:
hearings before a subcommittee of the Committee on Government
Operations, House of Representatives, Ninety-ninth Congress,
first session, July 9 and 10, 1985. Washington: U.S.G.P.O.,
1985.

U.S. Congress. House. Committee on Government Operations.
Manpower and Housing Subcommittee. Equal Employment Opportunity Commission's Handling of Pay Equity Cases: hearings
before a subcommittee of the Committee on Government Operations, House of Representatives, Ninety-eighth Congress, second
session, February 29 and March 14, 1984. Washington:
U.S.G.P.O., 1984.

U.S. Congress. House. Committee on Government Operations.
Manpower and Housing Subcommittee. The Women's Bureau; Is
It Meeting the Needs of Women Workers?: hearing before a Sub-
committee on the Committee on Government Operations, House of
Representatives, Ninety-eighth Congress, second session, July
26, 1934. Washington: U.S.G.P.O., 1984.

U.S. Congress. House. Committee on International Relations.
Subcommittee on International Organizations. International Wom-
en's Issues: hearing and briefing before the Subcommittee on
International Organizations and on International Development of
the Committee on International Relations, House of Representatives, Ninety-fifth Congress, second session, March 8 and 22,
1978. Washington: U.S.G.P.O., 1978.

U.S. Congress. House. Committee on Interstate and Foreign Commerce. Subcommittee on Consumer Protection and Finance.
Nondiscrimination in Insurance: hearings before the Subcommittee
on Consumer Protection and Finance of the Committee on Interstate

and Foreign Commerce, House of Representatives, Ninety-sixth
Congress, second session, on H.R. 100 ... August 21 and 28,
1980. Washington: U.S.G.P.O., 1981.

U.S. Congress. House. Committee on Interstate and Foreign Commerce. Subcommittee on Health and the Environment. Adolescent
Health Services, and Pregnancy Prevention Care Act of 1978:
hearing before the Subcommittee on Health and the Environment
of the Committee on Interstate and Foreign Commerce, House of
Representatives, Ninety-fifth Congress, second session, on H.R.
12146 ... June 28, 1978. Washington: U.S.G.P.O., 1978.

U.S. Congress. House. Committee on Interstate and Foreign Com-
merce. Subcommittee on Oversight and Investigations. Nurse
Midwifery: Consumers' Freedom of Choice: hearing before the
Subcommittee on Oversight and Investigations of the Committee
on Interstate and Foreign Commerce, House of Representatives,
Ninety-sixth Congress, second session, December 18, 1980.
Washington: U.S.G.P.O., 1981.

U.S. Congress. House. Committee on Post Office and Civil Serv-
ice. Subcommittee on Census and Population. Demographics of
Adolescent Pregnancy in the United States: joint hearing before
the Subcommittee on Census and Population of the Committee on
Post Office and Civil Service and the Subcommittee on Health and
the Environment of the Committee on Energy and Commerce,
House of Representatives, Ninety-ninth Congress, first session,
April 30, 1985. Washington: U.S.G.P.O., 1985.

U.S. Congress. House. Committee on Post Office and Civil Service. Subcommittee on Civil Service. Federal Government Affirmative Action Policies and Programs: joint hearing before the
Subcommittee on Civil Service of the Committee on Post Office
and the Subcommittee on Civil and Constitutional Rights of the
Committee on the Judiciary, House of Representatives, Ninety-
eighth Congress, first session, December 16, 1983. Washington:
U.S.G.P.O., 1984.

U.S. Congress. House. Committee on Post Office and Civil Service. Subcommittee on Compensation and Employee Benefits.
Federal Pay Equity Act of 1984: hearings before the Subcommittee on Compensation and Employee Benefits of the Committee on
Post Office and Civil Service, House of Representatives, Ninety-
eighth Congress, second session, on H.R. 4599 ... H.R. 5092....
Washington: U.S.G.P.O., 1984. 2 vols.

U.S. Congress. House. Committee on Post Office and Civil Serv-
ice. Subcommittee on Compensation and Employee Benefits.
Options for Conducting a Pay Equity Study of Federal Pay and
Classification Systems: hearings before the Subcommittee on
Compensation and Employee Benefits of the Committee on Post

Office and Civil Service, House of Representatives, Ninety-ninth Congress, first session, March 28, April 4, May 2, 30, and June 18, 1985. Washington: U.S.G.P.O., 1985.

U.S. Congress. House. Committee on Post Office and Civil Service. Subcommittee on Human Resources. Pay Equity: Equal Pay for Work of Comparable Value: joint hearings before the Subcommittee on Human Resources, Civil Service, Compensation and Employee Benefits of the Committee on Post Office and Civil Service, House of Representatives, Ninety-seventh Congress, second session. Washington: U.S.G.P.O., 1983. 2 vols.

U.S. Congress. House. Committee on Post Office and Civil Service. Subcommittee on Investigations. Sexual Harrassment in the Federal Government; hearings before the Subcommittee on Investigations of the Committee on Post Office and Civil Service, House of Representatives, Ninety-sixth Congress, first session, October 23, November 1, 12, 1979. Washington: U.S.G.P.O., 1980. 2 vols.

U.S. Congress. House. Committee on Post Office and Civil Service. Subcommittee on Postal Personnel and Modernization. Equal Employment Opportunity and Sexual Harassment in the Postal Service; hearing before the Subcommittee on Postal Personnel and Modernization of the Committee on Post Office and Civil Service, House of Representatives, Ninety-sixth Congress, second session, October 27, 1980. Washington: U.S.G.P.O., 1981.

U.S. Congress. House. Committee on Post Office and Civil Service. Subcommittee on Postal Personnel and Modernization. Racial Discrimination and Sexual Harassment in U.S. Postal Service: hearings before the Subcommittee on Postal Personnel and Modernization of the Committee on Post Office and Civil Service, House of Representatives, Ninety-seventh Congress, first session, July 1, 1981. Washington: U.S.G.P.O., 1982.

U.S. Congress. House. Committee on Science and Technology. Subcommittee on Domestic and International Scientific Planning, Analysis, and Cooperation. Research into Violent Behavior: Domestic Violence: hearings before the Subcommittee on Domestic and International Scientific Planning, Analysis, and Cooperation of the Committee on Science and Technology, House of Representatives, Ninety-fifth Congress, second session, February 14, 15, 16, 1978. Washington: U.S.G.P.O., 1978.

U.S. Congress. House. Committee on Science and Technology. Subcommittee on Domestic and International Scientific Planning, Analysis, and Cooperation. Research into Violent Behavior: Overview and Sexual Assaults: hearings before the Subcommittee on Domestic and International Scientific Planning, Analysis, and Cooperation of the Committee on Science and Technology,

House of Representatives, Ninety-fifth Congress, second session, January 10, 11, 12, 1978. Washington: U.S.G.P.O., 1978.

U.S. Congress. House. Committee on Small Business. National Commission on Women's Business Ownership, H.R. 3832: hearing before the Committee on Small Business, House of Representatives, Ninety-eighth Congress, second session, Washington, D.C., April 12, 1984. Washington: U.S.G.P.O., 1984.

U.S. Congress. House. Committee on Small Business. Subcommittee on General Oversight and Minority Enterprise. Women in Business: hearing before the Subcommittee on General Oversight and Minority Enterprise of the Committee on Small Business, House of Representatives, Ninety-sixth Congress, second session, Washington, D.C., September 18, 1980. Washington: U.S.G.P.O., 1980.

U.S. Congress. House. Committee on the Budget. Task Force on Entitlements, Uncontrollables, and Indexing. Women and Children in Poverty: hearing before the Task Force on Entitlements, Uncontrollables, and Indexing of the Committee on the Budget, House of Representatives, Ninety-eighth Congress, first session, October 27, 1983. Washington: U.S.G.P.O., 1984.

U.S. Congress. House. Committee on the Judiciary. Birth Control: hearings before the Committee on the Judiciary, House of Representatives, Seventy-third Congress, second session, on H.R. 5978, January 18, 19, 1934. Washington: U.S.G.P.O., 1934.

U.S. Congress. House. Committee on the Judiciary. Subcommittee on Civil and Constitutional Rights. Equal Rights Amendment Extension: hearings before the Subcommittee on Civil and Constitutional Rights of the Committee on the Judiciary, House of Representatives, Ninety-fifth Congress, first and second sessions, on H.J. Res 638. Washington: U.S.G.P.O., 1978.

U.S. Congress. House. Committee on the Judiciary. Subcommittee on Civil and Constitutional Rights. Proposed Constitutional Amendments on Abortion: hearings before the Subcommittee on Civil and Constitutional Rights of the Committee on the Judiciary House of Representatives, Ninety-fourth Congress, second session. Washington: U.S.G.P.O., 1976. 2 vols.

U.S. Congress. House. Committee on the Judiciary. Subcommittee on Courts, Civil Liberties, and the Administration of Justice. The Female Offender--1979-80: hearings before the Subcommittee on Courts, Civil Liberties, and the Administration of Justice of the Committee on the Judiciary, House of Representatives, Ninety-sixth Congress, first session, on the Female Offender--1979-80,

October 10, and 11, 1979. Washington: U.S.G.P.O., 1981. 2 vols.

U.S. Congress. House. Committee on the Judiciary. Subcommittee on Criminal Justice. Privacy of Rape Victims: hearing before the Subcommittee on Criminal Justice of the Committee on the Judiciary, House of Representatives, Ninety-fourth Congress, second session, on H.R. 14666 and Other Bills to Amend the Federal Rules of Evidence to Provide for the Protection of the Privacy of Rape Victims, July 29, 1976. Washington: U.S.G.P.O., 1976.

U.S. Congress. House. Committee on Veterans' Affairs. Select Subcommittee to Review WASP Bills. To Provide Recognition to the Women's Air Force Service Pilots for Their Service during World War II By Deeming Such Service to Have Been Active Duty in the Armed Forces of the United States for Purposes of Laws Administered by the Veterans Administration: hearing before a Select Subcommittee of the Committee on Veterans' Affairs, House of Representatives, Ninety-fifth Congress, first session... September 20, 1977. Washington: U.S.G.P.O., 1977.

U.S. Congress. House. Committee on Veterans' Affairs. Subcommittee on Hospitals and Health Care. VA Health Care for Women and H.R. 1137: hearings before the Subcommittee on Hospitals and Health Care of the Committee on Veterans' Affairs, House of Representatives, Ninety-eighth Congress, first session, March 3, 1983. Washington: U.S.G.P.O., 1983.

U.S. Congress. House. Committee on Veterans' Affairs. Subcommittee on Oversight and Investigations. Implementation of Title IV of Public Law 95-202, Relating to WASPS and Simularly Situated Groups: hearings before the Subcommittee on Oversight and Investigations of the Committee on Veterans' Affairs, House of Representatives, Ninety-seventh Congress, first session, September 29, 1981. Washington: U.S.G.P.O., 1981.

U.S. Congress. House. Committee on Ways and Means. Birth Control: hearings before the Committee on Ways and Means, House of Representatives, Seventy-second Congress, first session, on H.R. 11082, May 19 and 20, 1932. Washington: U.S.G.P.O., 1932.

U.S. Congress. House. Committee on Ways and Means. Economic Equity Act and Related Tax and Pension Reform: hearing before the Committee on Ways and Means, House of Representatives, Ninety-eight Congress, first session, October 25, 1983. Washington: U.S.G.P.O., 1984.

U.S. Congress. House. Committee on Ways and Means. Subcommittee on Public Assistance and Unemployment Compensation.

AFDC and Social Service Bills and Related Oversight Issues:
hearings before the Subcommittee on Public Assistance and Unemployment Compensation of the Committee on Ways and Means,
Ninety-eighth Congress, first session, July 18, 1983. Washington: U.S.G.P.O., 1984.

U.S. Congress. House. Committee on Ways and Means. Subcommittee on Public Assistance and Unemployment Compensation.
Teenage Pregnancy Issues: hearing before the Subcommittee
on Public Assistance and Unemployment Compensation of the
Committee on Ways and Means, House of Representatives, Ninety-
ninth Congress, first session, May 7, 1985. Washington:
U.S.G.P.O., 1985.

U.S. Congress. House. Committee on Ways and Means. Subcommittee on Social Security. Social Security Dependents' Benefits:
field hearing before the Subcommittee on Social Security of the
Committee on Ways and Means, House of Representatives, Ninety-
sixth Congress, second session, July 28, 1980, Falls Church,
Virginia. Washington: U.S.G.P.O., 1980.

U.S. Congress. House. Committee on Ways and Means. Subcommittee on Social Security. Treatment of Men and Women Under
The Social Security Program: hearings before the Subcommittee
on Social Security of the Committee on Ways and Means, House
of Representatives, Ninety-sixth Congress, first session, November 1 and 2, 1979. Washington: U.S.G.P.O., 1980.

U.S. Congress. House. Select Committee on Aging. Problems of
Aging Women: hearing before the Select Committee on Aging,
House of Representatives, Ninety-seventh Congress, second session, July 26, 1982, Omaha, Nebraska. Washington: U.S.G.P.O.,
1982.

U.S. Congress. House. Select Committee on Aging. Women's Pen-
sion Equity: hearing before the Select Committee on Aging,
House of Representatives, Ninety-eighth Congress, first session,
June 14, 1983. Washington: U.S.G.P.O., 1983.

U.S. Congress. House. Select Committee on Aging. Subcommittee
on Health and Long-Term Care. Elder Abuse: hearing before
the Subcommittee on Health and Long-Term Care of the Select
Committee on Aging, House of Representatives, Ninety-ninth
Congress, first session, May 10, 1985. Washington: U.S.G.P.O.,
1985.

U.S. Congress. House. Select Committee on Aging. Subcommittee
on Health and Long-Term Care. Progress in Controlling Breast
Cancer: hearing before the Subcommittee on Health and Long-
Term Care of the Select Committee on Aging, House of Representatives, Ninety-eighth Congress, second session, June 28,
1984. Washington: U.S.G.P.O., 1984.

U.S. Congress. House. Select Committee on Aging. Subcommittee on Retirement Income and Employment. The Impact of Reagan Economics on Aging Women: Oregon: hearing before the Subcommittee on Retirement Income and Employment of the Select Committee on Aging, House of Representatives, Ninety-seventh Congress, second session, September 1, 1982, Portland, Oregon. Washington: U.S.G.P.O., 1983.

U.S. Congress. House. Select Committee on Aging. Subcommittee on Retirement Income and Employment. National Policy Proposals Affecting Midlife Women: hearings before the Subcommittee on Retirement Income and Employment of the Select Committee on Aging, House of Representatives, Ninety-sixth Congress, first session, May 7 and 8, 1979. Washington: U.S.G.P.O., 1979.

U.S. Congress. House. Select Committee on Aging. Subcommittee on Retirement Income and Employment. Task Force on Social Security and Women. Earnings Sharing Implementation Plan: hearing before the Task Force and Social Security and Women of the Subcommittee on Retirement Income and Employment and the Select Committee on Aging, House of Representatives, Ninety-eighth Congress, second session, April 12, 1984. Washington: U.S.G.P.O., 1984.

U.S. Congress. House. Select Committee on Aging. Subcommittee on Retirement Income and Employment. Task Force on Social Security and Women. Inequities Toward Women in the Social Security System: hearing before the Task Force on Social Security and Women of the Subcommittee on Retirement Income and Employment and the Select Committee on Aging, House of Representatives, Ninety-eight Congress, first session, September 22, 1983. Washington: U.S.G.P.O., 1983.

U.S. Congress. House. Select Committee on Aging. Subcommittee on Retirement Income and Employment. Task Force on Social Security and Women. Treatment of Women Under Social Security: hearings before the Task Force on Social Security and Women of the Subcommittee on Retirement Income and Employment and the Select Committee on Aging, House of Representatives, Ninety-sixth Congress, first session, hearings held in Washington and Cleveland, May 16, 1979, June 3, 1980. Washington: U.S.G.P.O., 1980. 4 vols.

U.S. Congress. House. Select Committee on Children, Youth, and Families. Children, Youth, and Families: beginning the assessment hearings before the Select Committee on Children, Youth, and Families, House of Representatives, Ninety-eighth Congress, first session, hearing held in Washington, D.C. on April 28, 1983. Washington: U.S.G.P.O., 1983.

U.S. Congress. House. Select Committee on Children, Youth, and

Families. Families in Crisis: the Private Sector Response: hearing before the Select Committee on Children, Youth, and Families, House of Representatives, Ninety-eighth Congress, first session, hearing held in Washington, D.C. on July 12, 1983. Washington: U.S.G.P.O., 1983.

U.S. Congress. House. Select Committee on Children, Youth, and Families. Families with Disabled Children: Issues for the 1980's: hearing before the Select Committee on Children, Youth, and Families, House of Representatives, Ninety-ninth Congress, first session, hearing held in Anaheim, CA, April 19, 1985. Washington: U.S.G.P.O., 1985.

U.S. Congress. House. Select Committee on Children, Youth, and Families. Teen Parents and Their Children, Issues and Programs: hearing before the Select Committee on Children, Youth, and Families, House of Representatives, Ninety-eighth Congress, first session, hearing held in Washington, D.C., on July 20, 1983. Washington: U.S.G.P.O., 1984.

U.S. Congress. House. Select Committee on Children, Youth, and Families. Violence and Abuse in American Families: hearing before the Select Committee on Children, Youth, and Families, House of Representatives, Ninety-eighth Congress, second session, hearing held in Washington, D.C., on July 14, 1984. Washington: U.S.G.P.O., 1985.

U.S. Congress. House. Select Committee on Population. Fertility and Contraception in America: hearings before the Select Committee on Population, House of Representatives, Ninety-fifth Congress, second session. Washington: U.S.G.P.O., 1978. 3 vols.

U.S. Congress. Joint Economic Committee. American Women: Three Decades of Change: hearing before the Joint Economic Committee, Congress of the United States, Ninety-eighth Congress, first session, November 9, 1983. Washington: U.S.G.P.O., 1984.

U.S. Congress. Joint Economic Committee. Economic Status of Women: hearing before the Joint Economic Committee, Congress of the United States, Ninety-seventh Congress, second session, February 3, 1982. Washington: U.S.G.P.O., 1982.

U.S. Congress. Joint Economic Committee. Problems of Working Women: hearing before the Joint Economic Committee, Congress of the United States, Ninety-eighth Congress, second session, April 3, 1984. Washington: U.S.G.P.O., 1984.

U.S. Congress. Joint Economic Committee. The Role of Older Women in the Work Force: hearing before the Joint Economic Committee, Congress of the United States, Ninety-eighth Congress, second session, June 6, 1984. Washington: U.S.G.P.O., 1984.

U.S. Congress. Joint Economic Committee. <u>Women in the Work</u>
<u>Force: Pay Equity</u>: hearing before the Joint Economic Commit-
tee, Congress of the United States, Ninety-eighth Congress,
second session, April 10, 1984. Washington: U.S.G.P.O.,
1984.

U.S. Congress. Joint Economic Committee. Subcommittee on Economic Growth and Stabilization. <u>American Women Workers in a</u>
<u>Full Employment Economy</u>: hearing before the Subcommittee on
Economic Growth and Stabilization of the Joint Economic Committee, Congress of the United States, Ninety-fifth Congress, first
session, September 16, 1977. Washington: U.S.G.P.O., 1978.

U.S. Congress. Joint Economic Committee. Subcommittee on Priorities and Economy in Government. <u>The Role of Women in the</u>
<u>Military</u>: hearings before the Subcommittee on Priorities and
Economy in Government of the Joint Economic Committee, Congress of the United States, Ninety-fifth Congress, first session,
July 22 and September 1, 1977. Washington: U.S.G.P.O., 1978.

U.S. Congress. Senate. Committee on Finance. <u>Potential Inequities</u>
<u>Affecting Women</u>: hearings before the Committee on Finance,
United States Senate, Ninety-eighth Congress, first session, on
S. 19 and S. 888, June 20, 21, and August 2, 1983. Washington:
U.S.G.P.O., 1983. 3 vols.

U.S. Congress. Senate. Committee on Finance. Subcommittee on
Social Security and Income Maintenance Programs. <u>Women's Ca-</u>
<u>reer Choice Equity Legislation</u>: hearing before the Subcommittee
on Social Security and Income Maintenance Programs of the Committee on Finance, United States Senate, Ninety-eighth Congress,
first session, July 28, 1983. Washington: U.S.G.P.O., 1983.

U.S. Congress. Senate. Committee on Foreign Relations. <u>Nomina-</u>
<u>tion of Hon. Millicent Fenwick</u>: hearing before the Committee on
Foreign Relations, United States Senate, Ninety-eighth Congress,
first session, on the nomination of Hon. Millicent Fenwick, of
New Jersey, for the rank of Ambassador, July 20, 1983. Washington: U.S.G.P.O., 1983.

U.S. Congress. Senate. Committee on Foreign Relations. <u>Women</u>
<u>in Development: Looking to the Future</u>: hearing before the
Committee on Foreign Relations, United States Senate, Ninety-
eighth Congress, second session, June 7, 1984. Washington:
U.S.G.P.O., 1984. 2 vols.

U.S. Congress. Senate. Committee on Human Resources. <u>Adoles-</u>
<u>cent Health, Services, and Pregnancy Prevention Care Act of</u>
<u>1978</u>: hearings before the Committee on Human Resources, United
States Senate, Ninety-fifth Congress, second session, on S.
2910 ... June 14, and July 12, 1978. Washington: U.S.G.P.O.,
1978.

U.S. Congress. Senate. Committee on Human Resources. Subcommittee on Alcoholism and Drug Abuse. Alcohol Labeling and Fetal Alcohol Syndrome, 1978: hearing before the Subcommittee on Alcoholism and Drug Abuse of the Committee on Human Resources, United States Senate, Ninety-fifth Congress, second session, on S. 1461 to Require a Health Warning on the Labels of Bottles Containing Alcohol Beverages, January 31, 1978. Washington: U.S.G.P.O., 1978.

U.S. Congress. Senate. Committee on Labor and Human Resources. Barrier to Adoption: hearings before the Committee on Labor and Human Resources, United States Senate, Ninety-ninth Congress, first session, June 25, and July 10, 1985. Washington: U.S.G.P.O., 1985.

U.S. Congress. Senate. Committee on Labor and Human Resources. The Coming Decade: American Women and Human Resources Policies and Programs, 1979: hearings before the Committee on Labor and Human Resources, United States Senate, Ninety-sixth Congress, first session. Washington: U.S.G.P.O., 1979. 2 vols.

U.S. Congress. Senate. Committee on Labor and Human Resources. Oversight of Family Planning programs, 1981: hearing before the Committee on Labor and Human Resources, United States Senate, Ninety-seventh Congress, first session, on Examination of the Role of the Federal Government in Birth Control, Abortion Referral, and Sex Education Programs, March 31, 1981. Washington: U.S.G.P.O., 1981.

U.S. Congress. Senate. Committee on Labor and Human Resources. Sex Discrimination in the Workplace, 1981: hearings before the Committee on Labor and Human Resources, United States Senate, Ninety-seventh Congress, first session, on Examination of Issues Affecting Women in Our Nation's Labor Force, January 28, and April 21, 1981. Washington: U.S.G.P.O., 1981.

U.S. Congress. Senate. Committee on Labor and Human Resources. Woman in Transition, 1983: hearing before the Committee on Labor and Human Resources, United States Senate, Ninety-eighth Congress, first session on Examination of Problems Faced by Women in Transition From Work Without Pay to Economic Self-sufficiency, November 8, 1983. Washington: U.S.G.P.O., 1984.

U.S. Congress. Senate. Committee on Labor and Human Resources. Subcommittee on Aging, Family, and Human Services. Oversight on Family Planning Programs under Title X of the Public Health Service Act, 1981: hearing before the Subcommittee on Aging, Family, and Human Services of the Committee on Labor and Human Resources, United States Senate, Ninety-seventh Congress, first session, on Oversight of the Role of the Federal Government

in Family Planning Administered under Title X of the Public
Health Service Act, June 23, and September 28, 1981. Washington: U.S.G.P.O., 1981.

U.S. Congress. Senate. Committee on Labor and Human Resources.
Subcommittee on Child and Human Development. Domestic Violence Prevention and Services Act, 1980: hearing before the
Subcommittee on Child and Human Development of the Committee
on Labor and Human Resources, United States Senate, Ninety-
sixth Congress, second session on S. 1843 ... and related bill,
February 6, 1980. Washington: U.S.G.P.O., 1980.

U.S. Congress. Senate. Committee on Labor and Human Resources.
Subcommittee on Education, Arts, and Humanities. Civil Rights
Act of 1984: joint hearing before the Subcommittee on Education, Arts, and Humanities and the Subcommittee on the Handicapped of the Committee on Labor and Human Resources, United
States Senate, Ninety-eighth Congress, second session, on S.
2568 ... Washington: U.S.G.P.O., 1984. 2 vols.

U.S. Congress. Senate. Committee on Labor and Human Resources.
Subcommittee on Family and Human Services. Adolescents in
Crisis: Parental Involvement: hearing before the Subcommittee
on Family and Human Services of the Committee on Labor and Human Resources, United States Senate, Ninety-eighth Congress,
second session, on Examining How Best to Help Adolescents with
Problems of Alcohol Abuse, Drug Dependence ... February 24,
1984. Washington: U.S.G.P.O., 1984.

U.S. Congress. Senate. Committee on Labor and Human Resources.
Subcommittee on Family and Human Services. Broken Families:
hearings before the Subcommittee on Family and Human Services
of the Committee on Labor and Human Resources, United States
Senate, Ninety-eighth Congress, first session, on Oversight on
the Breakdown of the Traditional Family Unit, Focusing on the
Effects of Divorce, Separation, and Conflict within Marriage on
Children and Women and Men, March 22 and 24, 1983. Washington: U.S.G.P.O., 1983. 2 vols.

U.S. Congress. Senate. Committee on Labor and Human Resources.
Subcommittee on Family and Human Services. Forum for Families:
Quality of American Family Life: hearing before the Subcommittee
on Family and Human Services of the Committee on Labor and
Human Resources, United States Senate, Ninety-eighth Congress,
first session, on Examination of Federal Policies Intended to Pre-
serve and Increase the Quality of American Family Life; a Prelude
to National Family Week and National Adoption Week, November
18, 1983. Washington: U.S.G.P.O., 1984.

U.S. Congress. Senate. Committee on Labor and Human Resources.
Subcommittee on Family and Human Services. Oversight on Family

Planning Programs under Title X of the Public Health Service Act, 1984: hearings before the Subcommittee on Family and Human Services of the Committee on Labor and Human Resources, United States Senate, Ninety-eighth Congress, second session, April 5, and May 1, 1984. Washington: U.S.G.P.O., 1984.

U.S. Congress. Senate. Committee on Labor and Human Resources. Subcommittee on Family and Human Services. Reauthorization of the Adolescent Family Life Demonstration Projects Act of 1981: hearings before the Subcommittee on Family and Human Services of the Committee on Labor and Human Resources, United States Senate, Ninety-eighth Congress, second session, April 24 and 26, 1984. Washington: U.S.G.P.O., 1985.

U.S. Congress. Senate. Committee on Labor and Human Resources. Subcommittee on Health and Scientific Research. Reappraisal of Mental Health Policy, 1979: hearing before the Subcommittee on Health and Scientific Research of the Committee on Labor and Human Resources, United States Senate, Ninety-sixth Congress, first session, February 7, 1979. Washington: U.S.G.P.O., 1979.

U.S. Congress. Senate. Committee on Labor and Human Resources. Subcommittee on Health and Scientific Research. Women in Science and Technology Equal Opportunity Act, 1979: hearing before the Subcommittee on Health and Scientific Research of the Committee on Labor and Human Resources, United States Senate, Ninety-sixth Congress, first session, on S. 568 ... August 1, 1979. Washington: U.S.G.P.O., 1979.

U.S. Congress. Senate. Committee on Labor and Human Resources. Subcommittee on Labor. Amending the Fair Labor Standards Act to Include Industrial Homework: hearing before the Subcommittee on Labor of the Committee on Labor and Human Resources, United States Senate, Ninety-Eighth Congress, second session, on S. 2145 ... February 9, 1984. Washington: U.S.G.P.O., 1984.

U.S. Congress. Senate. Committee on Labor and Human Resources. Subcommittee on Labor. Retirement Equity Act of 1983: hearing before the Subcommittee on Labor of the Committee on Labor and Human Resources, United States Senate, Ninety-eighth Congress, first session, on S. 19 and related bills, October 4, 1982. Washington: U.S.G.P.O., 1983.

U.S. Congress. Senate. Committee on Small Business. Federal Contracting Opportunities for Minority and Women-Owned Businesses: An Examination of the 8(d) Subcontracting Program: hearings before the Committee on Small Business, United States Senate, Ninety-eighth Congress, first session, on Federal Contracting Opportunities for Minority and Women-Owned Businesses; an Examination of the 8(d) Subcontracting Program, Tacoma, Washington, December 21, 1983. Washington: U.S.G.P.O., 1984.

U.S. Congress. Senate. Committee on Small Business. Women Entrepreneurs: Their Success and Problems: hearing before the Committee on Small Business, United States Senate, Ninety-eighth Congress, second session, on Women Entrepreneurs, Their Success and Problems, Eugene, Oregon, May 30, 1984. Washington: U.S.G.P.O., 1984.

U.S. Congress. Senate. Committee on the Judiciary. Birth Control: hearings before a subcommittee of the Committee on the Judiciary, United States Senate, Seventy-first Congress, third session, on S. 4582. Washington: U.S.G.P.O., 1931.

U.S. Congress. Senate. Committee on the Judiciary. Birth Control: hearings before a subcommittee of the Committee on the Judiciary, United States Senate, Seventy-second Congress, first session, on S. 4436, a bill to amend section 305(a) of the Tariff Act of 1930, and sections 211, 245, and 312 of the Criminal Code as amended, May 12, 19, and 20, 1932. Washington: U.S.G.P.O., 1932.

U.S. Congress. Senate. Committee on the Judiciary. Birth Control: hearings before a subcommittee of the Committee on the Judiciary, United States Senate, Seventy-third Congress, second session, on S. 1842, a bill to amend sections 211, 245, and 312 of the Criminal Code, as amended, March 1, 20, and 27, 1934. Washington: U.S.G.P.O., 1934.

U.S. Congress. Senate. Committee on the Judiciary. Subcommittee on Criminal Law. Impact of Media Coverage of Rape Trials: hearing before the Subcommittee on Criminal Law of the Committee on the Judiciary, United States Senate, Ninety-eighth Congress, second session, on Oversight of the Effect of Publicity on the Victims in Rape Cases, and the Right of the Press to Have Access to Such Proceedings, April 24, 1984. Washington: U.S.G.P.O., 1985.

U.S. Congress. Senate. Committee on the Judiciary. Subcommittee on Juvenile Justice. Effect of Pornography on Women and Children: hearings before the Subcommittee on Juvenile Justice of the Committee on the Judiciary, United States Senate, Ninety-eighth Congress, second session, on Oversight on Pornography ... Child Abuse, Child Molestation, and Problems of Conduct Against Women, Washington, D.C., August 8, September 12, and 25, and October 20, 1984; Pittsburgh, PA, October 18, 1984. Washington: U.S.G.P.O., 1985.

U.S. Congress. Senate. Committee on the Judiciary. Subcommittee on Juvenile Justice. Juvenile Rape Victims: hearing before the Subcommittee on Juvenile Justice of the Committee on the Judiciary, United States Senate, Ninety-ninth Congress, first session, on the Problems of Juvenile Victims in Sexual Assault Cases, April 24, 1985. Washington: U.S.G.P.O., 1985.

U.S. Congress. Senate. Committee on the Judiciary. Subcommittee on Juvenile Justice. Teenage Suicide: hearing before the Subcommittee on Juvenile Justice of the Committee on the Judiciary, United States Senate, Ninety-eighth Congress, second session, on Oversight on the Factors That May Lead to Teenage Suicide, and What May Be Done to Prevent That Tragedy, October 3, 1984. Washington: U.S.G.P.O., 1985.

U.S. Congress. Senate. Committee on the Judiciary. Subcommittee on Separation of Powers. The Human Life Bill: hearings before the Subcommittee on Separation of Powers of the Committee on the Judiciary, United States Senate, Ninety-seventh Congress, first session, on S. 158 ... April 23, 24, May 20, 21, June 1, 10, 12 and 18, 1982. Washington: U.S.G.P.O., 1982. 2 vols.

U.S. Congress. Senate. Committee on the Judiciary. Subcommittee on the Constitution. Civil Rights Act of 1984: hearings before the Subcommittee of the Constitution of the Committee on the Judiciary, United States Senate, Ninety-eighth Congress, second session, on S. 2568 ... May 30, and June 5, 1984. Washington: U.S.G.P.O., 1984.

U.S. Congress. Senate. Committee on the Judiciary. Subcommittee on the Constitution. Constitutional Amendments Relating to Abortion: hearings before the Subcommittee on the Constitution of the Committee on the Judiciary, United States Senate, Ninety-seventh Congress, first session ... Washington: U.S.G.P.O., 1983. 2 vols.

U.S. Congress. Senate. Committee on the Judiciary. Subcommittee on the Constitution. The Impact of the Equal Rights Amendment: hearings before the Subcommittee on the Constitution of the Committee on the Judiciary, United States Senate, Ninety-eighth Congress, first and second sessions, on S.J. Res. 10 ... Washington: U.S.G.P.O., 1985. 2 vols.

U.S. Congress. Senate. Committee on the Judiciary. Subcommittee on the Constitution. Legal Ramifications of the Human Life Amendment: hearings before the Subcommittee on the Constitution of the Committee on the Judiciary, United States Senate, Ninety-eighth Congress, first session on S.J. Res. 3 ... February 28, and March 7, 1983. Washington: U.S.G.P.O., 1983.

U.S. Congress. Senate. Committee on the Judiciary. Subcommittee to Investigate Juvenile Delinquency. Protection of Children Against Sexual Exploitation: hearings before the Subcommittee to Investigate Juvenile Delinquency of the Committee on the Judiciary, United States Senate, Ninety-fifth Congress, first session, Chicago, IL, May 27, 1977, Washington, D.C., June 16, 1977. Washington: U.S.G.P.O., 1978.

U.S. Congress. Senate. Committee on Veterans' Affairs. Recognition for Purposes of VA Benefits: hearing before the Committee on Veterans' Affairs, United States Senate, Ninety-fifth Congress, first session, on S. 247, S. 1414, S. 129, and related bills, May 25, 1977. Washington: U.S.G.P.O., 1977.

U.S. Congress. Senate. Committee on Veterans' Affairs. Veteran's Health Care and Programs Improvement Act of 1983: hearings before the Committee on Veterans' Affairs, United States Senate, Ninety-eighth Congress, first session ... March 9, and 10, 1983. Washington: U.S.G.P.O., 1983.

U.S. Congress. Senate. Select Committee on Small Business. Women-In-Business Programs in the Federal Government: hearing before the Select Committee on Small Business, United States Senate, Ninety-sixth Congress, second session ... May 29, 1980. Washington: U.S.G.P.O., 1980.

U.S. Congress. Senate. Special Committee on Aging. Adapting Social Security to a Changing Work Force: hearing before the Special Committee on Aging, United States Senate, Ninety-sixth Congress, first session, Washington, D.C., November 28, 1979. Washington: U.S.G.P.O., 1980.

U.S. Congress. Senate. Special Committee on Aging. Prospects For Better Health For Older Women: hearing before the Special Committee on Aging, United States Senate, Ninety-ninth Congress, first session, Toledo, OH, April 15, 1985. Washington: U.S.G.P.O., 1985.

U.S. Congress. Senate. Special Committee on Aging. Women in Our Aging Society: hearing before the Special Committee on Aging, United States Senate, Ninety-eighth Congress, second session, Columbus, OH, October 8, 1984. Washington: U.S.G.P.O., 1985.

U.S. Department of Health, Education, and Welfare. Secretary's Advisory Committee on the Rights and Responsibilities of Women. Child Care and the Working Woman: report and recommendations of the Secretary's Advisory Committee on the Rights and Responsibilities of Women, 1975. Washington: U.S.G.P.O., 1975.

U.S. Equal Employment Opportunity Commission. Hearings Before the United States Equal Employment Opportunity Commission on Job Segregation and Wage Discrimination. Washington: The Commission, 1980.

U.S. Health Resources Administration. Division of Nursing. Prospectives for Nursing: A Symposium. Hyattsville, MD: Department of Health and Human Services, Public Health Service, Health Resources Administration, Bureau of Health Professions, Division of Nursing, 1980.

U.S. National Commission on the Observance of International Women's Year. The Spirit of Houston: the First National Women's Conference: an official report to the President, the Congress, and the People of the United States. Washington: U.S.G.P.O., 1978.

U.S. Women's Bureau. Native American Women and Equal Opportunity: How to Get Ahead in the Federal Government. U.S. Department of Labor, Women's Bureau. Washington: U.S.G.P.O., 1979.

Victorian Women; A Documentary Account of Women's Lives in Nineteenth-Century England, France, and the United States, edited by Erna Olafson Hellerstein, Leslie Parker Hume, and Karen M. Offen. Stanford, CA: Stanford University Press, 1981.

Walker, Alice. In Search of Our Mother's Gardens: Womanist Prose. New York: Harcourt Brace Jovanovich, 1983.

Warner, Anne R. Health Womenpower: Attaining Greater Influence of Women in the Health Care System: a report of the regional conference, October 12-14, 1977, New York City/prepared by Anne R. Warner, the National Health Council. Washington: U.S.G.P.O., 1979.

We Shall Be Heard: Women Speakers in America, 1828-Present, edited by Patricia Scileppi Kennedy and Gloria Hartmann O'Sheilds. Dubuque, IA: Kendall/Hunt Pub. Co., 1983.

The Web of Southern Social Relations: Women, Family, and Education, edited by Walter J. Fraser, Jr., R. Frank Saunders, Jr., and John Wakelyn. Athens: University of Georgia Press, 1985.

Webster, Margaret. Shakespeare and the Modern Theatre. The fifth lecture on the Helen Kenyon lectureship at Vassar College, delivered June 1, 1944. Poughkeepsie, NY: n.p., 1944.

Welty, Eudora. One Writer's Beginnings. Cambridge, MA: Harvard University Press, 1984.

Western Regional Civil Rights and Women's Rights Conference (4th: 1977: San Francisco, CA) Recent Developments, New Opportunities in Civil Rights and Women's Rights: a report of the proceedings of the Western Regional Civil Rights and Women's Conference IV/sponsored by the United States Commission on Civil Rights in San Francisco, CA, June 29-July 1, 1977. Washington: The Commission, 1977.

The Woman in Management: Career and Family Issues, edited by Jennie Farley. Ithaca, NY: ILR Press, New York State School of Industrial and Labor Relations, Cornell University, 1983.

Womanguides: Readings Toward a Feminist Theology, compiled by
Rosemary Radford Ruether. Boston: Beacon Press, 1985.

A Woman's Choices: the Relief Society Legacy Lectures, edited by
Barbara B. Smith (et al.). Salt Lake City: Deseret, 1984.

Woman's "True" Profession: Voices from the History of Teaching,
edited by Nancy Hoffman. Old Westbury, NY: The Feminist
Press; New York: McGraw-Hill, 1981.

Women: A Developmental Perspective: proceedings of a research
conference, edited by Phyllis W. Berman, and Estelle R. Ramey.
Bethesda, MD: U.S. Department of Health and Human Services,
Public Health Service, National Institutes of Health, 1982.

Women and Educational Leadership, edited by Sari Knopp Biklen and
Marylin B. Brannigan. Lexington, MA: Lexington Books, 1980.

Women and Health: the Politics of Sex in Medicine, edited by Elizabeth Fee. Farmingdale, NY: Baywood, 1983.

Women and Health in America: Historical Readings, edited by Judith
Walzer Leavitt. Madison: University of Wisconsin Press, 1984.

Women and Men: Changing Roles, Relationships, and Receptions:
report of a workshop, edited by Libby A. Carter and Anne Firor
with Wendy Martyne. Palo Alto, CA: Aspen Institute for Humanistic Studies, 1976.

Women and Men: The Consequences of Power: A Collection of New
Essays: selected papers from the National Bicentennial Conference, Pioneers for Century III, April 22-25, 1976, Cincinnati,
OH, edited by Dana V. Heller and Robin Ann Aheals. Cincinnati: University of Cincinnati, Office of Women's Studies, 1977.

Women and Minorities in Science: Strategies for Increasing Participation, edited by Sheila M. Humphreys. Boulder, CO: Published by Westview Press for the American Association for the
Advancement of Science, 1982.

Women and Psychotherapy: An Assessment of Research and Practice, edited by Annette M. Brodsky and Rachel T. Hare-Mustin.
New York: Gulford, 1980.

Women and Technological Change in Developing Countries, edited by
Roslyn Dauber and Melinda L. Cain. Boulder, CO: Published
by Westview Press for the American Association for the Advancement of Science, 1982.

Women and the News, edited by Laurily Keir Epstein. New York:
Hastings House, 1978.

Women and the Word: Sermons, edited by Helen Gray Crotwell.
   Philadelphia: Fortress Press, 1978.

Women, Feminist Identity, and Society in the 1980's: selected papers, edited by Myriam Dbiaz-Diocaretz and Iris M. Zavala.
   Amsterdam; Philadelphia: Benjamins, 1985.

Women in Action: speeches and panel discussion of the Conference-
   Workshop, March 26, 1969. Ann Arbor: Center for Continuing
   Education of Women, University of Michigan, 1969.

Women in Crisis Conference (1st: 1979: New York, NY). Women
   in Crisis, edited by Penelope Russianoff; sponsored by Women
   In Crisis, Inc. New York: Human Sciences Press, 1981.

Women in Engineering: Beyond Recruitment: the proceedings of the
   Conference held June 22 to 25, 1975, Cornell University, Ithaca,
   New York, edited by Mary Diederich Ott and Nancy A. Reese.
   Ithaca, NY: Cornell University, 1975.

Women in Latin America: an anthology from Latin American Perspectives, edited by Eleanor B. Leacock. Riverside, CA: Latin
   American Perspectives, 1979.

Women in Latin American Literature: A Symposium: Women in Latin
   America: Their Role as Writers and Their Image in Fiction, by
   Martha Paley Frencescato. Jorge Amado's Heroines and the Ideological Double Standard, by Daphne Patai. Manuel Puig's Heartbreak Tango: Women and Mass Culture, by Ellen McCracken.
   Amherst, MA: International Area Studies Program, University
   of Massachusetts at Amherst, 1979.

Women in Management: Environment and Role, edited by Milton L.
   Shuch. Indianapolis, IN: Bobbs-Merrill, 1981.

Women in New Worlds: Historical Perspectives on the Wesleyan
   Tradition, edited by Hilah F. Thomas and Rosemary Skinner
   Keller. Nashville, TN: Abingdon, 1981-82. 2 vols.

Women in Organizations: Barriers and Breakthroughs, edited by
   Joseph J. Pilotta. Prospect Heights, IL: Waveland Press, 1983.

Women in Scientific and Engineering Professions, edited by Violet
   B. Haas and Carolyn C. Perrucci, with the assistance of Jean
   E. Brenchley. Ann Arbor: University of Michigan Press, 1984.

Women in the Judiciary: A Symposium for Women Judges, edited by
   Marilyn McCoy Roberts and David Rhein. Williamsburg, VA:
   National Center for State Courts, 1983.

Women in the Work Force, edited by H. John Bernardin. New York:
   Praeger, 1982.

Women in the Workplace, edited by Phyllis A. Wallace. Boston: Auburn House, 1982.

Women in the Workplace: Effects on Families, edited by Kathryn M. Borman, Daisy Quarm, and Sarah Gideonse. Norwood, NJ: Ablex, 1984.

Women in Theatre: Compassion & Hope, edited by Karen Malpede. New York: Drama Book Publishers, 1983.

Women of America; A History, by Carol Ruth Berkin and Mary Beth Norton. Boston: Houghton Mifflin, 1979.

Women of the Word: Contemporary Sermons by Women Clergy, by Janice M. Bracket (et al.), edited by Charles D. Hackett. Atlanta, GA: Susan Hunter, 1985.

Women Organizing: An Anthology, by Bernice Cummings and Victoria Schuck. Metuchen, NJ: Scarecrow Press, 1979.

Women, Power, and Political Systems, edited by Margherita Rendel with the assistance of Georgina Ashworth. New York: St. Martin's Press, 1981.

Women, State, and Party in Eastern Europe, edited by Sharon L. Wolchik and Alfred G. Meyer. Durham, NC: Duke University Press, 1985.

Women, the Arts, and the 1920s in Paris and New York, edited by Kenneth W. Wheeler and Virginia Lee Lussier. New Brunswick, NJ: Transaction Books, 1982.

Women, the Family, and Freedom: the debate in documents, edited by Susan Groag Bell and Karen M. Offen. Stanford, CA: Stanford University Press, 1983. 2 vols.

Women Workers in fifteen Countries: essays in honor of Alice Hanson Cook, edited by Jennie Farley. Ithaca, NY: ILR Press, New York State School of Industrial and Labor Relations, Cornell University, 1985.

Women's America: Refocusing the Past, edited by Linda K. Kerber and Jane DeHart Mathews. New York: Oxford University Press, 1982.

Women's Folklore, Women's Culture, edited by Rosan A. Jordan and Susan J. Kalcik. Philadelphia: University of Pennsylvania Press, 1985.

Women's Lives: New Theory, Research and Policy, edited by Dorothy G. McGuigan. Ann Arbor: University of Michigan, Center for Continuing Education of Women, 1980.

Women's Spirit Bonding, edited by Janet Kalven and Mary I. Buckley. New York: Pilgrim Press, 1984.

Women's Studies: An Interdisciplinary Collection, edited by Kathleen O'Connor Blumhagen and Walter D. Johnson. Westport, CT: Greenwood Press, 1978.

Women's Travel Issues: Research Needs and Priorities: conference proceedings and papers/U.S. Department of Transportation, Research and Special Programs Administration. Washington: U.S.G.P.O., 1980.

The Writer on Her Work, edited by Janet Sternburg. New York: Norton, 1980.

Ye Are Free to Choose, edited by Maren M. Mouritsen. Provo, UT: Brigham Young University Publications, 1981.

Young Women and Employment: What We Know and Need to Know About the School-To-Work Transition: report of a conference. Washington: U.S. Department of Labor, Employment and Training Administration, Women's Bureau, 1978.

Zak, Michele Wender. Women and the Politics of Culture: Studies in the Sexual Economy, by Michele Wender Zak and Patricia A. Moots. New York: Longman, 1983.

The Zero People: Essays on Life, edited by Jeff Lane Hensley. Ann Arbor, MI: Servant Books, 1983.

AUTHOR INDEX

Aal, Deborah.
"Statement." In U.S. Congress. House. Select Committee on Children, Youth, and Families. Violence and Abuse in American Families, p. 14-18.

Abernethy, Ann Greenawalt.
"Unbinding for Life." In Spinning a Sacred Yarn, p. 3-8.

Abramowitz, Elizabeth A.
"Statement on Behalf of the President." In U.S. Women's Bureau. Native American Women and Equal Opportunity, p. 2.

Abrams, Ann Uhry.
"Frozen Goddess: The Image of Women in Turn-of-the-Century American Art." In Conference on the History of Women (1977: St. Paul, MN). Woman's Being, Woman's Place, p. 93-108.

Abramson, Edith R.
"Statement." In U.S. Congress. House. Committee on Ways and Means. Subcommittee on Social Security. Social Security Dependents' Benefits, p. 52.

Abzug, Bella S.
"Making Change." In Women in Crisis Conference (1st: 1979: New York, NY). Women in Crisis, p. 236-42.
"Speech by Bella Abzug, Presiding Officer." In U.S. National Committee on the Observance of International Women's Year. The Spirit of Houston, p. 217-219.
"Statement." In U.S. Congress. House. Committee on Armed Services. Subcommittee on Military Personnel. Hearings on H.R. 6569, Registration of Women. Washington: U.S.G.P.O., 1981, p. 66-76.
"Statement." In U.S. Congress. Senate. Committee on Labor and Human Resources. The Coming Decade, p. 443-46, 480-2.
"Statement." In U.S. Congress. Senate. Committee on the Judiciary. Subcommittee on the Constitution. Constitutional Amendments Relating to Abortion, v. 1, p. 1147-50.

Acevedo, Raydean.
 "Statement." In U.S. Congress. Senate. Committee on the
  Judiciary. Subcommittee on the Constitution. Constitutional
  Amendments Relating to Abortion, v. 1, p. 1045-46.

Acord, Lea.
 "Statement." In U.S. Congress. House. Committee on Post
  Office and Civil Service. Subcommittee on Compensation and
  Employee Benefits. Federal Pay Equity Act of 1984, pt. 1,
  p. 221-23.

Acosta, Katherine.
 "Testimony." In U.S. Commission on Civil Rights. Hearing before the U.S. Commission on Civil Rights held in Denver,
  1976, p. 231-33.

Addams, Jane.
 "Account of Her Interview with the Foreign Ministers of Europe
  (Carnegie Hall, N.Y., 9 July 1915)." In My Country is the
  Whole World, p. 86-7.
 "Child Labor Legislation--A Requisite for Industrial Efficiency."
  In Addams, Jane Addams on Education, p. 124-135.
 "Patriotism and Pacifists in War Time." In Addams, Peace and
  Bread in Time of War. Printed with Patriotism and Pacifists
  in War Time. Garland, 1971, p. 1-23.
 "The Public School and the Immigrant Child." In Addams, Jane
  Addams on Education, p. 136-42.
 "Recreation as a Public Function in Urban Communities." In
  Addams, Jane Addams on Education, p. 186-91.
 "Speech at Carnegie Hall, New York, 9 July, 1915." In My
  Country is the Whole World, p. 86-7.
 "The Subjective Necessity for Social Settlements." In Addams,
  Jane Addams on Education, p. 49-63. Also in Outspoken
  Women, p. 2-9.

Adherns, Diane.
 "Statement." In U.S. Congress. Senate. Committee on Labor
  and Human Resources. Subcommittee on Family and Human
  Services. Broken Families, pt. 2, p. 275-80.

Adler, Rachel.
 "A Mother in Israel: Aspects of the Mother-Role in Jewish Myth."
  In Beyond Androcentrism, p. 237-55.

Adlon, Suzanne Kunkel.
 "Sex Differences in Adjustment of Widowhood." In Women's Lives,
  p. 239-45.

Ahmad, Sharon E.
 "U.S.-Canada Relations." Dept. of State Bulletin, 80 (October
  1980), 20-3.

Aikens, Joan D.
"Working With the Federal Election Commission: Some Proposed Changes." Vital Speeches, 47 (February 15, 1981), 275-77.

Alake, Zakiya.
"Personal Report to the Conference on Women and Poverty in Massachusetts." Women's Studies Quarterly, 13 (Summer 1985), 8.

Albert, Ethel M.
"The Unmothered Woman." In The Challenge to Women, p. 34-50.

Albert, Margie.
"Testimony." In U.S. Commission on Civil Rights. Hearing Before the U.S. Commission on Civil Rights held in Chicago, 1974, p. 256-7, 259-65, 267-69.

Alden, Leslie.
"Statement." In U.S. Congress. House. Committee on Ways and Means. Subcommittee on Social Security. Social Security Dependents' Benefits, p. 26-9.

Aldrich, Michele.
"Statement." In Symposium on Minorities and Women in Science and Technology (1981: Washington, DC). Symposium on Minorities and Women in Science and Technology, p. 17-19.

Alexander, Cheryl S.
"Women as Victims of Crime." In The Changing Risk of Disease in Women, p. 81-7.

Alexander, Florence Hicks.
"Statement." In U.S. Congress. House. Committee on Government Operations. Manpower and Housing Subcommittee. The Women's Bureau, p. 201-3.

Alexander, Lenora Cole.
"Statement." In U.S. Congress. House. Committee on Government Operations. Manpower and Housing Subcommittee. The Women's Bureau, p. 115-22.
"Statement." In U.S. Congress. Joint Economic Committee. Problems of Working Women, p. 23-30.
"Testimony." In U.S. Congress. Senate. Committee on Labor and Human Resources. Woman in Transition 1983, p. 3-8.

Alford, Brenda.
"Statement." In U.S. Congress. House. Committee on Small Business. National Commission on Women's Business Ownership, p. 14-16.

Alford, Carolyn.
"Statement." In U.S. Congress. House. Select Committee on

Aging. Subcommittee on Health and Long-Term Care. Progress in Controlling Breast Cancer, p. 45-9.

Allen, Anita L.
"Women and Their Privacy: What Is at Stake?" In Beyond Domination, p. 233-49.

Allen, Christine Garside.
"Who Was Rebekah? 'On Me Be the Curse, My Son.'" In Beyond Androcentrism, p. 183-215.

Allen, Clara L.
"Statement." In U.S. Congress. Senate. Committee on Labor and Human Resources. The Coming Decade, pt. 2, p. 2-6.

Allen, Marylee.
"Statement." In U.S. Congress. House. Committee on Ways and Means. Subcommittee on Public Assistance and Unemployment Compensation. AFDC and Social Service Bills and Related Oversight Issues, p. 172-74.

Allen, Paula Gunn.
"Answering the Deer: Genocide and Continuance in American Indian Women's Poetry." In Coming to Light, p. 223-32.

Alley, Marilyn L.
"Statement." In U.S. Congress. House. Committee on Post Office and Civil Service. Subcommittee on Postal Personnel and Modernization. Racial Discrimination and Sexual Harassment in U.S. Postal Service, p. 13-17.
"Testimony." In U.S. Congress. House. Committee on Post Office and Civil Service. Subcommittee on Postal Personnel and Modernization. Equal Employment Opportunity and Sexual Harassment in the Postal Service, p. 73-75.

Allison, Dorothy.
"Public Silence, Private Terror." In Pleasure and Danger, p. 103-114.

Alpers, Svetlana.
"Art History and Its Exclusions: The Example of Dutch Art." In Feminism and Art History, p. 183-99.

Althouse, Lavonne.
"Love's Winning Circle (Easter)." In Women and the Word, p. 65-9.

Altman, Meryl.
"Everything They Always Wanted You To Know: The Ideology of Popular Sex Literature." In Pleasure and Danger, p. 115-130.

Ambrogi, Donna.
  "Excerpted Testimony from the Northern California Hearings on
    the Feminization of Poverty." Signs, 10 (Winter 1984), 401-2.

American, Sadie.
  "Organization." In U.S. Congress. Joint Economic Committee.
    The American Woman, p. 427-31.

Ampola, Mary G.
  "Prenatal Diagnosis." In The Custom-Made Child?, p. 75-80.

Amrane, Djamila.
  "Algeria: Anticolonial War." In Female Soldiers--Combatants or
    Noncombatants?, p. 123-36.

Anderson, Dianne Luce.
  "Jeanie Drake: A South Carolina Writer Overlooked." In Rey-
    nolds Conference (2nd: 1975: University of South Carolina).
    South Carolina Women Writers, p. 1-13.

Anderson, Livina Field.
  "Mary Fielding Smith: Her Ox Goes Marching On." In Blue-
    prints for Living, v.2, p. 2-13.

Anderson, Susan B.
  "Statement." In U.S. Congress. House. Select Committee on
    Aging. Problems of Aging Women, p. 116-9.

Andrulis, Marilyn.
  "Statement." In U.S. Congress. Senate. Select Committee on
    Small Business. Women-In-Business Programs in the Federal
    Government, p. 38-41.
  "Testimony. In U.S. Congress. House. Committee on Small
    Business. Subcommittee on General Oversight and Minority
    Enterprises. Women in Business, p. 113-7.

Anglin, Mary.
  "Redefining the Family and Women's Status Within the Family:
    The Case of Southern Appalachia." In Feminist Visions, p.
    110-18.

Anthony, Susan Brownell.
  "Address of Susan B. Anthony," also known as the "Constitu-
    tional Argument." In We Shall Be Heard, p. 78-87.
  "Constitutional Argument." In Stanton, Elizabeth Cady Stanton,
    p. 152-65.
  "Demand for Party Recognition." In Outspoken Women, p. 11-16.
  "Guaranteed to Us and Our Daughters Forever." In Women's
    America, p. 205-8.
  "Homes of Single Women." In Stanton, Elizabeth Cady Stanton,
    p. 146-51.

"Response to the NAWSA Resolution Disavowing The Woman's
Bible." In Stanton, Elizabeth Cady Stanton, p. 243-44.
"Suffrage and the Working Woman." In Stanton, Elizabeth Cady
Stanton, p. 139-45.
"Woman Wants Bread, Not the Ballot!" In Zak, Michele, Women
and the Politics of Culture, p. 351-4.

Antler, Joyce.
"Culture, Service, and Work: Changing Ideals of Higher Educa-
tion for Women." In The Undergraduate Woman, p. 15-42.
"Was She a Good Mother? Some Thoughts on a New Issue for
Feminist Biography." In Berkshire Conference on the History
of Women (5th: 1982: Vassar College). Women and the
Structure of Society, p. 53-66.

Antonucci, Toni.
"The Need for Female Role Models in Education." In Women and
Educational Leadership, p. 185-96.

Apodaca, Pauline.
"Migrant Workers: A Report from the Clinic." In Health Needs
of the World's Poor Women, p. 61-3.

Aptheker, Bettina.
"On 'The Damnation of Women': W. E. B. DuBois and a Theory
for Woman's Emancipation." In Aptheker, Woman's Legacy,
p. 77-88.
"Quest for Dignity: Black Women in the Professions, 1865-1900."
In Aptheker, Woman's Legacy, p. 89-110.
"Woman Suffrage and the Crusade Against Lynching, 1890-1920."
In Aptheker, Woman's Legacy, p. 53-76.

Archer, Leonie J.
"The Role of Jewish Women in the Religion, Ritual and Cult of
Graeco-Roman Palestine." In Images of Women in Antiquity,
p. 273-87.

Armstrong, Virginia.
"Statement." In U.S. Congress. House. Committee on Post Of-
fice and Civil Service. Subcommittee on Investigations.
Sexual Harassment in the Federal Government, pt. 1, p. 134-5.

Arnold, Marilyn.
"Pornography, Romance, and the Paradox of Freedom." In Ye
Are Free to Choose, p. 50-62.
"Reading and Loving Literature." In Blueprints for Living, v.
2, p. 61-73.

Aroskar, Mila A.
"Toward 1999: Probing Ethical Dilemmas in Nursing's Future."
In Prospectives for Nursing, p. 11-6.

Arri, Julia K.
    "Testimony." In U.S. Congress. Senate. Special Committee on
        Aging. Adapting Social Security to a Changing Work Force,
        p. 62-66.

Ashley, Mary Jane.
    "Women, Alcohol, and the Risk of Disease." In The Changing
        Risk of Disease in Women, p. 89-105.

Astin, Helen Stavridou.
    "Patterns of Women's Occupations." In Psychology of Women, p.
        257-83.

Atwell, Mary Welek.
    "Elsie Dinsmore Haunting the Minds of Millions of Women." In
        Conference on "Scholars and Women" (1981: University of
        Maryland). Women's Studies and the Curriculum, p. 147-57.

Auchincloss, Eva.
    "Statement." In U.S. Congress. Senate. Committee on the
        Judiciary. Subcommittee on the Constitution. Civil Rights
        Act of 1984, p. 356-58.

Auerbach, Nina.
    "Dorothy Sayers and the Amazons." Feminist Studies, 3 (1976),
        54-62.
    "The Materfamilias: Power and Presumption." In Women and
        Men, p. 132-39.

Auerbach, Sylvia.
    "Personal Economics for Today's Woman." In Women in Manage-
        ment, p. 15-30.

Austin, Severa.
    "Plenary Session: Intervention/Service Delivery Systems." In
        Women in Crisis Conference (1st: 1979: New York, NY).
        Women in Crisis, p. 108-15.

Avery, Mary Ellen.
    "Statement." In U.S. Congress. Senate. Committee on the
        Judiciary. Subcommittee on Separation of Powers. The Hu-
        man Life Bill, p. 78-9.

Avery, Valeen Tippets.
    "Emma Smith: An Unknown Sister." In Blueprints for Living,
        v. 2, p. 25-31.

Avner, Judith I.
    "Statement." In U.S. Congress. Senate. Committee on Finance.
        Potential Inequities Affecting Women, pt. 2, p. 103-5.

Axelsen, Diana E.
    "Decisions About Handicapped Newborns: Values and Proce-
        dures." In The Custom-Made Child?, p. 135-44.

Babbott, Joan.
    "Statement." In U.S. Congress. Senate. Committee on Labor
        and Human Resources. Oversight on Family Planning Pro-
        grams, p. 217-8.

Bacon, Sylvia.
    "Statement." In U.S. Congress. House. Committee on the
        Judiciary. Subcommittee on Criminal Justice. Privacy of
        Rape Victims, p. 25-30.
    "H.R. 14666 The Privacy Protection for Rape Victims Act of
        1976." Women Lawyers Journal, 63 (Winter 1977), 10-2.

Bader, Jean.
    "Statement." In U.S. Congress. House. Select Committee on
        Aging. Subcommittee on Retirement Income and Employment.
        Impact of Reagan Economics on Aging Women, p. 23-5.

Badran, Margot.
    "Contamination in Practice." In Health Needs of the World's Poor
        Women, p. 98-102.

Baer, Peggy.
    "Statement." In California. Legislature. Joint Committee on
        Legal Equality. Women in the Justice System, p. 76-7.

Bagnal, Anne.
    "Statement." In U.S. Congress. House. Committee on Ways
        and Means. Subcommittee on Social Security. Treatment of
        Men and Women Under the Social Security Program, p. 178-83.

Bailey, Patricia P.
    "Thanks for the Gender Gap." Ms., 12 (March 1984), 118.

Bailyn, Lotte.
    "The Apprenticeship Model of Organizational Careers: A Re-
        sponse to Changes in the Relation Between Work and Family."
        In Women in the Workplace, p. 45-58.

Baird, Shirley.
    "Statement." In U.S. Congress. Senate. Committee on Small
        Business. Federal Contracting Opportunities for Minority and
        Women-Owned Businesses, p. 107-9.

Baker, Kathy.
    "Statement." In U.S. Congress. House. Committee on the

Budget. Task Force on Entitlements, Uncontrollables, and Indexing. Women and Children in Poverty, p. 10-13.

Bako, Yolanda.
    "Networking." In Report of the YWCA National Consultation for Programs on Domestic Violence, p. 30-32.
    "Statement." In U.S. Congress. House. Committee on Science and Technology. Subcommittee on Domestic and International Scientific Planning, Analysis, and Cooperation, Research into Violent Behavior: Overview and Sexual Assaults, p. 650-57.

Balch, Emily Greene.
    "Human Nature Seems to Me Like the Alps." In Balch, Beyond Nationalism, p. 193.
    "The Many-Sided Approach to World Organization: Private, Functional, Governmental or the Political Expression of World Unity (Part II of Nobel Lecture, 1948)." In Balch, Beyond Nationalism, p. 231-38.
    "Nobel Lecture" (April 7, 1948-Oslo, Norway)." Bulletin of the Atomic Scientists, 35, (April 1979), 1.
    "The Self-Defeating Character of Coercion." In Balch, Beyond Nationalism, p. 220-22.
    "The Slow Growth Toward a World Community. Part I of Nobel Lecture, Oslo, 1948." In Balch, Beyond Nationalism, p. 131-38.
    "Temptations to Neo-Imperialism." In Balch, Beyond Nationalism, p. 182.
    "The Time to Make Peace." In Outspoken Women, p. 17-20.
    "Towards a Planetary Civilization." In Balch, Beyond Nationalism, p. 162-64.
    "The United Nations: What It Is and What It May Be." In Balch, Beyond Nationalism, p. 127-30.
    "What It Means to Be an American." In Balch, Beyond Nationalism, p. 34-40.

Baldwin, Pat.
    "Statement." In U.S. Congress. Senate. Committee on Labor and Human Resources. Sex Discrimination in the Workplace, 1981, p. 511.

Baldwin, Wendy H.
    "Statement." In U.S. Congress. House. Committee on Post Office and Civil Service. Subcommittee on Census and Population. Demographics of Adolescent Pregnancy in the United States, p. 27-9.
    "Statement." In U.S. Congress. House. Select Committee on Children, Youth, and Families. Teen Parents and Their Children, p. 8-12.
    "Statement." In U.S. Congress. House. Select Committee on Population. Fertility and Contraception, pt. 2, p. 3-12.
    "Testimony." In U.S. Congress. House. Committee on Education

and Labor. Subcommittee on Select Education. Adolescent
Pregnancy, p. 23-4.
"Testimony." In U.S. Congress. Senate. Committee on Human
Resources. Adolescent Health, Services and Pregnancy Pre-
vention and Care Act of 1978, p. 203-5.

Ballard, Bettina.
"Women and Fashion." In Cooper Union for the Advancement of
Science and Art, Women, Society and Sex, p. 229-48.

Ballif, Jae R.
"Welcome (to Panel on Mormon Women: A Response to the World)."
In Blueprints For Living, p. 90-1.

Bane, Mary Jo.
"The American Divorce Rate: What Does It Mean? What Should
We Worry About?" In The Challenge of Change, p. 181-98.
"Statement." In U.S. Congress. House. Committee on Ways
and Means. Subcommittee on Public Assistance and Unemploy-
ment Compensation. Teenage Pregnancy Issues, p. 70-2.

Bankart, Brenda.
"From Our Work and Experience: Questions for the Academy."
In GLCA Women's Studies Conference (6th: 1980). Toward
a Feminist Transformation of the Academy, II, p. 1-3.

Barajas, Gloria.
"Statement." In U.S. Congress. House. Committee on Post Of-
fice and Civil Service. Subcommittee on Compensation and
Employee Benefits. Options for Conducting a Pay Equity
Study, p. 640-2.

Barazzone, Esther L.
"Women and the Scottish Enlightenment." In Sisterhood Surveyed, p. 56-63.

Bardwick, Judith M.
"The Seasons of a Woman's Life." In Women's Lives, p. 35-57.

Barlow, Sally.
"A Response, and More Questions." In Blueprints For Living,
p. 107-11.

Barnes, Carolyn.
"Strengthening Voltaic Women's Roles in Development (Upper
Volta)." In International Conference on Women and Food
(1978: University of Arizona). A Conference on the Role of
Women in Meeting Basic Food and Water Needs in Developing
Countries, p. 71-4.

Barnes, Hazel E.
"Apologia Pro Vita Mae. The Ideal Portrait of a University
Teacher." Vital Speeches, 47 (May 15, 1981), 473-5.

Barnes, Helen B.
"Reproduction, Obstetric Care, and Infertility." In Women: A
Developmental Perspective, p. 255-8.
"Response (to the Depo-Provera Weapon)." In Birth Control and
Controlling Birth, p. 117-20.
"Statement." In U.S. Congress. House. Select Committee on
Population. Fertility and Contraception in America, pt. 3,
p. 4-5.

Barr, Jennifer.
"Statement." In U.S. Congress. Senate. Committee on the
Judiciary. Subcommittee on Criminal Law. Impact of Media
Coverage of Rape Trials, p. 51-4.

Barrett, Nancy Smith.
"Comment on 'New Evidence on the Dynamics of Female Labor
Supply.'" In Conference on Women in the Labor Market
(1977: Barnard College). Women in the Labor Market, p.
111-6.

Barry, Kathleen.
"Beyond Pornography: From Defensive Politics to Creating a
Vision." In Take Back the Night, p. 307-12.

Barry, Lenora.
"Report of the General Investigator, 1887." In Victorian Women,
p. 401-3.
"Report of the General Investigator, 1889." In Victorian Women,
p. 403-4.

Barstow, Anne Llewellyn.
"An Ambiguous Legacy: Anglican Clergy Wives After the Reformation." In Women in New Worlds, v. 2, p. 97-111.

Bart, Pauline B.
"Dirty Books, Dirty Films, and Dirty Data." In Take Back the
Night, p. 204-17.

Bartlett, Linda.
"Coping with Illegal Sex Discrimination." In The Woman In Management, p. 40-4.

Bass, Charlotta.
"It Is the Call of All My People And To My People." National
Guardian, 4 (April 2, 1952), 3.

Battistella, Alison.
  "Statement." In U.S. Congress. House. Select Committee on
    Children, Youth, and Families. Children, Youth, and Fam-
    ilies, p. 76.

Bauer, Mary.
  "Testimony." In U.S. Congress. Senate. Committee on Labor
    and Human Resources. Women in Transition, 1983, p. 101-2.

Baum, Joanne.
  "Coping Patterns in Widowhood." In Women's Lives, p. 247-55.

Baumann, Marie.
  "Two Features of 'Women's Speech?'" In Conference on the So-
    ciology of the Languages of American Women (1976: New
    Mexico State University). Proceedings, p. 33-40.

Bay, Edna.
  "Summary of Panel on Developing Country Women's Perceptions
    of Food/Nutrition Problems." In International Conference on
    Women and Food (1978: University of Arizona). A Confer-
    ence on the Role of Women in Meeting Basic Food and Water
    Needs in Developing Countries, p. 43-4.

Bayne, Susan.
  "Statement." In U.S. Congress. House. Select Committee on
    Population. Fertility and Contraception in America, p. 239-42.

Bazemore, Agnes.
  "Statement." In U.S. Congress. House. Committee on Ways
    and Means. Subcommittee on Social Security. Treatment of
    Men and Women Under the Social Security Program, p. 129-30.

Bean, Joan P.
  "The Development of Psychological Androgyny: Early Childhood
    Socialization." In Conference on Non-Sexist Early Childhood
    Education (1976: Arden House). Perspectives on Non-Sexist
    Early Childhood Education, p. 94-100.

Beaudry, Jo.
  "Testimony." In U.S. Congress. Senate. Committee on the
    Judiciary. Subcommittee on Criminal Law. Impact of Media
    Coverage of Rape Trials, p. 71-3.

Beerhalter, Barbara.
  "Statement." In U.S. Congress. House. Committee on Post
    Office and Civil Service. Subcommittee on Compensation and
    Employee Benefits. Federal Pay Equity Act of 1984, pt. 2,
    p. 139-41.

Behr, Marion R.
  "Statement." In U.S. Congress. Senate. Committee on Labor

and Human Resources. Subcommittee on Labor. Amending the Fair Labor Standards Act to Include Industrial Homework, p. 78-81.

Belcher, La Rue.
  "Testimony." In U.S. Commission on Civil Rights. Hearing before the U.S. Civil Rights Committee held at Denver, 1976, p. 380-1, 387-8.

Bell, Carolyn Shaw.
  "Implementing Safety and Health Regulations for Women in the Workplace." In Feminist Studies, 5 (Summer 1979), 286-301.
  "Panel Discussion of Societal Responsibilities as Seen By Women." In Conference on Women and the Workplace (1976: Washington, DC). Conference on Women and the Workplace, p. 316-20.
  "Statement." In U.S. Congress. Joint Economic Committee. Problems of Working Women, p. 67-72.

Bell, Connie.
  "Statement." In U.S. Congress. Senate. Committee on Finance. Potential Inequities Affecting Women, pt. 2, p. 178-9.

Bell, Elouise.
  "All Write, All Write." In Blueprints For Living, v. 2, p. 74-81.

Bell, Susan Groag.
  "Christiane De Pizan (1364-1430): Humanism and the Problem of a Studious Woman." Feminist Studies, 3 (1976), 173-84.

Bellamy, Carol.
  "Keynote Address." In Warner, Anne R. Health Womenpower, p. 11-6.
  "Problems of Older Women: Implementing Public Policy Change." In Older Women in the City, p. 183-88.
  "Statement." In U.S. Congress. House. Committee on Education and Labor. Oversight on the Impact of the Administration Fiscal 1986 Budget Proposals on Programs Under the Jurisdiction of the Committee on Education and Labor. Washington: U.S.G.P.O., 1985, p. 148-76.
  "Statement." In U.S. Congress. House. Committee on Government Operations. Government Activities and Transportation Subcommittee. Federal Support For Urban Mass Transit--New York and Chicago. Washington: U.S.G.P.O., 1985, p. 10-21.
  "Statement." In U.S. Congress. House. Committee on Government Operations. Intergovernmental Relations and Human Resources Subcommittee. The Federal Response to the Homeless Crisis. Washington: U.S.G.P.O., 1985, p. 653-74.
  "Statement." In U.S. Congress. House. Committee on Ways and Means. Subcommittee on Oversight. Impact of the Administration's Proposed Budget Cuts on Children. Washington: U.S.G.P.O., 1982, p. 72-80.

"Statement." In U.S. Congress. House. Select Committee on
Aging. Subcommittee on Retirement Income and Employment.
Administration's Plan to Eliminate Older Workers Jobs Program.
Washington: U.S.G.P.O., 1982, p. 95-8.
"Statement." In U.S. Congress. Senate. Committee on Environ-
ment and Public Works. Infrastructure and Jobs. Washington:
U.S.G.P.O., 1983, pt. 2, p. 231-37.
"Statement." In U.S. Congress. Senate. Committee on Labor
and Human Resources. Subcommittee on Employment, Poverty,
and Migratory Labor. Youth Employment and Welfare Reform
Jobs, 1980. Washington: U.S.G.P.O., 1980, p. 244-87.
"Statement." In U.S. Congress. Senate. Committee on the
Judiciary. Subcommittee on Separation of Powers. The Hu-
man Life Bill, p. 758-66.

Bellanca, Dorothy Jacobs.
"Sister Dorothy Jacobs Bellanca, Union Leader, Makes a Report:
1940." In The American Jewish Woman, p. 798-801.

Belle, Deborah.
"Mothers and Their Children: A Study of Low-Income Families."
In The Evolving Female, p. 74-91.

Beller, Andrea H.
"The Impact of Equal Employment Opportunity Laws on the Male-
Female Earnings Differential. In Conference on Women in the
Labor Market (1977: Barnard College). Women in the Labor
Market, p. 304-30.
"Occupational Segregation and the Earnings Gap." In Compar-
able Worth: Issues for the Eighties, p. 15-18.
"Testimony." In U.S. Equal Employment Opportunity Commission.
Hearing Before the U.S. Equal Employment Opportunity Com-
mission on Job Segregation and Wage Discrimination, p. 293-
304.
"Trends in Occupational Segregation by Sex and Race, 1960-
1981." In Sex Segregation in the Workplace, p. 11-26.

Bellinger, Mary Ann.
"Upright But Not Uptight." In Those Preachin' Women, p. 69-76.

Bellows, Barbara L.
"'My Children, Gentlemen, Are My Own': Poor Women, the Urban Elite and the Bonds of Obligation in Antebellum Charleston." In The Web of Southern Social Relations, p. 52-71.

Belovitch, Tamara E.
"The Experience of Abortion." In The Evolving Female, p. 92-
106.

Bem, Sandra Lipsitz.
"Beyond Androgyny: Some Presumptuous Prescriptions for a
Liberated Sexual Identity." In Psychology of Women, p. 1-23.

Bendix, Helga M.
"Rights of a Handicapped Neonate: What Every Parent and Professional Should Know." In The Custom-Made Child?, p. 147-54.

Bendor, Jan.
"Statement." In U.S. Congress. House. Committee on Science and Technology. Subcommittee on Domestic and International Scientific Planning, Analysis, and Cooperation. Research Into Violent Behavior: Overview and Sexual Assaults, p. 436-41.

Benesch, Joan S.
"Statement." In U.S. Congress. House. Select Committee on Population. Fertility and Contraception in America, pt. 2, p. 102-11.

Benjamin, Jessica.
"The Bonds of Love: Rational Violence and Erotic Domination." In The Future of Difference, p. 41-66.

Bennett, Sheila Kishler.
"Undergraduates and Their Teachers: An Analysis of Student Evaluations of Male and Female Instructors." In The Undergraduate Woman, p. 251-74.

Bennett, Stephanie M.
"The Re-Entry Woman. Prospects and Challenges." Vital Speeches, 46 (June 1, 1980), 502-5.

Benson, Lucy Wilson.
"Antarctica: 10th Meeting of Treaty Consultative Parties." Dept. of State Bulletin, 79 (November 1979), 22-3.
"Munitions Sales to Saudi Arabia." Dept. of State Bulletin, 80 (March 1980), 63-4.
"Science and Technology; Their Interaction with Foreign Policy." Dept. of State Bulletin, 78 (October 1978), 54-6.
"Science and Technology: U.S. Approach to the UNCSTD." Dept. of State Bulletin, 79 (September 1979), 58-60.

Benson, Susan Porter.
"Women in Retail Sales Work: The Continuing Dilemma in Service." In My Troubles Are Going To Have Trouble With Me, p. 113-23.

Bentley, Helen Delich.
"Statement." In U.S. Congress. House. Committee on Appropriations. Subcommittee on Energy and Water Development. Energy and Water Development Appropriations for 1986. Washington: U.S.G.P.O., 1985, pt. 8, p. 469-518.

Benton, Marjorie.
  "Statement." In U.S. Congress. House. Select Committee on
  Children, Youth, and Families. Children, Youth, and Families,
  p. 68.

Bere, Phyllis.
  "Testimony." In U.S. Commission on Civil Rights. Hearing Before the U.S. Commission on Civil Rights held in Chicago,
  1974, v. 1, p. 404-8.

Beresford, Terry.
  "Statement." In U.S. Congress. Senate. Committee on the
  Judiciary. Subcommittee on the Constitution. Constitutional
  Amendments Relating to Abortion, v. 1, p. 273-6.

Bergen, Polly.
  "Blueprint For the Top Manager--Me." In Women In Management,
  p. 1-14.

Berger, Brigitte.
  "Occupational Segregation and the Earnings Gap." In Comparable
  Worth: Issues for the Eighties, p. 26-8.
  "Statement." In U.S. Congress. Senate. Committee on Labor
  and Human Resources. Subcommittee on Family and Human
  Services. Broken Families, pt. 2, p. 358-61.

Berggren, Anne-Marie.
  "Education and Equality for Women." In Cornell Conference on
  Women (1969: Cornell University). Proceedings, p. 43-4, 46.
  "Is the Question of Women A Political Question?" In Cornell
  Conference on Women (1969: Cornell University). Proceed-
  ings, p. 21, 26-8.

Berglin, Linda.
  "Statement." In U.S. Congress. House. Committee on Post Office and Civil Service. Subcommittee on Compensation and
  Employee Benefits. Federal Pay Equity Act of 1984, pt. 2,
  p. 176-78.

Bergman, Sherrie S.
  "Library Resources on Women." In Toward a Balanced Curriculum, p. 127-34.

Bergmann, Barbara R.
  "The Economic Case for Comparable Worth." In Comparable Worth:
  New Directions for Research, p. 71-85.
  "The Housewife and Social Security Reform: A Feminist Perspec-
  tive." In A Challenge to Social Security, p. 229-34.
  "Statement." In U.S. Congress. Joint Economic Committee.
  American Women: Three Decades of Change, p. 32-5.
  "Statement." In U.S. Congress. Joint Economic Committee.

Economic Status of Women, p. 69-73.
"Testimony." In U.S. Equal Employment Opportunity Commis-
sion. Hearing Before the U.S. Equal Employment Opportunity
Commission on Job Segregation and Wage Discrimination, p.
305-17.
"Testimony." In U.S. Congress. House. Select Committee on
Aging. Subcommittee on Retirement Income and Employment.
Task Force on Social Security and Women. Treatment of Wom-
en Under Social Security, p. 130-33.
"The United States of America." In Women Workers in Fifteen
Countries, p. 170-75.

Berkeley, Kathleen C.
"'Colored Ladies Also Contributed': Black Women's Activities
from Benevolence to Social Welfare, 1866-1896." In The Web
of Southern Social Relations, p. 181-203.

Berkman, Joyce Avrech.
"Historical Styles of Contraceptive Advocacy." In Birth Control
and Controlling Birth, p. 27-36.

Berman, Joan R. Saks.
"Ethical Feminist Perspectives of Dual Relationships with Clients."
In Handbook of Feminist Therapy, p. 287-96.

Bernard, Jessie.
"Ground Rules for Marriage: Perspectives on the Pattern of an
Era." In The Challenge of Change, p. 97-122.

Bernhardt, Marybeth.
"Statement." In U.S. Congress. House. Committee on Small
Business. National Commission on Women's Business Owner-
ship, p. 19-22.

Bernikow, Louise.
"From Our Work and Experience: Questions for the Academy."
In GLCA Women's Studies Conference (6th: 1980). Toward
a Feminist Transformation of the Academy, II, p. 3-5.

Bernstein, Alison.
"Curriculum Reform, Or What Do You Mean, 'Our College Should
Have a Feminist Curriculum?'" In GLCA Women's Studies
Conference (5th: 1979). Toward a Feminist Transformation
of the Academy, p. 59-61.

Berrio, Margaret.
"Sex Differences in Choices of Toy and Modes of Play in Nursery
School." In GLCA Women's Studies Conference (4th: 1978:
Rochester, Indiana). Structure of Knowledge, p. 33-6.

Berry, Mary Frances.
"Deliberately Fraught With Difficulties: New Light on the History

of Constitutional Amendments and the Prospects for Women's Rights." Women's Studies Quarterly, 14 (Spring 1985), 2-7.

"Statement." In U.S. Congress. House. Committee on Education and Labor. Civil Rights Act of 1984, p. 93-5.

"Statement." In U.S. Congress. House. Committee on Government Operations. Manpower and Housing Subcommittee. Equal Employment Opportunity Commission's Handling of Pay Equity Cases, p. 271-3.

"Statement." In U.S. Congress. Committee on Post Office and Civil Service. Subcommittee on Compensation and Employee Benefits. Options for Conducting a Pay Equity Study, p. 583-6.

"Statement." In U.S. Congress. Senate. Committee on Labor and Human Resources. The Coming Decade, p. 720-22.

Bertina, Beverly.
"Statement." In U.S. Congress. House. Select Committee on Children, Youth, and Families. Families With Disabled Children, p. 3-6.

Bertrom, Linda.
"Testimony." In U.S. Commission on Civil Rights. Hearings Before the U.S. Commission on Civil Rights held in Denver, 1976, p. 476-7.

Berube, Susan C.
"Statement." In U.S. Congress. House. Committee on Government Operations. Intergovernmental Relations and Human Resources Committee. Barrier to Self-Sufficiency for Single Female Heads of Families, p. 422-25.

Bethune, Mary McLeod.
"The Association for the Study of Negro Life and History: Its Contributions to Our Modern Life." The Journal of Negro History, 20 (October 1935), 406-10.

"A Century of Progress of Negro Women." In Outspoken Women, p. 22-3.

"Clarifying Our Vision With the Facts." The Journal of Negro History, 23 (January 1938), 10-15.

"The Negro in Retrospect and Prospect." The Journal of Negro History, 35 (January 1950), 9-19.

Betz, Cheryl Y.
"Testimony." In U.S. Commission on Civil Rights. Hearing Before the U.S. Commission on Civil Rights held in Denver, 1976, p. 378-80.

Betz, Helen M.
"Testimony." In U.S. Congress. Senate. Committee on the Judiciary. Birth Control (1934), p. 63-4.

Bielby, Denise Del Vento.
"Career Commitment of Female College Graduates: Conceptualization and Measurement Issues." In The Undergraduate Woman, p. 337-50.

Bilinkoff, Jodi.
"The Holy Woman and the Urban Community in Sixteenth-Century Avila." In Berkshire Conference on the History of Women (5th: 1982: Vassar College). Women and the Structure of Society, p. 74-82.

Bingham, Eula.
"Conference Preview." In Conference on Women and the Workplace (1976: Washington, DC). Conference on Women and the Workplace, p. 2-4.
"Should the Congress Enact S. 2153 to Amend the Occupational Safety and Health Act." Congressional Digest, 59 (August-September 1980), 209, 211, 213.

Bird, Caroline M.
"Testimony." In U.S. Equal Employment Opportunity Commission. Hearings Before the U.S. Equal Employment Opportunity Commission on Job Segregation and Wage Discrimination, p. 111-26.
"Two Paycheck Power. Redesigning Jobs Around People." Vital Speeches, 46 (January 15, 1980), 202-5.

Bissette, Brenda K.
"The North Carolina Rape Kit Program." In Forensic Science Symposium on the Analysis of Sexual Assault Evidence (1983: Quantico, VA). Proceedings, p. 121.

Blair, Francine D.
"Occupational Segregation and Labor Market Discrimination." In Sex Segregation in the Workplace, p. 117-43.

Blair, Patricia W.
"The Women and Health Connection." In Health Needs of the World's Poor Women, p. 85-7.

Blake, Judith.
"Demographic Revolution and Family Evolution: Some Implications for American Women." In Women: A Developmental Perspective, p. 299-312.

Blanchard, Evelyn Lance.
"Observations on Social Work with American Indian Women." In NASW Conference on Social Work Practice With Women (1st: 1980: Washington, DC). Women, Power, and Change, p. 96-103.
"Organizing American Indian Women." In Conference on the

Educational and Occupational Needs of American Indian Women
(1976: Albuquerque, NM). Conference on the Educational
and Occupational Needs of American Indian Women, p. 123-39.

Blanchard, Mary Lou.
"Testimony." In U.S. Congress. House. Committee on Inter-
state and Foreign Commerce. Subcommittee on Health and the
Environment. Adolescent Health Services, p. 354-56.

Bland, Laurel L.
"Statement." In U.S. Congress. Senate. Committee on Small
Business. Federal Contracting Opportunities For Minority
and Women-Owned Businesses, p. 109-10.

Blank, Helen.
"Statement." In U.S. Congress. House. Committee on Govern-
ment Operations. Intergovernmental Relations and Human
Resources Subcommittee. Barrier to Self-Sufficiency for Single
Female Heads of Families, p. 177-83.
"Statement." In U.S. Congress. House. Committee on Ways
and Means. Economic Equity Act and Related Tax and Pen-
sion Reform, p. 151-52.
"Statement." In U.S. Congress. Joint Economic Committee.
Problems of Working Women, p. 97-101.
"Statement." In U.S. Congress. Senate. Committee on Finance.
Potential Inequities Affecting Women, pt. 2, p. 187-8.

Blau, Francine D.
"Concluding Remarks." In Sex Segregation in the Workplace, p.
310-19.
"The Impact of the Unemployment Rate on Labor Force Entries
and Exits." In Conference on the National Longitudinal Sur-
veys of Mature Women (1978: U.S. Dept. of Labor). Women's
Changing Roles At Home and On the Job, p. 263-86.
"Occupational Segregation and Labor Market Discrimination." In
Sex Segregation In the Workplace, p. 117-43.

Blaunstein, Phyllis.
"Testimony." In U.S. Congress. House. Committee on Energy
and Commerce. Subcommittee on Health and the Environment.
Health and the Environment Miscellaneous, pt. 3, p. 958-9.

Blechman, Elaine A.
"Behavior Therapies." In Women and Psychotherapy, p. 217-44.

Bleser, Carol K.
"The Perrys of Greenville: A Nineteenth-Century Marriage."
In The Web of Southern Social Relations, p. 72-89.

Block, Jeanne H.
"Another Look at Sex Differentiation in the Socialization Behaviors

of Mothers and Fathers." In Psychology of Women, p. 29-87.
"Psychological Development of Female Children and Adolescents."
In Women: A Developmental Perspective, p. 107-24.

Block, Marilyn.
"Testimony." In U.S. Congress. House. Select Committee on
Aging. Subcommittee on Retirement Income and Employment.
Task Force on Social Security and Women. Treatment of Wom-
en Under Social Security, p. 48-52.

Blockwick, Jessma.
"Testimony." In U.S. Congress. Senate. Committee on Human
Resources. Adolescent Health, Services, p. 443-46.

Bloom, Anne R.
"Israel: The Longest War." In Female Soldiers, p. 137-62.

Bloomquist, Karen L.
"The Yes That Heals Our Paralysis." In Women and the Word,
p. 22-5.

Bloomrosen, Meryl.
"Testimony." In U.S. Congress. House. Committee on Energy
and Commerce. Subcommittee on Health and the Environment.
Health and the Environment Miscellaneous, pt. 4, p. 427-8.

Blos, Joan W.
"Newbery Medal Acceptance." Horn Book, 56 (1980), 369-73.

Blum, Barbara B.
"Statement." In U.S. Congress. House. Committee on the
Budget. Task Force on Entitlements, Uncontrollables, and
Indexing. Women and Children in Poverty, p. 89-91.
"Statement." In U.S. Congress. House. Committee on Ways
and Means. Subcommittee on Public Assistance and Unemploy-
ment Compensation. Teenage Pregnancy Issues, p. 137-39.
"Testimony." In U.S. Congress. Senate. Committee on Human
Resources. Adolescent Health, Services, and Pregnancy Pre-
vention Care Act of 1978, p. 334-40.

Blume, Sheila B.
"Motivation and the Alcoholic Women." In Conference on Women
in Crisis (1st: 1979: New York, NY). Women in Crisis, p.
128-32.
"Testimony." In U.S. Congress. House. Committee on Energy
and Commerce. Subcommittee on Health and the Environment.
Health and the Environment Miscellaneous, pt. 5, p. 440-42.

Bodek, Evelyn Gordon.
"Salonieres and Bluestockings: Educated Obsolescence and Ger-
minating Feminist." Feminist Studies, 3 (1976), 185-99.

Bogdan, Janet.
    "The Transition from Parenting to Working and Parenting." In
    <u>Women and Educational Leadership</u>, p. 209-22.

Boggs, Elizabeth M.
    "Statement." In U.S. Congress. Senate. Committee on Finance.
    <u>Potential Inequities Affecting Women</u>, pt. 2, p. 199-200.

Boggs, Lindy (Corrine C.).
    "Statement." In U.S. Congress. House. Committee on Appro-
      priations. Subcommittee on Energy and Water Development.
      <u>Energy and Water Development Appropriations for 1984</u>.
      Washington: U.S.G.P.O., 1984, pt. 8, p. 1156-75.
    "Statement." In U.S. Congress. House. Committee on Appro-
      priations. Subcommittee on the Departments of Labor, Health
      and Human Services, Education, and Related Agencies. <u>De-
      partments of Labor, Health and Human Services, Education,
      and Related Agencies Appropriations for 1982</u>. Washington:
      U.S.G.P.O., 1981, pt. 8, p. 13-30.
    "Statement." In U.S. Congress. House. Committee on Appro-
      priations. Subcommittee on the Departments of Labor, Health
      and Human Services, Education, and Related Agencies. <u>De-
      partments of Labor, Health and Human Services, Education,
      and Related Agencies Appropriations for 1983</u>. Washington:
      U.S.G.P.O., 1982, pt. 8, p. 754-73.
    "Statement." In U.S. Congress. House. Committee on Appro-
      priations. Subcommittee on the Departments of Labor, Health
      and Human Services, Education, and Related Agencies. <u>De-
      partments of Labor, Health and Human Services, Education,
      and Related Agencies Appropriations for 1984</u>. Washington:
      U.S.G.P.O., 1983, pt. 8, p. 107-28.
    "Statement." In U.S. Congress. House. Committee on Appro-
      priations. Subcommittee on the Departments of Labor, Health,
      and Human Services, Education, and Related Agencies. <u>De-
      partments of Labor, Health and Human Services, Education,
      and Related Agencies Appropriations for 1985</u>. Washington:
      U.S.G.P.O., 1984, pt. 3, p. 443-54.
    "Statement." In U.S. Congress. House. Committee on Appro-
      priations. Subcommittee on the Departments of Labor, Health
      and Human Services, Education, and Related Agencies. <u>De-
      partments of Labor, health and Human Services, Education,
      and Related Agencies Appropriations for 1986</u>. Washington:
      U.S.G.P.O., 1985, pt. 10, p. 824-38.
    "Statement." In U.S. Congress. House. Committee on Appro-
      priations. Subcommittee on the Department of the Interior
      and Related Agencies. <u>Department of the Interior and Related
      Agencies Appropriations for 1984</u>. Washington: U.S.G.P.O.,
      1983, pt. 12, p. 904-48.
    "Statement." In U.S. Congress. House. Committee on Appro-
      priations. Subcommittee on Department of Transportation and
      Related Agencies Appropriations. <u>Federal Aviation Administration</u>

Plan For Office and Facility Consolidation. Washington:
U.S.G.P.O., 1984, p. 37-41.
"Statement." In U.S. Congress. House. Committee on Banking,
Finance, and Urban Affairs. Subcommittee on Housing and
Community Development. Federal Flood Insurance--1983.
Washington: U.S.G.P.O., 1983, p. 19-41.
"Statement." In U.S. Congress. House. Committee on Educa-
tion and Labor. Oversight on the Federal Role in Education.
Washington: U.S.G.P.O., 1985, pt. 1, p. 15-8.
"Statement." In U.S. Congress. House. Committee on Educa-
tion and Labor. Subcommittee on Employment Opportunities.
Oversight Hearings on Equal Employment Opportunity and Af-
firmative Action. Washington: U.S.G.P.O., 1985, v. 1, p.
157-62.
"Statement." In U.S. Congress. House. Committee on Energy
and Commerce. Subcommittee on Fossil and Synthetic Fuels.
Energy Security Policy. Washington: U.S.G.P.O., 1985,
p. 404-5.
"Statement." In U.S. Congress. House. Committee on Energy
and Commerce. Subcommittee on Health and the Environment.
Pregnancy-Related Health Services, p. 46-7.
"Statement." In U.S. Congress. House. Committee on Energy
and Commerce. Subcommittee on Oversight and Investigations.
Infant Mortality Rates: Failure to Close the Black-White Gap.
Washington: U.S.G.P.O., 1984, p. 24-8.
"Statement." In U.S. Congress. House. Committee on Govern-
ment Operations. Government Information, Justice, and Agri-
culture Subcommittee. Review of the Administration's Drug
Interdiction Efforts. Washington: U.S.G.P.O., 1983, p.
386-7.
"Statement." In U.S. Congress. House. Committee on Interior
and Insular Affairs. Subcommittee on Mining, Forest Manage-
ment, and Bonneville Power Administration. Consideration of
Legislation to Restrict the Department of the Interior's Oil and
Gas Leasing Program on the Outer Continental Shelf. Wash-
ington: U.S.G.P.O., 1984, p. 228-31.
"Statement." In U.S. Congress. House. Committee on Interior
and Insular Affairs. Subcommittee on Public Lands and Na-
tional Parks. Public Land Management Policy. Washington:
U.S.G.P.O., 1983, pt. 9, p. 46-9.
"Statement." In U.S. Congress. House. Committee on Merchant
Marine and Fisheries. Subcommittee on Merchant Marine.
Competitive Shipping and Shipbuilding Act of 1983. Washing-
ton: U.S.G.P.O., 1983, p. 25-36.
"Statement." In U.S. Congress. House. Committee on Merchant
Marine and Fisheries. Subcommittee on Merchant Marine.
Maritime Redevelopment. Washington: U.S.G.P.O., 1983,
p. 406.
"Statement." In U.S. Congress. House. Committee on Merchant
Marine and Fisheries. Subcommittee on Merchant Marine. Port
Development. Washington: U.S.G.P.O., 1983, v. 1, p. 27-30.

"Statement." In U.S. Congress. House. Committee on Merchant Marine and Fisheries. Subcommittee on Merchant Marine. <u>United States Public Health Service Hospitals and Clinics</u>. Washington: U.S.G.P.O., 1981, p. 364-6.

"Statement." In U.S. Congress. House. Committee on Post Office and Civil Services. Subcommittee on Compensation and Employee Benefits. <u>Federal Pay Equity Act of 1984</u>, pt. 2, p. 93-4.

"Statement." In U.S. Congress. House. Committee on Public Works and Transportation. Subcommittee on Aviation. <u>DOT / FAA Proposed New Policy for Airports in the Metropolitan Washington Area</u>. Washington: U.S.G.P.O., 1980, p. 311-15.

"Statement." In U.S. Congress. House. Committee on Public Works and Transportation. Subcommittee on Water Resources. <u>Proposed Water Resources Development Projects of the U.S. Army Corps of Engineers</u>. Washington: U.S.G.P.O., 1983, p. 1807-18.

"Statement." In U.S. Congress. House. Committee on Science and Technology. Subcommittee on Domestic and International Scientific Planning, Analysis, and Cooperation. <u>Research into Violent Behavior: Domestic Violence</u>, p. 4-7.

"Statement." In U.S. Congress. House. Committee on Small Business. <u>National Commission on Women's Business Ownership</u>, p. 35-8.

"Statement." In U.S. Congress. House. Committee on Small Business. Subcommittee on General Oversight and Minority Enterprise. <u>Women In Business</u>, p. 9-10.

"Statement." In U.S. Congress. House. Committee on Veterans' Affairs. Select Subcommittee to Review WASP Bills. <u>To Provide Recognition to the Women's Air Force...</u>, p. 231-33.

"Statement." In U.S. Congress. House. Committee on Veterans' Affairs. Subcommittee on Hospitals and Health Care. <u>VA 5-year Major Medical Facilities Construction Plans</u>. Washington: U.S.G.P.O., 1981, p. 34-8.

"Statement." In U.S. Congress. House. Select Committee on Aging. <u>Long-Term Care for the Elderly: Louisiana's Experience</u>. Washington: U.S.G.P.O., 1985, p. 506.

"Statement." In U.S. Congress. House. Select Committee on Children, Youth, and Families. <u>Families in Crisis</u>, p. 1-2.

"Statement." In U.S. Congress. Joint Economic Committee. <u>Economic Status of Women</u>, p. 6.

"Statement." In U.S. Congress. Senate. Committee on Commerce, Science, and Transportation. Subcommittee on Merchant Marine. <u>Cargo Preference</u>. Washington: U.S.G.P.O., 1984, p. 61-9.

"Statement." In U.S. Congress. Senate. Committee on Environment and Public Works. Subcommittee on Water Resources. <u>Water Resource Projects in Louisiana</u>. Washington: U.S.G.P.O., 1983, p. 2-5.

Bohachevsky-Chomiak, Martha.
"Ukrainian Feminism in Interwar Poland." In Women, State, and Party in Eastern Europe, p. 82-97.

Boland, Janet.
"Statement." In U.S. Congress. House. Committee on Post Office and Civil Service. Subcommittee on Compensation and Employee Benefits. Federal Pay Equity Act of 1984, pt. 2, p. 170-3.

Bolin, Winifred D. Wandersee.
"American Woman and the Twentieth-Century Work Force: The Depression Experience." In Conference on the History on Women (1977: St. Paul, MN). Woman's Being, Woman's Place, p. 296-312.

Bolton, Frances P.
"Statement." In U.S. Congress. House. Committee on Veterans' Affairs. Select Subcommittee to Review WASP Bills. To Provide Recognition to the Women's Air Force..., p. 103-7.
"Treatment of Indians in South Africa." Department of State Bulletin, 29 (November 23, 1953), 728-30.

Bonder, Evelyn.
"Testimony." In U.S. Congress. House. Select Committee on Aging. Subcommittee on Retirement Income and Employment. Task Force on Social Security and Women. Treatment of Women Under Social Security, p. 153.

Bonder, Gloria.
"The Educational Process of Women's Studies in Argentina: Reflections on Theory and Technique." In Gendered Subjects, p. 64-77.

Boneparth, Ellen.
"Evaluating Women's Studies: Academic Theory and Practice." In Women's Studies, p. 21-9.

Bonner, Deanne.
"Women as Caregivers." Women's Studies Quarterly, 13 (Summer 1985), 11.

Bonsaro, Carol A.
"Affirmative Action and the Continuing Majority: Women of All Races and Minority Men." In Covert Discrimination and Women in the Sciences, p. 45-63.
"Women's Rights, ERA, and After." In Western Regional Civil Rights and Women's Rights Conference (4th: 1977: San Francisco, CA). Recent Development, p. 68-78.

Booker, Marjorie Leeper.
"A Prescription for Humility." In Those Preachin' Women, p. 85-92.

Bordin, Ruth.
"A Baptism of Power and Liberty": The Women's Crusade of 1873-1874." In Conference on the History of Women (1977: St. Paul, MN). Woman's Being, Woman's Place, p. 283-95.

Boroviak, Darlene L.
"The Social Sciences: Establishing Gender as a Category." In Toward a Balanced Curriculum, p. 42-8.

Boulding, Elise.
"Integration into What? Reflections on Development Planning for Women-Alternatives to Integration for Women." In Women and Technological Change in Developing Countries, p. 9-32.

Bouquard, Marilyn Lloyd see Lloyd, Marilyn

Bowen, Louise De Koven.
"Address at Juvenile Protective Association Dinner." In Bowen, Speeches, Addresses and Letters, p. 800-2.
"Address on the Juvenile Protective Association of Chicago." In Bowen, Speeches, Addresses and Letters, p. 448-66.
"Address to Woman's City Club." In Bowen, Speeches, Addresses and Letters, p. 814-7.
"Annual Meeting of the J.P.A. 'Nobody Cared.'" In Bowen, Speeches, Addresses and Letters, p. 764-7.
"Annual Meeting of United Charities." In Bowen, Speeches, Addresses and Letters, p. 430-2.
"Before the Resolutions Committee of the Republican National Convention." In Bowen, Speeches, Addresses and Letters, p. 234-6.
"Birth Control." In Bowen, Speeches, Addresses and Letters, p. 817-8.
"Campaign Against Segregation." In Bowen, Speeches, Addresses and Letters, p. 725-6.
"Campaign to Elect Mr. Robert Hall McCormick, Alderman." In Bowen, Speeches, Addresses and Letters, p. 473-5.
"Can Children Afford It?" In Bowen, Speeches, Addresses and Letters, p. 795-9.
"Child Labor Amendment." In Bowen, Speeches, Addresses and Letters, p. 695-8.
"Christmas." In Bowen, Speeches, Addresses and Letters, p. 97-100.
"Dedication of Boys' Club Building Hull-House." In Bowen, Speeches, Addresses and Letters, p. 114-7.
"Dedication of Children's Building Mary Crane Nursery, Hull-House." In Bowen, Speeches, Addresses and Letters, p. 108-13.

and Letters, p. 62-7.

"The Juvenile Court." (1913) In Bowen, Speeches, Addresses and Letters, p. 286-306.

"Lessons from Other Lands for the Conduct of Life in Ours." In Bowen, Speeches, Addresses and Letters, p. 101-7.

"Mary Rozet Smith Memorial." In Bowen, Speeches, Addresses and Letters, p. 832-3.

"Mass Meeting." In Bowen, Speeches, Addresses and Letters, p. 731-3.

"Mass Meeting of Women Voters to Protest Against the Spoils System and to Discuss and Adopt a Woman's Municipal Platform." In Bowen, Speeches, Addresses and Letters, p. 375-84.

"Mass Meeting, Woman's Roosevelt Republican Club." In Bowen, Speeches, Addresses and Letters, p. 761-2.

"Meeting on High Cost of Living." In Bowen, Speeches, Addresses and Letters, p. 528-9.

"A Memorial Day in the Country." In Bowen, Speeches, Addresses and Letters, p. 838-42.

"Mexico." In Bowen, Speeches, Addresses and Letters, p. 45-58.

"The Minimum Wage." In Bowen, Speeches, Addresses and Letters, p. 228-31.

"Money-Raising for Campaign." In Bowen, Speeches, Addresses and Letters, p. 684-90.

"National Urban League Annual Conference." In Bowen, Speeches, Addresses and Letters, p. 629-32.

"A Nature Talk." In Bowen, Speeches, Addresses and Letters, p. 72-84.

"The Need of Protective Work in Illinois." In Bowen, Speeches, Addresses and Letters, p. 577-601.

"The Need of Recreation." In Bowen, Speeches, Addresses and Letters, p. 144-51.

"Needed Legislation Suggested by Experiences in the Lower North District." In Bowen, Speeches, Addresses and Letters, p. 132-36.

"New Year's Talk." In Bowen, Speeches, Addresses and Letters, p. 334-7.

"On to the Polls!" In Bowen, Speeches, Addresses and Letters, p. 428-30.

"Opening of Hull-House Woman's Club." In Bowen, Speeches, Addresses and Letters, p. 68-70.

"Opening Remarks at the Speakers Institute, Woman's Department Fair Price Commission. January 20th, 1920." In Bowen, Speeches, Addresses and Letters, p. 525-7.

"Pan-American Congress of Women. Political Status of Women." In Bowen, Speeches, Addresses and Letters, p. 658-62.

"Pan-American Congress of Women. Prevention of Traffic in Women." In Bowen, Speeches, Addresses and Letters, p. 656-8.

"Pan-American Congress of Women. Welcome to Child Welfare Conference." In Bowen, Speeches, Addresses and Letters, p. 652-3.

"Pan-American Congress of Women. Women in Industry." In
Bowen, Speeches, Addresses and Letters, p. 654-5.
"Political Meeting." (1916) In Bowen, Speeches, Addresses and
Letters, p. 477-9.
"President's Address." (1916) In Bowen, Speeches, Addresses
and Letters, p. 433-42.
"President's Address." (1917) In Bowen, Speeches, Addresses
and Letters, p. 467-73.
"President's Address--Juvenile Protection Association." (1919)
In Bowen, Speeches, Addresses and Letters, p. 507-18.
"President's Address to Juvenile Protective Association." (1922)
In Bowen, Speeches, Addresses and Letters, p. 643-6.
"President's Address to Juvenile Protective Association." (1924)
In Bowen, Speeches, Addresses and Letters, p. 734-9.
"President's Address to Juvenile Protective Association." (1925)
In Bowen, Speeches, Addresses and Letters, p. 748-52.
"The Primary Elections Campaign." In Bowen, Speeches, Ad-
dresses and Letters, p. 768-74.
"Protest Against Endorsement of Certain Candidates." In Bowen,
Speeches, Addresses and Letters, p. 740-1.
"Protest Against Endorsement of Governor Len Small." In Bowen,
Speeches, Addresses and Letters, p. 726-7.
"Remarks at Farewell Dinner to Sherman C. Kingsley." In Bow-
en, Speeches, Addresses and Letters, p. 445-7.
"Remarks at Mass Meeting." (1922) In Bowen, Speeches, Ad-
dresses and Letters, p. 690-2.
"Remarks by the President Before Juvenile Protective Associa-
tion." In Bowen, Speeches, Addresses and Letters, p. 601-
10.
"Remarks: Conference of State Chairman. Woman's Committee,
Council of National Defense." In Bowen, Speeches, Ad-
dresses and Letters, p. 475-6.
"The Renewal of Life." In Bowen, Speeches, Addresses and
Letters, p. 85-93.
"The Rights of Children." In Bowen, Speeches, Addresses and
Letters, p. 93-7.
"Report of Nominating Committee to Juvenile Protective Associa-
tion." In Bowen, Speeches, Addresses and Letters, p. 833-6.
"Report of the Districts Committee." In Bowen, Speeches, Ad-
dresses and Letters, p. 827-32.
"Report on the Pan-American Congress." (League of Women Vot-
ers) In Bowen, Speeches, Addresses and Letters, p. 667-70.
"Report on the Pan-American Congress." (Woman's City Club)
In Bowen, Speeches, Addresses and Letters, p. 664-7.
"Roosevelt Club Banquet." In Bowen, Speeches, Addresses and
Letters, p. 728-30.
"Roosevelt Club Luncheon." (1921) In Bowen, Speeches, Ad-
dresses and Letters, p. 692-4.
"Roosevelt Club Luncheon." (1926) In Bowen, Speeches, Ad-
dresses and Letters, p. 777-9.
"Ruth Hanna McCormick for Congressman-at-Large." In Bowen,

Speeches, Addresses and Letters, p. 804-7.

"Second Woman's World Fair." In Bowen, Speeches, Addresses and Letters, p. 779-80.

"Segregation." In Bowen, Speeches, Addresses and Letters, p. 723-5.

"Speech Before Chicago Association of Commerce." In Bowen, Speeches, Addresses and Letters, p. 619-23.

"Speech Delivered Before the Hamilton Club." In Bowen, Speeches, Addresses and Letters, p. 536-40.

"Substitute for the Saloon." In Bowen, Speeches, Addresses and Letters, p. 501-2.

"Talk to Junior League." In Bowen, Speeches, Addresses and Letters, p. 482-7.

"Talk to Probation Officers, Cook County Juvenile Court." In Bowen, Speeches, Addresses and Letters, p. 117-22.

"Talk to Students in Miss Harris School and Presentation of Medals." In Bowen, Speeches, Addresses and Letters, p. 681-4.

"Ten Years of Work." In Bowen, Speeches, Addresses and Letters, p. 540-58.

"To Welcome Back the Boys of Hull-House Boy's Club and Hull-House Band." In Bowen, Speeches, Addresses and Letters, p. 519-21.

"Two Years of Effort." In Bowen, Speeches, Addresses and Letters, p. 488-95.

"United Charities Luncheon." In Bowen, Speeches, Addresses and Letters, p. 787-9.

"Urging Election of Mr. Alexander A. McCormick as President of Board of Cook County Commissioners." In Bowen, Speeches, Addresses and Letters, p. 237-9.

"A Visit in Constantinople." In Bowen, Speeches, Addresses and Letters, p. 27-45.

"What There Is For Women To Do In Chicago." In Bowen, Speeches, Addresses and Letters, p. 306-33.

"Wolf in Sheep's Clothing." In Bowen, Speeches, Addresses and Letters, p. 372-5.

"Woman's City Club." In Bowen, Speeches, Addresses and Letters, p. 365-72.

"Woman's City Club Dinner." In Bowen, Speeches, Addresses and Letters, p. 632-4.

"Woman's Roosevelt Republican Club Banquet to Mr. and Mrs. Nicholas Longworth." In Bowen, Speeches, Addresses and Letters, p. 762-3.

"Woman's Roosevelt Republican Club Luncheon to Vice-President Dawes." In Bowen, Speeches, Addresses and Letters, p. 763-4.

"Woman's Roosevelt Republican Club Reception and Tea." In Bowen, Speeches, Addresses and Letters, p. 761-2.

"The Woman's World Fair." In Bowen, Speeches, Addresses and Letters, p. 752-7.

Bowles, Gloria.
"Is Women's Studies An Academic Discipline?" In Theories of
Women's Studies, p. 1-11.

Bowman, Barbara T.
"Sexism and Racism in Education." In Conference on Non-Sexist
Early Childhood Education (1976: Arden House). Perspectives
on Non-Sexist Early Childhood Education, p. 25-39.

Bowman, Heidi.
"Statement." In U.S. Congress. House. Select Committee on
Children, Youth, and Families. Children, Youth and Families,
p. 70-1.

Boxer, Barbara.
"Statement." In U.S. Congress. House. Committee on Appro-
priations. Subcommittee on the Departments of Labor, Health
and Human Services, Education, and Related Agencies. De-
partments of Labor, Health and Human Services, Education,
and Related Agencies Appropriations for 1984. Washington:
U.S.G.P.O., 1983, pt. 9, p. 392-7.
"Statement." In U.S. Congress. Committee on Appropriations.
Subcommittee on the Department of the Interior and Related
Agencies. Department of the Interior and Related Agencies
Appropriations for 1984. Washington: U.S.G.P.O., 1983,
pt. 12, p. 253-64.
"Statement." In U.S. Congress. House. Committee on Appro-
priations. Subcommittee on the Department of the Interior
and Related Agencies. Department of the Interior and Re-
lated Agencies Appropriations for 1986. Washington:
U.S.G.P.O., 1985, p. 1223-8.
"Statement." In U.S. Congress. House. Committee on Appro-
priations. Subcommittee on Department of Transportation and
Related Agencies Appropriations. Department of Transporta-
tion and Related Agencies Appropriations for 1984. Washing-
ton: U.S.G.P.O., 1983, pt. 7, p. 687-701.
"Statement." In U.S. Congress. House. Committee on Armed
Services. Subcommittee on Military Installations and Facilities.
Hearing on H.R. 1816 (H.R. 2972) to Authorize Certain Con-
struction at Military Installations for Fiscal Year 1984, and
For Other Purposes... Washington: U.S.G.P.O., 1983, p.
854-9.
"Statement." In U.S. Congress. House. Committee on Armed
Services. Subcommittee on Military Installations and Facilities.
Hearings on H.R. 4931 (H.R. 5704), to Authorize Certain
Construction at Military Installations for Fiscal Year 1985, and
For Other Purposes. Washington: U.S.G.P.O., 1984, p.
762-72.
"Statement." In U.S. Congress. House. Committee on Energy
and Commerce. Subcommittee on Energy Conservation and
Power. Auto Fuel Efficiency Standards. Washington:

U.S.G.P.O., 1983, p. 4-5.

"Statement." In U.S. Congress. House. Committee on Foreign Affairs. Proposal to Ban Nuclear Testing. Washington: U.S.G.P.O., 1985, p. 43-54.

"Statement." In U.S. Congress. House. Committee on Government Operations. Commerce, Consumer, and Monetary Affairs Subcommittee. Federal Response to Criminal Misconduct By Bank Officers, Directors, and Insiders. Washington: U.S.G.P.O., 1984, pt. 1, p. 167-70.

"Statement." In U.S. Congress. House. Committee on Government Operations. Intergovernmental Relations and Human Resources Subcommittee. Federal Response to AIDS. Washington: U.S.G.P.O., 1983, p. 4-5, 257.

"Statement." In U.S. Congress. House. Committee on Government Operations. Manpower and Housing Subcommittee. The Women's Bureau, p. 18-20.

"Statement." In U.S. Congress. House. Committee on House Administration. Task Force on Elections. Campaign Finance Reform. Washington: U.S.G.P.O., 1984, p. 439-50.

"Statement." In U.S. Congress. House. Committee on Interior and Insular Affairs. Subcommittee on Mining, Forest Management, Bonneville Power Administration. Consideration of Legislation to Restrict the Department of the Interior's Oil and Gas Leasing Program on the Outer Continental Shelf. Washington: U.S.G.P.O., 1984, p. 16-8.

"Statement." In U.S. Congress. House. Committee on Merchant Marine and Fisheries. Subcommittee on the Panama Canal/ Outer Continental Shelf. Offshore Oil and Gas Oversight. Washington: U.S.G.P.O., 1984, p. 13-6.

"Statement." In U.S. Congress. House. Committee on Post Office and Civil Service. Subcommittee on Compensation and Employee Benefits. Federal Employees Health Benefits Reform Act of 1983. Washington: U.S.G.P.O., 1984, p. 237-41.

"Statement." In U.S. Congress. House. Committee on Post Office and Civil Service. Subcommittee on Compensation and Employee Benefits. Federal Pay Equity Act of 1984, pt. 2, p. 92-3.

"Statement." In U.S. Congress. House. Committee on Public Works and Transportation. Subcommittee on Public Buildings and Grounds. Potential Health Hazards Associated with the Use of Asbestos- Containing Material in Public and Private Facilities. Washington: U.S.G.P.O., 1984, p. 25-7.

"Statement." In U.S. Congress. House. Committee on Public Works and Transportation. Subcommittee on Surface Transportation. Highway Needs in the Santa Rosa, CA Region. Washington: U.S.G.P.O., 1985, p. 116-8.

"Statement." In U.S. Congress. House. Committee on Small Business. Small Business Administration Disaster Assistance Programs. Washington: U.S.G.P.O., 1983, p. 6-13.

"Statement." In U.S. Congress. House. Committee on Small Business. Subcommittee on General Oversight and the

Economy. <u>Competition in Federal Procurement</u>. Washington:
U.S.G.P.O., 1984, p. 5-18.
"Statement." In U.S. Congress. House. Committee on Veterans'
Affairs. Subcommittee on Compensation, Pension, and Insur-
ance. <u>H.R. 1961--Vietnam Veterans Agent Orange Relief Act</u>.
Washington: U.S.G.P.O., 1983, p. 96-100.
"Statement." In U.S. Congress. Senate. Committee on the
Budget. <u>Economic Impact of the FY 1986 Budget Proposals
on the State of Indiana</u>. Washington: U.S.G.P.O., 1985,
p. 14-7.

Boyd-Franklin, Nancy.
"Black Family Life-Styles: A Lesson in Survival." In <u>Class,
Race, and Sex</u>, p. 189-99.

Boyle, Patricia.
"Testimony." In U.S. Congress. House. Committee on the
Judiciary. Subcommittee on Criminal Justice. <u>Privacy of
Rape Victims</u>, p. 77-84.

Brackbill, Yvonne.
"Drugs, Birth, and Ethics." In <u>Birth Control and Controlling
Birth</u>, p. 175-82.

Bracken, Janice M.
"Advent III." In <u>Women of the Word</u>, p. 22-5.
"Lent I." In <u>Women of the Word</u>, p. 26-9.
"Pentecost VI." In <u>Women of the Word</u>, p. 30-3.

Bradford, Naomi.
"Testimony." In U.S. Commission on Civil Rights. <u>Hearing
Before the U.S. Commission on Civil Rights held in Denver,
1976</u>, p. 276-80, 284.

Bradley, Valerie Jo.
"It Happened on My Birthday." In Miniconsultation on the Mental and Physical Health Problems of Black Women (1974:
Washington, DC). <u>Miniconsultation on the Mental and Physical Health Problems of Black Women</u>, p. 103-10.

Bradshaw, Gail M.
"Statement." In U.S. Congress. House. Committee on Educa-
tion and Labor. Subcommittee on Employment Opportunities.
<u>Oversight Hearings on Equal Employment Opportunity and
Affirmative Action</u>, pt. 2, p. 185-7.

Bradshaw, Roxanne.
"Statement." In U.S. Congress. House. Committee on Post Of-
fice and Civil Service. Subcommittee on Compensation and
Employee Benefits. <u>Options for Conducting a Pay Equity
Study</u>, p. 642-4.

Brady, Katherine.
"Statement." In U.S. Congress. Senate. Committee on the
Judiciary. Subcommittee on Juvenile Justice. Effect of
Pornography on Women and Children, p. 55-66.

Branca, Patricia.
"Image and Reality: The Myth of the Idle Victorian Women."
In Clio's Consciousness Raised, p. 179-89.

Brandwein, Ruth A.
"Toward Androgyny in Community and Organizational Practice."
In NASW Conference on Social Work Practice With Women (1st:
1980: Washington, DC). Women, Power, and Change, p.
158-70.

Brannan, Emora T.
"A Partnership of Equality: The Marriage and Ministry of John
and Mary Goucher." In Women in New Worlds, v. 2, p. 132-
47.

Braun, Betty.
"Statement." In U.S. Congress. House. Select Committee on
Aging. Problems of Aging Women, p. 18-20.

Brazile, Donna.
"Statement." In U.S. Congress. House. Committee on Post Of-
fice and Civil Service. Subcommittee on Compensation and
Employee Benefits. Options for Conducting a Pay Equity
Study, p. 637-9.

Breen, Aviva.
"Statement." In U.S. Congress. House. Committee on Government Operations. Intergovernmental Relations and Human Resources Subcommittee. Barriers to Self-Sufficiency for Single
Female Heads of Families, p. 208-11.

Breen, Edith.
"Toward Freedom and Self-Determination: New Directions in Mental Health Services." In Toward the Second Decade, p. 83-92.

Brenzel, Barbara.
"Lancaster Industrial School for Girls: A Social Portrait of a
Nineteenth-Century Reform School for Girls." Feminist Studies,
3 (1976), 40-53.

Brereton, Virginia Lieson.
"Preparing Women for the Lord's Work: The Story of Three
Methodist Training Schools, 1880-1940." In Women in New
Worlds, v. 1, p. 178-99.

Brewer, Margaret A.
"Statement." In U.S. Congress. House. Committee on Armed

Services. Subcommittee on Military Personnel. <u>Women in the Military</u>, p. 331-3.

Bricker-Jenkins, Mary.
"Statement." In U.S. Congress. Senate. Committee on the Judiciary. Subcommittee on the Constitution. <u>Constitutional Amendments Relating to Abortion</u>, v. 1, p. 1140-3.

Bridenthal, Renate.
"The Family: The View From a Room of Her Own." In <u>Rethinking the Family</u>, p. 225-39.
"Notes Toward a Feminist Dialectic." In <u>Class, Race, and Sex</u>, p. 3-9.

Briggs, Sheila.
"Images of Women and Jews in Nineteenth-and Twentieth-Century German Theology." In <u>Immaculate & Powerful</u>, p. 226-259.

Brinton, Louise A.
"Etiologic Factors for Invasive and Noninvasive Cervical Abnormalities." In <u>The Changing Risk of Disease in Women</u>, p. 199-210.

Brinton, Sally Peterson.
"The Blessing of Music in the Home." In <u>A Woman's Choices</u>, p. 79-85.

Briscoe, Anne M.
"Scientific Sexism: The World of Chemistry." In <u>Women in Scientific and Engineering Professions</u>, p. 147-59.
"Statement." In U.S. Congress. Senate. Committee on Labor and Human Resources. Subcommittee on Health and Scientific Research. <u>Women in Science and Technology Equal Opportunity Act, 1979</u>, p. 75-9.

Brookins, Louise.
"Statement." In U.S. Congress. House. Committee on Ways and Means. Subcommittee on Public Assistance and Unemployment Compensation. <u>AFDC and Social Service Bills and Related Oversight Issues</u>, p. 110-12.

Brooks, Evelyn.
"The Feminist Theology of the Black Baptist Church, 1880-1900." In <u>Class, Race, and Sex</u>, p. 31-59.

Brookshire, Karla.
"Testimony." In U.S. Commission on Civil Rights. <u>Hearing Before the U.S. Commission on Civil Rights held at Denver, 1976</u>, p. 161-63.

Brophy, Alice M.
  "Older Women in New York City--Today and Tomorrow." In
  Older Women in the City, p. 1-15.

Brothers, Joyce.
  "Testimony." In U.S. Congress. House. Select Committee on
  Aging. Subcommittee on Retirement Income and Employment.
  National Policy Proposals Affecting Midlife Women, p. 7-19.

Broude, Norma.
  "Degas's 'Misogyny.'" In Feminism and Art History, p. 247-69.
  "Miriam Schapiro and 'Femmage': Reflections on the Conflict
  Between Decoration and Abstraction in Twentieth-Century
  Art." In Feminism and Art History, p. 315-29.

Brown, Anna V.
  "Statement." In U.S. Congress. Senate. Special Committee on
  Aging. Women in Our Aging Society, p. 78-84.

Brown, Clair Vickery.
  "Home Production for Use in a Market Economy." In Rethinking
  the Family, p. 151-67.

Brown, Cynthia G.
  "Statement." In U.S. Congress. House. Committee on Educa-
  tion and Labor. Civil Rights Act of 1984, p. 71-2.
  "Statement." In U.S. Congress. Senate. Committee on Labor
  and Human Resources. Subcommittee on Education, Arts and
  Humanities. Civil Rights of 1984, p. 375-7.

Brown, Helen S.
  "Statement." In U.S. Congress. House. Select Committee on
  Aging. Subcommittee on Retirement Income and Employment.
  Task Force on Social Security and Women. Treatment of Wom-
  en Under Social Security, v. 3, p. 48-9.

Brown, Joan.
  "Is the Question of Women a Political Question?" In Cornell Con-
  ference on Women (1969: Cornell University). Proceedings,
  p. 31.
  "Child Bearing, Child Rearing, Abortion and Contraception."
  In Cornell Conference on Women (1969: Cornell University).
  Proceedings, p. 56-7.

Brown, Judie.
  "Statement." In U.S. Congress. Senate. Committee on Labor
  and Human Resources. Oversight on Family Planning Programs, p. 118-9.
  "Testimony." In U.S. Congress. House. Committee on Energy
  and Commerce. Subcommittee on Health and the Environment.
  Health and the Environment Miscellaneous, pt. 3, p. 513-14.

Brown, Karen McCarthy.
"Why Women Need the War God." In Women's Spirit Bonding,
p. 190-201.

Brown, Laura.
"Ethics and Business Practice in Feminist Therapy." In Handbook of Feminist Therapy, p. 297-304.

Brown, Lynne H.
"Involvement of Students in Research Projects." In Women in
Engineering--Beyond Recruitment, p. 98-105.

Brown, Marcia.
"Caldecott Medal Acceptance." Horn Book, 59 (1983), 414-22.

Brown, Marsha D.
"Career Plans of College Women: Patterns and Influences." In
The Undergraduate Women, p. 303-36.

Brown, Myrtle L.
"Black Women's Nutritional Problems." In Women: A Developmental Perspective,p. 167-78.

Brown, Nan M.
"The Mind of the Insecure." In Those Preachin' Women, p. 61-8.

Brown, Norma E.
"Statement." In U.S. Congress. House. Committee on Armed
Services. Subcommittee on Military Personnel. Women in the
Military, p. 330-1.

Brown, Olympia.
"Address on Woman Suffrage (n.d.: after 1909)." In Brown,
Suffrage and Religious Principle, p. 154-8.
"Christian Charity: A Doctrinal Sermon for Universalists (February 18, 1872)." In Brown, Suffrage and Religious Principle, p. 79-88.
"Crime and the Remedy (September 22, 1893)." In Brown, Suffrage and Religious Principle, p. 131-8.
"Hand of Fellowship (February 19, 1868)." In Brown, Suffrage
and Religious Principle, p. 67-9.
"On Foreign Rule." In Zak, Michele, Women and the Politics of
Culture, p. 363-5.
"On Margaret Fuller." In Brown, Suffrage and Religious Principle, p. 53-8.
"The Opening Doors (September 12, 1920)." In Brown, Suffrage
and Religious Principle, p. 167-73.
"United States Citizenship (August 9, 1893)." In Brown, Suffrage and Religious Principle, p. 121-30.
"Where Is the Mistake? (February 21, 1890)." In Brown, Suffrage and Religious Principle, p. 112-20.

"Woman's Place in the Church (May 10, 1869)." In Brown, Suf-
frage and Religious Principle, p. 70-8.
"Woman's Suffrage (August 29, 1888)." In Brown, Suffrage and
Religious Principle, p. 109-11.
"Women and Skepticism (January 25, 1885)." In Brown, Suffrage
and Religious Principle, p. 99-108.

Brown, Patricia A.
"My Ministry as a Parish Secretary." In Conference on Women
and Lay Ministry (1976: St. Michel's Church, Milton, MA).
Conference on Women and Lay Ministry, p. 2-3.

Brown, Quincalee.
"Statement." In U.S. Congress. House. Committee on Post Office and Civil Service. Subcommittee on Compensation and
Employee Benefits. Federal Pay Equity Act of 1984, pt. 1,
p. 77-9.

Brown, Rita Mae.
"Violence." In Brown, R., A Plain Brown Rapper, p. 25-6.

Brown, Sue.
"Testimony." In U.S. Congress. Senate. Committee on the
Judiciary. Subcommittee on Juvenile Justice. Effect of Por-
nography on Women and Children, p. 182-4.

Brubaker, Cynthia C.
"Statement." In U.S. Congress. House. Committee on Ways
and Means. Economic Equity Act and Related Tax and Pension Reform, p. 174-5.

Brumberg, Joan Jacobs.
"The Case of Ann Hasseltine Judson: Missionary, Hagiography
and Female Popular Culture, 1815-1850." In Women in New
Worlds, v.2, p. 234-48.
"The Ethnological Mirror: American Evangelical Women and Their
Heathen Sisters, 1870-1910." In Berkshire Conference on the
History of Women (5th: 1982: Vassar College). Women and
the Structure of Society, p. 108-28.

Brummond, Naomi.
"Statement." In U.S. Congress. House. Committee on Ways
and Means. Subcommittee on Social Security. Treatment of
Men and Women Under the Social Security Program, p. 126-9.

Brunauer, Ester Caukin.
"Statement." In U.S. Congress. House. Committee on Foreign
Affairs. American Neutrality Policy, p. 378-87.

Brunson, Dorothy E.
"Statement." In U.S. Congress. House. Committee on Small

Business. National Commission on Women's Business Ownership, p. 48-9.

Bryant, Barbara Everett.
  "Statement." In U.S. Congress. Senate. Committee on the
  Judiciary. Subcommittee on the Constitution. Constitutional
  Amendments Relating to Abortion, v. 1, p. 936-8, 997-1001.

Bryant, Connie.
  "Statement." In U.S. Congress. House. Committee on Post
  Office and Civil Service. Subcommittee on Compensation and
  Employee Benefits. Options for Conducting a Pay Equity
  Study, p. 429-30.

Bryant, Donna.
  "Statement." In U.S. Congress. House. Committee on Ways
  and Means. Subcommittee on Public Assistance and Unemployment Compensation. Teenage Pregnancy Issues, p. 147-52.

Bryant, Ruth.
  "Inflation: The Seven Percent Solution. A Less Expansive Government." Vital Speeches, 46 (June 15, 1980), 520-22.

Bryce, Dorotea Lowe.
  "Issues in Afro-Hispanic Development." In Immigrants and Refugees in a Changing Nation, p. 125-32.

Buchanan, Mary I.
  "Excerpted Testimony From the Southern California Hearings on
  the Feminization of Poverty." Signs, 10 (Winter, 1984), 404.
  "Women, Poverty, and Economic Justice." In Women's Spirit
  Bonding, p. 3-10.

Buckley, Priscilla.
  "Speech at National Review's Thirtieth Anniversary Dinner."
  National Review, 37 (December 31, 1985), 126.

Bucknell, Susan.
  "Testimony." In U.S. Equal Employment Opportunity Commission.
  Hearings Before the U.S. Equal Employment Opportunity Com-
  mission on Job Segregation and Wage Discrimination, p. 443-58.

Buechler, Jan.
  "Statement." In U.S. Congress. House. Committee on Ways
  and Means. Subcommittee on Social Security. Treatment of
  Men and Women Under Social Security Program, p. 123-5.

Bunch, Charlotte.
  "Lesbianism and Erotica in Pornographic America." In Take Back
  the Night, p. 91-4.
  "Not For Lesbians Only." In Building Feminist Theory, p. 67-73.

"Speech at the National Women's Political Caucus Conference, July 1981." Ms, 10 (October, 1981), 94.

Bunting, Mary I.
  "The University's Responsibility in Educating Women for Leadership." In Education of Women for Social and Political Leadership, p. 40-50.

Burch, Beverly.
  "Another Perspective on Merger in Lesbian Relationships." In Handbook of Feminist Therapy, p. 100-9.

Burgess, Anne.
  "Statement." In U.S. Congress. House. Committee on Science and Technology. Subcommittee on Domestic and International Scientific Planning, Analysis, and Cooperation. Research into Violent Behavior: Overview and Sexual Assaults, p. 376-91.
  "Testimony." In U.S. Congress. Senate. Committee on the Judiciary. Subcommittee on Juvenile Justice. Effect of Pornography on Women and Children, p. 122-25.

Burgess, Geneva.
  "Statement." In U.S. Congress. House. Committee on Education and Labor. Subcommittee on Labor-Management Relations. Pension Equity for Women, p. 52-4.
  "Statement." In U.S. Congress. Senate. Committee on Finance. Potential Inequities Affecting Women, pt. 1, p. 243-4.

Burke, Carolyn G.
  "The New Poetry and the New Women: Mina Loy." In Coming To Light, p. 37-57.
  "Rethinking the Maternal." In The Future of Difference, p. 107-14.

Burke, Mary.
  "How Women Can Make a Difference." In International Conference on Women and Food (1978: University of Arizona). A Conference on the Role of Women in Meeting Basic Food and Water Needs in Developing Countries. p. 131-3.
  "Session Summary." In International Conference on Women and Food (1978: University of Arizona). A Conference on the Role of Women in Meeting Basic Food and Water Needs in Developing Countries. p. 159-62.

Burke, N. Peggy.
  "Power and Power Plays: Women as Leaders." Vital Speeches, 45 (January 15, 1979), 207.

Burke, Yvonne Braithwaite.
  "Economic Strength Is What Counts." In Women Organizing, p. 210-20.

Burks, Esther Lee.
"Career Interruptions and Perceived Discrimination Among Women Students in Engineering and Science." In Women in Engineering--Beyond Recruitment, p. 134-40.

Burlage, Dorothy D.
"Judaeo-Christian Influences on Female Sexuality." In Sexist Religion and Women in the Church, p. 93-116.

Burnett, K. Patricia.
"An Alternative Approach to Travel Demand Modeling: Constraints-Oriented Theories and Societal Roles." In Women's Travel Issues, p. 633-79.

Burnett, Marilou.
"Knots In the Family Tie." In Toward the Second Decade, p. 59-70.

Burris, Carol.
"Testimony." In U.S. Commission on Civil Rights. Hearing Before the U.S. Commission on Civil Rights held in Chicago, 1974, v. 1, p. 390-7.
"Testimony." In U.S. Congress. House. Select Committee on Aging. Subcommittee on Retirement Income and Employment. Task Force on Social Security and Women. Treatment of Women Under Social Security, p. 65.

Burstein, Karen.
"Notes from a Political Career." In Women Organizing, p. 49-60.

Burstyn, Joan N.
"Historical Perspectives on Women in Educational Leadership." In Women and Educational Leadership, p. 65-76.

Burt, Martha R.
"Statement." In U.S. Congress. House. Committee on Post Office and Civil Service. Subcommittee on Census and Population. Demographics of Adolescent Pregnancy in the United States, p. 62-5.
"Statement." In U.S. Congress. House. Committee on Science and Technology. Subcommittee on Domestic and International Scientific Planning, Analysis and Cooperation. Research into Violent Behavior: Overview and Sexual Assaults, p. 305-22.
"Testimony." In U.S. Congress. House. Committee on Energy and Commerce. Subcommittee on Health and Environment. Health and the Environment Miscellaneous, pt. 3, p. 976-7.

Burtle, Vasanti.
"Therapeutic Anger in Women." In Handbook of Feminist Therapy, p. 71-9.

Burton, Delores.
"Statement." In U.S. Congress. House. Committee on Post Office and Civil Service. Subcommittee on Compensation and Employee Benefits. Federal Pay Equity Act of 1984, pt. 1, p. 235-6.

Burton, Sala.
"Statement." In U.S. Congress. House. Committee on Appropriations. Subcommittee on the Departments of Labor, Health and Human Services, Education, and Related Agencies. Departments of Labor, Health and Human Services, Education, and Related Agencies Appropriations for 1986. Washington: U.S.G.P.O., 1985, pt. 9, p. 1-7.
"Statement." In U.S. Congress. Senate. Committee on Energy and Natural Resources. Subcommittee on Public Lands and Reserved Water. California Wilderness Act of 1983. Washington: U.S.G.P.O., 1984, p. 148-52.
"Statement." In U.S. Congress. House. Committee on Public Works and Transportation. Subcommittee on Public Buildings and Grounds. Potential Health Hazards Associated with the Use of Asbestos Containing Material in Public and Private Facilities. Washington: U.S.G.P.O., 1984, p. 4-25, 309.
"Statement." In U.S. Congress. House. Committee on the Judiciary. Subcommittee on Administrative Law and Governmental Relations. Japanese-American and Aleutian Wartime Relocation. Washington: U.S.G.P.O., 1985, p. 20-3.
"Statement." In U.S. Congress. House. Select Committee on Aging. Medicare and Acupuncture. Washington: U.S.G.P.O., 1984, p. 2-3.
"Statement." In U.S. Congress. House. Select Committee on Children, Youth, and Families. Child Care, Exploring Private and Public Sector Approaches. Washington: U.S.G.P.O., 1985, p. 3.

Butler, Alice.
"Individual Woman's Need of Birth Control." In American Birth Control Conference (1st: 1921: New York). Birth Control: What It Is, How It Works, What It Will Do, p. 37-9.

Butler, Johnnella E.
"The Humanities: Redefining the Canon." In Toward a Balanced Curriculum, p. 35-41.

Butler, Marylou.
"Guidelines for Feminist Therapy." In Handbook of Feminist Therapy, p. 32-8.

Byrd, Arkie.
"Statement." In U.S. Congress. House. Committee on Education and Labor. Subcommittee on Employment Opportunities. Oversight Hearings on the OFCCP's Proposed Affirmative

Action Regulations, p. 95-7.
"Statement." In U.S. Congress. House. Committee on Post Office and Civil Service. Subcommittee on Human Resources. Pay Equity, pt. 1, p. 102.
"Statement." In U.S. Congress. Senate. Committee on Labor and Human Resources. Sex Discrimination in the Workplace, 1981, p. 233-4.

Byrnes, Eleanor.
"Dual Career Couples: How the Company Can Help." In The Woman in Management, p. 49-53.

Byron, Beverly.
"Statement." In U.S. Congress. House. Committee on Appropriations. Subcommittee on the Department of the Interior and Related Agencies. Department of the Interior and Related Agencies Appropriations for 1984. Washington: U.S.G.P.O., 1983, pt. 12, p. 151-2.
"Statement." In U.S. Congress. House. Committee on Appropriations. Subcommittee on Department of the Interior and Related Agencies. Department of the Interior and Related Agencies Appropriations for 1985. Washington: U.S.G.P.O., 1984, pt. 1, p. 140-3.
"Statement." In U.S. Congress. House. Committee on Armed Services. Technology Transfer Panel. Technology Transfer. Washington: U.S.G.P.O., 1984, p. 265-71.
"Statement." In U.S. Congress. House. Committee on Energy and Commerce. Subcommittee on Fossil and Synthetic Fuels. Natural Gas Issues. Washington: U.S.G.P.O., 1983, p. 1005-18.
"Statement." In U.S. Congress. House. Committee on Post Office and Civil Service. Subcommittee on Compensation and Employee Benefits. Civil Service Amendments of 1984 and Merit Pay Improvement Act. Washington: U.S.G.P.O., 1984, p. 20-2.

Bystrom, Marcia J.
"Statement." In U.S. Congress. House. Committee on Small Business. Subcommittee on General Oversight and Minority Enterprise. Women in Business, p. 27-8.

Cabrera-Drinane, Suleika.
"Developing Meaningful Roles for Minority Women." In Older Women in the City, p. 178-82.

Cadden, Joan.
"Questions and Reflections on Science for Women." In GLCA Women's Studies Conference (6th: 1980). Toward a Feminist Transformation of the Academy, II, p. 57-61.

Cahn, Anne H.
"The Economic Consequences of the Arms Race." In U.S. National Commission on the Observance of International Women's Year. The Spirit of Houston, p. 236-8.

Cain, Melinda L.
"Java, Indonesia: The Introduction of Rice Processing Technology." In Women and Technological Change in Developing Countries, p. 127-37.

Cain, Pamela Stone.
"Commentary." In Sex Segregation in the Workplace, p. 87-90.
"Prospects for Pay Equity in a Changing Economy." In Comparable Worth: New Directions for Research, p. 137-65.

Calderone, Mary S.
"Above and Beyond Politics: The Sexual Socialization of Children." In Pleasure and Danger, p. 131-7.
"Nothing Less Than the Truth Will Do, For We Have Nowhere To Go But Forward." In Today's Girl: Tomorrow's Woman, p. 26-30.

Caldicott, Helen Mary.
"A Commitment to Life. Acceptance Speech at American Humanist Association Annual Conference." In Humanist, 42 (September/October 1982), 6-11.
"Nuclear War--the Human Dimension." In U.S. National Commission on the Observance of International Women's Year. The Spirit of Houston, p. 241.
"We Are the Curators of Life on Earth." In Representative American Speeches: 1982-83, p. 72-80.

Callahan, Pat.
"Statement." In U.S. Congress. House. Committee on Education and Labor. Subcommittee on Labor-Management Relations. Legislative Hearing on Pension Equity for Women, p. 57-9.

Calloway, Doris Howes.
"Food/Nutrition in the Third World: An Overview." In International Conference on Women and Food (1978: University of Arizona). A Conference on the Role of Women in Meeting Basic Food and Water Needs in Developing Countries, p. 35-40.

Campanella, Connie.
"Testimony." In U.S. Congress. House. Committee on the Judiciary. Subcommittee on Civil and Constitutional Rights. Equal Rights Amendment Extension, p. 400-6.

Campbell, Jane L.
"Statement." In U.S. Congress. House. Committee on Post Office and Civil Service. Subcommittee on Compensation and

Employee Benefits. Options for Conducting a Pay Equity
Study, p. 183-7.
"Testimony." In U.S. Congress. House. Select Committee on
Aging. Subcommittee on Retirement Income and Employment.
Task Force on Social Security and Women. Treatment of
Women Under Social Security, p. 150-2.

Campbell, Nancy Duff.
"Statement." In U.S. Congress. House. Committee on Ways
and Means. Economic Equity Act and Related Tax and Pen-
sion Reform, p. 158-9.
"Statement." In U.S. Congress. House. Committee on Ways
and Means. Subcommittee on Social Security. Treatment of
Men and Women Under the Social Security Program, p. 168-70.
"Testimony." In U.S. Congress. House. Select Committee on
Aging. Subcommittee on Retirement Income and Employment.
Task Force on Social Security and Women. Treatment of Wom-
en Under Social Security, v. 1, p. 100-2, v. 3, p. 31-5.

Campbell, Penelope.
"Sub-Saharan Africa: Foreign Policy Dilemmas for the Reagan
Administration." Vital Speeches, 47 (January 1, 1981), 186-8.

Campbell, Ruth.
"Statement." In U.S. Congress. House. Select Committee on
Aging. Subcommittee on Retirement Income and Employment.
Task Force on Social Security and Women. Treatment of
Women Under Social Security, v. 4, p. 137-9.

Candela, Christine.
"Statement." In U.S. Congress. House. Committee on Ways
and Means. Subcommittee on Social Security. Treatment of
Men and Women Under the Social Security Program, p. 198-
200.
"Testimony." In U.S. Congress. House. Select Committee on
Aging. Subcommittee on Retirement Income and Employment.
National Policy Proposals Affecting Midlife Women, p. 79-80.
"Testimony." In U.S. Congress. House. Select Committee on
Aging. Subcommittee on Retirement Income and Employment.
Task Force on Social Security and Women. Treatment of
Women Under Social Security, p. 60-2.

Candy, Sandra Gibbs.
"Social Support for Women in Transitions: Conceptual Considerations." In Women's Lives, p. 221-7.

Canellos, Georgia.
"Testimony." In U.S. Congress. Joint Economic Committee.
Subcommittee on Economic Growth and Stabilization. American
Women Workers in a Full Employment Economy, p. 54-5.

Cannon, Elaine A.
  "Daughters of God." In Blueprints For Living, p. 69-76.
  "Finding Our Peace on Earth." In A Woman's Choices, p. 171-84.

Cannon, Katie G.
  "On Remembering Who We Are." In Those Preachin' Women, p.
  43-50.

Cantor, Marjorie H.
  "Income Inadequacy of Older Women." In Older Women in the
  City, p. 16-32.

Cappelli, Denise.
  "Vocational Rehabilitation: Options For Women." In Women in
  Crisis Conference (1st: 1979: New York, NY). Women in
  Crisis, p. 225-8.

Carbon, Susan.
  "Women on the State Bench: Their Characteristics and Attitudes
  About Judicial Selection." In Women in the Judiciary, p. 14-
  16.

Carden, Patricia.
  "The Woman Student in Russia." In The Role and Status of
  Women in the Soviet Union, p. 57-9.

Cardin, Shoshana.
  "Testimony." In U.S. Congress. House. Select Committee on
  Aging. Subcommittee on Retirement Income and Employment.
  Task Force on Social Security and Women. Treatment of Wom-
  en Under Social Security, p. 134-7.

Cardman, Francine.
  "Tradition, Hermeneutics and Ordination." In Sexism and Church
  Law, p. 58-81.

Carlberg, Gwendolyn Jo M.
  "Statement." In U.S. Congress. Senate. Committee on Labor
  and Human Resources. Sex Discrimination in the Workplace,
  1981, p. 542-7.

Carlo, Carmen.
  "Credit & Financial Problems of Older Women." In Older Women
  in the City, p. 53-65.

Carlson, Carole.
  "America--Finished Or Unfinished." In Spinning a Sacred Yarn,
  p. 9-14.

Carlton, Wendy.
  "Perfectability and the Neonate: The Burden of Expectations on

Mothers and Their Health Providers." In The Custom-Made Child?, p. 129-34.

Carpenter, Liz.
"Commissioner Liz Carpenter: Faces and Voices." In U.S. National Commission on the Observance of International Women's Year. The Spirit of Houston, p. 221-2.
"God, But We're Getting Smart." In Women Organizing, p. 321-8.
"Speech at the National Women's Political Caucus Conference, July, 1981." Ms, 10 (October 1981), 91.
"Statement." In U.S. Congress. Senate. Committee on Labor and Human Resources. The Coming Decade, p. 11-6.

Carpenter, M. Kathleen.
"Statement." In U.S. Congress. House. Committee on Armed Services. Subcommittee on Military Personnel. Women in the Military, p. 294-5.

Carque, Patricia A.
"The Wait of Pregnancy." In Spinning a Sacred Yarn, p. 15-9.

Carr, Marilyn.
"Technologies Appropriate for Women: Theory, Practice and Policy." In Women and Technological Change in Developing Countries, p. 193-203.

Carroll, Berenice A.
"Feminist Politics and Peace." In The Role of Women in Conflict and Peace, p. 61-9.

Carroll, Maureen P.
"A Homily for the Feast of Teresa of Avila." In Spinning a Sacred Yarn, p. 20-4.

Carson, Julie.
"The Rumpelstiltskin Syndrome: Sexism in American Naming Traditions." In Women & Men, p. 64-73.

Carter, Judy.
"Speech by Judy Carter." In U.S. National Commission on the Observance of International Woman's Year. The Spirit of Houston, p. 224.

Carter, Marie.
"Myths and Realities." In Training Conference (1st: 1984: Washington, DC). Interagency Committee on Women in Federal Law Enforcement, p. 33-36.

Carter, Norene.
"A Lay Theological Perspective." In Conference on Women and Lay Ministry (1976: St. Michel's Church, Milton, MA). Women and Lay Ministry, p. 23-31.

Carter, Rosalynn Smith.
    "As the Delegate from Georgia, Said...; Address, November 19,
       1976." MH, 60 (Winter 1977), 14.
    "Mrs. Carter Visits Thailand." Department of State Bulletin, 80
       (January 1980), 6-7.
    "Speech by First Lady Rosalyn Carter." In U.S. National Com-
       mission on the Observance of International Woman's Year.
       The Spirit of Houston, p. 219-20.
    "Statement." In U.S. Congress. Senate. Committee on Labor
       and Human Resources. Subcommittee on Health and Scientific
       Research. Reappraisal of Mental Health Policy, 1979, p. 5-8.
    "Toward a More Caring Society; Excerpts from Address, August
       25, 1977." MH, 61 (Summer 1977), 3-5.

Casias, Stella.
    "Testimony." In U.S. Commission on Civil Rights. Hearing Be-
       fore the U.S. Commission on Civil Rights held in Denver,
       1976, p. 428, 431-2.

Cassedy, Ellen.
    "Testimony." In U.S. Equal Employment Opportunity Commission.
       Hearings Before the U.S. Equal Employment Opportunity Com-
       mission on Job Segregation and Wage Discrimination, p. 423-42.

Casserly, Patricia Lund.
    "Factors Affecting Female Participation in Advanced Placement
       Programs in Mathematics, Chemistry, and Physics." In Hyman
       Blumberg Symposium on Research in Early Childhood Educa-
       tion (8th: 1976: Johns Hopkins University). Women and the
       Mathematical Mystique, p. 138-63.

Catania, Susan.
    "Statement." In U.S. Congress. Senate. Committee on Foreign
       Relations. Women in Development, p. 77-83.

Catt, Carrie Chapman.
    "Address to the Seventh Congress of the International Woman
       Suffrage Alliance at Budapest, 15 June 1913." In Women,
       the Family, and Freedom, v. 2, p. 245.
    "Mrs. Catt's International Address." In Women, the Family, and
       Freedom, v. 2, p. 234-36.
    "Is Woman Suffrage Progressing?" In We Shall Be Heard, p.
       189-95.
    "Why Are Only Women Compelled to Prove Themselves?" (1915)
       In Outspoken Women, p. 24-7.

Cauchear, Mary.
    "Statement." In U.S. Congress. House. Select Committee on
       Aging. Subcommittee on Retirement Income and Employment.
       Task Force on Social Security and Women. Treatment of
       Women Under Social Security, v. 3, p. 68-9.

Ceballos, Jaqui.
"The Future of Women." In Cornell Conference on Women (1969: Cornell University). Proceedings, p. 63.

Celender, Ivy M.
"Careers in Industry for Scientifically Trained Women." In Expanding the Role of Women in the Sciences, p. 179-89.

Cerda, Gloria.
"Testimony." In U.S. Commission on Civil Rights. Hearing Before the U.S. Commission on Civil Rights Held in Chicago, 1974, v. 1, p. 42-50.

Chai, Alice.
"Korean Women in Hawaii, 1903-1945: The Role of Methodism in Their Liberation and in Their Participation in the Korean Independence Movement." In Women in New Worlds, v. 1, p. 328-44.

Chambers, (Mother) Bessie, R.S.C.J.
"Psychological Effects of Segregation." In Split-Level Lives, p. 43-51.

Chambers, Marjorie Bell.
"A Summing Up." In Today's Girls: Tomorrow's Women, p. 80-1.
"What Do You Wish to Accomplish? Genius Is the Ability to Light One's Own Fire." Vital Speeches, 45 (August 15, 1979), 670-1.

Chambers-Schiller, Lee.
"The Single Woman: Family and Vocation Among Nineteenth-Century Reformers." In Conference on the History of Women (1977: St. Paul, MN). Woman's Being, Woman's Place, p. 334-50.

Chancey, Virginia Crawford.
"Motivation of Women to Leadership: Results of a Survey." In Education of Women for Social and Political Leadership, p. 81-4.

Chandler, Effie L.
"Testimony." In U.S. Congress. House. Committee on Post Office and Civil Service. Subcommittee on Postal Personnel and Modernization. Equal Employment Opportunity and Sexual Harassment in the Postal Service, p. 81-2.

Chaney, Elsa.
"Testimony." In U.S. Congress. House. Committee on International Relations. Subcommittee on International Organizations. International Women's Issues, p. 7-12.

Chang, Maria Hsia.
    "United States Relations With Taiwan. A Critical Review of the
    Taiwan Relations Act." Vital Speeches, 51 (June 15, 1985),
    530-3.

Chapman, Jane Roberts.
    "Testimony." In U.S. Congress. House. Committee on the
    Judiciary. Subcommittee on Courts, Civil Liberties, and the
    Administration of Justice. The Female Offender--1979-80,
    p. 85-8.

Chapman, Martha.
    "Testimony." In U.S. Congress. House. Committee on Energy
    and Commerce. Subcommittee on Health and the Environment.
    Health and the Environment Miscellaneous, pt. 5, p. 274-6.

Chapple, Joyce F.
    "Statement." In U.S. Congress. Senate. Special Committee on
    Aging. Women in Our Aging Society, p. 62-7.

Chase-Anderson, Marilyn.
    "Statement." In U.S. Congress. Senate. Committee on the
    Judiciary. Subcommittee on the Constitution. Civil Rights
    Act of 1984, p. 71-3.

Chavez, Linda.
    "Statement." In U.S. Congress. Senate. Committee on Labor
    and Human Resources. Subcommittee on Education, Arts and
    Humanities. Civil Rights Act of 1984, pt. 1, p. 17-22, pt.
    21, p. 8-10.

Chayes, Antonia Handler.
    "The Rewards and Obstacles of Community Involvement." In
    Women in Action, p. 1-6.
    "Statement." In U.S. Congress. House. Committee on Armed
    Services. Subcommittee on Military Personnel. Women in the
    Military, p. 53-73.
    "Statement." In U.S. Congress. House. Committee on Veter-
    ans' Affairs. Select Subcommittee to Review WASP Bills.
    To Provide Recognition to the Women's Air Force..., p. 261-6.
    "Testimony." In U.S. Congress. Joint Economic Committee.
    Subcommittee on Priorities and Economy in Government. The
    Role of Women in the Military, p. 9-12.
    "Testimony." In U.S. Congress. Senate. Committee on the
    Judiciary. Subcommittee on the Constitution. The Impact
    of the Equal Rights Amendment, pt. 1, p. 283-8.

Cherry, Violet Padayachi.
    "The Role of the Family in Teenage Pregnancy: Support or
    Sabotage." In Women in Crisis Conference (1st: 1979: New
    York, NY). Women in Crisis Conference, p. 156-71.

Chinoy, Helen Krich.
"Suppressed Desires: Women in the Theater." In Women, the Arts, and the 1920s in Paris and New York, p. 126-32.

Chisholm, Shirley.
"Statement." In U.S. Congress. House. Committee on Agriculture. Subcommittee on Department Investigations, Oversight, and Research. Grants for Certain Purposes to 1890 Land-Grant Colleges. Washington: U.S.G.P.O., 1980, p. 4-11.
"Statement." In U.S. Congress. House. Committee on Education and Labor. Impact of Administration's Economic Proposals on Programs Under the Jurisdiction of the Education and Labor Committee. Washington: U.S.G.P.O., 1981, p. 240-70.
"Statement." In U.S. Congress. House. Committee on Education and Labor. Subcommittee on Human Resources. Oversight Hearing on the Head Start Program. Washington: U.S.G.P.O., 1982, p. 55-65.
"Statement." In U.S. Congress. House. Committee on Education and Labor. Subcommittee on Human Resources. Oversight Hearing on the Office of Juvenile Justice and Delinquency Prevention. Washington: U.S.G.P.O., 1982, p. 53-5.
"Statement." In U.S. Congress. House. Committee on Education and Labor. Subcommittee on Postsecondary Education. Budget Allocation for the Endowments for the Arts and Humanities, and Museums and Libraries. Washington: U.S.G.P.O., 1981, p. 77-85.
"Statement." In U.S. Congress. House. Committee on Education and Labor. Subcommittee on Postsecondary Education. Guaranteed Student Loan and Civil Rights Enforcement. Washington: U.S.G.P.O., 1984, p. 8-13.
"Statement." In U.S. Congress. House. Committee on Education and Labor. Subcommittee on Postsecondary Education. Oversight on Higher Education Budget Fiscal Years 1981 and 1982. Washington: U.S.G.P.O., 1983, p. 16-31.
"Statement." In U.S. Congress. House. Committee on Post Office and Civil Service. Subcommittee on Census and Population. Immigration Reform and Control Act of 1982. Washington: U.S.G.P.O., 1983, p. 16-21.
"Statement." In U.S. Congress. House. Committee on Post Office and Civil Service. Subcommittee on Census and Population. Oversight Hearings on the 1980 Census. Washington: U.S.G.P.O., 1980, pt. 23, p. 26-7.
"Statement." In U.S. Congress. House. Committee on the Judiciary. Subcommittee on Crime. LEAA Reauthorization. Washington: U.S.G.P.O., 1981, pt. 2, p. 1097-1110.
"Statement." In U.S. Congress. House. Committee on Ways and Means. Subcommittee on Public Assistance and Unemployment Compensation. Administration's Proposed Savings in Unemployment Compensation, Public Assistance, and Social Services Programs. Washington: U.S.G.P.O., 1981, p. 44-9.

"Statement." In U.S. Congress. Senate. Committee on Banking, Housing, and Urban Affairs. Cross-Industry Takeovers Between Commercial Banks and Thrift Institutions. Washington: U.S.G.P.O., 1980, p. 139-81.

"Statement." In U.S. Congress. Senate. Committee on the Judiciary. Subcommittee on Immigration and Refugee Policy. United States as a Country of Mass First Asylum. Washington: U.S.G.P.O., 1982, p. 109-19.

Chodorow, Nancy.
"Gender, Relation, and Difference in Psychoanalytic Perspective." In The Future of Difference, p. 3-16.

Christ, Carol P.
"Feminist Liberation Theology and Yahweh as Holy Warrior: An Analysis of Symbol." In Women's Spirit Bonding, p. 202-12.
"Feminist Studies in Religion and Literature: A Methodological Reflection." In Beyond Androcentrism, p. 35-51.
"Why Women Need the Goddess: Phenomenological, Psychological, and Political Reflections." In The Politics of Women's Spirituality, p. 71-86.

Cisler, Cindy.
"Child Bearing, Child Rearing, Abortion, and Contraception." In Cornell Conference on Women (1969: Cornell University). Proceedings, p. 51-2, 57.
"Education and Equality for Women." In Cornell Conference on Women (1969: Cornell University). Proceedings, p. 38.

Clamar, Aphrodite.
"Stepmothering: Fairy Tales and Reality." In Handbook of Feminist Therapy, p. 159-69.

Clapp, Margaret.
"Realistic Education for Women." Journal of the American Association of University Women, (Summer 1950) 199-202.

Clark, Helen S.
"Statement." In U.S. Congress. House. Select Committee on Aging. Problems of Aging Women, p. 10-12.

Clark, Linda.
"The Day's Own Trouble." In Spinning a Sacred Yarn, p. 25-30.

Clarke, Mary E.
"Statement." In U.S. Congress. House. Committee on Armed Services. Subcommittee on Military Personnel. Women in the Military, p. 328-9.

Clauss, Carin.
"Statement." In U.S. Congress. House. Committee on Education

and Labor. Subcommittee on Employment Opportunities.
Oversight Hearings on Equal Employment Opportunity and Affirmative Action, pt. 2, p. 7-17.

Cleary, Beverly.
"Newbery Medal Acceptance." Horn Book, 60 (1984), 429-38.

Cleland, Virginia.
"Prospectives for Nursing: Old Dreams, New Visions." In
Prospectives for Nursing, p. 1-9.

Clement, Jacqueline.
"Sex Bias in School Administration." In Women and Educational
Leadership, p. 131-8.

Clement, Mary.
"Statement." In U.S. Congress. Senate. Committee on Labor
and Human Resources. Subcommittee on Labor. Amending
the Fair Labor Standards Act to Include Industrial Homework,
p. 17, 25-6.

Clinton, Catherine.
"Caught in the Web of the Big House: Women and Slavery." In
The Web of Southern Social Relations, p. 19-34.

Clusen, Ruth C.
"The League of Women Voters and Political Power." In Women
Organizing, p. 112-32.

Coates, Susan.
"Sex Differences in Field Independence Among Preschool Children." In Sex Differences in Behavior, p. 259-74.

Cobb, Jewel Plummer.
"Filters for Women in Science." In Expanding the Role of Women
in the Sciences, p. 236-48.
"Planning Strategies for Women in Scientific Professions." In
Women in Scientific and Engineering Professions, p. 75-85.
"Statement." In Symposium on Minorities and Women in Science
and Technology (1981: Washington, DC). Symposium on
Minorities and Women in Science and Technology, p. 67-8.

Cocciolone, Denise.
"Statement." In U.S. Congress. Senate. Committee on Labor
and Human Resources. Subcommittee on Aging, Family, and
Human Services. Oversight on Family Planning Programs Under Title X of the Public Health Service Act, 1981, p. 110-1.

Coffey, Margaret.
"One Family's Decision: A Leave of Absence." In The Woman
in Management, p. 61-4.

Cohen, Sylvan H.
   "Feminism as a Sophisticated Concept: Good News, Bad News,
      and Old News." In Sisterhood Surveyed, p. 93-104.

Col, Jeannie Marie.
   "Women's Employment Networks: Strategies for Development."
      In Women, Power, and Political Systems, p. 184-94.

Colbert, Evelyn.
   "Poison Gas Use in Indochina." Department of State Bulletin,
      80 (March 1980), 43-5.

Cole, Eunice.
   "Statement." In U.S. Congress. House. Committee on Post
      Office and Civil Service. Subcommittee on Compensation and
      Employee Benefits. Federal Pay Equity Act of 1984, pt. 2,
      p. 107-10.
   "Statement." In U.S. Congress. House. Committee on Post
      Office and Civil Service. Subcommittee on Human Resources.
      Pay Equity, pt. 1, p. 266-70.

Cole-Alexander, Lenora.
   "Statement." In U.S. Congress. House. Committee on Foreign
      Affairs. Subcommittee on Human Rights and International
      Organizations. U.S. Contribution to the U.N. Decade for
      Women, p. 9-12.

Coleman, Teresa.
   "Testimony." In U.S. Congress. House. Committee on Energy
      and Commerce. Subcommittee on Health and the Environment.
      Health and the Environment Miscellaneous, pt. 3, p. 640-1.

Collins, Cardiss.
   "Statement." In U.S. Congress. House. Committee on Appro-
      priations. Subcommittee on Department of the Interior and
      Related Agencies. Department of the Interior and Related
      Agencies Appropriations for 1985. Washington: U.S.G.P.O.,
      1984, p. 558-78.
   "Statement." In U.S. Congress. House. Committee on Educa-
      tion and Labor. Subcommittee on Employment Opportunities.
      Oversight Hearings on Equal Employment Opportunity and
      Affirmative Action. Washington: U.S.G.P.O., 1982, v. 2,
      p. 4-7.
   "Statement." In U.S. Congress. House. Committee on Educa-
      tion and Labor. Subcommittee on Labor-Management Relations.
      Legislative Hearing on Pension Equity for Women, p. 24-7.
   "Statement." In U.S. Congress. House. Committee on Energy
      and Commerce. Subcommittee on Health and the Environment.
      Mobile Source Provisions. Washington: U.S.G.P.O., 1982,
      p. 1345-8.
   "Statement." In U.S. Congress. House. Committee on Science

and Technology. Subcommittee on Science, Research, and Technology. Proposed Dismantling of the U.S. Fire Administration. Washington: U.S.G.P.O., 1982, p. 30-6.

"Statement." In U.S. Congress. House. Committee on the Judiciary. Subcommittee on Crime. Federal Antitampering Act. Washington: U.S.G.P.O., 1984, p. 5-13.

"Statement." In U.S. Congress. Senate. Committee on Labor and Human Resources. Nomination: Hearing on William J. Bennett, of North Carolina, to be Secretary, Department of Education, January 28, 1985. Washington: U.S.G.P.O., 1985, p. 78-96.

Collins, Judy.
"Statement." In U.S. Congress. Senate. Committee on the Judiciary. Subcommittee on Separation of Powers. The Human Life Bill, p. 974-8.

Collins, Mary Jean.
"Statement." In U.S. Congress. House. Select Committee on Aging. Subcommittee on Retirement Income and Employment. Task Force on Social Security and Women. Inequities Toward Women in the Social Security System, p. 84-7.

Colten, Mary Ellen.
"Heroin Addiction Among Women." In Women's Lives, p. 337-43.

Comini, Alessandra.
"Gender or Genius? The Women Artists of German Expressionism." In Feminism and Art History, p. 271-91.

Compton, Geraldine.
"Statement." In U.S. Congress. House. Committee on Ways and Means. Economic Equity Act and Related Tax and Pension Reform, p. 143-4.

Comstock, Ada Louise.
"Inaugural Address." School and Society, 18 (November 10, 1923), 541-6.

Conable, Charlotte W.
"Testimony." In U.S. Congress. House. Select Committee on Aging. Subcommittee on Retirement Income and Employment. National Policy Proposals Affecting Midlife Women, p. 55-7.

Condren, Mary.
"Patriarchy and Death." In Women's Spirit Bonding, p. 173-89.

Conibear, Shirley.
"Women as a High-Risk Population." In Conference on Women and the Workplace (1976: Washington, DC). Women and the Workplace, p. 168-73.

Connell, Elizabeth B.
    "The Pill: Risks and Benefits." In Hormonal Contraceptives,
        Estrogens, and Human Welfare, p. 1-6.
    "Testimony." In U.S. Congress. House. Committee on the
        Judiciary. Subcommittee on Civil and Constitutional Rights.
        Proposed Constitutional Amendments on Abortion, p. 446-50.

Conniff, Maura.
    "Statement." In U.S. Congress. House. Select Committee on
        Children, Youth, and Families. Children, Youth, and Fami-
        lies, p. 73.

Connors, Denise.
    "Response (to Unnatural Selection: On Choosing Children's
        Sex)." In The Custom-Made Child?, p. 205-8.

Conoley, Jane Close.
    "The Psychology of Leadership: Implications for Women." In
        Women and Educational Leadership, p. 35-46.

Conway, Jill Ker.
    "Margaret Sanger and American Reform." In Margaret Sanger
        Centennial Conference (1979: Northampton, MA). Margaret
        Sanger Centennial Conference, p. 7-11.
    "A Proper Perspective." In Today's Girls: Tomorrow's Women,
        p. 10-7.
    "Statement." In U.S. Congress. Senate. Committee on Labor
        and Human Resources. The Coming Decade, p. 430-3.

Conway, M. Margaret.
    "Women as Voluntary Political Activists: A Review of Recent
        Empirical Research." In Women Organizing, p. 289-303.

Cook, Alice H.
    "Collective Bargaining as a Strategy for Achieving Equal Oppor-
        tunity and Equal Pay: Sweden and West Germany." In Equal
        Employment Policy for Women, p. 53-78.
    "Vocational Training, the Labor Market, and the Unions." In
        Equal Employment Policy for Women, p. 199-225.

Cook, Beverly Blair.
    "The Dual Role of Women Judges." In Women in the Judiciary,
        p. 7-9.
    "Sex Discrimination in Politics and the All-Male Club." In Women
        in the Judiciary, p. 17-22.
    "Will Women Judges Make a Difference in Women's Legal Rights?
        A Prediction from Attitudes and Simulated Behaviour." In
        Women, Power, and Political Systems, p. 216-39.

Cook, Blanche Wiesen.
    "Women and Politics: The Obscured Dimension." In Women, the
        Arts, and the 1920s in Paris and New York, p. 147-52.

Cook, Constance.
  "Child Bearing, Child Rearing, Abortion, and Contraception."
    In Cornell Conference on Women (1969: Cornell University).
    Proceedings, p. 52-4, 57.

Cook, Katsi.
  "A Native American Response." In Birth Control and Controlling
    Birth, p. 251-8.

Cooke, Flora J.
  "Fundamental Considerations Underlying the Curriculum of the
    Francis W. Parker School." In National Society for the Study
    of Education. Twenty-Sixth Yearbook. The Foundations and
    Technique of Curriculum-Construction. Bloomington, IL:
    Public School Publishing Company, 1926.

Coon, Jane.
  "South Asia--Old Problems, New Challenges." Department of
    State Bulletin, 80 (April 1980), 61-2.

Cooney, Barbara.
  "Caldecott Medal Acceptance." Horn Book, 56 (1980), 378-82.

Cooper, Donna L.
  "Statement." In U.S. Congress. House. Select Committee on
    Population. Fertility and Contraception in America, pt. 3,
    p. 17-21.

Cooper, Helen.
  "Testimony." In U.S. Commission on Civil Rights. Hearing Be-
    fore the U.S. Commission on Civil Rights Held in Chicago,
    1974, v. 1, p. 51, 57-80.

Cooper, Mary Anderson.
  "Statement." In U.S. Congress. House. Committee on Ways
    and Means. Subcommittee on Public Assistance and Unemploy-
    ment Compensation. AFDC and Social Service Bills and Re-
    lated Oversight Issues, p. 120-5.

Cooper, Maudine.
  "Statement." In U.S. Congress. House. Committee on Educa-
    tion and Labor. Subcommittee on Employment Opportunities.
    Oversight Hearing on the OFCCP's Proposed Affirmative Action
    Regulations, p. 352-5.

Coopersmith, Esther.
  "U.S. Contributions to the UNHCR." Department of State Bul-
    letin, 80 (April 1980), 68-9.

Copley, Helen K.
  "General Spirit of the People. A Free Press and the Judiciary."

Vital Speeches, 46 (January 1, 1980), 169-72.
"The Wiring of America. The New Information Age." Vital
Speeches, 48 (June 15, 1982), 535-8.

Corbett, Katharine T.
"Louisa Catherine Adams: The Anguished 'Adventures of a No-
body.'" In Conference on the History of Women (1977: St.
Paul, MN). Woman's Being, Woman's Place, p. 67-84.

Corcoran, Mary E.
"Sex-Based Wage Differentials." In Women's Lives, p. 179-93.
"Testimony." In U.S. Equal Employment Opportunity Commission.
Hearing Before the U.S. Equal Employment Opportunity Com-
mission on Job Segregation and Wage Discrimination, p. 274-92.
"Work Experience, Labor Force Withdrawals, and Women's Wages:
Empirical Results Using the 1976 Panel of Income Dynamics."
In Conference on Women in the Labor Market (1977: Barnard
College). Women in the Labor Market, p. 216-45.

Cordova, Dorothy L.
"Educational Alternatives for Asian-Pacific Women." In Confer-
ence on the Educational and Occupational Needs of Asian-
Pacific-American Women (1976: San Francisco, CA). Confer-
ence on the Educational and Occupational Needs of Asian-
Pacific-American Women, p. 135-56.

Corea, Gena.
"The Depo-Provera Weapon." In Birth Control and Controlling
Birth, p. 107-116.

Correa, Gladys.
"Puerto Rican Women in Education and Potential Impact on Occu-
pational Patterns." In Conference on the Educational and
Occupational Needs of Hispanic Women (1976: Denver, CO
and Washington, DC). Conference on the Educational and
Occupational Needs of Hispanic Women, p. 47-64.

Costain, Anne N.
"Lobbying for Equal Credit." In Women Organizing, p. 82-110.

Costanza, Margaret "Midge."
"Speech by Honorable Margaret 'Midge' Costanza, Assistant to
the President." In U.S. National Commission on the Observance of International Women's Year. The Spirit of Houston,
p. 232.

Costello, Cynthia B.
"'We're Worth It! Work!' Work, Culture and Conflict at the Wis-
consin Education Association Insurance Trust." Feminist
Studies, 11 (Fall 1985), 497-518.

Coston, Carol.
"A Feminist Approach to Alternative Enterprises." In Women's
Spirit Bonding, p. 336-44.

Cota, Kathleen.
"Statement." In U.S. Congress. House. Committee on Post Office and Civil Service. Subcommittee on Compensation and
Employee Benefits. Federal Pay Equity Act of 1984, pt. 2,
p. 166.

Cotera, Martha.
"Women in Power." In International Women's Year Conference on
Women in Public Life (1975: Lyndon Baines Johnson Library).
Women in Public Life, p. 26-7.

Cotner, Suone.
"Statement." In U.S. Congress. Senate. Committee on Labor
and Human Resources. The Coming Decade, p. 555-8.

Cott, Nancy F.
"The Women's Studies Program: Yale University." In Toward a
Balanced Curriculum, p. 91-7.
"Young Women in the Second Great Awakening in New England."
Feminist Studies, 3 (1976), 15-29.

Cotton, Kitty.
"Statement." In U.S. Congress. House. Committee on Armed
Services. Military Personnel and Compensation Subcommittee.
Benefits for Former Spouses of Military Members, pt. 1, p.
35-6.

Couch, Beatriz Melano.
"Suffering and Hope." In Women and the Word, p. 114-23.

Cowan, Ann Bunzel.
"Session Summary." In International Conference on Women and
Food (1978: University of Arizona). A Conference on the
Role of Women in Meeting Basic Food and Water Needs in De-
veloping Countries, p. 89-92.

Cowan, Belita.
"Ethical Problems in Government-Funded Contraceptive Research."
In Birth Control and Controlling Birth, p. 37-46.

Cowan, Ruth Schwartz.
"A Case Study of Technological And Social Change: The Wash-
ing Machine and the Working Wife." In Clio's Consciousness
Raised, p. 245-52.

Cox, Rachel Dunaway.
"Marriage and the Family." In The Role and Status of Women in
the Soviet Union, p. 130-36.

Coyner, Sandra.
   "Women's Studies as an Academic Discipline: Why and How to
      Do It." In Theories of Women's Studies, p. 18-40.

Craft, Carolyn R.
   "Promoting the Humanities. The Image Problems." Vital
      Speeches, 48 (January 1, 1982), 180-4.

Crandall, Catherine A.
   "Testimony." In U.S. Commission on Civil Rights. Hearing Be-
      fore the U.S. Commission on Civil Rights Held in Denver,
      1976, p. 290.

Craven, Delle Mullen.
   "The Unpublished Diaries of Mary Morangne Davis." In Rey-
      nolds Conference (2nd: 1975: University of South Carolina).
      South Carolina Women Writers, p. 15-25.

Crawford, Sandra.
   "Statement." In U.S. Congress. Committee on Education and
      Labor. Subcommittee on Select Education. Hearing on Domes-
      tic Violence, p. 56-60.
   "Statement." In U.S. Congress. House. Committee on Ways
      and Means. Subcommittee on Public Assistance and Unemploy-
      ment Compensation. AFDC and Social Service Bills and Re-
      lated Oversight Issues, p. 155-60.
   "Statement." In U.S. Congress. Senate. Committee on Finance.
      Potential Inequities Affecting Women, pt. 2, p. 282-4.

Criley, Florence L.
   "Testimony." In U.S. Commission on Civil Rights. Hearing Be-
      fore the U.S. Commission on Civil Rights Held in Chicago,
      1974, v. 2, p. 179-87.

Crisswell, Jo Ann.
   "Testimony." In U.S. Congress. House. Committee on Energy
      and Commerce. Subcommittee on Health and the Environment.
      Health and the Environment Miscellaneous, pt. 3, p.633-4.

Crist, Miriam J.
   "Winifred L. Chappel: Everybody on the Left Knew Her." In
      Women in New Worlds, v. 1, p. 362-78.

Crockett-Cannon, Margaret W.
   "What Do You Want Me To Do For You?" In Spinning a Sacred
      Web, p. 31-5.

Croll, Kyle J.
   "Health Problems of Native Americans." In Health Needs of the
      World's Poor Women, p. 64-6.

Cross, Nancy Jewell.
 "Statement." In California. Legislature. Joint Committee on
  Legal Equality. <u>Women in the Justice System</u>, p. 104-20,
  171-7.

Crotwell, Helen Gray.
 "Broken Community (The Seventh Sunday of Easter)." In <u>Women</u>
  <u>and the Word</u>, p. 124-31.

Cruz, Christina.
 "Statement." In California. Legislature. Joint Committee on
  Legal Equality. <u>Women in the Justice System</u>, p. 177-83.

Cruz, Rebecca.
 "Testimony." In U.S. Commission on Civil Rights. <u>Hearing Be-</u>
  <u>fore the U.S. Commission on Civil Rights Held in Chicago,</u>
  <u>1974</u>, v. 1, p. 40-1, 48-9.
 "Welcoming Statement." In U.S. Commission on Civil Rights.
  <u>Hearing Before the U.S. Commission on Civil Rights Held in</u>
  <u>Chicago, 1974</u>, v. 1, p. 25-6.

Cuellar, Rosa.
 "Response (to Woman-Controlled Birth Control)." In <u>Birth Con-</u>
  <u>trol and Controlling Birth</u>, p. 79-80.

Culler, Jeanne.
 "Panel Discussion of Societal Responsibilities as Seen by Women."
  In Conference on Women and the Workplace (1976: Washington,
  DC). <u>Women and the Workplace</u>, p. 303-5.

Culley, Margo.
 "Anger and Authority in the Introductory Women's Studies Classroom." In <u>Gendered Subjects</u>, p. 209-17.

Culpepper, Emily Erwin.
 "Reflections: Uncovering Patriarchal Agendas and Exploring
  Woman-Oriented Values." In <u>The Custom-Made Child?</u>, p.
  301-10.
 "Sex Preselection: Discussion Moderator's Remarks." In <u>The</u>
  <u>Custom-Made Child?</u>, p. 213-4.

Cummerton, Joan M.
 "Homophobia and Social Work Practice With Lesbians." In NASW
  Conference on Social Work Practice With Women (1st: 1980:
  Washington, DC). <u>Women, Power, and Change</u>, p. 104-13.

Cunneen, Sally.
 "Women: Living Wholly/Holy in a Fractured World." In <u>Spinning</u>
  <u>a Sacred Yarn</u>, p. 36-44.

Cunningham, Mary E.
"Productivity and the Corporate Culture. A Return to Balance."
Vital Speeches, 47 (April 1, 1981), 363-7.

Curran, Hilda.
"Testimony." In U.S. Equal Employment Opportunity Commission.
Hearings Before the U.S. Equal Employment Opportunity Com-
mission on Job Segregation and Wage Discrimination, p. 835-49.

Curtis, Carla.
"Statement." In U.S. Congress. Senate. Committee on Finance.
Potential Inequities Affecting Women, pt. 2, p. 206-8.

Curtis, Lynn.
"Statement." In U.S. Congress. House. Committee on Science
and Technology. Subcommittee on Domestic and International
Scientific Planning, Analysis, and Cooperation. Research into
Violent Behavior: Overview and Sexual Assaults, p. 134-43.

Cutler, Mary S.
"What a Woman Librarian Earns." In The Role of Women in Librarianship, p. 13-5.

Daly, Mary.
"Theology After the Demise of God the Father: A Call for the
Castration of Sexist Religion." In Sexist Religion and Women
in the Church, p. 125-42.

Damschroder, Deanne.
"Statement." In U.S. Congress. Senate. Special Committee on
Aging. Prospects for Better Health for Older Women, p. 50-2.

Daniel, Margaret Truman.
"The Remarkable Man from Missouri: Harry S. Truman." In
Representative Speeches, 1984-1985, p. 151-4.

Daniels, Anna Kaplan.
"A Comparative Study of Birth Control Methods with Special Reference to Spermatoxins." In International Birth Control Conference (7th: 1930: Zurich). (Reports and Papers), p.
104-11.
"Development of Feminist Networks in the Professions." In Expanding the Role of Women in the Sciences, p. 215-27.

Daniels, Arlene.
"W.E.A.L.: The Growth of a Feminist Organization." In Women
Organizing, p. 133-51.

Darlington-Hope, Marion.
"Women of Color and the Feminization of Poverty." Women's Studies Quarterly, 13 (Summer 1985), 10-11.

Darner, Karen.
"Statement." In U.S. Congress. House. Committee on Ways and Means. Subcommittee on Social Security. Social Security Dependents' Benefits, p. 36-9.

Darrow, Margaret H.
"French Noblewomen and the New Domesticity, 1750-1850." Feminist Studies, 5 (Spring 1979), 41-65.

Datan, Nancy.
"The Lost Cause: The Aging Woman in American Feminism." In Toward the Second Decade, p. 119-28.

Dauber, Roslyn.
"Applying Policy Analysis to Women and Technology: A Framework for Consideration." In Women and Technological Change in Developing Countries, p. 237-51.

Daugherty, Mary Lee.
"The Sacrament of Serpent Handling." In Beyond Androcentrism, p. 139-57.

Daum, Annette.
"Sisterhood Is Powerful." In Spinning a Sacred Yarn, p. 45-51.

Davidoff, Lenore.
"Class and Gender in Victorian England: The Diaries of Arthur J. Munby and Hannah Cullwick." Feminist Studies, 5 (Spring 1979), 87-141.

Davidson, Diane.
"Statement." In U.S. Congress. Senate. Committee on Small Business. Women Entrepreneurs, p. 54-6.

Davis, Anne J.
"Statement." In U.S. Congress. House. Committee on Ways and Means. Subcommittee on Public Assistance and Unemployment Compensation. Teenage Pregnancy Issues, p. 82-5.
"Diethylstilbestrol: An Interdisciplinary Analysis: Overview." In The Custom-Made Child?, p. 21-2.

Davis, Carolyne K.
"Statement." In U.S. Congress. House. Committee on Energy and Commerce. Subcommittee on Health and Environment. Health Budget Proposals, p. 154-6.

Davis, Christine.
"Testimony." In U.S. Congress. House. Committee on Interstate and Foreign Commerce. Subcommittee on Consumer Protection and Finance. Nondiscrimination in Insurance, p. 111-13.

Davis, Dolores A.
"Testimony." In U.S. Congress. House. Select Committee on Aging. Subcommittee on Retirement Income and Employment. National Policy Proposals Affecting Midlife Women, p. 83-4.
"Testimony." In U.S. Congress. House. Select Committee on Aging. Subcommittee on Retirement Income and Employment. Task Force on Social Security and Women. Treatment of Women Under Social Security, p. 94-6.

Davis, Jessica G.
"Statement." In U.S. Congress. Senate. Committee on the Judiciary. Subcommittee on Separation of Powers. The Human Life Bill, p. 106-8.

Davis, Karen.
"Statement." In U.S. Congress. House. Committee on Energy and Commerce. Subcommittee on Health and Environment. Health Budget Proposals, p. 18-21.

Davis, Mollie C.
"The Countess of Huntingdon: A Leader in Missions for Social and Religious Reform." In Women in New Worlds, v. 2, p. 162-75.

Davis, Natalie Zemon.
"Gender and Genre: Women as Historical Writers, 1400-1820." In Beyond Their Sex, p. 153-82.
"Men, Women and Violence: Some Reflections on Equality." In The Role of Women in Conflict and Peace, p. 19-29.
"Women's History" in Transition: the European Case." Feminist Studies, 3 (1976), 83-103.

Davis, Patricia E.
"The Best Is Yet To Be." In Spinning a Sacred Yarn, p. 52-7.

Davis, Sandra O.
"Assertiveness: A Key to Achievement." In Women in Engineering--Beyond Recruitment, p. 49-51.

Davis, Susan A.
"Statement." In U.S. Congress. House. Committee on Small Business. National Commission on Women's Business Ownership, p. 51-3.

Davis, Suzanne.
"Statement." In U.S. Congress. House. Committee on Armed

Services. Military Personnel and Compensation Subcommittee. Benefits for Former Spouses of Military Members, pt. 2, p. 22-5.

Dawson, Kathy.
"Excerpted Testimony from the Southern California Hearings on the Feminization of Poverty." Signs, 10 (Winter, 1984), 409-10.

Dawson-Brown, Claire.
"Testimony." In U.S. Congress. Senate. Committee on the Judiciary. Subcommittee on Juvenile Justice. Effect of Pornography on Women and Children, p. 46-54.

Day, Lee Provancha.
"Talents Bring Joy." In Ye Are Free To Choose, p. 98-101.

De Cleyre, Voltairine.
"The Economic Tendency of Freethought." In Freedom, Feminism, and the State, p. 311-22.

De Lange, Janice M.
"Depression in Women: Explanations and Prevention." In NASW Conference on Social Work Practice with Women (1st: 1980: Washington, DC). Women, Power, and Change, p. 17-26.

De Neely, Yolanda Agular.
"Statement." In U.S. Congress. Senate. Committee on Labor and Human Resources. The Coming Decade, pt. 2, p. 99-101.

De Salvo, Jackie.
"Class, Gender, and Religion: A Theoretical Overview and Some Political Implications." In Women's Spirit Bonding, p. 11-34.

Dean, Sara.
"Testimony." In U.S. Congress. House. Select Committee on Aging. Subcommittee on Retirement Income and Employment. Task Force on Social Security and Women. Treatment of Women Under Social Security, p. 126-9.

Deaux, Kay.
"Internal Barriers." In Women in Organizations, p. 11-22.

Deconcini, Susan Hurley.
"Testimony." In U.S. Congress. House. Select Committee on Aging. Subcommittee on Retirement Income and Employment. National Policy Proposals Affecting Midlife Women, p. 61-2.

Decrow, Karen.
"Is the Question of Woman a Political Question?" In Cornell Conference on Women (1969: Cornell Conference). Proceedings, p. 33.

Decter, Midge.
   "Expanding World Freedom: the Self-Deception of the West."
      Vital Speeches, 47 (September 15, 1981), 723-6.
   "Statement." In U.S. Congress. Senate. Committee on Labor
      and Human Resources. Subcommittee on Family and Human
      Services. Broken Families, pt. 2, p. 5-7.

Dehardt, Doris C.
   "Can a Feminist Therapist Facilitate Clients' Heterosexual Rela-
      tionships?" In Handbook of Feminist Therapy, p. 170-82.

Delaney, Carol.
   "The Legacy of Abraham." In Beyond Androcentrism, p. 217-35.

Delaney, Geraldine.
   "Statement." In U.S. Congress. Committee on Labor and Human
      Resources. The Coming Decade, pt. 2, p. 80-3.

Delk, Yvonne V.
   "Singing the Lord's Song." In Those Preachin' Women, p. 51-60.
   "Statement." In U.S. Congress. Senate. Committee on Finance.
      Potential Inequities Affecting Women, pt. 1, p. 251-3.

Denecke, Audrey.
   "Statement." In U.S. Congress. House. Committee on Educa-
      tion and Labor. Subcommittee on Employment Opportunities.
      Oversight Hearings on Equal Employment Opportunity and Af-
      firmative Action, pt. 2, p. 189-90.

Denham, Priscilla L.
   "It's Hard to Sing the Song of Deborah." In Spinning a Sacred
      Yarn, p. 58-64.

Denmark, Florence L.
   "Women in Psychology in the United States." In Expanding the
      Role of Women in the Sciences, p. 65-78.

Dennett, Jan.
   "Statement." In U.S. Congress. Senate. Committee on Labor
      and Human Resources. Subcommittee on Family and Human
      Services. Forum for Families, p. 15-6.

Denny, Alice.
   "Excerpted Testimony from the Northern California Hearings on
      the Feminization of Poverty." Signs, 10 (Winter 1984), 398-
      401.

Denton, Cynthia.
   "Statement." In U.S. Congress. House. Committee on Post Of-
      fice and Civil Service. Subcommittee on Compensation and Em-
      ployee Benefits. Federal Pay Equity Act of 1984, pt. 1, p.
      250-1.

"Statement." In U.S. Congress. House. Committee on Post Office and Civil Service. Subcommittee on Human Resources. Pay Equity, pt. 1, p. 620-3.

Derian, Patricia M.
"Critique of Reagan Administration Human Rights Policy." In Women Leaders in American Politics, p. 374-9.
"Four Treaties Pertaining to Human Rights." Department of State Bulletin, 80 (January 1980), 31-2.
"Human Rights and International Law." Department of State Bulletin, 81 (January 1981), 21-3.
"Human Rights Conditions in Non-Communist Asia." Department of State Bulletin, 80 (May 1980), 30-2.
"Human Rights in South Africa." Department of State Bulletin, 80 (October 1980), 56-9.
"Missing and Disappeared Persons." Department of State Bulletin, 80 (February 1980), 37-9.
"Patricia Derian on Human Rights in Latin America." In Women Leaders in American Politics, p. 354-62. Same As: "Review of Human Rights in Latin America." Department of State Bulletin, 80 (October 1980), 51-5.
"Western Hemisphere: the Role of Human Rights Policy in Arms Transfers." Department of State Bulletin, 78 (November 1978), 51-4.

Derrig, Nancy L.
"Statement." In U.S. Congress. Senate. Committee on Labor and Human Resources. Subcommittee on Child and Human Development. Domestic Violence Prevention and Services Act, 1980, p. 187-90.

Derryck, Vivian Lowery.
"Statement." In U.S. Congress. Senate. Committee on Foreign Affairs. Women in Development, p. 37-40.

Deshazer, Mary.
"'My Scourge, My Sister': Louise Bogan's Muse." In Coming To Light, p. 92-104.

Detre, Katherine.
"Hypertension in Women--A Review." In The Changing Risk of Disease in Women, p. 243-55.

Devanesan, Mona.
"Statement." In U.S. Congress. Senate. Committee on Labor and Human Resources. The Coming Decade, pt. 2, p. 87-90.

Devesa, Susan S.
"Time Trends of Cancer Incidence and Mortality Among Women." In The Changing Risk of Disease in Women, p. 169-83.

Devilbiss, Lydia Allen.
"Medical Aspects of Birth Control." In American Birth Control Conference (1st: 1921: New York). Birth Control: What It Is, How It Works, What It Will Do, p. 39-45.

Devlin, Suzanne.
"Myths and Realities." In Training Conference (1st: 1984: Washington, DC). Interagency Committee on Women in Federal Law Enforcement, p. 39-41.

DeVries, Chris.
"Statement." In U.S. Congress. House. Committee on Post Office and Civil Service. Subcommittee on Compensation and Employee Benefits. Options for Conducting a Pay Equity Study, p. 434-5.

Dewine, Sue.
"Breakthrough: Making It Happen with Women's Networks." In Women in Organizations, p. 85-101.

Diamond, Irene.
"Exploring the Relationship Between Female Candidacies and the Women's Movement." In Women Organizing, p. 241-52.
"Pornography and Repression: A Reconsideration of 'Who' and 'What.'" In Take Back the Night, p. 187-203.
"Women, Representation and Public Policy: Reflections for the Future." In Women's Lives, p. 439-44.

Dickie, Jane.
"Women's Studies and the Re-vision of Liberal Education: 'What Is A Nice Girl/Boy Like You Doing Here?'" In GLCA Women's Studies Conference (7th: 1981). Toward a Feminist Transformation of the Academy, III, p. 66-7.

Dickinson, Anna E.
"Why Colored Men Should Enlist." In We Shall Be Heard, p. 100-2.

Didion, Joan.
"Why I Write." In The Writer on Her Work, p. 17-25.

Diehl, Joanne Feit.
"At Home With Loss; Elizabeth Bishop and the American Sublime." In Coming to Light, p. 123-37.

Diener, Margaret.
"Testimony." In U.S. Congress. House. Committee on Energy and Commerce. Subcommittee on Health and the Environment. Health and the Environment Miscellaneous, pt. 2, p. 85-8.

Dill, Bonnie Thornton.
"'On the Hem of Life': Race, Class, and the Prospects for Sisterhood." (1920) In Class, Race, and Sex, p. 173-88.

Dilla, Harriette A.
"The Greater Freedom by Birth Control." In American Birth
Control Conference (1st: 1921: New York). Birth Control:
What It Is, How It Works, What It Will Do, p. 74-82.

Dillman, Caroline M.
"Methodologies on Integration of Scholarship About Women Into
Sociology Courses." In Conference on "Scholars and Women"
(1981: University of Maryland). Women's Studies and the
Curriculum, p. 197-202.

Dimen, Muriel.
"Politically Correct? Politically Incorrect?" In Pleasure and
Danger, p. 138-48.

Distefano, Anna.
"Feminist Counseling." In GLCA Women's Studies Conference
(7th: 1981). Towards a Feminist Transformation of the
Academy, III, p. 27-31.

Dix, Dorothea.
"On Behalf of the Insane Poor in Kentucky." In Outspoken
Women, p. 29-38.

Dixon, Marlene.
"Chicanas and Mexicanas in a Transnational Working Class." In
The Future of Women, p. 146-80.

Dobrof, Rose.
"The Family Relationships and Living Arrangements of Older
Women." In Older Women in the City, p. 142-52.

Dobson, Jualynne.
"Nineteenth-Century A.M.E. Preaching Women: Cutting Edge of
Women's Inclusion in Church Polity." In Women in New World,
v. 1, p. 276-89.

Dolch, Debra.
"Statement." In U.S. Congress. House. Selecting Committee
on Aging. Subcommittee on Health and Long-Term Care.
Elder Abuse, p. 19.

Dole, Elizabeth Hanford.
"Statement." In U.S. Congress. House. Committee on Appro-
priations. Subcommittee on Department of Transportation and
Related Agencies Appropriations. Department of Transportation

and Related Agencies Appropriations for 1984. Washington:
U.S.G.P.O., 1983, pt. 3, p. 1-100.

"Statement." In U.S. Congress. House. Committee on Appropriations. Subcommittee on Department of Transportation and
Related Agencies Appropriations. Department of Transportation and Related Agencies Appropriations for 1985. Washington:
U.S.G.P.O., 1984, pt. 7, p. 1-110.

"Statement." In U.S. Congress. House. Committee on Appropriations. Subcommittee on Department of Transportation and
Related Agencies Appropriations. Department of Transportation and Related Agencies Appropriations for 1986. Washington:
U.S.G.P.O., 1985, pt. 1, p. 1-158.

"Statement." In U.S. Congress. House. Committee on Energy
and Commerce. Subcommittee on Commerce, Transportation,
and Tourism. Administration's Proposal to Eliminate Amtrack
Funding. Washington: U.S.G.P.O., 1985, p. 159-220.

"Statement." In U.S. Congress. House. Committee on Merchant
Marine and Fisheries. Subcommittee on Coast Guard and
Navigation. Coast Guard Oversight. Washington: U.S.G.P.O.,
1984, p. 5-26.

"Statement." In U.S. Congress. House. Committee on Merchant
Marine and Fisheries. Subcommittee on Merchant Marine.
Merchant Marine Miscellaneous. Washington: U.S.G.P.O.,
1983, p. 77-90.

"Statement." In U.S. Congress. House. Committee on Public
Works and Transportation. Subcommittee on Aviation. Review
of Airline Deregulation and Sunset of the Civil Aeronautics
Board (Organization and Procedures to be Followed by the De-
partment of Transportation in Administering Its Responsibilities
After Sunset of the Civil Aeronautics Board). Washington:
U.S.G.P.O., 1984, p. 6-128.

"Statement." In U.S. Congress. House. Committee on Public
Works and Transportation. Subcommittee on Investigations
and Oversight. Status of the Air Traffic Control System.
Washington: U.S.G.P.O., 1984, p. 3-32.

"Statement." In U.S. Congress. Committee on Public Works
and Transportation. Subcommittee on Surface Transportation.
Surface Transportation Issues. Washington: U.S.G.P.O.,
1984, p. 1042-69.

"Statement." In U.S. Congress. House. Committee on Science
and Technology. Subcommittee on Space Science and Applications. The Expendable Launch Vehicle Commercialization Act.
Washington: U.S.G.P.O., 1984, p. 2-41.

"Statement." In U.S. Congress. House. Committee on Ways
and Means. Alternatives to the Heavy Vehicle Use Tax.
Washington: U.S.G.P.O., 1984, p. 4-28.

"Statement." In U.S. Congress. Senate. Committee on Appropriations. Subcommittee on Transportation and Related Agencies. Department of Transportation and Related Agencies
Appropriations for Fiscal Year 1984. Washington: U.S.G.P.O.,
1983, v. 1, p. 1-106.

"Statement." In U.S. Congress. Senate. Committee on Appropriations. Subcommittee on Transportation and Related Agencies. Department of Transportation and Related Agencies Appropriations for Fiscal Year 1985. Washington:
U.S.G.P.O., 1984, v. 2, p. 1-93.
"Statement." In U.S. Congress. Senate. Committee on Commerce, Science, and Transportation. Motor Carrier Act of
1980. Washington: U.S.G.P.O., 1984, p. 2-12.
"Statement." In U.S. Congress. Senate. Committee on Commerce, Science, and Transportation. Nomination--DOT.
Washington: U.S.G.P.O., 1983, p. 6-47.
"Statement." In U.S. Congress. Senate. Committee on Com-
merce, Science, and Transportation. Sale of Conrail.
Washington: U.S.G.P.O., 1985, p. 6-42.
"Statement." In U.S. Congress. Senate. Committee on Com-
merce, Science, and Transportation. Subcommittee on Surface
Transportation. Alcohol and Drug Abuse on Railroads. Wash-
ington: U.S.G.P.O., 1984, p. 2-20.
"Statement." In U.S. Congress. Senate. Committee on Environ-
ment and Public Works. Testimony of Elizabeth Hanford Dole.
Washington: U.S.G.P.O., 1983, p. 7-55.
"Statement." In U.S. Congress. Senate. Committee on Finance.
Alternative to Tax on the Use of Heavy Trucks. Washington:
U.S.G.P.O., 1984, p. 18-38.

Donchin, Anne.
"Concepts of Women in Psychoanalytic Theory: The Nature-
Nurture Controversy Revisited." In Beyond Domination, p.
89-103.

Donnelly, Elaine.
"Statement." In U.S. Congress. House. Committee on Armed
Services. Subcommittee on Military Personnel. Hearings on
H.R. 6569, Registration of Women, p. 99-102.
"Statement." In U.S. Congress. House. Committee on Ways
and Means. Subcommittee on Social Security. Treatment of
men and Women Under the Social Security Program, p. 111-6.

Donohue, Mary V.
"Report and Discussion on Recommendations in the Sex Discrimi-
nation Report." In Western Regional Civil Rights and Women's
Rights Conference (4th: 1977: San Francisco, CA). Recent
Developments, p. 141-2.

Dorman, Lesley.
"Testimony." In U.S. Congress. House. Select Committee on
Aging. Subcommittee on Retirement Income and Employment.
National Policy Proposals Affecting Midlife Women, p. 44-9.

Dorrill, Marion J.
"The Identification and Distribution of ABH and Lewis Substance

in Vaginal Secretions." In Forensic Science Symposium on the Analysis of Sexual Assault Evidence (1983: Quantico, VA). Proceedings, p. 91-99.

Dougherty, Mary Agnes.
"The Social Gospel According to Phoebe: Methodist Deaconesses in the Metropolis, 1885-1918." In Women in New Worlds, v. 1, p. 200-16.

Douglas, Ann.
"Willa Cather: A Problematic Ideal." In Women, the Arts, and the 1920s in Paris and New York, p. 14-9.

Douglas, Joan.
"A Developmental Study of Sex Differences in Mathematics and Reading Avoidance." In Conference on "Scholars and Women" (1981: University of Maryland). Women's Studies and the Curriculum, p. 179-84.

Douglas, Mary Ann.
"The Role of Power in Feminist Therapy: A Reformulation." In Handbook of Feminist Therapy, p. 241-9.

Douglas, Sally.
"Statement." In U.S. Congress. House. Committee on Post Office and Civil Service. Subcommittee on Compensation and Employee Benefits. Options for Conducting a Pay Equity Study, p. 527, 531-32.

Douglass, Jane Dempsey.
"The Foundation and Significance of Christian Freedom." In Douglass, Women, Freedom, and Calvin, p. 11-23.
"Freedom in God's Order." In Douglass, Women, Freedom, and Calvin, p. 24-41.
"Freedom in Obedience." In Douglass, Women, Freedom, and Calvin, p. 108-22.
"Women's Freedom in Church Order: Calvin in the Medieval and Renaissance Context." In Douglass, Women, Freedom, and Calvin, p. 66-82.
"Women's Freedom in Church Order: Calvin in the Reformation Context." In Douglass, Women, Freedom, and Calvin, p. 83-107.
"Women's Freedom in Church Order: Calvin's View." In Douglass, Women, Freedom, and Calvin, p. 42-65.

Douvan, Elizabeth.
"Family Roles in a Twenty-Year Perspective." In The Challenge of Change, p. 199-217.
"Sex Difference in Aggression and Dominance." In The Role of Women in Conflict and Peace, p. 9-17.
"Toward a New Policy for the Family." In Women's Lives, p. 391-5.

Doyle, Jean.
"Statement." In U.S. Congress. Senate. Committee on the Judiciary. Subcommittee on the Constitution. Constitutional Amendments Relating to Abortion, v. 1, p. 1210-12.

Dresselhaus, Mildred S.
"Responsibilities of Women Faculty in Engineering Schools." In Women in Scientific and Engineering Professions, p. 128-34.

Driscoll, Gertrude P.
"Women Without Men." In Cooper Union for the Advancement of Science and Art. In Women, Society and Sex, p. 53-65.

Driscoll, Pat.
"Statement." In U.S. Congress. House. Select Committee on Children, Youth, and Families. Teen Parents and Their Children, p. 126-7, 133-4, 155.

Drissell, Kayleen.
"Career Conflicts and Solutions." In Training Conference (1st: 1984: Washington, DC). Interagency Committee on Women in Federal Law Enforcement, p. 53-7.

Dryfoos, Joy G.
"Statement." In U.S. Congress. Committee on the Judiciary. Subcommittee on the Constitution. Constitutional Amendments Relating to Abortion, v. 1, p. 378-85.
"Statement." In U.S. Congress. House. Select Committee on Population. Fertility and Contraception in America, pt. 2, p. 113-22.

Dubeck, Paula.
"Influential Alliances: Cincinnati Women in the Political Arena, 1920-1945." In Women & Men, p. 287-99.

DuBois, Barbara.
"Passionate Scholarship. Notes on Values, Knowing and Method in Feminist Social Science." In Theories of Women's Studies II, p. 11-24.

DuBois, Ellen.
"The Limitations of Sisterhood: Elizabeth Cady Stanton and Division in the American Suffrage Moment, 1875-1902." In Berkshire Conference on the History of Women (5th: 1982: Vassar College). Women and the Structure of Society, p. 160-9.
The Radicalism of the Woman Suffrage Movement: Notes Toward the Reconstruction of Nineteenth-Century Feminism." Feminist Studies, 3 (1976), 63-71.

DuCrocq, Francoise.
"The London Biblewomen and Nurses Missions, 1857-1880: Class

Relations/Women's Relations." In Berkshire Conference on the History of Women (5th: 1982: Vassar College). Women and the Structure of Society, p. 98-107.

Duffe, Nikki N.
"Reaching the Middle Class Female." In Women in Crisis Conference (1st: 1979: New York, NY). Women in Crisis, p. 64-8.

Duggan, Lisa.
"The Social Enforcement of Heterosexuality and Lesbian Resistance in the 1920s." In Class, Race, and Sex, p. 75-92.

Dujon, Diane.
"Bring It Back to the People You're Researching." Women's Studies Quarterly, 13 (Summer 1985), 13.
"Overcoming Barriers to Education." Women's Studies Quarterly, 13 (Summer 1985) 13.

Dulansey, Mary Anne L.
"Session Summary." In International Conference on Women and Food (1978: University of Arizona). A Conference on the Role of Women in Meeting Basic Food And Water Needs in Developing Countries, p. 135-6.

Dumas, Bethany K.
"Male-Female Conversational Interaction Cues: Using Data From Dialect Surveys." In Conference on the Sociology of the Languages of American Women (1976: New Mexico State University). Proceedings, p. 41-52.

Duncan, Carol.
"Happy Mothers and Other New Ideas in Eighteenth-Century French Art." In Feminism and Art History, p. 201-19.
"Virility and Domination in Early Twentieth-Century Vanguard Painting." In Feminism and Art History, p. 293-313.

Dunham, Vera S.
"The Changing Image of Women in Soviet Literature." In The Role and Status of Women in the Soviet Union, p. 60-97.

Dunkle, Margaret.
"Statement." In U.S. Congress. House. Committee on Government Operations. Intergovernmental Relations and Human Resources Subcommittee. Barriers to Self-Sufficiency for Single Female Heads of Families, p. 220-4.
"Statement." In U.S. Congress. Senate. Committee on Labor and Human Resources. Subcommittee on Health and Scientific Research. Women in Science and Technology Equal Opportunity Act, 1980, p. 50-2.

Dunlap, Mary.
"Resistance to the Women's Movement in the United States. The

ERA Controversy as Prototype." In <u>Toward the Second Decade</u>, p. 163-70.

Dunning, (Mrs.) George A.
"Testimony." In U.S. Congress. House. Committee on Ways and Means. <u>Birth Control (1932)</u>, p. 64-5.

Durchholz, Pat.
"Women in A Man's World: The Female Engineers." In <u>Women & Men</u>, p. 214-30.

Duskin, Betty.
"Testimony." In U.S. Congress. House. Select Committee on Aging. Subcommittee on Retirement Income and Employment. Task Force on Social Security and Women. <u>Treatment of Women Under Social Security</u>, p. 87-9.

Duxbury, Mitzi.
"Testimony." In U.S. Congress. House. Committee on Energy and Commerce. Subcommittee on Health and the Environment. <u>Health and the Environment Miscellaneous</u>, pt. 5, p. 799-801.

Dworkin, Andrea.
"Pornography and Grief." In <u>Take Back the Night</u>, p. 286-91.
"Testimony." In U.S. Congress. Senate. Committee on the Judiciary. Subcommittee on Juvenile Justice. <u>Effect of Pornography on Women and Children</u>, p. 227-9.

Dydo, Ulla E.
"To Have the Winning Language: Texts and Contexts of Gertrude Stein." In <u>Coming to Light</u>, p. 58-73.

Dye, Nancy Schrom.
"Clio's American Daughters: Male History, Female Reality." In <u>Prism of Sex</u>, p. 9-31.
"Creating a Feminist Alliance: Sisterhood and Class Conflict in the New York Women's Trade Union League, 1903-1914." <u>Feminist Studies</u>, 2 (1975), 24-38.
"Feminism or Unionism? The New York Women's Trade Union League and the Labor Movement." <u>Feminist Studies</u>, 3 (1976), 111-25.
"Mary Breckenridge, the Frontier Nursing Service, and the Introduction of Nurse-Midwifery in the United States." In <u>Women and Health in America</u>, p. 327-43.

Dyer, Carolyn Stewart.
"The Costs of Freedom of the Press." In <u>Representative American Speeches: 1983-84</u>, p. 140-52.

East, Catherine.
"Statement." In U.S. Congress. House. Committee on Govern-
ment Operations. Manpower and Housing Subcommittee. The
Women's Bureau, p. 104.
"Statement." In U.S. Congress. House. Committee on Ways
and Means. Economic Equity Act and Related Tax and Pen-
sion Reform, p. 58-60.
"Statement." In U.S. Congress. House. Committee on Ways
and Means. Subcommittee on Social Security. Social Security
Dependents' Benefits, p. 52-4.
"Statement." In U.S. Congress. Select Committee on Aging.
Subcommittee on Retirement Income and Employment. Task
Force on Social Security and Women. Security and Women.
Inequities Toward Women in the Social Security System, p.
112-4.
"Testimony." In U.S. Equal Employment Opportunity Commission.
Hearings Before the U.S. Equal Employment Opportunity Com-
mission on Job Segregation and Wage Discrimination, p. 94-110.
"Testimony." In U.S. Congress. House. Committee on Inter-
state and Foreign Commerce. Subcommittee on Consumer Pro-
tection and Finance. Nondiscrimination in Insurance, p. 268-9.

Eastman, Crystal.
"Feminism: A Statement Read at the First Feminist Congress in
the United States, New York, March 1, 1919." In Eastman,
Crystal Eastman on Women & Revolution, p. 49-51.
"Political Equality League (Report on the Wisconsin Suffrage Cam-
paign)." In Eastman, Crystal Eastman on Women & Revolution,
p. 66-70.
"The Three Essentials for Accident Prevention." In Eastman,
Crystal Eastman on Women & Revolution, p. 280-90.
"We Have the Vote, Now We Can Begin." In Outspoken Women,
p. 39-42.

Eaton, Shannon.
"Statement." In U.S. Congress. House. Committee on Post Of-
fice and Civil Service. Subcommittee on Human Resources.
Pay Equity, pt. 1, p. 319-21.

Ebeling, Elizabeth.
"Statement." In U.S. Congress. House. Committee on Energy
and Commerce. Subcommittee on Health and the Environment.
Pregnancy-Related Health Services, p. 265-6.

Echols, Alice.
"The Taming of the Id: Feminist Sexual Politics, 1968-83." In
Pleasure and Danger, p. 50-72.

Eddy, Mary Baker.
"Christian Health." (1886) In Outspoken Women, p. 44-50.

Edelman, Marian Wright.
"Commencement Address, Bryn Mawr College, May 15, 1982." In I Am Honored To Be Here Today, p. 69-77.

Edmonds, Juanita.
"Testimony." In U.S. Congress. Senate. Committee on Labor and Human Resources. Women in Transition, 1983, p. 53-5.

Edwards, Jane.
"Statement." In U.S. Congress. Senate. Committee on Labor and Human Resources. Barriers to Adoption, p. 241-3.

Edwards, Lynn.
"Statement." In U.S. Congress. House. Committee on Post Office and Civil Service. Subcommittee on Compensation and Employee Benefits. Options for Conducting a Pay Equity Study, p. 196-8.

Edwards, Maureen.
"Neonatology: Directions and Goals." In The Custom-Made Child?, p. 123-8.

Ehrenreich, Barbara.
"Luncheon Address." In Warner, Anne R. Health Womenpower, p. 55-9.

Eidson, Elaine.
"Statement." In U.S. Congress. House. Committee on Armed Services. Subcommittee on Military Personnel. Hearings on H.R. 6569, Registration of Women, p. 2-5.

Eidson, Geraldine.
"Testimony." In U.S. Congress. House. Select Committee on Aging. Subcommittee on Retirement Income and Employment. National Policy Proposal Affecting Midlife Women, p. 81-2.
"Testimony." In U.S. Congress. House. Select Committee on Aging. Subcommittee on Retirement Income and Employment. Task Force on Social Security and Women. Treatment of Women Under Social Security, p. 69-73.

Eisenstein, Zillah.
"Antifeminism and the Right." In Class, Race, and Sex, p. 111-25.

Ekman, Rosalind.
"Women and the Changing Norms of Health and Disease." In Conference on "Scholars and Women" (1981: University of Maryland). Women's Studies and the Curriculum, p. 77-84.

Ekstrom, Susan Cope.
"A Report on Birth in Three Cultures." In Birth Control and Controlling Birth, p. 213-22.

Eliason, Claudia Furhiman.
  "Making You and Your Child Successful." In A Woman's
    Choices, p. 69-78.

Ellis, Effie O'Neal.
  "Statement." In U.S. Congress. House. Select Committee on
    Children, Youth, and Families. Teen Parents and Their Chil-
    dren, p. 100-2.

Ellis, Katherine.
  "Paradise Lost: the Limits of Domesticity in the Nineteenth-
    Century Novel." Feminist Studies, 2 (1975), 55-63.

Ellis, Tottie.
  "Statement." In U.S. Congress. House. Committee on Armed
    Services. Subcommittee on Military Personnel. Women in the
    Military, p. 249-52.
  "Statement." In U.S. Congress. House. Committee on Ways
    and Means. Subcommittee on Social Security. Treatment of
    Men and Women Under the Social Security Program, p. 183-86.

Elmendorf, Mary L.
  "Changing Role of Maya Mothers and Daughters." In Women and
    Technological Change in Developing Countries, p. 149-79.
  "Women, Water, and Waste: Beyond Access." In Health Needs
    of the World's Poor Women, p. 93-5.

Elmer, Elizabeth.
  "Statement." In U.S. Congress. House. Select Committee on
    Children, Youth, and Families. Families in Crisis, p. 106-9.

Elshtain, Jean Bethke.
  "Methodological Sophistication and Conceptual Confusion: A
    Critique of Mainstream Political Science." In Prism of Sex,
    p. 229-51.

Emerson, Bettye.
  "Testimony." In U.S. Commission on Civil Rights. Hearing Be-
    fore the U.S. Commission on Civil Rights Held in Denver,
    1976, p. 300-2, 316.

Emery, Jean.
  "Testimony." In U.S. Commission on Civil Rights. Hearing Be-
    fore the U.S. Commission on Civil Rights Held in Denver,
    1976, p. 450-6, 59-60, 61-2.

Endres, Karen A.
  "Mary Moragne's The British Partizan." In Reynolds Conference
    (2nd: 1975: University of South Carolina). South Carolina
    Women Writers, p. 27-45.

Engelsman, Joan Chamberlain.
  "The Legacy of Georgia Harkness." In Women in New Worlds,
    v. 2, p. 338-58.

England, Paula.
  "Occupational Segregation and the Earnings Gap." In Compar-
    able Worth: Issues for the Eighties, p. 21-5.

Englund, Jan.
  "Testimony." In U.S. Congress. House. Committee on Energy
    and Commerce. Subcommittee on Health and the Environment.
    Health and the Environment Miscellaneous, pt. 7, p. 68-79.

Enloe, Cynthia H.
  "Women Textile Workers in the Militarization of Southeast Asia."
    In Perspectives on Power, p. 73-86.

Ensor, Phyllis.
  "Testimony." In U.S. Congress. House. Committee on Energy
    and Commerce. Subcommittee on Health and the Environment.
    Health and the Environment Miscellaneous, pt. 4, p. 301-2.

Epstein, Cynthia Fuchs.
  "The Role Strain of Balancing Political and Professional Respon-
    sibilities with Family and Personal Responsibilities." In Women
    in the Judiciary, p. 10-3.

Erhart, Robin
  "DES and Drugs in Pregnancy: A Consumer Reaction." In The
    Custom-Made Child?, p. 47-50.

Erkut, Sumru.
  "Social Psychology Looks at But Does Not See the Undergraduate
    Woman." In The Undergraduate Woman, p. 183-204.

Erlich, Susie.
  "Caucus Report of the Northwest Region." In Western Regional
    Civil Rights and Women's Rights Conference (4th: 1977:
    San Francisco, CA). Recent Developments, p. 143-5.

Ermath, Elizabeth.
  "Fictional Consensus and Female Casualties." In The Represen-
    tation of Women in Fiction, p. 1-18.

Ernster, Virginia L.
  "Risk Factors for Benign and Malignant Breast Disease." In
    The Changing Risk of Disease in Women, p. 185-98.

Escalante, Alicia.
  "Testimony." In U.S. Commission on Civil Rights. Hearing

Before the U.S. Commission on Civil Rights Held in Chicago, 1974, v. 1, p. 123-9.

Espin, Oliva M.
"Cultural and Historical Influences on Sexuality in Hispanic/Latin Women: Implications for Psychotherapy." In Pleasure and Danger, p. 149-64.

Estabrook, Leigh S.
"Women's Work in the Library/Information Sector." In My Troubles Are Going To Have Trouble with Me, p. 160-72.

Etter, Carolyn.
"Testimony." In U.S. Commission on Civil Rights. Hearing Before the U.S. Commission on Civil Rights Held in Denver, 1976, p. 178-9.

Everhart, Janet S.
"Maggie Newton Van Cott: The Methodist Episcopal Church Considers the Question of Women Clergy." In Women in New Worlds, v. 2, p. 300-17.

Ewell, Yvonne.
"Viable Alternatives to Traditional Education for Minorities and Women." In Young Women and Environment, p. 48-9.

Fabricant, Carole.
"Pope's Portraits of Women: The Tyranny of the Pictorial Eye." In Women & Men, p. 74-91.

Fadeley, Nancie.
"Statement." In U.S. Congress. House. Select Committee on Aging. Subcommittee on Retirement Income and Employment. Impact of Reagan Economics on Aging Women, p. 6-8.

Falco, Mathea.
"Narcotics: Successes in International Drug Control." Department of State Bulletin, 79 (August 1979), 50-3.

Falk, Joyce Duncan.
"The New Technology for Research in European Women's History: 'Online' Bibliographies." Signs, 9 (Autumn 1983), 120-33.

Falk, Nancy Auer.
"Draupadi and the Dharma." In Beyond Androcentrism, p. 89-113.

Falvey, Mary C.
"Testimony." In U.S. Congress. Senate. Select Committee on

Aging. <u>Adapting Social Security to a Changing Work Force</u>, p. 54-61.

Farenthold, Frances T.
"Women in Power." In International Women's Year Conference on Women in Public Life (1975: Lyndon Baines Johnson Library). <u>Women in Public Life</u>, p. 22-3.

Farnham, Marynia.
"The Lost Sex." In Cooper Union for the Advancement of Science and Art. <u>Women, Society and Sex</u>, p. 33-52.

Farris, Barbara.
"Statement." In U.S. Congress. House. Committee on Post Office and Civil Service. Subcommittee on Compensation and Employee Benefits. <u>Options for Conducting a Pay Equity Study</u>, p. 178-9.

Fasal, Elfriede.
"Estrogen and Breast Cancer." In <u>Hormonal Contraceptives, Estrogens, and Human Welfare</u>, p. 85-98.

Fasciona, Josephine.
"Can We Afford to Say 'Good Morning'? Mixing People and Computers in the Workplace." <u>Vital Speeches</u>, 48 (February 15, 1982), 277-80.

Faunce, Patricia Spencer.
"Teaching Feminist Therapies: Integrating Feminist Therapy, Pedagogy, and Scholarship." In <u>Handbook of Feminist Therapy</u>, p. 309-20.

Fausto-Sterling, Anne.
"The New Research on Women: How Does It Affect the Natural Sciences?" <u>Women's Studies Quarterly</u>, 13 (Summer 1985), 30-2.

Faver, Catherine A.
"Generational and Life-Cycle Effects on Women's Achievement Orientation." In <u>Women's Lives</u>, p. 111-3.

Fee, Elizabeth.
"From Voluntary Motherhood to Planned Parenthood: Perspectives on the Birth Control Movement in America." In Margaret Sanger Centennial Conference (1979: Northampton, MA). <u>Margaret Sanger Centennial Conference</u>, p. 51-9.
"The Sexual Politics of Victorian Social Anthropology." In <u>Clio's Consciousness Raised</u>, p. 86-102.

Feiger, Lynn D.
"Statement." In U.S. Congress. House. Committee on Post

Office and Civil Service. Subcommittee on Civil Service. Federal Government Affirmative Action Policies and Programs, p. 32-5.

Feinsgold, Ellen B.
"Speech." In Women's Travel Issues, p. 733-8.

Feinstein, Dianne.
"Women in Politics: Time for a Change." In Representative American Speeches: 1983-1984, p. 99-103.

Feistritzer, Emily C.
"Statement." In U.S. Congress. Senate. Committee on Labor and Human Resources. Subcommittee on Education, Arts and Humanities. Civil Rights Act of 1984, pt. 2, p. 199-201.

Feit, Rona F.
"Organizing for Political Power: The National Women's Political Caucus." In Women Organizing, p. 184-208.

Feldberg, Roslyn L.
"Comparable Worth: Toward Theory and Practice in the United States." Signs, 10 (Winter 1984), 311-28.

Feldman, Margaret.
"Psychological Differences Between Men and Women." In Cornell Conference on Women (1969: Cornell University). Proceedings, p. 71-9.

Fennema, Elizabeth.
"Sex-Related Differences in Mathematics Achievement: Where and Why." In Hyman Blumberg Symposium on Research in Early Childhood Education (8th: 1976: Johns Hopkins University). Women and the Mathematical Mystique, p. 76-93.

Fenton, Ann.
"Testimony." In U.S. Commission on Civil Rights. Hearing Before the U.S. Commission on Civil Rights Held in Denver, 1976, p. 456-7.

Fenwick, Millicent.
"Statement." In U.S. Congress. House. Committee on Education and Labor. Subcommittee on Select Education. Hearings on Foreign Languages and International Studies. Washington: U.S.G.P.O., 1980, p. 18-23.
"Statement." In U.S. Congress. House. Committee on Public Works and Transportation. Subcommittee on Surface Transportation. Examining Current Conditions in the Trucking Industry and the Possible Necessity for Change in the Manner and Scope of Its Regulations. Washington: U.S.G.P.O., 1980, pt. 3, p. 4-5-10.

"Statement." In U.S. Congress. House. Committee on Public
Works and Transportation. Subcommittee on Water Resources.
Proposed Water Resources Development Projects of the U.S.
Army Corps of Engineers. Washington: U.S.G.P.O., 1982,
p. 1665-8.
"Statement." In U.S. Congress. House. Committee on Veter-
ans' Affairs. Subcommittee on Education, Training, and Em-
ployment. Veterans Employment Programs. Washington:
U.S.G.P.O., 1981, p. 9-11.
"Statement." In U.S. Congress. House. Committee on Ways
and Means. Advisability of a Tax Reduction in 1980 Effective
for 1981. Washington: U.S.G.P.O., 1980, v. 1, p. 216-22.
"Statement." In U.S. Congress. House. Select Committee on
Aging. Subcommittee on Retirement Income and Employment.
Task Force on Social Security and Women. Treatment of
Women Under Social Security, v. 4, p. 17-8.
"Statement." In U.S. Congress. Senate. Committee on Agri-
culture, Nutrition, and Forestry. Subcommittee on Foreign
Agricultural Policy. Cargo Preference Laws as They Relate
to Public Law 480. Washington: U.S.G.P.O., 1981, p. 1-3.
"Statement." In U.S. Congress. Senate. Committee on Foreign
Relations. Nomination of Hon. Millicent Fenwick, p. 5-10.
"Statement." In U.S. Congress. Senate. Committee on the
Judiciary. Subcommittee on Juvenile Justice. Alternative
Disposition to Juvenile Incarceration. Washington:
U.S.G.P.O., 1983, p. 2-3.
"Statement." In U.S. Congress. Senate. Committee on the
Judiciary. Subcommittee on Separation of Powers. The
Human Life Bill, p. 178-80.

Feral, Josette.
"The Powers of Difference." In The Future of Difference, p.
88-94.

Ferge, Zsuzsa.
"Explicit and Comprehensive Family Policy: Hungary." In Inter-
national Working Party of Family Policy (1977: Arden House).
Family Policy, p. 68-90.

Ferguson, Nancy.
"Summary of Panel on Food/Nutrition Problems--Impact on Women
and Women's Role in Interventions to Solve Them." In Inter-
national Conference on Women and Food (1978: University of
Arizona). A Conference on the Role of Women in Meeting
Basic Food and Water Needs in Developing Countries, p. 41-2.

Fernandez Kelly, Maria Patricia.
"Maquiladoras: The View From the Inside." In My Troubles
Are Going To Have Trouble With Me, p. 229-46.

Fernandez-Mattei, Margarita.
"Statement." In U.S. Congress. Senate. Committee on Labor

and Human Resources. Subcommittee on Family and Human
Services. Reauthorization of the Adolescent Family Life Demonstration Projects Act of 1981, p. 222-4.

Ferrante, Joan M.
"The Education of Women in the Middle Ages in Theory, Fact,
and Fantasy." In Beyond Their Sex, p. 9-42.

Ferraro, Geraldine A.
"Acceptance Speech. Delivered at the Democratic National Con-
vention, San Francisco, California, July 19, 1984." Vital
Speeches, 50 (August 15, 1984), 644-6. Also in Historic
Documents of 1984, p. 655-8.
"Controversy Over the Federal Budget Deficit." Congressional
Digest, 63 (February 1984), 56, 58.
"Speech at the National Women's Political Caucus Conference,
July, 1981." Ms, 10 (October 1981), 94.
"Statement." In U.S. Congress. House. Committee on Appro-
priations. Subcommittee on the Departments of Labor, Health
and Human Services, Education, and Related Agencies. De-
partments of Labor, Health and Human Services, Education,
and Related Agencies Appropriations for 1982. Washington:
U.S.G.P.O., 1981, pt. 9, p. 662-7.
"Statement." In U.S. Congress. House. Committee on Education and Labor. Subcommittee on Labor-Management Relations. Hearing on Pension Legislation. Washington:
U.S.G.P.O., 1983, p. 141-7.
"Statement." In U.S. Congress. House. Committee on Education and Labor. Subcommittee on Labor-Management Relations.
Pension Equity for Women, p. 26-8.
"Statement." In U.S. Congress. House. Committee on Energy
and Commerce. Subcommittee on Commerce, Transportation,
and Tourism. Hazardous Materials Transportation Act Author-
ization, Fiscal Year 1982. Washington: U.S.G.P.O., 1981,
p. 3-11.
"Statement." In U.S. Congress. House. Committee on Energy
and Commerce. Subcommittee on Oversight and Investigations.
DOE Enforcement: RIF'S and Budget Reductions. Washing-
ton: U.S.G.P.O., 1981, v. 2, p. 11-4.
"Statement." In U.S. Congress. House. Committee on Govern-
ment Operations. Manpower and Housing Subcommittee. Equal
Employment Opportunity Commission's Handling of Pay Equity
Cases, p. 17-20.
"Statement." In U.S. Congress. House. Committee on House
Administration. Task Force on Elections. Campaign Finance
Reform. Washington: U.S.G.P.O., 1984, p. 203-19.
"Statement." In U.S. Congress. House. Committee on Post Of-
fice and Civil Service. Subcommittee on Compensation and
Employee Benefits. Civil Service Spouse Retirement Equity
Act. Washington: U.S.G.P.O., 1984, p. 9-11.
"Statement." In U.S. Congress. House. Committee on Post

Office and Civil Service. Subcommittee on Human Resources. Pay Equity, p. 1-3.

"Statement." In U.S. Congress. House. Committee on Public Works and Transportation. Subcommittee on Public Buildings and Grounds. To Provide Improved Protection for Foreign Diplomatic Missions. Washington: U.S.G.P.O., 1982, p. 33-40.

"Statement." In U.S. Congress. House. Committee on Public Works and Transportation. Subcommittee on Surface Transportation. Review of the Implementation of the Surface Transportation Assistance Act of 1982. Washington: U.S.G.P.O., 1983, p. 470-1.

"Statement." In U.S. Congress. House. Committee on Small Business. Subcommittee on General Oversight and Minority Enterprise. Women in Business, p. 4-5.

"Statement." In U.S. Congress. House. Committee on the Budget. Task Force on Entitlements, Uncontrollables, and Indexing. Women and Children in Poverty, p. 3-4.

"Statement." In U.S. Congress. House. Committee on the Judiciary. Subcommittee on Immigration, Refugees, and International Law. INS Oversight/Authorization. Washington: U.S.G.P.O., 1981, p. 107-12.

"Statement." In U.S. Congress. House. Committee on Ways and Means. Economic Equity Act and Related Tax and Pension Reform, p. 21-3.

"Statement." In U.S. Congress. House. Committee on Ways and Means. Subcommittee on Social Security. Financing Problems of the Social Security System. Washington: U.S.G.P.O., 1983, pt. 1, p. 33-9.

"Statement." In U.S. Congress. House. Committee on Ways and Means. Subcommittee on Trade. Miscellaneous Tariff and Trade Bills. Washington: U.S.G.P.O., 1982, p. 300-2.

"Statement." In U.S. Congress. House. Select Committee on Aging. Subcommittee on Retirement Income and Employment. Task Force on Social Security and Women. Treatment of Women Under Social Security, v. 1, p. 3-4, v. 3, p. 14, v. 4, p. 3-4.

"Statement." In U.S. Congress. Senate. Committee on Commerce, Science, and Transportation. Subcommittee on Surface Transportation. Tandem Truck Safety Act of 1984. Washington: U.S.G.P.O., 1984, p. 9-14.

"Statement." In U.S. Congress. Senate. Committee on Finance. Potential Inequities Affecting Women, pt. 2, p. 61-3.

"Statement." In U.S. Congress. Senate. Committee on Governmental Affairs. Subcommittee on Civil Service, Post Office, and General Services. Flexitime (Alternative Work Schedule) Legislation. Washington: U.S.G.P.O., 1982, p. 2-7.

"Statement." In U.S. Congress. Senate. Committee on Labor and Human Resources. Subcommittee on Labor. Retirement Equity Act of 1983, p. 14-16.

"Who Will Fight for the Worth of Women's Work? Women in

Leadership Can Make a Difference." Vital Speeches, 49 (November 15, 1982), 70-3.

"Women in Leadership Can Make a Difference." In Representative American Speeches: 1982-1983, p. 198-206.

Ferree, Myra Marx.
"Sacrifice, Satisfaction, and Social Change: Employment and the Family." In My Troubles Are Going to Have Trouble With Me, p. 61-79.

Ferrell, Dolores.
"Statement." In California. Legislature. Joint Committee on Legal Equality. Women in the Justice System, p. 44-52.

Ferris, Carolyn.
"The Women's Movement as Catalyst for Change in Obstetrical Care Service." In Women: A Developmental Perspective, p. 271-82.

Ferron, Roberta.
"Special Workshop Report on Sex Discrimination." In Western Regional Civil Rights and Women's Rights Conference (4th: 1977: San Francisco, CA). Recent Developments, p. 140.

"State and Local Agencies' Workshop Report on Legal Questions Involved in the Sunshine Act, Freedom of Information Act, and the Privacy Act." In Western Regional Civil Rights and Women's Rights Conference (4th: 1977: San Francisco, CA). Recent Developments, p. 137-9.

Fertig, Beverly.
"Testimony." In U.S. Congress. House. Committee on Energy and Commerce. Subcommittee on Health and the Environment. Health and the Environment Miscellaneous, pt. 3, p. 303-4.

Fethke, Carol Carde Oliven.
"Living Too Long, Dying Too Young, and Disability for the Homemaker." In Women's Lives, p. 405-15.

Fiedler, Bobbi.
"Statement." In U.S. Congress. House. Committee on Appropriations. Subcommittee on the Department of the Interior and Related Agencies. Department of the Interior and Related Agencies Appropriations for 1984. Washington: U.S.G.P.O., 1983, pt. 12, p. 123-33.

"Statement." In U.S. Congress. House. Committee on Appropriations. Subcommittee on Department of the Interior and Related Agencies. Department of the Interior and Related Agencies Appropriations for 1985. Washington: U.S.G.P.O., 1984, p. 504-9.

"Statement." In U.S. Congress. House. Committee on Appropriations. Subcommittee on Department of Transportation and

Related Agencies Appropriations. <u>Department of Transporta-</u>
<u>tion and Related Agencies Appropriations for 1984</u>. Washing-
ton: U.S.G.P.O., 1983, pt. 7, p. 264-8.
"Statement." In U.S. Congress. House. Committee on Appro-
priations. Subcommittee on Department of Transportation and
Related Agencies Appropriations. <u>Department of Transporta-</u>
<u>tion and Related Agencies Appropriations for 1985</u>. Washing-
ton: U.S.G.P.O., 1984, pt. 7, p. 863-89.
"Statement." In U.S. Congress. House. Committee on Appro-
priations. Subcommittee on Energy and Water Development.
<u>Energy and Water Development Appropriations, for 1982</u>.
Washington: U.S.G.P.O., 1981, pt. 9, p. 1001-7.
"Statement." In U.S. Congress. House. Committee on Appro-
priations. Subcommittee on Energy and Water Development.
<u>Energy and Water Development Appropriatons for 1983</u>.
Washington: U.S.G.P.O., 1982, pt. 7, p. 1-18.
"Statement." In U.S. Congress. House. Committee on Appro-
priations. Subcommittee on Energy and Water Development.
<u>Energy and Water Development Appropriations for 1984</u>.
Washington: U.S.G.P.O., 1983, pt. 8, p. 2046-66.
"Statement." In U.S. Congress. House. Committee on Armed
Services. Subcommittee on Military Installations and Facilities.
<u>Hearing on H.R. 1816 (H.R. 2972) to Authorize Certain Con-</u>
<u>struction at Military Installations for Fiscal Year 1984, and</u>
<u>for Other Purposes</u>. Washington: U.S.G.P.O., 1983, p.
871-9.
"Statement." In U.S. Congress. House. Committee on Interior
and Insular Affairs. Subcommittee on Public Lands and Na-
tional Parks. <u>Public Land Management Policy</u>. Washington:
U.S.G.P.O., 1985, pt. 9, p. 199-204.
"Statement." In U.S. Congress. House. Committee on the
Budget. Task Force on Entitlements, Uncontrollables, and
Indexing. <u>Women and Children in Poverty</u>, p. 4-5.
"Statement." In U.S. Congress. House. Committee on the
Judiciary. Subcommittee on Civil and Constitutional Rights.
<u>School Desegregation</u>. Washington: U.S.G.P.O., 1982, p.
98-117.
"Statement." In U.S. Congress. House. Committee on Ways
and Means. <u>Economic Equity Act and Related Tax and Pension</u>
<u>Reform</u>, p. 50-2.
"Statement." In U.S. Congress. House. Committee on Ways
and Means. Subcommittee on Trade. <u>Options to Improve the</u>
<u>Trade Remedy Laws</u>. Washington: U.S.G.P.O., 1983, p.
847-50.
"Statement." In U.S. Congress. House. Speaker's Commission
on Pages. <u>Hearings Before the Speaker's Commission on Pages</u>.
Washington: U.S.G.P.O., 1982, pt. 1, p. 109-16.
"Statement." In U.S. Congress. Senate. Committee on Appropriations. Subcommittee on Energy and Water Development.
<u>Energy and Water Development Appropriations for Fiscal Year</u>
<u>1982</u>. Washington: U.S.G.P.O., 1982, pt. 3, p. 2386-2438.

"Statement." In U.S. Congress. Senate. Committee on Appropriations. Subcommittee on Energy and Water Development. Energy and Water Development Appropriations for Fiscal Year 1983. Washington: U.S.G.P.O., 1983, pt. 3, p. 1313-22.

"Statement." In U.S. Congress. Senate. Committee on Appropriations. Subcommittee on Energy and Water Development. Energy and Water Development Appropriations for Fiscal Year 1984. Washington: U.S.G.P.O., 1983, pt. 3, p. 2464-2522.

"Statement." In U.S. Congress. Senate. Committee on Appropriations. Subcommittee on Transportation and Related Agencies. Department of Transportation and Related Agencies Appropriations for Fiscal Year 1984. Washington: U.S.G.P.O., 1983, pt. 1, p. 1063-7.

"Statement." In U.S. Congress. Senate. Committee on Appropriations. Subcommittee on Transportation and Related Agencies. Department of Transportation and Related Agencies Appropriations for Fiscal Year 1985. Washington: U.S.G.P.O., 1984, pt. 3, p. 470-8.

"Statement." In U.S. Congress. Senate. Committee on Energy and Natural Resources. Subcommittee on Public Lands and Reserved Water. Miscellaneous Resolutions, Conveyances, Trail Study Designations, Ceiling Increase and Boundary Adjustments in Units of the National Park System and On Public Lands. Washington: U.S.G.P.O., 1984, p. 155-7.

"Statement." In U.S. Congress. Senate. Committee on Labor and Human Resources. Private Sector Initiatives. Washington: U.S.G.P.O., 1984, p. 16-31.

Fiedler, Maureen.
"The Congressional Ambitions of Female Political Elites." In Women Organizing, p. 253-88.

Fields, Marjory.
"Statement." In U.S. Congress. House. Committee on Science and Technology. Subcommittee on Domestic and International Scientific Planning, Analysis, and Cooperation. Research into Violent Behavior: Domestic Violence, p. 262-72.

Fierst, Edith U.
"Discussion (of Supplemental OASI Benefits to Homemakers)." In A Challenge to Social Security, p 66-72.

"Statement." In U.S. Congress. House. Committee on Ways and Means. Subcommittee on Social Security. Social Security Dependents' Benefits, p. 16-8.

"Statement." In U.S. Congress. House. Select Committee on Aging. Subcommittee on Retirement Income and Employment. Task Force on Social Security and Women. Inequities Toward Women in the Social Security System, p. 123-5.

"Statement." In U.S. Congress. House. Select Committee on Aging. Subcommittee on Retirement Income and Employment. Task Force on Social Security and Women. Treatment of Women Under Social Security, v. 1, p. 121-5, v. 4, p. 132-4.

Fimbres, Martha Molina.
"The Chicana in Transition." In NASW Conference on Social Work Practice with Women (1st: 1980: Washington, DC). Women, Power, and Change, p. 89-95.

Fineshriber, Phyllis.
"Testimony." In U.S. Congress. House. Select Committee on Aging. Subcommittee on Retirement Income and Employment. Task Force on Social Security and Women. Treatment of Women Under Social Security, p. 211-20.

Finkelstein, Norma.
"Innovative Alcoholism Programs for Women." In Women in Crisis Conference (1st: 1979: New York, NY). Women in Crisis, p. 122-7.

Finn, Judith B.
"Statement." In U.S. Congress. House. Select Committee on Aging. Subcommittee on Retirement Income and Employment. Task Force on Social Security and Aging. Inequities Toward Women in the Social Security System, p. 150-3.
"Statement." In U.S. Congress. Senate. Committee on Labor and Human Resources. Sex Discrimination in the Workplace, p. 428-31.
"Testimony." In U.S. Congress. Senate. Committee on the Judiciary. Subcommittee on the Constitution. The Impact of The Equal Rights Amendment, pt. 1, p. 828-32.

Finne, Grace.
"What Can International Development Banks Do?" In International Conference on Women and Food (1978: University of Arizona). A Conference on the Role of Women in Meeting Basic Food and Water Needs in Developing Countries, p. 137-42.

Fiorenza, Elisabeth Schussler.
"Claiming the Center: A Critical Feminist Theology of Liberation." In Women's Spirit Bonding, p. 293-309.

Fippinger, Grace J.
"This Is a Very Good Time. Seek Out the Problems." Vital Speeches, 46 (January 15, 1980), 222-4.

Fire Thunder, Celia.
"Excerpted Testimony From the Southern California Hearings on the Feminization of Poverty." Signs, 10 (Winter 1984), 406-8.

Fischer, Mary Ellen.
"Women in Romanian Politics: Elena Ceausescu, Pronatalism, and the Promotion of Women." In Women, State, and Party in Eastern Europe, p. 121-37.

Fisher, Marguerite.
    "The Future of Women in America." In Cornell Conference on
        Women (1969: Cornell University). Proceedings, p. 61.

Fitch, (Mrs.) George A.
    "Statement." In U.S. Congress. House. Committee on Foreign
        Affairs. American Neutrality Policy, p. 401-8.

Fitzpatrick, Beatrice."
    "Statement." In U.S. Congress. House. Committee on Small
        Business. Subcommittee on General Oversight and Minority
        Enterprise. Women in Business, p. 127-45.
    "Statement." In U.S. Congress. House. Committee on Small
        Business. Women-In-Business Programs in the Federal Gov-
        ernment, p. 95-101.

Fitzpatrick, Mary Anne.
    "Effective Interpersonal Communication for Women of the Corpora-
        tion: Think Like a Man, Talk Like a Lady." In Women in
        Organizations, p. 73-84.

Flanagan, Hallie.
    "Opening Address, Federal Theatre Production Conference,
        Poughkeepsie, July 1936." In Women in Theatre, p. 182-7.

Flanders, Jane.
    "The Fallen Woman in Fiction." In Feminist Visions, p. 97-109.

Flax, Jane.
    "Mother-Daughter Relationships: Psychodynamics, Politics, and
        Philosophy." In The Future of Difference, p. 20-38.

Fleming, Jacqueline.
    "Sex Differences in the Educational and Occupational Goals of
        Black College Students: Continued Inquiry Into the Black
        Matriarchy Theory." In The Challenge of Change, p. 297-316.
    "Sex Differences in the Impact of College Environments on Black
        Students." In The Undergraduate Woman, p. 229-50.

Fleming, Jane P.
    "Statement." In U.S. Congress. House. Committee on Educa-
        tion and Labor. Subcommittee on Employment Opportunities.
        Oversight Hearings on Equal Employment Opportunity and
        Affirmative Action, pt. 1, p. 189-95.
    "Statement." In U.S. Congress. Senate. Committee on Labor
        and Human Resources. Sex Discrimination in the Workplace,
        1981, p. 34-5.
    "Testimony." In U.S. Equal Employment Opportunity Commission.
        Hearings Before the U.S. Equal Employment Opportunity Com-
        mission on Job Segregation and Wage Discrimination, p. 411-22.
    "Testimony." In U.S. Congress. House. Select Committee on

Aging. Subcommittee on Retirement Income and Employment. National Policy Proposals Affecting Midlife Women, p. 87-8.

Flitcraft, Anne.
"Statement." In U.S. Congress. House. Committee on Science and Technology. Subcommittee on Domestic and International Scientific Planning, Analysis and Cooperation. Research into Violent Behavior: Domestic Violence, p. 239-45.

Flournoy, Fay.
"Statement." In U.S. Congress. House. Committee on Ways and Means. Subcommittee on Social Security. Social Security Dependents' Benefits, p. 46-7.

Flower, Ruth.
"Statement." In U.S. Congress. House. Committee on Ways and Means. Subcommittee on Public Assistance and Unemployment Compensation. AFDC and Social Service Bills and Related Oversight Issues, p. 138-40.

Flynn, Bonnie.
"Statement." In U.S. Congress. House. Committee on Education and Labor. Subcommittee on Select Education. Hearing on Domestic Violence, p. 31-2.

Flynn, Elizabeth Gurley.
"Statement at the Smith Act Trial." In We Shall Be Heard, p. 239-44.
"The Truth About the Paterson Strike." In Outspoken Women, p. 52-61.

Fodor, Iris Goldstein.
"Assertiveness Training for the Eighties: Moving Beyond the Personal." In Handbook of Feminist Therapy, p. 257-65.

Foley, Kathleen M.
"Testimony." In U.S. Congress. House. Committee on Energy and Commerce. Subcommittee on Health and the Environment. Health and the Environment Miscellaneous, pt. 2, p. 599-601.

Foley, M. Nadine, O.P.
"A Homily for Midnight Mass (Christmas)." In Women and the Word, p. 47-53.
"Woman in Vatican Documents--1960 to the Present." In Sexism and Church Law, p. 82-108.

Follis, Anne.
"Panel Discussion." In Public Forum on Women's Rights and Responsibilities (1978: Las Vegas, NV). Public Forum on Women's Rights and Responsibilities, p. 8-9.

Forbush, Janet Bell.
"Testimony." In U.S. Congress. House. Committee on Education and Labor. Subcommittee on Select Education. Adolescent Pregnancy, p. 103-5.
"Testimony." In U.S. Congress. Senate. Committee on Human Resources. Adolescent Health, Services and Pregnancy Prevention Care Act of 1978, p. 278-81.

Ford, Betty.
"Speech by Betty Ford, National Commissioner and Former First Lady." In U.S. National Commission on the Observance of International Women's Year. The Spirit of Houston, p. 220-1.

Ford, Kimberly.
"Gospel Principles and Women." In Blueprints for Living, p. 103-6.

Forisha, Barbara L.
"Assessing the Atmosphere: Education and Career Success in Academic Women." In Women's Lives, p. 347-61.

Forman, Maxine.
"Statement." In U.S. Congress. House. Select Committee on Aging. Subcommittee on Retirement Income and Employment. Task Force on Social Security and Women. Inequities Toward Women in the Social Security System, p. 22-6.

Forrest, Jacqueline Darroch.
"Statement." In U.S. Congress. House. Committee on Energy and Commerce. Subcommittee on Health and the Environment. Pregnancy-Related Health Services, p. 322-4.
"Statement." In U.S. Congress. House. Committee on Post Office and Civil Service. Subcommittee on Census and Population. Demographics of Adolescent Pregnancy in the United States, p. 46-9.

Fortmann, Louise.
"The Plight of the Invisible Farmer: the Effect of National Agricultural Policy on Women in Africa." In Women and Technological Change in Developing Countries, p. 205-14.

Fortune, Marie M.
"My God, My God, Why Have You Forsaken Me?" In Spinning a Sacred Yarn, p. 65-71.

Fossedal, Ruth.
"Testimony." In U.S. Congress. Senate. Committee on Labor and Human Resources. Women in Transition 1983, p. 89-91.

Foster, Abby Kelley.
"It Is the Pulpit Who Casts Out 'Impure' Women." In Outspoken

Frederickson, Mary E.
    "Shaping a New Society: Methodist Women and Industrial Reform
    in the South, 1880-1940." In Women in New Worlds, v. 1,
    p. 345-61.

Freedman, Anne E.
    "Testimony." In U.S. Congress. Senate. Committee on the
    Judiciary. Subcommittee on the Constitution. The Impact of
    The Equal Rights Amendment, pt. 1, p. 451-5.

Freeman, Frankie M.
    "Statement." In U.S. Commission on Civil Rights. Hearing Be-
    fore the U.S. Commission on Civil Rights Held in Chicago,
    1974, v. 1, 4-5, v. 2, p. 2-4, 12-14, 116-18.
    "Statement." In U.S. Commission on Civil Rights. Hearing Be-
    fore the U.S. Commission on Civil Rights Held in Denver,
    1976, p. 2-5.

Freeman, Jo.
    "Testimony." In U.S. Equal Employment Opportunity Commission.
    Hearings Before the U.S. Equal Employment Opportunity Com-
    mission on Job Segregation and Wage Discrimination, p. 655-67.

Freeze, Karen Johnson.
    "Medical Education for Women in Austria: A Study in the Politics
    of the Czech Women's Movement in the 1890s." In Women,
    State, and Party in Eastern Europe, p. 51-63.

French, Julie.
    "Testimony." In U.S. Congress. House. Select Committee on
    Aging. Subcommittee on Retirement Income and Employment.
    Task Force on Social Security and Women. Treatment of
    Women Under Social Security, p. 89-90.

Frenier, Mariam Darce.
    "The Effects of the Chinese Revolution on Women and Their Fam-
    ilies.: In Berkshire Conference on the History of Women (5th:
    1982: Vassar College). Women and the Structure of Society,
    p. 232-52.

Friedan, Betty.
    "The Crisis in Women's Identity." In We Shall Be Heard, p. 316-
    25.
    "Education and Equality for Women." In Cornell Conference on
    Women (1969: Cornell University). Proceedings, p. 44-6, 49.
    "How Do Men Look at Women." In Cornell Conference on Women
    (1969: Cornell University). Proceedings, p. 8-10, 12, 13.
    "Is the Question of Women a Political Question?" In Cornell
    Conference on Women (1969: Cornell University). Proceed-
    ings, p. 17-18, 22-23.
    "Statement." In U.S. Congress. Senate. Committee on Labor

and Human Resources. <u>Broken Families</u>, pt. 2, p. 349-54.
"Testimony." In U.S. Congress. House. Select Committee on
Aging. Subcommittee on Retirement Income and Employment.
<u>National Policy Proposals Affecting Midlife Women</u>, p. 71-9.

Friedensohn, Doris.
"From Our Work and Experience: Questions for the Academy."
In GLCA Women's Studies Conference (6th: 1980). <u>Towards</u>
<u>a Feminist Transformation of the Academy II</u>, p. 7-10.

Friedlander, Lynn.
"The Worship of Woman in Courtly Love and Rock and Roll." In
<u>Women & Men</u>, p. 92-110.

Friedman, Jean E.
"Piety and Kin: The Limits of Antebellum Southern Women's Reform." In Berkshire Conference on the History of Women
(5th: 1982: Vassar College). <u>Women and the Structure of</u>
<u>Society</u>, p. 12-9.
"Women's History and the Revision of Southern History." In
<u>Sex, Race, and the Role of Women in the South</u>, p. 3-12.

Friedman, Susan Stanford.
"Authority in the Feminist Classroom: A Contradiction in Terms?"
In <u>Gendered Subjects</u>, p. 203-98.
"'I Go Where I Love': An Intertextual Study of H.D. and Adri-
enne Rich." In <u>Coming to Light</u>, p. 233-53.

Frieze, Irene Hanson.
"Psychological Barriers for Women in Sciences: Internal and
External." In <u>Covert Discrimination and Women in the Sci-
ences</u>, p. 65-95.

Fritsche, Joann M.
"Moving Beyond the Curriculum: The 'Political' Value of an Integration Strategy." In <u>Toward a Balanced Curriculum</u>, p.
117-23.

Frye, Marilyn.
"Lesbian Feminism and the Gay Rights Movement: Another View
of Male Supremacy, Another Separatism." In Frye, Marilyn.
<u>The Politics of Reality</u>, p. 128-51.
"On Being White: Thinking Toward a Feminist Understanding
of Race and Race Supremacy." In Frye, <u>The Politics of Real-
ity</u>, p. 110-27.
"Some Reflections on Separatism and Power." In Frye, <u>The
Politics of Reality</u>, p. 95-109.

Fuchs, Jo-Ann P.
"Female Eroticism in <u>The Second Sex</u>." In <u>Feminist Studies</u>, 6
(Summer 1980), 304-13.

Fujii, Haron M.
"Elderly Pacific Island and Asian-American Women: A Framework for Understanding." In Conference on the Educational and Occupational Needs of Asian-Pacific-American Women (1976: San Francisco, CA.). Conference on the Educational and Occupational Needs of Asian-Pacific-American Women, p. 343-58.

Futrell, Mary Hatwood.
"Education. A Capital Investment." Vital Speeches, 50 (June 1, 1984), 504-6.
"Statement." In U.S. Congress. House. Committee on Education and Labor. Civil Rights Act of 1984, p. 160-3.
"Statement." In U.S. Congress. House. Committee on Post Office and Civil Service. Subcommittee on Compensation and Employee Benefits. Federal Pay Equity Act of 1984, pt. 1, p. 41-3.

Gaines, Roberta.
"Testimony." In U.S. Congress. House. Select Committee on Aging. Subcommittee on Retirement Income and Employment. National Policy Proposals Affecting Midlife Women, p. 89-98.

Galler, Janina.
"Statement." In U.S. Congress. Senate. Committee on Labor and Human Resources. Subcommittee on Aging, Family, and Human Services. Oversight on Family Planning Programs Under Title X of the Public Health Service Act, 1981, p. 128-30.

Galler, Roberta.
"The Myth of the Perfect Body." In Pleasure and Danger, p. 165-72.

Gallop, Jane.
"Psychoanalysis in France." In The Future of Difference, p. 114-9.

Gampel, Gwen Victor.
"The Planter's Wife Revisited: Women, Equity Law, and the Chancery Court in Seventeenth-Century Maryland." In Berkshire Conference on the History of Women (5th: 1982: Vassar College). Women and the Structure of Society, p. 20-35.

Garcia, Frieda.
"The Cult of Virginity." In Conference on the Educational and Occupational Needs of Hispanic Women (1976: Denver, CO and Washington, DC). Conference on the Educational and Occupational Needs of Hispanic Women, p. 64-74.

Gardiner, Judith.
"The Heroine as Her Author's Daughter." In Women & Men, p.
140-8.

Gardner, Eileen.
"Statement." In U.S. Congress. Senate. Committee on Labor
and Human Resources. Subcommittee on Education, Arts and
Humanities. Civil Rights Act of 1984, pt. 1, p. 353-4.

Gardner, Tracey A.
"Racism in Pornography and the Women's Movement." In Take
Back the Night, p. 105-14.

Garrard, Mary D.
"Artemisia and Susanna." In Feminism and Art History, p. 147-
71.

Gascon, Barbara.
"Testimony." In U.S. Congress. Senate. Committee on Labor
and Human Resources. Women in Transition 1983, p. 155-8.

Gaskin, Ina May.
"Community Alternatives to High Technology Birth." In Birth
Control and Controlling Birth, p. 223-30.

Gasper, Jo Ann.
"Statement." In U.S. Congress. House. Committee on Foreign
Affairs. Subcommittee on Human Rights and International
Organizations. U.S. Contribution to the U.N. Decade for
Women, p. 27-9.
"Statement." In U.S. Congress. House. Committee on Ways
and Means. Subcommittee on Public Assistance and Unem-
ployment Compensation. Teenage Pregnancy Issues, p. 59-62.

Gaston, Caroline.
"Statement." In U.S. Congress. Senate. Committee on Human
Resources. Adolescent Health, Services, and Pregnancy
Prevention Care Act of 1978, p. 139-42.

Gates, Mary M.
"The Changing Role of Women in Voluntarism. Individual Growth
and Worth." Vital Speeches, 47 (May 1, 1981), 436-9.

Gavett, Patricia.
"Statement." In U.S. Congress. Senate. Committee on the
Judiciary. Subcommittee on the Constitution. Constitutional
Amendments Relating to Abortion, v. 1, p. 1023-4.

Gaynor, Florence.
"Health Services Administration." In Warner, Anne R. Health
Womenpower, p. 17-23.

Gearhart, Sally.
"Womanpower: Energy Re-Sourcement." In The Politics of Women's Spirituality, p. 194-206.

Geller, Laura.
"Can Isaac and Ishmael Be Reconciled?" In Spinning a Sacred Yarn, p. 77-87.

Gentry, Cathleen M.
"Statement." In U.S. Congress. House. Select Committee on Population. Fertility and Contraception in America, p. 98-105.

George, Yolanda Scott.
"Affirmative Action Programs That Work." In Women and Minorities in Science, p. 87-98.

Germain, Carel.
"Casework and Science: A Historical Encounter." In Charlotte Towle Memorial Symposium on Comparative Theoretical Approaches to Casework Practice (1969: University of Chicago). Theories of Social Casework, p. 3-32.

Gerster, Carolyn.
"Statement." In U.S. Congress. Senate. Committee on the Judiciary. Subcommittee on Separation of Powers. The Human Life Bill, p. 962-5, 1029-34.

Gianturco, Adriana.
"Speech." In Women's Travel Issues, p. 743-56.

Gibbons, Lillian K.
"The Challenge for Health Care Providers." In Health Needs of the World's Poor Women, p. 103-4.

Gibbs, (Mrs.) Rufus M.
"Testimony." In U.S. Congress. Senate. Committee on the Judiciary. Birth Control (1932), p. 121.
"Testimony." In U.S. Congress. House. Committee on the Judiciary. Birth Control (1934), p. 130-1.
"Testimony." In U.S. Congress. Senate. Committee on the Judiciary. Birth Control (1934), p. 111-2.

Giele, Janet Zollinger.
"Crossovers: New Themes in Adult Roles and the Life Cycle." In Women's Lives, p. 3-15.

Gifford, Carolyn Deswarte.
"For God and Home and Native Land: The W.C.T.U.'s Image of Woman in the Late Nineteenth Century." In Women in New Worlds, v. 1, p. 310-27.

Gilbert, Lucia Albino.
"Feminist Therapy." In Women and Psychotherapy, p. 245-66.

Gilbert, Melissa.
"Statement." In U.S. Congress. House. Committee on Energy and Commerce. Subcommittee on Health and the Environment. Pregnancy-Related Health Services, p. 259.

Gilbert, Sandra M.
"In Yeats's House: The Death and Resurrection of Sylvia Plath." In Coming to Light, p. 145-66.
"My Name Is Darkness: The Poetry of Self-Definition." In Women & Men, p. 372-85.

Gilkes, Cheryl Townsend.
"From Slavery to Social Welfare: Racism and the Control of Black Women." In Class, Race, and Sex, p. 288-300.
"Together and In Harness: Women's Traditions in the Sanctified Church." Signs, 10 (Summer 1985), 678-99.

Gillespie, Joanna Bowen.
"The Sun in Their Domestic System: The Mother in Early Nineteenth-Century Methodist Sunday School Lore." In Women in New Worlds, v. 2, p. 45-59.

Gillespie-Woltemade, Nellice.
"The Feminist Academy and Third World Women." In GLCA Women's Studies Conference (5th: 1979). Toward a Feminist Transformation of the Academy, p. 19-27.

Gilligan, Carol.
"Do Changes in Women's Rights Change Women's Moral Judgments?" In The Challenge of Change, p. 39-60.
"In A Different Voice: Women's Conceptions of Self and Morality." In The Future of Difference, p. 274.
"Restoring the Missing Text of Women's Development to Life Cycle Theories." In Women's Lives, p. 17-33.

Gilman, Charlotte Perkins.
"The Humanness of Women." (1910) In Outspoken Women, p. 66-9.
"The Social Body and Soul." In We Shall Be Heard, p. 213-17.
"Testimony." In U.S. Congress. House. Committee on Ways and Means. Birth Control, (1932), p. 55-7.

Gimbutas, Marija.
"Women and Culture in Goddess-Oriented Old Europe." In The Politics of Women's Spirituality, p. 22-31.

Ginsberg, Elaine.
"Playwrights, Poets, and Novelists: Sisters Under the Skin." In Toward the Second Decade, p. 35-40.

Ginsberg, Faye.
    "The Body Politic: The Defense of Sexual Restriction by Anti-
    Abortion Activists." In Pleasure and Danger, p. 173-88.

Ginsburg, Ruth Bader.
    "Realizing the Equality Principle." In Social Justice & Prefer-
    ential Treatment, p. 135-53.
    "Statement." In U.S. Congress. House. Committee on the
    Judiciary. Subcommittee on Civil and Constitutional Rights.
    Equal Rights Amendment Extension, p. 262-85.
    "Women 's Right to Full Participation in Shaping Society's Course:
    an Evolving Constitutional Precept." In Toward the Second
    Decade, p. 171-88.

Glazer, Nona Y.
    "Paid and Unpaid Work: Contradictions in American Women's
    Lives Today." In Women in the Workplace, p. 169-86.

Gleason, Jane.
    "Statement." In U.S. Congress. House. Select Committee on
    Aging. Subcommittee on Retirement Income and Employment.
    Impact of Reagan Economics on Aging Women, p. 40-1.

Godbold, Ruth.
    "Statement." In U.S. Congress. House. Committee on Educa-
    tion and Labor. Subcommittee on Labor-Management Relations.
    Pension Equity for Women, p. 54-5.

Godley, Anita.
    "Statement." In U.S. Congress. Senate. Committee on Labor
    and Human Resources. Subcommittee on Family and Human
    Service. Forum for Families, p. 38-9.

Godley, Aquilla Laverna.
    "Statement." In U.S. Congress. Senate. Committee on Labor
    and Human Resources. Subcommittee on Family and Human
    Services. Forum for Families, p. 39-40.

Gojack, Mary.
    "Panel Discussion." In Public Forum on Women's Rights and Re-
    sponsibilities (1978: Las Vegas, NV). Public Forum on
    Women's Rights and Responsibilities, p. 9-11.

Gold, Ellen B.
    "Epidemiology of Pituitary Adenomas." In The Changing Risk of
    Disease in Women, p. 153-67.

Goldberg, Evelyn L.
    "Health Effects of Becoming Widowed." In The Changing Risk
    of Disease in Women, p. 49-63.

Golden, Renny.
"White Women and Racism." In Women's Spirit Bonding, p. 97-105.

Goldenberg, Edie N.
"An Overview of Access to the Media." In Women and the News, p. 50-63.

Goldenberg, Naomi R.
"Jung After Feminism." In Beyond Androcentrism, p. 53-65.

Goldfarb, Sally F.
"Statement." In U.S. Congress. House. Committee on Ways and Means. Economic Equity Act and Related Tax and Pension Reform, p. 158-9.

Goldin, Claudia.
"Factual Overview: Women in the Work Force." In Comparable Worth: Issues for the 80's, p. 2-14.

Goldman, Emma.
"Address to the Jury, July, 1917." In We Shall Be Heard, p. 225-33.
"Emma Goldman's Defense." The Masses, 8 (June, 1916), 27.
"Preparedness: The Road to Universal Slaughter." (1915) In Outspoken Women, p. 71-5.

Goldman, Karla.
"Statement." In U.S. Congress. House. Committee on Armed Services. Subcommittee on Military Personnel. Hearings on H.R. 6569, Registration of Women, p. 120-2.

Goldsberry, Barbara.
"Statement." In U.S. Congress. House. Committee on Post Office and Civil Service. Subcommittee on Compensation and Employee Benefits. Options for Conducting a Pay Equity Study, p. 201-3.

Goldsmid, Paula.
"Curriculum Reform, or What Do You Mean, 'Our College Should Have a Feminist Curriculum'?" In GLCA Women's Studies Conference (5th: 1979). Towards a Feminist Transformation of the Academy, p. 52-9.
"In-House Resources." In Toward a Balanced Curriculum, p. 170-2.

Goldsmith, Judy.
"Gender Gap '84--Women Reject Reagan." National NOW Times, 16 (August, 1983), 5, 8.
"Statement." In U.S. Congress. House. Committee on Armed Services. Subcommittee on Military Personnel. Hearings on

H.R. 6569, Registration of Women, p. 78-80.
"Statement." In U.S. Congress. House. Committee on Educa-
tion and Labor. Civil Rights Act of 1984, p. 147-9.
"Statement." In U.S. Congress. House. Committee on Post
Office and Civil Service. Subcommittee on Compensation and
Employee Benefits. Federal Pay Equity Act of 1984, pt. 1,
p. 37-40.
"Statement." In U.S. Congress. House. Committee on Post
Office and Civil Service. Subcommittee on Compensation and
Employee Benefits. Options for Conducting a Pay Equity
Study, p. 230-2.
"Statement." In U.S. Congress. House. Committee on the
Judiciary. Subcommittee on Courts, Civil Liberties, and the
Administration of Justice. Judiciary Implications of Draft
Registration--1980. Washington: U.S.G.P.O., 1980, p. 19-27.
"Testimony." In U.S. Congress. Senate. Committee on the
Judiciary. Subcommittee on Juvenile Justice. Effect of
Pornography on Women and Children, p. 150-4.

Goldstein, Naomi.
"Statement." In U.S. Congress. Senate. Committee on the
Judiciary. Subcommittee on Separation of Powers. The Hu-
man Life Bill, p. 1051-6.

Goldston, Sudie M.
"Statement." In U.S. Congress. Senate. Committee on Veterans' Affairs. Veterans' Health Care and Programs Improvement, p. 231-2.

Gomberg, Edith S. Lisansky.
"Learned Helplessness, Depression, and Alcohol Problems of
Women." In Women in Crisis Conference (1st: 1979: New
York, NY). Women in Crisis, p. 38-43.
"Risk Factors Related to Alcohol Problems Among Women: Prone-
ness and Vulnerability." In Alcoholism and Alcohol Abuse
Among Women: Research Issues, p. 83-114.

Gonzales, Sylvia.
"Chicana Evolution." In Conference on the Educational and
Occupational Needs of Hispanic Women (1979: Denver, CO
and Washington, DC). Conference on the Educational and
Occupational Needs of Hispanic Women, p. 179-85.
"La Chicana: An Overview." In Conference on the Educational
and Occupational Needs of Hispanic Women (1979: Denver,
CO and Washington, DC). Conference on the Educational
and Occupational Needs of Hispanic Women, p. 186-212.
"The White Feminist Movement: The Chicana Perspective." In
Women's Studies, p. 65-74.

Gonzalez, Nancie L.
"Professional Women in Developing Nations: The United States

and the Third World Compared." In Women in Scientific and
Engineering Professions, p. 19-42.

Goode, Millicent P.
"Statement." In U.S. Congress. House. Committee on Educa-
tion and Labor. Subcommittee on Labor-Management Relations.
Pension Equity for Women, p. 49-51.

Goodin, Joan M.
"Statement." In U.S. Congress. Senate. Committee on Labor
and Human Resources. The Coming Decade, p. 179-84.
"Statement." In U.S. Congress. Senate. Committee on Labor
and Human Resources. Sex Discrimination in the Workplace,
1981, p. 13-14, 24-5.
"Testimony." In U.S. Equal Employment Opportunity Commission.
Hearings Before the U.S. Equal Employment Opportunity Commission on Job Segregation and Wage Discrimination, p. 459-67.

Goodman, Jill Laurie.
"Testimony." In U.S. Congress. Joint Economic Committee.
Subcommittee on Priorities and Economy in Government. The
Role of Women in the Military, p. 72-5.

Goodwin, Fannie L.
"Statement." In U.S. Congress. House. Select Committee on
Aging. Problems of Aging Women, p. 8-9.

Gordon, Bette.
"Variety: The Pleasure in Looking." In Pleasure and Danger,
p. 189-203.

Gordon, Diana R.
"Crime: The Citizen Connection. Criminal Justice." Vital
Speeches, 49 (May 1, 1983), 432-4.

Gordon, Linda.
"From Voluntary Motherhood to Planned Parenthood: Perspectives
on the Birth Control Movement in America." In Margaret
Sanger Centennial Conference (1979: Northampton, MA).
Margaret Sanger Centennial Conference, p. 32-43.
"Voluntary Motherhood: the Beginnings of Feminist Birth Control
Ideas in the United States." In Clio's Consciousness Raised,
p. 54-68.
"Why Nineteenth-Century Feminists Did Not Support 'Birth Con-
trol' and Twentieth-Century Feminist Do: Feminism, Repro-
duction, and the Family." In Rethinking the Family, p. 40-53.

Gordon, Lynn D.
"Co-Education on Two Campuses: Berkeley and Chicago, 1890-
1912." In Conference on the History of Women (1977: St.
Paul, MN). Woman's Being, Woman's Place, p. 171-93.

Gordon, Nancy M.
  "Comment on 'Bargaining Analyses of Household Decisions.'" In
    Conference on Women in the Labor Market (1977: Barnard).
    Women in the Labor Market, p. 171-93.
  "Statement." In U.S. Congress. Senate. Committee on Labor
    and Human Resources. The Coming Decade, p. 26-8.
  "Testimony." In U.S. Congress. Senate. Special Committee
    on Aging. Adapting Social Security to a Changing Work
    Force, p. 36-41.

Gordus, Jeanne Prial.
  "Women in CETA: The Social Context of Public Service Employ-
    ment." In Women's Lives, p. 195-203.

Goren, Suzane.
  "Luncheon Address." In Warner, Anne R. Health Womenpower,
    p. 36-45.

Gorie, Margaret.
  "Statement." In U.S. Congress. House. Select Committee on
    Aging. Subcommittee on Retirement Income and Employment.
    Task Force on Social Security and Women. Treatment of
    Women Under Social Security, v. 3, p. 64-6.

Gosch, Noreen N.
  "Testimony." In U.S. Congress. Senate. Committee on the
    Judiciary. Subcommittee on Juvenile Justice. Effect of
    Pornography on Women and Children, p. 67-9.

Gough, Paddy W.
  "The Female Engineering Student: What Makes Her Tick." In
    Women in Engineering--Beyond Recruitment, p. 52-60.

Gould, Carol C.
  "Private Rights and Public Virtues: Women, the Family, and
    Democracy." In Beyond Domination, p. 3-18.

Gould, Sara K.
  "Statement." In U.S. Congress. House. Committee on Govern-
    ment Operations. Intergovernmental Relations and Human
    Resources Subcommittee. Barriers to Self-Sufficiency for
    Single Female Heads of Families, p. 577-80.

Gouma-Peterson, Thalia.
  "Three Decades of Reminiscences About Women in the Academy."
    In GLCA Women's Studies Conference (6th: 1980). Toward
    the Feminist Transformation of the Academy II, p. 73-6.

Graber, Doris A.
  "Agenda-Setting: Are There Women's Perspectives?" In Women
    and the News, p. 15-37.

Gradford, Judy.
    "Caregivers' Wages." <u>Women's Studies Quarterly</u>, 13 (Summer
        1985), 11.

Graham, Marian.
    "Personal Report to the Conference on Women and Poverty in
        Massachusetts." <u>Women's Studies Quarterly</u>, 13 (Summer
        1985), 7.

Graham, Patricia Albjerg.
    "The Cult of True Womanhood. Past and Present." <u>Vital
        Speeches</u>, 49 (April 15, 1983), 400-7.

Grant, Elinor.
    "Statement." In California. Legislature. Joint Committee on
        Legal Equality. <u>Women in the Justice System</u>, p. 121-55.

Grant, Jacquelyn.
    "A Black Response to Feminist Theology." In <u>Women's Spirit
        Bonding</u>, p. 117-24.

Grant, Mary H.
    "Domestic Experience and Feminist Theory: The Case of Julia
        Ward Howe." In Conference on the History of Women (1977:
        St. Paul, MN). <u>Woman's Being, Women's Place</u>, p. 220-32.

Grasso, Ella T.
    "Budget Address by Governor Ella T. Grasso; Joint Session of
        Connecticut General Assembly, Hall of the House, State Capi-
        tol." In Connecticut. General Assembly. House. <u>Journal</u>.
        Hartford, 1980, p. 54-7.
    "Budget Message to the Connecticut General Assembly by Ella T.
        Grasso, February 4, 1976." In Connecticut. General Assem-
        bly. House. <u>Journal</u>. Hartford, 1976, p. 34-7.
    "Budget Message to the Connecticut General Assembly by Gov-
        ernor Ella Grasso, February 10, 1978." In Connecticut.
        General Assembly. House. <u>Journal</u>. Hartford, 1978, p.
        58-64.
    "Governor's Message. State of the State Address to the Con-
        necticut General Assembly, January 5, 1977." In Connecticut.
        General Assembly. House. <u>Journal</u>. Hartford, 1977, p.
        96-100.
    "Inaugural Message to the Connecticut General Assembly by Gov-
        ernor Ella T. Grasso, January 8, 1975." In Connecticut.
        General Assembly. House. <u>Journal</u>. Hartford, 1975, p.
        61-5.
    "Inaugural Message to the Connecticut General Assembly by Gov-
        ernor Ella Grasso, January 3, 1979." In Connecticut. Gen-
        eral Assembly. House. <u>Journal</u>. Hartford, 1979, p. 72-4.

Gray, Alice.
    "Testimony." In U.S. Commission on Civil Rights. <u>Hearing</u>

before the U.S. Commission on Civil Rights Held in Chicago, 1974, v. 1, p. 427-8.

Gray, Kimi O.
"Statement." In U.S. Congress. House. Committee on Government Operations. Intergovernmental Relations and Human Resources Subcommittee. Barrier to Self-Sufficiency for Single Female Heads of Families, p. 488-91.

Gray, Mary Jane.
"An Obstetrician's Perspective." In Birth Control and Controlling Birth, p. 259-60.

Gray, Mary W.
"Statement." In U.S. Congress. Committee on Education and Labor. Subcommittee on Labor-Management Relations. Pension Equity for Women, p. 72-3.
"Statement." In U.S. Congress. House. Committee on Post Office and Civil Service. Subcommittee on Compensation and Employee Benefits. Federal Pay Equity Act of 1984, pt. 2, p. 100-2.
"Statement." In U.S. Congress. Senate. Committee on Labor and Human Resources. Subcommittee on Labor. Retirement Equity Act of 1983, p. 117-9.

Gray, Naomi T.
"Sterilization and the Black Female: An Historical Perspective." In Miniconsultation on the Mental and Physical Health Problems of Black Women (1977: Washington, DC). Miniconsultation on the Mental and Physical Health Problems of Black Women, p. 80-90.

Gray, Nellie.
"Statement." In U.S. Congress. Senate. Committee on the Judiciary. Subcommittee on the Constitution. Constitutional Amendments Relating to Abortion, v. 1, p. 1172-4.

Gray, Warlene.
"Statement." In U.S. Congress. Senate. Committee on Finance. Potential Inequities Affecting Women, pt. 2, p. 126-8.

Green, Nancy.
"Female Education and School Competition: 1820-1850." In Conference on the History of Women (1977: St. Paul, MN). Woman's Being, Woman's Place, p. 127-41.

Green, Virginia.
"A Japanese Experience." ISIS Women's World, no. 8 (December, 1985), 8-9.

Greenberg, Jeanne.
"A Profile of the Successful High-Tech Salesperson. The Client

Is Sophisticated and Knowledgeable." <u>Vital Speeches</u>, 51
(May 15, 1985), 477-9.

Greenberg, Selma.
"Preschool and the Politics of Sexism." In Conference on Non-
Sexist Early Childhood Education (1976: Arden House).
<u>Perspectives on Non-Sexist Early Childhood Education</u>, p.
40-56.

Greenberger, Marcia D.
"The Effectiveness of Federal Laws Prohibiting Sex Discrimination
in Employment in the United States." In <u>Equal Employment</u>
<u>Policy for Women</u>, p. 108-27.
"Statement." In U.S. Congress. House. Committee on Educa-
tion and Labor. <u>Civil Rights Act of 1984</u>, p. 271-5.
"Statement." In U.S. Congress. Senate. Committee on Labor
and Human Resources. Subcommittee on Education, Arts, and
Humanities. <u>Civil Rights Act of 1984</u>, pt. 1, p. 177-83.
"Statement." In U.S. Congress. Senate. Committee on Labor
and Human Resources. Subcommittee on Labor. <u>Retirement</u>
<u>Equity Act of 1983</u>, p. 138-9.
"Statement." In U.S. Congress. Senate. Committee on the
Judiciary. Subcommittee on the Constitution. <u>Civil Rights</u>
<u>Act of 1984</u>, p. 40-2.

Greene, Bernadette.
"Testimony." In U.S. Congress. House. Committee on Energy
and Commerce. Subcommittee on Health and the Environment.
<u>Health and the Environment Miscellaneous</u>, pt. 4, p. 306-8.

Greene, Maxine.
"Equality and Inviolability: An Approach to Compensatory Justice." In <u>Social Justice & Preferential Treatment</u>, p. 176-98.

Greenfield, Louise S.
"Testimony." In U.S. Congress. House. Committee on Energy
and Commerce. Subcommittee on Health and the Environment.
<u>Health and the Environment Miscellaneous</u>, pt. 6, p. 223-5.

Gregory, Eileen.
"The Formality of Memory: A Study of Literary Manuscripts of
Mary Boykin Chesnut." In Reynolds Conference (2nd: 1975:
University of South Carolina). <u>South Carolina Women Writers</u>,
p. 229-43.

Gribskov, Margaret.
"Feminism and the Woman School Administrator." In <u>Women and</u>
<u>Educational Leadership</u>, p. 77-92.

Griffen, Joyce.
"A Cross-Cultural Investigation of Behavioral Changes at Menopause." In <u>Women's Studies</u>, p. 47-53.

Griffin, Gail.
    "Still Crazy After All These Years: The Uses of Madness in
    Women's Fiction." In GLCA Women's Studies Conference
    (7th: 1981). Towards a Feminist Transformation of the
    Academy III, p. 18-26.

Griffith, Elisabeth.
    "Elizabeth Cady Stanton on Marriage and Divorce: Feminist
    Theory and Domestic Experience." In Conference on the
    History of Women (1977: St. Paul, MN). Woman's Being,
    Woman's Place, p. 233-52.

Griffiths, Martha.
    "Power--How To Get It And How to Use It." In International
    Women's Year Conference on Women in Public Life (1975:
    Lyndon Baines Johnson Library). Women in Public Life, p.
    31.
    "Testimony." In U.S. Congress. House. Select Committee on
    Aging. Subcommittee on Retirement Income and Employment.
    Task Force on Social Security and Women. Treatment of Wom-
    en Under Social Security, p. 27-9.

Griffiths-Boris, Norma J.
    "Statement." In U.S. Congress. House. Committee on Veter-
    ans' Affairs. Subcommittee on Hospitals and Health Care.
    VA Health Care For Women, p. 30-2.

Grimke, Angelina E.
    "The North, Go On! Go On!" (1863) In Outspoken Women, p.
    77-9.
    "Speech in Pennsylvania Hall." In We Shall Be Heard, p. 26-30.

Grindal, Gracia.
    "Both Boxes." In Spinning a Sacred Yarn, p. 88-92.

Gross, Rita M.
    "Androcentrism and Androgyny in the Methodology of History of
    Religions." In Beyond Androcentrism, p. 7-21.

Grossman, Carol Burroughs.
    "Statement." In U.S. Congress. House. Committee on Armed
    Services. Military Personnel and Compensation Subcommittee.
    Benefits for Former Spouses of Military Members, pt. 2, p.
    1-3.
    "Statement." In U.S. Congress. Senate. Committee on Labor
    and Human Resources. Sex Discrimination in the Workplace,
    1981, p. 219-21.

Grossmann, Atina.
    "Crisis, Reaction, and Resistance; Women in Germany in the 1920s
    and 1930s." In Class, Race, and Sex, p. 60-74.

Grune, Joy Ann.
  "Comparable Worth as a Remedy for Sex Discrimination." In
    Comparable Worth: Issue for the 80's, p. 108-11.
  "Statement." In U.S. Congress. Senate. Committee on Labor
    and Human Resources. The Coming Decade, p. 184-6.

Grygelko, Marilee.
  "Federal Support: Understanding and Utilizing the Federal Dol-
    lar." In Women in Crisis Conference (1st: 1979: New York,
    NY). Women in Crisis, p. 257-9.

Gubar, Susan.
  "The Birth of the Artist as Heroine: (Re)production, the Kunst-
    lerroman Tradition, and the Fiction of Katharine Mansfield."
    In The Representation of Women in Fiction, p. 19-59.
  "Mother, Maiden, and the Marriage of Death: Women Writers and
    an Ancient Myth." In Women & Men, p. 386-97.

Gueron, Judith M.
  "Statement." In U.S. Congress. House. Committee on Govern-
    ment Operations. Intergovernmental Relations and Human Re-
    sources Subcommittee. Barriers to Self-Sufficiency for Single
    Female Heads of Families, p. 100-3.

Gullahorn, Jeanne E.
  "Sex-Related Factors in Cognition and in Brain Lateralization."
    In Psychology and Women: In Transition, p. 9-35.

Gullett, Gayle.
  "City Mothers, City Daughters, and the Dance Hall Girls: The
    Limits of Female Political Power in San Francisco, 1913." In
    Berkshire Conference on the History of Women (5th: 1982:
    Vassar College). Women and the Structure of Society, p.
    149-58.

Gump, Janice Porter.
  "Reality and Myth: Employment and Sex Role Ideology in Black
    Women." In Psychology of Women, p. 349-80.

Guninan, Mary Beth.
  "Testimony." In U.S. Commission on Civil Rights. Hearing Be-
    fore the U.S. Commission on Civil Rights Held in Chicago,
    1974, v. 1, p. 408-9.

Gurieva, Diana M.
  "Statement." In U.S. Congress. House. Committee on Energy
    and Commerce. Subcommittee on Health and the Environment.
    Pregnancy-Related Health Services, p. 280-4.

Gustafson, Jamie R.
  "Dry Bones and Rolled Stones." In Spinning a Sacred Yarn,
    p. 93-7.

Guttentag, Marcia.
"The Social Psychology of Sex-Role Intervention." In Conference on Non-Sexist Early Childhood Education (1976: Arden
House). Perspectives on Non-Sexist Early Childhood Education, p. 71-8.

Gutwirth, Madelyn.
"The Education of Germaine de Stael, or Rousseau Betrayed."
In Sisterhood Surveyed, p. 64-71.

Guyker, Ellen.
"Statement." In U.S. Congress. Senate. Committee on the
Judiciary. Subcommittee on Criminal Law. Impact of Media
Coverage of Rape Trials, p. 48-50.

Gwizdak, Linda.
"Personal Report to the Conference on Women and Poverty in
Massachusetts." Women's Studies Quarterly, 13 (Summer
1985), 7.

Haas, Rae M.
"Special Interest Report on Qualitative Approach to Budgeting."
In Western Regional Civil Rights and Women's Rights Conference (4th: 1977: San Francisco, CA). Recent Developments,
p. 122-3.

Haber, Barbara.
"Women in the Old and New Left: The Evolution of a Political
Issue?" Feminist Studies, 5 (Fall 1979), 417-30.

Hacker, Helen.
"Testimony." In U.S. Equal Employment Opportunity Commission.
Hearing Before the U.S. Equal Employment Opportunity Commission on Job Segregation and Wage Discrimination, p. 164-
78.

Hackett, Jo Ann.
"In the Days of Jael: Reclaiming the History of Women in Ancient
Israel." In Immaculate & Powerful, p. 15-38.

Haener, Dorothy.
"Testimony." In U.S. Equal Employment Opportunity Commission.
Hearings Before the U.S. Equal Employment Opportunity Commission on Job Segregation and Wage Discrimination, p. 791-
800.

Hageman, Alice L.
"Women and Missions: The Cost of Liberation." In Sexist Religion and Women in the Church, p. 167-94.

Hague, Betsy.
"Testimony." In U.S. Congress. Health. Subcommittee on Energy and Commerce. Subcommittee on Health and the Environment. Health and the Environment Miscellaneous, pt. 2, p. 557-8.

Hahn, Emily.
"Salonist and Chronicles." In Women, the Arts, and the 1920s in Paris and New York, p. 56-64.

Haines, Patricia Foster.
"Coeducation and the Development of Leadership Skills in Women: Historical Perspectives from Cornell University, 1868-1900." In Women and Educational Leadership, p. 112-27.

Haley, Margaret.
"Why Teachers Should Organize." In Woman's "True" Profession, p. 289-95.

Hall, Betty Jean.
"Statement." In U.S. Congress. Senate. Committee on Labor and Human Resources. Sex Discrimination in the Workplace, 1981, p. 501-5.

Hall, Diana Long.
"Academics, Bluestockings, and Biologists: Women at the University of Chicago, 1892-1932." In Expanding the Role of Women in the Science, p. 300-20.

Hall, Jacquelyn H.
"Statement." In U.S. Congress. Senate. Committee on Labor and Human Resources. The Coming Decade, p. 653-8.
"Stereotypes and Stigma: Barrier to Recovery." In Women in Crisis Conference (1st: 1979: New York, NY). Women in Crisis, p. 229-34.

Hall, Katie.
"Statement." In U.S. Congress. House. Committee on Appropriations. Subcommittee on Energy and Water Development. Energy and Water Development Appropriations for 1984. Washington: U.S.G.P.O., 1983, pt. 7, p. 404-18.
"Statement." In U.S. Congress. House. Committee on Appropriations. Subcommittee on the Department of the Interior and Related Agencies. Department of the Interior and Related Agencies Appropriations for 1984. Washington: U.S.G.P.O., 1983, pt. 12, p. 314-20.

Hall, Rubye M.
"Statement." In U.S. Congress. Senate. Committee on Labor and Human Resources. Subcommittee on Labor. Retirement Equity Act of 1983, p. 49-50.

Hallaren, Mary A.
   "Statement." In U.S. Congress. Joint Economic Committee.
      Subcommittee on Priorities and Economy in Government. The
      Role of Women in the Military, p. 89-90.

Hallett-Weller, Irene.
   "Testimony." In U.S. Commission on Civil Rights. Hearing Be-
      fore the U.S. Commission on Civil Rights Held in Chicago,
      1974, v. 2, p. 274-6.

Halley, Janet E.
   "Harmonious Sister, Voice and Verse": Women and Fiction in
      Milton's Early Verse." In Sisterhood Surveyed, p. 49-55.

Halloran, Jeane M.
   "Testimony." In U.S. Congress. House. Committee on Energy
      and Commerce. Subcommittee on Health and the Environment.
      Health and the Environment Miscellaneous, pt. 6, p. 280-2.

Hally, Eloise.
   "Easter VI." In Women of the Word, p. 42-5.
   "Lent III." In Women of the Word, p. 37-41.
   "Pentecost XXVI." In Women of the Word, p. 46-50.

Halpern, Rose.
   "Testimony." In U.S. Congress. Senate. Committee on the
      Judiciary. Birth Control, (1934), p. 65-6.

Halpern, Susan.
   "The Mythology of Rape." In Women in Crisis Conference (1st:
      1979: New York, NY). Women in Crisis, p. 145-7.

Halttunen, Karen.
   "The Domestic Drama of Louisa May Alcott." Feminist Studies,
      10 (Summer 1984), 233-54.

Halverson, Jill.
   "Excerpted Testimony from the Southern California Hearings on
      the Feminization of Poverty." Signs, 10 (Winter 1984), 403-4.

Hambrick, Margaret C.
   "The Realities of Women Correctional Officers in Male Correctional
      Institutions." In Training Conference (1st: 1984: Washing-
      ton, DC). Interagency Committee on Women in Law Enforce-
      ment, p. 18-22.

Hamburg, Beatrix A.
   "The Psychobiology of Sex Differences: An Evolutionary Per-
      spective." In Sex Differences in Behavior, p. 373-92.

Hamilton, Edith.
   "Address to the Athenians." In Hamilton, The Ever-Present

Hansen, Susan.
"Statement." In U.S. Congress. House. Committee on Education and Labor. Subcommittee on Select Education. Hearing on Domestic Violence, p. 33-7.

Haraway, Donna J.
"Class, Race, Sex, Scientific Objects of Knowledge: A Socialist-Feminist Perspective on the Social Construction of Productive Nature and Some Political Consequences." In Women in Scientific And Engineering Professions, p. 212-29.

Hardesty, Nancy A.
"Just As I Am." In Women and the Word, p. 6-11.
"Minister as Prophet? or As Mother?: Two Nineteenth-Century Models." In Women in New Worlds, v. 1, p. 88-101.

Harding, Sandra.
"Is Gender a Variable in Conceptions of Rationality? A Survey of Issues." In Beyond Domination, p. 43-63.

Hardy, Dorcas R.
"Statement." In U.S. Congress. Senate. Committee on Labor and Human Resources. Barrier to Adoption, p. 335-8.
"Statement." In U.S. Congress. Senate. Committee on Labor and Human Resources. Subcommittee on Family and Human Services. Broken Families, pt. 2, p. 224-9.

Hardy, Harriet L.
"Acceptance by Dr. Hardy (of the Second Award of the Society for Occupational and Environmental Health)." In Conference on Women and the Workplace (1976: Washington, DC). Women and Workplace, p. 353-7.

Hardy, Janet B.
"Statement." In U.S. Congress. House. Select Committee on Population. Fertility and Contraception in America, pt. 2, p. 203-6.
"Statement." In U.S. Congress. Senate. Committee on Labor and Human Resources. Subcommittee on Family and Human Services. Reauthorization of the Adolescent Family Life Demonstrations Project of 1981, p. 125-7.
"Testimony." In U.S. Congress. House. Committee on Education and Labor. Subcommittee on Select Education. Adolescent Pregnancy, p. 39, 50-1.
"Testimony." In U.S. Congress. House. Committee on Energy and Commerce. Subcommittee on Health and the Environment. Health and the Environment Miscellaneous, pt. 3, p. 903-4.
"Testimony." In U.S. Congress. Senate. Committee on Human Resources. Adolescent Health, Services, and Pregnancy Prevention Care Act of 1978, p. 156-7.

Hareven, Tamara K.
"The Family and Gender Roles in Historical Perspective." In
Women and Men: Changing Roles, p. 93-118.

Hargreaves, Mary W. M.
"Darkness Before the Dawn: the Status of Working Women in
the Depression Years." In Conference on Women's History
(1976: Washington, DC). Clio Was a Woman, p. 178-88.

Harley, Sharon.
"Black Women in A Southern City: Washington, D.C., 1890-
1920." In Sex, Race, and the Role of Women in the South,
p. 59-74.

Harm, Mary Gay.
"The Mission of the YWCA." In Report of the YWCA National
Consultation for Programs on Domestic Violence, p. 1-2.

Harman, Lillian.
"Some Problems of Social Freedom." In Freedom, Feminism, and
the State, p. 192-201.

Harmon, Elaine D.
"Statement." In U.S. Congress. House. Committee on Veter-
ans' Affairs. Subcommittee on Oversight and Investigations.
Implementation of Title IV of Public Law 95-202, Relating to
WASPS and Similarly Situated Groups, p. 7-12.

Harper, Anne L.
"From Voluntary Motherhood to Planned Parenthood: Perspec-
tives on the Birth Control Movement in America." In Mar-
garet Sanger Centennial Conference (1979: Northampton,
MA). Margaret Sanger Centennial Conference, p. 29-30.
"Human Sexuality: New Insights From Women's History." In
Feminist Visions, p. 170-83.
"Reproductive Freedom Today: The Legacy of Margaret Sanger."
In Margaret Sanger Centennial Conference (1979: Northamp-
ton, MA). Margaret Sanger Centennial Conference, p. 12-28.

Harper, Frances.
"Liberty for Slaves." In Outspoken Women, p. 80-2.

Harragan, Betty Lehan.
"Women and Men at Work: Jockeying for Position." In The Woman in Management, p. 12-20.

Harris, Evergie.
"Statement." In U.S. Congress. House. Select Committee on
Aging. Subcommittee on Retirement Income and Employment.
Impact of Reagan Economics on Aging Women, p. 50-1.

Harris, Mary Mitchell.
  "Predicting the Null in Women's Research with Black Populations."
    In Conference on "Scholars and Women" (1981: University of
    Maryland). Women's Studies and the Curriculum, p. 173-8.

Harris, Patricia Roberts.
  "Religion and Politics: a Commitment to a Pluralistic Society."
    Vital Speeches, 47 (November 1, 1980), 50-3.
  "The Role of the American Intellectual Community in Redefining
    Our National Purpose: Americans Don't Trust Their Leaders."
    Vital Speeches, 45 (July 15, 1979), 600-4.

Harrison, Anna J.
  "Implications of Equality." In Expanding the Role of Women in
    the Sciences, p. 190-6.

Harrison, Beppie.
  "A Deliberate Choice: Staying At Home." In A Woman's Choices,
    p. 54-68.

Harrison, Beverly Wildung.
  "The Equal Rights Amendment: A Moral Analysis." In Harrison,
    Making the Connections, p. 167-73.
  "The Power of Anger in the Work of Love. Christian Ethics for
    Women and Other Strangers." In Harrison, Making the Con-
    nections, p. 3-21.
  "Sexism and the Contemporary Church: When Evasion Becomes
    Complicity." In Sexist Religion and Women in the Church,
    p. 195-216.
  "Sexism and the Language of Christian Ethics." In Harrison,
    Making the Connections, p. 22-41.

Hart, Barbara J.
  "Statement." In U.S. Congress. Senate. Committee on Labor
    and Human Resources. Subcommittee on Child and Human
    Development. Domestic Violence Prevention and Services Act,
    1980, p. 223-6.

Hartford, Beverly S.
  "Phonological Differences in the English of Adolescent Chicanas
    and Chicanos." In Conference on the Sociology of the Lan-
    guages of American Women (1976: New Mexico State Univer-
    sity). Proceedings, p. 73-80.

Hartman, Maryann.
  "A Descriptive Study of the Language of Men and Women Born in
    Maine Around 1900 As It Reflects the Lakoff Hypotheses in
    'Language and Women's Place.'" In Conference on the Sociol-
    ogy of the Languages of American Women (1976: New Mexico
    State University). Proceedings, p. 81-90.

Hartmann, Heidi I.
"Statement." In U.S. Congress. House. Committee on Post
Office and Civil Service. Subcommittee on Human Resources.
Pay Equity, pt. 1, p. 190-2.
"Statement." In U.S. Congress. Joint Economic Committee.
Women in the Work Force, p. 2-8.

Hartmann, Susan M.
"Women in the Military Service." In Conference on Women's His-
tory (1976: Washington, DC). Clio Was a Woman, p. 195-205.
"Women's Organizations During World War II: the Interaction of
Class, Race, and Feminism." In Conference on the History
of Women (1977: St. Paul, MN). Woman's Being, Woman's
Place, p. 313-28.

Hartsock, Nancy C. M.
"Feminism, Power, and Change: A Theoretical Analysis." In
Women Organizing, p. 2-24.

Harvey, Brett.
"No More Nice Girls." In Pleasure and Danger, p. 204-9.

Harvey, Susan Ashbrook.
"Women in Early Syrian Christianity." In Images of Women in
Antiquity, p. 288-98.

Hass, Violet B.
"Evolving Views of Women's Professional Roles." In Women in
Scientific and Engineering Professions, p. 230-40.

Hatwood-Futrell, Mary.
"Statement." In U.S. Congress. House. Committee on Post
Office and Civil Service. Subcommittee on Human Resources.
Pay Equity, pt. 1, p. 234-7.

Hauserman, Nancy R.
"The American Homemaker: Policy Proposals." In Women's
Lives, p. 397-403.

Havelock, Christine Mitchell.
"Mourners on Greek Vases; Remarks on the Social History of
Women." In Feminism and Art History, p. 45-61.

Hawkins, Paula.
"Choices in a Nation of Alternatives." In Ye Are Free to Choose,
p. 32-40.
"Statement." In U.S. Congress. House. Committee on Government Operations. Government Information, Justice and Agriculture Subcommittee. Continued Review of the Administration's Drug Interdiction Efforts. Washington: U.S.G.P.O.,
1984, p. 171-8.

"Statement." In U.S. Congress. House. Committee on Interior and Insular Affairs. Subcommittee on Public Lands and National Parks. Additions to the National Wilderness Preservation System. Washington: U.S.G.P.O., 1982, pt. 5, p. 35-43.

"Statement." In U.S. Congress. House. Committee on Post Office and Civil Services. Subcommittee on Postal Personnel and Modernization. Photography and Biography of Missing Child.... Washington: U.S.G.P.O., 1985, p. 30-6.

"Statement." In U.S. Congress. House. Committee on the Judiciary. Subcommittee on Civil and Constitutional Rights. Missing Children's Act. Washington: U.S.G.P.O., 1982, p. 2-10.

"Statement." In U.S. Congress. House. Committee on the Judiciary. Subcommittee on Crime. Trademark Counterfeiting Act of 1984. Washington: U.S.G.P.O., 1985, p. 144-51.

"Statement." In U.S. Congress. House. Committee on Veterans' Affairs. Subcommittee on Hospitals and Health Care. Hospital Care and Medical Services to Eligible Veterans in the State of Florida. Washington: U.S.G.P.O., 1982, p. 4-6.

"Statement." In U.S. Congress. Senate. Committee on Appropriations. Subcommittee on Energy and Water Development. Energy and Water Development Appropriations for Fiscal Year 1984. Washington: U.S.G.P.O., 1983, pt. 3, p. 2423.

"Statement." In U.S. Congress. Senate. Committee on Appropriations. Subcommittee on the Department of the Treasury, U.S. Postal Service, and General Government Appropriations. Drug Threat to Arizona and the Southwest Border. Washington: U.S.G.P.O., 1984, p. 8-10.

"Statement." In U.S. Congress. Senate. Committee on Appropriations. Subcommittee on Departments of Labor, Health and Human Services, Education, and Related Agencies. Youth Drug Abuse in New York. Washington: U.S.G.P.O., 1983, p. 4-5.

"Statement." In U.S. Congress. Senate. Committee on Banking, Housing, and Urban Affairs. Federal Reserve Board Membership and Structure. Washington: U.S.G.P.O., 1982, p. 29-35.

"Statement." In U.S. Congress. Senate. Committee on Banking, Housing, and Urban Affairs. Subcommittee on Securities. Regulation of Government Securities. Washington: U.S.G.P.O., 1985, p. 40-1.

"Statement." In U.S. Congress. Senate. Committee on Energy and Natural Resources. Subcommittee on Public Lands and Reserved Water. Prohibiting Phosphate in the Osceola National Forest, Florida. Washington: U.S.G.P.O., 1982, p. 35-43.

"Statement." In U.S. Congress. Senate. Committee on Energy and Natural Resources. Subcommittee on Energy Conservation and Supply. Outer Continental Shelf Leasing Activities. Washington: U.S.G.P.O., 1984, p. 32-45.

"Statement." In U.S. Congress. Senate. Committee on Finance. Child Support Enforcement Program Reform Proposals.

Washington: U.S.G.P.O., 1984, p. 14-25.
"Statement." In U.S. Congress. Senate. Committee on Finance.
Nominations of Margaret M. Heckler and John A. Svahn.
Washington: U.S.G.P.O., 1983, p. 3.
"Statement." In U.S. Congress. Senate. Committee on Finance.
Potential Inequities Affecting Women, pt. 2, p. 3-5.
"Statement." In U.S. Congress. Senate. Committee on Foreign
Relations. Radio Broadcasting to Cuba. Washington:
U.S.G.P.O., 1983, pt. 1, p. 374-5, 490-2.
"Statement." In U.S. Congress. Senate. Committee on Foreign
Relations. Subcommittee on International Economic Policy.
Unitary Tax. Washington: U.S.G.P.O., 1985, p. 7-10.
"Statement." In U.S. Congress. Senate. Committee on Labor
and Human Resources. Subcommittee on Labor. Retirement
Equity Act of 1983, p. 10-12.
"Statement." In U.S. Congress. Senate. Committee on the
Judiciary. Confirmation Hearings on Federal Appointments.
Washington: U.S.G.P.O., 1984, pt. 2, p. 33-4, 61-4.
"Statement." In U.S. Congress. Senate. Committee on the
Judiciary. Confirmation of Federal Judges. Washington:
U.S.G.P.O., 1982, pt. 2, p. 71-2.
"Statement." In U.S. Congress. Senate. Committee on the
Judiciary. Subcommittee on on Immigration and Refugee
Policy. Immigration Emergency Legislation. Washington:
U.S.G.P.O., 1985, p. 105-8.
"Statement." In U.S. Congress. Senate. Committee on the
Judiciary. Subcommittee on Immigration and Refugee Policy.
Immigration Emergency Powers. Washington: U.S.G.P.O.,
1983, p. 37-41.
"Statement." In U.S. Congress. Senate. Committee on the
Judiciary. Subcommittee on Immigration and Refugee Policy.
Immigration Reform and Control Act. Washington:
U.S.GP.O., 1983, p. 8-14.
"Statement." In U.S. Congress. Senate. Committee on the
Judiciary. Subcommittee on Immigration and Refugee Policy.
Refugee Act Reauthorization. Washington: U.S.G.P.O.,
1983, p. 226-30.
"Statement." In U.S. Congress. Senate. Committee on the
Judiciary. Subcommittee on Juvenile Justice. Child Kidnap-
ping. Washington: U.S.G.P.O., 1983, p. 2-13.
"Statement." In U.S. Congress. Senate. Committee on the
Judiciary. Subcommittee on Juvenile Justice. Exploited and
Missing Children. Washington: U.S.G.P.O., 1983, p. 57-9.
"Statement." In U.S. Congress. Senate. Committee on the
Judiciary. Subcommittee on Juvenile Justice. Missing Chil-
dren's Assistance Act. Washington: U.S.G.P.O., 1984, p.
17-18.
"Statement." In U.S. Congress. Senate. Committee on the
Judiciary. Subcommittee on Juvenile Justice. Serial Murders.
Washington: U.S.G.P.O., 1984, p. 10-14.
"Statement." In U.S. Congress. Senate. Committee on the

Judiciary. Subcommittee on Patents, Copyrights, and Trademarks. The Free Market Copyright Royalty Act of 1983. Washington: U.S.G.P.O., 1985, p. 54-61.
"Testimony." In U.S. Congress. Senate. Committee on Labor and Human Resources. Women in Transition 1983, p. 119-20.

Hawley, Carol Ann.
"Fortifying Ourselves Against Evil." In Ye Are Free To Choose, p. 102-4.

Haynes, Janice.
"Statement." In U.S. Congress. House. Select Committee on Children, Youth, and Families. Families in Crisis, p. 16-7.

Hays, Maxine.
"Statement." In U.S. Congress. Senate. Committee on Small Business. Women Entrepreneurs, p. 2-5.

Haywood, Doris P.
"Statement." In U.S. Congress. House. Committee on Post Office and Civil Service. Subcommittee on Human Resources. Pay Equity, pt. 1, p. 192-7.

Heagstedt, Nina.
"Testimony." In U.S. Congress. Joint Economic Committee. Subcommittee on Economic Growth and Stabilization. American Women Workers in a Full Employment Economy, p. 20-3.

Heckler, Margaret M.
"Congresswoman Margaret M. Heckler's Speech." In U.S. Department of Health, Education, and Welfare. Secretary's Advisory Committee on the Rights and Responsibilities of Women. Child Care and Working Women, p. 39-44.
"HHS Secretary on AIDS, June 14, 1983." In Historic Documents of 1983, p. 535-41.
"Speech by Congresswomen Margaret M. Heckler." In U.S. National Commission on the Observance of International Women's Year. The Spirit of Houston, p. 226-7.
"Statement." In U.S. Congress. House. Committee on Appropriations. Subcommittee on Energy and Water Development. Energy and Water Development Appropriations for 1983. Washington: U.S.G.P.O., 1982, pt. 8, p. 1569-92.
"Statement." In U.S. Congress. House. Committee on Appropriations. Subcommittee on the Departments of Labor, Health and Human Services, Education, and Related Agencies. Departments of Labor, Health and Human Services, Education, and Related Agencies Appropriations for 1984. Washington: U.S.G.P.O., 1983, pt. 2, p. 1-165.
"Statement." In U.S. Congress. House. Committee on Appropriations. Subcommittee on the Departments of Labor, Health and Human Services, Education, and Related Agencies.

Child Support Enforcement Program Reform Proposals. Washington: U.S.G.P.O., 1984, p. 32-61.

"Statement." In U.S. Congress. Senate. Committee on Finance. Nominations of Margaret M. Heckler and John A. Svahn. Washington: U.S.G.P.O., 1983, p. 4-42.

"Statement." In U.S. Congress. Senate. Committee on Finance. Subcommittee on Social Security and Income Maintenance Programs. Proposed Restructure of the Child Support Enforcement Program. Washington: U.S.G.P.O., 1984, p. 9-43.

"Statement." In U.S. Congress. Senate. Committee on Governmental Affairs. Permanent Subcommittee on Investigations. The Role of the Entertainment Industry in Deglamorizing Drug Use. Washington: U.S.G.P.O., 1985, p. 3-27.

"Statement." In U.S. Congress. Senate. Committee on Labor and Human Resources. Health Care Cost: Defining the Issues, 1983. Washington: U.S.G.P.O., 1983, p. 26-76.

"Statement." In U.S. Congress. Senate. Committee on Labor and Human Resources. Margaret M. Heckler, To Be Secretary, Department of Health and Human Services--Additional Consideration. Washington: U.S.G.P.O., 1983, p. 4-106.

"Statement." In U.S. Congress. Senate. Committee on Labor and Human Resources. Subcommittee on Aging. Oversight on Treatment of Alzheimer's Disease, 1983. Washington: U.S.G.P.O., 1983, p. 20-35.

"Statement." In U.S. Congress. Senate. Committee on Labor and Human Resources. Subcommittee on the Handicapped. Services for Mentally Retarded Persons. Washington: U.S.G.P.O., 1984, p. 32-57.

"Statement." In U.S. Congress. Senate. Committee on the Budget. First Concurrent Resolution on the Budget--Fiscal Year 1985. Washington: U.S.G.P.O., 1984, pt. 3, p. 99-171.

"Statement." In U.S. Congress. Senate. Committee on Veterans' Affairs. Recognition for Purposes of VA Benefits, p. 42-4.

"Testimony." In U.S. Congress. House. Committee on Energy and Commerce. Subcommittee on Health and the Environment. Health and the Environment Miscellaneous, pt. 3, p. 447-52.

"Testimony." In U.S. Congress. Joint Economic Committee. Subcommittee on Economic Growth and Stabilization. American Women Workers in a Full Employment Economy, p. 15-6.

Heffernan, Esther.
"Testimony." In U.S. Congress. House. Committee on the Judiciary. Subcommittee on Courts, Civil Liberties, and the Administration of Justice. The Female Offender--1979-80, p. 93, 97-105.

Heffernan, Sister Mary Esther, O.P.
"Equality and 'The System.'" In Split-Level Lives, p. 103-23.

Height, Dorothy I.
"Statement." In U.S. Congress. House. Committee on Ways and Means. Subcommittee on Public Assistance and Unemployment Compensation. Teenage Pregnancy Issues, p. 21-2.
"Statement." In U.S. Congress. Senate. Committee on Labor and Human Resources. Sex Discrimination in the Workplace, 1981, p. 176-8.
"Testimony." In U.S. Congress. House. Committee on International Relations. Subcommittee on International Organizations. International Women's Issues, p. 43-6.
"Testimony." In U.S. Congress. House. Committee on the Judiciary. Subcommittee on Civil and Constitutional Rights. Equal Rights Amendment Extension, p. 396-9.

Heilbrun, Carolyn G.
"Androgyny and the Psychology of Sex Differences." In The Future of Difference, p. 258-65.
"Louisa May Alcott: The Influence of Little Women." In Women, the Arts, and the 1920s in Paris and New York, p. 20-6.

Hein, Hilde.
"Liberating Philosophy: An End to the Dichotomy of Matter and Spirit." In Beyond Domination, p. 123-41.

Heller, Valerie.
"Testimony." In U.S. Congress. Senate. Committee on the Judiciary. Subcommittee on Juvenile Justice. Effect of Pornography on Women and Children, p. 163-8.

Hellwig, Monika K.
"Christian Women in a Troubled World." In Hellwig, Christian Women in a Troubled World, p. 1-54.
"The Expectation and the Birth (The Fourth Sunday in Advent)." In Women and the Word, p. 42-6.

Helson, Ravenna Mathews.
"The Creative Woman Mathematician." In Hyman Blumburg Symposium on Research in Early Childhood Education (8th: 1976: Johns Hopkins University). Women and the Mathematical Mystique, p. 23-54.
"Creativity in Women." In Psychology of Women, p. 553-604.

Hemmings-Gapihan, Grace S.
"Baseline Study for Socio-Economic Evaluation of Tangaye Solar Site." In Women and Technological Change in Developing Countries, p. 139-48.

Hendee, Laura L.
"Testimony." In U.S. Commission on Civil Rights. Hearings Before the U.S. Commission on Civil Rights Held in Denver, 1976, p. 184-8.

Henderson, Darcell.
   "Statement." In U.S. Congress. House. Committee on Ways
   and Means. Subcommittee on Public Assistance and Unemployment Compensation. Teenage Pregnancy Issues, p. 47.

Hendricks, Maureen Calista.
   "Feminist Spirituality in Jewish and Christian Traditions." In
   Handbook of Feminist Therapy, p. 135-46.
   "Feminist Therapy with Women and Couples Who Are Infertile."
   In Handbook of Feminist Therapy, p. 147-58.

Hendrixson, Carolyn.
   "Statement." In U.S. Congress. House. Committee on Post
   Office and Civil Service. Subcommittee on Compensation and
   Employee Benefits. Federal Pay Equity Act of 1984, pt. 2,
   p. 173-4.

Hepburn, Katharine Houghton.
   "Testimony." In U.S. Congress. House. Committee on Ways
   and Means. Birth Control, (1932) p. 4-5.
   "Testimony." In U.S. Congress. House. Committee on the
   Judiciary. Birth Control, (1934) p. 5.
   "Testimony." In U.S. Congress. Senate. Committee on the
   Judiciary. Birth Control, (1931) p. 2.
   "Testimony." In U.S. Congress. Senate. Committee on the
   Judiciary. Birth Control, (1932) p. 5-6.
   "Testimony." In U.S. Congress. Senate. Committee on the
   Judiciary. Birth Control, (1934) p. 4-5.

Herbert, Myra A.
   "Testimony." In U.S. Congress. Senate. Committee on the
   Judiciary. Subcommittee on Juvenile Justice. Teenage Sui-
   cide, p. 45-7.

Herlands, Rosalind L.
   "Biological Manipulations for Producing and Nurturing Mammalian
   Embryos." In The Custom-Made Child?, p. 231-40.

Herman, Alexis M.
   "Statement." In U.S. Congress. House. Committee on Govern-
   ment Operations. Manpower and Housing Subcommittee. The
   Women's Bureau, p. 97-9.
   "Statement." In U.S. Congress. Senate. Committee on Labor
   and Human Relations. The Coming Decade, p. 269-72.
   "Testimony." In U.S. Equal Employment Opportunity Commission.
   Hearings Before the U.S. Equal Employment Opportunity Com-
   mission on Job Segregation and Wage Discrimination, p. 343-51.
   "Testimony." In U.S. Congress. House. Select Committee on
   Aging. Subcommittee on Retirement Income and Employment.
   National Policy Proposals Affecting Midlife Women, p. 34-44.

Herman, Debra.
"Does Equality Mean Sameness? A Historical Perspective on the College Curriculum for Women with Reflections on the Current Situation." In Feminist Visions, p. 149-57.

Hernandez, Antonia.
"Statement." In U.S. Congress. House. Committee on Education and Labor. Subcommittee on Employment Opportunities. Oversight Hearings on the OFCCP's Proposed Affirmative Actions Regulations, p. 167-9, 181-2.

Herre, Saundra R.
"Statement." In U.S. Congress. House. Committee on Small Business. National Commission on Women's Business Ownership, p. 51-60.
"Statement." In U.S. Congress. Senate. Select Committee on Small Business. Women-In-Business Programs in the Federal Government, p. 4-7.

Herrick, Allison.
"Statement." In U.S. Congress. House. Committee on Foreign Affairs. Subcommittee on Human Rights and International Organizations. U.S. Contribution to the U.N. Decade for Women, p. 108-10.

Herrin, Judith.
"In Search of Byzantine Women: Three Avenues of Approach." In Images of Women in Antiquity, p. 167-89.

Hersh, Blanche Glassman.
"The 'True Women' and the 'New Women' in Nineteenth-Century America: Feminists-Abolitionists and a New Concept of True Womanhood." In Conference on the History of Women (1977: St. Paul, MN). Woman's Being, Woman's Place, p. 271-82.

Hershey, Lenore.
"Communicating and Managing the Media Challenge." In Women in Management, p. 31-41.

Hertz, Judith.
"Testimony." In U.S. Congress. House. Committee on the Judiciary. Subcommittee on Civil and Constitutional Rights. Equal Rights Amendment Extension, p. 296-8.

Hess, Beth.
"The 'New Breed' of Old People." In Older Women in the City, p. 153-62.

Hewitt, Gloria C.
"The Status of Women in Mathematics." In Expanding the Role of Women in the Sciences, p. 100-9.

Heyward, Carter.
  "Being 'In Christ?'" In Heyward, Our Passion for Justice, p.
    94-9.
  "Compassion." In Heyward, Our Passion for Justice, p. 234-42.
  "The Covenant: A Meditation on Jewish and Christian Roots."
    In Heyward, Our Passion for Justice, p. 175-8.
  "The Enigmatic God." In Heyward, Our Passion for Justice, p.
    24-32. Also in Spinning a Sacred Yarn, p. 107-115.
  "Gay Pride Day." In Heyward, Our Passion for Justice, p. 179-
    83.
  "God or Mammon?" In Heyward, Our Passion for Justice, p.
    132-6.
  "Judgment." In Heyward, Our Passion for Justice, p. 201-10.
  "Liberating the Body." In Heyward, Our Passion for Justice,
    p. 137-47.
  "Limits of Liberalism: Feminism in Moral Crisis." In Heyward,
    Our Passion for Justice, p. 153-74.
  "Living in the Struggle." In Heyward, Our Passion for Justice,
    p. 248-53.
  "Must 'Jesus Christ' Be a Holly Terror?--Using Christ as a
    Weapon Against the Jews, Women, Gays, and Just About Every-
    body Else." In Heyward, Our Passion for Justice, p. 211-21.
  "On Behalf of Women Priests." In Heyward, Our Passion for Jus-
    tice, p. 3-5.
  "On El Salvador." In Heyward, Our Passion for Justice, p. 3-5.
  "Passion." In Heyward, Our Passion for Justice, p. 19-23.
  "Priesthood (The Ordination of Doug Clark)." In Women and the
    Word, p. 76-85.
  "Redefining Power." In Heyward, Our Passion for Justice, p.
    116-22.
  "Sexual Fidelity." In Heyward, Our Passion for Justice, p. 184-
    99.

Higashi, Sumiko.
  "Cinderella v. Statistics: The Silent Movie Heroine as a Jazz-
    Age Working Girl." In Conference on the History of Women
    (1977: St. Paul, MN). Woman's Being, Woman's Place, p.
    109-26.

Higginbotham, Elizabeth.
  "Laid Bare by the System: Work and Survival for Black and
    Hispanic Women." In Class, Race, and Sex, p. 200-15.

Higgins, Doria.
  "Child Bearing, Child Rearing, Abortion and Contraception." In
    Cornell Conference on Women (1969: Cornell University.)
    Proceedings, p. 55-6.

Higgins, Millicent W.
  "Changing Patterns of Smoking and Risk of Disease." In The
    Changing Risk of Disease in Women, p. 65-79.

Higgs, Cathy.
"Statement." In U.S. Congress. House. Committee on Small
Business. Subcommittee on General Oversight and Minority
Enterprise. Women in Business, p. 120-7.

Hill, Ann Corinne.
"Protection of Women Workers and the Courts: A Legal Case
History." Feminist Studies, 5 (Summer 1979), 247-73.

Hill, Frances.
"Statement." In U.S. Congress. House. Select Committee on
Aging. Subcommittee on Health and Long-Term Care. Elder
Abuse, p. 82-4.

Hill, Kathleen Spangler.
"Work Requirements for AFDC Mothers." In NASW Conference on
Social Work Practice With Women (1st: 1980: Washington,
DC). Women, Power, and Change, p. 137-45.

Hill, Shirley Y.
"Introduction: The Biological Consequences." In Alcoholism
and Alcohol Abuse Among Women, p. 45-62.

Hilton, Mary N.
"Greetings." In U.S. Women's Bureau. Native American Women
and Equal Opportunity, p. 3.
"Priorities as Viewed from a Federal Agency." In Conference on
the National Longitudinal Surveys of Mature Women (1978:
U.S. Department of Labor). Women's Changing Roles at Home
and on the Job, p. 309-10.

Hilty, Deborah.
"From Our Work and Experience: Questions for the Academy."
In GLCA Women's Studies Conference (6th: 1980). Towards
a Feminist Transformation of the Academy II, p. 5-7.

Hinding, Andrea.
"An Abundance of Riches: the Women's History Sources Survey."
In Conference on Women's History (1976: Washington, DC).
Clio Was a Woman, p. 23-9.

Hirano, Irene.
"Statement." In U.S. Congress. House. Committee on Educa-
tion and Labor. Subcommittee on Employment Opportunities.
Oversight Hearings on Equal Employment Opportunity and
Affirmative Action, pt. 2, p. 450-3.

Hirata, Lucie Cheng.
"Social Mobility of Asian Women in America: A Critical Review."
In Conference on the Educational and Occupational Needs of
Asian-Pacific-American Women (1976: San Francisco, CA).

Conference on the Educational and Occupational Needs of
Asian-Pacific-American Women, p. 323-42.

Hoagland, Sarah.
"On the Reeducation of Sophie." In Women's Studies, p. 13-20.

Hobby, Ovita Culp.
"Statement." In U.S. Congress. House. Committee on Veterans' Affairs. Select Subcommittee to Review WASP Bills.
To Provide Recognition to the Women's Air Force Service, p.
89-93.

Hock, Carolyn.
"Residential Location and Transportation Analyses: Married
Women Workers." In Women's Travel Issues, p. 285-303.

Hodgkins, Gael.
"Sedna: Images of the Transcendent in an Eskimo Goddess."
In Beyond Androcentrism, p. 305-13.

Hodgman, Joan E.
"Pregnancy Outcome, Neonatal Mortality." In Women: a Development Perspective, p. 259-70.

Hoffman, Lois W.
"Childbearing and the Woman's Role." In Women & Men, p. 239-
50.
"Social Change and Its Effects on Parents and Children: Limitations to Knowledge." In Women: A Developmental Perspective, p. 313-24.

Hofmann, Adele D.
"Testimony." In U.S. Congress. Senate. Committee on Human
Resources. Adolescent Health, Services, and Pregnancy Pre-
vention Care Act of 1978, p. 511-14.
"Today's Girls: Human Sexuality--Comments." In Today's Girls:
Tomorrow's Women, p. 35.

Hofrichter, Frima Fox.
"Judith Leyster's Proposition--Between Virtue and Vice." In
Feminism and Art History, p. 173-81.

Hoisington, Elizabeth.
"Statement." In U.S. Congress. House. Committee on Armed
Services. Subcommittee on Military Personnel. Women in the
Military, p. 231-5.

Holden, Karen C.
"Supplemental OASI Benefits to Homemakers Through Current
Spouse Benefits, A Homemaker's Credit, and Child-Care Drop-
Out Years." In A Challenge to Social Security, p. 41-65.

Holland, Patricia T.
"Pure Hearts and Pure Homes." In Ye Are Free to Choose, p. 63-70.
"Women and the Priesthood." In Blueprints for Living, v. 2, p. 40-8.

Hollibaugh, Amber.
"Desire for the Future: Radical Hope in Passion and Pleasure." In Pleasure and Danger, p. 401-10.

Hollinshead, May.
"Health Professional Education." In Warner, Anne R. Health Womenpower, p. 30-5.

Hollis, Florence.
"The Psychosocial Approach to the Practice of Casework." In Charlotte Towle Memorial Symposium on Comparative Theoretical Approaches to Casework Practice (1969: University of Chicago). Theories of Social Casework, p. 33-75.

Holly, Ella Louise.
"Statement." In U.S. Congress. Senate. Special Committee on Aging. Women in Our Aging Society, p. 60-2.

Holm, Jeanne M.
"Statement." In U.S. Congress. House. Committee on Armed Services. Subcommittee on Military Personnel. Women in the Military, p. 2-13.
"Testimony." In U.S. Congress. Joint Economic Committee. Subcommittee on Priorities and Economy in Government. The Role of Women in the Military, p. 90-4.

Holmes, Deborah.
"Statement." In U.S. Congress. Senate. Committee on Small Business. Women Entrepreneurs, p. 75-7.

Holmes, Helen Bequaert.
"A Feminist Analysis of the Universal Declaration of Human Rights." In Beyond Domination, p. 250-64.

Holmes, Julia A.
"Statement." In U.S. Congress. House. Committee on Education and Labor. Subcommittee on Employment Opportunities. Oversight Hearings on the OFCCP's Proposed Affirmative Action Regulations, p. 197-201.
"Statement." In U.S. Congress. Committee on Post Office and Civil Service. Subcommittee on Human Resources. Pay Equity, pt. 1, p. 115-20.

Holmstrom, Engin I.
"The New Pioneers ... Women Engineering Students." In Women in Engineering--Beyond Recruitment, p. 19-27.

Holt, Marjorie
    "Statement." In U.S. Congress. House. Committee on Appro-
    priations. Subcommittee on Department of the Interior and
    Related Agencies. Department of the Interior and Related
    Agencies Appropriations for 1983. Washington: U.S.G.P.O.,
    1982, pt. 7, p. 71-3.
    "Statement." In U.S. Congress. House. Committee on Armed
    Services. Subcommittee on Military Installations and Facilities.
    Hearing on H.R. 3278 and H.R. 3017: Criteria for Sizing
    Military Medical Facilities. Washington: U.S.G.P.O., 1983,
    p. 8-10.
    "Statement." In U.S. Congress. Committee on Armed Services.
    Subcommittee on Military Personnel. Women in the Military,
    p. 297-8.
    "Statement." In U.S. Congress. House. Committee on the Dis-
    trict of Columbia. Lottery Initiative. Washington:
    U.S.G.P.O., 1981, p. 22-9.
    "Statement." In U.S. Congress. House. Committee on Veter-
    ans' Affairs. Subcommittee on Hospitals and Health Care.
    VA Medical Construction Program. Washington: U.S.G.P.O.,
    1983, p. 4-5.

Holtzman, Elizabeth.
    "Statement." In U.S. Congress. House. Committee on Inter-
    state and Foreign Commerce. Subcommittee on Health and the
    Environment. Drug Regulation Reform--Oversight: New Drug
    Approval Process. Washington: U.S.G.P.O., 1980, pt. 1,
    p. 3-6.
    "Statement." In U.S. Congress. House. Committee on Science
    and Technology. Subcommittee on Energy Development and
    Applications. H.R. 4382--Energy Management Partnership Act.
    Washington: U.S.G.P.O., 1980, pt. 1, p. 63-4.

Holtzman, Joan Hirsch.
    "DES: Ten Points of Controversy." In The Custom-Made Child?,
    p. 51-6.

Homma-True, Reiko.
    "Mental Health Issues Among Asian-American Women." In Confer-
    ence on the Educational and Occupational Needs of Asian-
    Pacific-American Women (1976: San Francisco, CA). Confer-
    ence on the Educational and Occupational Needs of Asian-
    Pacific-American Women, p. 65-88

Honeycutt, Karen.
    "Clara Zetkin: A Socialist Approach to the Problems of Woman's
    Oppression." Feminist Studies, 3 (1976), 131-44.

Hong, Heather.
    "Statement." In U.S. Congress. House. Select Committee on
    Aging. Problems of Aging Women, p. 33-5.

Honig, Alice Sterling.
"Child Care Options and Decisions: Facts and Figurings for
Families." In Women in the Workplace, p. 89-111.

Honig, Emily.
"Burning Incense, Pledging Sisterhood: Communities of Women
Workers in the Shanghai Cotton Mills, 1919-1949." Signs, 10
(Summer 1985), 700-14.

Hooker, Edith Houghton.
"Address of Welcome." In American Birth Control Conference
(1st: 1921: New York). Birth Control: What It Is, How
It Works, What It Will Do, p. 12-4.

Hooker, Eva.
"History of a Weekend." In GLCA Women's Studies Conference
(6th: 1980). Toward a Feminist Transformation of the
Academy II, p. 77-8.

Hoover, Theressa.
"Black Women and the Churches: Triple Jeopardy." In Sexist
Religion and Women in the Church, p. 63-76.
"Testimony." In U.S. Congress. House. Committee on the
Judiciary. Subcommittee on Civil and Constitutional Rights.
Proposed Constitutional Amendments on Abortion, p. 322-6.

Hopkins, Esther A. H.
"A Certain Restlessness." In Expanding the Role of Women in
the Sciences, p. 173-8.
"Alternative Development of a Scientific Career." In Women in
Scientific and Engineering Professions, p. 137-46.

Horansky, Ruby.
"Statement." In U.S. Congress. House. Committee on Energy
and Commerce. Subcommittee on Health and the Environment.
Health and the Environment Miscellaneous, pt. 2, p. 755-7.

Hornig, Lilli S.
"Professional Women in Transition." In Women in Scientific and
Engineering Professions, p. 43-58.
"Response to The Social Scene: Isolation and Frustration." In
Women in Engineering--Beyond Recruitment, p. 77-8.
"Scientific Sexism." In Expanding the Role of Women in the Sci-
ences, p. 125-33.

Hoskins, Betty B.
"Manipulative Reproductive Technologies: Overview." In The
Custom-Made Child?, p. 227-30.

Hough, Eleanor.
"Testimony." In U.S. Congress. House. Committee on Ways and
Means. Birth Control, (1932) p. 83-4.

Houston, Nezarine.
  "Testimony." In U.S. Commission on Civil Rights. Hearing Before the U.S. Commission on Civil Rights Held in Chicago, 1974, v. 1, p. 423-4.

Howard, Carole.
  "Moving Into Senior Management. Progress? Yes; Success, Sometimes." Vital Speeches, 51 (December 15, 1984), 148-50.

Howard, Marion.
  "Statement." In U.S. Congress. House. Committee on Energy and Commerce. Subcommittee on Health and the Environment. Pregnancy-Related Health Services, p. 142-4.
  "Statement." In U.S. Congress. Senate. Committee on Labor and Human Resources. Subcommittee on Family and Human Services. Reauthorization of the Adolescent Family Life Demonstration Projects Act of 1981, p. 84-7.

Howard, Maureen.
  "City of Words." In Women, the Arts, and the 1920s in Paris and New York, p. 42-8.

Howe, Carol.
  "Statement." In U.S. Congress. Senate. Committee on Labor and Human Resources. Subcommittee on Family and Human Services. Adolescents in Crisis, p. 116-20.

Howe, Florence.
  "American Literature and Women's Lives." In Howe, Myths of Coeducation, p. 285-306.
  "Breaking the Disciplines." In GLCA Women's Studies Conference (4th: 1978: Rochester, Indiana). Structure of Knowledge, p. 1-10. Also In Howe, Myths of Coeducation, p. 221-30.
  "Feminism and the Education of Women." In Howe, Myths of Coeducation, p. 175-87.
  "Feminism and the Study of Literature." In Howe, Myths of Coeducation, p. 188-205.
  "Feminism, Fiction, and the Classroom." In Howe, Myths of Coeducation, p. 47-64.
  "Feminist Scholarship: the Extent of the Revolution." In Learning Our Way, p. 98-111. Also In Howe, Myths of Coeducation, p. 270-84. Also In Liberal Education and the New Scholarship on Women, p. 5-21.
  "The Future of Women's Colleges." In Howe, Myths of Coeducation, p. 125-38.
  "Literary and Literature." In Howe, Myths of Coeducation, p. 111-24.
  "Myths of Coeducation." In Howe, Myths of Coeducation, p. 206-20.
  "The Past Ten Years: A Critical Retrospective." In Howe, Myths of Coeducation, p. 231-445.

"The Power of Education: Change in the Eighties." In Howe, Myths of Coeducation, p. 246-58.
"Sex-Role Stereotypes Start Early." In Howe, Myths of Coeducation, p. 65-77.
"Teaching in the Modern Languages." In Howe, Myths of Coeducation, p. 38-46.
"Why Educate Women?" In Howe, Myths of Coeducation, p. 18-27.
"Why Educate Women? The Responses of Wellesley and Stanford." In Howe, Myths of Coeducation, p. 259-69.
"Women and the Power of Education." In Conference on "Scholars and Women" (1981: University of Maryland). Women's Studies and the Curriculum, p. 17-28.
"Women's Studies and Social Change." In Howe, Myths of Coeducation, p. 78-110.

Howe, Julia Ward.
"Is Polite Society Polite?" In We Shall Be Heard, p. 173-83.
"Julia Ward Howe Addresses the Massachusetts Legislature." In Women Leaders in American Politics, p. 206-7.

Howe, Sharon M.
"A Legislative Perspective." In Conference on the National Longitudinal Surveys of Mature Women (1978: U.S. Department of Labor). Women's Changing Roles at Home and On the Job, p. 311-2.

Howell, Mary C.
"The New Feminism and the Medical School Milieu." In Expanding the Role of Women in the Sciences, p. 210-4.

Howett, Catherine M.
"Careers in Landscape Architecture: Recovering for Women What the 'Ladies' Won and Lost." In Feminist Visions, p. 139-48.

Hricko, Andrea.
"Panel Discussion of Societal Responsibilities as Seen By Women." In Conference on Women and the Workplace (1976: Washington, DC). Women and the Workplace, p. 310-12.

Hsu, Lily.
"Statement." In U.S. Congress. House. Select Committee on Aging. Subcommittee on Health and Long-Term Care. Elder Abuse, p. 18-9.

Hubbard, Louisa.
"Lady School Managers." In International Women's Year Conference on Women in Public Life (1975: Lyndon Baines Johnson Library). Women in Public Life, p. 265-6.

Hubbard, Marilyn French.
"Statement." In U.S. Congress. Senate. Select Committee on

Small Business. Women-In-Business Programs in the Federal
Government, p. 11-4.

Hubbard, Ruth.
"The Case Against In Vitro Fertilization and Implantation." In
The Custom-Made Child?, p. 259-62.
"Feminism in Academia: Its Problematic and Problems." In Expanding the Role of Women in the Sciences, p. 249-56.
"Should Professional Women Be Like Professional Men?" In Women in Scientific and Engineering Professions, p. 205-11.

Huber, Joan.
"The Future of Parenthood: Implications of Declining Fertility."
In Women & Men, p. 333-51.

Huebner, Ruby.
"Statement." In U.S. Congress. House. Select Committee on
Aging. Problems of Aging Women, p. 17-8.

Huggard, Marianne.
"Women as Agents of Change." In International Conference on
Women and Food (1978: University of Arizona). A Conference on the Role of Women in Meeting Basic Food and Water
Needs in Developing Countries, p. 129-30.

Hughes, Sarah T.
"Women in Power." In International Women's Year Conference on
Women in Public Life (1975: Lyndon Baines Johnson Library).
Women in Public Life, p. 23-4.

Huikamp, Sister Julia.
"Testimony." In U.S. Commission on Civil Rights. Hearing Before the U.S. Commission on Civil Rights Held in Chicago,
1974, v. 1, p. 26-9, 31, 33-8.

Hulen, Patricia Lux.
"Simultaneous Electrophoresis of Phosphogluecomutase (PGM) and
Peptidase A (PepA)." In Forensic Science Symposium on the
Analysis of Sexual Assault Evidence (1983: Quantico, VA).
Proceedings, p. 129.

Hulett, Josephine.
"Testimony." In U.S. Commission on Civil Rights. Hearing Before the U.S. Commission on Civil Rights Held in Chicago,
1974, v. 1, p. 233-42.

Hulka, Barbara S.
"Estrogens and Endometrial Cancer." In The Changing Risk of
Disease in Women, p. 211-20.

Humez, Jean M.
"'My Spirit Eye': Some Functions of Spiritual and Visionary

Experience in the Lives of Five Black Women Preachers, 1810-
1880." In Berkshire Conference on the History of Women
(5th: 1982: Vassar College). Women and the Structure of
Society, p. 129-43.

Humphrey, Muriel.
"Statement." In U.S. Congress. House. Committee on the
Judiciary. Subcommittee on Civil and Constitutional Rights.
Equal Rights Amendment Extension, p. 6-8.

Humphreys, Sarah C.
"Public and Private Interest in Classical Athens." In Humphreys,
The Family, Women, and Death, p. 22-32.

Humphreys, Sheila M.
"Effectiveness of Science Career Conferences." In Women and
Minorities in Science, p. 165-86.

Hunt, Linda.
"Cygnets and Ducklings: George Eliot and the Problem of Female
Community." In Sisterhood Surveyed, p. 42-8.

Hunt, Mary E.
"Political Oppression and Creative Survival." In Women's Spirit
Bonding, p. 164-72.
"A Political Perspective." In Women's Spirit Bonding, p. 249-54.

Hunt, Vilma R.
"A Brief History of Women Workers and Hazards of the Work-
place." Feminist Studies, 5 (Summer 1979), 274-85.
"Radiation Exposure and Protection." In Conference on Women
and the Workplace (1976: Washington, DC). Women and the
Workplace, p. 196-201.

Hunter, Frances C.
"Testimony." In U.S. Equal Employment Opportunity Commission.
Hearing Before the U.S. Equal Employment Opportunity Com-
mission on Job Segregation and Wage Discrimination, p. 260-73.

Hunter, Nan D.
"Testimony." In U.S. Congress. House. Committee on Energy
and Commerce. Subcommittee on Health and the Environment.
Health and the Environment Miscellaneous, pt. 3, p. 934-7.

Hunter, Sue.
"Statement." In U.S. Congress. Senate. Committee on Finance.
Potential Inequities Affecting Women, pt. 2, p. 142-3.

Hutar, Patricia.
"Statement." In U.S. Congress. Senate. Committee on Foreign
Relations. Women in Development, p. 48-9.

Hutchinson, Anne.
    "The Examination of Mrs. Anne Hutchinson." In Outspoken Wom-
        en, p. 83-4.

Hutchinson, Barbara B.
    "Statement." In U.S. Congress. House. Committee on Post
        Office and Civil Service. Subcommittee on Compensation and
        Employee Benefits. Federal Pay Equity Act of 1984, pt. 1,
        p. 207-11.
    "Statement." In U.S. Congress. House. Committee on Post
        Office and Civil Service. Subcommittee on Compensation and
        Employee Benefits. Options for Conducting a Pay Equity
        Study, p. 357-9.
    "Statement." In U.S. Congress. House. Committee on Post
        Office and Civil Service. Subcommittee on Human Resources.
        Pay Equity, pt. 1, p. 511-14, 519-20.

Hutchinson, Callie.
    "Statement." In U.S. Congress. House. Committee on Ways
        and Means. Subcommittee on Public Assistance and Unem-
        ployment Compensation. AFDC and Social Service Bills and
        Related Oversight Issues, p. 112-14.

Huws, Ursula.
    "Demystifying New Technology." ISIS, 28 (September 1983),
        4-6.

Hyman, Trina Schart.
    "Caldecott Medal Acceptance." Horn Book, 61 (1985), 410-21.

Hymes, Viola H.
    "The State Commission for Women--Its Scope and Purpose." In
        Education of Women for Social and Political Leadership, p. 51-6.

Ilchman, Alice Stone.
    "The Public Purposes of Private Colleges." In Representative
        American Speeches, 1981-1982, p. 102-11.

Iron, Pamela.
    "Testimony." In U.S. Congress. House. Committee on Energy
        and Commerce. Subcommittee on Health and the Environment.
        Health and the Environment Miscellaneous, pt. 5, p. 90.

Ivera, Silva.
    "The Need for an Anthropological and Cognitive Approach to the
        Education of Hispanic Women." In Conference on the Educa-
        tional and Occupational Needs of Hispanic Women (1976: Den-
        ver, CO and Washington, DC). Conference on the Educational
        and Occupational Needs of Hispanic Women, p. 277-89.

Jacker, Corinne.
  "Better Than a Shriveled Huck: New Forms for the Theatre."
  In Toward the Second Decade, p. 25-34.

Jackson, Dana.
  "Workshop Report on Housing and Community Development." In
  Western Regional Civil Rights and Women's Right Conference
  (4th: 1977: San Francisco, CA). Recent Developments, p.
  111-4.

Jackson, Ethel J.
  "Two Projects in Rural North Carolina, U.S.A." In Health Needs
  of the World's Poor Women, p. 142-7.

Jackson, Frances L.
  "Testimony." In U.S. Congress. House. Committee on Energy
  and Commerce. Subcommittee on Health and the Environment.
  Health and the Environment Miscellaneous, pt. 3, p. 856-8.

Jackson, Jacqueline.
  "Statement." In U.S. Congress. House. Committee on Post
  Office and Civil Service. Subcommittee on Compensation and
  Employee Benefits. Federal Pay Equity Act of 1984, pt. 1,
  p. 21-4.

Jackson, Jacquelyne J.
  "Death Rate Trends of Black Females, United States, 1964-1978."
  In Women: A Developmental Perspective, p. 23-48.

Jackson, Shirley A.
  "From Clerk-Typist to Research Physicist." In Expanding the
  Role of Women in the Sciences, p. 296-9.

Jacksteit, Mary.
  "Statement." In U.S. Congress. House. Committee on Post
  Office and Civil Service. Subcommittee on Investigations.
  Sexual Harassment in the Federal Government, pt. 1, p. 109-
  11.

Jacobs, Sylvia M.
  "Three Afro-American Women: Missionaries in Africa, 1882-1904."
  In Women in New Worlds, v. 2, p. 268-80.

Jacobsen, Florence S.
  "Our Heritage." In Blueprints for Living, p. 26-30.

Jacobsen, Genevieve.
  "Statement." In U.S. Congress. House. Select Committee on
  Aging. Problems of Aging Women, p. 6-7.

Jacoby, Robin Miller.
"The Women's Trade Union League and American Feminism."
Feminist Studies, 3 (1976), 126-40.

Jacox, Ada.
"Testimony." In U.S. Equal Employment Opportunity Commission. Hearings Before the U.S. Equal Employment Opportunity Commission on Job Segregation and Wage Discrimination,
p. 510-26.

Jacquette, Jane S.
"Legitimizing Political Women: Expanding Options for Female
Political Elites in Latin America." In Perspectives on Power,
p. 27-36.

Jaggar, Alison.
"Human Biology in Feminist Theory: Sexual Equality Reconsidered." In Beyond Domination, p. 21-42.

James, Edith.
"Edith Bolling Wilson: A Documentary View." In Conference on
Women's History (1976: Washington, DC). Clio Was A Woman,
p. 234-40.

James, Jennifer.
"Prostitution and Sexual Violence." In Women in Crisis Conference (1st: 1979: New York, NY). Women in Crisis, p.
176-217.

James, M. S. R.
"Women and Their Future in Library Work." In The Role of
Women in Librarianship, p. 29-33.

James, Sally.
"State and Local Agencies' Workshop Report on Basic Skills for
Monitoring Civil Rights Compliance." In Western Regional
Civil Rights and Women's Rights Conference (4th: 1977:
San Francisco, CA). Recent Developments, p. 137.

Jancar, Barbara W.
"Women in the Opposition in Poland and Czechoslovakia in the
1970s." In Women, State, and Party in Eastern Europe, p.
168-85.
"Yugoslavia: War of Resistance." In Female Soldiers, p. 85-106.

Janeway, Elizabeth.
"Women and the Uses of Power." In The Future of Difference,
p. 327-44.

Janiewski, Dolores.
"Sisters Under Their Skins: Southern Working Women, 1880-

1950." In Sex, Race, and the Role of Women in the South, p. 13-36.

Jann, Rebecca C.
"What They Should Have Told Me When I Was A Senior. Learn to Spell and Write Please." Vital Speeches,, 50 (November 1, 1983), 51-2.

Jarzynski, Teresa.
"Testimony." In U.S. Congress. House. Committee on Energy and Commerce. Subcommittee on Health and the Environment. Health and the Environment Miscellaneous, pt. 3, p. 643.

Jayaratne, Toby.
"The Value of Quantitative Methodology for Feminist Research." In Theories of Women's Studies II, p. 47-67.

Jeanette, Doris.
"Feminism, The Future Of?" In Handbook of Feminist Therapy, p. 39-46.

Jefferson, Mildred F.
"Statement." In U.S. Congress. House. Committee on the Judiciary. Subcommittee on Civil and Constitutional Rights. Proposed Constitutional Amendments on Abortion, p. 452-4.
"Statement." In U.S. Congress. House. Select Committee on Population. Fertility and Contraception in America, p. 108-15.
"Statement." In U.S. Congress. Senate. Committee on Labor and Human Resources. Subcommittee on Family and Human Services. Reauthorization of the Adolescent Family Life Demonstration Project Act of 1981, p. 168-72.
"Statement." In U.S. Congress. Senate. Committee on the Judiciary. Subcommittee on Separation of Powers. The Human Life Bill, p. 112-4.

Jeffrey, Julie Roy.
"Ministry Through Marriage: Methodist Clergy Wives on the Trans-Mississippi Frontier." In Women in New Worlds, v. 1, p. 143-60.

Jeffrey, Mildred.
"Panel Discussion." In Public Forum on Women's Rights and Responsibilities (1978: Las Vegas, NV). Public Forum on Women's Rights and Responsibilities,p. 11-2.
"Testimony." In U.S. Congress. House. Committee on the Judiciary. Subcommittee on Civil and Constitutional Rights. Equal Rights Amendment Extension, p. 386-93.
"Testimony." In U.S. Congress. House. Select Committee on Aging. Subcommittee on Retirement Income and Employment. Task Force on Social Security and Women. Treatment of Women Under Social Security, p. 66-7.

Jenks, Marjorie.
"Statement." In U.S. Congress. Senate. Special Committee on Aging. Women in Our Aging Society, p. 25-7.

Jensen, Patricia A.
"Statement." In U.S. Congress. House. Committee on Education and Labor. Subcommittee on Elementary, Secondary, and Vocational Education. Hearing on Women's Educational Equity Act, p. 114-6.
"Statement." In U.S. Congress. House. Committee on Foreign Affairs. Subcommittee on Human Rights and International Organization. U.S. Contribution to the U.N. Decade for Women, p. 97-9.

Jermany, Catherine.
"Testimony." In U.S. Commission on Civil Rights. Hearing Before the U.S. Commission on Civil Rights Held in Chicago, 1974, v. 1, p. 119-23, 132-4.

Jerome, Elizabeth.
"A Physician's View of the Adolescent Woman." In Today's Girls: Tomorrow's Women, p. 26-34.

Jett-Ali, Joyce.
"Traditional Birth Attendants and the Need for Training." In Health Needs of the World's Poor Women, p. 120-5.

Jiminez-Vazquez, Rosa.
"Social Issues Confronting Hispanic American Women." In Conference on the Educational and Occupational Needs of Hispanic Women (1976: Denver, CO and Washington, DC). Conference on the Educational and Occupational Needs of Hispanic Women, p. 213-50.

Johns, Ruth C.
"Testimony." In U.S. Commission on Civil Rights. Hearing Before the U.S. Commission on Civil Rights Held in Denver, 1976, p. 437-8.

Johnson, Barbara.
"Statement." In California. Legislature. Joint Committee on Legal Equality. Women in the Justice System, p. 94-103.

Johnson, Billie Sewell.
"Statement." In U.S. Congress. Senate. Special Committee on Aging. Prospects for Better Health for Older Women, p. 8-12.

Johnson, Dewaran.
"Statement." In U.S. Congress. House. Committee on Ways and Means. Subcommittee on Public Assistance and Unemployment. Teenage Pregnancy Issues, p. 127-30.

"Statement." In U.S. Congress. House. Committee on Educa-
tion and Labor. Subcommittee on Employment Opportunities.
Oversight Hearing on the Job Training Partnership Act.
Washington: U.S.G.P.O., 1985, p. 2-17.

"Statement." In U.S. Congress. House. Committee on Energy
and Commerce. Subcommittee on Commerce, Transportation,
and Tourism. Implementation of the Superfund Program.
Washington: U.S.G.P.O., 1984, p. 11-5.

"Statement." In U.S. Congress. House. Committee on Ways
and Means. Subcommittee on Public Assistance and Unemployment Compensation. Teenage Pregnancy Issues, p. 11-5.

"Testimony." In U.S. Congress. House. Committee on Energy
and Commerce. Subcommittee on Health and the Environment.
Health and the Environment Miscellaneous, pt. 3, p. 432-3.

Johnson, Pam McAllister.
"Being a Manager in a Multicultural World." In The Woman in
Management, p. 37-9.

Johnson, Rebecca.
"A Historical Addendum." In Women's Spirit Bonding, p. 75-84.

Johnson, Sonia.
"Statement." In U.S. Congress. House. Committee on Post
Office and Civil Service. Subcommittee on Compensation and
Employee Benefits. Federal Pay Equity Act of 1984, pt. 1,
p. 110-1.

"Testimony." In U.S. Congress. House. Committee on the
Judiciary. Subcommittee on Civil and Constitutional Rights.
Equal Rights Amendment Extension, p. 307-10.

Johnson, Stephanie.
"Statement." In U.S. Congress. House. Committee on Energy
and Commerce. Subcommittee on Health and the Environment.
Pregnancy-Related Health Services, p. 357-9.

Johnson, Suzan D.
"God's Woman." In Those Preachin' Women, p. 119-26.

Johnson, Virginia E.
"Welcome and Opening Remarks." In Ethical Issues in Sex Therapy and Research, v. 2, p. 183-4.

Jones, Anne Goodwyn.
"Southern Literary Women as Chroniclers of Southern Life." In
Sex, Race, and the Role of Women in the South, p. 75-94.

Jones, Barbara A.
"Introductory Remarks on Work and Family Roles." In Conference on the National Longitudinal Surveys of Mature Women
(1978: U.S. Department of Labor). Proceedings, p. 123-8.

Jones, Diane Carlson.
"Power Structures and Perceptions of Power Holders in Same-Sex Groups of Young Children." In Biopolitics and Gender, p. 147-64.

Jones, Doris.
"Statement." In U.S. Congress. House. Committee on Post Office and Civil Service. Subcommittee on Compensation and Employee Benefits. Options for Conducting a Pay Equity Study, p. 180-2.

Jones, E. Claiborne.
"Lent V." In Women of the Word, p. 54-5.
"Pentecost XIV." In Women of the Word, p. 56-9.
"Sermon to the Seniors." In Women of the Word, p. 60-2.

Jones, Judith Burns.
"Statement." In U.S. Congress. House. Select Committee on Children, Youth, and Families. Teen Parents and Their Children, p. 112-7.

Jones, Judith E.
"Statement." In U.S. Congress. House. Select Committee on Population. Fertility and Contraception in America, pt. 2, p. 126-9.

Jones, Linda R. Wolf.
"Statement." In U.S. Congress. House. Committee on Ways and Means. Subcommittee on Public Assistance and Unemployment Compensation. AFDC and Social Service Bills and Related Oversight Issues, p. 188-91.

Jones, (Mother) Mary Harris.
"Agitation, The Greatest Factor for Progress--Speech in Memorial Hall, Toledo, March 24, 1903." In Jones, Mother Jones Speaks, p. 95-9.
"An Appeal for Striking Miners--Speech at American Federation of Labor Convention, Philadelphia, November 13, 1914." In Jones, Mother Jones Speaks, p. 259-62.
"An Appeal to Cooper Miners to Organize--Speech at Red Jacket, Michigan, April 18, 1905." In Jones, Mother Jones Speaks, p. 112-6.
"Appeal to the Cause of Miners in the Pine Creek District." In Outspoken Women, p. 85-97.
"Background to West Virginia's Bloodiest Mine War--Speech at United Mine Workers Convention, September 26, 1921." In Jones, Mother Jones Speaks, p. 329-47.
"Barbarous West Virginia--Five Speeches to Striking Coal Miners, Charleston and Montgomery, West Virginia. August 1, 4, 15, September 6, 21, 1912." In Jones, Mother Jones Speaks, p. 152-221.

"Be True to the Principles of Our Forefathers--Speech at Special Convention, United Mine Workers of America, July 19, 1902." In Jones, Mother Jones Speaks, p. 83-90.

"Dialogue With a Judge--Report of Remarks in Federal Court, Parkersburg, West Virginia, July 24, 1902." In Jones, Mother Jones Speaks, p. 81-2.

"Don't Give the Master Class Any Weapon to Strike You With-- Speech at United Mine Workers Convention, 1911." In Jones, Mother Jones Speaks, p. 140-51

"I Urge the Unity of Working People Everywhere Regardless of Political Philosophy--Speeches at the Third Congress, Pan- American Federation of Labor, Mexico City, January 13, 1921." In Jones, Mother Jones Speaks, p. 320-8.

"I Want to Give the Nation a More Highly Developed Citizenship --Speech at Carnegie Hall, New York City, May 27, 1913." In Jones, Mother Jones Speaks, p. 222-5.

"I Want to See More Alex Howats and I Want to Live Long Enough to Develop Them--Speech at United Mine Workers Convention, 1922." In Jones, Mother Jones Speaks, p. 348-59.

"If You Want to See Brutal Autocracy, Come With Me to the Steel Centers--Speeches at United Mine Workers Conventions, September 9, 1919." In Jones, Mother Jones Speaks, p. 303-15.

"I'm a Bolshevist from the Bottom of My Feet to the Top of My Head--Speech to Steel Strikers and Their Wives, Gary, Indi- ana, October 23, 1919." In Jones, Mother Jones Speaks, p. 316-9.

"The I.W.W. Convention--Remarks at Founding Convention of the Industrial Workers of the World, Chicago, July 7, 1905." In Jones, Mother Jones Speaks, p. 117-9.

"Labor's Memorial Day--Speech at Seattle, May 30, 1914." In Jones, Mother Jones Speaks, p. 245-9.

"Lay Down Your Picks and Shovels and Quit Work!--Reports of Speech to Miners at Clarksburg, West Virginia, June 20, 1902." In Jones, Mother Jones Speaks, p. 78-80.

"Let Us Have a Strike, A Strike to Strike the Kaiser Off the Throne--Speech at United Mine Workers Convention, 1919." In Jones, Mother Jones Speaks, p. 291-302.

"The Lives of the Coal Miners--Speech Delivered Summer, 1897, During Strike in West Virginia." In Jones, Mother Jones Speaks, p. 73-6.

"My Epitaph--Speech at Convention, United Mine Workers of America, January, 1901." In Jones, Mother Jones Speaks, p. 77-8.

"My Old Eyes Can See the Coming of Another Day--Speech at Conference of Farmer-Labor Party, Chicago, July 3, 1923." In Jones, Mother Jones Speaks, p. 360-5.

"Not an Industrial War, But a Civil War--Speech at Labor Tem- ple, Vancouver, Canada, June 10, 1914." In Jones, Mother Jones Speaks, p. 250-6.

"A Plea for a Strike Settlement--Speech at United Mine Workers

Waistmakers on Strike, New York City, December 9, 1909."
In Jones, Mother Jones Speaks, p. 136-7.

"To Be in Prison Is No Disgrace--Appeal from Cell, Walsenburg,
Colorado, March 31, 1914." In Jones, Mother Jones Speaks,
p. 238-44.

"Tribute to Italian Miners--Speech Before New York City Central
Federated Union, August 7, 1904." In Jones, Mother Jones
Speaks, p. 109-11.

"The Tyranny of Mexico--Speech at People's Forum, Brooklyn,
New York, December 12, 1909." In Jones, Mother Jones
Speaks, p. 138-9.

"The Wail of the Children--Speech at Coney Island During March
of the Mill Children, July 28, 1903." In Jones, Mother Jones
Speaks, p. 100-3.

"We Must Stand Together--Speech at Meeting of Miners, Louis-
ville, Colorado, November 21, 1903." In Jones, Mother Jones
Speaks, p. 104-8.

"Women are Fighters--Speech Before Central Labor Council of
Cincinnati, July 23, 1902." In Jones, Mother Jones Speaks,
p. 91-4.

"You Are Less Free Than the Negroes Were Before the Civil
War!--Speech to Striking Coal Miners, Walsenburg, Colorado,
October 27, 1913." In Jones, Mother Jones Speaks, p.
236-7.

"You Can't Fool My Boys, Mr. Rockefeller--Speech at Cooper
Union, New York City, January 28, 1915." In Jones, Mother
Jones Speaks, p. 263-7.

"You Don't Need a Vote to Raise Hell!" In Zak, Michele. Wom-
en and the Politics of Culture, p. 355-6.

"You Ought to be Out Raising Hell!--Speeches to New York City
Striking Carmen and Their Wives, October 4, 6, 1916."
In Jones, Mother Jones Speaks, p. 287-90.

"You Women Must Organize If You Want Your Men to Earn a De-
cent Living Wage--Speech on Behalf of Striking Street Car
Workers, El Paso, Texas, August 16, 1916." In Jones,
Mother Jones Speaks, p. 284-6.

Jones, Mildred B.
"Statement." In U.S. Congress. House. Task Force on Social
Security and Women. Treatment of Women Under Social Secur-
ity, v. 4, p. 175-7.

Jones, Tiffini.
"Statement." In U.S. Congress. House. Select Committee on
Children, Youth, and Families. Children, Youth, and Fami-
lies, p. 71-2.

Jones, Tricia S.
"Sexual Harassment in the Organization." In Women in Organizations, p. 23-38.

Jordan, Amy.
"Testimony." In U.S. Commission on Civil Rights. Hearing Before the U.S. Commission on Civil Rights Held in Denver, 1976, p. 475-6.

Jordan, Barbara.
"Keynote Speech by Congresswoman Barbara Jordan." In U.S. National Commission on the Observance of International Women's Year. The Spirit of Houston, p. 223.
"Who Then Will Speak for the Common Good?" In We Shall Be Heard, p. 332-5.

Jordan, Nancy.
"Testimony." In U.S. Commission on Civil Rights. Hearing Before the U.S. Commission on Civil Rights Held in Denver, 1976, p. 359-61.

Jordan, Ruth.
"Statement." In U.S. Congress. Senate. Committee on the Judiciary. Subcommittee on the Constitution. Constitutional Amendments Relating to Abortion, v. 1, p. 1105-7.

Jorge, Angela.
"Issues of Race and Class in Women's Studies: A Puerto Rican Woman's Thoughts." In Class, Race, and Sex, p. 216-20.

Jorgensen, Valerie.
"Adolescent Contraception." In Hormonal Contraceptives, Estrogens, and Human Welfare, p. 107-12.

Joseph, Rachel A.
"Testimony." In U.S. Congress. House. Committee on Energy and Commerce. Subcommittee on Health and the Environment. Health and the Environment Miscellaneous, pt. 5, p. 163-4.

Joyer, Paulette.
"Statement." In U.S. Congress. Senate. Committee on the Judiciary. Subcommittee on the Constitution. Constitutional Amendments Relating to Abortion, v. 1, p. 1157-8.

Joyner, Nancy Douglas.
"Statement." In U.S. Congress. Senate. Committee on Labor and Human Resources. The Coming Decade, p. 704-6.

Joynes, Margot.
"Testimony." In U.S. Congress. Senate. Committee on Labor and Human Resources. Women in Transition, 1983, p. 124-8.

Kahn, Diana Grossman.
"Interdisciplinary Studies and Women's Studies: Questioning

Answers and Creating Questions." In GLCA Women's Studies Conference (4th: 1978: Rochester, Indiana). Structures of Knowledge, p. 20-4.

Kahne, Hilda.
"Women and Social Security: Social Policy Adjusts to Social Change." In Conference on "Scholars and Women" (1981: University of Maryland). Women's Studies and the Curriculum, p. 87-93.

Kahr, Madlyn Millner.
"Delilah." In Feminism and Art History, p. 119-45.

Kamerman, Sheila B.
"Work and Family in Industrialized Societies." Signs, 4 (Summer 1979), 632-50.

Kampen, Natalie Boymel.
"Social Status and Gender in Roman Art: The Case of the Saleswoman." In Feminism and Art History, p. 63-77.

Kane, M. Theresa.
"Statement to Pope John Paul II: Be Mindful of the Intense Suffering and Pain." In Images of Women in American Popular Culture, p. 428-9.

Kane, Roslyn D.
"The Occupational Choices of Young Women as Affected by Schools and Parents." In Young Women and Employment, p. 31-7.

Kanter, Rosabeth Moss.
"The Impact of Organizational Structure: Models and Methods for Change." In Equal Employment Policy for Women, p. 311-28.
"Women Managers: Moving Up in a High Tech Society." In The Woman in Management, p. 21-36.

Kanuk, Leslie.
"Regulating the Ocean Shipping Industry. Where Are We Going and How Do We Get There?" Vital Speeches, 45 (July 1, 1979), 572-6.
"The Role of Regulatory Agencies in the Eighties. A Fully Integrated Transportation System." Vital Speeches, 46 (March 1, 1980), 315-20.

Kaplan, Adele.
"Statement." In U.S. Congress. Senate. Committee on Labor and Human Resources. The Coming Decade, pt. 2, p. 41-7.

Kaplan, Helen S.
  "Training of Sex Therapists." In Ethical Issues in Sex Therapy
  and Research, p. 182-8.

Kapp, Ardeth Greene.
  "Drifting, Dreaming, Directing." In Blueprints for Living, p.
  77-88.

Kaptur, Marcy.
  "Controversy Over the Federal Budget Deficit." Congressional
  Digest, 63 (February 1984), 58, 60, 62.
  "Statement." In U.S. Congress. House. Committee on Agriculture. Long-Term Farm Policy to Succeed the Agriculture
  and Food Act of 1981. Washington: U.S.G.P.O., 1984, pt.
  9, p. 950-4.
  "Statement." In U.S. Congress. House. Committee on Agriculture. Subcommittee on Domestic Marketing, Consumer Relations and Nutrition. Emergency Food Assistance and Com-
  modity Distribution Act of 1983. Washington: U.S.G.P.O.,
  1983, p. 13-5.
  "Statement." In U.S. Congress. House. Committee on Appropriations. Subcommittee on Energy and Water Development.
  Energy and Water Development Appropriations for 1985.
  Washington: U.S.G.P.O., 1984, pt. 3, p. 259-75.
  "Statement." In U.S. Congress. House. Committee on Appro-
  priations. Subcommittee on Energy and Water Development.
  Energy and Water Development Appropriations for 1986.
  Washington: U.S.G.P.O., 1985, pt. 9, p. 1840-6.
  "Statement." In U.S. Congress. House. Committee on Appro-
  priations. Subcommittee on the Department of the Interior
  and Related Agencies. Department of the Interior and Re-
  lated Agencies Appropriations for 1986. Washington:
  U.S.G.P.O., 1985, pt. 10, p. 983-8.
  "Statement." In U.S. Congress. House. Committee on Post
  Office and Civil Service. Subcommittee on Compensation and
  Employee Benefits. Federal Pay Equity Act of 1984, pt. 1,
  p. 17-8.
  "Statement." In U.S. Congress. House. Committee on Ways
  and Means. Subcommittee on Public Assistance and Unemployment Compensation. Federal Supplemental Compensation Pro-
  gram. Washington: U.S.G.P.O., 1985, p. 184-94.
  "Statement." In U.S. Congress. House. Committee on Ways
  and Means. Subcommittee on Public Assistance and Unemploy-
  ment Compensation. Proposals to Improve the Federal-State
  Unemployment Insurance System. Washington: U.S.G.P.O.,
  1985, p. 73-85.
  "Statement." In U.S. Congress. House. Committee on Ways
  and Means. Subcommittee on Trade. Miscellaneous Tariff and
  Trade Bills. Washington: U.S.G.P.O., 1985, p. 749-51.
  "Statement." In U.S. Congress. House. Select Committee on
  Aging. Subcommittee on Retirement Income and Employment.

Task Force on Social Security and Women. Inequities Toward
Women in the Social Security System, p. 122-3.
"Statement." In U.S. Congress. Senate. Committee on Environ-
ment and Public Works. Subcommittee on Water Resources.
Omnibus Water Resources Legislation. Washington:
U.S.G.P.O., 1983, pt. 1, p. 221-2.
"Statement." In U.S. Congress. Senate. Special Committee on
Aging. Prospects for Better Health in Older Women, p. 5-6.

Karmel, Roberta S.
"A Skeptical Regulator Looks at the Future of Regulation: To
Look at the General Public Welfare in the Whole Economy."
Vital Speeches, 45 (February 1, 1979), 238-42.

Karowe, Marjorie.
"Statement." In U.S. Congress. House. Committee on Post
Office and Civil Service. Subcommittee on Human Resources.
Pay Equity, pt. 1, p. 527, 37-9.

Kassebaum, Nancy Landon.
"Is the Proposed Anti-Apartheid Act of 1985 Sound Policy?"
Congressional Digest, 64 (October 1985), 233, 235, 237.
"Statement." In U.S. Congress. House. Committee on Foreign
Affairs. Subcommittee on Human Rights and International
Organizations. The U.S. Role in the United Nations. Wash-
ington: U.S.G.P.O., 1984, p. 4-19.
"Statement." In U.S. Congress. Joint Economic Committee.
Economic Status of Women, p. 23-5.
"Statement." In U.S. Congress. Senate. Committee on Com-
merce, Science and Transportation. Nomination--DOT ...
On Nomination of Elizabeth H. Dole, to be Secretary, Depart-
ment of Transportation, January 26, 1983. Washington:
U.S.G.P.O., 1983, p. 4.
"Statement." In U.S. Congress. Senate. Committee on Energy
and Natural Resources. Natural Gas Legislation. Washington:
U.S.G.P.O., 1983, pt. 2, p. 179-88.
"Statement." In U.S. Congress. Senate. Committee on Energy
and Natural Resources. Subcommittee on Energy and Mineral
Resources. Strategic Petroleum Reserve Program. Washing-
ton: U.S.G.P.O., 1981, pt. 2, p. 301-21.
"Statement." In U.S. Congress. Senate. Committee on Finance.
Child Support Enforcement Program Reform Proposals. Wash-
ington: U.S.G.P.O., 1984, p. 17-25.
"Statement." In U.S. Congress. Senate. Committee on Finance.
Potential Inequities Affecting Women, pt. 1, p. 63-4.
"Statement." In U.S. Congress. Senate. Committee on Finance.
Subcommittee on Taxation and Debt Management. Airport and
Airway Tax Measures. Washington: U.S.G.P.O., 1981, p.
35-40.
"Statement." In U.S. Congress. Senate. Committee on Labor
and Human Resources. Subcommittee on Labor. Retirement

Equity Act of 1983, p. 198-200.
"Statement." In U.S. Congress. Senate. Committee on the
Judiciary. Subcommittee on the Constitution. Bail Reform.
Washington: U.S.G.P.O., 1982, p. 79-81.
"Statement." In U.S. Congress. Senate. Special Committee on
Aging. Adapting Social Security to a Changing Work Force,
p. 1-3.

Kasun, Jacqueline R.
"Statement." In U.S. Congress. Senate. Committee on Labor
and Human Resources. Oversight of Family Planning Programs, 1981, p. 86-8.

Katz, Lillian G.
"Teacher Education and Non-Sexist Early Childhood Education."
In Conference on Non-Sexist Early Childhood Education (1976:
Arden House). Perspectives on Non-Sexist Early Childhood
Education, p. 57-61.

Katzenellenbogen, Benita.
"Cellular Actions of Estrogens and Oral Contraceptive Sex Steroid
Hormones." In Hormonal Contraceptives, Estrogens, and Hu-
man Welfare, p. 45-56.

Kavinoky, Nadina.
"California Public Health and Mothers' Clinics." In International
Birth Control Conference (7th: 1930: Zurich). Practice of
Contraception, p. 205-8.

Kay, Herma Hill.
"Statement." In U.S. Congress. Senate. Committee on the
Judiciary. Subcommittee on the Constitution. Constitutional
Amendments Relating to Abortion, v. 1, p. 766-9.

Keeley, Kathryn Szymoniak.
"Statement." In U.S. Congress. House. Committee on Govern-
ment Operations. Intergovernmental Relations and Human
Resources Subcommittee. Barriers to Self-Sufficiency for
Single Female Heads of Families, p. 587-9.

Keller, Candace.
"Testimony." In U.S. Congress. House. Committee on Energy
and Commerce. Subcommittee on Health and the Environment.
Health and the Environment Miscellaneous, pt. 5, p. 337-9.

Keller, Helen.
"Strike Against War." In We Shall Be Heard, p. 253-7.

Keller, Margaret.
"Testimony." In U.S. Congress. Senate. Committee on Labor
and Human Resources. Women in Transition, 1983, p. 117-8.

Keller, Rosemary Skinner.
> "Creating a Sphere for Women: The Methodist Episcopal Church,
> 1869-1906." In Women in New Worlds, v. 1, p. 246-60.
> "This Ministry: God's Mercy ... Our Hope." In Spinning a
> Sacred Yarn, p. 116-22.

Kelley, Florence.
> "The Child, the State, and the Nation." In Outspoken Women,
> p. 98-101.

Kelley, Mary.
> "At War With Herself; Harriet Beecher Stowe as Woman in Con-
> flict Within the Home." In Conference on the History of
> Women (1977: St. Paul, MN). Woman's Being, Woman's Place,
> p. 201-19.

Kelley, Maryellen R.
> "Commentary: The Need to Study the Transformation of Job
> Structures." In Sex Segregation in the Workplace, p. 261-4.
> "Testimony." In U.S. Equal Employment Opportunity Commission.
> Hearings Before the U.S. Equal Employment Opportunity Com-
> mission on Job Segregation and Wage Discrimination, p. 373-92.

Kellogg, Susan.
> "Aztec Women in the Sixteenth Century: Kinship and Religion."
> In Conference on "Scholars and Women" (1981: University of
> Maryland). Women's Studies and the Curriculum, p. 129-35.

Kelly, Casey.
> "Testimony." In U.S. Commission on Civil Rights. Hearing Be-
> fore the U.S. Commission on Civil Rights Held in Chicago,
> 1974, v. 2, p. 260-2, 270-1.

Kelly, Gertrude.
> "State Aid to Science." In Freedom, Feminism, and the State,
> p. 275-84.

Kelly, Joan.
> "The Doubled Vision of Feminist Theory: A Postscript to the
> 'Woman and Power' Conference." Feminist Studies, 5 (Spring
> 1979), 216-27.
> "Early Feminist Theory and the Querelle Des Femmes, 1400-1789."
> Signs, 8 (Autumn 1982), 4-28.

Kelly, Patricia.
> "Statement." In U.S. Congress. Senate. Committee on Finance.
> Potential Inequities Affecting Women, pt. 2, p. 233.

Kelly-Dreiss, Susan.
> "Statement." In U.S. Congress. House. Committee on Education
> and Labor. Subcommittee on Select Education. Hearing on
> Domestic Violence, p. 37-9.

Kelsey, Jennifer L.
"Epidemiology of Osteoporosis." In The Changing Risk of Disease in Women, p. 287-98.

Kelty, Miriam F.
"Ethical Issues and Requirements for Sex Research with Humans: Confidentiality." In Ethical Issues in Sex Therapy and Research, p. 84-105.

Kendall, Elizabeth.
"Women and Dance." In Women, the Arts, and the 1920s in Paris and New York, p. 133-7.

Kenen, Regina H.
"A Look at Prenatal Diagnosis Within the Context of Changing Parental and Reproductive Norms." In The Custom-Made Child?, p. 67-74.

Kennedy, Florynce.
"If You Want to Know Where the Apathy Is, You're Probably Sitting On It." In Kennedy, Color Me Flo, p. 116-20.
"Most People Are Not Taught to Understand That the Two O'Clock Orgasm Leads to the Three O'Clock Feeding." In Kennedy, Color Me Flo, p. 97-9.
"The Question Arises ... Whether All Lawyers Are the Same. This Is Like Asking Whether Everything That Gets Into a Sewer Is Garbage." In Kennedy, Color Me Flo, p. 129-36.
"Show the Power Structure That You're Prepared to Kick Your Mother and Father, And They'll Find You Relevant, Because Business and Government Are in Loco Parentis to the Oppressed Individual." In Kennedy, Color Me Flo, p. 84-9.
"Silence Is Collaboration, and Rape Without Struggle Is No Rape, It's Just a Bad Screw." In Kennedy, Color Me Flo, p. 89-96.

Kennelly, Barbara Bailey.
"Statement." In U.S. Congress. House. Committee on Appropriations. Subcommittee on Department of the Interior and Related Agencies. Department of the Interior and Related Agencies Appropriations for 1983. Washington: U.S.G.P.O., 1982, pt. 7, p. 389-94.
"Statement." In U.S. Congress. House. Committee on Appropriations. Subcommittee on Department of Transportation and Related Agencies Appropriations. Department of Transportation and Related Agencies Appropriations for 1983. Washington: U.S.G.P.O., 1982, pt. 7, p. 556-82.
"Statement." In U.S. Congress. House. Committee on Energy and Commerce. Subcommittee on Health and the Environment. Health Financing. Washington: U.S.G.P.O., 1985, pt. 11, p. 413-5.
"Statement." In U.S. Congress. Senate. Committee on Commerce, Science, and Transportation. Subcommittee on Surface

Transportation. <u>Tandem Truck Safety Act of 1984</u>. Washington: U.S.G.P.O., 1984, p. 16-9.

"Statement." In U.S. Congress. Senate. Committee on Finance. <u>Child Support Enforcement Program Reform Proposals</u>. Washington: U.S.G.P.O., 1984, p. 8-11.

"Statement." In U.S. Congress. Senate. Committee on Finance. <u>Potential Inequities Affecting Women</u>, pt. 2, p. 64-6.

Kern, Coralee Smith.
"Statement." In U.S. Congress. Senate. Committee on Labor and Human Resources. Subcommittee on Labor. <u>Amending the Fair Labor Standards Act to Include Industrial Homework</u>, p. 89-92.

Keshena, Rita.
"Relevancy of Tribal Interests and Tribal Diversity in Determining the Educational Needs of American Indians." In Conference on the Educational and Occupational Needs of American Indian Women (1976: Albuquerque, NM). <u>Conference on the Educational and Occupational Needs of American Indian Women</u>, p. 231-49.

Kessler, Carol F.
"Communities of Sisters: Utopian Fiction by U.S. Women, 1970-1980." In <u>Sisterhood Surveyed</u>, p. 79-87.

Kessler-Harris, Alice.
"Where Are the Organized Women Workers." <u>Feminist Studies</u>, 3 (1976), 92-110.

Key, Mary Louise.
"Statement." In U.S. Congress. House. Select Committee on Children, Youth, and Families. <u>Violence and Abuse in American Families</u>, p. 9-12.

Keys, Martha.
"Statement." In U.S. Congress. House. Committee on Post Office and Civil Service. Subcommittee on Compensation and Employee Benefits. <u>Federal Pay Equity Act of 1984</u>, pt. 1, p. 32-6.

"Statement." In U.S. Congress. House. Committee on Ways and Means. Subcommittee on Social Security. <u>Treatment of Men and Women Under the Social Security Program</u>, p. 133-9.

"Statement." In U.S. Congress. House. Select Committee on Aging. Subcommittee on Retirement Income and Employment. Task Force on Social Security and Women. <u>Treatment of Women Under Social Security</u>, pt. 1, p. 11-5, pt. 3, p. 4-6.

"Statement." In U.S. Congress. Special Committee on Aging. <u>Adapting Social Security to a Changing Work Force</u>, p. 27-35.

Keyserling, Mary Dublin.
  "New Realities in Women's Work Lives: Some Challenges to Ac-
    tion." In Today's Girls: Tomorrow's Women, p. 40-4.

Kidder, Alice E.
  "Transportation Problems of Low Income Women as Members of
    the Transportation Disadvantaged." In Women's Travel Issues,
    p. 689-90.

Kidwell, Clara Sue.
  "The Status of American Indian Women in Higher Education." In
    Conference on the Educational and Occupational Needs of
    American Indian Women (1976: Albuquerque, NM). Confer-
    ence on the Educational and Occupational Needs of American
    Indian Women, p. 83-121.

Kievit, Mary.
  "Statement." In U.S. Congress. Senate. Committee on Labor
    and Human Resources. The Coming Decade, p. 753-7.

Kilbreth, Mary G.
  "Testimony." In U.S. Congress. Senate. Committee on the
    Judiciary. Birth Control, (1932) p. 122-7.

Kilburn, Kaye.
  "Women in the Textile Industry." In Conference on Women and
    the Workplace (1976: Washington, DC). Conference on Wom-
    en and the Workplace, p. 189-95.

Kim, Bok-Lim C.
  "Asian Wives of U.S. Servicemen: Women in Triple Jeopardy."
    In Conference on the Educational and Occupational Needs of
    Asian-Pacific-American Women (1976: San Francisco, CA).
    Conference on the Educational and Occupational Needs of
    Asian-Pacific-American Women, p. 359-79.

Kimball, Camilla E.
  "Keys for a Woman's Progression." In Blueprints for Living, p.
    17-25.
  "The Rewards of Correct Choice." In Ye Are Free To Choose,
    p. 10-8.

Kimball, Gayle.
  "From Motherhood to Sisterhood: The Search for Female Reli-
    gious Imagery in Nineteenth and Twentieth Century Theology."
    In Beyond Androcentrism, p. 259-68.

King, Coretta Scott.
  "Coretta Scott King's Remarks." In Historic Documents of 1983,
    p. 887-8.

"Opportunities Masquerade as Problems." In My Country Is the Whole World, p. 183-4.

King, Gertrude.
"Women Clerks." In International Women's Year Conference on Women in Public Life (1975: Lyndon Baines Johnson Library). Women in Public, p. 104-5.

King, Margaret L.
"Book-Lined Cells: Women and Humanism in the Early Italian Renaissance." In Beyond Their Sex, p. 66-90.

King, Nancy R.
"Statement." In U.S. Congress. House. Select Committee on Aging. Subcommittee on Retirement Income and Employment. Task Force on Social Security and Women. Treatment of Women Under Social Security, pt. 4, p. 144-7.
"Statement." In U.S. Congress. Joint Economic Committee. The Role of Older Women in the Work Force, p. 77-82.

King, Nestra.
"Making the World Live: Feminism and the Domination of Nature." In Women's Spirit Bonding, p. 56-64.

King, Patricia.
"Recent Developments with Respect to Equal Opportunities in Higher Educational Programs." In Western Regional Civil Rights and Women's Right Conference (4th: 1977: San Francisco, CA). Recent Developments, p. 49-53.

King-Reynolds, Winnetta Ann.
"Statement." In U.S. Congress. Senate. Committee on Labor and Human Resources. Subcommittee on Health and Scientific Research. Women in Science and Technology Equal Opportunity Act, 1980, p. 40-2.

Kinoy, Susan.
"The Aging Within the Structure: Some Thoughts on Legislative and Social Action Implications." In Older Women in the City, p. 163-6.

Kinzer, Nora Scott.
"Testimony." In U.S. Congress. Committee on Veterans' Affairs. Veterans' Health Care and Programs Improvement, p. 315-6.

Kipp, Rita Smith.
"The Feminist Critique: Plans and Prospects." In GLCA Women's Studies Conference (4th: 1978: Rochester, Indiana). Structure of Knowledge, p. 49-53.
"Have Women Always Been Unequal?" In GLCA Women's Studies

Conference (5th: 1979). Towards a Feminist Transformation of the Academy, p. 12-8.

Kirkpatrick, Jeanne J.
"Beyond Sadat." In Kirkpatrick, The Reagan Phenomenon, p. 137-44.
"Central America: Nicaragua and Her Neighbors." In Kirkpatrick, The Reagan Phenomenon, p. 183-93.
"Central America: Sandino Betrayed I." In Kirkpatrick, The Reagan Phenomenon, p. 194-7.
"Central America: Sandino Betrayed II." In Kirkpatrick, The Reagan Phenomenon, p. 198-206.
"Condemning Israel: The Iraqi Reactor." In Kirkpatrick, The Reagan Phenomenon, p. 131-4.
"Delegitimizing Israel." In Kirkpatrick, The Reagan Phenomenon, p. 126-30.
"Exacerbating Problems." In Kirkpatrick, The Reagan Phenomenon, p. 135-6.
"Gaining Strength and Respect in the World. A Strong Steady Policy." Vital Speeches, 50 (March 1, 1984), 290-1.
"Golan Again." In Kirkpatrick, The Reagan Phenomenon, p. 124-5.
"Human Rights and Wrongs in the United Nations." In Kirkpatrick, The Reagan Phenomenon, p. 46-53.
"Human Rights in Afghanistan." In Kirkpatrick, The Reagan Phenomenon, p. 70-6.
"Human Rights in El Salvador." In Kirkpatrick, The Reagan Phenomenon, p. 54-61.
"Human Rights in Nicaragua." In Kirkpatrick, The Reagan Phenomenon, p. 62-9.
"Ideas and Institutions." In Kirkpatrick, The Reagan Phenomenon, p. 39-45.
"International Conference on Assistance to Africa's Refugees." Department of State Bulletin, 81 (June 1981), 58-9.
"Israel as Scapegoat." In Kirkpatrick, The Reagan Phenomenon, p. 109-18.
"Kirkpatrick's Remarks (U.N. on Israeli Raid)." In Historic Documents of 1981, p. 515-8.
"Managing Freedom." In Kirkpatrick, The Reagan Phenomenon, p. 209-12.
"A Miserable Resolution." In Kirkpatrick, The Reagan Phenomenon, p. 119-23.
"The Peace Process Continued." In Kirkpatrick, The Reagan Phenomenon, p. 145-52.
"Personal Virtues, Public Vices." In Kirkpatrick, The Reagan Phenomenon, p. 213-8.
"The Problem of the United Nations." In Kirkpatrick, The Reagan Phenomenon, p. 92-8.
"Problems of the Alliance." In Kirkpatrick, The Reagan Phenomenon, p. 174-82.
"Promoting Free Elections." In Representative American

Speeches: 1982-83, p. 161-70.

"The Reagan Phenomenon and the Liberal Tradition." In Kirkpatrick, The Reagan Phenomenon, p. 3-16.

"Reagan Policies and Black American Goals for Africa." In Kirkpatrick, The Reagan Phenomenon, p. 17-27.

"The Reagan Reassertion of Western Values." In Kirkpatrick, The Reagan Phenomenon, p. 28-36.

"Redefining Asian-American Ties." In Kirkpatrick, The Reagan Phenomenon, p. 169-73.

"Security Council Meets to Consider Israeli Raid: Statement." Department of State Bulletin, 81 (August 1981), 84-5.

"Southern Africa: Fair Play for Namibia." In Kirkpatrick, The Reagan Phenomenon, p. 163-4.

"Southern Africa: Fair Play for South Africa." In Kirkpatrick, The Reagan Phenomenon, p. 167-8.

"Southern Africa: Namibia, the United Nations, and the United States." In Kirkpatrick, The Reagan Phenomenon, p. 155-62.

"Southern Africa: Solving the Problem of Namibia." In Kirkpatrick, The Reagan Phenomenon, p. 165-6.

"Standing Alone." In Kirkpatrick, The Reagan Phenomenon, p. 79-91.

"U.S. Foreign Policy. The Difference Between Superpowers." Vital Speeches, 50 (May 15, 1984), 454-6.

"The U.S. Role in the United Nations." In Kirkpatrick, The Reagan Phenomenon, p. 99-106.

"The U.S. Role in the United Nations. Our Lack of a Coherent National Purpose." Vital Speeches, 48 (August 1, 1982), 610-2.

Kiryluk, Carol.
"The Single Woman: Moving Up by Moving Around." In The Woman in Management, p. 45-8.

Kistiakowsky, Vera.
"Women in Physics and Astronomy." In Expanding the Role of Women in the Sciences, p. 35-47.

Kittay, Eva Feder.
"Pornography and the Erotics of Domination." In Beyond Domination, p. 145-74.

Klaaren, Mary D.
"Realism and Hope." In Spinning a Sacred Yarn, p. 123-6.

Klaus, Hanna.
"Statement." In U.S. Congress. Senate. Committee on Labor and Human Resources. Oversight on Family Planning Programs, p. 126-8.

Klay, Robin.
"Analyzing Discrimination Against Women in the Labor Market--A

Few Lessons From John Stuart Mill." In GLCA Women's
Studies Conference (7th: 1981). Towards a Feminist Transformation of the Academy III, p. 61-5.

Klein, Ann.
"Statement." In U.S. Congress. Senate. Committee on Labor
and Human Resources. Subcommittee on Child and Human Development. Domestic Violence Prevention and Services Act,
1980, p. 209-10.

Klein, Frieda.
"The Transportation Implications of Women's Fear of Assault."
In Women's Travel Issues, p. 479-84.

Klein, Joan Dempsey.
"Statement." In California. Legislature. Joint Committee on
Legal Equality. Women in the Justice System, p. 3-10.

Klenke-Hamel, Karen.
"Causal Determinant of Job Satisfaction in Dual Career Couples."
In Women in the Work Force, p. 183-204.

Kligman, Gail.
"The Rites of Women: Oral Poetry, Ideology, and the Socializa-
tion of Peasant Women in Contemporary Romania." In Women,
State, and Party in Eastern Europe, p. 323-43.

Kline, Jennie.
"Environmental Exposures and Spontaneous Abortion." In The
Changing Risk of Disease in Women, p. 127-38.

Knight, Carolyn Ann.
"The Survival of the Unfit." In Those Preachin' Women, p. 27-
34.

Knowles, Eleanor.
"The Scriptures: A Personal Odyssey." In A Woman's Choices,
p. 148-58.

Knowles, Jane.
"Statement." In U.S. Congress. Senate. Committee on Foreign
Affairs. Women in Development, p. 73-5.

Kobell, Ruth E.
"Statement." In U.S. Congress. House. Committee on Ways
and Means. Subcommittee on Social Security. Treatment of
Men and Women Under the Social Security Program, p. 164-5.

Kocher, Joann.
"Career Conflicts and Solutions." In Training Conference (1st:
1984: Washington, DC). Interagency Committee on Women in
Federal Law Enforcement, p. 50-3.

Kohen, Janet A.
"Widowhood and Well-Being." In Women's Lives, p. 303-7.

Kohlstedt, Sally Gregory.
"Single-Sex Education and Leadership: The Early Years of Simmons College." In Women and Educational Leadership, p. 93-112.

Kolker, Ann.
"Statement." In U.S. Congress. Senate. Committee on Foreign Affairs. Potential Inequities Affecting Women, pt. 2, p. 255-6.

Kolmerton, Carol.
"The Myth of Sexual Egalitarian Communities: New Harmony and Brook Farm Revisited." In Conference on "Scholars and Women" (1981: University of Maryland). Women's Studies and the Curriculum, p. 137-45.

Komarovksy, Mirra.
"Dilemmas of Masculinity in a Changing World." In Psychology and Women: In Transition, p. 71-81.
"Women's Roles: Problems and Polemics." In The Challenge to Women, p. 20-33.

Koole, Florine.
"Statement." In U.S. Congress. House. Committee on Post Office and Civil Service. Subcommittee on Compensation and Employee Benefits. Federal Pay Equity Act of 1984, pt. 1, p. 105-10.
"Statement." In U.S. Congress. House. Committee on Post Office and Civil Service. Subcommittee on Compensation and Employee Benefits. Options for Conducting a Pay Equity Study, p. 420-3.

Koop, Martha.
"Response to the Social Scene: Isolation and Frustration." In Women in Engineering--Beyond Recruitment, p. 80.

Kopec, Jeanne.
"Testimony." In U.S. Commission on Civil Rights. Hearing Before the U.S. Commission on Civil Rights Held in Denver, 1976, p. 458.

Kopp, Sister Mary Audrey, S.N.J.M.
"The Myth of Race." In Split-Level Lives, p. 137-55.

Koppel, Flora.
"Establishing Interdisciplinary Treatment Networks." In Women in Crisis Conference (1st: 1979: New York, NY). Women in Crisis, p. 247-51.

Korenbrot, Carol.
"Value Conflicts in Biomedical Research into Future Contraceptives." In Birth Control and Controlling Birth, p. 47-54.

Korner, Anneliese F.
"Methodological Considerations in Studying Sex Differences in the Behavioral Functioning of Newborns." In Sex Differences in Behavior, p. 197-207.

Kostalos, Mary.
"Statement." In U.S. Congress. Senate. Committee on Labor and Human Resources. Subcommittee on Health and Scientific Research. Women in Science and Technology Equal Opportunity Act, 1980, p. 187-8.

Kotelchuck, Ronda.
"Is the Question of Women a Political Question?" In Cornell Conference on Women (1969: Cornell University). Proceedings, p. 28-9.

Kragelund, Louise.
"Personal Report to the Conference on Women and Poverty in Massachusetts." Women's Studies Quarterly, 13 (Summer 1985), 8.

Kramer, Joyce Marie.
"Urban Indians, A Neglected Group." In Health Needs of the World's Poor Women, p. 67-72.

Kraus, Irene.
"Light and Help and Human Kindness. The Importance of Caring." Vital Speeches, 46 (July 15, 1980), 596-7.

Kravetz, Diane.
"Consciousness-Raising and Self-Help." In Women and Psychotherapy, p. 268-84.

Kreinberg, Nancy.
"Equals: Working with Educators--." In Women and Minorities in Science, p. 39-54.

Krekel, Sylvia.
"Placement of Workers in High-Risk Areas--A Workers' Viewpoint." In Conference on Women and the Workplace (1976: Washington, DC). Conference on Women and the Workplace, p. 124-6.

Kreps, Juanita M.
"Women in a Changing Economy." In Woman in Management, p. 1-11.

Kreuger, Roberta L.
"Loyalty and Betrayal: Iseut and Brangein in the Tristan Romances of Beroul and Thomas." In Sisterhood Surveyed, p. 72-8.

Krickus, Mary Ann.
"The Status of East European Women in the Family: Tradition and Change." In Conference on the Educational and Occupational Needs of White Ethnic Women (1978: Boston, MA). Conference on the Educational and Occupational Needs of White Ethnic Women, p. 76-100.

Krieter, Nancy.
"Testimony." In U.S. Equal Employment Opportunity Commission. Hearings Before the U.S. Equal Employment Opportunity Commission on Job Segregation and Wage Discrimination, p. 527-37.

Kruger, Barbara.
"No Progress in Pleasure." In Pleasure and Danger, p. 210-6.

Krupsak, Mary Anne.
"The Decision to Become Politically Involved." In Women in Management, p. 51-4.

Kryzak, Rose.
"The Plight of Older Women in Retirement." In Older Women in the City, p. 82-4.

Kubler-Ross, Elisabeth.
"Death Does Not Exist." In We Shall Be Heard, p. 342-53.

Kuharski, Mary Ann.
"Statement." In U.S. Congress. Senate. Committee on Labor and Human Resources. Subcommittee on Family and Human Services. Forum for Families, p. 11-4.

Kuhn, Maggie.
"Statement." In U.S. Congress. House. Select Committee on Aging. Subcommittee on Retirement Income and Employment. Task Force on Social Security and Women. Treatment of Women Under Social Security, pt. 3, p. 10-2.

Kump, Eileen Gibbons.
"The Bread and Milk of Living." In A Woman's Choices, p. 98-111.

Kunin, Madelaine M.
"Statement." In U.S. Congress. House. Committee on Ways and Means. Subcommittee on Public Assistance and Unemployment Compensation. Amendments to the FDC Quality Control Program. Washington: U.S.G.P.O., 1985, p. 7-22.

"Statement." In U.S. Congress. Senate. Committee on Agriculture, Nutrition, and Forestry. Reauthorization of the Agriculture and Food Act to 1981. Washington: U.S.G.P.O., 1985, pt. 3, p. 66-9.

"Statement." In U.S. Congress. Senate. Committee on Environment and Public Works. Environmental Progress and Issues in the State of Vermont. Washington: U.S.G.P.O., 1985, p. 2-6.

Kurtz, Maxine.
"Statement." In U.S. Congress. House. Committee on Post Office and Civil Service. Subcommittee on Human Resources. Pay Equity, pt. 1, p. 599-601.

Kushner, Rose.
"Statement." In U.S. Congress. House. Select Committee on Aging. Subcommittee on Health and Long-Term Care. Progress in Controlling Breast Cancer, p. 49-52.

Kutzke, Elizabeth S.
"Statement." In U.S. Congress. Senate. Committee on Science and Technology. Subcommittee on Domestic and International Scientific Planning, Analysis, and Cooperation. Research into Violent Behavior: Overview and Sexual Assaults, p. 530-2, 549, 553-70, 595-6.

La Prade, Von.
"Statement." In U.S. Congress. House. Select Committee on Aging. Subcommittee on Health and Long-Term Care. Elder Abuse, p. 88-9.

Labalme, Patricia H.
"Women's Roles in Early Modern Venice: An Exceptional Case." In Beyond Their Sex, p. 129-52.

Ladky, Ann.
"Testimony." In U.S. Commission on Civil Rights. Hearings Before the U.S. Commission on Civil Rights Held in Chicago, 1974, pt. 2, p. 48-54, 262-5, 268-70, 272.

Lafresche, Susette.
"The Plight of the Ponca Indians." In Outspoken Women, p. 102-5.

Laise, Carol.
"American Women and American Foreign Policy." In International Women's Year Conference on Women in Public Life (1975: Lyndon Baines Johnson Library). Women in Public Life, p. 12-4.

Lall, Betty G.
"What Disarmament Policy for the United States?" In U.S. National Commission on the Observance of International Women's Year. The Spirit of Houston, p. 238-40.

Lambert, Jean.
"Becoming Human: A Contextual Approach to Decisions About Pregnancy and Abortion." In Feminism and Process Thought, p. 106-37.

Lamp, Virginia P.
"Statement." In U.S. Congress. House. Committee on Post Office and Civil Service. Subcommittee on Compensation and Employee Benefits. Options for Conducting a Pay Equity Study, p. 302-4, 307-10.

Lamphere, Louise.
"Bringing the Family to Work: Women's Culture on the Shop Floor." Feminist Studies, 11 (Fall 1985), 519-40.
"The Economic Struggles of Female Factory Workers: A Comparison of French, Polish and Portuguese Immigrants." In Conference on the Educational and Occupational Needs of White Ethnic Women (1978: Boston, MA). Conference on the Educational and Occupational Needs of White Ethnic Women, p. 129-52.
"On the Shop Floor: Multi-Ethnic Unity Against the Conglomerate." In My Troubles Are Going to Have Trouble With Me, p. 247-63.

Lanam, Linda L.
"Testimony." In U.S. Congress. House. Committee on Energy and Commerce. Subcommittee on Health and the Environment. Health and the Environment Miscellaneous, pt. 4, p. 92-3.

Lane, Ann J.
"Keynote Address: Friends for Half a Century: The Relationship of Charlotte Perkins Gilman and Grace Channing Stetson." In Sisterhood Surveyed, p. 4-11.

Lang, Nancy.
"Statement." In U.S. Congress. House. Committee on Ways and Means. Subcommittee on Social Security. Treatment of Men and Women Under the Social Security Program, p. 200-2.

Langer, Sandra L.
"Against the Grain: A Working Feminist Art Criticism." In Feminist Visions, p. 84-96.

Langlois, Janet L.
"Belle Gunness, The Lady Bluebeard: Narrative Use of a Deviant Woman." In Women's Folklore, Women's Culture, p. 109-24.

Lansburgh, (Mrs.) Mark.
"Testimony." In U.S. Congress. Senate. Committee on the
Judiciary. Birth Control, (1934), p. 68-9.

Lapham, E. Virginia Sheppard.
"Living With an Impaired Neonate and Child: A Feminist Issue."
In The Custom-Made Child?, p. 155-64.

Lapidus, Gail W.
"The Soviet Union." In Women Workers In Fifteen Countries, p.
13-31.

Largen, Mary Ann.
"Statement." In U.S. Congress. House. Committee on Post
Office and Civil Service. Subcommittee on Investigations.
Sexual Harassment in the Federal Government, pt. 1, p. 38,
43-53.
"Statement." In U.S. Congress. House. Committee on Science
and Technology. Subcommittee on Domestic and International
Scientific Planning, Analysis, and Cooperation. Research into
Violent Behavior: Overview and Sexual Assaults, p. 499-516.
"Testimony." In U.S. Congress. House. Committee on the
Judiciary. Subcommittee on Criminal Justice. Privacy of
Rape Victims, p. 35-48.

Lashof, Joyce C.
"Forces Impacting on the Policymaker." In Birth Control and
Controlling Birth, p. 269-74.
"Statement." In U.S. Congress. House. Select Committee on
Population. Fertility and Contraception in America, p. 67-87.

Lasky, Ella.
"Psychotherapists' Ambivalence About Fees." In Handbook of
Feminist Therapy, p. 250-6.

Latinis, Barbara.
"Statement." In U.S. Congress. House. Select Committee on
Population. Fertility and Contraception in America, pt. 3,
p. 25-7.

Latzko, Trudy.
"Statement." In U.S. Congress. House. Select Committee on
Children, Youth, and Families. Families with Disabled Chil-
dren, p. 51-4.

Laurence, Iris May.
"Statement." In U.S. Congress. House. Select Committee on
Aging. Subcommittee on Retirement Income and Employment.
Impact of Reagan Economics on Aging Women, p. 42-5.

Laurie, Leslie Tarr.
"Statement." In U.S. Congress. Senate. Committee on Labor and Human Resources. Subcommittee on Aging, Family, and Human Services. Oversight on Family Planning Programs Under Title X of the Public Health Service Act, 1981, p. 94-8.
"Testimony." In U.S. Congress. Senate. Committee on Human Resources. Adolescent Health, Services and Pregnancy Prevention Care Act of 1978, p. 197.

Lautzenheiser, Barbara J.
"Testimony." In U.S. Congress. House. Committee on Interstate and Foreign Commerce. Subcommittee on Consumer Protection and Finance. Nondiscrimination in Insurance, p. 58-67.

Lawlor, Mary.
"Statement." In U.S. Congress. House. Committee on Armed Services. Subcommittee on Military Personnel. Women in the Military, p. 244-9.

Lawrence, Gloria.
"Funding." In Report of the YWCA National Consultation for Programs on Domestic Violence, p. 28-9.

Laws, Judith Long.
"Work Motivation and Work Behavior of Women: New Perspectives." In Psychology of Women, p. 285-348.

Lazar, Joyce.
"Plenary Session: Intervention/Service Delivery Systems." In Women in Crisis Conference (1st: 1979: New York, NY). Women in Crisis, p. 116-21.

Le Doeuff, Michele.
"Simone de Beauvoir and Existentialism." Feminist Studies, 6 (Summer 1980), 277-89.

Leacock, Eleanor.
"Women, Development, and Anthropological Facts and Fictions." In Women in Latin America, p. 7-16.

Lear, Julia Graham.
"Women's Health Needs in the United States." In Health Needs of the World's Poor Women, p. 53-7.

Lease, Mary E.
"The Red Dragon of Wall Street Vs. the Farmer." In Outspoken Women, p. 106-7.

Lebacqz, Karen.
"The Ethicist in Policymaking." In Birth Control and Controlling Birth, p. 283-7.

Lee, Dorothy D.
"To Be or Not To Be: Notes on the Meaning of Maternity." In
The Challenge to Women, p. 51-62.

Lee, Karen.
"Myths and Realities." In Training Conference (1st: 1984:
Washington, DC). Interagency Committee on Women in Fed-
eral Law Enforcement, p. 30-3.

Lee, Maryat.
"Legitimate Theatre Is Illegitimate." In Toward the Second Decade, p. 11-24.

Lee, Sirkka Tuomi.
"The Role of Learning in the Lives of Finnish and Other Ethnic
Women and a Proposal for Self-Education." In Conference on
the Educational and Occupational Needs of White Ethnic Women
(1978: Boston, MA). Conference on the Educational and Occupational Needs of White Ethnic Women, p. 101-14.

Lee, Susan Dye.
"Evangelical Domesticity: The Woman's Temperance Crusade of
1873-1874." In Women in New Worlds, v. 1, p. 293-309.

Lee, Suzanne.
"Personal Report to the Conference on Women and Poverty in
Massachusetts." Women's Studies Quarterly, 13 (Summer
1985), 8.

Lee, Valerie.
"Lucille Clifton: Black Feminist Poet." In GLCA Women's Studies
Conference (6th: 1980). Towards a Feminist Transformation
of the Academy II, p. 17-23.

Leeper, Pat.
"Statement." In U.S. Congress. Senate. Committee on Veterans'
Affairs. Recognition for Purposes of VA Benefits, p. 139-46.

Lefkowitz, Mary R.
"Influential Women." In Images of Women in Antiquity, p. 49-64.

Lehnhard, Mary Nell.
"Testimony." In U.S. Congress. House. Committee on Energy
and Commerce. Subcommittee on Health and the Environment.
Health and the Environment Miscellaneous, pt. 4, p. 488-90.

Leidholdt, Dorchen.
"Testimony." In U.S. Congress. Senate. Committee on the
Judiciary. Subcommittee on Juvenile Justice. Effect of
Pornography on Women and Children, p. 55-9.

Lemkau, Jeanne Parr.
"Women and Employment: Some Emotional Hazards." In The
Evolving Female, p. 107-37.

Lemlich, Clara.
"Address at Cooper Union in April, 1912." Life and Labor,
(July 1912), 216-7.
"Senators vs. Working Women." In Eisenstein, Sarah. Give Us
Bread But Give Us Roses, p. 159-60.

Lenhoff, Donna R.
"Statement." In U.S. Congress. House. Committee on Post
Office and Civil Service. Subcommittee on Investigations.
Sexual Harassment in the Federal Government, pt. 1, p. 3-12,
32-8.
"Statement." In U.S. Congress. Senate. Committee on Finance.
Potential Inequities Affecting Women, pt. 2, p. 80-3.
"Statement." In U.S. Congress. Senate. Committee on Labor
and Human Resources. Sex Discrimination in the Workplace,
1981, p. 234-8, 314-6.
"Testimony." In U.S. Equal Employment Opportunity Commis-
sion. Hearings Before the Equal Employment Opportunity
Commission on Job Segregation and Wage Discrimination, p.
565-6.

Lenhoff, Nora.
"Statement." In U.S. Congress. House. Select Committee on
Aging. Subcommittee on Retirement Income and Employment.
Impact of Reagan Economics on Aging Women, p. 61-2.

Lennert, Midge.
"Statement." In California. Legislature. Joint Committee on
Legal Equality. Women in the Justice System, p. 184-95.

Leonard, Karen.
"Women and Social Change in Modern India." Feminist Studies,
3 (1976), 117-30.

Leone, Rose.
"The Stigmatized Woman." In Women in Crisis Conference (1st:
1979: New York, NY). Women in Crisis, p. 44-8.

Lerman, Hannah.
"Some Barriers to the Development of a Feminist Theory of Personality." In Handbook of Feminist Therapy, p. 5-12.

Lerner, Elinor.
"Jewish Involvement in the New York City Woman Suffrage Movement." In Berkshire Conference on the History of Women
(5th: 1982: Vassar College). Women and the Structure of
Society, p. 191-205.

Lerner, Gerda.
 "Black Women in the United States: A Problem in Historiography
  and Interpretation." In Lerner, The Majority Finds Its Past,
  p. 63-82.
 "The Challenge of Women's History." In Liberal Education and
  the New Scholarship on Women, p. 39-47. Also In Lerner,
  The Majority Finds Its Past, p. 83-93.
 "Just a Housewife." In Lerner, The Majority Finds Its Past,
  p. 129-44.
 "Placing Women in History: Definitions and Challenges."
  Feminist Studies, 3 (Fall 1975), 5-14. Also In Lerner, The
  Majority Finds Its Past, p. 145-59.
 "The Political Activities of Antislavery Women." In Lerner, The
  Majority Finds Its Past, p. 112-28.

Levick, Marsha.
 "Testimony." In U.S. Congress. Senate. Committee on the
  Judiciary. Subcommittee on the Constitution. The Impact
  of the Equal Rights Amendment, pt. 2, p. 49-55.

Levin, Doris E.
 "Statement." In U.S. Congress. House. Select Committee on
  Aging. Subcommittee on Health and Long-Term Care. Pro-
  gress in Controlling Breast Cancer, p. 38-9.

Levine, Carol.
 "Depo-Provera: Some Ethical Questions About a Controversial
  Contraceptive." In Birth Control and Controlling Birth, p.
  101-6.

Levine, Jacqueline K.
 "An Appeal to Admit Women into the Hierarchy of Decision-
  Makers: 1972." In The American Jewish Woman, p. 902-7.

Levine, Lena.
 "Women's Changing Role in Marriage." In Cooper Union for the
  Advancement of Science and Art. Women, Society and Sex,
  p. 103-15.

Lewis, Barbara A.
 "Sexism in Treatment." In Women in Crisis Conference (1st:
  1979: New York, NY). Women in Crisis, p. 85-91.
 "Women in Development Planning: Advocacy, Institutionalization
  and Implementation." In Perspectives on Power, p. 102-18.

Lewis, Helen.
 "Statement." In U.S. Congress. House. Committee on Post
  Office and Civil Service. Subcommittee on Investigations.
  Sexual Harassment in the Federal Government, pt. 1, p. 53-4,
  64-9.

Lewis, Joann.
  "The Sixth Day. We Can't Go Back." Vital Speeches, 48 (July 1, 1982), 571-5.

Lewis, Margaret.
  "Cosa Rica/Oregon Cooperative Nutrition Projects." In International Conference on Women and Food (1978: University of Arizona). A Conference on the Role of Women in Meeting Basic Food and Water Needs in Developing Countries, p. 79-82.

Lewis, Ruth R.
  "Statement." In U.S. Congress. House. Committee on Ways and Means. Subcommittee on Social Security. Social Security Dependents' Benefits, p. 56-7.

Lewter-Simmons, Margie.
  "Our Spiritual Account." In Those Preachin' Women, p. 113-8.

Liburdi, Lillian C.
  "Speech." In Women's Travel Issues, p. 757-66.

Lichtman, Judith L.
  "Statement." In U.S. Congress. Senate. Committee on Labor and Human Resources. Subcommittee on Education, Arts and Humanities. Civil Rights Act of 1984, pt. 1, p. 291-4.
  "Testimony." In U.S. Equal Employment Opportunity Commission. Hearings Before the U.S. Equal Employment Opportunity Commission on Job Segregation and Wage Discrimination, p. 550-67.

Lieberman, Deborah.
  "Testimony." In U.S. Congress. House. Committee on the Judiciary. Subcommittee on Criminal Justice. Privacy of Rape Victims, p. 55-61.

Liebert, Mary Ann.
  "Statement." In U.S. Congress. House. Committee on Energy and Commerce. Subcommittee on Health and the Environment. Pregnancy-Related Health Services, p. 104-6.

Liebschutz, Sarah F.
  "Republican Women and the Future of the Republican Party." In Women Organizing, p. 304-18.

Lief, Beth.
  "Statement." In U.S. Congress. Senate. Committee on the Judiciary. Subcommittee on the Constitution. Constitutional Amendments Relating to Abortion, pt. 1, p. 1112-4.

Lightfoot, Sara Lawrence.
  "Socialization and Education of Young Black Girls in Schools." In Conference on the Educational and Occupational Needs of

Black Women (1975: Washington, DC). Conference on the Educational and Occupational Needs of Black Women, pt. 2, p. 3-29. Also In Women and Educational Leadership, p. 139-64.

Lim, Linda Y. C.
"Women's Work in Multinational Electronics Factories." In Women and Technological Change in Developing Countries, p. 181-90.

Lindsey, Karen.
"Women and the Draft." In Reweaving the Web of Life, p. 322-5.

Linn, Mary.
"Statement." In U.S. Congress. House. Select Committee on Aging. Subcommittee on Retirement Income and Employment. Impact of Reagan Economics on Aging Women, p. 47-8.

Lipman-Blumen, Jean.
"A Crisis Perspective on Emerging Health Roles: A Paradigm for the Entry of Women Into New Occupational Roles." In Women Organizing, p. 345-62.
"Emerging Patterns of Female Leadership in Formal Organizations, Or Must the Female Leader Go Formal?" In The Challenge of Change, p. 61-91.

Liss, Lora.
"Testimony." In U.S. Equal Employment Opportunity Commission. Hearings Before the U.S. Equal Employment Opportunity Commission on Job Segregation and Wage Discrimination, p. 179-95.

Litten, Betty.
"Statement." In U.S. Congress. Senate. Committee on Labor and Human Resources. Subcommittee on Education, Arts and Humanities. Civil Rights Act of 1984, pt. 1, p. 393-4.

Little, Frances.
"Statement." In U.S. Congress. House. Committee on Ways and Means. Subcommittee on Social Security. Treatment of Men and Women Under the Social Security Program, p. 121-3.

Littlejohn, Virginia.
"Statement." In U.S. Congress. House. Committee on Small Business. National Commission on Women's Business Ownership, p. 28-30.
"Statement." In U.S. Congress. Senate. Select Committee on Small Business. Women-In-Business Programs in the Federal Government, p. 87-9.

Littleton, Camille S.
"Epiphany VIII." In Women of the Word, p. 65-7.
"Lent IV." In Women of the Word, p. 68-9.
"Pentecost VI." In Women of the Word, p. 70-2.

Litwak, Eleanor.
"Problems in Pension Systems as Specifically Related to Women Retirees." In Older Women in the City, p. 44-52.

Livermore, Mary A.
"What Shall We Do With Our Daughters." In We Shall Be Heard, p. 160-66.

Lloyd, Marilyn.
"Statement." In U.S. Congress. House. Committee on Armed Services. Subcommittee on Investigations. Status of Inventory of Uranium at Department of Energy Oak Ridge Nuclear Weapon Production Facility. Washington: U.S.G.P.O., 1984, p. 2.
"Statement." In U.S. Congress. House. Committee on Government Operations. Government Activities and Transportation Subcommittee. Program to Increase Sales of Federal Surplus Real Property. Washington: U.S.G.P.O., 1984, p. 171-84.
"Statement." In U.S. Congress. House. Committee on Government Operations. Intergovernmental Relations and Human Resources Subcommittee. Joint Funding Simplification Act of 1974. Washington: U.S.G.P.O., 1980, p. 4-16.
"Statement." In U.S. Congress. House. Committee on Public Works and Transportation. Subcommittee on Water Resources. The Effect of TVA Electric Rates on Homeowners, Business, and Industrial Activities, Contracting Out Policies, the Fertilizer Center Activities, and the TVA Board Structure and Functions. Washington: U.S.G.P.O., 1982, p. 7-8.
"Statement." In U.S. Congress. House. Committee on Science and Technology. Subcommittee on Energy Development and Applications. The Status of Synthetic Fuels and Cost-Shared Energy R&D Facilities. Washington: U.S.G.P.O., 1984, p. 2-18.
"Statement." In U.S. Congress. House. Committee on Science and Technology. Subcommittee on Investigations and Oversight. West Valley Cooperative Agreement. Washington: U.S.G.P.O., 1981, p. 3-6.
"Statement." In U.S. Congress. House. Committee on Science and Technology. Subcommittee on Investigations and Oversight. Review of the Department of Energy's Health and Mortality Study. Washington: U.S.G.P.O., 1983, p. 101-2.
"Statement." In U.S. Congress. House. Committee on Ways and Means. Treasury's Temporary and Proposed Regulations Relating to Recordkeeping for Automobiles and Certain Other Property. Washington: U.S.G.P.O., 1985, p. 42-4.
"Statement." In U.S. Congress. House. Select Committee on Aging. Subcommittee on Retirement Income and Employment. Task Force on Social Security and Women. Treatment of Women Under Social Security, p. 5-6.
"Statement." In U.S. Congress. Senate. Committee on the Budget. Impact of the President's FY 1986 Budget Proposals

on the Tennessee Economy, p. 88-91.
"Statement." In U.S. Congress. Senate. Committee on the
   Judiciary. Confirmation Hearings on Federal Appointments
   ... to the Federal Judiciary and the Department of Justice.
   Washington: U.S.G.P.O., pt. 1, p. 215.
"Statement." In U.S. Congress. Senate. Committee on the
   Judiciary. Confirmation Hearings on Federal Appointments.
   Washington: U.S.G.P.O., 1985, pt. 3, p. 468-72, 494-6.

Lloyd-Jones, Esther.
   "Education for Reentry Into the Labor Force." In Conference on
   Work in the Lives of Married Women (1957: Columbia Univer-
   sity). Work in the Lives of Married Women, p. 27-40.

Lo Sasso, Rosann.
   "Testimony." In U.S. Commission on Civil Rights. Hearing Before the U.S. Commission on Civil Rights Held in Chicago,
   1974, pt. 1, p. 412-9.

Locke, Elaine.
   "Antenatal Diagnosis: The Physician-Patient Relationship." In
   The Custom-Made Child?, p. 81-8.

Locke, Mamie.
   "Sexism and Racism: Obstacles to the Development of Black
   Women in South Africa." In Feminist Visions, p. 119-29.

Lockheed, Marlaine E.
   "Sex Bias in Aptitude and Achievement Tests Used in Higher
   Education." In The Undergraduate Woman, p. 99-126.

Lockwood, Belva Ann.
   "The Political Rights of Women." In We Shall Be Heard, p. 136-8.

Lockwood, Collette.
   "Statement." In U.S. Congress. House. Select Committee on
   Children, Youth, and Families. Children, Youth and Families,
   p. 74-5.

Loden, Marilyn.
   "Networking: It Can Change Your Life." Vital Speeches, 47
   (August 1, 1981), 613-6.

Loewenstein, Sophie Freud.
   "Passion as a Mental Health Hazard." In The Evolving Female,
   p. 45-73.
   "Toward Choice and Differentiation in the Midlife Crisis of Wom-
   en." In The Evolving Female, p. 158-88.

Lofquist, Ethel.
   "Statement." In U.S. Congress. House. Select Committee on

Aging. Subcommittee on Retirement Income and Employment.
Impact of Reagan Economics on Aging Women, p. 54-5.

Logan, Rebecca L.
"Ectogenesis and Ideology." In The Custom-Made Child?, p.
291-94.

Lomax-Cooke, Carolyn.
"The Speaker and the Ghost. The Speaker Is the Speech."
Vital Speeches, 48 (December 1, 1981), 125-8.

Long, Cathy.
"Federal Equitable Pay Practices Act." Congressional Record,
99th Congress, 1st session, 1985, 131, pt. 133, H8531-32.
"Latin America." Congressional Record, 99th Congress, 1st
session, 1985, 131, pt. 49, H2460.

Longino, Helen.
"Scientific Objectivity and Feminist Theorizing." In Conference
on "Scholars and Women" (1981: University of Maryland).
Women's Studies and the Curriculum, p. 33-41.

Lonsdale, Eileen M.
"Statement." In U.S. Congress. Joint Economic Committee.
The Role of Older Women in the Work Force, p. 46-9.

Loo, Fe V.
"Asian Women in Professional Health Schools, With Emphasis on
Nursing." In Conference on the Educational and Occupational
Needs of Asian-Pacific-American Women (1976: San Francisco,
CA). Conference on the Educational and Occupational Needs
of Asian-Pacific-American Women, p. 105-34.

Lopata, Helena Znaniecki.
"Women's Travel Issues: American Patterns." In Women's Travel
Issues, p. 681-2.

Lorde, Audre.
"Age, Race, Class, and Sex: Women Redefining Difference."
In Lorde, Sister Outsider, p. 114-23.
"Learning from the 60s." In Lorde, Sister Outsider, p. 134-44.
"The Master's Tools Will Never Dismantle the Master's House."
In Lorde, Sister Outsider, p. 110-13.
"Poetry Is Not a Luxury." In The Future of Difference, p. 125.
"The Transformation of Silence Into Language and Action." In
Lorde, Sister Outsider, p. 40-4.
"The Uses of Anger: Women Responding to Racism." In Lorde,
Sister Outsider, p. 124-33. Also in Women's Studies Quarter-
ly, 9 (Fall, 1981), 7.
"Uses of the Erotic: The Erotic as Power." In Lorde, Sister
Outsider, p. 53-9. Also In Take Back the Night, p. 295-300.

Lott, Juanita Tamayo.
"Keynote Address." In Conference on the Educational and Occupational Needs of Asian-Pacific-American Women (1976:
San Francisco, CA). Conference on the Educational and Occupational Needs of Asian-Pacific-American Women, p. 9-16.

Lowry, I. Elaine.
"Organizing Neighborhood Women for Political and Social Action."
In Conference on the Educational and Occupational Needs of
White Ethnic Women (1978: Boston, MA). Conference on the
Educational and Occupational Needs of White Ethnic Women,
p. 55-61.

Lubetkin, Rebecca.
"Statement." In U.S. Congress. Senate. Committee on Labor
and Human Resources. The Coming Decade, p. 767-71.

Lubic, Ruth Watson.
"Testimony." In U.S. Congress. House. Committee on Inter-
state and Foreign Commerce. Subcommittee on Oversight and
Investigations. Nurse Midwifery: Consumer's Freedom of
Choice, p. 72-6.

Luce, Clare Booth.
"Is the New Morality Destroying America?" In We Shall Be Heard,
p. 287-97.

Luce, Judith Dickson.
"Ethical Issues Relating to Childbirth as Experience by the Birth-
ing Woman and Midwife." In Birth Control and Controlling
Birth, p. 239-44.

Luckey, Charlotte.
"Statement." In U.S. Congress. House. Select Committee on
Aging. Subcommittee on Retirement Income and Employment.
Task Force on Social Security and Women. Inequities Toward
Women in the Social Security System, p. 145-7.

Lukas, Theresa A.
"Integrating Women in Development: Programming in AID." In
Health Needs of the World's Poor Women, p. 159-60.

Luke, Barbara.
"Statement." In U.S. Congress. Senate. Committee on Human
Resources. Subcommittee on Alcoholism and Drug Abuse.
Alcohol Labeling and Fetal Alcohol Syndrome, 1978, p. 183-5.

Luker, Kristin.
"Response (to Woman-Controlled Birth Control)." In Birth Control and Controlling Birth, p. 81-4.

Luomala, Nancy.
  "Matrilineal Reinterpretation of Some Egyptian Sacred Cows."
    In Feminism and Art History, p. 19-31.

Lutter, Judy Mahle.
  "The Minnesota Experience: Continuing Education for Women,
    1960 to 1978." In Women's Lives, p. 363-71.

Lynch, Felicia.
  "A View From the Funding Agencies." In Toward a Balanced
    Curriculum, p. 159-162.

Lyons, Elizabeth T.
  "Statement." In U.S. Congress. Senate. Committee on Labor
    and Human Resources. The Coming Decade, pt. 2, p. 35-41.

Mabry, Hannelore.
  "The New Women's Movement and the Party and Trade Union
    Question." In German Feminism, p. 324-8.

Mabry, Ruth.
  "Testimony." In U.S. Commission on Civil Rights. Hearing Be-
    fore the U.S. Commission on Civil Rights Held in Chicago,
    1974, pt. 1, p. 29-30, 32-3, 38-9.

Maccoby, Eleanor E.
  "Effects Upon Children of their Mothers' Outside Employment."
    In Conference on Work in the Lives of Married Women (1957:
    Columbia University). Work in the Lives of Married Women,
    p. 150-72.
  "Woman's Sociobiological Heritage: Destiny or Free Choice?" In
    Psychology and Women: In Transition, p. 147-65.

MacDonald, Carolyn T.
  "An Experiment in Mathematics Education at the College Level."
    In Hyman Blumberg Symposium on Research on Early Child-
    hood Education (8th: Johns Hopkins University). Women and
    the Mathematical Mystique, p. 115-37.

Machung, Anne.
  "Word Processing: Forward for Business, Backward for Women."
    In My Troubles Are Going To Have Trouble With Me, p. 124-39.

MacKinnon, Catharine A.
  "Testimony." In U.S. Congress. Senate. Committee on the
    Judiciary. Subcommittee on Juvenile Justice. Effects of
    Pornography on Women and Children, p. 232-4.

Macklin, Ruth.
  "Confidentiality in Sex Therapy." In Ethical Issues in Sex

Therapy and Research, v. 2, p. 346-53.
"Designated Discussion (Ethical Requirement for Sex Research in Humans)." In The Evolving Female, p. 69-73.

Macleod, Jennifer S.
"Testimony." In U.S. Congress. Joint Economic Committee. Subcommittee on Economic Growth and Stabilization. American Women Workers in a Full Employment Economy, p. 11-5.

Macy, Joanna Rodgers.
"Perfection of Wisdom: Mother of All Buddhas." In Beyond Androcentrism, p. 315-33.

Madar, Olga.
"Testimony." In U.S. Congress. House. Select Committee on Aging. Subcommittee on Retirement Income and Employment. Task Force on Social Security and Women. Treatment of Women Under Social Security, p. 106-9.

Madden, Janice Fanning.
"Comment on 'Occupational Segregation Among Women.'" In Conference on Women in the Labor Market (1977: Barnard College). Women in the Labor Market, p. 157-8.
"Testimony." In U.S. Equal Employment Opportunity Commission. Hearings Before the U.S. Equal Employment Opportunity Commission on Job Segregation and Wage Discrimination, p. 318-28.

Madden, Sister Loretta Ann, S.L.
"Challenge to the Churches." In Split-Level Lives, p. 9-25.

Maddox, Violet.
"Statement." In U.S. Congress. House. Committee on Post Office and Civil Service. Subcommittee on Compensation and Employee Benefits. Options for Conducting A Pay Equity Study, p. 194-5.

Madison, Avril J.
"Statement." In U.S. Congress. Joint Economic Committee. Problems of Working Women, p. 142-7.
"Statement." In U.S. Congress. Senate. Committee on Labor and Human Resources. Sex Discrimination in the Workplace, 1981, p. 35-7.
"Testimony." In U.S. Congress. Senate. Committee on Labor and Human Resources. Women in Transition, 1983, p. 52-7.

Maher, Frances.
"Appropriate Teaching Methods for Integrating Women." In Toward a Balanced Curriculum, p. 101-8.

Maher, Mary Denis.
"Statement." In U.S. Congress. House. Select Committee on

Aging. Subcommittee on Retirement Income and Employment. Task Force on Social Security and Women. Treatment of Women Under Social Security, v. 3, p. 56-8.

Mainardi, Patricia.
"Quilts: The Great American Art." In Feminism and Art History, p. 331.

Mainker, Marlene Crosby.
"Self-Power and Leadership." In Women in Crisis Conference (1st: 1979: New York, NY). Women in Crisis, p. 252-6.

Majcher, Jane.
"Testimony." In U.S. Congress. House. Committee on Energy and Commerce. Subcommittee on Health and the Environment. Health and the Environment Miscellaneous, pt. 4, p. 359.

Major, Bessie.
"Statement." In U.S. Congress. House. Select Committee on Aging. Subcommittee on Retirement Income and Employment. Task Force on Social Security and Women. Treatment of Women Under Social Security, pt. 3, p. 64.

Major, Gerene D.
"Prenatal Diagnosis: Overview." In The Custom-Made Child?, p. 65-6.

Makarushka, Julia Loughlin.
"Workers' Compensation: The Long-Term Consequences of Work-Related Injury for Women." In Conference on Women and the Workplace (1976: Washington, DC). Conference on Women and the Workplace, p. 292-301.

Makward, Christiane.
"To Be Or Not to Be ... A Feminist Speaker." In The Future of Difference, p. 95-104.

Malcom, Shirley Mahaley.
"Statement." In U.S. Congress. Senate. Committee on Labor and Human Resources. Subcommittee on Health and Scientific Research. Women in Science and Technology Equal Opportunity Act, 1980, p. 49-50.

Mallan, Lucy.
"Women's Incomes as Workers and Dependents." In Women Organizing, p. 221-38.

Mallett, Connie.
"Statement." In U.S. Congress. House. Committee on Ways and Means. Economic Equity Act and Related Tax and Pension Reform, p. 180-3.

"Statement." In U.S. Congress. Senate. Committee on Labor and Human Resources. Subcommittee on Family and Human Services. Broken Families, p. 249-54.

Malpede, Karen.
"A Talk for the Conference on Feminism & Militarism." In Reweaving the Web of Life, p. 200-8.

Mangan, Sister Mary, S.L.
"Unwritten History." In Split-Level Lives, p. 87-101.

Manis, Jean.
"Transition to Work: Who Is Satisfied and Who Is Not?" In Women's Lives, p. 283-9.

Mankin, Helen Douglas.
"Statement." In U.S. Congress. House. Committee on Armed Services. Select Subcommittee to Review WASP Bills. To Provide Recognition to the Women's Air Force, p. 154-60.

Mann, Alice B.
"Lazarus, Come Forth (Lent)." In Women and the Word, p. 60-4.

Mann, Dorothy.
"Statement." In U.S. Congress. Senate. Committee on Labor and Human Resources. Oversight on Family Planning Programs, p. 179-81.
"Testimony." In U.S. Congress. House. Committee on Energy and Commerce. Subcommittee on Health and the Environment. Health and the Environment Miscellaneous, pt. 3, p. 534-5.

Mansfield, Sue.
"Strategy, Fear and the Atom. The Goddess of Defense." Vital Speeches, 50 (March 1, 1984), 305-8.

Mapp, Patricia.
"Testimony." In U.S. Commission on Civil Rights. Hearing Before the U.S. Commission on Civil Rights Held in Chicago, 1974, v. 1, p. 303-11, 315-6.

Marchiano, Linda (Lovelace).
"Testimony." In U.S. Congress. Senate. Committee on the Judiciary. Subcommittee on Juvenile Justice. Effect of Pornography on Women and Children, p. 178-80.

Marcus, Jane.
"Liberty, Sorority, Misogyny." In The Representation of Women in Fiction, p. 60-97.

Marks, Lynn.
"Testimony." In U.S. Congress. Senate. Committee on the

Judiciary. Subcommittee on Criminal Law. <u>Impact of Media Coverage of Rape Trials</u>, p. 61-4.

Marks, Patricia.
"Statement." In U.S. Congress. Senate. Committee on Finance. <u>Potential Inequities Affecting Women</u>, pt. 1, p. 65-6.

Markson, Elizabeth W.
"Statement." In U.S. Congress. Joint Economic Committee. <u>The Role of Older Women in the Work Force</u>, p. 8-11.

Markus, Hazel.
"Work, Women and Well-Being: A Cognitive Approach." In <u>Women's Lives</u>, p. 269-81.

Marrett, Cora Bagley.
"On the Evolution of Women's Medical Societies." In <u>Women and Health in America</u>, p. 429-37.
"Statement." In Symposium on Minorities and Women in Science and Technology (1981: Washington, DC). <u>Symposium on Minorities and Women in Science and Technology</u>, p. 4-6.

Marshall, Mary A.
"Statement." In U.S. Congress. House. Committee on Ways and Means. Subcommittee on Social Security. <u>Social Security Dependent's Benefits</u>, p. 3-5.

Marshall, Paule.
"Emerging Ones." In <u>Breaking the Sequence</u>, p. 28-35.

Marshner, Connaught.
"Statement." In U.S. Congress. Senate. Committee on Labor and Human Resources. <u>Oversight on Family Planning Programs</u>, p. 148-52.

Martelet, Penny.
"The Woman's Land Army, World War I." In Conference on Women's History (1976: Washington, DC). <u>Clio Was a Woman</u>, p. 136-46.

Martin, Beverly.
"The Black Woman in America." In Cornell Conference on Women (1969: Cornell University). <u>Proceedings</u>, p. 85-6, 90, 91.

Martin, Elaine.
"Role Conflicts for Women in Positions of Authority." In GLCA Women's Studies Conference (6th: 1980). <u>Towards a Feminist Transformation of the Academy II</u>, p. 28-35.

Martin, Joan M.
"Testimony." In U.S. Congress. House. Committee on the

Judiciary. Subcommittee on Civil and Constitutional Rights.
Equal Rights Amendment Extension, p. 291-6.

Martin, Judith.
Common Courtesy: In Which Miss Manners Solves the Problem
That Baffled Mr. Jefferson. New York: Atheneum, 1985,
p. 3-70.

Martin, Lynn.
"Statement." In U.S. Congress. House. Committee on Educa-
tion and Labor. Subcommittee on Employment Opportunities.
Hearings on Job Creation Proposals. Washington:
U.S.G.P.O., 1983, p. 177-94.
"Statement." In U.S. Congress. House. Committee on Energy
and Commerce. Subcommittee on Fossil and Synthetic Fuels.
Natural Gas Issues. Washington: U.S.G.P.O., 1983, pt. 2,
p. 995-1001.
"Statement." In U.S. Congress. House. Committee on Public
Works and Transportation. Subcommittee on Surface Trans-
portation. Examining the Nation's Immediate and Long-Term
Surface Transportation Capital Needs. Washington:
U.S.G.P.O., 1981, p. 1327-35.
"Statement." In U.S. Congress. House. Committee on Public
Works and Transportation. Subcommittee on Surface
Transportation. Surface Transportation Assistance Act
Amendments. Washington: U.S.G.P.O., 1981, p. 201-25.
"Statement." In U.S. Congress. House. Speaker's Commission
on Pages. Hearings Before the Speaker's Commission on
Pages. Washington: U.S.G.P.O., 1982, pt. 1, p. 202-13.
"Statement." In U.S. Congress. Senate. Committee on Agri-
culture, Nutrition and Forestry. Subcommittee on Rural De-
velopment, Oversight, and Investigations. Oversight on General Farm and Food Programs. Washington: U.S.G.P.O.,
1985, p. 47-50.
"Statement." In U.S. Congress. Senate. Committee on Foreign
Relations. U.S. Machine Tool Industry: Its Relations to National Security. Washington: U.S.G.P.O., 1984, p. 11-6.
"Statement." In U.S. Congress. Senate. Committee on Governmental Affairs. Subcommittee on Energy, Nuclear Prolifera-
tion, and Government Processes. Federal Regulation. Washington: U.S.G.P.O., 1981, pt. 1, p. 5-6.

Martinez, Arabella.
"Listen to the Children. A Focus on Issues Raised During the
International Year of the Child." Vital Speeches, 46 (October
15, 1979), 18-21.

Martinez, Diane Ida.
"Innovative Approaches: Meeting the Needs of Women Faculty in
the Eighties." In Expanding the Role of Women in the Sciences, p. 268-75.

Martinez, Vilma S.
  "Proposed Sanctions Against Employers of Illegal Aliens." Con-
    gressional Digest, 60 (October 1981), 241, 243, 245, 247, 249,
    251, 253.
  "Statement." In U.S. Congress. House. Committee on Educa-
    tion and Labor. Subcommittee on Employment Opportunities.
    Oversight Hearings on Equal Employment Opportunity and Af-
    firmative Action, pt. 1, p. 59-66.

Maslin, Audrey.
  "A Typology of Motives and Attitudes Toward Women's Roles
    Among Black and White Older Undergraduate Women at an
    Urban University." In Conference on "Scholars and Women"
    (1981: University of Maryland). Women's Studies and the
    Curriculum, p. 185-9.

Mason, Karen Oppenheim.
  "Commentary: Strober's Theory of Occupational Sex Segregation."
    In Sex Segregation in the Workplace, p. 157-70.

Mason, Priscilla.
  "From the Salutatory Oration, Delivered by Miss Priscilla Mason,
    May 15, 1793." In Women of America, p. 89-91.

Massinga, Ruth W.
  "Statement." In U.S. Congress. House. Committee on Govern-
    ment Operations. Intergovernmental Relations and Human Re-
    sources Subcommittee. Barriers to Self-Sufficiency for Single
    Female Heads of Families, p. 524-7.
  "Statement." In U.S. Congress. House. Committee on Ways
    and Means. Subcommittee on Public Assistance and Unemploy-
    ment Compensation. Teenage Pregnancy Issues, p. 74-8.

Masson, Veneta.
  "An Example of Holist Care (Washington, DC)." In Health Needs
    of the World's Poor Women, p. 107-10.

Masters, Billie.
  "Speech by Billie Masters, Chair, National American Indian and
    Alaskan Native Women's Conference." In U.S. National Com-
    mission on the Observance of International Women's Year.
    The Spirit of Houston, p. 232-3.

Mater, Catherine.
  "Statement." In U.S. Congress. Senate. Committee on Small
    Business. Women Entrepreneurs, p. 43-8.

Mathews, Linda.
  "Chinese Contradictions: We Ought To Be Cautious Toward
    China." Vital Speeches, 47 (August 1, 1981), 628-32.

Matulis, Sherry.
  "Statement." In U.S. Congress. Senate. Committee on the
    Judiciary. Subcommittee on the Constitution. Constitutional
    Amendments Relating to Abortion, v. 1, p. 1158-60.

Maves, Barbara.
  "Statement." In U.S. Congress. Senate. Committee on Labor
    and Human Resources. Oversight of Family Planning Pro-
    grams, 1981, p. 32-4, 55-78, 73-82.

Max, Claire Ellen.
  "Career Paths for Women in Physics." In Women and Minorities
    in Science, p. 99-118.

Maxwell, Colleen.
  "The Traditional Role of the Mormon Woman." In Blueprints for
    Living, p. 112-5.

Mayer, Linda.
  "Testimony." In U.S. Commission on Civil Rights. Hearing Be-
    fore the U.S. Commission on Civil Rights Held in Chicago,
    1974, v. 2, p. 170-1.

Mayer, Mary J.
  "The Older Woman: Work Roles and Mandatory Retirement." In
    Older Women in the City, p. 33-43.

Mayerson, Arlene B.
  "Statement." In U.S. Congress. House. Committee on Educa-
    tion and Labor. Civil Rights Act of 1984, p. 281-4.
  "Statement." In U.S. Congress. Senate. Committee on the
    Judiciary. Subcommittee on the Constitution. Civil Rights
    Act of 1984, p. 23-5.

Maymi, Carmen R.
  "Women in the Labor Force." In Women: A Developmental Per-
    spective, p. 181-206.

Mayne, Judith.
  "The Woman at the Keyhole: Women's Cinema and Feminist Criti-
    cism." In Re-Vision, p. 49-66.

Mayrand, Theres.
  "Response (to Ethics and Reproductive Technology)." In The
    Custom-Made Child?, p. 249-52.

Mazo, Judith F.
  "Statement." In U.S. Congress. House. Committee on Ways
    and Means. Economic Equity Act and Related Tax and Pen-
    sion Reform, p. 101-3.

McAdoo, Harriet.
    "Statement." In U.S. Congress. House. Committee on the
        Budget. Task Force on Entitlements, Uncontrollables and
        Indexing. Women and Children in Poverty, p. 73-8.
    "Statement." In U.S. Congress. Senate. Committee on Labor
        and Human Resources. Subcommittee on Family and Human
        Services. Broken Families, p. 239-47.

McAfee, Naomi J.
    "Women in Engineering Revisited." In Expanding the Role of
        Women in the Sciences, p. 94-9.
    "You've Come a Long Way Baby: The Myth and the Reality."
        In Women in Scientific and Engineering Professions, p. 160-9.

McArthur, Leslie Zebrowitz.
    "Social Judgment Biases in Comparable Worth Analysis." In
        Comparable Worth: New Directions for Research, p. 53-70.

McBee, Mary Louise.
    "The Values Development Dilemma." In Lloyd-Jones Symposium
        (1979: University of Georgia Continuing Education Center).
        Rethinking College Responsibilities for Values, p. 1-8.

McBroom, Elizabeth.
    "Socialization and Social Casework." In Charlotte Towle Memorial
        Symposium on Comparative Theoretical Approaches to Casework
        Practice (1969: University of Chicago). Theories of Social
        Casework, p. 313-51.

McCabe, Carol.
    "Testimony." In U.S. Commission on Civil Rights. Hearings Be-
        fore the U.S. Commission on Civil Rights Held In Chicago,
        1974, v. 1, p. 1-13.

McCambridge, Ruth.
    "The Coalition of Battered Women's Service Groups." Women's
        Studies Quarterly, 13 (Summer 1985), 12-3.

McCartney, Marion.
    "Testimony." In U.S. Congress. House. Committee on Inter-
        state and Foreign Commerce. Subcommittee on Oversight and
        Investigations. Nurse Midwifery: Consumers' Freedom of
        Choice, p. 59-61.

McChesney, Kathleen.
    "Myths and Realities." In Training Conference (1st: 1984:
        Washington, DC). Interagency Committee on Women in Fed-
        eral Law Enforcement, p. 23-5.

McClain, Mary Ann.
    "Testimony." In U.S. Commission on Civil Rights. Hearing

Before the U.S. Commission on Civil Rights Held in Denver,
p. 40-8-10, 417-20.

McClean, Gail Pepper.
"Testimony." In U.S. Congress. House. Committee on Energy
and Commerce. Subcommittee on Health and the Environment.
Health and the Environment Miscellaneous, pt. 3, p. 60-1.

McClendon, Sarah.
"Statement." In U.S. Congress. House. Committee on Veterans'
Affairs. Subcommittee on Hospitals and Health Care. VA
Health Care for Women, p. 8-10.

McConnel-Ginet, Sally.
"Difference and Language: A Linguist's Perspective." In The
Future of Difference, p. 157-64.

McConnell, Nancy F.
"Testimony." In U.S. Congress. House. Committee on Energy
and Commerce. Subcommittee on Health and the Environment.
Health and the Environment Miscellaneous, pt. 3, p. 951-3.

McCord, Ramona.
"Statement." In U.S. Congress. Senate. Committee on Labor
and Human Resources. Subcommittee on Family and Human
Services. Forum for Families, p. 58.

McCourt, Kathleen.
"Irish, Italian, and Jewish Women at the Grassroots Level: A
Historical and Sociological Perspective." In Conference on
the Educational and Occupational Needs of White Ethnic Women
(1978: Boston, MA). Conference on the Educational and
Occupational Needs of White Ethnic Women, p. 153-79.

McCoy, Carla.
"Statement." In U.S. Congress. House. Select Committee on
Children, Youth, and Families. Children, Youth, and Fam-
ilies, p. 72-3.

McCracken, Ellen.
"Manuel Puig's Heartbreak Tango: Women and the Mass Culture."
In Women in Latin American Literature, p. 37-54.

McDonald, Nancy.
"Statement." In U.S. Congress. House. Committee on Science
and Technology. Subcommittee on Domestic and International
Scientific Planning, Analysis, and Cooperation. Research into
Violent Behavior: Overview and Sexual Assaults, p. 409-25.

McElderry, Betty.
"Statement." In U.S. Congress. Senate. Committee on Labor

and Human Resources. Subcommittee on Labor. Retirement
Equity Act of 1983, p. 39-41.

McEnamy, Gina.
"Housewife, Mother, and Parish Volunteer." In Conference on
Women and Lay Ministry (1976: St. Michel's Church, Milton,
MA). Women and Lay Ministry, p. 4-7.

McFadden, Ophelia.
"Statement." In U.S. Congress. House. Committee on Post
Office and Civil Service. Subcommittee on Compensation and
Employee Benefits. Federal Pay Equity Act of 1984, pt. 2,
p. 114-5.
"Statement." In U.S. Congress. House. Committee on Post
Office and Civil Service. Subcommittee on Compensation and
Employee Benefits. Federal Pay Equity Act of 1984, pt. 2,
p. 114-5.

McGee, Elizabeth A.
"Statement." In U.S. Congress. House. Select Committee on
Children, Youth, and Families. Teen Parents and Their
Children, p. 80-3.

McGee, Mary.
"In Celebration of Heroes and Nobodies." In Spinning a Sacred
Yarn, p. 127-31.

McGee, Sandra F.
"Right-Wing Female Activists in Buenos Aires, 1900-1932." In
Berkshire Conference on the History of Women (5th: 1982:
Vassar College). Women and the Structure of Society, p.
85-97.

McGeorge, Jo Ann.
"Women and Policy Making in the Housing Area." In Women's
Lives, p. 423-6.

McGibbon, Nancy.
"Statement." In U.S. Congress. House. Committee on Post
Office and Civil Service. Subcommittee on Compensation and
Employee Benefits. Federal Pay Equity Act of 1984, pt. 2,
p. 179-81.

McGill-Jackson, Deborah.
"To Set at Liberty." In Those Preachin' Women, p. 35-42.

McGlauflin, Deborah.
"Mainstreaming Refugee Women's Economic Development." In
Immigrants and Refugees in a Changing Nation, p. 111-6.

McGoldrick, Rita C.
"Testimony." In U.S. Congress. House. Committee on the

Judiciary. Birth Control, (1934) p. 141-4.
"Testimony." In U.S. Congress. House. Committee on Ways
and Means. Birth Control, (1932) p. 85-7.
"Testimony." In U.S. Congress. Senate. Committee on the
Judiciary. Birth Control, (1931) p. 68-70.
"Testimony." In U.S. Congress. Senate. Committee on the
Judiciary. Birth Control, (1932) p. 115-7.

McGrath, Eileen.
"Government Publications for Women's Studies Research: An Introduction." In GLCA Women's Studies Conference (6th:
1980). Towards a Feminist Transformation of the Academy II,
p. 66-70.

McGrath, Mary Jean.
"What Can Private Institutions, Particularly Cooperatives Do?"
In International Conference on Women and Food (1978: Uni-
versity of Arizona). A Conference on the Role of Women in
Meeting Basic Food and Water Needs in Developing Countries,
p. 143-57.

McHenry, Ramona.
"Testimony." In U.S. Commission on Civil Rights. Hearing Before the U.S. Commission on Civil Rights Held in Denver,
p. 180-2, 189-91.

McHugh, (Mrs.) Tucker.
"Education and Equality for Women." In Cornell Conference on
Women (1969: Cornell University). Proceedings, p. 47.

McIlwee, Judith S.
"Work Satisfaction Among Women in Non-Traditional Occupations."
In Conference on
"Scholars and Women" (1981: University of Maryland). Women's
Studies and the Curriculum, p. 95-109.

McIntosh, Peggy.
"Interactive Phases of Curricular Re-Vision." In Towards a
Balanced Curriculum, p. 25-34.

McIntosh, Sharon.
"Testimony." In U.S. Congress. House. Committee on Energy
and Commerce. Subcommittee on Health and the Environment.
Pregnancy-Related Health Services, p. 258.

McKee, Frances E.
"Statement." In U.S. Congress. House. Committee on Armed
Services. Subcommittee on Military Personnel. Women in the
Military, p. 329-30.

McKenna, Margaret.
"The View from the White House." In Conference on the National

Longitudinal Surveys of Mature Women (1978: U.S. Department of Labor). Women's Changing Roles at Home and on the Job, p. 313-4.

McKenna, Theresa.
"Statement." In U.S. Congress. House. Committee on Ways and Means. Subcommittee on Social Security. Social Security Dependents' Benefits, p. 11-3.

McKinlay, Lynn A.
"To Love Our God." In Ye Are Free to Choose, p. 41-9.

McKinley, Robin.
"Newbery Medal Acceptance." Hornbook, 61 (1985), 395-405.

McLean, Helen V.
"Psychological Roles for Women in Public Affairs." In Education of Women for Social and Political Leadership, p. 31-9.

McLellan, Lib.
"Is the Question of Women a Political Question?" In Cornell Conference on Women (1969: Cornell University). Proceedings, p. 18-9.

McMahon, Sarah Lynne.
"Women in Marital Transition." In Women and Psychotherapy, p. 365-84.

McNamara, Jo Ann.
"Sexual Equality and the Cult of Virginity in Early Christian Thought." Feminist Studies, 3 (1976), 145-58.

McPherson, Aimee Semple.
"The Cat and the Canary." In We Shall Be Heard, p. 264-71.

McSteen, Martha.
"Statement." In U.S. Congress. House. Select Committee on Aging. Subcommittee on Retirement Income and Employment. Task Force on Social Security. Earnings Sharing Implementation Plan, p. 5-8.

Mead, Margaret.
"A Comment on the Role of Women in Agriculture." In AAAS Seminar on Women in Development. Women in World Development, p. 9-11.
"One Aspect of Male and Female." In Cooper Union for the Advancement of Science and Art. Women, Society and Sex, p. 15-32.
"Speech by Honorable Margaret Mead." In U.S. National Commission on the Observance of International Women's Year. The Spirit of Houston, p. 230-1.

Meagher, Katherine.
"Women in Relation to Orders and Jurisdiction." In Sexism and Church Law, p. 21-42.

Mears, Judith.
"Testimony." In U.S. Congress. House. Committee on the Judiciary. Subcommittee on Civil and Constitutional Rights. Proposed Constitutional Amendments on Abortion, p. 93-8.

Mecklenburg, Marjory.
"Statement." In U.S. Congress. House. Select Committee on Population. Fertility and Contraception in America, pt. 2, p. 131-7.
"Testimony." In U.S. Congress. House. Committee on Education and Labor. Subcommittee on Select Education. Adolescent Pregnancy, p. 105-7.
"Testimony." In U.S. Congress. House. Committee on Energy and Commerce. Subcommittee on Health and the Environment. Health and the Environment Miscellaneous, pt. 3, p. 837-40.
"Testimony." In U.S. Congress. Senate. Committee on Human Resources. Adolescent Health, Services and Pregnancy Prevention Care Act of 1978, p. 428-31.

Medicine, Beatrice.
"The Interaction of Culture and Sex Roles in the Schools." In Conference on the Educational and Occupational Needs of American Indian Women (1976: Albuquerque, NM). Conference on the Educational and Occupational Needs of American Indian Women, p. 141-57.

Mednick, Martha T. Shuch.
"The New Psychology of Women: A Feminist Analysis." In Psychology and Women: In Transition, p. 189-211.
"Women and the Psychology of Achievement: Implications for Personal and Social Change." In U.S. Congress. Joint Economic Committee. Women in the Work Force, p. 48-69.

Meehan, Sister Maria Eucharia, C.S.J.
"Residence and Race." In Split-Level Lives, p. 125-35.

Meehan, Mary.
"Statement." In U.S. Congress. Senate. Committee on the Judiciary. Subcommittee on Separation of Powers. The Human Life Bill, p. 1014-7.

Mendelson, Johanna S. R.
"Statement." In U.S. Congress. House. Committee on Ways and Means. Economic Equity Act and Related Tax and Pension Reform, p. 95-7.
"Statement." In U.S. Congress. Senate. Committee on Finance. Potential Inequities Affecting Women, pt. 2, p. 118-9.

Mendez, Doris.
　"Statement." In U.S. Congress. House. Select Committee on
　　Aging. Problems of Aging Women, p. 125-7.

Menken, Jane.
　"Statement." In U.S. Congress. House. Select Committee on
　　Population. Fertility and Contraception in America, p. 3-9.

Menning, Barbara.
　"In Defense of In Vitro Fertilization." In The Custom-Made
　　Child?, p. 263-8.

Mentzer, Nancy.
　"Testimony." In U.S. Commission on Civil Rights. Hearing Be-
　　fore the U.S. Commission on Civil Rights Held in Denver,
　　p. 469-70.

Mercer, Ethel.
　"Statement." In U.S. Congress. Senate. Special Committee on
　　Aging. Prospects for Better Health for Older Women, p. 20-1.

Merriam, Eve.
　"Creating Feminist Work." In A Panel Discussion from The Schol-
　　ar and the Feminist V, p. 11-6.
　"Woman's Expectation: Mirage or Reality." In The Challenge to
　　Women, p. 5-19.

Merrill, Barbara.
　"Testimony." In U.S. Commission on Civil Rights. Hearing Be-
　　fore the U.S. Commission on Civil Rights Held in Chicago,
　　v. 1, p. 258-9, 64, 270.

Merrill, Marlene.
　"Archives and Women's History Research." In GLCA Women's
　　Studies Conference (6th: 1980). Towards a Feminist Trans-
　　formation of the Academy II, p. 71-2.

Merry, Marilyn.
　"Statement." In U.S. Congress. House. Committee on Post
　　Office and Civil Service. Subcommittee on Compensation and
　　Employee Benefits. Options for Conducting a Pay Equity
　　Study, p. 198-200.

Messinger, Ruth W.
　"Postintervention and Support Systems." In Women in Crisis
　　Conference (1st: 1979: New York, NY). Women in Crisis,
　　p. 243-6.
　"Women in Power and Politics." In The Future of Difference,
　　p. 318-23.

Metress, Eileen.
   "Statement." In U.S. Congress. Senate. Special Committee on
   Aging. Prospects for Better Health for Older Women, p. 13-9.

Meyer, Carol H.
   "Issues for Women in a 'Woman's' Profession." In NASW Conference on Social Work Practice With Women (1st: 1980: Washington, DC). Women, Power, and Change, p. 197-205.

Meyer, Elizabeth.
   "Statement." In U.S. Congress. House. Select Committee on
   Aging. Subcommittee on Retirement Income and Employment.
   Impact of Reagan Economics on Aging Women, p. 5-6.

Meyer, Jan.
   "Statement." In U.S. Congress. House. Committee on Appro-
   priations. Subcommittee on Energy and Water Development.
   Energy and Water Development Appropriations for 1986.
   Washington: U.S.G.P.O., 1985, pt. 9, 1074-1104.

Meyer, Katherine A.
   "Testimony." In U.S. Congress. House. Committee on Energy
   and Commerce. Subcommittee on Health and the Environment.
   Health and the Environment Miscellaneous, pt. 6, p. 14-5.

Meyer, Rosemary.
   "Statement." In U.S. Congress. Senate. Committee on the
   Judiciary. Subcommittee on the Constitution. Constitutional
   Amendments Relating to Abortion, v. 1, p. 1002-4.

Michel, Andree.
   "Projected Future Employment and Leadership Needs and Areas."
   In Changing Roles of Women in Industrial Societies, p. 138-63.

Michel, Harriet.
   "The Federal Government and the War on Youth Employment."
   In Young Women and Employment, p. 73-6.

Middlebrook, Diane Wood.
   "'I Tapped My Own Head:' The Apprenticeship of Anne Sexton."
   In Coming to Light, p. 195-213.

Middletown-Jeter, Verona.
   "Statement." In U.S. Congress. House. Select Committee on
   Children, Youth, and Families. Families in Crisis, p. 60-3.

Mikulski, Barbara A.
   "Statement." In General Farm Bill of 1981. Washington:
   U.S.G.P.O., 1981, pt. 2, p. 314-20.
   "Statement." In U.S. Congress. House. Committee on Appro-
   priations. Subcommittee on Foreign Operations and Related

Programs. Foreign Assistance and Related Programs Appropriations for 1982. Washington: U.S.G.P.O., 1981, pt. 1,
p. 25-94.

"Statement." In U.S. Congress. House. Committee on Appro-
priations. Subcommittee on the Departments of Commerce,
Justice, and State, the Judiciary, and Related Agencies.
Department of Commerce, Justice, and State, the Judiciary,
and Related Agencies Appropriations for 1986. Washington:
U.S.G.P.O., 1985, pt. 8, p. 260-94.

"Statement." In U.S. Congress. House. Committee on Education and Labor. Subcommittee on Human Resources. Author-
izations for Head Start, Follow Through, Community Services,
and Establish Child Care Information and Referral Services.
Washington: U.S.G.P.O., 1985, p. 23-4.

"Statement." In U.S. Congress. House. Committee on Education and Labor. Subcommittee on Human Resources. Hearing
on Child Care Information and Referral Services Act. Washington: U.S.G.P.O., 1984, p. 8-9.

"Statement." In U.S. Congress. House. Committee on Energy
and Commerce. Subcommittee on Fossil and Synthetic Fuels.
Natural Gas Issues. Washington: U.S.G.P.O., 1983, pt. 2,
v. 2, p. 1001-3.

"Statement." In U.S. Congress. House. Committee on Foreign
Affairs. Subcommittee on Inter-American Affairs. U.S. Policy
Toward El Salvador. Washington: U.S.G.P.O., 1981, p. 3-7.

"Statement." In U.S. Congress. House. Committee on Interstate and Foreign Commerce. Subcommittee on Consumer Protection and Finance. Nondiscrimination in Insurance, p. 53-7.

"Statement." In U.S. Congress. House. Committee on Inter-
state and Foreign Commerce. Subcommittee on Oversight and
Investigations. Nurse Midwifery: Consumers' Freedom of
Choice, p. 2-4.

"Statement." In U.S. Congress. House. Committee on Post
Office and Civil Service. Subcommittee on Compensation and
Employee Benefits. Federal Pay Equity Act of 1984, pt. 1,
p. 15-7.

"Statement." In U.S. Congress. House. Committee on Public
Works and Transportation. Subcommittee on Water Resources.
Improved Operation, Maintenance, and Financing of the Na-
tion's Water Transportation System.... Washington:
U.S.G.P.O., 1983, p. 2-5.

"Statement." In U.S. Congress. House. Committee on Ways
and Means. Impact of the Administration's Budget Cuts.
Washington: U.S.G.P.O., 1982, p. 45-6.

"Statement." In U.S. Congress. House. Committee on Ways
and Means. Advisability of a Tax Reduction in 1980 Effective
for 1981. Washington: U.S.G.P.O., 1980, pt. 1, p. 244-50.

"Statement." In U.S. Congress. House. Committee on Ways
and Means. Subcommittee on Health. Administration's Proposed Elimination of the Office of Direct Reimbursement at the
Health Care Financing Administration. Washington:

U.S.G.P.O., 1984, p. 23-4.

"Statement." In U.S. Congress. House. Committee on Ways and Means. Subcommittee on Health. Health Care Cost Control Act of 1983. Washington: U.S.G.P.O., 1984, p. 7-11.

"Statement." In U.S. Congress. House. Committee on Ways and Means. Subcommittee on Select Revenue Measures. Exclusion for Group Legal Services Plans and Miscellaneous Tax Bills. Washington: U.S.G.P.O., 1984, p. 203-6.

"Statement." In U.S. Congress. House. Committee on Ways and Means. Subcommittee on Social Security. Treatment of Men and Women Under the Social Security Program, p. 46-9.

"Statement." In U.S. Congress. House. Select Committee on Aging. Subcommittee on Retirement Income and Employment. Task Force on Social Security and Women. Treatment of Women Under Social Security, pt. 1, p. 6-9, pt. 4, p. 5-6.

"Statement." In U.S. Congress. Senate. Committee on Commerce, Science, and Transportation. Professional Sports Team Community Protection Act. Washington: U.S.G.P.O., 1984, p. 27-33.

"Statement." In U.S. Congress. Senate. Committee on Labor and Human Resources. Subcommittee on Child and Human Development. Domestic Violence Prevention and Services Act, 1980, p. 53-5.

Mikus, Karen C.
"Psychological Correlates of Early Family Formation." In Women's Lives, p. 117-25.

Miles, Pauline.
"Opening Remarks." In Warner, Anne R. Health Womenpower, p. 1-3.

Miller, Deborah.
"Statement." In U.S. Congress. House. Committee on Post Office and Civil Service. Subcommittee on Compensation and Employee Benefits. Options for Conducting a Pay Equity Study, p. 492-4.

Miller, Nancy K.
"Creating Feminist Work." In A Panel Discussion from The Scholar and the Feminist V, p. 17-21.

"Mastery, Identity and the Politics of Work: A Feminist Teacher in the Graduate Classroom." In Gendered Subjects, p. 195-200.

"Writing (from) the Feminine: George Sand and the Novel of Female Pastoral." In The Representation of Women in Fiction, p. 124-51.

Miller, Tobie.
"Testimony." In U.S. Congress. House. Committee on Energy and Commerce. Subcommittee on Health and the Environment. Health and the Environment Miscellaneous, pt. 4, p. 53-5.

Millett, Kate.
"Beyond Politics? Children and Sexuality." In Pleasure and Danger, p. 217-24.
"Education and Equality for Women." In Cornell Conference on Women (1969: Cornell University). Proceedings, p. 37, 41-2, 43.
"How Do Men Look at Women?" In Cornell Conference on Women (1969: Cornell University). Proceedings, p. 3-6.
"Is the Question of Women a Political Question?" In Cornell Conference on Women (1969: Cornell University). Proceedings, p. 15-6, 22.

Mills-Morton, Clara.
"The Blessings and Burdens of the Divinely Chosen." In Those Preachin' Women, p. 93-100.

Milstein, Bonnie.
"Statement." In U.S. Congress. Senate. Committee on Labor and Human Resources. Subcommittee on Education, Arts and Humanities. Civil Rights Act of 1984, pt. 1, p. 334-7.

Milton, Catherine.
"Holistic Approaches for Women." In Women in Crisis Conference (1st: 1979: New York, NY). Women in Crisis p. 77-9.

Miner, Myrtilla.
"The School for Colored Girls." In O'Connor, Ellen M. Myrtilla Miner: a Memoir. The School for Colored Girls: an address, by Mrytilla Miner. New York: Arno Press, 1969, p. 3-9.

Minge, Wanda.
"The Industrial Revolution and the European Family: 'Childhood' as a Market for Family Labor." In Women's Work, p. 13-24.

Mink, Patsy.
"Speech at the National Women's Political Caucus Conference, July, 1981." Ms., 10 (October 1981), 94.
"Speech by Honorable Patsy Mink, Assistant Secretary of State (Former Congresswoman and Co-sponsor PL 94-167)." In U.S. National Conference on the Observance of International Women's Year. The Spirit of Houston, p. 227-8.

Minich, Elizabeth Kamarck.
"Curriculum Reform, or What Do You Mean, 'Our Colleges Should Have a Feminist Curriculum'?" In GLCA Women's Studies Conference (5th: 1979). Toward a Feminist Transformation of the Academy, p. 61-2.
"A Feminist Critique of the Liberal Arts." In Liberal Education and the New Scholarship on Women, p. 22-38.
"Friends and Critics: The Feminist Academy." In GLCA Women's Studies Conference (5th: 1979). Towards a Feminist

Transformation of the Academy, p. 1-11. Also in Learning Our Way, p. 317-29.

"The Meaning of 'Human' In the Humanities." In Conference on Women's Studies and the Humanities (1983: University of North Carolina at Greensboro). Equity and Excellence, p. 9-18.

Mitchell, Carol.
"Damnation and Stereotyping in Joke Telling." In Women and Men, p. 298-310.

Mitchell, Juliet.
"Feminity, Narrative and Psychoanalysis." In Mitchell, Women, the Longest Revolution, p. 287-94.

"Feminism and Feminity at the Turn of the Century." In Mitchell, Women, the Longest Revolution, p. 115-24.

"Feminism as a Political Movement." In Mitchell, Women, the Longest Revolution, p. 91-103.

"Psychoanalysis: A Humanist Humanity or a Linguist Science?" In Mitchell, Women, the Longest Revolution, p. 233-47.

"The Question of Femininity and the Theory of Psychoanalysis." In Mitchell, Women, the Longest Revolution, p. 295-313.

"Romantic Love." In Mitchell, Women, the Longest Revolution, p. 103-114.

"What Is Feminism?" In Mitchell, Women, the Longest Revolution, p. 79-91.

"Women and Equality." In Mitchell, Women, the Longest Revolution, p. 55-76.

Mitgang, Iris.
"Statement." In U.S. Congress. Senate. Committee on Labor and Human Resources. Sex Discrimination in the Workplace, 1981, p. 112-6.

"Statement." In U.S. Congress. Senate. Committee on Labor and Human Resources. Subcommittee on Child and Human Development. Domestic Violence Prevention and Services Act, 1980, p. 251.

Mixer, Madeline H.
"Statement." In U.S. Congress. House. Committee on Government Operations. Manpower and Housing Subcommittee. The Women's Bureau, p. 25-8.

Mobley, Sadie.
"Statement." In U.S. Congress. House. Committee on the Budget. Task Force on Entitlements, Uncontrollables, and Indexing. Women and Children in Poverty, p. 7-9.

Moe, Ann M.
"The Future Is Now for Business and Industry. Leadership: Management Catalyst for the Eighties." Vital Speeches, 50

(February 1, 1984), 236-9.

"Women and Work. A Time for New Strategies." Vital Speeches, 49 (September 1, 1983), 699-701.

Moen, Cynthia A.
"Testimony." In U.S. Congress. House. Select Committee on Aging. Subcommittee on Retirement Income and Employment. Task Force on Social Security and Women. Treatment of Women Under Social Security, p. 159.

Moffat, (Mrs.) Douglass.
"Testimony." In U.S. Congress. Senate. Committee on the Judiciary. Birth Control, (1931) p. 24.

Mollenkott, Virginia Ramey.
"The Ephesians' Vision: Universal Justice." In Spinning A Sacred Yarn, p. 132-43.

Mondale, Joan.
"Statement." In U.S. Congress. House. Committee on Post Office and Civil Service. Subcommittee on Compensation and Employee Benefits. Federal Pay Equity Act of 1984, pt. 1, p. 24-5.

Monsman, Diana.
"Statement." In U.S. Congress. House. Committee on Foreign Affairs. American Neutrality Policy, p. 582-3.

Monteiro, Helen.
"The Hunger Emergency." Women's Studies Quarterly, 13 (Summer 1985), 12.

Montgomery, Betty Jane.
"Statement." In U.S. Congress. House. Committee on Post Office and Civil Service. Subcommittee on Civil Service. Federal Government Affirmative Action Policies and Programs, p. 37-9.

Mooney, Chris.
"Testimony." In U.S. Congress. House. Committee on Education and Labor. Subcommittee on Select Education. Adolescent Pregnancy, p. 56, 61-2.

Moore, Emily.
"Statement." In U.S. Congress. House. Select Committee on Population. Fertility and Contraception in America, pt. 2, p. 53-62.
"Statement." In U.S. Congress. Senate. Committee on the Judiciary. Subcommittee on the Constitution. Constitutional Amendments Relating to Abortion, pt. 1, p. 1188-90.

Moore, Kristin A.
"The Social and Economic Consequences of Teenage Childbearing." In Young Women and Employment, p. 18-9.
"Statement." In U.S. Congress. House. Select Committee on Population. Fertility and Contraception in America, pt. 2, p. 34-8.
"Testimony." In U.S. Congress. Senate. Committee on Human Resources. Adolescent Health, Services and Pregnancy Prevention Care Act of 1978, p. 253-4.

Moore, Laverne.
"Statement." In U.S. Congress. House. Select Committee on Aging. Subcommittee on Retirement Income and Employment. Impact of Reagan Economics on Aging Women, p. 45-7.

Moore, Mamie.
"Testimony." In U.S. Commission on Civil Rights. Hearing Before the U.S. Commission on Civil Rights Held in Chicago, pt. 1, p. 347-55.

Morantz, Regina Markell.
"Feminism, Professionalism, and Germs: A Study of the Thought of Mary Putnam Jacobi and Elizabeth Blackwell." In Berkshire Conference on the History of Women (5th: 1982: Vassar College). Women and the Structure of Society, p. 170-85.
"The Lady and Her Physician." In Clio's Consciousness Raised, p. 38-51.
"Making Women Modern: Middle-Class Women and Health Reform in 19th-Century America." In Women and Health in America, p. 346-58.

Morfino, Gina.
"Statement." In U.S. Congress. House. Select Committee on Children, Youth, and Families. Children, Youth, and Families, p. 75-6.

Morgan, Robin.
"International Feminism: A Call for Support of the Three Marias." In Morgan, Going Too Far, p. 202-8.
"Lesbianism and Feminism: Synonyms or Contradictions?" In Morgan, Going Too Far, p. 173-88.
"The Proper Study of Womankind: on Women's Studies." In Morgan, Going Too Far, p. 189-201.

Morisey, Muriel.
"Statement." In U.S. Congress. House. Committee on Education and Labor. Subcommittee on Employment Opportunities. Oversight Hearings on the OFCCP's Proposed Affirmative Action Regulations, p. 79-81.

Morris, (Mrs.) Ralph B.
    "Women and Politics." In Cooper Union for the Advancement of
    Sciences and Art. Women, Society and Sex, p. 195-212.

Morris, Lonnie Holtzman.
    "Testimony." In U.S. Congress. House. Committee on Inter-
    state and Foreign Commerce. Subcommittee on Oversight and
    Investigations. Nurse Midwifery: Consumers' Freedom of
    Choice, p. 55-9.

Morton, Nelle.
    "Preaching the Word." In Sexist Religion and Women in the
    Church, p. 29-46.

Moses, Margaret L.
    "Testimony." In U.S. Equal Employment Opportunity Commission.
    Hearings Before the U.S. Equal Employment Opportunity Com-
    mission on Job Segregation and Wage Discrimination, p. 224-43.

Moss, Anne.
    "Statement." In U.S. Congress. House. Committee on Educa-
    tion and Labor. Subcommittee on Labor-Management Relations.
    Pension Equity for Women, p. 82-3.
    "Statement." In U.S. Congress. House. Committee on Ways
    and Means. Economic Equity Act and Related Tax and Pen-
    sion Reform, p. 130-1.
    "Statement." In U.S. Congress. Joint Economic Committee.
    The Role of Older Women in the Work Force, p. 67-9.
    "Statement." In U.S. Congress. Senate. Committee on Finance.
    Potential Inequities Affecting Women, pt. 1, p. 98-9.
    "Statement." In U.S. Congress. Senate. Committee on Labor
    and Human Resources. Subcommittee on Labor. Retirement
    Equity Act of 1983, p. 151-3.

Moss, Lauree E.
    "Feminist Body Psychotherapy." In Handbook of Feminist Ther-
    apy, p. 80-90.

Moss, Thelma.
    "Testimony." In U.S. Congress. House. Committee on Small
    Business. Subcommittee on General Oversight and Minority
    Enterprise. Women in Business, p. 117-9.
    "Statement." In U.S. Congress. Senate. Select Committee on
    Small Business. Women-In-Business Programs in the Federal
    Government, p. 83.

Mossberg, Barbara Antonina Clarke.
    "Sylvia Plath's Baby Book." In Coming to Light, p. 182-94.

Motes, Rosa Peffly.
    "The Pacific Northwest: Changing Role of the Pastor's Wife Since
    1840." In Women in New Worlds, v. 2, p. 148-61.

Mott, Lucretia.
"Abuses and Uses of the Bible. Sermon Delivered at Cherry
Street Meeting, Philadelphia, November 4, 1849." In Mott,
Lucretia Mott: Her Complete Speeches, p. 123-34.
"The Argument That Women Do Not Want to Vote. Address De-
livered to the American Equal Rights Association, New York,
May 9-10, 1867." In Mott, Lucretia Mott: Her Complete
Speeches, p. 287-90.
"Discourse on Woman. Delivered in Philadelphia, December 17,
1849." In Mott, Lucretia Mott: Her Complete Speeches, p.
143-62. Also In We Shall Be Heard, p. 15-22.
"Do Not Keep Still. Remarks Delivered at the Woman's Rights
Convention, Syracuse, New York, September 8-9, 1852."
In Mott, Lucretia Mott: Her Complete Speeches, p. 195-6.
"Doctrine Concerning Death. Remarks Delivered at the Funeral
of Mrs. Johnson, 1872." In Mott, Lucretia Mott: Her Com-
plete Speeches, p. 367-8.
"The Duty of Prayer and Its Effects. Sermon Delivered at
Cherry Street Meeting, Philadelphia, October 14, 1849."
In Mott, Lucretia Mott: Her Complete Speeches, p. 115-22.
"An Encouraging View as to What Has Already Been Effected.
Remarks Delivered at the Seventh National Woman's Rights
Convention, New York, November 25-26, 1856." In Mott,
Lucretia Mott: Her Complete Speeches, p. 227-33.
"A Faithful Testimony Against Bearing Arms. Remarks Delivered
at the Meeting of the Pennsylvania Peace Society, Abington,
Pennsylvania, September 19, 1875." In Mott, Lucretia Mott:
Her Complete Speeches, p. 375-8.
"The Free Religious Association and the Advance It Has Made.
Extracts from Reports of Addresses Delivered at the Annual
Meetings of the Free Religious Association, Boston, 1870,
1871, 1872, 1873, 1875." In Mott, Lucretia Mott: Her Com-
plete Speeches, p. 359-65.
"Going to the Root of the Matter. Remarks Delivered at the
Pennsylvania Peace Society at Its Second Anniversary, Novem-
ber 19-20, 1868." In Mott, Lucretia Mott: Her Complete
Speeches, p. 311-4.
"I Am No Advocate of Passivity. Remarks Delivered at the
Twenty-Fourth Annual Meeting of the Pennsylvania Anti-
Slavery Society, October 25-26, 1860." In Mott, Lucretia
Mott: Her Complete Speeches, p. 261-2.
"I Am Not Here as a Representative of Any Sect. Remarks De-
livered at a Meeting Held in Boston, May 30, 1867." In Mott,
Lucretia Mott: Her Complete Speeches, p. 291-7.
"Improving Our Hearts and Enlarging Our Souls. Sermon Deli-
vered at Cherry Street Meeting, Philadelphia, September 16,
1849." In Mott, Lucretia Mott: Her Complete Speeches, p.
101-6.
"Infinite Source of Good. Remarks Delivered at the Fifteenth
Annual Meeting of Pennsylvania Anti-Slavery Society, West
Chester, Pennsylvania, October 25-26, 1852." In Mott,

Lucretia Mott: Her Complete Speeches, p. 197-8.
"Keep Yourselves From Idols. Sermons Delivered at Cherry
   Street Meeting, Philadelphia, March 27, 1850." In Mott,
   Lucretia Mott: Her Complete Speeches, p. 171-9.
"Laboring to Obtain the Divine Kingdom. Remarks Delivered to
   the Executive Committee on the Pennsylvania Peace Society,
   November 17, 1877." In Mott, Lucretia Mott: Her Complete
   Speeches, p. 391-2.
"Law of Progress. Speech Delivered at the Fourteenth Annual
   Meeting of the American Anti-Slavery Society, New York,
   May 9, 1848." In Mott, Lucretia Mott: Her Complete Speeches,
   p. 71-9.
"The Laws in Relation to Women. Remarks Delivered at the Na-
   tional Women's Rights Convention, Cleveland, Ohio, October
   5-7, 1853." In Mott, Lucretia Mott: Her Complete Speeches,
   p. 211-25.
"Likeness to Christ. Sermon Delivered at Cherry Street Meeting,
   Philadelphia, September 30, 1849." In Mott, Lucretia Mott:
   Her Complete Speeches, p. 107-13.
"Luther's Will. Remarks Delivered at a Woman's Rights Meeting,
   West Chester, Pennsylvania, June 2, 1852." In Mott, Lucretia
   Mott: Her Complete Speeches, p. 191-3.
"The Mothers Should Depart and Give Place to the Children.
   Remarks Delivered at the Eleventh National Woman's Rights
   Convention, New York, May 10, 1866." In Mott, Lucretia
   Mott: Her Complete Speeches, p. 267-70.
"The Natural Instincts of Man Are For Peace. Remarks Deli-
   vered at a Special Meeting of the Universal Peace Union, Cam-
   den, New Jersey, September 16, 1877." In Mott, Lucretia
   Mott: Her Complete Speeches, p. 389-90.
"The Necessity of Our Cause. Speech Delivered at the Meeting
   of the Pennsylvania Anti-Slavery Society, Philadelphia, Novem-
   ber 22, 1866." In Mott, Lucretia Mott: Her Complete Speeches,
   p. 283-5.
"No Greater Joy Than to See These Children Walking in the Anti-
   Slavery Path. Speech Delivered to the American Anti-Slavery
   Society at Its Third Decade Meeting, Philadelphia, December
   3-4, 1863." In Mott, Lucretia Mott: Her Complete Speeches,
   p. 263-6.
"One Standard of Goodness and Truth. Sermon Delivered at
   Bristol, Pennsylvania, June 6, 1860." In Mott, Lucretia Mott:
   Her Complete Speeches, p. 253-60.
"Place Woman in Equal Power. Remarks Delivered at the Thirti-
   eth Anniversary of the Seneca Fall Convention, July, 1878."
   In Mott, Lucretia Mott: Her Complete Speeches, p. 393.
"The Principles of the Co-Equality of Woman With Man. Remarks
   Delivered at the Woman's Rights Convention, New York,
   September 6-7, 1853." In Mott, Lucretia Mott: Her Complete
   Speeches, p. 203-10.
"Progress of the Religious World. Remarks Delivered to the Anti-
   Sabbath Convention, Boston, March 23-24, 1848." In Mott,

September 1-2, 1853." In Mott, <u>Lucretia Mott: Her Complete Speeches</u>, p. 199-201.

"The Truth of God ... The Righteousness of God. Sermon Delivered at Marlboro Chapel, Boston, September 23, 1841." In Mott, <u>Lucretia Mott: Her Complete Speeches</u>, p. 25-34.

"Unity of Spirit in the Bond of Peace. Sermon Delivered at Cherry Street Meeting, Philadelphia, September 2, 1849." In Mott, <u>Lucretia Mott: Her Complete Speeches</u>, p. 95-100.

"A Warlike Spirit. Remarks Delivered at the Woman's Peace Festival, Philadelphia, June 2, 1876." In Mott, <u>Lucretia Mott: Her Complete Speeches</u>, p. 379-83.

"We Have Food While Others Starve. Sermon Delivered at Cherry Street Meeting, Philadelphia, March 31, 1850." In Mott, <u>Lucretia Mott: Her Complete Speeches</u>, p. 181-9.

"When the Heart Is Attuned to Prayer. Discourse Delivered at the Second Unitarian Church, Brooklyn, New York, November 24, 1867." In Mott, <u>Lucretia Mott: Her Complete Speeches</u>, p. 299-310.

"Why Should Not Woman Seek to be a Reformer?" In <u>Outspoken Women</u>, p. 108-14.

"Worship in Spirit and in Truth. Discourse Delivered at Friends Meeting, Fifteenth Street, New York City, November 11, 1866." In Mott, <u>Lucretia Mott: Her Complete Speeches</u>, p. 271-81.

Moulton, Ruth.
"Psychological Challenges Confronting Women in the Sciences." In <u>Expanding the Role of Women in the Sciences</u>, p. 321-35.

Mouritsen, Maren M.
"Scholars of the Scriptures." In <u>Blueprints for Living</u>, v. 2, p. 119-28.
"Welcome (to a Panel on Mormon Women: A Response to the World)." In <u>Blueprints for Living</u>, v. 1, p. 92-3.

Mudd, Emily Hartshorne.
"The Historical Background of Ethical Considerations in Sex Research and Sex Therapy." In <u>Ethical Issues in Sex Therapy and Research</u>, p. 1-10.

Mueller, Kate Hevner.
"Education: The Realistic Approach." In <u>The Challenge to Women</u>, p. 111-29.

Muhlenfeld, Elisabeth S.
"Literary Elements in Mary Chesnut's Journal." In Reynolds Conference (2nd: 1975: University of South Carolina). <u>South Carolina Women Writers</u>, p. 245-83.
"Of Paradigm and Paradox: The Case of Mary Boykin Chesnut." In <u>Feminist Visions</u>, p. 130-8.

Mukhopadhyay, Carol.
  "Sati or Shakti: Women, Culture and Politics in India." In
    Perspectives on Power, p. 11-26.

Mulcahy, Elena Berezaluce.
  "Latinas in Educational Leadership: Chicago, Illinois." In Con-
    ference on the Educational and Occupational Needs of Hispanic
    Women (1976: Denver, CO and Washington, DC). Conference
    on the Educational and Occupational Needs of Hispanic Women,
    p. 75-86.

Mulhauser, Karen.
  "Statement." In U.S. Congress. House. Select Committee on
    Population. Fertility and Contraception in America, p. 116-9.
  "Testimony." In U.S. Congress. House. Committee on Educa-
    tion and Labor. Subcommittee on Select Education. Adoles-
    cent Pregnancy, p. 117-20.

Mullay, Camilla.
  "Peace Forever--And Now. John Paul II's Teaching on Peace
    and Peace-Making." Vital Speeches, 49 (April 1, 1983), 373-7.

Mullings, Leith.
  "Uneven Development: Class, Race, and Gender in the United
    States Before 1900." In Women's Work, p. 41-57.

Munter, Carol.
  "Fat and the Fantasy of Perfection." In Pleasure and Danger,
    p. 225-31.

Murphree, Mary C.
  "Brave New Office: The Changing World of the Legal Secretary."
    In My Troubles Are Going to Have Trouble With Me, p. 140-
    59.

Murphy, Angela.
  "Statement." In U.S. Congress. House. Select Committee on
    Aging. Problems of Aging Women, p. 9-10.

Murphy, Evelyn F.
  "Statement." In U.S. Congress. House. Committee on Ways
    and Means. Economic Equity Act and Related Tax and Pen-
    sion Reform, p. 147-9.

Murphy, Ruth E.
  "Statement." In U.S. Congress. Senate. Committee on Finance.
    Potential Inequities Affecting Women, pt. 2, p. 249-50.

Murphy, Suzanne.
  "Statement." In U.S. Congress. House. Committee on the

Budget. Task Force on Entitlements, Uncontrollables, and Indexing. Women and Children in Poverty, p. 5-7.

Murray, Linda Rae.
"Statement." In U.S. Congress. Senate. Committee on Labor and Human Resources. Subcommittee on Health and Scientific Research. Women in Science and Technology Equal Opportunity Act, 1979, p. 72-5.

Muscari, Ann.
"Statement." In U.S. Congress. Senate. Committee on Finance. Potential Inequities Affecting Women, p. 217-8.

Muscato, Pam.
"Statement." In U.S. Congress. Senate. Committee on Small Business. Women Entrepreneurs, p. 37-42.

Musil, Caryn McTighe.
"A Screen of Blooms." National Women's Studies Associations Perspectives, 3 (Fall, 1985), 3-6.

Myers, Margaret.
"Testimony." In U.S. Equal Employment Opportunity Commission. Hearings Before the U.S. Equal Employment Opportunity Commission on Job Segregation and Wage Discrimination, p. 602-10.

Myers, Toby.
"Statement." In U.S. Congress. House. Committee on Science and Technology. Subcommittee on Domestic and International Scientific Planning, Analysis, and Cooperation. Research into Violent Behavior: Domestic Violence, p. 184-5.

Nalepka, Joyce.
"Statement." In U.S. Congress. Senate. Committee on Labor and Human Resources. Subcommittee on Family and Human Services. Adolescents in Crisis, p. 94-7.

Nanez, Clotilde Falcon.
"Hispanic Clergy Wives: Their Contribution to United Methodism in the Southwest, Later Nineteenth Century to the Present." In Women in New Worlds, v. 1, p. 161-77.

Nation, Carry.
"Prohibition or Abolition--What It Means." In Outspoken Women, p. 115-7.

Near, Holly.
"Speaking Out." In My Country Is the Whole World, p. 252, 254.

Neary, Denise.
"Statement." In U.S. Congress. Senate. Committee on the Judiciary. Subcommittee on the Constitution. Constitutional Amendments Relating to Abortion, v. 1, p. 1120-2.

Neblett, Renee.
"The Black Women in America." In Cornell Conference on Women (1969: Cornell University). Proceedings, p. 83-4, 88, 90-1.

Nelms, Dorothy.
"Statement." In U.S. Congress. House. Committee on Post Office and Civil Service. Subcommittee on Investigations. Sexual Harassment in the Federal Government, pt. 1, p. 114-8, 121-8.
"Testimony." In U.S. Equal Employment Opportunity Commission. Hearings Before the U.S. Equal Employment Opportunity Commission on Job Segregation and Wage Discrimination, p. 425-42.

Nelson, Christine.
"Job: The Confessions of a Suffering Person." In Spinning a Sacred Yarn, p. 144-8.

Nentwig, M. Ruth.
"Technical Aspects of Sex Preselection." In The Custom-Made Child?, p. 181-6.

Nerad, Lori.
"Statement." In U.S. Congress. House. Committee on Energy and Commerce. Subcommittee on Health and the Environment. Pregnancy-Related Health Service, p. 260-1.

Nestle, Joan.
"The Feminine Question." In Pleasure and Danger, p. 232-41.

Netherton, Jean.
"Statement." In U.S. Congress. Joint Economic Committee. The Role of Older Women in the Work Force, p. 2-8.

Neville, Gwen Kennedy.
"Religious Socialization of Women Within U.S. Subcultures." In Sexism Religion and Women in the Church, p. 77-92.

Newell, Barbara W.
"Impact for Change: Students in Action." In Women in Action, p. 25-8.

Newman, Susan K.
"Statement." In U.S. Congress. Senate. Committee on Government Affairs. Permanent Subcommittee on Investigations. The Role of the Entertainment Industry in Deglamorizing Drug Use. Washington: U.S.G.P.O., 1985, p. 35-60.

Nichols, Patricia C.
  "Black Women in the Rural South: Conservative and Innovative."
    In Conference on the Sociology of the Languages of American
    Women (1976: New Mexico State University). Proceedings,
    p. 103-14.

Nicholson, Linda.
  "Feminist Theory: The Private and the Public." In Beyond
    Domination, p. 221-30.

Nieto, Consuelo.
  "Chicana Identity: Interaction of Culture and Sex Roles." In
    Conference on the Educational and Occupational Needs of
    Hispanic Women (1976: Denver, CO and Washington, DC).
    Conference on the Educational and Occupational Needs of
    Hispanic Women, p. 251-76.

Nieva, Veronica F.
  "The Feminization of the Labor Force: Research for Industrial/
    Organizational Psychology." In The Changing Composition of
    the Workforce, p. 77-104.

Nievera, Fe C.
  "Some Effects of Childrearing Practices on the Value Systems of
    Asian-American Women." In Conference on the Educational
    and Occupational Needs of Asian-Pacific-American Women
    (1976: San Francisco, CA). Conference on the Educational
    and Occupational Needs of Asian-Pacific-American Women, p.
    39-64.

Nightingale, Demetra Smith.
  "Statement." In U.S. Congress. House. Committee on Govern-
    ment Operations. Intergovernmental Relations and Human Re-
    sources Subcommittee. Barriers to Self-Sufficiency for Single
    Female Heads of Families, p. 18-23.

Nin, Anaïs.
  "The Artist as Magician." In Nin, A Woman Speaks, p. 181-96.
  "Furrawn." In Nin, A Woman Speaks, p. 200-6.
  "A New Center of Gravity." In Nin, A Woman Speaks, p. 1-5.
  "The Personal Life Deeply Lived." In Nin, A Woman Speaks,
    p. 148-62.
  "Proceed from the Dream." In Nin, A Woman Speaks, p. 115-31.
  "Refusal to Despair." In Nin, A Woman Speaks, p. 6-18.
  "The Unveiling of Woman." In Nin, A Woman Speaks, p. 79-95.
  "Women Reconstructing the World." In Nin, A Woman Speaks,
    p. 35-56.

Nishi, Setsuko Mitsunaga.
  "Chairperson's Report." In Conference on the Educational and
    Occupational Needs of Asian-Pacific-American Women (1976:

San Francisco, CA). Conference on the Educational and Occupational Needs of Asian-Pacific-American Women, p. 160-80.

Nixon, Janet.
"Statement." In U.S. Congress. House. Select Committee on Aging. Subcommittee on Health and Long-Term Care. Progress in Controlling Breast Cancer, p. 43-5.

Noble, Sallie.
"Testimony." In U.S. Commission on Civil Rights. Hearing Before the U.S. Commission on Civil Rights Held in Chicago, v. 2, p. 278-82.

Nochlin, Linda.
"Lost and Found: Once More the Fallen Woman." In Feminism and Art History, p. 221-45.

Noel, Rachel.
"Testimony." In U.S. Commission on Civil Rights. Hearing Before the U.S. Commission on Civil Rights Held in Denver, p. 7-17.
"Welcoming Statement." In U.S. Commission on Civil Rights. Hearing Before the U.S. Commission on Civil Rights Held in Denver, p. 5-7.

Nolan-Haley, Jacqueline.
"Statement." In U.S. Congress. House. Committee on the Judiciary. Subcommittee on Civil and Constitutional Rights. Proposed Constitutional Amendments on Abortion, p. 261-7.

Norsigian, Judy.
"Response (To Woman-Controlled Birth Control)." In Birth Control and Controlling Birth, p. 85-8.
"Statement." In U.S. Congress. House. Select Committee on Population. Fertility and Contraception in America, pt. 3, p. 71-4, 76-7, 82-5.
"Testimony." In U.S. Congress. House. Committee on Interstate and Foreign Commerce. Subcommittee on Oversight and Investigations. Nurse Midwifery: Consumers' Freedom of Choice, p. 18-22.

Nortell, Eleanor Tomlinson.
"Testimony." In U.S. Commission on Civil Rights. Hearing Before the U.S. Commission on Civil Rights Held in Chicago, v. 1, p. 424-6.

North, Jeanne Foote.
"Women Participants in the Food Marketing System in West Africa." In International Conference on Women and Food (1978: University of Arizona). A Conference on the Role of Women in Meeting Basic Food and Water Needs in Developing Countries, p. 103-12.

North, Jeryl.
    "Statement." In U.S. Congress. Senate. Select Committee on
        Aging. Women in Our Aging Society, p. 28-9.

Norton, Eleanor Holmes.
    "Opening Statement." In U.S. Equal Employment Opportunity
        Commission. Hearings Before the U.S. Equal Employment
        Opportunity Commission on Job Segregation and Wage Dis-
        crimination, p. 1-10.
    "Speech at the National Women's Political Caucus Conference,
        July, 1981." Ms., 10 (October 1981), 92-3.
    "Statement." In U.S. Congress. House. Committee on Educa-
        tion and Labor. Subcommittee on Employment Opportunities.
        Oversight Hearings on Equal Employment Opportunity and
        Affirmative Action, pt. 1, p. 99-106.
    "Statement." In U.S. Congress. House. Committee on Post
        Office and Civil Service. Subcommittee on Human Resources.
        Pay Equity, pt. 1, p. 39-50.
    "Statement." In U.S. Congress. House. Committee on Post
        Office and Civil Service. Subcommittee on Investigations.
        Sexual Harassment in the Federal Government, pt. 1, p. 40-
        9, 90-8.
    "Statement." In U.S. Congress. House. Committee on the
        Budget. Task Force on Entitlements, Uncontrollables, and
        Indexing. Women and Children in Poverty, p. 30-6.
    "Statement." In U.S. Congress. Senate. Committee on Labor
        and Human Resources. Sexual Discrimination in the Work-
        place, 1981, p. 465-74, 535-40.
    "Women in Crisis: The Issues." In Women in Crisis Conference
        (1st: 1979: New York, NY) Women in Crisis, p. 24-31.

Norton, Mary T.
    "Testimony." In U.S. Congress. House. Committee on Ways
        and Means. Birth Control, (1932) p. 66-70.
    "Testimony." In U.S. Congress. House. Committee on the
        Judiciary. Birth Control, (1934) p. 147-50.
    "Testimony." In U.S. Congress. Senate. Committee on the
        Judiciary. Birth Control, (1931) p. 50-3.

Norwood, Janet.
    "The Facts of Life for a Teen-Aged Girl." In Young Women and
        Employment, p. 7-10.
    "Statement." In U.S. Congress. House. Committee on Post
        Office and Civil Service. Subcommittee on Human Resources.
        Pay Equity, p. 51-7, 62-4.

Noschese, Christine.
    "Ethnic Women and the Media." In Conference on the Educational
        and Occupational Needs of White Ethnic Women (1978: Boston
        MA). Conference on the Educational and Occupational Needs
        of White Ethnic Women, p. 41-53.

Novello, Dorothy J.
"Prospectives for Nursing: Forces for Forecasting: Organizational Issues." In U.S. Health Resources Administration. Division of Nursing. Prospectives for Nursing, p. 25-8.

Nuland-Ames, Linda.
"Statement." In U.S. Congress. House. Committee on Ways and Means. Subcommittee on Social Security. Social Security Dependents' Benefits, p. 23-5.

Nuss, Shirley A.
"The Role of Women in Underdeveloped Countries: Some Sociological Issues Concerning Conflict and Peace." In The Role of Women in Conflict and Peace, p. 71-81.

Nussbaum, Karen.
"Statement." In U.S. Congress. House. Committee on Post Office and Civil Service. Subcommittee on Human Resources. Pay Equity, pt. 1, p. 87-90.
"Statement." In U.S. Congress. Senate. Committee on Labor and Human Resources. Sex Discrimination in the Workplace, 1981, p. 29-30.

Oakar, Mary Rose.
"Statement." In General Farm Bill of 1981. Washington: U.S.G.P.O., 1981, pt. 2, p. 5-8.
"Statement." In U.S. Congress. House. Committee on Agriculture. Subcommittee on Domestic Marketing, Consumer Relations, and Nutrition. Review of the Surplus Commodity Distribution Program. Washington: U.S.G.P.O., 1984, p. 27-8.
"Statement." In U.S. Congress. House. Committee on Appropriations. Subcommittee on Department of Transportation and Related Agencies Appropriations. Department of Transportation and Related Agencies Appropriations for 1985. Washington: U.S.G.P.O., 1984, pt. 7, p. 651-6.
"Statement." In U.S. Congress. House. Committee on Appropriations. Subcommittee on the Department of the Interior and Related Agencies. Department of the Interior and Related Agencies Appropriations for 1986. Washington: U.S.G.P.O., 1985, pt. 11, p. 1229-35.
"Statement." In U.S. Congress. House. Committee on Banking, Finance, and Urban Affairs. How the Financial System Can Best Be Shaped to Meet the Needs of the American People: Financial Deregulation. Washington: U.S.G.P.O., 1984, p. 320-56.

"Statement." In U.S. Congress. House. Committee on Education and Labor. Subcommittee on Postsecondary Education. The Soviet-Eastern European Research and Training Act of 1983. Washington: U.S.G.P.O., 1984, p. 27-31.

"Statement." In U.S. Congress. House. Committee on Energy and Commerce. Subcommittee on Fossil and Synthetic Fuels. Natural Gas Issues. Washington: U.S.G.P.O., 1983, p. 979-86.

"Statement." In U.S. Congress. House. Committee on Foreign Affairs. Subcommittee on Inter-American Affairs. U.S. Policy Toward El Salvador. Washington: U.S.G.P.O., 1981, p. 7-16.

"Statement." In U.S. Congress. House. Committee on Government Operations. Government Information, Justice, and Agriculture Subcommittee. Review of USDA's Surplus Dairy Products Donation Program. Washington: U.S.G.P.O., 1983, p. 8-9.

"Statement." In U.S. Congress. House. Committee on Government Operations. Manpower and Housing Subcommittee. Equal Employment Opportunity Commission's Handling of Pay Equity Cases, p. 3-4.

"Statement." In U.S. Congress. House. Committee on Merchant Marine and Fisheries. Subcommittee on Panama Canal/Outer Canal Zone Area. Washington: U.S.G.P.O., 1984, p. 9-11.

"Statement." In U.S. Congress. House. Committee on Post Office and Civil Service. Subcommittee on Compensation and Employee Benefits. Federal Pay Equity Act of 1984, pt. 2, p. 131-3.

"Statement." In U.S. Congress. House. Committee on Post Office and Civil Service. Subcommittee on Compensation and Employee Benefits. Options for Conducting a Pay Equity Study, p. 19-22, 151-2, 207-10, 451-2, 555-8.

"Statement." In U.S. Congress. House. Committee on Post Office and Civil Service. Subcommittee on Human Resources. Fair Reduction in Force Practices Act of 1984. Washington: U.S.G.P.O., 1985, p. 38-45.

"Statement." In U.S. Congress. House. Committee on Post Office and Civil Service. Subcommittee on Human Resources. Federal Employees Flexible and Compressed Work Schedules Act. Washington: U.S.G.P.O., 1985, p. 50-3.

"Statement." In U.S. Congress. House. Committee on Post Office and Civil Service. Subcommittee on Human Resources. Pay Equity, pt. 1, p. 4-5.

"Statement." In U.S. Congress. House. Committee on Public Works and Transportation. Subcommittee on Surface Transportation. Review of the Implementation of the Surface Transportation Assistance Act of 1982. Washington: U.S.G.P.O., 1983, p. 195-200.

"Statement." In U.S. Congress. House. Committee on Public Works and Transportation. Subcommittee on Water Resources. Proposed Water Resources Development Projects of the U.S.

Army Corps of Engineers. Washington: U.S.G.P.O., 1982, p. 1820-30.

"Statement." In U.S. Congress. House. Committee on the Judiciary. Subcommittee on Civil and Constitutional Rights. School Desegregation. Washington: U.S.G.P.O., 1981, p. 600-11.

"Statement." In U.S. Congress. House. Committee on Ways and Means. Subcommittee on Health. Administration's Proposed Budget Cuts Affecting the Medicare Programs. Washington: U.S.G.P.O., 1982, p. 289-94.

"Statement." In U.S. Congress. House. Committee on Ways and Means. Subcommittee on Public Assistance and Unemployment Compensation. The Administration's Proposal for Additional Weeks of Unemployment Compensation. Washington: U.S.G.P.O., 1980, p. 44-6.

"Statement." In U.S. Congress. House. Committee on Ways and Means. Subcommittee on Social Security. Financing Problems of the Social Security System. Washington: U.S.G.P.O., 1983, p. 53-8.

"Statement." In U.S. Congress. House. Committee on Ways and Means. Subcommittee on Social Security. Social Security as an Independent Agency. Washington: U.S.G.P.O., 1985, p. 122-7.

"Statement." In U.S. Congress. House. Committee on Ways and Means. Subcommittee on Social Security. Social Security Financing Issues. Washington: U.S.G.P.O., 1981, p. 65-6.

"Statement." In U.S. Congress. House. Committee on Ways and Means. Subcommittee on Social Security. Treatment of Men and Women Under the Social Security Program, p. 20-5.

"Statement." In U.S. Congress. House. Select Committee on Aging. Subcommittee on Health and Long-Term Care. Elder Abuse, p. 4.

"Statement." In U.S. Congress. House. Select Committee on Aging. Subcommittee on Health and Long-Term Care. Progress in Controlling Breast Cancer, p. 37-8.

"Statement." In U.S. Congress. House. Select Committee on Aging. Subcommittee on Retirement Income and Employment. National Policy Proposals Affecting Midlife Women, p. 5-6.

"Statement." In U.S. Congress. House. Select Committee on Aging. Subcommittee on Retirement Income and Employment. Task Force on Social Security and Women. Inequities Toward Women in the Social Security System, p. 1-3.

"Statement." In U.S. Congress. House. Select Committee on Aging. Subcommittee on Retirement Income and Employment. Task Force on Social Security and Women. Earning Sharing Implementation Plan, p. 1-2.

"Statement." In U.S. Congress. House. Select Committee on Aging. Subcommittee on Retirement Income and Employment. Task Force on Social Security and Women. Treatment of Women Under Social Security, v. 1, p. 1-3, v. 3, p. 1-2, v. 4, p. 1-3.

"Statement." In U.S. Congress. Senate. Committee on Labor and Human Resources. Subcommittee on Aging. Alzheimer's Disease and Related Disorders. Washington: U.S.G.P.O., 1985, p. 3-4.

"Statement." In U.S. Congress. Senate. Special Committee on Aging. Women in Our Aging Society, p. 4-5.

"Testimony." In U.S. Congress. Senate. Special Committee on Aging. Adapting Social Security to a Changing Work Force, p. 5-14.

O'Bannon, Helen B.
"The Social Scene: Isolation and Frustration." In Women in Engineering--Beyond Recruitment, p. 69-76.

Oberstar, Jo.
"Testimony." In U.S. Congress. House. Select Committee on Aging. Subcommittee on Retirement Income and Employment. National Policy Proposals Affecting Midlife Women, p. 53-5.

Obitko, Maryellen.
"Custodians of a House of Resistance: Black Women Respond to Slavery." In Women & Men, p. 256-69.

O'Brien, Sharon.
"Tomboyism and Adolescent Conflict: Three Nineteenth-Century Case Studies." In Conference on the History of Women (1977: St. Paul, MN). Woman's Being, Woman's Place, p. 351-72.

Ochshorn, Judith.
"The Contest Between Androgyny and Patriarchy in Early Western Tradition." In Feminist Visions, p. 66-83.

"Reclaiming Our Past." In Women's Spirit Bonding, p. 281-92.

O'Connell, Marjorie A.
"Statement." In U.S. Congress. House. Committee on Ways and Means. Economic Equity Act and Related Tax and Pension Reform, p. 87-9.

"Statement." In U.S. Congress. Senate. Committee on Finance. Potential Inequities Affecting Women, pt. 1, p. 197-8.

O'Connor, Reena.
"Excerpted Testimony from the Southern California Hearings on the Feminization of Poverty." Signs, 10 (Winter 1984), 408-9.

O'Connor, Sandra Day.
"Statement." In U.S. Congress. Senate. Committee on the Judiciary. Nomination of Sandra Day O'Connor. Washington: U.S.G.P.O., 1982, p. 57-113, 115-221, 237-55.

"Testimony of Sandra Day O'Connor (Before Senate Judiciary Committee, September 9, 10, and 11, 1981 on Her Appointment to the Supreme Court)." In Historic Documents of 1981, p. 579-90.

O'Donnell, Saranne Price.
"Distress from the Press: Antifeminism in the Editorials of James Monroe Buckley, 1880-1912." In Women in New Worlds, v. 2, p. 76-93.

Oesterle, Patricia M.
"Working Couples and Child Care." In The Woman in Management, p. 54-6.

Oettinger, Katherine Brownell.
"Maternal Employment and Children. In Conference on Work in the Lives of Married Women (1957: Columbia University). Work in the Lives of Married Women, p. 133-49.

O'Farrell, Brigid.
"Women and Nontraditional Blue Collar Jobs in the 1980s." In Women in the Workplace, p. 135-68.

O'Hare, Kate Richards.
"Farewell Address of a Socialist." In Outspoken Women, p. 118-22. Also in O'Hare, Kate Richards O'Hare, p. 194-201.
"Good Morning! Mr. American Citizen." In O'Hare, Kate Richards O'Hare, p. 165-70.
"Speech Delivered in Court by Kate Richards O'Hare Before Being Sentenced by Judge Wade." In O'Hare, Kate Richards O'Hare, p. 170-81.

O'Hern, Elizabeth M.
"Women in the Biological Sciences." In Expanding the Role of Women in the Sciences, p. 110-24.

Olson, Laura Katz.
"Sex-Linked Values: Their Impacts on Women in Engineering." In Women's Studies, p. 87-100.

Omolade, Barbara.
"Black Women and Feminism." In The Future of Difference, p. 247-56.

Oneglia, Stewart B.
"Keynote Address." In Public Forum on Women's Rights and Responsibilities (1978: Las Vegas, NV). Public Forum on Women's Rights and Responsibilities, p. 3-6.

O'Neill, Alyse.
"Statement." In U.S. Congress. House. Committee on Ways and Means. Subcommittee on Social Security. Treatment of Men and Women Under the Social Security Program, p. 116, 118-20.

O'Neill, June.
"Comparable Worth as a Remedy for Sex Discrimination." In

Comparable Worth: Issue for the 80's, p. 11-5.
"Statement." In U.S. Congress. Joint Economic Committee.
American Women: Three Decades of Change, p. 44-9.

O'Reilly, Jane.
"Speech at the National Women's Political Caucus Conference,
July, 1981." Ms., 10 (October 1981), 93.

O'Reilly, Leonora.
"Leonora O'Reilly's Congressional Statement." In Eisenstein,
Sarah. Give Us Bread But Give Us Roses, p. 155-6.
"Women's Opportunities in the Civil Service." In Outspoken
Women, p. 123-6.

Oren, Laura.
"The Welfare of Women in Laboring Families: England, 1860-
1950." In Clio's Consciousness Raised, p. 226-40.

Orijel, Joanne.
"Testimony." In U.S. Congress. House. Committee on Energy
and Commerce. Subcommittee on Health and the Environment.
Health and the Environment Miscellaneous, pt. 5, p. 288-9.

O'Riordan, Anne.
"Statement." In U.S. Congress. House. Select Committee on
Aging. Subcommittee on Health and Long-Term Care. Elder
Abuse, p. 89-90.

Orr, Bea N.
"Statement." In U.S. Congress. Senate. Committee on Labor
and Human Resources. Subcommittee on Education, Arts and
Humanities. Civil Rights Act of 1984, p. 394-5.

Ortega, Katherine Davalos.
"Keynote Address at the Republican National Convention."
Vital Speeches, 50 (September 15, 1984), 712-3.

Ortiz, Francisca Garcia.
"Address to the First Feminist Congress in Mexico, 1916." Signs,
5 (Autumn 1979), 197-9.

Osako, Masako Murakami.
"The Effects of Asian-American Kinship Systems on Women's Edu-
cational and Occupational Attainment." In Conference on the
Educational and Occupational Needs of Asian-Pacific-American
Women (1976: San Francisco, CA). Conference on the Edu-
cational and Occupational Needs of Asian-Pacific-American
Women, p. 211-36.

Oschshorn, Judith.
"The Contest Between Androgyny and Patriarchy in Early Western
Traditions." In Feminist Visions, p. 66-87.

Osofsky, Joy.
"Education and Equality for Women." In Cornell Conference on
Women (1969: Cornell University). Proceedings, p. 39-40,
43.

Osterman, Gail Bryant.
"Does Becoming a Parent Mean Falling Off the Fast Track?" In
The Woman in Management, p. 57-60.

Ostriker, Alicia.
"The Thieves of Language: Women Poets and Revisionist Myth-
making." In Coming to Light, p. 10-36.

Ott, Mary Diederich.
"Attitudes and Experiences of Freshman Engineers at Cornell."
In Women in Engineering--Beyond Recruitment, p. 13-8.

Ottley, Joann.
"A Musical Stewardship--Teacher of Life." In A Woman's
Choices, p. 86-97.

Overly, Cathy.
"Statement." In U.S. Congress. House. Committee on Post
Office and Civil Service. Subcommittee on Compensation
and Employee Benefits. Options for Conducting a Pay Equity
Study, p. 545-7.

Owens, Margaret R.
"Career Conflicts and Solutions." In Training Conference (1st:
1984: Washington, DC). Interagency Committee on Women
in Federal Law Enforcement, p. 60-3.

Page, Carol A.
"Charlotte Manye Maxeke: Missionary and Educator in South
Africa, 1901-1930." In Women in New Worlds, v. 2, p. 281-9.

Pais, Sara Via.
"Shapes of the Feminine Experience in Art." In Women, the
Arts, and the 1920s in Paris and New York, p. 49-55.

Palast, Geri.
"Statement." In U.S. Congress. House. Committee on Educa-
tion and Labor. Subcommittee on Labor-Management Relations.
Legislative Hearing on Pension Equity for Women, p. 39-40.
"Statement." In U.S. Congress. House. Committee on Ways
and Means. Economic Equity Act and Related Tax and Pen-
sion Reform, p. 66-8.
"Testimony." In U.S. Congress. House. Committee on Energy
and Commerce. Subcommittee on Health and the Environment.
Health and the Environment Miscellaneous, pt. 4, p. 74-5.

Palmer, Emily.
  "Testimony." In U.S. Congress. House. Committee on Educa-
    tion and Labor. Adolescent Pregnancy, p. 51-6.
  "Testimony." In U.S. Congress. Senate. Committee on Human
    Resources. Adolescent Health, Services, and Pregnancy Pre-
    vention Care Act of 1978, p. 461-4.

Palmer, Phyllis Marynick.
  "Housework and Domestic Labor: Racial and Technological
    Change." In My Troubles Are Going to Have Trouble With
    Me, p. 80-91.
  "Testimony." In U.S. Equal Employment Opportunity Commission.
    Hearings Before the U.S. Equal Employment Opportunity Com-
    mission on Job Segregation and Wage Discrimination, p. 196-
    213.
  "White Women/Black Women: The Dualism of Female Identity and
    Experience in the United States." Feminist Studies, 9 (Spring
    1983), 151-70.

Palmer, Sally.
  "The Wounded Healer." In Spinning a Sacred Yarn, p. 149-52.

Panzini, Marianne.
  "Statement." In U.S. Congress. Senate. Committee on Labor
    and Human Resources. The Coming Decade, p. 614-6.

Papanek, Hanna.
  "The Differential Impact of Programs and Policies on Women in
    Development." In Women and Technological Change in De-
    veloping Countries, p. 215-27.
  "Low-Income Countries." In Women Workers in Fifteen Countries,
    p. 81-8.

Parker, Brenda.
  "Speech by Brenda Parker, President, Future Homemakers of
    America." In U.S. National Commission on the Observance
    of International Women's Year. The Spirit of Houston, p. 233.

Parlee, Mary Brown.
  "Psychological Aspects of Menstruation, Childbirth, and Meno-
    pause." In Psychology of Women, p. 179-238.

Parr, Carol C.
  "Statement." In U.S. Congress. House. Committee on Armed
    Services. Subcommittee on Military Personnel. Women in the
    Military, p. 201-10.
  "Testimony." In U.S. Congress. Joint Economic Committee.
    Subcommittee on Priorities and Economy in Government. The
    Role of Women in the Military, p. 97-102.

Parr, Joyce.
  "The Art of Quilting: Thoughts From a Contemporary Quilter."

In GLCA Women's Studies Conference (7th: 1981). <u>Towards a Feminist Transformation of the Academy III</u>, p. 47-51.
"Effects of Isolation on the Woman Artist." In GLCA Women's Studies Conference (5th: 1979). <u>Towards a Feminist Transformation of the Academy</u>, p. 31-3.

Parsons, Jacqueline.
"The Effects of Teachers' Expectancies and Attribution of Students' Expectancies of Success in Mathematics." In <u>Women's Lives</u>, p. 373-9.

Parsons, Kathryn Pyne.
"Moral Revolution." In <u>Prism of Sex</u>, p. 189-227.

Parturier, Francoise.
"Is the Question of Women a Political Question?" In Cornell Conference on Women (1969: Cornell University). <u>Proceedings</u>, p. 31-2.

Paschall, Eliza.
"Statement." In U.S. Congress. Senate. Committee on Labor and Human Resources. <u>Sex Discrimination in the Workplace</u>, p. 451-4.

Pasternak, Beatrice.
"Created in Her Image." In <u>Spinning a Sacred Yarn</u>, p. 153-8.

Patai, Daphne.
"Jorge Amado's Heroines and the Ideological Double Standard." In <u>Women in Latin American Literature</u>, p. 15-36.

Paterson, Katherine.
"Newbery Medal Acceptance." <u>Horn Book</u>, 57 (1981), 385-93.

Patton, Carolyn.
"Statement." In U.S. Congress. Senate. Committee on Small Business. <u>Federal Contracting Opportunities for Minority and Women-Owned Business</u>, p. 19-21.

Paul, Alice.
"Forming the Woman's Party." In <u>Outspoken Women</u>, p. 127-9.

Payne, Joyce.
"Black Women in Urban Schools." In <u>Women & Men</u>, p. 196-213.

Peacock, Carol.
"The Massachusetts Experiment Towards Equal Service for Girls." In <u>Today's Girls: Tomorrow's Women</u>, p. 67-9.
"Young Female Offenders in Massachusetts: Toward Leaving the Juvenile Justice System Successfully." In Women in Crisis Conference (1st: 1979: New York, NY). <u>Women in Crisis</u>, p. 218-20.

Peak, Jane.
"Statement." In U.S. Congress. House. Committee on Ways and Means. Subcommittee on Social Security. Treatment of Men and Women Under the Social Security Program, p. 191-7.

Peissachowitz, Nelly A.
"Advisability of Maintaining People in Their Own Homes." In Older Women in the City, p. 135-41.

Pendergrass, Virginia.
"Stress in the Lives of Female Law Enforcement Officials." In Training Conference (1st: 1984: Washington, DC). Interagency Committee on Women in Federal Law Enforcement, p. 15-8.

Penfield, Pauline.
"Testimony." In U.S. Congress. House. Select Committee on Aging. Subcommittee on Retirement Income and Employment. Task Force on Social Security and Women. Treatment of Women Under Social Security, p. 167-8.

Penman, Robbie.
"Testimony." In U.S. Congress. House. Select Committee on Aging. Subcommittee on Retirement Income and Employment. Task Force on Social Security and Women. Treatment of Women Under Social Security, p. 161.

Perdue, Theda.
"Southern Indians and the Cult of True Womanhood." In The Web of Southern Social Relations, p. 35-51.

Perlman, Helen Harris.
"The Problem-Solving Model in Social Casework." In Charlotte Towle Memorial Symposium on Comparative Theoretical Approaches to Casework Practice (1969: University of Chicago). Theories of Social Casework, p. 129-79.

Perlman, Nancy D.
"Testimony." In U.S. Congress. House. Committee on Post Office and Civil Service. Subcommittee on Human Resources. Pay Equity, pt. 1, p. 64-72.
"Testimony." In Hearings Before the U.S. Equal Employment Opportunity Commission on Job Segregation and Wage Discrimination, p. 643-54.

Perreault, Geraldine.
"Contemporary Feminist Perspectives on Women and Higher Education." In Beyond Domination, p. 283-309.

Perrucci, Carolyn C.
"Central Issues Facing Women in the Science-Based Professions." In Women in Scientific and Engineering Professions, p. 1-16.

Perun, Pamela J.
"The Undergraduate Woman: Theme and Variations." In The
Undergraduate Woman, p. 3-14.

Perry, Bonita L.
"Three Career Traps for Women. Caution: Your Career May
Be Hazardous to Your Health." Vital Speeches, 48 (November
15, 1981), 76-9.

Petchesky, Rosalind Pollack.
"Reproduction and Class Divisions Among Women." In Class,
Race and Sex, p. 221-42.

Peters, Laura Alice.
"Statement." In U.S. Congress. Senate. Committee on Labor
and Human Resources. The Coming Decade, pt. 2, p. 101-3.

Peterson, Esther.
"Statement." In U.S. Congress. House. Committee on Agricul-
ture. Subcommittee on Dairy and Poultry. Nitrite Restriction
on Poultry. Washington: U.S.G.P.O., 1978, p. 10-20.
"Statement." In U.S. Congress. House. Committee on Agriculture. Subcommittee on Domestic Marketing, Consumer Rela-
tions, and Nutrition. Nutrition Education. Washington:
U.S.G.P.O., 1977, p. 149-62.
"Statement." In U.S. Congress. House. Committee on Appro-
priations. Subcommittee on HUD-Independent Agencies.
Department of Housing and Urban Development--Independent
Agencies Appropriations for 1980. Washington: U.S.G.P.O.,
1979, pt. 1, p. 329-71.
"Statement." In U.S. Congress. House. Committee on Govern-
ment Operations. Commerce, Consumer, and Monetary Affairs
Subcommittee. U.S. Export of Banned Products. Washington:
U.S.G.P.O., 1978, p. 2-32.
"Statement." In U.S. Congress. House. Committee on Govern-
ment Operations. Legislation and National Security Subcom-
mittee. Agency for Consumer Protection. Washington:
U.S.G.P.O., 1977, p. 38-53.
"Statement." In U.S. Congress. House. Committee on Inter-
state and Foreign Commerce. Subcommittee on Consumer
Protection and Finance. Installation of Passive Restraints in
Automobiles. Washington: U.S.G.P.O., 1978, p. 239-45.
"Statement." In U.S. Congress. House. Committee on Inter-
state and Foreign Commerce. Subcommittee on Health and
the Environment. Food Safety and Nutrition Amendments of
1978. Washington: U.S.G.P.O., 1978, p. 99-106.
"Statement." In U.S. Congress. House. Committee on Science
and Technology. Subcommittee on Domestic and International
Scientific Planning, Analysis and Cooperation. Nutrition-
Related Oversight Review. Washington: U.S.G.P.O., 1977,
p. 566-77.

"Statement." In U.S. Congress. House. Committee on the Budget. Task Force on Inflation. Hearings Before the Task Force on Inflation of the Committee on the Budget.... Washington: U.S.G.P.O., 1979, pt. 2, p. 179-85.

"Statement." In U.S. Congress. House. Committee on the Judiciary. Subcommittee on Courts, Civil Liberties, and the Administration of Justice. Resolution of Minor Disputes. Washington: U.S.G.P.O., 1979, p. 64-74.

"Statement." In U.S. Congress. Senate. Committee on Agriculture, Nutrition, and Forestry. Subcommittee on Nutrition. Nutrition Labeling and Information. Washington: U.S.G.P.O., 1978, pt. 1, p. 13-24.

"Statement." In U.S. Congress. Senate. Committee on Appropriations. Subcommittee on HUD-Independent Agencies. Department of House and Urban Development and Certain Independent Agencies Appropriations for Fiscal Year 1980. Washington: U.S.G.P.O., 1979, pt. 1, p. 105-30.

"Statement." In U.S. Congress. Senate. Committee on Banking, Housing, and Urban Affairs. Subcommittee on Consumer Affairs. Electronic Fund Transfer Consumer Protection Act. Washington: U.S.G.P.O., 1977, p. 3-7.

"Statement." In U.S. Congress. Senate. Committee on Commerce, Science, and Transportation. Household Goods Transportation Act of 1979. Washington: U.S.G.P.O., 1979, p. 32-9, 355-68.

"Statement." In U.S. Congress. Senate. Committee on Commerce, Science, and Transportation. Subcommittee for Consumers. Cost of Government Regulations to the Consumer. Washington: U.S.G.P.O., 1978, p. 76-93.

"Statement." In U.S. Congress. Senate. Committee on Commerce, Science, and Transportation. Subcommittee for Consumers. Oversight of the Federal Trade Commission. Washington: U.S.G.P.O., 1979, p. 167-77.

"Statement." In U.S. Congress. Senate. Committee on Commerce, Science, and Transportation. Subcommittee for Consumers. Passive Restraint Rule. Washington: U.S.G.P.O., 1977, p. 343-9.

"Statement." In U.S. Congress. Senate. Committee on Energy and Natural Resources. Subcommittee on Parts and Recreation. Eleanor Roosevelt National Historic Site. Washington: U.S.G.P.O., 1977, p. 19-20.

"Statement." In U.S. Congress. Senate. Committee on Governmental Affairs. The Consumer Protection Act of 1977. Washington: U.S.G.P.O., 1977, p. 4-12.

"Statement." In U.S. Congress. Senate. Committee on the Judiciary. Subcommittee on Antitrust and Monopoly. Public Impact of Natural Gas Price Deregulation. Washington: U.S.G.P.O., 1977, p. 18-20.

"Statement." In U.S. Congress. Senate. Committee on the Judiciary. Subcommittee on Antitrust, Monopoly, and Business Rights. Energy Antimonopoly Act of 1979. Washington: U.S.G.P.O., 1979, pt. 2, p. 627-33.

Peterson, Grethe Ballif.
"Priesthood and Sisterhood: an Equal Partnership." In Blueprints for Living, v. 2, p. 49-56.

Peurala, Alice.
"Statement." In U.S. Congress. House. Committee on Education and Labor. Subcommittee on Employment Opportunities. Oversight Hearings on Equal Employment Opportunity and Affirmative Action, pt. 2, p. 96-7.

Pfafflin, Sheila M.
"Equal Opportunity for Women in Science." In Expanding the Role of Women in the Sciences, p. 341-4.
"Statement." In Symposium on Minorities and Women in Science and Technology (1981: Washington, DC). Symposium on Minorities and Women in Science and Technology, p. 47-9.

Pharr, Susan J.
"Tea and Power: The Anatomy of a Conflict." In Perspectives on Power, p. 37-49.

Phelps, Edith B.
"Keynote." In Today's Girls: Tomorrow's Women, p. 6-9.
"A Look Ahead." In Today's Girls: Tomorrow's Women, p. 82-3.

Phelps, Jamie.
"Racism and the Bonding of Women." In Women's Spirit Bonding, p. 70-4.

Phillips, Elizabeth.
"The Prickly Art of Housekeeping: Reading Emily Dickinson." In Conference on Women's Studies and the Humanities (1983: University of North Carolina at Greensboro). Equity and Excellence, p. 19-23.

Phillips, Ruth M.
"Women in Medicine." In Toward the Second Decade, p. 49-58.

Pian, Canta.
"Immigration of Asian Women and the Status of Recent Asian Women Immigrants." In Conference on the Educational and Occupational Needs of Asian-Pacific-American Women (1976: San Francisco, CA). Conference on the Educational and Occupational Needs of Asian-Pacific-American Women, p. 181-210.

Piercy, Day.
"Statement." In U.S. Congress. House. Committee on Education and Labor. Subcommittee on Employment Opportunities. Oversight Hearings on Equal Employment Opportunity and Affirmative Action, pt. 2, p. 44-6.
"Statement." In U.S. Congress. House. Committee on Education

and Labor. Subcommittee on Employment Opportunities.
Oversight Hearings on the OFCCP's Proposed Affirmative Action Regulations, p. 249-53.

Pierre, (Mrs.) Hubert Werthman.
"Statement." In U.S. Congress. House. Committee on Armed
Services. Subcommittee on Military Personnel. Women in the
Military, p. 222-3.

Pilpel, Harriet F.
"Statement." In U.S. Congress. House. Select Committee on
Population. Fertility and Contraception in America, pt. 2,
p. 137-44.
"Testimony." In U.S. Congress. House. Committee on the
Judiciary. Subcommittee on Civil and Constitutional Rights.
Proposed Constitutional Amendments on Abortion, p. 188-95.

Pines, Marion.
"Statement." In U.S. Congress. Senate. Committee on Labor
and Human Resources. The Coming Decade, p. 572-5.

Pinotti, Mary.
"Is the Question of Women a Political Question?" In Cornell
Conference on Women (1969: Cornell University). Proceedings, p. 19-20.
"The Isolation of the Housewife in the Suburbs." In Cornell
Conference on Women (1969: Cornell University). Proceedings, p. 61-3.

Pittman, Karen Johnson.
"Statement." In U.S. Congress. House. Committee on Ways
and Means. Subcommittee on Public Assistance and Unemployment Compensation. Teenage Pregnancy Issues, p. 114-20.

Plaskow, Judith.
"Anti-Semitism: The Unacknowledged Racism." In Women's
Spirit Bonding, p. 89-96.
"The Feminist Transformation of Theology." In Beyond Androcentrism, p. 23-33.

Plummer, Mary W.
"The Training of Women as Librarians." In The Role of Women
in Librarianship, p. 26-9.

Plunkett, Marcia W.
"Meanings of Work for Mothers." In Women's Lives, p. 95-9.

Podojil, Toni.
"Testimony." In U.S. Congress. House. Select Committee on
Aging. Subcommittee on Retirement Income and Employment.
Task Force on Social Security and Women. Treatment of Women Under Social Security, p. 160.

Podgregin, Letty Cottin.
"Non-Sexist Parenting at Home and at School." In Conference
on Non-Sexist Early Childhood Education (1976: Arlen
House). Perspectives on Non-Sexist Early Childhood Education, p. 113-21.

Pomeroy, Sarah B.
"Infanticide in Hellenistic Greece." In Images of Women in
Antiquity, p. 207-22.

Poovey, Mary.
"Persuasion and the Promises of Love." In The Representation
of Women in Fiction, p. 152-79.

Pope, Lois A.
"Statement." In U.S. Congress. House. Select Committee on
Aging. Subcommittee on Health and Long-Term Care. Elder
Abuse, p. 29-30.

Popkin, Susan Brandeis.
"Bat Mitzvah Address of a Young Aristocrat: 1977." In The
American Jewish Woman, p. 976-7.

Porcino, Jane.
"Testimony." In U.S. Congress. House. Select Committee on
Aging. Subcommittee on Retirement Income and Employment.
National Policy Proposals Affecting Midlife Women, p. 85-6.

Porter, Elsa A.
"An Experiment in Part-Time Employment of Professionals in the
Federal Government." In Women in Action, p. 11-6.
"Testimony." In U.S. Congress. Joint Economic Committee.
Subcommittee on Economic Growth and Stabilization. American
Women Workers in a Full Employment Economy, p. 17-20.

Porter, Natalie.
"New Perspectives on Therapy Supervision." In Handbook of
Feminist Therapy, p. 332-43.

Porter, Sandra V.
"Representing the 80 Percent: Needs of the Pink and Blue Col-
lar Woman Worker." In Women's Lives, p. 417-21.
"Statement." In U.S. Congress. Committee on Government Op-
erations. Manpower and Housing Subcommittee. The Women's
Bureau, p. 91-2.
"Statement." In U.S. Congress. House. Committee on Post
Office and Civil Service. Subcommittee on Human Resources.
Pay Equity, pt. 1, p. 125-6.

Portis, Kattie.
"Closing Session." Women's Studies Quarterly, 13 (Summer 1985),
13-4.

Portnoy, Mindy.
 "Statement." In U.S. Congress. Senate. Committee on the
 Judiciary. Subcommittee on the Constitution. Constitutional
 Amendments Relating to Abortion, v. 1, p. 1051-3.

Potter, Jane.
 "Statement." In U.S. Congress. House. Select Committee on
 Aging. Problems of Aging Women, p. 75-80.

Powledge, Tabitha M.
 "Unnatural Selection: On Choosing Children's Sex." In The
 Custom-Made Child?, p. 193-200.

Poyadue, Florence M.
 "Statement." In U.S. Congress. House. Select Committee on
 Children, Youth, and Families. Families with Disabled Chil-
 dren, p. 55-61.

Poythress, Mary.
 "Statement." In U.S. Congress. House. Committee on Post
 Office and Civil Service. Subcommittee on Postal Personnel
 and Modernization. Racial Discrimination and Sexual Harassment in U.S. Postal Service, p. 44-7.

Praeger, Roberta.
 "Personal Report to the Conference on Women and Poverty in
 Massachusetts." Women's Studies Quarterly, 13 (Summer
 1985), 6.

Praeger, Susan.
 "Shifting Perspectives on Marital Property Law." In Rethinking
 the Family, p. 111-30.

Pratt, Peggy.
 "Statement." In U.S. Congress. House. Committee on Educa-
 tion and Labor. Subcommittee on Employment Opportunities.
 Oversight Hearings on Equal Employment Opportunity and
 Affirmative Action, pt. 2, p. 477-8.

Preciado De Burciaga, Cecilia.
 "Panel Discussion." In Public Forum on Women's Rights and Responsibilities (1978: Las Vegas, NV). Public Forum on Wom-
 en's Rights and Responsibilities, p. 7-8.

Pressar, Arlene.
 "Testimony." In U.S. Congress. House. Committee on Energy
 and Commerce. Subcommittee on Health and Environment.
 Health and the Environment Miscellaneous, pt. 2, p. 761-2.

Presser, Harriet B.
 "Statement." In U.S. Congress. House. Select Committee on

Punnett, Laura.
"Women-Controlled Research." In Birth Control and Controlling
Birth, p. 61-70.

Purcell, Mary.
"Statement." In U.S. Congress. Senate. Committee on the
Judiciary. Subcommittee on the Constitution. Constitutional
Amendments Relating to Abortion, v. 1, p. 1040-3.

Purdy, Laura M.
"Integrating Women's Studies Perspectives Into the Philosophy
Curriculum." In Conference on "Scholars and Women" (1981:
University of Maryland). Women's Studies and the Curriculum,
p. 207-9.

Purdy, Virginia C.
"National Archives Resources for Research in the History of
American Women." In Conference on Women's History (1976:
Washington, DC). Clio Was a Woman, p. 31-44.

Putnam, Linda L.
"Lady You're Trapped: Breaking Out of Conflict Cycles." In
Women in Organizations, p. 39-54.

Putney, Gail Jackson.
"Children: In Dreams Come Unexpected Responsibilities." In
The Challenge to Women, p. 73-85.

Quaglio, Francine.
"Religion as an Instrument of Social Control." In Class, Race,
and Sex, p. 301-7.

Quarm, Daisy.
"Sexual Inequality: the High Cost of Leaving Parenting to Wom-
en." In Women in the Workplace, p. 187-208.

Queen, Renee.
"Towards Liberating Toys: You Are What You Play." In Conference on Non-Sexist Early Childhood Education (1976: Arden House). Perspectives on Non-Sexist Early Childhood
Education, p. 62-8.

Quick, Tamara M.
"Personal Revelation." In Blueprints for Living, v. 2, p. 108-18.

Quinlan, Alice.
"Statement." In U.S. Congress. House. Committee on Armed
Services. Military Personnel and Compensation Subcommittee.
Benefits for Former Spouses of Military Members, pt. 2, p.
7-12.

"Statement." In U.S. Congress. House. Select Committee on Aging. Subcommittee on Retirement Income and Employment. Task Force on Social Security and Women. Inequities Toward Women in the Social Security System, p. 60-3.

Quinn, Mary Joy.
"Statement." In U.S. Congress. House. Select Committee on Aging. Subcommittee on Health and Long-Term Care. Elder Abuse, p. 85-7.

Rachner, Mary Jane.
"Statement." In U.S. Congress. House. Committee on Post Office and Civil Service. Subcommittee on Compensation and Employee Benefits. Federal Pay Equity Act of 1984, pt. 2, p. 187-8.

Radetsky, Martha.
"Testimony." In U.S. Commission on Civil Rights Hearing Before the U.S. Commission on Civil Rights Held in Denver, p. 474-5.

Ramaley, Judith A.
"Strategies for Change: A Summary." In Expanding the Role of Women in the Sciences, p. 228-33.

Ramey, Estelle R.
"The Natural Capacity for Health in Women." In Women: A Developmental Perspective, p. 3-12.

Randall, Carrie.
"Testimony." In U.S. Congress. Senate. Committee on Human Resources. Subcommittee on Alcoholism and Drug Abuse. Alcohol Labeling and Fetal Alcohol Syndrome, 1978, p. 169-72.

Rankin, Jeannette.
"Statement." In U.S. Congress. House. Committee on Foreign Affairs. American Neutrality Policy, p. 229-31.

Ransom, Gail S.
"Chafing Dish, Apron Strings." In Spinning a Sacred Yarn, p. 159-62.

Rapoport, Lydia.
"Crisis Intervention as a Mode of Brief Treatment." In Charlotte Towle Memorial Symposium on Comparative Theoretical Approaches to Casework Practice (1969: University of Chicago). Theories of Social Casework, p. 265-311.

Raskin, Ellen.
    "Newbery Medal Acceptance." Horn Book, 55 (1979), 385-91.

Rasmus, Carolyn J.
    "The Gift and Power of the Holy Ghost." In A Woman's Choices,
        p. 33-41.
    "Women in the Light of the Gospel." In Blueprints for Living,
        p. 121-25.

Ratner, Ronnie Steinberg.
    "Equal Employment Policy for Women: Summary of Themes and
        Issues." In Equal Employment Policy for Women, p. 419-42.
    "The Policy and Problem: Overview of Seven Countries." In
        Equal Employment Policy for Women, p. 1-52.

Rauseenbush, Esther.
    "Education and Equality for Women." In Cornell Conference on
        Women (1969: Cornell University). Proceedings, p. 35-7,
        44, 49-50.

Rave, Elizabeth.
    "Pornography: The Leveler of Women." In Handbook of Feminist
        Therapy, p. 226-36.

Rawles, Beth.
    "The Media and Their Effect on Black Images." In Conference
        on the Educational and Occupational Needs of Black Women
        (1975: Washington, DC). Conference on the Educational
        and Occupational Needs of Black Women, v. 2, p. 227-52.

Rawlings, Edwina.
    "Myths and Realities." In Training Conference (1st: 1984:
        Washington, DC). Interagency Committee on Women in Fed-
        eral Law Enforcement, p. 37-8.

Rayburn, Carole A.
    "Three Women from Moab." In Spinning a Sacred Yarn, p. 163-
        71.

Raymond, Janice G.
    "Sex Preselection: Introduction." In The Custom-Made Child?,
        p. 177-80.
    "Sex Preselection: A Response." In The Custom-Made Child?,
        p. 209-12.

Raymond, M. Susan Ueber.
    "Paying for Women's Health Services: A Financial Dilemma."
        In Health Needs of the World's Poor Women, p. 88-90.

Reach, Barbara.
    "Statement." In U.S. Congress. Senate. Committee on the

Judiciary. Subcommittee on the Constitution. Constitutional Amendments Relating to Abortion, v. 1, p. 1049-51.

Redlinger, Wendy.
"Mother's Speech to Children in Bilingual Mexican-American Homes." In Conference on the Sociology of the Languages of American Women (1976: New Mexico State University). Proceedings, p. 119-30.

Reder, Nancy.
"Statement." In U.S. Congress. House. Committee on Government Operations. Manpower and Housing Subcommittee. Equal Employment Opportunity Commission's Handling of Pay Equity Cases, p. 223-6.
"Statement." In U.S. Congress. House. Committee on Post Office and Civil Service. Subcommittee on Compensation and Employee Benefits. Federal Pay Equity Act of 1984, pt. 1, p. 69-72.

Reed, Carolyn.
"Testimony." In U.S. Equal Employment Opportunity Commission. Hearing Before the U.S. Equal Employment Opportunity Commission on Job Segregation and Wage Discrimination, p. 214-23.
"Testimony." In U.S. Congress. House. Select Committee on Aging. Subcommittee on Retirement Income and Employment. Task Force on Social Security and Women. Treatment of Women Under Social Security, p. 99-100.

Reed, Evelyn.
"How Women Lost Control of Their Destiny and How They Can Regain It." In Reed, Problems of Women's Liberation, p. 48-63.
"Women and the Family: a Historical View." In Reed, Problems of Women's Liberation, p. 12-27.
"Women: Caste, Class or Oppressed Sex?" In Reed, Problems of Women's Liberation, p. 64-76.

Reed, Kay.
"Testimony." In U.S. Commission on Civil Rights. Hearing Before the U.S. Commission on Civil Rights Held in Denver, p. 457-8, 460.

Reed, Mary E.
"Peasant Women of Croatia in the Interwar Years." In Women, State, and Party in Eastern Europe, p. 99-112.

Reed, Willie.
"Testimony." In U.S. Commission on Civil Rights. Hearing Before the U.S. Commission on Civil Rights Held in Chicago, v. 1, p. 419-22.

Regan, Agnes S.
  "Testimony." In U.S. Congress. House. Committee on the
    Judiciary. Birth Control, (1934) p. 172.
  "Testimony." In U.S. Congress. Senate. Committee on the
    Judiciary. Birth Control, (1931) p. 61-2.
  "Testimony." In U.S. Congress. Senate. Committee on the
    Judiciary. Birth Control, (1932) p. 114-5.
  "Testimony." In U.S. Congress. Senate. Committee on the
    Judiciary. Birth Control, (1934) p. 123-6.

Reid, Inez Smith.
  "Health Issues Facing Black Women." In Conference on the
    Educational and Occupational Needs of Black Women (1975:
    Washington, DC). Conference on the Educational and Occu-
    pational Needs of Black Women, v. 2, p. 203-24.
  "How Powerful Is Powerful? The Women's Movement and the
    Four Black Congresswomen." In Women Organizing, p. 24-46.

Reid, Marlene.
  "Statement." In U.S. Congress. House. Committee on Post
    Office and Civil Service. Subcommittee on Compensation and
    Employee Benefits. Federal Pay Equity Act of 1984, pt. 2,
    p. 185-7.

Reid, Pamela T.
  "Socialization of Black Female Children." In Women: A Develop-
    mental Perspective, p. 137-56.

Reinecker, Jeannette.
  "Statement." In U.S. Congress. House. Select Committee on
    Population. Fertility and Contraception in America, p. 242-8.

Reingold, Eve.
  "Black Suicide in San Francisco." In Miniconsultation on the
    Mental and Physical Health Problems of Black Women (1974:
    Washington, DC). Miniconsultation on the Mental and Physical
    Health Problems of Black Women, p. 111-20.

Reinharz, Shulamit.
  "Experimental Analysis: A Contribution to Feminist Research."
    In Theories of Women's Studies II, p. 68-97.

Reisinger, Mary.
  "Statement." In U.S. Congress. House. Select Committee on
    Aging. Subcommittee on Retirement Income and Employment.
    Impact of Reagan Economics on Aging Women, p. 21.

Reiss, Mary-Ann.
  "Rosa Mayreder (1858-1938) Pioneer of Austrian Feminism." In
    Sisterhood Surveyed, p. 88-92.

Reivitz, Linda.
  "Women's Achievements Towards Equality. In 1985 We're Both
    Secretaries." Vital Speeches, 52 (November 15, 1985), 88-91.

Remick, Helen.
  "Beyond Equal Pay for Equal Work: Comparable Worth in the
    State of Washington." In Equal Employment Policy for Women,
    p. 405-18.
  "Testimony." In U.S. Equal Employment Opportunity Commission.
    Hearings Before the U.S. Equal Employment Opportunity Com-
    mission on Job Segregation and Wage Discrimination, p. 818-24,
    828-34.

Renfro, Sue T.
  "Statement." In U.S. Congress. House. Committee on Ways
    and Means. Subcommittee on Social Security. Social Security
    Dependents' Benefits, p. 58.

Reno, Virginia P.
  "Discussion (of Earnings Sharing: Incremental and Fundamental
    Reform)." In A Challenge to Social Security, p. 92-100.

Repetto, Margherita.
  "The Development of Women's Liberation in Italy After World War
    II." In GLCA Women's Studies Conference (4th: 1978:
    Rochester, Indiana). Structure of Knowledge, p. 41-8.

Resh, Mary.
  "Feminist Therapy with the Woman Over 50." In Handbook of
    Feminist Therapy, p. 191-8.

Resnik, Judith.
  "Testimony." In U.S. Congress. House. Committee on the
    Judiciary. Subcommittee on Courts, Civil Liberties, and the
    Administration of Justice, The Female Offender--1979-80, p. 157-66.

Reuben, Elaine.
  "Toward a Feminist Transformation of the Academy: The Search
    for Wholeness, Again." In GLCA Women's Studies Conference
    (6th: 1980). Towards a Feminist Transformation of the
    Academy II, p. 11-6.

Reuss, Margaret.
  "Testimony." In U.S. Congress. House. Select Committee on
    Aging. Subcommittee on Retirement Income and Employment.
    National Policy Proposals Affecting Midlife Women, p. 57-9.

Reuss, Patricia.
  "Statement." In U.S. Congress. House. Committee on Finance.
    Potential Inequities Affecting Women, pt. 1, p. 74-6.

Reverby, Susan.
"Neither For the Drawing Room Nor For the Kitchen: Private Duty Nursing in Boston, 1873-1920." In Women and Health in America, p. 454-66.

Reynolds, Nancy Clark.
"Statement." In U.S. Congress. House. Committee on Foreign Affairs. Subcommittee on Human Rights and International Organizations. U.S. Contribution to the U.N. Decade for Women, p. 2-5.
"Statement." In U.S. Congress. Senate. Committee on Foreign Relations. Women in Development, p. 14-8.

Reynolds, W. Ann.
"Change. An Imperative for Higher Education." Vital Speeches, 50 (April 15, 1984), 397-400.
"What Is Right With Our Public Schools." In Representative American Speeches: 1983-84, p. 15-26. Also in Vital Speeches, 49 (September 1, 1983), 695-9.

Ricardo-Campbell, Rita.
"Major Issues in National Health Policy. Policy to Encourage Primary Research." Vital Speeches, 46 (October 1, 1980), 744-6.
"Social Security: New Directions. Have You Really Paid For Your Benefits." Vital Speeches, 48 (November 1, 1981), 52-6.
"Statement." In U.S. Congress. House. Select Committee on Aging. Subcommittee on Retirement Income and Employment. Task Force on Social Security and Women. Treatment of Women Under Social Security, v. 4, p. 76-82.

Rice, Patricia.
"Women Out of the Myths and Into Focus." In Women and the News, p. 38-49.

Rich, Adrienne.
"Commencement Address, Smith College, 1979." In I Am Honored To Be Here Today, p. 207-13. Also in Images of Women in American Popular Culture, p. 117-23.
"Keynote Address: Disobedience Is What NWSA Is Potentially About." Women's Studies Quarterly, 9 (Fall, 1981), 4.
"Notes Toward a Politics of Location." In Women, Feminist Identity, and Society in the 1980's, p. 7-22.
"Taking Women Students Seriously." In Gendered Subjects, p. 21-8.

Rich, Dorothy.
"Statement." In U.S. Congress. Senate. Committee on Labor and Human Resources. Subcommittee on Family and Human Services. Broken Families, p. 110-13.

Richards, Caroline.
"The Emergence of Women in Twentieth-Century Chilean History and Literature." In GLCA Women's Studies Conference (7th: 1981). <u>Towards a Feminist Transformation of the Academy III</u>, p. 1-8.

Richards, Evelyn.
"Statement." In U.S. Congress. House. Committee on Ways and Means. Subcommittee on Social Security. <u>Treatment of Men and Women Under the Social Security Program</u>, p. 175-8.

Richardson, Sally K.
"Statement." In U.S. Congress. House. Committee on Armed Services. Subcommittee on Military Personnel. <u>Women in the Military</u>, p. 159-62, 192-200.

Richman, Julia.
"Women Wage-Workers: With Reference to Directing Immigrants." In <u>The American Jewish Woman</u>, p. 421-7.

Richmond, Mary E.
"Address to Students of the New York School of Philanthropy." In Richmond, <u>The Long View</u>, p. 232-3.
"Adequate Relief." In Richmond, <u>The Long View</u>, p. 326-8.
"Attitudes Toward Charitable Giving." In Richmond, <u>The Long View</u>, p. 229-31.
"Book and Reading." In Richmond, <u>The Long View</u>, p. 19-28.
"Charitable Co-operation." In Richmond, <u>The Long View</u>, p. 186-202.
"Charity and Homemaking." In Richmond, <u>The Long View</u>, p. 77-85.
"The College and the Community." In Richmond, <u>The Long View</u>, p. 382-4.
"The Concern of the Community With Marriage." In Richmond, <u>The Long View</u>, p. 602-16.
"Criticism and Reform in Charity." In Richmond, <u>The Long View</u>, p. 43-55.
"The Family and the Social Worker." In Richmond, <u>The Long View</u>, p. 262-7.
"A Forward Look." In Richmond, <u>The Long View</u>, p. 234-7.
"Friendly Visiting." In Richmond, <u>The Long View</u>, p. 254-61.
"The Friendly Visitor." In Richmond, <u>The Long View</u>, p. 39-42.
"How Social Workers Can Aid Housing Reform." In Richmond, <u>The Long View</u>, p. 320-5.
"Industrial Conditions and the Charity Worker." In Richmond, <u>The Long View</u>, p. 238-40.
"The Interrelation of Social Movements." In Richmond, <u>The Long View</u>, p. 285-91.
"Lessons Learned in Baltimore." In Richmond, <u>The Long View</u>, p. 292-300.
"The Long View." In Richmond, <u>The Long View</u>, p. 468-73.

"Married Vagabonds." In Richmond, The Long View, p. 70-6.

"Medical and Social Co-operation." In Richmond, The Long View, p. 338-42.

"The Need of a Training School in Applied Philanthropy." In Richmond, The Long View, p. 99-104.

"Of the Art of Beginning in Social Work." In Richmond, The Long View, p. 309-19.

"Our Relation to the Churches." In Richmond, The Long View, p. 115-9.

"A Plea for Poetry." In Richmond, The Long View, p. 147-50.

"The Profession and Practice of Begging." In Richmond, The Long View, p. 56-68.

"The Relation of Output to Intake." In Richmond, The Long View, p. 329-37.

"Report to the Mayor of Baltimore." In Richmond, The Long View, p. 127-30.

"The Retail Method of Reform." In Richmond, The Long View, p. 214-21.

"The Social Case Work Side of Probation and Parole." In Richmond, The Long View, p. 402-5.

"The Social Case Worker in a Changing World." In Richmond, The Long View, p. 374-81.

"The Social Case Worker's Task." In Richmond, The Long View, p. 397-401.

"Some Next Steps in Social Treatment." In Richmond, The Long View, p. 484-91.

"Some Relations of Family Case Work to Social Progress." In Richmond, The Long View, p. 526-35.

"To the Volunteers of 1915." In Richmond, The Long View, p. 365-73.

"The Training of Charity Workers." In Richmond, The Long View, p. 86-98.

"War and Family Solidarity." In Richmond, The Long View, p. 447-59.

Riddle, Dorothy I.
"Politics, Spirituality, and Models of Change." In The Politics of Women's Spirituality, p. 373-81.

Ridgway, Rozanne L.
"CSCE Review Meeting in Madrid." Department of State Bulletin, 80 (November 1980), 49-51.

"Extension of MFN Waivers for China, Hungary, Romania." Department of State Bulletin, 80 (December 1980), 40-1.

Ridings, Dorothy S.
"Advocating the People's Interest in Washington. An Agenda for Better Government." Vital Speeches, 51 (June 1, 1985), 485-90.

Rinehart, Barbara.
"Concrete Services: A Response to Mental Health Needs?" In Older Women in the City, p. 130-4.

Rini, Meg.
"Testimony." In U.S. Congress. State. Committee on Human Resources. Adolescent Health, Services and Pregnancy Prevention Care Act of 1978, p. 442-3.

Rivera, Elba.
"Personal Reports to the Conference on Women and Poverty in Massachusetts." Women Studies Quarterly, 13 (Summer 1985), 6.

Rivlin, Alice M.
"Statement." In U.S. Congress. House. Select Committee on Children, Youth, and Families. Children, Youth, and Families, p. 11-5.

Robb, Lynda Johnson.
"Testimony." In U.S. Equal Employment Opportunity Commission. Hearings Before the U.S. Equal Employment Opportunity Commission on Job Segregation and Wage Discrimination, p. 10-20.
"Testimony." In U.S. Congress. House. Select Committee on Aging. Subcommittee on Retirement Income and Employment. Task Force on Social Security and Women. Treatment of Women Under Social Security, p. 114-6.

Robbins, Jean Hamerman.
"The Appointment Hassle: Clues About Women's Themes of Separation-Individuation." In Handbook of Feminist Therapy, p. 22-31.

Robe, Lucy Barry.
"Pregnancy and Drinking." In Women in Crisis Conference (1st: 1979: New York, NY). Women in Crisis, p. 172-5.

Roberts, Nanette M.
"Last at the Cross." In Spinning a Sacred Yarn, p. 172-80.

Robertson, Adelle F.
"Continuing Education: A Vital Process for Women." In Toward the Second Decade, p. 71-82.

Robinson, Cheryl.
"Testimony." In U.S. Congress. House. Committee on the Judiciary. Subcommittee on Criminal Justice. Privacy of Rape Victims, p. 49-51.

Robinson, Gertrude Joch.
"Women, Media Access and Social Control." In Women and the News, p. 87-108.

Robinson, Jill.
　　"Statement." In U.S. Congress. Senate. Committee on Labor
　　　and Human Relations. The Coming Decade, p. 640-2.

Robinson, Lillian S.
　　"Women, Media, and the Dialectics of Resistance." In Class,
　　　Race, and Sex, p. 308-24.

Robinson, Patricia Murphy.
　　"The Historical Repression of Women's Sexuality." In Pleasure
　　　and Danger, p. 251-66.

Roby, Pamela Ann.
　　"Toward Full Equality: More Job Education for Women." In
　　　Conference on the Educational and Occupational Needs of
　　　Black Women (1975: Washington, DC). Conference on the
　　　Educational and Occupational Needs of Black Women, v. 2,
　　　p. 33-68.

Rocha, Barbara.
　　"Statement." In California. Legislature. Joint Committee on
　　　Legal Equality. Women in the Justice System, p. 88-93.

Rock, Diana.
　　"Statement." In U.S. Congress. House. Committee on Post
　　　Office and Civil Service. Subcommittee on Compensation and
　　　Employee Benefits. Federal Pay Equity Act of 1984, pt. 1,
　　　p. 129-31.
　　"Statement." In U.S. Congress. House. Committee on Post
　　　Office and Civil Service. Subcommittee on Compensation and
　　　Employee Benefits. Options for Conducting a Pay Equity
　　　Study, p. 465-8.

Rockefeller, Sharon Percy.
　　"Statement." In U.S. Congress. Senate. Committee on Labor
　　　and Human Resources. The Coming Decade, p. 130-6.

Rockwell, Virginia.
　　"Testimony." In U.S. Commission on Civil Rights. Hearing Be-
　　　fore the U.S. Commission on Civil Rights Held in Denver, p.
　　　282-3.

Rodriguez, Elsa.
　　"Statement." In U.S. Congress. House. Committee on Armed
　　　Services. Military Personnel and Compensation Subcommittee.
　　　Benefits for Former Spouses of Military Members, pt. 1, p.
　　　50-1.

Rodriguez, Helen.
　　"Concluding Remarks (on Depo-Provera and Sterilization Abuse)."
　　　In Birth Control and Controlling Birth, p. 125-8.

Rodriguez-Mendoza, Amalia.
"Caucus Report of the Western Region." In Western Regional
Civil Rights and Women's Rights Conference (4th: 1977:
San Francisco, CA). Recent Developments, p. 147.

Rodriguez-Trias, Helen.
"Health Care Delivery." In Warner, Anne. Health Womenpower,
p. 24-9.
"Problems and Priorities of Poor, Culturally Different Parents."
In Conference on Non-Sexist Early Childhood Education (1976:
Arden House). Perspectives on Non-Sexist Early Childhood
Education, p. 122-7.

Rogal, Margaret L.
"Subject Access to Works on Women." In GLCA Women's Studies
Conference (6th: 1980). Towards a Feminist Transformation
of the Academy II, p. 62-5.

Rogers, Edith Nourse.
"Statement." In U.S. Congress. House. Committee on Veterans' Affairs. Select Subcommittee to Review WASP Bills. To
Provide Recognition to the Women's Air Force Service. p. 62,
173.

Rogers, Kim Lacy.
"Relicts of the New World: Conditions of Widowhood in Seventeenth-Century New England." In Conference on the History
of Women (1977: St. Paul, MN). Woman's Being, Woman's
Place, p. 26-52.

Rogers, Mary F.
"The Swaying Scales of Balance. Liberal Learning and Varieties
of Practicality." Vital Speeches, 51 (March 1, 1985), 318-20.

Rogin, Carole M.
"Statement." In U.S. Congress. House. Committee on Ways
and Means. Economic Equity Act and Related Tax and Pension Reform, p. 161-2.

Rolls, Karen.
"Statement." In U.S. Congress. Senate. Committee on Small
Business. Women Entrepreneurs, p. 48-52.

Rooks, Judith.
"Testimony." In U.S. Congress. House. Committee on Inter-
state and Foreign Commerce. Subcommittee on Oversight and
Investigations. Nurse Midwifery: Consumers' Freedom of
Choice, p. 145-8.

Roosevelt, Eleanor.
"Address at Conference on Educational Programs for Veterans."

Education for Victory, 3 (April 20, 1945), 1-3.
"Adoption of Declaration of Human Rights." In We Shall Be Heard, p. 278-80.
"Before the Democratic National Convention." In Representative American Speeches, 1956-57, p. 109-13.
"Children of School Age." School Life, 18 (March 1933), 121.
"Civil Liberties, the Individual and the Community; Speech, March 14, 1940." Reference Shelf, 14 (1940), 173-82.
"Communist Charges Against U.S. Territorial Policies." Department of State Bulletin, 27 (December 29, 1952), 1032-3.
"The Human Factor in the Developing of International Understanding." In Colgate Lectures in Human Relations. Hamilton, NY: Colgate University, 1949, p. 3-17.
"Human Rights and Human Freedom." New York Times Magazine, (March 24, 1946), 21.
"In Service of Truth; Excerpt from an Address, June 19, 1955." Nation, 131 (July 9, 1955), 37.
"Is a UN Charter Review Conference Advisable Now?" Congressional Digest, 34 (November 1955), 275.
"The Meaning of Democracy. An Address Before the National Institute of Government, May 4, 1940." Congressional Record, v. 86, pt. 96, May 15, 1940, p. 2959-60.
"Progress Toward Completion of Human Rights Covenants." Department of State Bulletin, 26 (June 30, 1952), 1024-8.
"Reply to Attacks on U.S. Attitude Toward Human Rights Covenant." Department of State Bulletin, 26 (January 14, 1952), 59-61.
"Restlessness of Youth: An Asset of Free Societies." Department of State Bulletin, 26 (January 21, 1952), 94-6.
"The Role of the Educator." Journal of the National Education Association, 33 (March 1944), 59-60.
"Social Responsibility for Individual Welfare." In Russell, James Earl. National Policies for Education, Health, and Social Services. Garden City, NY: Doubleday, 1955, p. xxxv-xxxvii.
"The U.N. and the Welfare of the World." National Parent-Teacher, 47 (June 1953), 14-6, 35.
"UN Deliberations on Draft Convention on the Political Rights of Women; Statements of December 12 and 15." Department of State Bulletin, 28 (January 5, 1953), 29-32.
"Universal Validity of Man's Right to Self-Determination; excerpt from Statement, November 18, 1952." Department of State Bulletin, 27 (December 8, 1952), 917-9.

Rose, Ernestine L.
"Addresses at Woman's Rights Convention in Syracuse, 1852." In The American Jewish Woman, p. 165-6.
"The Necessity for the Utter Extinction of Slavery." In Outspoken Women, p. 130-4.
"Speech at 2nd National Woman's Rights Convention in Worcester, 1851." In The American Jewish Woman, p. 163-5.

"Speech on Slavery, Flushing, Long Island, August 4, 1853."
In The American Jewish Woman, p. 166-9.
"Speech of Mrs. E. L. Rose, May 1860." In We Shall Be Heard,
p. 57-9.

Rosen, Margie.
"Testimony." In U.S. Commission on Civil Rights. Hearing Before the U.S. Commission on Civil Rights Held in Chicago,
v. 1, p. 409-10.

Rosenberg, Dorothy.
"The Emancipation of Women in Fact and Fiction: Changing Roles
in GDR Society and Literature." In Women, State, and Party
in Eastern Europe, p. 344-61.

Rosenberg, Jan.
"Feminism, the Family and the New Right." In Class, Race, and
Sex, p. 126-37.

Rosenberg, Rosalind.
"In Search of Woman's Nature, 1850-1920." Feminist Studies, 3
(1976), 141-54.

Rosenfeld, Rachel A.
"Academic Career Mobility for Women and Men Psychologists."
In Women in Scientific and Engineering Professions, p. 89-127.
"Job Changing and Occupational Sex Segregation: Sex and Race
Comparison." In Sex Segregation in the Workplace, p. 56-86.

Rosenstein, Betty.
"Statement." In Symposium on Minorities and Women in Science
and Technology (1981: Washington, DC). Symposium on
Minorities and Women in Science and Technology, p. 72-6.

Rosewater, Lynne Bravo.
"Feminist Interpretation of Traditional Testing." In Handbook of
Feminist Therapy, p. 266-73.
"Schizophrenic, Borderline, or Battered?" In Handbook of Fem-
inist Therapy, p. 215-25.

Rosoff, Jeannie I.
"Statement." In U.S. Congress. House. Select Committee on
Population. Fertility and Contraception in America, p. 88-93.

Ross, Catherine.
"Measuring the Distributional Impact of Transportation Service
on Women." In Women's Travel Issues, p. 683-4.

Ross, Jo Anne B.
"Statement." In U.S. Congress. House. Committee on Government Operations. Intergovernmental Relations and Human

Resources Subcommittee. Barriers to Self-Sufficiency for Single Female Heads of Families, p. 126-30.

"Statement." In U.S. Congress. House. Committee on Ways and Means. Subcommittee on Public Assistance and Unemployment Compensation. AFDC and Social Service Bills and Related Oversight Issues, p. 5-9.

Ross, Ofelia Gonzalez.
"Testimony." In U.S. Commission on Civil Rights. Hearing Before the U.S. Commission on Civil Rights Held in Chicago, p. 410-12.

Rossi, Alice S.
"Social Trends and Women's Lives--1965-1985." In Changing Roles of Women in Industrial Societies, p. 64-100.

Rossman, Marge.
"Statement." In U.S. Congress. House. Committee on Small Business. Subcommittee on General Oversight and Minority Enterprise. Women in Business, p. 112-3.

Rothchild, Nina.
"Factual Overview: Current Comparable Worth Proposals at the Federal, State, and Local Levels." In Comparable Worth: Issue for the 80's, p. 73-5.

"Statement." In U.S. Congress. House. Committee on Post Office and Civil Service. Subcommittee on Compensation and Employee Benefits. Federal Pay Equity Pay of 1984, pt. 2, p. 135-8.

"Statement." In U.S. Congress. House. Committee on Post Office and Civil Service. Subcommittee on Compensation and Employee Benefits. Options for Conducting a Pay Equity Study, p. 104-6.

Rothenberg, Paula S.
"Feminist Issues and Feminist Attitudes: Teaching Today's Students." In Sisterhood Surveyed, p. 105-6.

"The Political Nature of Relations Between the Sexes." In Beyond Domination, p. 204-20.

Rothman, Flora.
"Reforming the 'System.'" In Today's Girls: Tomorrow's Women, p. 64-6.

Rothschild, Joan.
"Technology, 'Women's Work' and the Social Control of Women." In Women, Power and Political Systems, p. 160-83.

Roukema, Margaret S.
"Statement." In U.S. Congress. House. Committee on Banking, Finance, and Urban Affairs. Subcommittee on Domestic Monetary

Policy. Analysis of Federal Reserve Policies as They Affect
Interest Rates and Credit Markets. Washington:
U.S.G.P.O., 1981, p. 2-3.
"Statement." In U.S. Congress. House. Committee on Educa-
tion and Labor. Subcommittee on Select Education. Over-
sight Hearing on Child Support Enforcement. Washington:
U.S.G.P.O., 1984, p. 3-5.
"Statement." In U.S. Congress. House. Committee on Educa-
tion and Labor. Subcommittee on Labor-Management Relations.
Pension Equity for Women, p. 24-5.
"Statement." In U.S. Congress. House. Committee on Public
Works and Transportation. Subcommittee on Water Resources.
Water Resources Problems Affecting the Northeast: the
Drought and Present and Future Water Supply Problems.
Washington: U.S.G.P.O., 1981, p. 4-5.
"Statement." In U.S. Congress. House. Committee on Ways
and Means. Subcommittee on Public Assistance and Unem-
ployment Compensation. Child Support Enforcement Legisla-
tion. Washington: U.S.G.P.O., 1984, p. 87-97.
"Statement." In U.S. Congress. Senate. Committee on Finance.
Child Support Enforcement Program Reform Proposals. Wash-
ington: U.S.G.P.O., 1984, p. 23-31.

Rounder, Rita.
"Ministry and the Life of Faith." In Conference on Women and
Lay Ministry (1976: St. Michel's Church, Milton, MA).
Women and Lay Ministry, p. 15-22.

Roundtree, Dovey.
"Testimony." In U.S. Congress. House. Committee on the
Judiciary. Subcommittee on Criminal Justice. Privacy of
Rape Victims, p. 67-76.

Roundtree, Jill.
"Testimony." In U.S. Commission on Civil Rights. Hearing Before the U.S. Commission on Civil Rights Held In Chicago,
v. 1, p. 428-9.

Roundtree, Martha.
"Statement." In U.S. Congress. House. Committee on the
Judiciary. Subcommittee on Courts, Civil Liberties, and the
Administration of Justice. Prayer in Public Schools and
Buildings--Federal Court Jurisdiction. Washington:
U.S.G.P.O., 1981, p. 383-402.

Rouse, Ina May.
"Testimony." In U.S. Congress. House. Select Committee on
Aging. Problems of Aging Women, p. 49-51.

Roylance, Susan.
"Statement." In U.S. Congress. Senate. Committee on Labor

and Human Resources. Oversight of Family Planning Programs, 1981, p. 231-5, 258-63.

Royle, Dorothy.
  "Statement." In U.S. Congress. House. Select Committee on
  Children, Youth, and Families. Children, Youth, and Families, p. 79.

Rozovsky, Fay A.
  "The Legal Aspects of the DES Case: What Can Be Done." In
  The Custom-Made Child?, p. 39-46.

Rubin, Gayle.
  "Thinking Sex: Notes for a Radical Theory of the Politics of
  Sexuality." In Pleasure and Danger, p. 267-319.

Ruckelshaus, Jill.
  "Speech at the National Women's Political Caucus Conference,
  July, 1981." Ms., 10 (October 1981), 94.
  "Speech by Jill Ruckelshaus, Former Presiding Officer, National
  Commission." In U.S. National Commission on the Observance
  of International Women's Year. The Spirit of Houston, p.
  225-6.

Ruether, Rosemary Radford.
  "Address at the Womanchurch Speakers Conference." In Woman-
  guides, p. 172-3.
  "Envisioning Our Hopes: Some Models of the Future." In Wom-
  en's Spirit Bonding, p. 325-35.
  "Sexism and Godtalk." In Women & Men, p. 409-25.
  "Sexism, Religion, and the Social and Spiritual Liberation of
  Women Today." In Beyond Domination, p. 107-22.
  "Statement." In U.S. Congress. Senate. Committee on the
  Judiciary. Subcommittee on Separation of Powers. The Hu-
  man Life Bill, p. 825-30.
  "Woman as Oppressed; Woman as Liberated in the Scriptures."
  In Spinning a Sacred Yarn, p. 181-6.
  "You Shall Call No Man Father: Sexism, Hierarchy and Libera-
  tion." In Women and the Word, p. 92-9.

Ruffin, Josephine St. Pierre.
  "Address to the First National Conference of Colored Women."
  In Images of Women in American Popular Culture, p. 400-3.

Ruggen, Barbara.
  "The Future of Women." In Cornell Conference on Women (1969:
  Cornell University). Proceedings, p. 63.

Rukeyser, Muriel.
  "The Education of a Poet." In The Writer on Her Work, p. 217-
  30.

Rupp, Leila.
"The Women's Community in the National Woman's Party, 1945 to the 1960s." Signs, 10 (Summer 1985), 715-40.

Rushing, Andrea Benton.
"Lucille Clifton: A Changing Voice for Changing Times." In Coming to Light, p. 214-22.

Russ, Anne J.
"Collegiate Women and Institutional Change, 1875-1920." In Conference on "Scholars and Women" (1981: University of Maryland). Women's Studies and the Curriculum, p. 123-7.

Russell, Brenda L.
"Statement." In U.S. Congress. House. Committee on Ways and Means. Subcommittee on Public Assistance and Unemployment Compensation. AFDC and Social Service Bills and Related Oversight Issues, p. 165-8.

Russell, Diane E. Haddock.
"How a Scientist Who Happens To Be Female Can Succeed in Academia." In Expanding the Role of Women in the Sciences, p. 283-95.
"Pornography and the Women's Liberation Movement." In Feminist Frontiers, p. 346-8. Also In Take Back the Night, p. 301-6.

Russell, Dorothy S.
"Mainstreaming Women's Studies Into Teacher Education." In Conference on "Scholars and Women" (1981: University of Maryland). Women's Studies and the Curriculum, p. 191-6.

Russell, Letty M.
"The Impossible Possibility." In Women and the Word, p. 86-91.
"Women and Ministry." In Sexist Religion and Women in the Church, p. 47-62.

Russell, Susan.
"Testimony." In U.S. Congress. House. Committee on Energy and Commerce. Subcommittee on Health and the Environment. Health and the Environment Miscellaneous, pt. 7, p. 419-20.

Russell, Valerie.
"Giving Thanks Or Making Do (Thanksgiving)." In Women and the Word, p. 35-41.

Russell-Young, Nancy.
"Statement." In U.S. Congress. House. Select Committee on Aging. Subcommittee on Retirement Income and Employment.

Impact of Reagan Economics on Aging Women, p. 48-9.

Russianoff, Penelope.
"Learned Helplessness." In Women in Crisis Conference (1st:
1979: New York, NY). Women in Crisis, p. 33-7.

Russo, Nancy Felipe.
"Beyond Adolescence: Some Suggested New Directions for Studying Female Development in the Middle and Later Years." In
Psychology of Women, p. 89-134.
"Statement." In U.S. Congress. Senate. Committee on Labor
and Human Relations. Sex Discrimination in the Workplace,
1981, p. 228-32.

Rutenberg, Taly.
"Learning Women's Studies." In Theories of Women's Studies,
p. 12-7.

Ruth, Sheila.
"Sexism, Patriarchy, and Feminism." In Women & Men, p.
47-60.

Rutherford, Thelma.
"Statement." In U.S. Congress. House. Select Committee on
Aging. Subcommittee on Retirement Income and Employment.
Task Force on Social Security and Women. Treatment of
Women Under Social Security, v. 3, p. 12-3.

Ruzek, Sheryl Burt.
"Ethical Issues in Childbirth Technology." In Birth Control and
Controlling Birth, p. 197-202.

Ryan, Angela Shen.
"Asian-American Women: A Historical and Cultural Perspectives."
In NASW Conference on Social Work Practice with Women (1st:
1980: Washington, DC). Women, Power, and Change, p.
78-88.

Ryan, Mary P.
"The Power of Women's Networks: A Case Study of Female Moral
Reform in Antebellum America." Feminist Studies, 5 (Spring
1979), 66-85.

Ryden, Hope.
"Testimony." In U.S. Congress. House. Committee on Energy
and Commerce. Subcommittee on Health and the Environment.
Health and the Environment Miscellaneous, pt. 7, p. 399-
400.

Sachs, Bernice Cohen.
"Changing Relationships Between Men and Women. Scope of the Problem." Vital Speeches, 50 (October 1, 1984), 757-62.

Sacks, Karen Brodkin.
"Computers, Ward Secretaries, and a Walkout in a Southern Hospital." In My Troubles Are Going To Have Trouble With Me, p. 173-90.
"Generations of Working-Class Families." In My Troubles Are Going To Have Trouble With Me, p. 15-38.
"An Overview of Women and Power in Africa." In Perspectives on Power, p. 1-10.
"Worlds in Collision or Ships Passing in the Night? The Impact of Feminist Theory on Anthropology." In Conference on Women's Studies and the Humanities (1983: University of North Carolina at Greensboro). Equity and Excellence, p. 24-9.

Sadler, Ann.
"Statement." In U.S. Congress. Senate. Committee on the Judiciary. Subcommittee on Juvenile Justice. Effect of Pornography on Women and Children, p. 276-80.

Saenz, Rita.
"Statement." In U.S. Congress. Senate. Committee on Labor and Human Resources. The Coming Decade, p. 581-3.

Safa, Helen I.
"Runaway Shops and Female Employment: the Search for Cheap Labor." Signs, 7 (Winter 1981), 418-33. Also in Women's Work, p. 58-71.

Safford, Florence.
"Realistic Assessment of the Needs of Older Women." In Older Women in the City, p. 122-3.

Saiving, Valerie C.
"Androgynous Life; A Feminist Appropriation of Process Thought." In Feminism and Process Thought, p. 11-31.

Salazar, Sandra A.
"Recommendations Regarding Latina Women." In Health Needs of the World's Poor Women, p. 58-60.

Saldich, Anne Rawley.
"Electronic Democracy. How TV Governs." Vital Speeches, 46 (June 1, 1980), 487-93.

Salk, Hilary.
"Response (to Benefits and Risks of Electronic Fetal Monitoring)." In Birth Control and Controlling Birth, p. 193-6.

Salladay, Susan Anthony.
    "Ethics and Reproductive Technology." In The Custom-Made
    Child?, p. 241-8.

Salmon, Ruth W.
    "Statement." In U.S. Congress. House. Committee on Energy
    and Commerce. Subcommittee on Health and the Environment.
    Pregnancy-Related Health Services, p. 126-30.

Samora, Betty.
    "Statement." In U.S. Congress. Senate. Committee on Labor
    and Human Resources. The Coming Decade, p. 184.

Sampey, Eleanor.
    "Statement." In U.S. Congress. House. Committee on Ways
    and Means. Subcommittee on Social Security. Social Security
    Dependents' Benefits, p. 58-9.

Sampson, Deborah.
    "An Address on Life as a Female Revolutionary Soldier." In
    Outspoken Women, p. 135-41.

Sanborn, Charlotte Feicht.
    "Etiology of Athletic Amenorrhea." In The Menstrual Cycle and
    Physical Activity, p. 45-54.

Sanchez, Peggy.
    "Statement." In U.S. Congress. Senate. Committee on Labor
    and Human Resources. Subcommittee on Family and Human
    Services. Reauthorization of the Adolescent Family Life Dem-
    onstration Projects Acts of 1981, p. 46-9.

Sancier, Betty.
    "Beyond Advocacy." In NASW Conference on Social Work Prac-
    tice with Women (1st: 1980: Washington, DC). Women,
    Power and Change, p. 186-96.

Sandage, Shirley.
    "Statement." In U.S. Congress. House. Committee on Educa-
    tion and Labor. Subcommittee on Labor-Management Relations.
    Pension Equity for Women, p. 59-62.
    "Statement." In U.S. Congress. Joint Economic Committee.
    The Role of Older Women in the Work Force, p. 21-5.
    "Statement." In U.S. Congress. Senate. Committee on Labor
    and Human Relations. Sex Discrimination in the Workplace,
    1981, p. 26-8.

Sandler, Bernice Resnick.
    "Women in Academe: Why It Still Hurts to Be a Woman in Labor."
    In Expanding the Role of Women in the Sciences, p. 14-26.

Sanger, Margaret Higgins.
　　"Address of Welcome." In International Birth Control Conference
　　　　(6th: New York: 1926). Reports and Papers, p. 3-8.
　　"The Children's Era." In International Birth Control Conference
　　　　(6th: 1926: New York). Reports and Papers, p. 53-8.
　　"Is Birth Control Moral?" In American Birth Control Conference
　　　　(1st: 1921: New York). Birth Control: What It Is, How It
　　　　Works, What It Will Do, p. 170-4.
　　"A Moral Necessity for Birth Control." In Outspoken Women,
　　　　p. 143-50.
　　"Opening Address." In American Birth Control Conference (1st:
　　　　1921: New York). Birth Control: What It Is, How It Works,
　　　　What It Will Do, p. 14-8.
　　"Should Legal Barriers Against Birth Control Be Removed?"
　　　　Congressional Digest, 10 (April 1931), 104-8.
　　"Testimony." In U.S. Congress. House. Committee on the
　　　　Judiciary. Birth Control, (1934) p. 6-9, 230-9.
　　"Testimony." In U.S. Congress. House. Committee on Ways
　　　　and Means. Birth Control, (1932) p. 6-16, 137-43.
　　"Testimony." In U.S. Congress. Senate. Committee on the
　　　　Judiciary. Birth Control, (1931) p. 2-5.
　　"Testimony." In U.S. Congress. Senate. Committee on the
　　　　Judiciary. Birth Control, (1932) p. 6-12, 135-8.
　　"Testimony." In U.S. Congress. Senate. Committee on the
　　　　Judiciary. Birth Control, (1934) p. 14-21, 149-51.

Sapienza, Joan.
　　"Statement." In U.S. Congress. Senate. Committee on Labor
　　　　and Human Resources. The Coming Decade, pt. 2, p. 96-7.

Sapiro, Virginia.
　　"Women's Studies and Political Conflict." In Prism of Sex, p.
　　　　253-65.

Sargent, M. E.
　　"Woman's Position in Library Science." In The Role of Women
　　　　in Librarianship, p. 16-7.

Sarrel, Lorna.
　　"Certification and Training of Sex Therapists." In Ethical Issues
　　　　in Sex Therapy and Research, v. 2, p. 288-91.

Saunders, Marguerite.
　　"The Double Bind: Minority Women." In Women in Crisis Con-
　　　　ference (1st: 1979: New York, NY). Women in Crisis, p.
　　　　49-55.

Sauvigne, Karen.
　　"Statement." In U.S. Congress. Senate. Committee on Labor
　　　　and Human Relations. Sex Discrimination in the Workplace,
　　　　1981, p. 511-5.

Sawatzky, Sharon Blessum.
    "Sometimes There's God, So Quickly." In <u>Spinning a Sacred Yarn</u>, p. 187-91.

Sawhill, Isabel V.
    "Black Women Who Head Families: Economic Needs and Economic Resources." In Conference on the Educational and Occupational Needs of Black Women (1975: Washington, DC). <u>Conference on the Educational and Occupational Needs of Black Women</u>, p. 169-79.
    "Comment on 'Male-Female Differentials.'" In Conference on Women in the Labor Market (1977: Barnard College). <u>Women in the Labor Market</u>, p. 352-55.
    "Conference Summary." In Conference on the National Longitudinal Surveys of Mature Women (1978: U.S. Department of Labor). <u>Women's Changing Roles at Home and on the Job</u>, p. 7-13.
    "Testimony." In U.S. Congress. Joint Economic Committee. Subcommittee on Economic Growth and Stabilization. <u>American Women Workers in a Full Employment Economy</u>, p. 3-5.
    "Testimony." In U.S. Congress. Senate. Committee on Labor and Human Resources. <u>The Coming Decade</u>, p. 535-7.

Scafidel, Beverly.
    "Caroline Carson." In Reynolds Conference (2nd: 1975: University of South Carolina). <u>South Carolina Women Writers</u>, p. 47-59.

Scanlon, Laura Polla.
    "Changing Needs of Ethnic Women in Higher Education." In Conference on the Educational and Occupational Needs of White Ethnic Women (1978: Boston, MA). <u>Conference on the Educational and Occupational Needs of White Ethnic Women</u>, p. 115-28.

Scanzoni, Letha Dawson.
    "The Great Chain of Being and the Chain of Command." In <u>Women's Spirit Bonding</u>, p. 41-55.
    "A Religious Perspective." In <u>Women's Spirit Bonding</u>, p. 243-8.

Schaffer, Jacqueline.
    "Testimony." In U.S. Commission on Civil Rights. <u>Hearing Before the U.S. Commission on Civil Rights Held in Chicago</u>, v. 2, p. 179-87.

Schain, Josephine.
    "Statement." In U.S. Congress. House. Committee on Foreign Affairs. <u>American Neutrality Policy</u>, p. 438-41.

Schaper, Donna.
    "The Movement of Suffering." In <u>Spinning a Sacred Yarn</u>, p. 192-8.

Schaudt, Yvonne V.
"Frontiers." In Spinning a Sacred Yarn, p. 199-202.

Schaus, Marilyn.
"Statement." In U.S. Congress. Senate. Committee on Labor
and Human Resources. Subcommittee on Family and Human
Services. Forum for Families, p. 34-5.

Scheirbeck, Helen Maynor.
"Current Educational Status of American Indian Girls." In
Conference on the Educational and Occupational Needs of
American Indian Women (1976: Albuquerque, NM). Confer-
ence on the Educational and Occupational Needs of American
Indian Women, p. 63-81.

Schepps, Mollie.
"Address at Cooper Union, April, 1912." Life and Labor, (July
1912), 215-6.

Scherago, Marcia.
"Testimony." In U.S. Congress. Senate. Committee on the
Judiciary. Subcommittee on Juvenile Justice. Teenage Sui-
cide, p. 2-3.

Schiller, Patricia.
"Competence of Sex Therapists." In Ethical Issues in Sex Therapy and Research, v. 2, p. 342-5.

Schirmer, Jennifer G.
"Women and Social Policy: Lessons from Scandinavia." In Perspectives on Power, p. 87-102.

Schissel, Lillian.
"Diaries of Frontier Women: On Learning to Read the Obscured
Patterns." In Conference on the History of Women (1977:
St. Paul, MN). Woman's Being, Woman's Place, p. 53-66.

Schlafly, Phyllis.
"Comparable Worth Is Unfair to Women and to Men." Daughters
of the American Revolution Magazine, 119 (November 1985),
768-70.
"Controversy Over the Equal Rights Amendment." In Images of
Women in American Popular Culture, p. 426-8.
"Schlafly Speech." In Historic Documents of 1982, p. 616-7.
"Statement." In U.S. Congress. House. Committee on Armed
Services. Subcommittee on Military Personnel. Women in the
Military, p. 235-8, 240-3.
"Statement." In U.S. Congress. House. Committee on Post
Office and Civil Service. Subcommittee on Compensation and
Employee Benefits. Federal Pay Equity Act of 1984, pt. 1,
p. 265-8.

"Statement." In U.S. Congress. House. Committee on Post
Office and Civil Service. Subcommittee on Compensation and
Employee Benefits. Options for Conducting a Pay Equity
Study, p. 453-6.
"Statement." In U.S. Congress. House. Committee on Ways
and Means. Subcommittee on Social Security. Treatment of
Men and Women Under the Social Security Program, p. 58-73.
"Statement." In U.S. Congress. Senate. Committee on Labor
and Human Resources. Sex Discrimination in the Workplace,
p. 396-9, 461-3.

Schlossberg, Nancy K.
"Testimony." In U.S. Congress. House. Select Committee on
Aging. Subcommittee on Retirement Income and Employment.
National Policy Proposals Affecting Midlife Women, p. 62-70.

Schmidt, Ruth.
"Women, Gender, and the Curriculum." In Toward a Balanced
Curriculum, p. 191-3.

Schmitz, Betty.
"From Issue to Action." In Toward a Balanced Curriculum, p.
157-8.
"Project on Women in the Curriculum: Montana State University."
In Toward a Balanced Curriculum, p. 80-90.

Schmotzer, Alice.
"Testimony." In U.S. Congress. House. Select Committee on
Aging. Subcommittee on Retirement Income and Employment.
Task Force on Social Security and Women. Treatment of
Women Under Social Security, p. 165-6.

Schmuck, Patricia A.
"Changing Women's Representation in School Management: A
Systems Perspective." In Women and Educational Leadership,
p. 239-59.

Schnaier, Jenny Ann.
"Statement." In U.S. Congress. House. Committee on Veterans'
Affairs. Subcommittee on Hospitals and Health Care, VA
Health Care for Women, p. 25-7.

Schneider, Claudine.
"Statement." In U.S. Congress. House. Committee on Appro-
priations. Subcommittee on the Department of the Interior
and Related Agencies. Department of the Interior and Re-
lated Agencies Appropriations for 1986. Washington:
U.S.G.P.O., 1985, pt. 10, p. 1159.
"Statement." In U.S. Congress. House. Committee on Appro-
priations. Subcommittee on the Departments of Commerce,
Justice, and State, the Judiciary, and Related Agencies.
Departments of Commerce, Justice, and State, the Judiciary,

and Related Agencies Appropriations for 1982. Washington: U.S.G.P.O., 1981, pt. 9, p. 686-90.

"Statement." In U.S. Congress. House. Committee on Education and Labor. Civil Rights Act of 1984, p. 57-9.

"Statement." In U.S. Congress. House. Committee on Education and Labor. Subcommittee on Labor-Management Relations. Pension Equity for Women, p. 34-5.

"Statement." In U.S. Congress. House. Committee on Education and Labor. Subcommittee on Postsecondary Education. Hearings on Higher Education Civil Rights Enforcement. Washington: U.S.G.P.O., 1984, p. 379-84.

"Statement." In U.S. Congress. House. Committee on Energy and Commerce. Subcommittee on Energy Conservation and Power. Clinch River: An Alternative Financing Plan. Washington: U.S.G.P.O., 1984, p. 42-55.

"Statement." In U.S. Congress. House. Committee on Energy and Commerce. Subcommittee on Energy Conservation and Power. Energy Assistance and the Elderly. Washington: U.S.G.P.O., 1982, p. 69-70.

"Statement." In U.S. Congress. House. Committee on Energy and Commerce. Subcommittee on Fossil and Synthetic Fuels. Synthetic Fuels Corporation and Oil Inventories Policy. Washington: U.S.G.P.O., 1982, p. 35-7.

"Statement." In U.S. Congress. House. Committee on Foreign Affairs. U.S. Foreign Policy and the Law of the Sea. Washington: U.S.G.P.O., 1982, p. 46-8.

"Statement." In U.S. Congress. House. Committee on Government Operations. Government Activities and Transportation Subcommittee. Program to Increase Sales of Federal Surplus Real Property. Washington: U.S.G.P.O., 1984, p. 191-8.

"Statement." In U.S. Congress. House. Committee on Interior and Insular Affairs. Subcommittee on Public Lands and Natural Parks. Public Land Management Policy. Washington: U.S.G.P.O., 1983, p. 18-25.

"Statement." In U.S. Congress. House. Committee on the Judiciary. Subcommittee on Administrative Law and Governmental Relations. Medical Malpractice Claims by Armed Forces Personnel. Washington: U.S.G.P.O., 1984, p. 16-27.

"Statement." In U.S. Congress. House. Committee on Veterans' Affairs. Legislative Presentation of the Military Order of the Purple Heart and AMVETS. Washington: U.S.G.P.O., 1981, p. 6-13.

"Statement." In U.S. Congress. House. Task Force on Social Security and Women. Treatment of Women Under Social Security, v. 3, p. 15.

Schneider, Rose.
   "Statement." In U.S. Congress. House. Select Committee on Aging. Subcommittee on Retirement Income and Employment. Task Force on Social Security and Women. Treatment of Women Under Social Security, v. 3, p. 52-3.

Schneiderman, Rose.
"Senators vs. Working Women." In Eisenstein, Sarah. Give Us Bread But Give Us Roses, p. 157-9.
"Speech on Suffrage." Life and Labor, (August 1912), 288.
"Under What Conditions Women Work." In Outspoken Women, p. 151-7.

Schoenrich, Edith.
"Testimony." In U.S. Congress. House. Committee on Energy and Commerce. Subcommittee on Health and the Environment. Health and the Environment Miscellaneous, pt. 5, p. 953-4.

Scholten, Catherine M.
"'On the Importance of the Obstetrick Art': Changing Customs of Childbirth in America, 1760-1825." In Women and Health in America, p. 142-54.

Schomp, Katherine.
"Testimony." In U.S. Commission on Civil Rights. Hearing Before the U.S. Commission on Civil Rights Held in Denver, p. 286-7.

Schor, Naomi.
"For a Restricted Thematics: Writing, Speech, and Difference in Madame Bovary." In The Future of Difference, p. 167.

Schramm, Patricia C.
"Statement." In U.S. Congress. House. Committee on Ways and Means. Subcommittee on Public Assistance and Unemployment Compensation. AFDC and Social Service Bills and Related Oversight Issues, p. 27-9.

Schramm, Sarah Slavin.
"Women's Studies: Its Focus, Idea Power, and Promise." In Women's Studies, p. 3-11.

Schroeder, Patricia.
"Great Expectations. From Abigail Adams to the White House." Vital Speeches, 50 (May 15, 1984), 472-4.
"Statement." In U.S. Congress. House. Committee on Appropriations. Subcommittee on the Departments of Commerce, Justice, and State, the Judiciary, and Related Agencies. Departments of Commerce, Justice, and State, the Judiciary, and Related Agencies Appropriations for 1985. Washington: U.S.G.P.O., 1984, pt. 11, p. 1-18.
"Statement." In U.S. Congress. House. Committee on Appropriations. Subcommittee on Energy and Water Development. Energy and Water Development Appropriations for 1983. Washington: U.S.G.P.O., 1982, pt. 7, p. 361-9.
"Statement." In U.S. Congress. House. Committee on Armed Services. Subcommittee on Military Compensation. Hearing

on H.R. 2817, H.R. 3677, and H.R. 6270, Legislation Related To Benefits for Former Spouse of a Military Retiree. Washington: U.S.G.P.O., 1980, p. 22-31.

"Statement." In U.S. Congress. House. Committee on Armed Services. Military Personnel and Compensation Subcommittee. Benefits for Former Spouses of Military Members, pt. 1, p. 15-7.

"Statement." In U.S. Congress. House. Committee on Education and Labor. Subcommittee on Employment Opportunities. Oversight Hearings on Equal Employment Opportunity and Affirmative Action, pt. 1, p. 156-7.

"Statement." In U.S. Congress. House. Committee on Education and Labor. Subcommittee on Employment Opportunities. Oversight Hearing on the Federal Enforcement of Equal Employment Opportunity Laws, p. 2-3.

"Statement." In U.S. Congress. House. Committee on Education and Labor. Subcommittee on Post Secondary Education. Guaranteed Student Loan and Civil Rights Enforcement. Washington: U.S.G.P.O., 1984, p. 6-13.

"Statement." In U.S. Congress. House. Committee on Education and Labor. Subcommittee on Postsecondary Education. Legislative Hearing: Regulations on the Solomon Amendment to the Defense Act of 1983. Washington: U.S.G.P.O., 1984, p. 13-20.

"Statement." In U.S. Congress. House. Committee on Energy and Commerce. Subcommittee on Health and the Environment. Pregnancy-Related Health Services, p. 48-50.

"Statement." In U.S. Congress. House. Committee on Energy and Commerce. Subcommittee on Telecommunications, Consumer Protection, and Finance. International Trade Issues in Telecommunications and Related Industries. Washington: U.S.G.P.O., 1983, p. 438-40.

"Statement." In U.S. Congress. House. Committee on Government Operations. Employment and Housing Subcommittee. Equal Employment Opportunity Commission Update: Policies on Pay Equity and Title VII Enforcement. Washington: U.S.G.P.O., 1985, p. 5-16.

"Statement." In U.S. Congress. House. Committee on Government Operations. Legislation and National Security Subcommittee. Administration Proposal Threatens First Amendment Rights of Government Grantees and Contractors. Washington: U.S.G.P.O., 1983, p. 19-24.

"Statement." In U.S. Congress. House. Committee on Government Operations. Manpower and Housing Subcommittee. Equal Employment Opportunity Commission's Handling of Pay Equity Cases, p. 319-22.

"Statement." In U.S. Congress. House. Committee on Interior and Insular Affairs. Subcommittee on Energy and the Environment. Reorganization of the Office of Surface Mining. Washington: U.S.G.P.O., 1981, p. 1-6, 93-4.

"Statement." In U.S. Congress. House. Committee on Interstate

and Foreign Commerce. Subcommittee on Consumer Protection
and Finance. Reciprocity in Investment. Washington:
U.S.G.P.O., 1981, p. 3-4.

"Statement." In U.S. Congress. House. Committee on Post
Office and Civil Service. Subcommittee on Civil Service.
Federal Government Affirmative Action Policies and Programs,
p. 1-2.

"Statement." In U.S. Congress. House. Committee on Post
Office and Civil Service. Subcommittee on Compensation and
Employee Benefits. Civil Service Spouse Retirement Equity
Act. Washington: U.S.G.P.O., 1984, p. 2-9.

"Statement." In U.S. Congress. House. Committee on Post
Office and Civil Service. Subcommittee on Compensation and
Employee Benefits. Federal Employees Health Benefits Reform
Act of 1983. Washington: U.S.G.P.O., 1984, p. 34-9.

"Statement." In U.S. Congress. House. Committee on Post
Office and Civil Service. Subcommittee on Compensation and
Employee Benefits. Federal Pay Equity Act of 1984. Wash-
ington: U.S.G.P.O., 1984, pt. 1, p. 7-10.

"Statement." In U.S. Congress. House. Committee on Post
Office and Civil Service. Subcommittee on Compensation and
Employee Benefits. Options for Conducting a Pay Equity
Study, p. 11-2.

"Statement." In U.S. Congress. House. Committee on Post
Office and Civil Service. Subcommittee on Compensation and
Employee Benefits. Revisions to H.R. 2300, the Civil Service
Spouse Retirement Equity Act. Washington: U.S.G.P.O.,
1984, p. 2-5.

"Statement." In U.S. Congress. House. Committee on Post
Office and Civil Service. Subcommittee on Human Resources.
Amend Ethics in Government Act of 1978. Washington:
U.S.G.P.O., 1984, p. 2-24.

"Statement." In U.S. Congress. House. Committee on Post
Office and Civil Service. Subcommittee on Human Resources.
Federal Employees Flexible and Compressed Work Schedules
Act. Washington: U.S.G.P.O., 1985, p. 9-12.

"Statement." In U.S. Congress. House. Committee on Public
Works and Transportation. Subcommittee on Public Buildings
and Grounds. Public Building Needs. Washington:
U.S.G.P.O., 1980, p. 12-8.

"Statement." In U.S. Congress. House. Committee on Public
Works and Transportation. Subcommittee on Water Resources.
Proposed Water Resources Development Projects of the U.S.
Army Corps of Engineers. Washington: U.S.G.P.O., 1982,
p. 1643-64.

"Statement." In U.S. Congress. House. Committee on Rules.
Subcommittee on the Legislative Process. Congressional Oversight of Federal Programs. Washington: U.S.G.P.O., 1983,
p. 15-25, 327-36.

"Statement." In U.S. Congress. House. Committee on Small
Business. Subcommittee on General Oversight and Minority

Enterprise. <u>Women in Business</u>, p. 14-5.

"Statement." In U.S. Congress. House. Committee on Ways and Means. <u>Economic Equity Act and Related Tax and Pension Reform</u>. Washington: U.S.G.P.O., 1984, p. 9-11.

"Statement." In U.S. Congress. House. Committee on Ways and Means. Subcommittee on Oversight. <u>Impact of the Administration's Budget Cuts on the Nation's Public Hospitals</u>. Washington: U.S.G.P.O., 1982, p. 4-5.

"Statement." In U.S. Congress. House. Committee on Ways and Means. Subcommittee on Public Assistance and Unemployment Compensation. <u>Administration's Fiscal Year 1983 Legislative Proposals for Unemployment Compensation and Public Assistance</u>. Washington: U.S.G.P.O., 1982, p. 426-31.

"Statement." In U.S. Congress. House. Committee on Ways and Means. Subcommittee on Public Assistance and Unemployment Compensation. <u>Child Support Enforcement Legislation</u>. Washington: U.S.G.P.O., 1984, p. 61-2.

"Statement." In U.S. Congress. House. Committee on Ways and Means. Subcommittee on Public Assistance and Unemployment Compensation. <u>Unemployment Compensation Bills</u>. Washington: U.S.G.P.O., 1980, p. 26-40.

"Statement." In U.S. Congress. House. Select Committee on Aging. Subcommittee on Retirement Income and Employment. <u>Administration's Plan to Eliminate Older Workers Jobs Program</u>. Washington: U.S.G.P.O., 1982, p. 28-32.

"Statement." In U.S. Congress. House. Select Committee on Aging. Subcommittee on Retirement Income and Employment. Task Force on Social Security and Women. <u>Inequities Toward Women in the Social Security Program</u>, p. 13-4.

"Statement." In U.S. Congress. House. Select Committee on Aging. Subcommittee on Retirement Income and Employment. Task Force on Social Security and Women. <u>Treatment of Women Under Social Security</u>, v. 4, p. 11-2.

"Statement." In U.S. Congress. Joint Economic Committee. <u>Economic Status of Women</u>, p. 16-8.

"Statement." In U.S. Congress. Senate. Committee on Armed Services. Subcommittee on Manpower and Personnel. <u>Uniformed Services Former Spouses Protection Act</u>. Washington: U.S.G.P.O., 1982, p. 24-9.

"Statement." In U.S. Congress. Senate. Committee on Finance. <u>Potential Inequities Affecting Women</u>, pt. 2, p. 58-9.

"Statement." In U.S. Congress. Senate. Committee on Labor and Human Resources. <u>The Coming Decade</u>, p. 629-31.

"Statement." In U.S. Congress. Senate. Committee on the Judiciary. <u>Presidential Nominations to the Civil Rights Commission</u>. Washington: U.S.G.P.O., 1984, p. 62-73.

Schub, Judy.

"Statement." In U.S. Congress. House. Committee on Education and Labor. Subcommittee on Labor-Management Relations.

Pension Equity for Women, p. 66-8.
"Statement." In U.S. Congress. House. Committee on Ways
and Means. Economic Equity Act and Related Tax and Pen-
sion Reform, p. 82-4.
"Statement." In U.S. Congress. House. Select Committee on
Aging. Subcommittee on Retirement Income and Employment.
Task Force on Social Security and Women. Inequities Toward
Women in the Social Security System, p. 67-9.
"Statement." In U.S. Congress. House. Select Committee on
Aging. Subcommittee on Retirement Income and Employment.
Task Force on Social Security and Women. Treatment of
Women Under Social Security, pt. 3, p. 28-9.
"Statement." In U.S. Congress. Senate. Committee on Finance.
Potential Inequities Affecting Women, pt. 1, p. 82-3.

Schulenburg, Jane Tibbetts.
"Clio's European Daughters: Myopic Modes of Perception." In
Prism of Sex, p. 33-53.

Schultz, Phyllis.
"Statement." In U.S. Congress. Senate. Committee on Labor
and Human Resources. Subcommittee on Child and Human
Development. Domestic Violence Prevention and Services Act,
1980, p. 77-9.

Schwarzer, Theresa F.
"The Changing Status of Women in the Geosciences." In Expanding the Role of Women in the Sciences, p. 48-64.

Schweber, Claudine A.
"But Some Were Less Equal ... The Fight for Women Jurors."
In Women Organizing, p. 329-44.
"Testimony." In U.S. Congress. House. Committee on the
Judiciary. Subcommittee on Courts, Civil Liberties, and the
Administration of Justice. The Female Offender--1979-80,
p. 73-8.

Schwerin, Susan.
"Testimony." In U.S. Commission on Civil Rights. Hearing Before the U.S. Commission on Civil Rights Held in Chicago,
v. 2, p. 265-7, 271.

Scott, Anne Firor.
"Are We the Women Our Grandmothers Were?" In Scott, Making
the Invisible Woman Visible, p. 337-52.
"Education and the Contemporary Woman." In Scott, Making the
Invisible Woman Visible, p. 353-60.
"Education of Women: the Ambiguous Reform." In Scott, Making
the Invisible Woman Visible, p. 298-312.
"Getting to Be A Notable Georgia Woman." In Scott, Making the
Invisible Woman Visible, p. 313-22.

"Historians Construct the Southern Woman." In Scott, Making the Invisible Woman Visible, p. 243-58. Also In Sex, Race, and the Role of Women in the South, p. 95-110.

"Old Wives' Tales." In Scott, Making the Invisible Woman Visible, p. 323-36.

"Woman's Place Is in the History Books." In Scott, Making the Invisible Woman Visible, p. 361-70.

"Womens' Perspective on the Patriarchy in the 1850s." In Scott, Making the Invisible Woman Visible, p. 175-89.

"Women's Voluntary Association in the Forming of American Society." In Scott, Making the Invisible Woman Visible, p. 279-94.

Scott, Gloria.
"Speech by Commissioner Gloria Scott." In U.S. National Commission on the Observance of International Women's Year. The Spirit of Houston, p. 217.

Scott, Martha L.
"Georgia Harkness: Social Activist and/or Mystic." In Women in New Worlds, v. 1, p. 117-40.

Scott, Melinda.
"Address at Cooper Union April 1912." Life and Labor, (June 1912), 190-1.

Scott, Patricia Bell.
"Black Women and the Work Experience." In Women's Lives, p. 169-77.

Scott, Peggy R.
"God Has a Master Plan for Your Life." In Those Preachin' Women, p. 107-12.

Scrivner, Ellen.
"Acculturating Women into Law Enforcement Careers." In Training Conference (1st: 1984: Washington, DC). Interagency Committee on Women in Federal Law Enforcement, p. 7-11.

Seaman, Barbara.
"Statement." In U.S. Congress. House. Select Committee on Population. Fertility and Contraception in America, pt. 3, p. 128-31.

"Statement." In U.S. Congress. Senate. Committee on Labor and Human Resources. Subcommittee on Health and Scientific Research. Women in Science and Technology Equal Opportunity Act, 1979, p. 63-8.

Secor, Cynthia.
"Gertrude Stein: The Complex Force of Her Femininity." In Women, the Arts, and the 1920s in Paris and New York, p. 27-35.

Seeman, Mary.
"Statement." In U.S. Congress. Senate. Committee on Small
Business. Women Entrepreneurs, p. 58-62.

Segal, Mady Wechsler.
"The Argument for Female Combatants." In Female Soldiers, p.
267-89.

Seidenberg, Faith.
"Is the Question of Women a Political Question?" In Cornell
Conference on Women (1969: Cornell University). Proceed-
ings, p. 20-1, 24, 29, 33.

Siedler-Feller, Doreen.
"A Feminist Critique of Sex Therapy." In Handbook of Feminist
Therapy, p. 119-30.

Siedman, Ann.
"Women and the Development of 'Underdevelopment': The African Experience." In Women and Technological Change in Developing Countries, p. 109-26.

Seizas, Judith.
"Reaching the Middle Class Alcoholic." In Women in Crisis Conference (1st: 1979: New York, NY). Women in Crisis, p.
69-75.

Seka (Ms.)
"Testimony." In U.S. Congress. Senate. Committee on the
Judiciary. Subcommittee on Juvenile Justice. Effect of
Pornography on Women and Children, p. 313-4.

Sells, Lucy W.
"Leverage for Equal Opportunity Through Mastery of Mathe-
matics." In Women and Minorities in Science, p. 7-26.
"The Mathematics Filter and the Education of Women and Minor-
ities." In Hyman Blumberg Symposium on Research in Early
Childhood Education (8th: 1976: Johns Hopkins University).
Women and the Mathematical Mystique, p. 66-75.

Seltzer, Mildred M.
"Statement." In U.S. Congress. Senate. Select Committee on
Aging. Women in Our Aging Society, p. 30-4.

Seltzer, Miriam.
"Research Perspectives for Programming to Meet the Needs of
Youth in Transition from School to Work." In Young Women
and Employment, p. 52-5.

Sen, Lalita.
"Travel Patterns and Behavior of Women in Urban Areas." In
Women's Travel Issues, p. 417-35.

Serbin, Lisa A.
"Teachers, Peers, and Play Preferences: An Environmental Approach to Sex Typing in the Preschool." In Conference on Non-Sexist Early Childhood Education (1976: Arden House). Perspectives on Non-Sexist Early Childhood Education, p. 79-93.

Serlin, Erica.
"Emptying the Nest: Women in the Launching Stage." In Women's Lives, p. 13-45.

Setta, Susan.
"Denial of the Female: Affirmation of the Feminine. The Father-Mother God of Mary Baker Eddy." In Beyond Androcentrism, p. 289-303.

Sewell, Sandra Serrano.
"Sterilization Abuse and Hispanic Women." In Birth Control and Controlling Birth, p. 121-4.

Sexton, Patricia Cayo.
"Where Women Find Work." In Young Women and Employment, p. 11-4.

Shadron, Virginia.
"The Laity Rights Movement, 1906-1918: Woman's Suffrage in the Methodist Episcopal Church, South." In Women in New Worlds, v. 1, p. 261-75.

Shaeffer, Ruth Gilbert.
"Improving Job Opportunities for Women from a U.S. Corporate Perspective." In Equal Employment Policy for Women, p. 277-310.

Shalala, Donna E.
"Speech." In Women's Travel Issues, p. 719-32.
"Statement." In U.S. Congress. Senate. Committee on Small Business. Women-In-Business Programs in the Federal Government, p. 144-6.
"Testimony." In U.S. Congress. Senate. Committee on the Judiciary. Subcommittee on the Constitution. The Impact of the Equal Rights Amendment, pt. 1, p. 113-6.

Shamana, Beverly J.
"Letting Go." In Those Preachin' Women, p. 101-6.

Shanley, Mary Lyndon.
"Individualism, Marriage, and the Liberal State: Beyond the Equal Rights Amendment." In Women Organizing, p. 363-87.

Shapiro-Perl, Nina.
"Resistance Strategies: The Routine Struggle for Bread and
    Roses." In My Troubles Are Going to Have Trouble With Me,
    p. 192-208.

Sharma, Arvind.
"Ramakrsna Paramahamsa: A Study in Mystic's Attitude Toward
    Women." In Beyond Androcentrism, p. 115-23.

Shaver, Anne.
"Women in Epic." In GLCA Women's Studies Conference (4th:
    1978: Rochester, Indiana). Structure of Knowledge, p. 37-
    40.

Shaw, Anna Howard.
"The Fate of Republics." In We Shall Be Heard, p. 201-6.
"The Heavenly Visitation." In Outspoken Women, p. 159-62.
"Presidential Address at the 1905 Convention of the National
    American Woman Suffrage Association, Portland, Oregon, June
    29, 1905." In Women, the Family, and Freedom, v. 2, p.
    140-1.
"Presidential Address at the 1906 Convention of the National
    American Woman Suffrage Association, Baltimore, Maryland,
    February 1906." In Women, the Family, and Freedom, v. 2,
    p. 141-3.

Shaw, Ethelrine.
"Professional Schools and Their Impact on Black Women." In
    Conference on the Educational and Occupational Needs of Black
    Women (1975: Washington, DC). Conference on the Educa-
    tional and Occupational Needs of Black Women, v. 2, p. 71-83.

Shaw, Lois B.
"Economic Consequences of Marital Disruption." In Conference
    on the National Longitudinal Surveys of Mature Women (1978:
    U.S. Department of Labor). Women's Changing Roles at Home
    and on the Job, p. 181-203.

Shaw, Nancy Stoller.
"Testimony." In U.S. Congress. House. Committee on the
    Judiciary. Subcommittee on Courts, Civil Liberties, and the
    Administration of Justice. The Female Offender--1979-80,
    p. 61-73.

Shearer, Beth.
"C/SEC: A Special-Interest Interpersonal Group Brings About
    Change." In Birth Control and Controlling Birth, p. 277-82.

Shed, Sarah K.
"Statement." In U.S. Congress. Joint Economic Committee.
    Problems of Working Women, p. 126-30.

Shepard, Anita.
"Statement." In U.S. Congress. House. Committee on the Budget. Task Force on Entitlements, Uncontrollables, and Indexing. Women and Children in Poverty, p. 9-10.

Shepro, Theresa Aragon.
"Impediments to Hispanic Women Organizing." In Conference on the Educational and Occupational Needs of Hispanic Women (1976: Denver, CO and Washington, DC). Conference on the Educational and Occupational Needs of Hispanic Women, p. 117-37.

Sherburne, Jane C.
"Testimony." In U.S. Congress. Senate. Committee on the Judiciary. Subcommittee on the Constitution. The Impact of the Equal Rights Amendment, pt. 1, p. 811-3.

Sherif, Carolyn Wood.
"Bias in Psychology." In Prism of Sex, p. 93-133.

Sherman, Claire Richter.
"Taking a Second Look: Observations on the Iconography of a French Queen, Jeanne de Bourbon (1338-1378)." In Feminism and Art History, p. 101-17.

Sherman, Julia A.
"Therapist Attitudes and Sex-Role Stereotyping." In Women and Psychotherapy, p. 35-66.

Shields, Laurie.
"Statement." In U.S. Congress. House. Select Committee on Aging. Subcommittee on Retirement Income and Employment. Task Force on Social Security and Women. Treatment of Women Under Social Security, v. 4, p. 173-5.

Shipp, Denese A.
"Statement." In U.S. Congress. House. Select Committee on Population. Fertility and Contraception in America, pt. 2, p. 207-11.
"Testimony." In U.S. Congress. House. Committee on Education and Labor. Subcommittee on Select Education. Adolescent Pregnancy, p. 67-9.

Shoong, Ellen.
"Testimony." In U.S. Congress. House. Committee on Education and Labor. Subcommittee on Employment Opportunities. Oversight Hearings on the OFCCP's Proposed Affirmative Action Regulations, p. 37-42, 46-62.

Short, Mary K.
"Statement." In U.S. Congress. House. Select Committee on

Children, Youth, and Families. Families with Disabled Children, p. 9-10.

Shriver, Eunice Kennedy.
"Testimony." In U.S. Congress. Senate. Committee on Human Resources. Adolescent Health, Services, and Pregnancy Prevention Care Act of 1978, p. 114-88.

Shteir, Ann B.
"Linnaeus's Daughters: Women and British Botany." In Berkshire Conference on the History of Women (5th: 1982: Vassar College). Women and the Structure of Society, p. 67-73.

Shulman, Gail B.
"View from the Back of the Synagogue: Women in Judaism." In Sexist Religion and Women in the Church, p. 143-66.

Shumway, Naomi M.
"Except You Become as Little Children." In Blueprints for Living, p. 62-8.

Siegel, Betty L.
"Knowledge with Commitment. Teaching Is the Central Task of the University." Vital Speeches, 50 (April 15, 1984), 394-7.

Siegel, Rachel Josefowitz.
"Beyond Homophobia: Learning to Work with Lesbian Clients." In Handbook of Feminist Therapy, p. 183-90.

Silver, Catherine Bodard.
"Salon, Foyer, Bureau: Women and the Professions in France." In American Journal of Sociology, 78 (January 1973), 836-51. Also in Clio's Consciousness Raised, p. 27-83.

Silverman, Kaja.
"Historie d'O: The Construction of a Female Subject." In Pleasure and Danger, p. 320-49.

Simmons, Althea T. L.
"Statement." In U.S. Congress. Senate. Committee on Labor and Human Resources. Subcommittee on Education, Arts and Humanities. Civil Rights Act of 1984, pt. 1, p. 274-7.
"Statement." In U.S. Congress. Senate. Committee on the Judiciary. Subcommittee on the Constitution. Civil Rights Act of 1984, p. 62-3.
"Testimony." In U.S. Congress. House. Committee on Interstate and Foreign Commerce. Subcommittee on Consumer Protection and Finance. Nondiscrimination in Insurance, p. 125-7.

Simmons, Delanne A.
   "Statement." In U.S. Congress. House. Select Committee on
   Aging. Problems of Aging Women, p. 120-2.

Simon, Bernece K.
   "Social Casework Theory: An Overview." In Charlotte Towle
   Memorial Symposium on Comparative Theoretical Approaches
   to Casework Practice (1969: University of Chicago). Theories of Social Casework, p. 353-95.

Sims, Anastatia.
   "Sisterhoods of Service: Women's Clubs and Methodist Women's
   Missionary Societies in North Carolina, 1890-1930." In Women
   in New Worlds, v. 2, p. 196-210.

Sims-Wood, Janet.
   "Resources in Black Women's Studies." In Toward a Balanced
   Curriculum, p. 135-41.

Sinclair, Laura.
   "Can Your Bones Live?" In Those Preachin' Women, p. 21-6.

Sizemore, Susan Johnson.
   "Testimony." In U.S. Congress. House. Committee on Inter-
   state and Foreign Commerce. Subcommittee on Oversight and
   Investigations. Nurse Midwifery: Consumers' Freedom of
   Choice, p. 48-53.

Sklar, Kathryn Kish.
   "Hull House in the 1890s: A Community of Women Reformers."
   Signs, 10 (Summer, 1985), 658-77.
   "The Last Fifteen Years: Historians' Changing Views of American
   Women in Religion and Society." In Women in New Worlds,
   v. 1, p. 48-65.

Slaughter, M. Jane.
   "Women and Socialism: the Case of Angelica Balabanoff." In
   Women's Studies, p. 55-63.

Sloan, Martha E.
   "Women in the Laboratory." In Women in Engineering--Beyond
   Recruitment, p. 88.

Smalley, Ruth E.
   "The Functional Approach to Casework Practice." In Charlotte
   Towle Memorial Symposium on Comparative Theoretical Ap-
   proaches to Casework Practice (1969: University of Chicago).
   Theories of Social Casework, p. 77-127.

Smeal, Eleanor Cutri.
   "Smeal Statement (on End of ERA Campaign)." In Historic

Documents of 1982, p. 613-5.
"Statement." In U.S. Congress. House. Committee on Education and Labor. Subcommittee on Employment Opportunities. Oversight Hearings on Equal Employment Opportunity and Affirmative Action, pt. 1, p. 84-92.
"Statement." In U.S. Congress. House. Committee on Ways and Means. Subcommittee on Social Security. Treatment of Men and Women Under the Social Security Program, p. 99-103.
"Statement." In U.S. Congress. House. Select Committee on Aging. Subcommittee on Retirement Income and Employment. Task Force on Social Security and Women. Treatment of Women Under Social Security, v. 1, p. 55-7, v. 3, p. 16-8, v. 4, p. 179-81.
"Statement." In U.S. Congress. Senate. Committee on Labor and Human Resources. Sex Discrimination in the Workplace, 1981, p. 178-84.
"Statement." In U.S. Congress. Senate. Committee on Labor and Human Resources. Subcommittee on Health and Scientific Research. Women in Science and Technology Equal Opportunity Act, 1979, p. 79-84.
"Statement." In U.S. Congress. Senate. Committee on the Judiciary. Nomination of Sandra Day O'Connor. Washington: U.S.G.P.O., 1982, p. 395-401.
"Statement." In U.S. Congress. Senate. Committee on the Judiciary. Confirmation Hearing on William French Smith, Nominee, to Be Attorney General. Washington: U.S.G.P.O., 1981, p. 93-108.
"Testimony." In U.S. Congress. House. Select Committee on Aging. Subcommittee on Retirement Income and Employment. National Policy Proposals Affecting Midlife Women, p. 24-34.

Smedley, Agnes.
"Birth Control Work in China." In International Birth Control Conference (7th: 1930: Zurich). Practice of Contraception, p. 283.

Smith, Aileen M.
"Congenital Minamata Disease: Methyl-Mercury Poisoning and Birth Defects in Japan." In Conference on Women and the Workplace (1976: Washington, DC). Conference on Women and the Workplace, p. 75-81.

Smith, Barbara.
"Racism and Women's Studies." In All the Women Are White, All the Blacks Are Men, But Some of Us Are Brave, p. 48-51.
"The Structure of Knowledge: A Feminist Perspective." In GLCA Women's Studies Conference (4th: 1978: Rochester, Indiana). Structure of Knowledge, p. 11-6.

Smith, Barbara B.
"Blueprints for Living." In Blueprints for Living, p. 32-43.

"Relief Society: A Story of New Beginnings." In A Woman's
Choices, p. 1-13.

Smith, Beverly.
"Statement." In U.S. Congress. Senate. Committee on Labor
and Human Resources. Subcommittee on Family and Human
Services. Forum for Families, p. 40-5.

Smith, Catherine.
"Mysticism and Feminism: Jacob Boehme and Jane Lead." In
Women & Men, p. 398-408.

Smith, Deborah K.
"Personal Choices." In The Woman in Management, p. 65-8.

Smith, Dorothy E.
"A Sociology for Women." In Prism of Sex, p. 135-87.

Smith, Elaine M.
"Mary McLeod Bethune and the National Youth Administration."
In Conference on Women's History (1976: Washington, DC).
Clio Was a Woman, p. 149-77.

Smith, Elise Fiber.
"Statement." In U.S. Congress. Senate. Committee on Foreign
Relations. Women in Development, p. 58-9.

Smith, Elske V. P.
"The Individual and the Institution." In Covert Discrimination
and Women in the Sciences, p. 7-35.

Smith, Heather.
"Statement." In U.S. Congress. Senate. Committee on Labor
and Human Resources. Subcommittee on Family and Human
Services. Forum for Families, p. 40.

Smith, Ida.
"A Woman's Role and Destiny." In Blueprints for Living, p. 98-
102.

Smith, Jane E.
"Testimony." In U.S. Congress. House. Committee on Energy
and Commerce. Subcommittee on Health and the Environment,
pt. 3, p. 28-9.

Smith, Janet E.
"Abortion as a Feminist Concern." In The Zero People, p. 77-95.

Smith, Janet Farrell.
"Rights-Conflict, Pregnancy, and Abortion." In Beyond Domination, p. 265-73.

Smith, Julie.
  "Testimony." In U.S. Congress. Senate. Committee on the
    Judiciary. Subcommittee on Juvenile Justice. Teenage Sui-
    cide, p. 12-3.

Smith, Margaret Chase.
  "Declaration of Conscience, June 1, 1950." In We Shall Be Heard,
    p. 304-8.
  "Declaration of Conscience II, June 1, 1970." In We Shall Be
    Heard, p. 309-11.

Smith, Maryann Yodelis.
  "Access to the Media: Balancing Feminism and the First Amend-
    ment." In Women and the News, p. 64-86.

Smith, Peggy.
  "Testimony." In U.S. Congress. Senate. Committee on the
    Judiciary. Subcommittee on Juvenile Justice. Effect of Por-
    nography on Women and Children, p. 174-7.

Smith, Princess Jackson.
  "Networking. What It Is, What I Can Do For You, How You Do
    It." Vital Speeches, 49 (September 15, 1983), 712-3.

Smith, Robbi.
  "Statement." In U.S. Congress. House. Committee on Armed
    Services. Subcommittee on Military Personnel. Hearings on
    H.R. 6569, Registration of Women, p. 61-3.
  "Statement." In U.S. Congress. House. Committee on Armed
    Services. Subcommittee on Military Personnel. Women in the
    Military, p. 282-7, 288-9.

Smith, Toulmin.
  "Discussion of The Training of Women as Librarians." In The
    Role of Women in Librarianship, p. 33-4.

Smith, Virginia.
  "Statement." In General Farm Bill of 1981. Washington:
    U.S.G.P.O., 1981, pt. 8, p. 112-4.
  "Statement." In U.S. Congress. House. Committee on Agricul-
    ture. Review of Agricultural Exports and Trade (Secretary
    John R. Block). Washington: U.S.G.P.O., 1984, p. 16-7.
  "Statement." In U.S. Congress. House. Committee on Agricul-
    ture. Ad Hoc Subcommittee on Grain Elevator Bankruptcy.
    Review of Grain Elevator Bankruptcies. Washington:
    U.S.G.P.O., 1983, p. 5-8.
  "Statement." In U.S. Congress. House. Committee on Agricul-
    ture. Subcommittee on Conservation, Credit, and Rural De-
    velopment. Miscellaneous Conservation. Washington:
    U.S.G.P.O., 1984, p. 310-2.
  "Statement." In U.S. Congress. House. Committee on

Agriculture. Subcommittee on Livestock and Graines. Imported Meat Inspection and Labeling. Washington: U.S.G.P.O., 1980, p. 29-32.
"Statement." In U.S. Congress. House. Committee on Agriculture. Subcommittee on Livestock, Dairy, and Poultry. Review of the Operation of the Imported Meat Inspection Program. Washington: U.S.G.P.O., 1984, p. 3-5, 26-8.
"Statement." In U.S. Congress. House. Committee on Appropriations. Subcommittee on Energy and Water Development. Energy and Water Development Appropriations for 1982. Washington: U.S.G.P.O., 1981, pt. 10, p. 1316-50.
"Statement." In U.S. Congress. House. Committee on Appropriations. Subcommittee on Energy and Water Development. Energy and Water Development Appropriations for 1985. Washington: U.S.G.P.O., 1984, pt. 8, p. 412-45.
"Statement." In U.S. Congress. House. Committee on Appropriations. Subcommittee on Military Construction Appropriations. Military Construction Appropriations for 1983. Washington: U.S.G.P.O., 1982, pt. 5, p. 417-20, 475-9.
"Statement." In U.S. Congress. House. Committee on Appropriations. Subcommittee on the Departments of Commerce, Justice, and State, the Judiciary, and Related Agencies. Departments of Commerce, Justice, and State, the Judiciary, and Related Agencies Appropriations for 1982. Washington: U.S.G.P.O., 1981, pt. 9, p. 325-32.
"Statement." In U.S. Congress. House. Committee on Appropriations. Subcommittee on the Departments of Commerce, Justice, and State, the Judiciary, and Related Agencies. Departments of Commerce, Justice, and State, the Judiciary, and Related Agencies Appropriations for 1986. Washington: U.S.G.P.O., 1985, pt. 1, p. 233-9.
"Statement." In U.S. Congress. House. Committee on Government Operations. Government Information, Justice, and Agriculture Subcommittee. The Impact of the FCC's Telephone Access Charge Decision. Washington: U.S.G.P.O., 1984, p. 679-95.
"Statement." In U.S. Congress. House. Committee on Merchant Marine and Fisheries. Subcommittee on Merchant Marine. Competitive Shipping and Shipbuilding Act of 1983. Washington: U.S.G.P.O., 1984, p. 93-9.
"Statement." In U.S. Congress. House. Committee on the Judiciary. Subcommittee on Courts, Civil Liberties, and the Administration of Justice. Marshals Service of Process. Washington: U.S.G.P.O., 1983, p. 28-46.
"Statement." In U.S. Congress. House. Committee on Veterans' Affairs. OMB Circular A-76--Contracting-Out in VA Facilities. Washington: U.S.G.P.O., 1982, p. 28-31.
"Statement." In U.S. Congress. House. Committee on Ways and Means. Advisability of a Tax Reduction in 1980 Effective for 1981. Washington: U.S.G.P.O., 1981, pt. 1, p. 234-7.
"Statement." In U.S. Congress. House. Committee on Ways

and Means. Financing Needs of the Highway Trust Fund for Fiscal Years 1983-1986. Washington: U.S.G.P.O., 1983, p. 196-201.

"Statement." In U.S. Congress. House. Committee on Ways and Means. Tax Aspects of the President's Economic Program. Washington: U.S.G.P.O., 1981, pt. 3, p. 1552-5.

"Statement." In U.S. Congress. House. Committee on Ways and Means. Subcommittee on Select Revenue Measures. Issues Arising Under the Payment-In-Kind Program. Washington: U.S.G.P.O., 1983, p. 55-6.

"Statement." In U.S. Congress. Senate. Committee on Commerce, Science, and Transportation. Subcommittee on Merchant Marine. Cargo Preference. Washington: U.S.G.P.O., 1984, p. 64-9.

"Statement." In U.S. Congress. Senate. Committee on Energy and Natural Resources. Subcommittee on Water and Power. Ground Water Recharge in the High Plains States, and Delivery of Water to the North Platte Irrigation Project. Washington: U.S.G.P.O., 1984, pt. 1, p. 37-9.

Smith-Rosenberg, Carroll.
"The New Woman and the New History." Feminist Studies, 3 (1976), 188-98.

"Puberty to Menopause: the Cycle of Femininity in Nineteenth-Century America." In Clio's Consciousness Raised, p. 23-34.

Smithson, Elaine.
"Statement." In U.S. Congress. House. Committee on Education and Labor. Subcommittee on Employment Opportunities. Oversight Hearing on the Federal Enforcement of Equal Employment Opportunity Laws, p. 76-8.

Smothers, Louise.
"Statement." In U.S. Congress. House. Committee on Education and Labor. Subcommittee on Employment Opportunities. Oversight Hearing on the Federal Enforcement of Equal Employment Opportunity Laws, p. 73-6.

"Statement." In U.S. Congress. House. Committee on the Post Office and Civil Service. Subcommittee on Investigations. Sexual Harassment in the Federal Government, pt. 1, p. 99-103, 105-11. '

Sneed, Michael.
"Statement." In U.S. Congress. Senate. Committee on the Judiciary. Subcommittee on Investigate Juvenile Delinquency. Protection of Children Against Sexual Exploitation, p. 57-64.

Snider, Yvonne B.
"Statement." In U.S. Congress. Senate. Select Committee on Small Business. Women-In-Business Programs in the Federal Government, p. 7-11.

Snow, Deborah.
  "Special Interest Report on Voting Rights." In Western Regional
    Civil Rights and Women's Rights Conference (4th: 1977:
    San Francisco, CA). Recent Developments, p. 132-4.

Snowe, Olympia J.
  "Statement." In U.S. Congress. House. Committee on Educa-
    tion and Labor. Civil Rights Act of 1984, p. 20-1.
  "Statement." In U.S. Congress. House. Committee on Educa-
    tion and Labor. Subcommittee on Labor Standards. Use and
    Control of Ethylene Oxide (EtO). Washington: U.S.G.P.O.,
    1984, p. 426-30.
  "Statement." In U.S. Congress. House. Committee on Govern-
    ment Operations. Manpower and Housing Subcommittee.
    Equal Employment Opportunity Commission's Handling of Pay
    Equity Cases, p. 8-10.
  "Statement." In U.S. Congress. House. Committee on Interior
    and Insular Affairs. Settlement of Indian Land Claims in the
    State of Maine. Washington: U.S.G.P.O., 1980, p. 25-27.
  "Statement." In U.S. Congress. House. Committee on Small
    Business. Subcommittee on General Oversight and Minority
    Enterprise. Women In Business, p. 6-7.
  "Statement." In U.S. Congress. House. Committee on Veterans'
    Affairs. Subcommittee on Hospitals and Health Care. Veter-
    ans' Administration's Research on Aging. Washington:
    U.S.G.P.O., 1984, p. 3-10.
  "Statement." In U.S. Congress. House. Committee on Ways
    and Means. Economic Equity Act and Related Tax and Pen-
    sion Reform. Washington: U.S.G.P.O., 1984, p. 11-5.
  "Statement." In U.S. Congress. House. Committee on Ways
    and Means. Subcommittee on Trade. Options to Improve the
    Trade Remedy Laws. Washington: U.S.G.P.O., 1983, p. 239-
    48.
  "Statement." In U.S. Congress. House. Select Committee on
    Aging. Subcommittee on Retirement Income and Employment.
    Task Force on Social Security and Women. Treatment of Wom-
    en Under Social Security, p. 4.
  "Statement." In U.S. Congress. Joint Economic Committee.
    American Women: Three Decades of Change, p. 1-2.
  "Statement." In U.S. Congress. Joint Economic Committee.
    Problems of Working Women, p. 1-2.
  "Statement." In U.S. Congress. Joint Economic Committee.
    The Role of Older Women in the Work Force, p. 1-2.
  "Statement." In U.S. Congress. Joint Economic Committee.
    Women in the Work Force, p. 1-2.
  "Statement." In U.S. Congress. Senate. Committee on Finance.
    Potential Inequities Affecting Women, pt. 2, p. 7-10.
  "Statement." In U.S. Congress. Senate. Committee on Labor
    and Human Resources. Subcommittee on Aging. Reauthoriza-
    tion of the Older Americans Act, 1984. Washington:
    U.S.G.P.O., 1984, pt. 2, p. 613-6.

Snyder, Dolores.
"Statement." In U.S. Congress. Senate. Special Committee on Aging. Women in Our Aging Society, p. 22-4.

Snyder, Mary.
"Testimony." In U.S. Commission on Civil Rights. Hearing Before the U.S. Commission on Civil Rights Held in Denver, p. 292-4, 297.

Soelle, Dorothee.
"The Children of Soweto." In Women and the Word, p. 110-3.

Sole, Yolanda Russinovich.
"Sociocultural and Sociopsychological Factors in Differential Language Retentiveness By Sex." In Conference on the Sociology of the Languages of American Women (1976: New Mexico State University). Proceedings, p. 137-54.

Solomon, Barbara Bryant.
"Social Work Values and Skills to Empower Women." In NASW Conference on Social Work Practice With Women (1st: 1980: Washington, DC). Women, Power, and Change, p. 206-14.

Solomon, Hannah G.
"Address to National Council of Jewish Women, Washington, 1902." In The American Jewish Woman, p. 436-40.

Solyom, (Mrs.) H. L.
"Testimony." In U.S. Congress. House. Committee on Ways and Means. Birth Control, (1932) p. 97.

Sommers, Tish.
"Statement." In U.S. Congress. Senate. Committee on Labor and Human Resources. The Coming Decade, p. 594-601.

Sorensen, Elaine Shaw.
"The Educated Woman Within Us." In A Woman's Choices, p. 24-32.

Sowards, Janie.
"Statement." In U.S. Congress. Senate. Committee on Labor and Human Resources. Subcommittee on Labor. Retirement Equity Act of 1983, p. 23-5.

Spaeth, Donna.
"Statement." In U.S. Congress. House. Select Committee on Population. Fertility and Contraception in America, p. 206-8.

Spafford, Belle S.
"The American Woman's Movement." In Blueprints for Living, p. 6-16.

Spancier, Betty.
"Beyond Advocacy." In NASW Conference on Social Work Prac-
tice With Women (1st: 1980: Washington, DC). Women,
Power, and Change, p. 186-96.

Spanier, Bonnie.
"The Natural Sciences: Casting a Critical Eye on 'Objectivity.'"
In Toward a Balanced Curriculum, p. 49-56.
"Toward a Balanced Curriculum: Wheaton College." In Toward
a Balanced Curriculum, p. 73-9.

Sparks, Caroline.
"Statement." In U.S. Congress. House. Committee on Science
and Technology. Subcommittee on Domestic and International
Scientific Planning, Analysis, and Cooperation. Research into
Violent Behavior: Overview and Sexual Assaults, p. 657-62,
666.

Spear, Ruth.
"Statement." In U.S. Congress. House. Select Committee on
Aging. Subcommittee on Health and Long-Term Care. Pro-
gress in Controlling Breast Cancer, p. 39-43.

Specter, Joan.
"Testimony." In U.S. Congress. Senate. Committee on the
Judiciary. Subcommittee on Juvenile Justice. Effect of
Pornography on Women and Children, p. 26-8.

Spellman, Gladys Noon.
"Statement." In U.S. Congress. House. Committee on Public
Works and Transportation. Subcommittee on Public Buildings
and Grounds. Art in Architecture. Washington: U.S.G.P.O.,
1980, p. 10-9.
"Statement." In U.S. Congress. House. Committee on Small
Business. Subcommittee on General Oversight and Minority
Enterprise. Women in Business, p. 3-4.
"Statement." In U.S. Congress. House. Committee on the Dis-
trict of Columbia. Subcommittee on Fiscal Affairs and Health,
Judiciary, Manpower, and Education and Metropolitan Affairs.
Miscellaneous Legislation. Washington: U.S.G.P.O., 1981,
p. 160-2.

Spence, Janet T.
"Traits, Roles, and the Concept of Androgyny." In Psychology
and Women: In Transition, p. 167-87.

Spencer, Dale.
"Theorising About Theorising." In Theories of Women's Studies
II, p. 119-22.

Spero, Joan.
"The North-South Dialogue." Department of State Bulletin, 80 (September 1980), 31-3.

Spigelmyer, Sharon.
"Statement." In U.S. Congress. House. Committee on Post Office and Civil Service. Subcommittee on Compensation and Employee Benefits. Options for Conducting a Pay Equity Study, p. 365-7, 369-71.

Spillers, Hortense J.
"Interstices: A Small Drama of Words." In Pleasure and Danger, p. 73-100.

Spinney, Eleanor.
"The Ministry of a Lay Associate." In Conference on Women and Lay Ministry (1976: St. Michel's Church, Milton, MA). Women and Lay Ministry, p. 8-10.

Sporberg, (Mrs.) William D.
"Women as a Social Force." In Cooper Union for the Advancement of Science and Art. Women, Society and Sex, p. 213-28.

Springer, Eugenia Franklin.
"The Emergence of Immigrant Women Artists." In Immigrants and Refugees in a Changing Nation, p. 117-24.

Srinivasan, Mangalam.
"Impact of Selected Industrial Technologies on Women in Mexico." In Women and Technological Change in Developing Countries, p. 89-108.

St. Martin, Darla.
"Statement." In U.S. Congress. Senate. Committee on the Judiciary. Subcommittee on the Constitution. Constitutional Amendments Relating to Abortion, v. 1, p. 1102-3.

Stadler, Quandra Prettyman.
"Visibility and Difference: Black Women in History and Literature--Pieces of a Paper and Some Ruminations." In The Future of Difference, p. 239-46.

Stahl, Angelique O.
"Palestinian Question: Assistance to Palestinians." Department of State Bulletin, 79 (February 1979), 64.
"Palestinian Question: Occupied Territories." Department of State Bulletin, 79 (February 1979), 63-4.

Stanton, Donna C.
"Language and Revolution: The Franco-American Dis-Connection." In The Future of Difference, p. 73.

Stanton, Elizabeth Cady.
"Fifteenth Amendment--Votes for Black Men Only?" In Women, the Family, and Freedom, v. 1, p. 494-500.
"Address Delivered at Seneca Falls, July 19, 1848." In Stanton, Elizabeth Cady Stanton, p. 27-35.
"Address of Welcome to the International Council of Women, March 25, 1888." In Stanton, Elizabeth Cady Stanton, p. 208-15.
"Address to the Founding Convention of the National American Woman Suffrage Association, February, 1890." In Stanton, Elizabeth Cady Stanton, p. 222-7.
"Address to the Legislature of New York on Women's Rights, February 14, 1854." In Stanton, Elizabeth Cady Stanton, p. 44-52.
"Appeal for the Maine Law, January 21, 1853." In Stanton, Elizabeth Cady Stanton, p. 40-3.
"The Case for Universal Suffrage." In Outspoken Women, p. 164-8.
"From Address to the New York State Legislature, 1860." In Gilbert S. Norton Anthology of Literature by Women, p. 344-7.
"Home Life." In Stanton, Elizabeth Cady Stanton, p. 131-8.
"The Solitude of Self." In Stanton, Elizabeth Cady Stanton, p. 246-54. Also in We Shall Be Heard, p. 66-75.
"Speech at Lawrence, Kansas, 1867." In Stanton, Elizabeth Cady Stanton, p. 113-8.
"Speech to the Anniversary of the American Anti-Slavery Society, 1860." In Stanton, Elizabeth Cady Stanton, p. 78-85.
"Speech to the McFarland-Richardson Protest Meeting, May, 1869." In Stanton, Elizabeth Cady Stanton, p. 125-30.

Staples, Emily Anne.
"Statement." In U.S. Congress. House. Select Committee on Children, Youth, and Families. Violence and Abuse in American Families, p. 37-41.

Staples, Sharon L.
"Stress: A Matter of Choice." In A Woman's Choices, p. 139-47.

Starbuck, Dorothy.
"Statement." In U.S. Congress. Senate. Committee on Veterans' Affairs. Recognition for Purposes of VA Benefits, p. 45-52.

Starhawk.
"Immanence: Uniting the Spiritual and Political." In Women's Spirit Bonding, p. 310-7.

Starrett, Barbara.
"The Metaphors of Power." In The Politics of Women's Spirituality, p. 185-93.

Stead, Bette Ann.
"Why Does the Secretary Hate Me and Other Laments of the

Professionally Educated Woman Employee." Vital Speeches, 48 (May 1, 1982), 438-40.

"Women and Men in Management. Getting Along." Vital Speeches, 46 (October 15, 1979), 10-16.

Steele, Diana A.
"Statement." In U.S. Congress. House. Committee on Armed Services. Subcommittee on Military Personnel. Hearings on H.R. 6569, Registration of Women, p. 40-3.

"Statement." In U.S. Congress. House. Committee on Armed Services. Subcommittee on Military Personnel. Women in the Military, p. 252-6, 268-70.

"Testimony." In U.S. Congress. House. Committee on Interstate and Foreign Commerce. Subcommittee on Consumer Protection and Finance. Nondiscrimination in Insurance, p. 246-9.

Steffey, Sue Ann.
"The Stuff That Covenant Is Made Of." In Women and the Word, p. 17-21.

Steiger, Janet.
"Testimony." In U.S. Congress. House. Select Committee on Aging. Subcommittee on Retirement Income and Employment. National Policy Proposals Affecting Midlife Women, p. 59-60.

Steiger, Joann M.
"Career Education: Who Needs It?" In Today's Girls: Tomorrow's Women, p. 45-9.

Steihm, Judith.
"Women and Citizenship: Mobilisation, Participation, Representation." In Women, Power, and Political Systems, p. 50-65.

Stein, Barbara.
"Statement." In U.S. Congress. House. Committee on Education and Labor. Subcommittee on Elementary, Secondary, and Vocational Education. Hearing on Women's Educational Equity Act, p. 68-71.

Stein, Eileen M.
"Statement." In U.S. Congress. House. Committee on Post Office and Civil Service. Subcommittee on Compensation and Employee Benefits. Options for Conducting a Pay Equity Study, p. 282-5.

"Statement." In U.S. Congress. Joint Economic Committee. Economic Status of Women, p. 102-5.

Stein, Gertrude.
"From Plays (Lectures in America)." In Women in Theatre, p. 157-62.

"The Gradual Making of the Making of Americans." In Stein,
Lectures in America, p. 135-61.
"Plays." In Stein, Lectures in America, p. 93-131.
"Poetry and Grammar." In Stein, Lectures in America, p. 209-46.
"Portraits and Repetition." In Stein, Lectures in America, p.
165-206.
"What Is English Literature?" In Stein, Lectures in America, p.
11-55.

Steinbacher, Roberta.
"Futuristic Implications of Sex Preselection." In The Custom-
Made Child?, p. 187-92.
"Sex Preselection: From Here to Fraternity." In Beyond Domina-
tion, p. 274-82.
"Statement." In U.S. Congress. House. Committee on Post Of-
fice and Civil Service. Subcommittee on Compensation and
Employee Benefits. Options for Conducting a Pay Equity
Study, p. 117-21.

Steinberg, Ronnie J.
"Comparable Worth Doctrine and Its Implementation." In Compar-
able Worth: Issues for the 80's, p. 55-9.
"Statement." In U.S. Congress. House. Committee on Post
Office and Civil Service. Subcommittee on Compensation and
Employee Benefits. Options for Conducting a Pay Equity
Study, p. 73-5.
"Statement." In U.S. Congress. House. Committee on Post
Office and Civil Service. Subcommittee on Human Resources.
Pay Equity, pt. 21, p. 539-43, 559-60.

Steinem, Gloria.
"Speech at the National Women's Political Caucus Conference,
July, 1981." Ms., 10 (October 1981), 93.

Steinmetz, Suzanne.
"Statement." In U.S. Congress. House. Committee on Science
and Technology. Subcommittee on Domestic and International
Scientific Planning, Analysis, and Cooperation. Research Into
Violent Behavior: Domestic Violence, p. 164-72.
"Statement." In U.S. Congress. House. Select Committee on
Aging. Subcommittee on Health and Long-Term Care. Elder
Abuse, p. 19-21.

Steinson, Barbara J.
"The Woman's Peace Party: New Departures and Old Arguments."
In The Role of Women in Conflict and Peace, p. 45-53.

Stelck, Kristin.
"Statement." In U.S. Congress. House. Committee on Govern-
ment Operations. Manpower and Housing Subcommittee. The
Women's Bureau, p. 218-20.

Stendahl, Krister.
"Enrichment or Threat? When the Eves Come Marching In." In
Sexist Religion and Women in the Church, p. 117-24.

Steorts, Nancy Harvey.
"Reg-U-Trends. Ten New Directions Transforming Project Safety
Regulation." Vital Speeches, 50 (November 15, 1983), 76-81.
"Testimony." In U.S. Congress. House. Committee on Energy
and Commerce. Subcommittee on Health and the Environment.
Health and the Environment Miscellaneous, pt. 7, p. 6-9,
765-7.

Stephenson, Wilda.
"Statement." In U.S. Congress. Senate. Committee on Labor
and Human Resources. The Coming Decade, p. 744-5.

Stere, Linda K.
"Feminist Assertiveness Training: Self-Esteem Groups as Skill
Training for Women." In Handbook of Feminist Therapy, p.
51-61.

Stern, Alvera.
"Statement." In U.S. Congress. House. Select Committee on
Children, Youth, and Families. Families in Crisis, p. 65-70.

Stern, Paula.
"Foreign Project Counterfeiting. Private Business Sometimes
Needs the Government." Vital Speeches, 51 (September 1,
1985), 674-7.
"Trade Problems in Agriculture. Will the Circle Be Unbroken?"
Vital Speeches, 51 (September 15, 1985), 725-8.

Stevens, Christine.
"Testimony." In U.S. Congress. House. Committee on Energy
and Commerce. Subcommittee on Health and the Environment.
Health and the Environment Miscellaneous, pt. 7, p. 373-4.

Stewart, Bonnie Ann.
"Session Summary." In International Conference on Women and
Food (1978: University of Arizona). A Conference on the
Role of Women in Meeting Basic Food and Water Needs in De-
veloping Countries, p. 63-70.

Stewart, Maria.
"African Rights and Liberty." In Outspoken Women, p. 169-73.

Stevens, Dottie.
"Organizing for Welfare Rights." Women's Studies Quarterly, 13
(Summer 1985), 11-2.

Stille, Darlene.
"Testimony." In U.S. Commission on Civil Rights. Hearings

Before the U.S. Commission on Civil Rights Held in Chicago,
pt. 1, p. 255-6, 65-6, 271, pt. 2, p. 44-8.

Stillman, Frances.
"Balancing Work, Family and Personal Lives." In Training Conference (1st: 1984: Washington, DC). Interagency Committee on Women in Federal Law Enforcement, p. 11-5.

Stimpson, Catharine R.
"Power, Presentations and the Presentable." In Women & Men,
p. 111-33.
"The Power to Name: Some Reflections on the Avant-Garde."
In Prism of Sex, p. 55-77.
"Scholarship About Women: The State of the Art." In Confer-
ence on "Scholars and Women" (1981: University of Maryland).
Women's Studies and the Curriculum, p. 7-15.
"Sex, Gender, and American Culture." In Women and Men:
Changing Roles, p. 201-44.
"Where Does Integration Fit: The Development of Women's
Studies." In Toward a Balanced Curriculum, p. 11-24.
"Women as Knowers." In Feminist Visions, p. 15-24.

Stitzel, Judith.
"Challenging Curricular Assumptions: Teaching and Studying
Women's Literature from a Regional Perspective." In Toward
the Second Decade, p. 141-8.

Stokes, Jeanette.
"Jesus, Son of David, Have Mercy on Me." In Women and the
Word, p. 12-6.

Stone, Elizabeth W.
"Statement." In U.S. Congress. House. Committee on Post
Office and Civil Service. Subcommittee on Human Resources.
Pay Equity, pt. 1, p. 755-59.

Stone, Hannah M.
"The Birth Control Clinical Research Bureau, New York." In
International Birth Control Conference (6th: 1926: New
York, NY). Reports and Papers, p. 199-204.
"Testimony." In U.S. Congress. House. Committee on the
Judiciary. Birth Control, (1934) p. 108-11.
"The Vaginal Occlusive Pessary." In International Birth Control
Conference (6th: 1926: New York, NY). Reports and Pa-
pers, p. 3-15.

Stone, Lucy.
"Disappointment Is the Lot of Women." In Zak, Michele. Women
and the Politics of Culture, p. 339-41.
"Nature and Revelation and Woman's Right to Vote." In Out-
spoken Women, p. 174-7.
"Taxation Without Representation." In We Shall Be Heard, p. 47-52.

Stone, Pauline Terrelonge.
    "Race, Sex, Age and Political Conservatism Among Partisan
       Elites." In Women's Lives, p. 427-38.

Stone, Valerie.
    "Testimony." In U.S. Congress. House. Committee on Energy
       and Commerce. Subcommittee on Health and the Environment.
       Health and the Environment Miscellaneous, pt. 5, p. 316-8.

Strandburg, Maria.
    "Testimony." In U.S. Commission on Civil Rights. Hearing Be-
       fore the U.S. Commission on Civil Rights Held in Denver, p.
       303-6, 311-5.

Straub, Eleanor F.
    "Women in the Civilian Labor Force." In Conference on Women's
       History (1976: Washington, DC). Clio Was a Woman, p.
       206-26.

Straumanis, Joan.
    "The Call for Feminist Theory: Will We Recognize the Answer."
       In GLCA Women's Studies Conference (6th: 1980). Towards
       a Feminist Transformation of the Academy II, p. 51-6.
    "The Feminist Critique: Plans and Prospects." In GLCA Wom-
       en's Studies Conference (4th: 1978: Rochester, Indiana).
       Structure of Knowledge, p. 58-60.
    "Generic 'Man' and Mortal Woman." In GLCA Women's Studies
       Conference (4th: 1978: Rochester, Indiana). Structure of
       Knowledge, p. 25-32.

Straus, Ellen Sulzberger.
    "The Telephone and the Microphone." In Women in Action, p.
       7-10.

Streeter, (Mrs.) Thomas W.
    "Statement." In U.S. Congress. House. Committee on Foreign
       Affairs. American Neutrality Policy, p. 122-4.

Strober, Myra H.
    "Market Work, Housework and Child Care: Burying Archaic
       Tenets, Building New Arrangements." In Women: A De-
       velopmental Perspective, p. 207-20.
    "Some Policy Research Issues Relating to Women's Employment."
       In Conference on the National Longitudinal Surveys of Mature
       Women (1978: U.S. Department of Labor). Women's Changing
       Roles at Home and on the Job, p. 301-8.
    "Toward a General Theory of Occupational Sex Segregation: the
       Case of Public School Teaching." In Sex Segregation in the
       Workplace, p. 144-56.
    "Women and Men in the World of Work: Present and Future."
       In Women and Men: Changing Roles, p. 119-52.

Strother, Dora Dougherty.
"Statement." In U.S. Congress. House. Committee on Veterans' Affairs. Select Subcommittee to Review WASP Bills. To Provide Recognition to the Women's Air Force, p. 340-4.
"Statement." In U.S. Congress. Senate. Committee on Veterans' Affairs. Recognition for Purposes of VA Benefits, p. 68-72.

Stuart, Martha.
"Welfare of the Client." In Ethical Issues in Sex Therapy and Research, v. 2, p. 353-7.

Stuchiner, Theresa B.
"Statement." In U.S. Congress. House. Committee on Education and Labor. Subcommittee on Labor-Management Relations. Legislative Hearing on Pension Equity for Women, p. 51-2.
"Statement." In U.S. Congress. Senate. Committee on Finance. Potential Inequities Affecting Women, pt. 1, p. 118-20.
"Statement." In U.S. Congress. Senate. Committee on Labor and Human Resources. Subcommittee on Labor. Retirement Equity Act of 1983, pt. 56-8, 60.

Sturgis, Christine.
"Testimony." In U.S. Commission on Civil Rights. Hearing Before the U.S. Commission on Civil Rights Held in Denver, p. 368, 371-6.

Sturlaugson, Mary Frances.
"Freedom to Become." In Ye Are Free to Choose, p. 105-7.

Suchocki, Marjorie.
"Openness and Mutuality in Process Thought and Feminist Action." In Feminism and Process Thought, p. 62-81.

Sullivan, Ann.
"Statement." In U.S. Congress. Senate. Committee on Labor and Human Resources. Subcommittee on Family and Human Resources. Subcommittee on Family and Human Resources. Reauthorization of the Adolescent Family Life Demonstration Projects Act of 1981, p. 210-2.

Sullivan, Sister Mary William.
"Statement." In U.S. Congress. Senate. Committee on Labor and Human Resources. Subcommittee on Family and Human Resources. Subcommittee on Family and Human Resources. Reauthorization of the Adolescent Family Life Demonstration Projects Act of 1981, p. 32-4.

Swacker, Marjorie.
"Women's Verbal Behavior at Learned and Professional Conference." In Conference on the Sociology of the Languages of American Women (1976: New Mexico State University). Pro-

ceedings, p. 155-60.

Swain, Martha H.
    "The Public Role of Southern Women." In Sex, Race, and the
    Role of Women in the South, p. 37-58.

Swallow, Helen.
    "Midwives in Many Settings." In Birth Control and Controlling
    Birth, p. 245-50.

Sweeney, Eileen.
    "Statement." In U.S. Congress. House. Select Committee on
    Aging. Subcommittee on Retirement Income and Employment.
    Task Force on Social Security and Women. Treatment of
    Women Under Social Security, v. 4, p. 123-5.

Swenson, Norma.
    "Response (to an Obstetrician's Perspective)." In Birth Control
    and Controlling Birth, p. 261-4.

Swift, Carolyn.
    "Statement." In U.S. Congress. House. Committee on Science
    and Technology. Subcommittee on Domestic and International
    Scientific Planning, Analysis, and Cooperation. Research into
    Violent Behavior: Overview and Sexual Assaults, p. 351-66.

Syler, Murrell.
    "Testimony." In U.S. Commission on Civil Rights. Hearing Be-
    fore the U.S. Commission on Civil Rights Held in Chicago,
    v. 1, p. 337-47.

Taber, Gisela.
    "Testimony." In U.S. Equal Employment Opportunity Commission.
    Hearings Before the U.S. Equal Employment Opportunity Com-
    mission on Job Segregation and Wage Discrimination, p. 813-8,
    824-6.

Taeuber, Irene B.
    "Dimensions of Living Space." In The Challenge to Women, p.
    130-45.

Taft, Shirley.
    "Statement." In U.S. Congress. House. Committee on Armed
    Services. Military Personnel and Compensation Subcommittee.
    Benefits for Former Spouses of Military Members, pt. 1, p.
    37-8.

Taimir, Lois M.
    "Men at Middle Age." In Women's Lives, p. 127-31.

Tanner, Doris B.
  "Statement." In U.S. Congress. House. Committee on Veterans'
  Affairs. Select Subcommittee to Review WASP Bills, p. 398,
  419-20.

Tarbel, Ida.
  "The History of the Standard Oil Company: The Oil War of
  1872." In Outspoken Women, p. 178-90.

Tarr-Whalen, Linda.
  "Statement." In U.S. Congress. Senate. Committee on the
  Judiciary. Subcommittee on the Constitution. Constitutional
  Amendments Relating to Abortion, v. 1, p. 1103-5.

Tate, Constance.
  "Statement." In Symposium on Minorities and Women in Science
  and Technology (1981: Washington, DC). Symposium on
  Minorities and Women in Science and Technology, p. 24-8.

Tate, Jean.
  "Statement." In U.S. Congress. Senate. Committee on Small
  Business. Women Entrepreneurs, p. 34-7.

Taub, Nadine.
  "Defining and Combating Sexual Harassment." In Class, Race,
  and Sex, p. 263-75.
  "Testimony." In U.S. Commission on Civil Rights. Hearing Before the U.S. Commission on Civil Rights Held in Chicago,
  v. 1, p. 110, 124, 129-32.

Taylor, Anita.
  "Talk, Future Shock and Futureshlock. Real Education Teachers
  Problem Solving." Vital Speeches, 51 (September 1, 1985),
  680-3.
  "Women as Leaders: The Skills at Which We Are So Uniquely
  Qualified." Vital Speeches, 50 (May 1, 1984), 445-8.

Taylor, Audrey.
  "Statement." In U.S. Congress. Senate. Committee on Finance.
  Potential Inequities Affecting Women, pt. 1, p. 217-8.

Taylor, Barbara.
  "'The Men Are As Bad As Their Masters...': Socialism, Feminism, and Sexual Antagonism in the London Tailoring Trade
  in the Early 1830s." Feminist Studies, 5 (Spring 1979), 7-40.
  "The Unique Employment Problems of Female Offenders Returning
  to the Community and Labor Market." In Women in Crisis
  Conference (1st: 1979: New York, NY). Women in Crisis,
  p. 221-4.

Taylor, Barbara Brown.
  "Pentecost II." In Women of the Word, p. 120-4.
  "Pentecost X." In Women of the Word, p. 125-9.
  "Pentecost XVIII." In Women of the Word, p. 130-4.

Taylor, Lily Ross.
  "The Assemblies in Their Settings: A Summary." In Taylor,
    Roman Voting Assemblies, p. 107-13.
  "Caesar's Propaganda and the Gallic Succession." In Taylor,
    Party Politics in the Age of Caesar, p. 157-61.
  "The Campaign for Election and Legislation." In Taylor, Party
    Politics in the Age of Caesar, p. 62-75.
  "Catonism and Caesarism." In Taylor, Party Politics in the Age
    of Caesar, p. 163-84.
  "Cato's Leadership of the Optimates." In Taylor, Party Politics
    in the Age of Caesar, p. 124-31.
  "The Centuriate Assembly in the Light of New Discoveries." In
    Taylor, Roman Voting Assemblies, p. 85-106.
  "Cicero and Sallust on the Reform of the State." In Taylor,
    Party Politics in the Age of Caesar, p. 152-6.
  "The Criminal Courts and the Rise of a New Man." In Taylor,
    Party Politics in the Age of Caesar, p. 98-118.
  "Methods of Voting and Places of Assembly of Centuries and
    Tribes." In Taylor, Roman Voting Assemblies, p. 34-58.
  "The Nature of the Assemblies: Ancient Sources and Modern
    Interpretations." In Taylor, Roman Voting Assemblies, p.
    1-14.
  "Nobles, Clients, and Personal Armies." In Taylor, Party Politics
    in the Age of Caesar, p. 25-49.
  "Optimates and Populares Before Catilines's Conspiracy." In
    Taylor, Party Politics in the Age of Caesar, p. 119-23.
  "Personalities and Programs." In Taylor, Party Politics in the
    Age of Caesar, p. 1-24.
  "Politics and the Public Priesthoods." In Taylor, Party Politics
    in the Age of Caesar, p. 90-7.
  "Pompey's Sole Consulship." In Taylor, Party Politics in the
    Age of Caesar, p. 148-51.
  "Propaganda and Public Opinion from 58 to 53 B.C." In Taylor,
    Party Politics in the Age of Caesar, p. 142-7.
  "Public Meetings in the Forum, on the Capitoline, and in the
    Circus Flaminius." In Taylor, Roman Voting Assemblies, p.
    15-33.
  "Religion and Divination in Politics." In Taylor, Party Politics
    in the Age of Caesar, p. 78-89.
  "The Removal of Cato." In Taylor, Party Politics in the Age of
    Caesar, p. 137-9.
  "The Role of the City Plebs and the Italians in the Voting." In
    Taylor, Party Politics in the Age of Caesar, p. 50-61.
  "The Thirty-Five Tribes and the Procedure in the Tribal Assem-
    blies." In Taylor, Roman Voting Assemblies, p. 59-84.
  "The Union of Cato's Enemies." In Taylor, Party Politics in the
    Age of Caesar, p. 132-6.

Taylor, Peggy.
"Placement of Workers in High-Risk Areas--A Legislative Viewpoint." In Conference on Women and the Workplace (1976:
Washington, DC). Conference on Women and the Workplace,
p. 127-32.

Taylor, Patricia P.
"Testimony." In U.S. Congress. House. Committee on the
Judiciary. Subcommittee on Courts, Civil Liberties, and the
Administration of Justice. The Female Offender--1979-80,
p. 29-33.

Taylor, Ruthie.
"Testimony." In U.S. Commission on Civil Rights. Hearing Before the U.S. Commission on Civil Rights Held in Chicago,
v. 2, p. 118-21.

Teague, Kathleen.
"Statement." In U.S. Congress. House. Committee on Armed
Services. Subcommittee on Military Personnel. Hearings on
H.R. 6569, Registration of Women, p. 103-5.

Tedesco, Marie.
"A Feminist Challenge to Darwinism: Antoinette L. B. Blackwell
on the Relations of the Sexes in Nature and Society." In
Feminist Visions, p. 27-30.

Tenant, Lucille.
"Statement." In U.S. Congress. House. Select Committee on
Aging. Subcommittee on Retirement Income and Employment.
Impact of Reagan Economics on Aging Women, p. 62-4.

Tenebaum, Betsy.
"'Gentle and Wavy and Graceful' Huck--An Androgynous Hero."
In Women & Men, p. 355-63.

Tennis, Diane.
"Suffering." In Spinning a Sacred Yarn, p. 203-7.

Tenopyr, Mary L.
"Implications of the Increasing Participation of Women in the Work
Force in the 1990's." In The Changing Composition of the
Workforce, p. 69-76.

Tentier, Leslie W.
"Work in the Lives of Married Women, 1900-1930." In Women &
Men, p. 184-95.

Ter Wisscha, Glennis.
"Statement." In U.S. Congress. House. Committee on Post
Office and Civil Service. Subcommittee on Compensation and

Employee Benefits. Federal Pay Equity Act of 1984, pt. 1,
p. 25-8.

Terrell, Mary Church.
"What It Means to be Colored in the Capital of the United States."
In Outspoken Women, p. 178-90.

Tessner, Elizabeth.
"Testimony." In U.S. Commission on Civil Rights. Hearings
Before the U.S. Commission on Civil Rights Held in Chicago,
v. 2, p. 273-7.

Thacker, Pat.
"Statement." In U.S. Congress. House. Select Committee on
Aging. Subcommittee on Retirement Income and Employment.
Impact of Reagan Economics on Aging Women, p. 21-3.

Thayne, Emma Lou.
"The Cat Fight and What Matters Most." In Blueprints for Living, v. 2, p. 58-60.

Theis, Fran.
"Statement." In U.S. Congress. House. Committee on Ways
and Means. Economic Equity Act and Related Tax and Pension
Reform, p. 125-7.

Theodore, Athena.
"Response to The Social Scene: Isolation and Frustration." In
Women in Engineering--Beyond Recruitment, p. 80-1.

Thomas, Julia.
"Ethics and Professionalism. The Integrated Way." Vital
Speeches, 49 (July 1, 1983), 558-62.

Thomas, M. Carey.
"Address to the Students at the Opening of the Academic Year
1899-1900." In Images of Women in American Popular Culture,
p. 48-51.
"Present Tendencies in Women College and University Education."
In Women, the Family, and Freedom, v. 2, p. 163-9.

Thomas, Marlo.
"Statement." In U.S. Congress. Senate. Committee on Labor
and Human Resources. The Coming Decade, p. 457-60, 484-5.

Thomas, Patricia.
"Statement." In U.S. Congress. House. Committee on Govern-
ment Operations. Manpower and Housing Subcommittee. The
Women's Bureau, p. 186-8.

Thomas, Shirley W.
"Women of Charity: Belle S. Spafford and Barbara B. Smith."
In A Woman's Choices, p. 14-23.

Thompson, Clara.
"Deviants Around 1912. Adler and Jung." In Thompson, Psychoanalysis, p. 153-71.
"Deviations and New Developments in the 1920's." In Thompson, Psychoanalysis, p. 172-92.
"The Ego and Character Structure." In Thompson, Psychoanalysis, p. 59-77.
"Evaluation of Freud's Biological Orientation." In Thompson, Psychoanalysis, p. 18-58.
"Freud's Cultural Orientation Compared with Modern Ideas of Culture." In Thompson, Psychoanalysis, p. 131-52.
"Recent Developments." In Thompson, Psychoanalysis, p. 193-224.
"Resistance and Transference." In Thompson, Psychoanalysis, p. 95-111.
"Therapy." In Thompson, Psychoanalysis, p. 225-43.
"Theories About Anxiety." In Thompson, Psychoanalysis, p. 112-30.
"Unconscious Processes and Repression." In Thompson, Psychoanalysis, p. 78-94.

Thompson, Melissa A.
"Controversy Over the Equal Rights Amendment." In Images of Women in American Popular Culture, p. 423-6.

Thompson, Rosemary.
"Statement." In U.S. Congress. Senate. Committee on Labor and Human Resources. Subcommittee on Child and Human Resources. Domestic Violence Prevention and Services Act, 1980, p. 220-3.

Thompson, Sharon.
"Search for Tomorrow: On Feminism and the Reconstruction of Teen Romance." In Pleasure and Danger, p. 350-84.

Thorman, Rose.
"Statement." In U.S. Congress. House. Committee on Armed Services. Subcommittee on Military Personnel. Women in the Military, p. 287-8.

Thorne, Barrie.
"Gender Imagery and Issues of War and Peace: The Case of the Draft Resistance Movement of the 1960's." In The Role of Women in Conflict and Peace, p. 55-9.

Thorne, W. M.
"Librarianship as a Career for Women." In The Role of Women in Librarianship, p. 84-6.

Threatt, Barbara.
  "Statement." In U.S. Congress. House. Select Committee on
    Aging. Subcommittee on Health and Long-Term Care. Pro-
    gress in Controlling Breast Cancer, p. 70-3.

Tice, Patricia.
  "Statement." In U.S. Congress. House. Committee on Ways
    and Means. Economic Equity Act and Related Tax and Pen-
    sion Reforms, p. 145-6.
  "Statement." In U.S. Congress. Senate. Committee on Finance.
    Potential Inequities Affecting Women, pt. 1, p. 248.

Tidball, M. Elizabeth.
  "To Use All Their Talents. Women Faculty and Their Effect on
    Women Students." Vital Speeches, 46 (April 1, 1980), 380-4.

Tiernan, Kip.
  "Closing Session." Women's Studies Quarterly, 13 (Summer 1985),
    14.
  "Urban Team Ministry." In Conference on Women and Lay Min-
    istry (1976: St. Michel's Church, Milton, MA). Women and
    Lay Ministry, p. 11-4.

Tilley, Barbara C.
  "Assessment of Risks from DES: An Analysis of Research on
    Those Exposed During Pregnancy or In Utero." In The
    Custom-Made Child?, p. 29-38.

Tilly, Louise A.
  "Paths of Proletarianization: Organization of Production, Sexual
    Division of Labor, and Women's Collective Action." Signs, 7
    (Winter 1981), 400-17. Also in Women's Work, p. 25-40.
  "Women and Collective Action in Europe." In The Role of Women
    in Conflict and Peace, p. 31-43.

Tilman-Blackston, Johnnie.
  "Excerpted Testimony From the Southern California Hearings on
    the Feminization of Poverty." Signs, 10 (Winter 1984), 405-6.

Tinker, Irene.
  "New Technologies for Food-Related Activities: An Equity
    Strategy." In Women and Technological Change in Developing
    Countries, p. 51-88.

Tischler, Bonni.
  "Myths and Realities." In Training Conference (1st: 1984:
    Washington, DC). Interagency Committee on Women in Federal
    Law Enforcement, p. 26-9.

Tobach, Ethel.
  "An Agenda to Further Expand the Role of Women in Science and

Technology." In <u>Expanding the Role of Women in the Sciences</u>, p. 336-40.

Tobias, Sheila.
"The Future of Women." In Cornell Conference on Women (1969: Cornell University). <u>Proceedings</u>, p. 64.
"Math Anxiety." In <u>Today's Girls: Tomorrow's Women</u>, p. 55-6.

Todd, Theresa M.
"Statement." In U.S. Congress. House. Committee on Ways and Means. Subcommittee on Social Security. <u>Treatment of Men and Women Under the Social Security Program</u>, p. 186, 190-1.

Tolpin, Martha.
"Wheaton's Assessment Process: A Case Study and Its Lessons." In <u>Toward a Balanced Curriculum</u>, p. 173-87.

Tom, Sally.
"Testimony." In U.S. Congress. House. Committee on Interstate and Foreign Commerce. Subcommittee on Oversight and Investigations. <u>Nurse Midwifery: Consumers' Freedom of Choice</u>, p. 5-6.

Torres, Teresa.
"Testimony." In U.S. Commission on Civil Rights. <u>Hearing by the U.S. Commission on Civil Rights held in Denver</u>, p. 163-4, 167-74.

Tovermale, Tara.
"Statement." In U.S. Congress. House. Select Committee on Children, Youth, and Families. <u>Children, Youth, and Families</u>, p. 79-80.

Trauner, Joan B.
"Testimony." In U.S. Congress. House. Committee on Energy and Commerce. Subcommittee on Health and the Environment. <u>Health and the Environment Miscellaneous</u>, pt. 4, p. 31-3.

Traxler, Margaret Ellen.
"Mary's Christmas Announces Freedom to Captives." In <u>Spinning a Sacred Yarn</u>, p. 208-11.

Traxler, Sister Mary Peter, S.S.N.D.
"Catholic Educational Dilemmas." In <u>Split-Level Lives</u>, p. 73-85.
"The Ministry of Presence." In <u>Split-Level Lives</u>, p. 1-7.

Trebbi, Diana.
"My Prayer 'Grows Up' as I Grow Older." In <u>Spinning a Sacred Yarn</u>, p. 212-7.

Trebilcock, Anne.
"Panel Discussion of Legal Requirements and Implications." In Conference on Women and the Workplace (1976: Washington, DC). Conference on Women and the Workplace, p. 335-40.

Tree, Marietta.
"The Dimensions of Citizenship--Demands of Political Leadership." In Education of Women for Social and Political Leadership, p. 3-10.

Trent, Kathryn.
"Testimony." In U.S. Congress. Senate. Committee on the Judiciary. Birth Control, (1934) p. 67.

Trescott, Martha M.
"Women Engineers in History: Profiles in Holism and Persistence." In Women in Scientific and Engineering Professions, p. 181-204.

Trible, Phyllis.
"The Opportunity of Oneliness (The Ordination of Mary Beale)." In Women and the Word, p. 70-5.

Triplette, Marianne.
"The Emerging Theory of Institutional Discrimination." In Conference on "Scholars and Women" (1981: University of Maryland). Women's Studies and the Curriculum, p. 111-21.

Troll, Lillian E.
"Meaningful Roles for Older Women." In Older Women in the City, p. 167-77.

Troxell, Barbara B.
"The No Which Enables Our Yes." In Women and the Word, p. 26-34.

Truth, Sojourner.
"Address on Woman's Rights." In Images of Women in American Popular Culture, p. 419-21.
"Ain't I a Woman?" In Gilbert, Sandra. Norton Anthology of Literature by Women, p. 253. Also in Outspoken Women, p. 197. Also in We Shall Be Heard, p. 92-3. Also in Zak, Michele. Women and the Politics of Culture, p. 153.
"And Ain't I a Woman?" In Women's America, p. 202-3.
"Equal Rights for All." In Outspoken Women, p. 198-9.
"Keeping the Thing Going While Things Are Stirring." In Gilbert, Sandra. Norton Anthology of Literature by Women, p. 255-6. Also in Zak, Michele. Women and the Politics of Culture, p. 350-1.
"Speech at Akron Women's Rights Convention, 1851." In Images of Women in American Popular Culture, p. 11-2. (Same as Ain't I a Woman?)

"What Time of Night It Is." In Gilbert, Sandra. Norton Anthology of Literature by Women, p. 254-5.

Tucker, Marna S.
"Testimony." In U.S. Congress. Senate. Committee on the Judiciary. Subcommittee on the Constitution. The Impact of the Equal Rights Amendment, pt. 1, p. 43-50.

Tunner, Ann Hamilton.
"Statement." In U.S. Congress. House. Committee on Veterans' Affairs. Select Subcommittee on Review WASP Bills. To Provide Recognition to the Women's Air Force, p. 256-61.

Turbitt, Coralie.
"Session Summary." In International Conference on Women and Food (1978: University of Arizona). A Conference on the Role of Women in Meeting Basic Food and Water Needs in Developing Countries, p. 127-8.
"Testimony." In U.S. Congress. House. Committee on International Relations. Subcommittee on International Organizations. International Women's Issues, p. 46-50.

Turnbull, Ann P.
"Statement." In U.S. Congress. House. Select Committee on Children, Youth, and Families. Families with Disabled Children, p. 17-22.

Turner, Carmen.
"Speech." In Women's Travel Issues, p. 767-79.

Turner, Patricia Russell.
"Statement." In U.S. Congress. Senate. Committee on Finance. Potential Inequities Affecting Women, pt. 2, p. 229.

Turner, Pauline.
"Statement." In U.S. Congress. House. Select Committee on Aging. Subcommittee on Retirement Income and Employment. Impact of Reagan Economics on Aging Women, p. 41-2.

Tuteur, Muriel.
"Testimony." In U.S. Commission on Civil Rights. Hearings Before the U.S. Commission on Civil Rights Held in Chicago, v. 1, p. 330-6.

Tyler, Jan L.
"Panel Discussion." In Public Forum on Women's Rights and Responsibilities (1978: Las Vegas, NV). Public Forum on Women's Rights and Responsibilities, p. 13-6.

Tyler, Mary.
"Statement." In U.S. Congress. House. Select Committee on Aging. Problems of Aging Women, p. 42-7.

Tyson, Cynthia H.
    "Communicating with Self and Others: A Model for Now and For
    the Future." Vital Speeches, 47 (October 15, 1980), 16-9.

Uehling, Barbara S.
    "Academics and Athletics: Creative Divorce or Reconciliation."
    Vital Speeches, 49 (June 1, 1983), 504-7.

Uhlig, Marylouise.
    "Statement." In U.S. Congress. House. Committee on Educa-
    tion and Labor. Subcommittee on Employment Opportunities.
    Oversight Hearing on the Federal Enforcement of Equal Em-
    ployment Opportunity Laws, p. 65-9.

Ullman, (Mrs.) Leon.
    "The Ladies' Hebrew Benevolent Society, Anniston, Alabama."
    In The American Jewish Woman, p. 208-12.

Umansky, Ellen M.
    "Reflections on the Creation of a Ritual Meal." In Women's Spirit
    Bonding, p. 351-2.

Underwood, Lorraine.
    "Statement." In U.S. Congress. Senate. Committee on Veter-
    ans' Affairs. Recognition for Purposes of VA Benefits, p.
    146-51.

Unger, Rhoda Kesler.
    "The Politics of Gender: A Review of Relevant Literature." In
    Psychology of Women, p. 461-518.

Vadas, Mary.
    "Statement." In U.S. Congress. House. Select Committee on
    Aging. Subcommittee on Retirement Income and Employment.
    Task Force on Social Security and Women. Treatment of
    Women Under Social Security, v. 3, p. 68.

Valuck, Dorothy.
    "Testimony." In U.S. Commission on Civil Rights. Hearing Be-
    fore the U.S. Commission on Civil Rights Held in Denver, p.
    425-8, 430-1.

Valentine, Bettylou.
    "Women on Welfare: Public Policy and Institutional Racism." In
    Class, Race, and Sex, p. 276-87.

Vance, Carole S.
"Pleasure and Danger: Toward a Politics of Sexuality." In
Pleasure and Danger, p. 1-26.

Vandegaer, Paula.
"Statement." In U.S. Congress. House. Select Committee on
Population. Fertility and Contraception in America, p. 208-25.

Van Devanter, Lynda M.
"Statement." In U.S. Congress. House. Committee on Veterans'
Affairs. Subcommittee on Hospitals and Health Care. VA
Health Care for Women, p. 4-7.
"Testimony." In U.S. Congress. Senate. Committee on Veter-
ans' Affairs. Veteran's Health Care and Programs Improve-
ment, p. 331-2.

Vann, Timothy.
"Statement." In U.S. Congress. Senate. Committee on Labor
and Human Resources. Subcommittee on Family and Human
Services. Forum for Families, p. 59-63.

Vaughan, Mary C.
"We Would Act as Well as Endure." In Women's America, p. 204-5.

Vaughn, Bonnie.
"Statement." In U.S. Congress. Senate. Committee on Labor
and Human Resources. The Coming Decade, p. 186-8.

Vellacott, Jo.
"Women, Peace & Power." In Reweaving the Web of Life, p. 31-
41.

Venegas, Hildreth.
"Greetings." In U.S. Women's Bureau. Native American Women
and Equal Opportunity, p. 5.

Vera, Veronica.
"Testimony." In U.S. Congress. Senate. Committee on the
Judiciary. Subcommittee on Juvenile Justice. Effect of
Pornography on Women and Children, p. 315-7.

Verbrugge, Lois M.
"Women's Social Roles and Health." In Women: A Developmental
Perspective, p. 49-78.

Verdesi, Elizabeth.
"Statement." In U.S. Congress. Senate. Committee on the
Judiciary. Subcommittee on the Constitution. Constitutional
Amendments Relating to Abortion, v. 1, p. 1143-5.

Verheyden-Hilliard, Mary Ellen.
    "Achieving the Dreams Beyond Tradition: Counseling White
        Ethnic American Girls." In Conference on the Educational
        and Occupational Needs of White Ethnic Women (1978: Bos-
        ton, MA). Conference on the Educational and Occupational
        Needs of White Ethnic Women, p. 210-31.
    "Assisting the School-To-Work Transition for Young Women:
        Who Needs the Counseling?" In Young Women and Employ-
        ment, p. 38-42.
    "Counseling: Potential Superbomb. Against Sexism." In To-
        day's Girls: Tomorrow's Women, p. 50-4.
    "Education, Girls, and Power." In Toward the Second Decade,
        p. 129-40.
    "Statement." In U.S. Congress. Joint Economic Committee.
        Economic Status of Women, p. 67-9.

Vermeulen, Joan.
    "Statement." In U.S. Congress. Senate. Committee on Labor
        and Human Resources. Sex Discrimination in the Workplace,
        1981, p. 532-4.

Vest, Mary Louise.
    "Testimony." In U.S. Commission on Civil Rights. Hearing Be-
        fore the U.S. Commission on Civil Rights Held in Denver,
        p. 475-6.

Vetter, Betty M.
    "Changing Patterns of Recruitment and Employment." In Women
        in Scientific and Engineering Professions, p. 59-74.
    "Labor Force Participation of Women Baccalaureates in Science."
        In Women and Minorities in Science, p. 27-38.
    "Statement." In U.S. Congress. Senate. Committee on Labor
        and Human Resources. Subcommittee on Health and Scientific
        Research. Women in Science and Technology Equal Employ-
        ment Opportunity Act, 1980, p. 12-3, 24-5.

Veve, Karen.
    "Statement." In U.S. Congress. House. Committee on Ways
        and Means. Subcommittee on Social Security. Social Security
        Dependents' Benefits, p. 20.

Vincent, Lisbeth J.
    "Statement." In U.S. Congress. House. Select Committee on
        Children, Youth, and Families. Families with Disabled Chil-
        dren, p. 12-4.

Viviano, Ann.
    "Testimony." In U.S. Equal Employment Opportunity Commission.
        Hearings Before the U.S. Equal Employment Opportunity Com-
        mission on Job Segregation and Wage Discrimination, p. 147-63.

Voigt, Cynthia.
"Newbery Medal Acceptance." Hornbook, 59 (1983), 401-9.

Viydanoff, Patricia.
"Work-Family Life Cycle Among Women." In Women's Lives, p. 61-7.

Vucanovich, Barbara F.
"Statement." In U.S. Congress. House. Committee on Appropriations. Subcommittee on Department of Transportation and Related Agencies Appropriations. Federal Aviation Administration Plan for Office and Facility Consolidation. Washington: U.S.G.P.O., 1984, p. 10-3.
"Statement." In U.S. Congress. House. Committee on Interior and Insular Affairs. Subcommittee on Public Lands and National Parks. Additions to the National Wilderness Preservation System. Washington: U.S.G.P.O., 1984, pt. 4, p. 194-206, 571-92.
"Statement." In U.S. Congress. House. Committee on Science and Technology. Subcommittee on Transportation, Aviation, and Materials. The 55-MPH Speed Limit. Washington: U.S.G.P.O., 1985, p. 13-7, 20.
"Statement." In U.S. Congress. House. Committee on the Judiciary. Subcommittee on Administrative Law and Governmental Relations. Regulatory Reform Act. Washington: U.S.G.P.O., 1983, p. 475-8.
"Statement." In U.S. Congress. Senate. Committee on Energy and Natural Resources. Subcommittee on Public Lands and Reserved Water. Federal Land Management Problems in Northern Nevada. Washington: U.S.G.P.O., 1984, p. 5-6.
"Statement." In U.S. Congress. Senate. Committee on the Environment and Public Works. Subcommittee on Transportation. Implementation of the Surface Transportation Assistance Act of 1982. Washington: U.S.G.P.O., 1984, p. 378-82.

Waber, Deborah P.
"The Meaning of Sex-Related Variation in Maturation Rate." In Psychology and Women: In Transition, p. 37-59.

Waelder, Catherine.
"Statement." In U.S. Congress. House. Committee on Post Office and Civil Service. Subcommittee on Compensation and Employee Benefits. Federal Pay Equity Act of 1984, pt. 1, p. 245-9.
"Statement." In U.S. Congress. House. Committee on Post Office and Civil Service. Subcommittee on Compensation and Employee Benefits. Pay Equity, pt. 1, p. 520-7.

Wainwright, Cheryl.
"Statement." In U.S. Congress. House. Committee on Post Office and Civil Service. Subcommittee on Compensation and Employee Benefits. Federal Pay Equity Act of 1984, pt. 1, p. 243-5.

Waite, Linda.
"Statement." In U.S. Congress. House. Select Committee on Population. Fertility and Contraception in America, p. 33-43.

Wakeman, Mary K.
"Affirming Diversity and Biblical Tradition." In Women's Spirit Bonding, p. 267-80.

Wald, Lillian.
"The Nurses' Settlement in New York." In Outspoken Women, p. 200-5.

Wald, Patricia M.
"Statement." In U.S. Congress. House. Committee on the Judiciary. Subcommittee on Civil and Constitutional Rights. Equal Rights Amendment Extension, p. 54-80.

Waldron, Ingrid.
"Employment and Women's Health: An Analysis of Causal Relationships." In Women and Health in America, p. 119-38.

Walker, Alice.
"Only Justice Can Stop a Curse." In In Search of Our Mother's Gardens, p. 338-42.
"Saving the Life That Is Your Own: The Importance of Models in the Artist's Life." In In Search of Our Mother's Gardens, p. 3-14.
"A Talk: Convocation 1972." In In Search of Our Mother's Gardens, p. 33-41.

Walker, Lenore E. Auerbach.
"Battered Women." In Women and Psychotherapy, p. 339-64.
"Feminist Forensic Psychology." In Handbook of Feminist Therapy, p. 274-84.
"Feminist Therapy with Victim/Survivors of Interpersonal Violence." In Handbook of Feminist Therapy, p. 203-14.
"Statement." In U.S. Congress. House. Committee on Science and Technology. Subcommittee on Domestic and International Scientific Planning, Analysis, and Cooperation. Research in Violent Behavior: Domestic Violence, p. 145-9.
"Statement." In U.S. Congress. Senate. Committee on Labor and Human Resources. Subcommittee on Child and Human Development. Domestic Violence Prevention and Services Act, 1980, p. 218-20.

Walker, Tillie.
"American Indian Children: Foster Care and Adoptions." In Conference on the Educational and Occupational Needs of American Indian Women (1976: Albuquerque, NM). Conference on the Educational and Occupational Needs of American Indian Women, p. 185-209.

Waler, Sue Sheridan.
"Widow and Ward: The Feudal Law of Child Custody in Medieval England." Feminist Studies, 3 (1976), 104-16.

Walkowitz, Judith R.
"Male Vice and Female Virtue: Feminism and the Politics of Prostitution in Nineteenth-Century Britain." In Class, Race, and Sex, p. 10-30.

Wall, Cheryl A.
"Poets and Versifiers, Signers, and Signifiers: Women of the Harlem Renaissance." In Women, the Arts, and the 1920s in Paris and New York, p. 74-98.

Wallace, Joan.
"Statement." In U.S. Congress. House. Committee on Education and Labor. Subcommittee on Employment Opportunities. Oversight Hearing on the Federal Enforcement of Equal Employment Opportunity Laws, p. 59-62.

Wallace, Molly.
"From the Valedictory Oration, Delivered by Miss Molly Wallace, June 20, 1792." In Women of America, p. 87-9.

Wallace, Phyllis A.
"Comment on Male-Female Wage Differentials." In Conference on Women in the Labor Market (1977: Barnard College). Women in the Labor Market, p. 256-61.
"Increased Labor Force Participation of Women and Affirmative Action." In Women in the Workplace, p. 1-24.

Wallace, Rita.
"Statement." In U.S. Congress. House. Committee on Post Office and Civil Service. Subcommittee on Compensation and Employee Benefits. Federal Pay Equity Act of 1984, pt. 1, p. 153-5.

Wallerstein, Judith S.
"Statement." In U.S. Congress. Senate. Committee on Labor and Human Resources. Subcommittee on Family and Human Services. Broken Families, p. 71-3.

Walling, Regis.
"Statement." In U.S. Congress. House. Select Committee on Population. Fertility and Contraception in America, p. 225-34.

Walsh, Bettianne.
"Statement." In U.S. Congress. Senate. Committee on Finance. Potential Inequities Affecting Women, pt. 2, p. 238-9.

Walsh, Julia M.
"Women's Role in the Private Sector in Investments." In Women in Management, p. 55-66.

Walsh, Lorena S.
"The Experiences and Status of Women in the Chesapeake, 1750-1775." In The Web of Southern Social Relations, p. 1-18.

Walsh, Michaela L.
"Statement." In U.S. Congress. Senate. Committee on Foreign Relations. Women in Development, p. 84-9.

Walstedt, Joyce J.
"An Exploration of Female Powerlessness: The Altruistic Other Orientation." In Women & Men, p. 153-67.

Ward, Ingeborg L.
"Sexual Behavior Differentiation: Prenatal Hormonal and Environmental Control." In Sex Differences in Behavior, p. 3-17.

Warden, Gail L.
"My Work and Welcome to It. An HMO's View of Strategic Planning in the Prospective Payment Environment." Vital Speeches, 51 (December 15, 1984), 150-4.

Wardle, Lynn D.
"Testimony." In U.S. Congress. Senate. Committee on the Judiciary. Subcommittee on the Constitution. The Impact of the Equal Rights Amendment, pt. 2, p. 2-9.

Wardman, Barbara.
"Testimony." In U.S. Congress. House. Committee on Energy and Commerce. Subcommittee on Health and the Environment. Health and the Environment Miscellaneous, pt. 5, p. 316-8.

Warner, Carolyn.
"Where There Is No Vision. The Death of Public and Private Education in America." Vital Speeches, 49 (January 15, 1983), 215-9.

Warnock, Donna.
"Patriarchy Is a Killer: What People Concerned About Peace and Justice Should Know." In Reweaving the Web of Life, p. 20-9.

Warren, Anna.
"Statement." In U.S. Congress. House. Committee on Post Office and Civil Service. Subcommittee on Compensation and

Employee Benefits. Options for Conducting a Pay Equity Study, p. 188-90.

Washbourn, Penelope.
"The Dynamics of Female Experiences: Process Models and Human Values." In Feminism and Process Thought, p. 83-105.

Waskel, Shirley.
"Statement." In U.S. Congress. House. Select Committee on Aging. Problems of Aging Women, p. 58-9.

Waters, Maxine.
"Statement." In U.S. Congress. House. Committee on Education and Labor. Subcommittee on Employment Opportunities. Oversight Hearings on Equal Employment Opportunity and Affirmative Action, pt. 2, p. 305-89.

Watkins, Bari J.
"Feminism: A Last Chance for the Humanities?" In Theories of Women's Studies, p. 41-7.
"On the Problem of the Real World: A Presentation to the Class of 1987." Vital Speeches, 50 (November 1, 1983), 45-8.

Watley, Louise.
"The Black Woman in America." In Cornell Conference on Women (1969: Cornell University). Proceedings, p. 85-88, 91.
"Child Bearing, Child Rearing, Abortion, and Contraception." In Cornell Conference on Women (1969: Cornell University). Proceedings, p. 55.

Wattleton, Faye.
"Statement." In U.S. Congress. Senate. Committee on Labor and Human Resources. Oversight of Family Planning Programs, 1981, p. 14-6, 42-56, 72-83.
"Statement." In U.S. Congress. Senate. Committee on the Judiciary. Subcommittee on the Constitution. Constitutional Amendments Relating to Abortion, v. 1, p. 1038-40.
"Testimony." In U.S. Congress. House. Committee on Energy and Commerce. Subcommittee on Health and the Environment. Health and the Environment Miscellaneous, pt. 3, p. 497-9.
"Testimony." In U.S. Congress. Senate. Committee on Human Resources. Adolescent Health, Services and Pregnancy Prevention Care Act of 1978, p. 192-6.

Watts, Meredith W.
"Biopolitics and Gender." In Biopolitics and Gender, p. 1-27.

Waxman, Margery.
"Statement." In U.S. Congress. House. Committee on Post Office and Civil Service. Subcommittee on Investigations. Sexual Harassment in the Federal Government, pt. 1, p. 158-61.

Way, Peggy Ann.
    "Fools, Clowns, and Temptations." In <u>Women and the Word</u>, p.
       100-9.
    "You Are Not My God, Jehovah." In <u>Spinning a Sacred Yarn</u>,
       p. 218-26.

Weaver, Ellen C.
    "Implications of Giving Woman a Greater Share of Academic De-
       cision-Making." In <u>Expanding the Role of Women in the Sci-</u>
       <u>ences</u>, p. 257-67.

Weaver, F. Ellen.
    "Cloister and Salon in Seventeenth Century Paris: Introduction
       to a Study in Women's History." In <u>Beyond Androcentrism</u>,
       p. 159-80.

Webb, Cathleen Crowell.
    "Statement." In U.S. Congress. Senate. Committee on the
       Judiciary. Subcommittee on Juvenile Justice. <u>Juvenile Rape</u>
       <u>Victims</u>, p. 14-5.

Webster, Margaret.
    "Shakespeare and the Modern Theatre." In Webster, Margaret.
       <u>Shakespeare and the Modern Theatre</u>, p. 5-24.

Webster, Paula.
    "The Forbidden: Eroticism and Taboo." In <u>Pleasure and Danger</u>,
       p. 385-98.

Weddington, Sarah.
    "Statement." In U.S. Congress. Senate. Committee on the
       Judiciary. Subcommittee on Separation of Powers. <u>The Hu-</u>
       <u>man Life Bill</u>, p. 944-7, 1025-7.
    "World Conference on the U.N. Decade for Women Held in Copen-
       hagen." <u>Department of State Bulletin</u>, 80 (November 1980),
       62-4.

Wedel, Cynthia.
    "The Story of the Transfiguration (Epiphany)." In <u>Women and</u>
       <u>the Word</u>, p. 54-9.

Wegner, Judith Welch.
    "Testimony." In U.S. Congress. Senate. Committee on the
       Judiciary. Subcommittee on the Constitution. <u>The Impact of</u>
       <u>the Equal Rights Amendment</u>, pt. 1, p. 878-83.

Weick, Ann.
    "Issues of Power in Social Work Practice." In NASW Conference
       on Social Work Practice With Women (1st: 1980: Washington,
       DC). <u>Women, Power, and Change</u>, p. 173-85.

Weinberg, Lisl.
  "Susie Weinberg: A Brand Plucked from the Burning." In U.S.
    Congress. Joint Economic Committee. The American Women,
    p. 791-6.

Weiner, Annette B.
  "Forgotten Wealth: Cloth and Women's Production in the Pacific."
    In Women's Work, p. 96-110.

Weiss, Carol H.
  "Introductory Remarks on What Policymakers Need to Know That
    Research Can Address." In Conference on the National
    Longitudinal Surveys of Mature Women (1978: U.S. Depart-
    ment of Labor). Women's Changing Roles at Home and On
    the Job, p. 295-300.
  "Getting to 'No' and Beyond." In Handbook of Feminist Therapy,
    p. 62-70.

Weissman, Myrna M.
  "Depression." In Women and Psychotherapy, p. 97-113.
  "The Treatment of Depressed Women: The Efficacy of Psycho-
    therapy." In The Evolving Female, p. 307-24.

Weitz, Judith.
  "Statement." In U.S. Congress. House. Committee on Energy
    and Commerce. Subcommittee on Health and Environment.
    Health Budget Proposals, p. 68-71.

Weitzel, Joan.
  "The Sparse Ghetto: Service Delivery in a Rural Area." In
    Women in Crisis Conference (1st: 1979: New York, NY).
    Women in Crisis, p. 56-63.

Wellman, Judith.
  "Women and Radical Reform in Antebellum Upstate New York:
    A Profile of Grassroots Female Abolitionists." In Conference
    on Women's History (1976: Washington, DC). Clio Was a
    Woman, p. 113-27.

Wells-Barnett, Ida.
  "Southern Horrors: Lynch Law in All Its Phases." In Out-
    spoken Women, p. 206-20.

Wells-Schooley, Jane.
  "Statement." In U.S. Congress. Senate. Committee on the
    Judiciary. Subcommittee on the Constitution. Constitutional
    Amendments Relating to Abortion, v. 1, p. 1122-6.

Welter, Barbara.
  "The Feminization of American Religion: 1800-1860." In Clio's
    Consciousness Raised, p. 137-52.

Welty, Eudora.
"Finding a Voice." In Welty, One Writer's Beginnings, p. 71-104.
"Learning to See." In Welty, One Writer's Beginnings, p. 41-69.
"Listening." In Welty, One Writer's Beginnings, p. 1-39.

Wernick, Ellen.
"The Concerns of the Labor Movement With Youth Programs for
Women." In Young Women and Employment, p. 66-7.
"Statement." In U.S. Congress. House. Committee on Govern-
ment Operations. Manpower and Housing Subcommittee. The
Women's Bureau, p. 175-8.
"Statement." In U.S. Congress. House. Committee on Post
Office and Civil Service. Subcommittee on Human Resources.
Pay Equity, pt. 1, p. 73-5.

Werth, Terry.
"Today Is All We Have." In Spinning a Sacred Yarn, p. 227-30.

Wertheimer, Barbara M.
"Leadership Training for Union Women in the United States:
Route to Equal Opportunity." In Equal Employment Policy
for Women, p. 226-41.

Wertheimer, Wendy J.
"Testimony." In U.S. Congress. House. Committee on Energy
and Commerce. Subcommittee on Health and the Environment.
Health and the Environment Miscellaneous, pt. 3, p. 224-5.

Wertz, Dorothy C.
"Man-Midwifery and the Rise of Technology: The Problems and
Proposals for Resolution." In Birth Control and Controlling
Birth, p. 147-66.

Wertz, Teyonda.
"Statement." In U.S. Congress. House. Committee on Educa-
tion and Labor. Subcommittee on Employment Opportunities.
Oversight Hearings on Equal Employment Opportunity and
Affirmative Action, pt. 2, p. 38-41.

West, Jessamyn.
"Commencement Address, Juniata College, May 24, 1981. Shar-
ing Your Being With Others--Through Words." In I Am
Honored to be Here Today, p. 299-304.

Westkott, Marcia.
"Women's Studies as a Strategy for Change: Between Criticism
and Vision." In Theories of Women's Studies II, p. 123-30.

Wetzel, Janice Wood.
"Redefining Concepts of Mental Health." In NASW Conference on
Social Work With Women (1st: 1980: Washington, DC).
Women, Power, and Change, p. 3-16.

Wexler, Jacqueline Grennan.
"Continuity in Executive Staffing: The Unanswered Question in Higher Education." Vital Speeches, 47 (December 1, 1980), 126-8.

Wheeler, Deborah.
"Testimony." In U.S. Commission on Civil Rights. Hearing Before the U.S. Commission on Civil Rights Held in Denver, p. 367-8, 374-8.

Whelchel, Marianne.
"'Phantasia for Elvira Shatayev' a Revolutionary Feminist Poem." In GLCA Women's Studies Conference (6th: 1980). Toward a Feminist Transformation of the Academy II, p. 24-7.

Whetsone, Gloria.
"Statement." In U.S. Congress. House. Committee on Education and Labor. Subcommittee on Select Education. Hearing on Domestic Violence, p. 39-41.

Whitbeck, Caroline.
"A Different Reality: Feminist Ontology." In Beyond Domination, p. 64-8.
"The Neonate: Introductory Remarks." In The Custom-Made Child?, p. 119-22.
"Response to Papers on Decisions About Handicapped Newborns: Values and Procedures." In The Custom-Made Child?, p. 145-6.

White, Barbara W.
"Black Women: The Resilient Victims." In NASW Conference on Social Work With Women (1st: 1980: Washington, DC). Women, Power, and Change, p. 69-77.

White, Diane.
"Statement." In U.S. Congress. Senate. Committee on Labor and Human Resources. Subcommittee on Education, Arts and Humanities. Civil Rights Act of 1984, p. 354-6.

White, Robin.
"Statement." In U.S. Congress. House. Committee on Ways and Means. Subcommittee on Public Assistance and Unemployment Compensation. Teenage Pregnancy Issues, p. 185-8.

Whiteman, Henrietta V.
"Insignificance of Humanity, 'Man Is Tampering With the Moon and the Stars': The Employment Status of American Indian Women." In Conference on the Educational and Occupational Needs of American Indian Women (1976: Albuquerque, NM). Conference on the Educational and Occupational Needs of American Indian Women, p. 37-61.

Whiting, Margaret.
    "CARE/Kenya Water Development Program." In International
      Conference on Women and Food (1978: University of
      Arizona). A Conference on the Role of Women in Meeting
      Basic Food and Water Needs in Developing Countries, p. 83-7.

Whitman, Marina v. N.
    "Black Hats, Economists and Societal Risk Assessment. Produc-
      tivity and Efficiency." Vital Speeches, 52 (December 1,
      1985), 115-8.

Whitney, Jeannie.
    "Testimony." In U.S. Commission on Civil Rights. Hearings
      Before the U.S. Equal Employment Opportunity Commission
      on Job Segregation and Wage Discrimination, p. 584-601.

Widdecombe, Judith.
    "Statement." In U.S. Congress. Senate. Committee on the
      Judiciary. Subcommittee on the Constitution. Constitutional
      Amendments Relating to Abortion, v. 1, p. 1020-2.

Widmann, Nancy.
    "Testimony." In U.S. Commission on Civil Rights. Hearing Be-
      fore the U.S. Commission on Civil Rights Held in Denver, p.
      434-7, 445.

Widnall, Sheila.
    "Response to The Social Scene: Isolation and Frustration." In
      Women in Engineering--Beyond Recruitment, p. 78-9.

Wiener, Marilyn.
    "Statement." In U.S. Congress. Senate. Committee on Labor
      and Human Resources. The Coming Decade, p. 401-4.

Wiersma, Jacquelyn.
    "Women's Mid-Life Career Change: Facilitating the Tasks of
      Mid-Life Transition." In Women's Lives, p. 207-19.

Wikler, Norma.
    "Overcoming the Obstacles to Women in Judicial Education." In
      Women in the Judiciary, p. 23-6.

Wilcox, Linda A.
    "Statement." In U.S. Congress. House. Committee on Govern-
      ment Operations. Intergovernmental Relations and Human
      Resources Subcommittee. Barriers to Self-Sufficiency for
      Single Female Heads of Families, p. 533-8.

Wilkins, Jan.
    "Statement." In U.S. Congress. Senate. Committee on the
      Judiciary. Subcommittee on the Constitution. Constitutional
      Amendments Relating to Abortion, v. 1, p. 1145-7.

Wilkinson, Doris Y.
"Minority Women: Social-Cultural Issues." In Women and Psychotherapy, p. 285-306.

Willard, Charity Cannon.
"A Fifteenth-Century View of Women's Role in Medieval Society:
Christine de Pizan's Livre Des Trois Vertus." In Role of
Women in the Middle Ages, p. 90-120.

Willard, Frances E.
"Temperance and Home Protection." In Outspoken Women, p.
221-6.
"A White Life for Two." In We Shall Be Heard, p. 146-54.

Willard, Nancy.
"Newbery Medal Acceptance." Horn Book, 58 (1982), 369-73.

Willard, Virginia J.
"Statement." In U.S. Congress. Senate. Committee on Small
Business. Women Entrepreneurs, p. 63-5.

Willenz, June A.
"Statement." In U.S. Congress. House. Committee on Veterans'
Affairs. Subcommittee on Hospital and Health Care, VA
Health Care For Women, p. 23-5.
"Testimony." In U.S. Congress. Senate. Committee on the
Judiciary. Subcommittee on the Constitution. The Impact of
the Equal Rights Amendment, pt. 1, p. 735-7.
"Testimony." In U.S. Congress. Senate. Committee on Veter-
ans' Affairs. Veterans' Health Care and Programs Improve-
ment Act of 1983, p. 316-8.

Willhoite, Betty.
"Statement." In U.S. Congress. House. Committee on Educa-
tion and Labor. Subcommittee on Employment Opportunities.
Oversight Hearings on Equal Employment Opportunity and
Affirmative Action, pt. 2, p. 79-80.

Williams, Agnes F.
"Transition from the Reservation to an Urban Setting and the
Changing Roles of American Indian Women." In Conference
on the Educational and Occupational Needs of American Indian Women (1976: Albuquerque, NM). Conference on the
Educational and Occupational Needs of American Indian Wom-
en, p. 251-83.

Williams, Consuelo M.
"Statement." In U.S. Congress. House. Committee on Educa-
tion and Labor. Subcommittee on Employment Opportunities.
Oversight Hearings on Equal Employment Opportunity and
Affirmative Action, pt. 2, p. 187-9.

Williams, Diane Rennay.
"Statement." In U.S. Congress. House. Committee on Post
Office and Civil Service. Subcommittee on Investigations.
Sexual Harassment in the Federal Government, pt. 1, p.
69-85.

Williams, Delores S.
"Women as Makers of Literature." In Women's Spirit Bonding,
p. 139-45.

Williams, Eva T.
"Pushing Out the Walls." In Women in Action, p. 17-20.

Williams, Karen Hastle.
"Statement." In U.S. Congress. House. Committee on Small
Business. Subcommittee on General Oversight and Minority
Enterprise. Women In Business, p. 35-43.

Williams, Louise A.
"Testimony." In U.S. Congress. House. Committee on Energy
and Commerce. Subcommittee on Health and the Environment.
Health and the Environment Miscellaneous, pt. 3, p. 653-4.

Williams, Mary.
"The Structure of Knowledge: A Feminist Perspective." In
GLCA Women's Studies Conference (4th: 1978: Rochester,
Indiana). The Structure of Knowledge, p. 16-9.

Williams, Mavis.
"Testimony." In U.S. Equal Employment Opportunity Commission.
Hearings Before the U.S. Equal Employment Opportunity Com-
mission on Job Segregation and Wage Discrimination, p. 403-10.

Williams, Odella Welch.
"Welcoming Statements." In U.S. Commission on Civil Rights.
Hearings Before the U.S. Commission on Civil Rights Held in
Chicago, v. 1, p. 6-8.

Williams, Sharon E.
"Studying War Some More." In Those Preachin' Women, p. 77-84.

Willis, Ellen.
"The Challenge of Profamily Politics: a Feminist Defense of Sexual Freedom." In Class, Race, and Sex, p. 325-38.

Wilpula, Sandra.
"Statement." In U.S. Congress. House. Select Committee on
Aging. Subcommittee on Retirement Income and Employment.
Task Force on Social Security and Women. Treatment of Wom-
en Under Social Security, v. 3, p. 58-9.

Wilsnack, Sharon C.
"Prevention and Education Research." In <u>Alcoholism and Alcohol Abuse Among Women</u>, p. 163-85.

Wilson, Boydena R.
"Glimpses of Muslim Urban Women in Classical Islam." In Berkshire Conference on the History of Women (5th: 1982: Vassar College). <u>Women and the Structure of Society</u>, p. 5-11.

Wilson, Elaine.
"Developing a Neighborhood-Based Health Facility." In Conference on the Educational and Occupational Needs of White Ethnic Women (1978: Boston, MA). <u>Conference on the Educational and Occupational Needs of White Ethnic Women</u>, p. 63-7.

Wilson, Joan Hoff.
"Hidden Riches: Legal Records and Women, 1750-1825." In Conference on the History of Women (1977: St. Paul, MN). <u>Woman's Being, Woman's Place</u>, p. 7-25.

Wilson, (Mrs.) John M.
"Statement." In U.S. Congress. House. Committee on Ways and Means. Subcommittee on Social Security. <u>Social Security Dependents' Benefits</u>, p. 60-2.

Wilson, Kathy.
"Statement." In U.S. Congress. Senate. Committee on the Judiciary. Subcommittee on the Constitution. <u>Constitutional Amendments Relating to Abortion</u>, v. 1, p. 1046-9.

Wilson, Lucy.
"The Opposition of the Vigilance Association." In International Women's Year Conference on Women in Public Life (1975: Lyndon Baines Johnson Library). <u>Women in Public Life</u>, p. 123-4.

Wilson, Lynn.
"My Voice ... And Many Others." In <u>Women's Spirit Bonding</u>, p. 240-2.

Wilson, Mercedes.
"Statement." In U.S. Congress. Senate. Committee on Labor and Human Resources. Subcommittee on Family and Human Services. <u>Reauthorization of the Adolescent Family</u>, p. 184-6.

Wilson, Susan.
"Testimony." In U.S. Commission on Civil Rights. <u>Hearing Before the U.S. Commission on Civil Rights Held in Chicago</u>, v. 1, p. 142-5, 152-6.

Winfield, Arleen.
"Testimony." In U.S. Commission on Civil Rights. Hearings Before the U.S. Commission on Civil Rights Held in Chicago, v. 1, p. 399-402.

Winger, Jeri J.
"Partners in Progress: Women in Community Service." In A Woman's Choices, p. 159-70.

Winship, Nate.
"Organizing Against Hunger." Women's Studies Quarterly, 13 (Summer 1985), 12.

Winslow, Mary Bowes.
"Leadership Training for Increased Effectiveness Among Women Educational Administrators: Two Local Models." In Women and Educational Leadership, p. 223-38.

Winsor, Mary.
"The Birth Control Movement in Europe." In American Birth Control Conference (1st: 1921: New York). Birth Control: What It Is, How It Works, What It Will Do, p. 51-7.

Wipper, Audrey.
"Riot and Rebellion Among African Women: Three Examples of Women's Political Clout." In Perspectives on Power, p. 50-72.

Wisman, Rosann.
"Statement." In U.S. Congress. House. Committee on Ways and Means. Subcommittee on Public Assistance and Unemployment Compensation. Teenage Pregnancy Issues, p. 40-3.

Withorn, Ann.
"Analysis and Action." Women's Studies Quarterly, 13 (Summer 1985), 9-10.

Witt, Mary L.
"Testimony." In U.S. Equal Employment Opportunity Commission. Hearing Before the U.S. Equal Employment Opportunity Commission on Job Segregation and Wage Discrimination, p. 127-46.

Witt, Shirley Hill.
"Native Women in the World of Work: An Overview." In U.S. Women's Bureau. Native American Women and Equal Opportunity, p. 8-15.

Woehrer, Carol.
"Family Roles and Identities of Scandinavian and German Women." In Conference on the Educational and Occupational Needs of White Ethnic Women (1978: Boston, MA). Conference on the Educational and Occupational Needs of White Ethnic Women, p. 180-209.

Wofford, Sunny K.
"Health Problems in the Airline Industries." In Conference on
Women and the Workplace (1976: Washington, DC). Confer-
ence on Women and the Workplace, p. 179-83.

Wolchik, Sharon L.
"Demography, Political Reform and Women's Issues in Czechoslo-
vakia." In Women, Power, and Political Systems, p. 135-50.
"The Precommunist Legacy, Economic Development, Social Trans-
formation, and Women's Roles in Eastern Europe." In Women,
State, and Party in Eastern Europe, p. 31-43.

Wolcott, Ilene.
"Response (to Forces Impacting on the Policymaker)." In Birth
Control and Controlling Birth, p. 275-6.
"Testimony." In U.S. Congress. Senate. Committee on Human
Resources. Adolescent Health, Services, and Pregnancy Pre-
vention Care Act of 1978, p. 561-4.

Wolf, Edna.
"Statement." In U.S. Congress. House. Select Committee on
Aging. Subcommittee on Retirement Income and Employment.
Task Force on Social Security and Women. Treatment of
Women Under Social Security, v. 3, p. 22.

Wolf, Margery.
"The People's Republic of China." In Women Workers in Fifteen
Countries, p. 33-47.

Wolf, Wendy C.
"Commentary (on Sex Typing in Occupational Socialization)."
In Sex Segregation in the Workplace, p. 233-4, 308-9.

Wolfe, Anne G.
"No Room at the Top." In The American Jewish Woman, p. 942-5.

Wolfe, Jean.
"Statement." In California. Legislature. Joint Committee on
Legal Equality. Women in the Justice System, p. 196-200.

Wolfe, Leslie.
"Statement." In U.S. Congress. House. Committee on Education and Labor. Subcommittee on Elementary, Secondary,
and Vocational Education. Hearing on Women's Educational
Equity Act, p. 150-5.

Wong, Germaine Q.
"Impediments to Asian-Pacific-American Women Organizing." In
Conference on the Educational and Occupational Needs of
Asian-Pacific-American (1976: San Francisco, CA). Confer-
ence on the Educational and Occupational Needs of Asian-
Pacific-American Women, p. 89-104.

Wood, Ann Douglas.
"'The Fashionable Diseases': Women's Complaints and Their
Treatment in Nineteenth-Century America." In Clio's Consciousness Raised, p. 1-18. Also in The Journal of Interdisciplinary History, 4 (Summer 1973), 25-52.

Wood, Rosemary.
"Health Problems Facing American Indian Women." In Conference
on the Educational and Occupational Needs of American Indian
Women (1976: Albuquerque, NM). Conference on the Educational and Occupational Needs of American Indian Women,
p. 159-83.

Woodhull, Victoria C.
"Constitutional Equality." In We Shall Be Heard, p. 108-29.
"The Principles of Social Freedom." In Outspoken Women, p.
227-51.

Woodman, Natalie Jane.
"Social Work with Lesbian Couples." In NASW Conference on
Social Work Practice With Women (1st: 1980: Washington,
DC). Women, Power, and Change, p. 114-24.

Woodruff, Constance.
"Statement." In U.S. Congress. House. Committee on Govern-
ment Operations. Manpower and Housing Subcommittee. The
Women's Bureau, p. 207-8.

Woodruff, Monica.
"Statement." In U.S. Congress. House. Committee on Ways
and Means. Subcommittee on Public Assistance and Unemployment Compensation. Teenage Pregnancy Issues, p. 47-8.

Woods, Bonnie.
"Historiogenic Art: Camouflage and Plumage." In GLCA Wom-
en's Studies Conference (5th: 1979). Towards a Feminist
Transformation of the Academy, p. 34-6.

Woods, Rilla.
"Statement." In U.S. Congress. House. Committee on Small
Business. Subcommittee on General Oversight and Minority
Enterprise. Women In Business, p. 25-7.

Woodward, Susan L.
"The Rights of Women: Ideology, Policy, and Social Change in
Yugoslavia." In Women, State, and Party in Eastern Europe,
p. 234-56.

Wright, Frances.
"Address, July 4, 1828." In We Shall Be Heard, p. 4-9.
"Of Free Enquiry." In Outspoken Women, p. 253-8.

Wright, Lucille Johnson.
"Testimony." In U.S. Congress. House. Select Committee on
Aging. Subcommittee on Retirement Income and Employment.
Task Force on Social Security and Women. Treatment of
Women Under Social Security, p. 146-50.

Wundram, Ina Jane.
"Sex Differences in the Brain: Implications for Curriculum
Change." In Feminist Visions, p. 158-69.

Wurf, Mildred Kiefer.
"Statement." In U.S. Congress. House. Committee on Ways
and Means. Subcommittee on Public Assistance and Unemployment Compensation. Teenage Pregnancy Issues, p. 181-3.
"Testimony." In U.S. Congress. Senate. Committee on Human
Resources. Adolescent Health, Services, and Pregnancy Prevention Care Act of 1978, p. 564-7.

Wyatt, Addie.
"Speech by Commissioner Addie Wyatt." In U.S. National Com-
mission on the Observance of International Women's Year.
The Spirit of Houston, p. 231.
"Statement." In U.S. Congress. House. Committee on Educa-
tion and Labor. Subcommittee on Labor-Management Relations.
Legislative Hearing on Pension Equity for Women, p. 33-6.

Yager, Elisabeth.
"Statement." In U.S. Congress. House. Committee on Educa-
tion and Labor. Subcommittee on Labor-Management Relations.
Pension Equity for Women, p. 55.

Yalom, Marilyn.
"Sylvia Plath, The Bell Jar, and Related Poems." In Coming to
Light, p. 167-81.

Yarros, Rachelle S.
"Experience with the Cervical Pessary." In International Birth
Control Conference (7th: 1930: Zurich). The Practice of
Contraception, p. 17.
"Testimony." In U.S. Congress. House. Committee on the
Judiciary. Birth Control, (1934) p. 92-5.

Yeamans, Robin.
"A Political-Legal Analysis of Pornography." In Take Back the
Night, p. 248-51.

Young, Carolyn.
"Testimony." In U.S. Commission on Civil Rights. Hearing Before the U.S. Commission on Civil Rights Held in Denver,
p. 413, 416.

Young, Dawn J.
   "All Thy Children Shall Be Taught." In A Woman's Choices, p.
   42-53.

Young, Jean C.
   "Statement." In U.S. Congress. Senate. Committee on Labor
   and Human Resources. The Coming Decade, p. 60-1.

Young, Lorie.
   "Testimony." In U.S. Commission on Civil Rights. Hearing Before the U.S. Commission on Civil Rights Held in Denver,
   p. 332, 337, 343, 344.

Young, Mary E.
   "Women Civilization, and the Indian Question." In Conference on
   Women's History (1976: Washington, DC). Clio Was a Woman,
   p. 98-110. Also in Women's America, p. 149-55.

Young, Ruth L.
   "Statement." In U.S. Congress. House. Committee on Veterans'
   Affairs. Subcommittee on Hospitals and Health Care. VA
   Health Care for Women, p. 28-30.

Young, Tasia.
   "Statement." In U.S. Congress. House. Committee on Post
   Office and Civil Service. Subcommittee on Compensation and
   Employee Benefits. Options for Conducting a Pay Equity
   Study, p. 139-41.

Young, Virginia C.
   "The Problem of the Delinquent Girl." In American Birth Con-
   trol Conference (1st: 1921: New York). Birth Control:
   What It Is, How It Works, What It Will Do, p. 60-6.

Zappi, Elda Gentili.
   "'If Eight Hours Seem Few to You...': Women Workers' Strikes
   in Italian Rice Fields, 1901-1906." In Berkshire Conference on
   the History of Women (5th: 1982: Vassar College). Women
   and the Structure of Society, p. 206-15.

Zavala, Iris M.
   "Concluding Remarks." In Women, Feminist Identity, and Society
   in the 1980's, p. 127-36.

Zavella, Patricia.
   "'Abnormal Intimacy': the Varying Work Networks of Chicana
   Cannery Workers." Feminist Studies, 11 (Fall 1985), 541-57.

Zeigler, Karen J.
   "Testimony." In U.S. Congress. House. Committee on Energy

and Commerce. Subcommittee on Health and the Environment. Health and the Environment Miscellaneous, pt. 3, p. 16-9.

Zeis, Sister Mary Eric, S.S.N.D.
"Forming a Christian Social Conscience." In Split-Level Lives, p. 27-41.

Zemotal, Linda.
"Travel Patterns of Women and Men Based on Stage in Family Life Cycle." In Women's Travel Issues, p. 687-8.

Ziadeh, May.
"Woman and Work." Signs, 5 (Winter 1979), 377-9.

Ziegler, Martha.
"Statement." In U.S. Congress. House. Select Committee on Children, Youth, and Families. Families with Disabled Children, p. 63-5.

Zimmer, Laurie.
"Education and Equality for Women." In Cornell Conference on Women (1969: Cornell University). Proceedings, p. 34, 41, 47.

Zimmerman, Joan G.
"Daughters of Main Street: Culture and the Female Community at Grinnell, 1884-1917." In Conference on the History of Women (1977: St. Paul, MN). Woman's Being, Woman's Place, p. 154-70.

Zimmerman, Mary.
"Alignment Strategies in Verbal Accounts of Problematic Conduct: The Case of Abortion." In Conference on the Sociology of the Languages of American Women (1976: New Mexico State University). Proceedings, p. 171-83.

Zuckerman, Ruth Jane.
"Testimony." In U.S. Congress. House. Committee on the Judiciary. Subcommittee on Civil and Constitutional Rights. Proposed Constitutional Amendments on Abortion, p. 222-30.

Zuckert, Catherine.
"Testimony." In U.S. Congress. Senate. Committee on the Judiciary. Subcommittee on the Constitution. The Impact of the Equal Rights Amendment, pt. 2, p. 96-101.

SUBJECT INDEX

ABORTION--U.S.
    Abzug, B. "Constitutional Amendments Relating to Abortion."
    Acevedo, R. "Statement."
    Avery, M. "Statement."
    Babbott, J. "Statement."
    Bellamy, C. "Statement."
    Belovitch, T. "The Experience of Abortion."
    Beresford, T. "Statement."
    Blaunstein, P. "Testimony."
    Blechman, E. "Behavior Therapies."
    Bloomrosen, M. "Testimony."
    Blume, S. "Testimony."
    Bricker-Jenkins, M. "Statement."
    Brown, J. "Statement."
    Brown, J. "Testimony."
    Bryant, B. "Statement."
    Burt, M. "Testimony."
    Chapman, M. "Testimony."
    Coleman, T. "Testimony."
    Collins, J. "Statement."
    Connell, E. "Testimony."
    Crisswell, J. "Testimony."
    Davis, J. "Statement."
    Diener, M. "Testimony."
    Doyle, J. "Statement."
    Dryfoos, J. "Statement."
    Duxbury, M. "Testimony."
    Englund, J. "Testimony."
    Ensor, P. "Testimony."
    Fenwick, M. "Statement."
    Fertig, B. "Testimony."
    Foley, K. "Testimony."
    Gavett, P. "Statement."
    Gerster, C. "Statement."
    Goldstein, N. "Statement."
    Gray, N. "Statement."
    Greene, B. "Testimony."
    Greenfield, L. "Testimony."
    Hague, B. "Testimony."
    Halloran, J. "Testimony."

350

ABORTION--U.S. (cont.)

Ruether, R. "Statement."
Russell, S. "Testimony."
Ryden, H. "Testimony."
St. Martin, D. "Statement."
Schoenrich, E. "Testimony."
Smith, J. "Testimony."
Smith, J. "Abortion as a Feminist Concern."
Steorts, N. "Testimony."
Stevens, C. "Testimony."
Stone, V. "Testimony."
Tarr-Whalen, L. "Statement."
Trauner, J. "Testimony."
Verdesi, E. "Statement."
Wardman, B. "Testimony."
Wattleton, F. "Statement." (2)
Wattleton, F. "Testimony."
Weddington, S. "Statement."
Wells-Schooley, J. "Statement."
Wertheimer, W. "Testimony."
Widdecombe, J. "Statement."
Wilkins, J. "Statement."
Williams, L. "Testimony."
Wilson, K. "Statement."
Zeigler, K. "Testimony."
Zuckerman, R. "Testimony."

ABUSED PARENTS

Baldwin, W. "Testimony."
Blanchard, M. "Testimony."
Blockwick, J. "Testimony."
Blum, B. "Testimony."
Dolch, D. "Statement."
Forbush, J. "Testimony."
Gaston, C. "Statement."
Hardy, J. "Testimony."
Hill, F. "Statement."
Hsu, L. "Statement."
Hofmann, A. "Testimony."
La Prade, V. "Statement."
Laurie, L. "Testimony."
Mecklenburg, M. "Testimony."
Moore, K. "Testimony."
Oakar, M. "Statement."
O'Riordan, A. "Statement."
Palmer, E. "Testimony."
Pope, L. "Statement."
Quinn, M. "Statement."
Rini, M. "Testimony."

ADOLESCENT MOTHERS

Baldwin, W. "Statement."
Bane, M. "Statement."
Blum, B. "Statement."
Boggs, L. "Statement."
Bryant, D. "Statement."
Davis, A. "Statement."
Driscoll, P. "Statement."
Ebeling, E. "Statement."
Ellis, E. "Statement."
Forrest, J. "Statement."
Gasper, J. "Statement."
Gilbert, M. "Statement."
Gurieva, D. "Statement."
Height, D. "Statement."
Henderson, D. "Statement."
Howard, M. "Statement."
Huiskamp, J. "Testimony."
Johnson, D. "Statement."
Johnson, N. "Statement."
Jones, J. "Statement."
Libert, M. "Statement."
Massinga, R. "Statement."
McGee, E. "Statement."
McIntosh, S. "Statement."
Nerad, L. "Statement."
Pittman, K. "Statement."
Preston, J. "Statement."
Salmon, R. "Statement."
Schroeder, P. "Statement."
White, R. "Statement."
Wisman, R. "Statement."
Woodruff, M. "Statement."
Wurf, M. "Statement."

ADOLESCENTS--U.S.--ALCOHOL USE

Howe, C. "Statement."
Nalepka, J. "Statement."

ADOPTION

Dennett, J. "Statement."
Edwards, J. "Statement."
Godley, A. "Statement."
Godley, A. "Statement."
Hardy, D. "Statement."
Kuharski, M. "Statement."

ADOPTION (cont.)
  McCord, R. "Statement."
  Schaus, M. "Statement."
  Smith, B. "Statement."
  Smith, H. "Statement."
  Vann, T. "Statement."

AERONAUTICS--U.S.--SAFETY MEASURES

  Boggs, L. "Statement."
  Dole, E. "Statement." (2)
  Johnson, N. "Statement."
  Kassebaum, N. "Statement."
  Vucanovich, B. "Statement."

AFFIRMATIVE ACTION PROGRAMS

  Boggs, L. "Statement."
  Bradshaw, G. "Statement."
  Collins, C. "Statement."
  Clauss, C. "Statement."
  Denecke, A. "Statement."
  Feiger, L. "Statement."
  Feingold, E. "Speech."
  Fleming, J. "Statement."
  Ginsburg, R. "Realizing the Quality Principle."
  Greene, M. "Equality and Inviolability."
  Hirano, I. "Statement."
  Martinez, V. "Statement."
  Montgomery, B. "Statement."
  Norton, E. "Statement."
  Peurala, A. "Statement."
  Piercy, D. "Statement."
  Pratt, P. "Statement."
  Schroeder, P. "Statement." (2)
  Smeal, E. "Statement."
  Waters, M. "Statement."
  Wertz, T. "Statement."
  Willhoite, B. "Statement."
  Williams, C. "Statement."

AFRO-AMERICAN CHILDREN--MORTALITY

  Boggs, L. "Statement."

AFRO-AMERICAN WOMEN

  Aptheker, B. "On 'The Damnation of Women.'"

AFRO-AMERICAN WOMEN (cont.)

Aptheker, B. "Quest for Dignity."

Aptheker, B. "Woman Suffrage and the Crusade Against Lynching, 1890-1920."

King, C. "Coretta Scott King Remarks."

Lorde, A. "Age, Race, Class, and Sex."

Lorde, A. "Learning from the 60s."

Lorde, A. "The Master's Tools Will Never Dismantle the Master's House."

Lorde, A. "The Transformation of Silence into Language and Action."

Lorde, A. "The Uses of Anger."

Lorde, A. "Uses of the Erotic."

Palmer, P. "White Women/Black Women."

Smith, B. "Racism and Women's Studies."

Walker, A. "Only Justice Can Stop a Curse."

Walker, A. "Saving the Life That Is Your Own."

Walker, A. "A Talk: Convocation 1972."

AFRO-AMERICAN WOMEN--EDUCATION

Bonder, G. "The Educational Process of Women's Studies in Argentina."

Culley, M. "Anger and Authority in the Introductory Women's Studies Classroom."

Friedman, S. "Authority in the Feminist Classroom."

Lightfoot, S. "Socialization and Education of Young Black Girls in Schools."

Miller, N. "Mastery, Identity and the Politics of Work."

Miner, M. "The School for Colored Girls."

Rawles, B. "The Media and Their Effect on Black Images."

Reid, I. "Health Issues Facing Black Women."

Rich, A. "Taking Women Students Seriously."

Roby, P. "Toward Full Equality."

Sawhill, I. "Black Women Who Head Families."

Shaw, E. "Professional Schools and Their Impact on Black Women."

AFRO-AMERICAN WOMEN--EMPLOYMENT

Darlington-Hope, M. "Women of Color and the Feminization of Poverty."

Lightfoot, S. "Socialization and Education of Young Black Girls in School."

Rawles, B. "The Media and Their Effect on Black Images."

Reid, I. "Health Issues Facing Black Women."

Roby, P. "Toward Full Equality."

Sawhill, I. "Black Women Who Head Families."

AFRO-AMERICAN WOMEN--HEALTH AND HYGIENE

    Bradley, V. "It Happened on My Birthday."
    Gray, N. "Sterilization and the Black Female."
    Reingold, E. "Black Suicide in San Francisco."

AFRO-AMERICAN WOMEN--HISTORY

    Lerner, G. "Black Women in the United States."
    Lerner, G. "The Challenge of Women's History."
    Lerner, G. "Community Work of Black Club Women."
    Lerner, G. "Just a Housewife."
    Lerner, G. "Placing Women In History."
    Lerner, G. "The Political Activities of Antislavery Women."

AFRO-AMERICAN WOMEN--SOUTHERN STATES

    Friedman, J. "Women's History of the Revision of Southern
      History."
    Harley, S. "Black Women in a Southern City."
    Janiewski, D. "Sisters Under Their Skins."
    Jones, A. "Southern Literary Women as Chroniclers of Southern
      Life."
    Scott, A. "Historians Construct the Southern Woman."
    Swain, M. "The Public Role of Southern Women."

AFRO-AMERICAN WOMEN--U.S.--ECONOMIC CONDITIONS

    Baker, K. "Statement."
    Blum, B. "Statement."
    Ferraro, G. "Statement."
    Fiedler, B. "Statement."
    McAdoo, H. "Statement."
    Mobley, S. "Statement."
    Murphy, S. "Statement."
    Norton, E. "Statement."
    Shepard, A. "Statement."

AFRO-AMERICANS--EDUCATION--U.S.

    Howe, F. "American Literature and Women's Lives."
    Howe, F. "Breaking the Disciplines."
    Howe, F. "Feminism and the Education of Women."
    Howe, F. "Feminism and the Study of Literature."
    Howe, F. "Feminism, Fiction, and the Classroom."
    Howe, F. "Feminist Scholarship."
    Howe, F. "The Future of Women's Colleges."

AFRO-AMERICANS--EDUCATION--U.S. (cont.)

 Howe, F. "Literacy and Literature."
 Howe, F. "Myths of Coeducation."
 Howe, F. "The Past Ten Years."
 Howe, F. "The Power of Education."
 Howe, F. "Sex-Role Stereotypes Start Early."
 Howe, F. "Teaching in the Modern Languages."
 Howe, F. "Why Educate Women?"
 Howe, F. "Why Educate Women: The Responses of Wellesley
  and Stanford."
 Howe, F. "Women's Studies and Social Change."

AFRO-AMERICANS--HISTORY

 Bethune, M. "The Association for the Study of Negro Life and
  History."
 Bethune, M. "Clarifying Our Vision With the Facts."
 Bethune, M. "The Negro in Retrospect and Prospect."

AGED--EMPLOYMENT--U.S.

 Bellamy, C. "Statement."
 Boggs, L. "Statement."
 Schroeder, P. "Statement."

AGED--MEDICAL CARE

 Oakar, M. "Statement."

AGED--U.S.--ABUSE OF--PREVENTION

 Dolch, D. "Statement."
 Hill, F. "Statement."
 Hsu, L. "Statement."
 La Prade, V. "Statement."
 Oakar, M. "Statement."
 O'Riordan, A. "Statement."
 Pope, L. "Statement."
 Quinn, M. "Statement."
 Schneider, C. "Statement."
 Steinmetz, S. "Statement."

AGED WOMEN--EMPLOYMENT--U.S.

 King, N. "Statement."
 Lonsdale, E. "Statement."

AGED WOMEN--EMPLOYMENT--U.S. (cont.)

Markson, E. "Statement."
Moss, A. "Statement."
Netherton, J. "Statement."
Sandage, S. "Statement."
Snowe, O. "Statement."

AGED WOMEN--HEALTH AND HYGIENE--U.S.

Johnson, B. "Statement."
Kaptur, M. "Statement."
Mercer, E. "Statement."
Metress, E. "Statement."

AGED WOMEN--NEW YORK

Bellamy, C. "Problems of Older Women."
Brophy, A. "Older Women in New York City--Today and Tomorrow."
Cabrera-Drinane, S. "Developing Meaningful Roles for Minority Women."
Cantor, M. "Income Inadequacy of Older Women."
Carlo, C. "Credit & Financial Problems of Older Women."
Dobrof, R. "The Family Relationships and Living Arrangements of Older Women."
Handkin, H. "Community Resources for the Elderly."
Hess, B. "The 'New Breed' of Old People."
Kinoy, S. "The Aging Within the Family Structure."
Kryzak, R. "The Plight of Older Women in Retirement."
Litwak, E. "Problems in Pension Systems as Specifically Related to Women Retirees."
Mayer, M. "The Older Woman."
Peissachowitz, N. "Advisability of Maintaining People In Their Own Homes."
Rinehart, B. "Concrete Services."
Safford, F. "Realistic Assessment of the Needs of Older Women."
Troll, Lillian E. "Meaningful Roles for Older Women."

AGED WOMEN--OREGON

Bader, J. "Statement."
Fadeley, N. "Statement."
Gleason, J. "Statement."
Harris, E. "Statement."
Laurence, I. "Statement."
Lenhoff, N. "Statement."
Linn, M. "Statement."
Lofquist, E. "Statement."

AGED WOMEN--OREGON (cont.)
    Meyer, E. "Statement."
    Moore, L. "Statement."
    Reisinger, M. "Statement."
    Russell-Young, N. "Statement."
    Tenant, L. "Statement."
    Thacker, P. "Statement."
    Turner, P. "Statement."

AGED WOMEN--UNITED STATES

    Anderson, S. "Statement."
    Braun, B. "Statement."
    Clark, H. "Statement."
    Hamon, E. "Statement."
    Hong, H. "Statement."
    Huebner, R. "Statement."
    Jacobsen, G. "Statement."
    Mendez, D. "Statement."
    Murphy, A. "Statement."
    Potter, J. "Statement."
    Rouse, I. "Statement."
    Simmons, D. "Statement."
    Tyler, M. "Statement."
    Waskel, S. "Statement."

AGED WOMEN--UNITED STATES--ECONOMIC CONDITIONS

    Brown, A. "Statement."
    Capple, J. "Statement."
    Jenks, M. "Statement."
    North, J. "Statement."
    Oakar, M. "Statement."
    Seltzer, M. "Statement."
    Snyder, D. "Statement."

AGENT ORANGE--PHYSIOLOGICAL EFFECTS

    Boxer, B. "Statement."

AGING--RESEARCH--UNITED STATES

    Snowe, O. "Statement."

AGRICULTURE

    Kaptur, M. "Statement."

AGRICULTURE (cont.)
  Kunin, M. "Statement."
  Lloyd, M. "Statement."
  Martin, L. "Statement."
  Mikulski, B. "Statement."
  Oakar, M. "Statement." (2)
  Smith, V. "Statement." (2)
  Stern, P. "Trade Problems in Agriculture."

AIDS

  Boxer, B. "Statement."
  Heckler, M. "Statement."

AIR TRAFFIC CONTROL--UNITED STATES

  Boggs, L. "Statement."
  Dole, E. "Statement."
  Johnson, N. "Statement."
  Kassebaum, N. "Statement."
  Vucanovich, B. "Statement."

ALCOHOL AND WOMEN

  Gomberg, E. "Risk Factors Related to Alcohol Problems Among
    Women."
  Hill, S. "Introduction: The Biological Consequences."
  Luke, B. "Statement."
  Randall, C. "Testimony."
  Wilsnack, S. "Prevention and Education Research."

ALEUTS--CLAIMS

  Boggs, L. "Statement."
  Burton, S. "Statement."

ALIEN LABOR--UNITED STATES

  Chisholm, S. "Statement."

ALZHEIMER'S DISEASE

  Heckler, M. "Statement."
  Oakar, M. "Statement."

AMERICAN LITERATURE--WOMEN AUTHORS

Anderson, D. "'Jeannie Drake.'"
Craven, D. "The Unpublished Diaries of Mary Moragne Davis."
Didion, J. "Why I Write."
Endres, K. "Mary Moragne's The British Partizan."
Gregory, E. "The Formality of Memory."
Hampton, A. "Sally Baxter Hampton."
Muhlenfeld, E. "Literary Elements in Mary Chesnut's Journal."
Nin, A. "The Artist as Magician."
Nin, A. "Furrawn."
Nin, A. "A New Center of Gravity."
Nin, A. "The Personal Life Deeply Lived."
Nin, A. "Proceed from the Dream."
Nin, A. "Refusal to Despair."
Nin, A. "The Unveiling of Woman."
Nin, A. "Women Reconstructing the World."
Rukeyser, M. "The Education of a Poet."
Scafidel, B. "Caroline Carson."
Stanton, E. "From Address to the New York State Legislature, 1860."
Stein, G. "The Gradual Making of the Making of Americans."
Stein, G. "Plays."
Stein, G. "Portraits and Repetition."
Stein, G. "What Is English Literature."
Truth, S. "Ain't I a Woman?"
Truth, S. "Keeping the Thing Going While Things Are Stirring."
Truth, S. "What Time of Night It Is."

AMERICAN ORATIONS--WOMEN AUTHORS--HISTORY--CASE STUDIES

Anthony, S. "Address of Susan B. Anthony."
Catt, C. "Is Woman Suffrage Progressing?"
Dickinson, A. "Why Colored Men Should Enlist."
Flynn, E. "Statement at the Smith Act Trial."
Foster, A. "Remarks of Abby Kelley, Before a Meeting of the Boston Female Anti-Slavery Society."
Friedan, B. "The Crisis in Women's Identity."
Gilman, C. "The Social Body and Soul."
Goldman, E. "Address to the Jury, July, 1917."
Grimke, A. "Speech in Pennsylvania Hall."
Howe, J. "Is Polite Society Polite?"
Jordan, B. "Who Then Will Speak For the Common Good?"
Keller, H. "Strike Against War."
Kubler-Ross, E. "Death Does Not Exist."
Livermore, M. "What Shall We Do With Our Daughters?"
Lockwood, B. "The Political Rights of Women."
Luce, C. "Is the New Morality Destroying America?"
McPherson, A. "The Cat and the Canary."
Mott, L. "Discourse on Women."

AMERICAN ORATIONS--WOMEN AUTHORS--HISTORY--CASE
    STUDIES (cont.)
Roosevelt, E. "Adoption of Declaration of Human Rights."
Rose, E. "Speech of Mrs. E. L. Rose, May, 1860."
Shaw, A. "The Fate of Republics."
Smith, M. "Declaration of Conscience, June 1, 1950."
Smith, M. "Declaration of Conscience II, June 1, 1970."
Stanton, E. "Solitude of Self."
Stone, L. "Taxation Without Representation."
Truth, S. "Ain't I a Woman?"
Willard, F. "A White Life for Two."
Woodhull, V. "Constitutional Equality."
Wright, F. "Address, July 4, 1828."

AMERICAN POETRY--WOMEN AUTHORS

Allen, P. "Answering the Deer."
Burke, C. "The New Poetry and the New Woman."
Deshazer, M. "'My Scourge, My Sister.'"
Diehl, J. "At Home With Loss."
Dydo, U. "To Have the Winning Language."
Friedman, S. "'I Go Where I Love.'"
Gilbert, S. "In Yeats's House."
Middlebrook, D. "'I Tapped My Own Head.'"
Mossberg, B. "Sylvia Plath's Baby Book."
Ostriker, A. "The Thieves of Language."
Rushing, A. "Lucille Clifton."
Yalom, M. "Sylvia Plath, The Bell Jar, and Related Poems."

ANTITRUST LAW--UNITED STATES

Chisholm, S. "Statement."

ASBESTOS--ENVIRONMENTAL ASPECTS--UNITED STATES

Boxer, B. "Statement."
Burton, S. "Statement."

ASIAN AMERICANS

Cordova, D. "Educational Alternatives of Asian-Pacific Women."
Fujii, H. "Elderly Pacific Island and Asian-American Women."
Hirata, L. "Social Mobility of Asian Women in America."
Homma-True, R. "Mental Issues Among Asian-American Women."
Kim, B. "Asian Wives of U.S. Servicemen."
Loo, F. "Asian Women in Professional Health Schools, With Em-
    phasis on Nursing."

ASIAN AMERICANS (cont.)

Lott, J. "Keynote Address."

Nievera, F. "Some Effects of Childrearing Practices on the Value Systems of Asian-American Women."

Nishi, S. "Chairperson's Report."

Osako, M. "The Effects of Asian-American Kinship Systems on Women's Educational and Occupational Attainment."

Pian, C. "Immigration of Asian Women and the Status of Recent Asian Women Immigrants."

Wong, G. "Impediments to Asian-Pacific-American Women Organizing."

ATOMIC WARFARE

Caldicott, H. "A Commitment to Life."
Caldicott, H. "Nuclear War."
Caldicott, H. "We Are the Curators of Life on Earth."
Mansfield, S. "Strategy, Fear and the Atom."

AUTOMOBILES

Boxer, B. "Statement."
Collins, C. "Statement."
Lloyd, M. "Statement."
Martin, L. "Statement."

BACCALAUREATE ADDRESSES

Edelman, M. "Commencement Address, Bryn Mawr College, May 15, 1982."
Rich, A. "Commencement Address, Smith College, 1979."
West, J. "Commencement Address, Juniata College, May 24, 1981."

BAIL--UNITED STATES

Kassebaum, N. "Statement."

BANK FAILURES

Boxer, B. "Statement."

BANKING LAW--UNITED STATES

Boxer, B. "Statement."

BANKING LAW--UNITED STATES (cont.)
Chisholm, S. "Statement."
Oakar, M. "Statement."

BENNETT, WILLIAM

Collins, C. "Statement."

BIRTH CONTROL

Babbott, J. "Statement."
Betz, H. "Testimony."
Brown, J. "Statement."
Butler, A. "Individual Woman's Need of Birth Control."
Cocciolone, D. "Statement."
Conway, J. "Margaret Sanger and American Reform."
Daniels, A. "A Comparative Study of Birth Control Methods
    with Special Reference to Spermatoxins."
Devilbiss, L. "Medical Aspects of Birth Control."
Dilla, H. "The Greater Freedom By Birth Control."
Dunning, (Mrs.) G. "Testimony."
Fee, E. "From Voluntary Motherhood to Planned Parenthood."
Galler, J. "Statement."
Gibbs, (Mrs.) R. "Testimony." (3)
Gilman, C. "Testimony."
Goldman, E. "Emma Goldman's Defense."
Gordon, L. "From Voluntary Motherhood to Planned Parenthood."
Halpern, R. "Testimony."
Hammond, B. "Statement."
Harper, A. "From Voluntary Motherhood to Planned Parenthood."
Harper, A. "Reproductive Freedom Today."
Hepburn, K. "Testimony." (5)
Hough, E. "Testimony."
Hooker, E. "Address of Welcome."
Kasun, J. "Statement."
Kavinoky, N. "California Public Health and Mothers' Clinics."
Kilbreth, M. "Testimony."
Klaus, H. "Statement."
Lansburgh, (Mrs.) M. "Testimony."
Laurie, L. "Statement."
Mann, D. "Statement."
Marshner, C. "Statement."
Maves, B. "Statement."
McGoldrick, R. "Testimony." (4)
Moffat, (Mrs.) D. "Testimony."
Norton, M. "Testimony." (3)
Regan, A. "Testimony." (4)
Roylance, S. "Statement."
Sanger, M. "Address of Welcome."

BIRTH CONTROL (cont.)

Sanger, M. "The Children's Era."
Sanger, M. "Is Birth Control Moral?"
Sanger, M. "Opening Address."
Sanger, M. "Should Legal Barriers Against Birth Control Be Removed?"
Sanger, M. "Testimony." (5)
Smedley, A. "Birth Control Work in China."
Solyom, (Mrs.) H. L. "Testimony."
Stone, H. "The Birth Control Clinical Research Bureau, New York."
Stone, H. "Testimony."
Stone, H. "The Vaginal Occlusive Pessary."
Trent, K. "Testimony."
Wattleton, F. "Statement."
Winsor, M. "The Birth Control Movement in Europe."
Yarros, R. "Experience with the Cervical Pessary."
Yarros, R. "Testimony."
Young, V. "The Problem of the Delinquent Girl."

BIRTH WEIGHT, LOW

Boggs, L. "Statement."
Ebeling, E. "Statement."
Forrest, J. "Statement."
Gilbert, M. "Statement."
Gurieva, D. "Statement."
Howard, M. "Statement."
Liebert, M. "Statement."
McIntosh, S. "Statement."
Nerad, L. "Statement."
Salmon, R. "Statement."
Schroeder, P. "Statement."

BLACK FAMILIES

Baker, K. "Statement."
Blum, B. "Statement."
Ferraro, G. "Statement."
Fiedler, B. "Statement."
McAdoo, H. "Statement."
Mobley, S. "Statement."
Murphy, S. "Statement."
Norton, E. "Statement."
Shepard, A. "Statement."

BREAST--CANCER

Alford, C. "Statement."

BREAST--CANCER (cont.)
   Kushner, R. "Statement."
   Levin, D. "Statement."
   Nixon, J. "Statement."
   Oakar, M. "Statement."
   Spear, R. "Statement."
   Threatt, B. "Statement."

BREEDER REACTORS

   Schneider, C. "Statement."

BROKEN HOMES

   Ahern, D. "Statement."
   Berger, B. "Statement."
   Decter, M. "Statement."
   Friedan, B. "Statement."
   Hardy, D. "Statement."
   Johnson, G. "Statement."
   Mallett, C. "Statement."
   McAdoo, H. "Statement."
   Rich, D. "Statement."
   Wallerstein, J. "Statement."

BUDGET--UNITED STATES

   Boxer, B. "Statement."
   Ferraro, G. "Controversy Over the Federal Budget Deficit."
   Hecker, M. "Statement." (2)
   Kaptur, M. "Controversy Over the Federal Budget Deficit."

CABLE TELEVISION

   Hawkins, P. "Statement."

CAMPAIGN FUNDS--UNITED STATES

   Boxer, B. "Statement."
   Ferraro, G. "Statement."
   Hecker, M. "Statement."

CAPITOL PAGES

   Fiedler, B. "Statement."
   Martin, L. "Statement."

CARGO PREFERENCE--UNITED STATES

Boggs, L. "Statement."
Smith, V. "Statement."

CHILD ABUSE--UNITED STATES

Aal, D. "Statement."
Hawkins, P. "Statement."
Key, M. "Statement."
Roukema, M. "Statement."
Sneed, M. "Statement."
Staples, E. "Statement."

CHILD HEALTH SERVICES--UNITED STATES

Davis, C. "Statement."
Davis, K. "Statement."
Weitz, J. "Statement."

CHILD MOLESTING--UNITED STATES

Brady, K. "Statement."
Brown, S. "Testimony."
Burgess, A. "Testimony."
Dawson-Brown, C. "Testimony."
Dworkin, A. "Testimony."
Frank, E. "Statement."
Goldsmith, J. "Testimony."
Gosch, N. "Testimony."
Heller, V. "Testimony."
Leidholdt, D. "Testimony."
MacKinnon, C. "Testimony."
Marchiano, L. "Testimony."
Sadler, A. "Statement."
Seka. "Testimony."
Smith, P. "Testimony."
Specter, J. "Testimony."
Vera, V. "Testimony."
Webb, C. "Statement."

CHILD REARING--UNITED STATES

Howe, C. "Statement."
Nalepka, J. "Statement."

CHILDREN IN PORNOGRPAHY

Brady, K. "Statement."
Brown, S. "Testimony."
Burgess, A. "Testimony."
Dawson-Brown, C. "Testimony."
Dworkin, A. "Testimony."
Goldsmith, J. "Testimony."
Gosch, N. "Testimony."
Hawkins, P. "Statement."
Heller, V. "Testimony."
Leidholdt, D. "Testimony."
MacKinnon, C. "Testimony."
Marchiano, L. "Testimony."
Sadler, A. "Statement."
Seka. "Testimony."
Smith, P. "Testimony."
Specter, J. "Testimony."
Vera, V. "Testimony."

CHILDREN OF DIVORCED PARENTS

Aherns, D. "Statement."
Berger, B. "Statement."
Decter, M. "Statement."
Friedan, B. "Statement."
Hardy, D. "Statement."
Johnson, G. "Statement."
Mallett, C. "Statement."
McAdoo, H. "Statement."
Rich, D. "Statement."
Wallerstein, J. "Statement."

CHILDREN'S LITERATURE

Blos, J. "Newbery Medal Acceptance."
Brown, M. "Caldecott Medal Acceptance."
Cooney, B. "Caldecott Medal Acceptance."
Cleary, B. "Newbery Medal Acceptance."
Halttunen, K. "The Domestic Drama of Louisa May Alcott."
Hyman, T. "Caldecott Medal Acceptance."
McKinley, R. "Newbery Medal Acceptance."
Paterson, K. "Newbery Medal Acceptance."
Raskin, E. "Newbery Medal Acceptance."
Voight, C. "Newbery Medal Acceptance."
Willard, N. "Newbery Medal Acceptance."

CHRISTIAN CHURCH

Hamilton, E. "The Way of the Church."

CHRISTIAN ETHICS

Harrison, B. "The Equal Rights Amendment."
Harrison, B. "The Power of Anger in the Work of Love."
Harrison, B. "Sexism and the Language of Christian Ethics."

CHURCH AND RACE PROBLEMS

Chambers, B. "Psychological Effects of Segregation."
Heffernan, M. "Equality and 'The System.'"
Kopp, M. "The Myth of Race."
Madden, L. "Challenge to the Churches."
Mangan, M. "Unwritten History."
Meehan, M. "Residence and Race."
Prince, M. "With All Deliberate Speed."
Traxler, M. "Catholic Educational Dilemmas."
Traxler, M. "The Ministry of Presence."
Zeis, M. "Forming a Christian Social Conscience."

CIVIL RIGHTS--UNITED STATES

Albert, M. "Testimony."
Bere, P. "Testimony."
Berry, M. "Statement."
Brown, C. "Statement." (2)
Burris, C. "Testimony."
Cerda, G. "Testimony."
Chavez, L. "Statement." (2)
Cooper, H. "Testimony."
Criley, F. "Testimony."
Cruz, R. "Testimony."
Cruz, R. "Welcoming Statement."
Feistritzer, E. "Statement."
Fraser, A. "Testimony."
Freeman, F. "Statement."
Futrell, M. "Statement."
Gardner, E. "Statement."
Ginsburg, R. "Realizing the Equality Principle."
Goldsmith, J. "Statement."
Gray, A. "Testimony."
Greenberger, M. "Statement." (2)
Greene, M. "Equality and Inviolability."
Guninan, M. "Testimony."
Hallett-Weller, I. "Testimony."

CIVIL RIGHTS--UNITED STATES (cont.)
    Houston, N. "Testimony."
    Hullett, J. "Testimony."
    Jermany, C. "Testimony."
    Kelley, C. "Testimony."
    Ladky, A. "Testimony."
    Lichtman, J. "Statement."
    Litten, B. "Statement."
    Lo Sasso, R. "Testimony."
    Mabry, R. "Testimony."
    Mapp, P. "Testimony."
    Mayer, L. "Testimony."
    Mayerson, A. "Statement."
    McCabe, C. "Testimony."
    Merrill, B. "Testimony."
    Milstein, B. "Statement."
    Moore, M. "Testimony."
    Noble, S. "Testimony."
    Nortell, E. "Testimony."
    Orr, B. "Statement."
    Reed, W. "Testimony."
    Rosen, M. "Testimony."
    Ross, O. "Testimony."
    Roundtree, J. "Testimony."
    Schaffer, J. "Testimony."
    Schneider, C. "Statement."
    Schwerin, S. "Testimony."
    Simmons, A. "Statement."
    Snowe, O. "Statement."
    Stille, D. "Testimony." (2)
    Syler, M. "Testimony."
    Taub, N. "Testimony."
    Taylor, R. "Testimony."
    Tessner, E. "Testimony."
    Tuteur, M. "Testimony."
    White, D. "Statement."
    Williams, O. "Welcoming Statement."
    Wilson, S. "Testimony."
    Winfield, A. "Testimony."

CIVIL SERVICE--UNITED STATES

    Byron, B. "Statement."
    Fenwick, M. "Statement."
    Schroeder, P. "Statement."

CIVIL SERVICE PENSIONS

    Ferraro, G. "Statement."
    Schroeder, P. "Statement."

COLLEGE TEACHERS

    Barnes, H. "Apologia Pro Vita."
    Tidball, M. "To Use All Their Talents."

COMMUNICATION

    Copley, H. "The Wiring of America."

COMPETITION, UNFAIR--UNITED STATES

    Fiedler, B. "Statement."

COMPUTERS

    Fasciona, J. "Can We Afford to Say 'Good Morning?'"

CONFLICT OF INTEREST--UNITED STATES

    Schroeder, P. "Statement."

CONJUGAL VIOLENCE--UNITED STATES

    Aal, D. "Statement."
    Bako, Y. "Statement."
    Bendor, J. "Statement."
    Boggs, L. "Statement."
    Burgess, A. "Statement."
    Burt, M. "Statement."
    Crawford, S. "Statement."
    Derrig, N. "Statement."
    Fields, M. "Statement."
    Flitcraft, A. "Statement."
    Flynn, B. "Statement."
    Hansen, S. "Statement."
    Hart, B. "Statement."
    Kelly-Dreiss, S. "Statement."
    Key, M. "Statement."
    Klein, A. "Statement."
    Kutzke, E. "Statement."
    Largen, M. "Statement."
    McDonald, N. "Statement."
    Mikulski, B. "Statement."
    Mitgang, I. "Statement."
    Myers, T. "Statement."
    Schultz, P. "Statement."

CONJUGAL VIOLENCE--UNITED STATES (cont.)
    Sparks, C. "Statement."
    Staples, E. "Statement."
    Steinmetz, S. "Statement."
    Thompson, R. "Statement."
    Walker, L. "Statement." (2)
    Whetstone, G. "Statement."

CONNECTICUT--GOVERNORS

    Grasso, E. "Budget Address by Governor Ella Grasso."
    Grasso, E. "Budget Message to the Connecticut General Assembly by Ella T. Grasso, February 4, 1976."
    Grasso, E. "Budget Message to the Connecticut General Assembly, by Governor Ella Grasso, February 10, 1978."
    Grasso, E. "Governor's Message."
    Grasso, E. "Inaugural Message to the Connecticut General Assembly by Governor Ella T. Grasso, January 8, 1975."
    Grasso, E. "Inaugural Message to the Connecticut General Assembly by Governor Ella Grasso, January 3, 1979."

CONSERVATISM

    Buckley, P. "Speech at National Review's Thirtieth Anniversary Dinner."
    Decker, M. "Expanding World Freedom."

CONSUMER PROTECTION

    Peterson, E. "Statement." (20)

CONTRACEPTION

    Baldwin, W. "Statement."
    Barnes, H. "Statement."
    Bayne, S. "Statement."
    Benesch, J. "Statement."
    Blanchard, M. "Testimony."
    Cooper, D. "Statement."
    Daniels, A. "A Comparative Study of Birth Control Methods with Special Reference to Spermatoxins."
    Dryfoos, J. "Statement."
    Gentry, C. "Statement."
    Hardy, J. "Statement."
    Jefferson, M. "Statement."
    Jones, J. "Statement."
    Kavinoky, N. "California Public Health and Mothers' Clinics."
    Lashof, J. "Statement."

CONTRACEPTIVES (cont.)
   Shearer, B. "C/SEC: A Special-Interest Interpersonal Group
      Brings About Change."
   Swallow, H. "Midwives in Many Settings."
   Swenson, N. "Response (to an Obstetrician's Perspective)."
   Wertz, D. "Man-Midwifery and the Rise of Technology."
   Wolcott, I. "Response (to Forces Impacting on the Policymaker)."

COTTAGE INDUSTRIES

   Behr, M. "Statement."
   Clement, M. "Statement."
   Kassenbaum, N. "Statement."
   Kern, C. "Statement."
   Pudvah, A. "Statement."

CRIME AND CRIMINALS

   Gordon, D. "Crime: The Citizen Connection...."

DAY CARE CENTERS

   Burton, S. "Statement."
   Fiedler, Bobbi. "Statement."
   Heckler, Margaret. "Congresswoman Margaret M. Heckler's
      Speech."
   Mikulski, Barbara. "Statement." (2)

DELINQUENT GIRLS

   Calderone, Mary. "Nothing Less Than the Truth Will Do, For
      We Have Nowhere To Go But Forward."
   Chambers, Marjorie. "A Summing Up."
   Conway, Jill. "A Proper Perspective."
   Hofmann, Adele. "Today's Girls."
   Jerome, Elizabeth. "A Physician's View of the Adolescent Wom-
      an."
   Keyserling, Mary. "New Realities in Women's Work Lives."
   Peacock, Carol. "The Massachusetts Experiment Toward Equal
      Service for Girls."
   Phelps, E. "Keynote."
   Phelps, E. "A Look Ahead."
   Rothman, F. "Reforming the 'System.'"
   Steiger, J. "Career Education."
   Tobias, S. "Math Anxiety."
   Verheyden-Hilliard, M. "Counseling."

DE PIZAN, CHRISTINE

   Bell, S. "Christine De Pizan (1364-1430)."

DESERTION AND NON-SUPPORT--UNITED STATES

   Hawkins, P. "Statement."
   Heckler, M. "Statement." (3)
   Kessbaum, N. "Statement."
   Kennelly, B. "Statement."
   Roukema, M. "Statement." (2)
   Schroeder, P. "Statement."

DISASTER RELIEF--UNITED STATES

   Boxer, B. "Statement."

DISCRIMINATION IN EDUCATION

   Chisholm, S. "Statement."
   Jensen, P. "Statement."
   Schneider, C. "Statement."
   Schroeder, P. "Statement."
   Stein, B. "Statement."
   Wolfe, L. "Statement."

DISCRIMINATION IN EMPLOYMENT

   Abramowitz, E. "Statement on Behalf of the President."
   Alley, M. "Statement."
   Beller, A. "Testimony."
   Bergman, B. "Testimony."
   Berry, M. "Statement."
   Bird, C. "Testimony."
   Boggs, L. "Statement."
   Bradshaw, G. "Statement."
   Bucknell, S. "Testimony."
   Byrd, A. "Statement."
   Cassedy, E. "Testimony."
   Clauss, C. "Statement."
   Collins, C. "Statement."
   Cooper, M. "Statement."
   Corcoran, M. "Testimony."
   Curran, H. "Testimony."
   Denecke, A. "Statement."
   East, C. "Testimony."
   Ferraro, G. "Statement."

DISCRIMINATION IN EMPLOYMENT (cont.)

Fleming, J. "Statement."
Fleming, J. "Testimony."
Freeman, J. "Testimony."
Goodin, J. "Testimony."
Goodwin, F. "Statement."
Hacker, H. "Testimony."
Haener, D. "Testimony."
Herman, A. "Testimony."
Hernandez, A. "Statement."
Hilton, M. "Greeting."
Hirano, I. "Statement."
Holmes, J. "Statement."
Hunter, F. "Testimony."
Jacox, A. "Testimony."
Johnson, E. "Testimony."
Kelley, M. "Testimony."
Krieter, N. "Testimony."
Lenhoff, D. "Testimony."
Lichtman, J. "Testimony."
Liss, L. "Testimony."
Madden, J. "Testimony."
Martinez, V. "Statement."
Morisey, M. "Statement."
Moses, M. "Testimony."
Myers, M. "Testimony."
Nelms, D. "Testimony."
Norton, E. "Opening Statement."
Norton, E. "Statement."
Oakar, M. "Statement."
Palmer, P. "Testimony."
Perlman, N. "Testimony."
Peurala, A. "Statement."
Piercy, D. "Statement." (2)
Poythress, M. "Statement."
Pratt, P. "Statement."
Reder, N. "Statement."
Reed, C. "Testimony."
Remick, H. "Testimony."
Robb, L. "Testimony."
Schroeder, P. "Statement." (2)
Shoong, E. "Testimony."
Smeal, E. "Statement."
Smithson, E. "Statement."
Smothers, L. "Statement."
Snowe, O. "Statement."
Taber, G. "Testimony."
Uhlig, M. "Statement."
Venegas, H. "Greeting."
Viviano, A. "Testimony."
Wallace, J. "Statement."

DISCRIMINATION IN EMPLOYMENT (cont.)
  Waters, M. "Statement."
  Wertz, T. "Statement."
  Whitney, J. "Testimony."
  Willhoite, B. "Statement."
  Williams, C. "Statement."
  Williams, M. "Testimony."
  Witt, M. "Testimony."
  Witt, S. "Native Women in the World of Work."

DISPLACED HOMEMAKERS--UNITED STATES

  Alexander, L. "Testimony."
  Bauer, M. "Testimony."
  Brothers, J. "Testimony."
  Candela, C. "Testimony."
  Conable, C. "Testimony."
  Davis, D. "Testimony."
  Deconcini, S. "Testimony."
  Dorman, L. "Testimony."
  Edmonds, J. "Testimony."
  Eidson, G. "Testimony."
  Fleming, J. "Testimony."
  Fossedal, R. "Testimony."
  Friedan, B. "Testimony."
  Gaines, R. "Testimony."
  Gascon, B. "Testimony."
  Hawkins, P. "Testimony."
  Herman, A. "Testimony."
  Joynes, M. "Testimony."
  Keller, M. "Testimony."
  Madison, A. "Testimony."
  Oakar, M. "Statement."
  Oberstar, J. "Testimony."
  Porcino, J. "Testimony."
  Reuss, M. "Testimony."
  Schlossberg, N. "Testimony."
  Smeal, E. "Testimony."
  Steiger, J. "Testimony."

DIVORCED WOMEN

  Ferraro, G. "Statement."
  Schroeder, P. "Statement." (3)

DOLE, ELIZABETH HANFORD

  Dole, E. "Statement." (2)
  Kassebaum, N. "Statement."

DOMESTIC RELATIONS--UNITED STATES

Aherns, D. "Statement."
Battistella, A. "Statement."
Benton, M. "Statement."
Berger, B. "Statement."
Bowman, H. "Statement."
Conniff, M. "Statement."
Friedan, B. "Statement."
Hardy, D. "Statement."
Johnson, G. "Statement."
Jones, T. "Statement."
Kramer, R. "Statement."
Lockwood, C. "Statement."
Mallett, C. "Statement."
McAdoo, H. "Statement."
McCoy, C. "Statement."
Morfino, G. "Statement."
Rich, D. "Statement."
Rivlin, A. "Statement."
Royle, D. "Statement."
Tovermale, T. "Statement."
Wallerstein, J. "Statement."

DRAFT REGISTRATION--UNITED STATES

Goldsmith, J. "Statement."
Schroeder, P. "Statement."

DRUG ABUSE

Hawkins, P. "Statement."

DRUG ADULTERATION

Collins, C. "Statement."

DRUGS

Holtzman, E. "Statement."

DUTY-FREE IMPORTATION--UNITED STATES

Ferraro, G. "Statement."
Kaptur, M. "Statement."

ECONOMIC ASSISTANCE, AMERICAN

Mikulski, B. "Statement." (2)
Oakar, M. "Statement."

EDUCATION

Chisholm, S. "Statement."
Futrell, M. "Education."
Reynolds, W. "Change."
Reynolds, W. "What Is Right with Our Public Schools."
Rogers, M. "The Swaying Scales of Balance."
Roosevelt, E. "Address at Conference on Educational Programs
    for Veterans."
Roosevelt, E. "Children of School Age."
Roosevelt, E. "The Human Factor in the Development of Inter-
    national Understanding."
Roosevelt, E. "The Role of the Educator."
Roosevelt, E. "Social Responsibility for Individual Welfare."
Siegel, B. "Knowledge with Commitment."
Taylor, A. "Talk, Future Shock and Futureshlock."
Uehling, B. "Academics and Athletics."
Watkins, B. "On the Problem of the Real World."
Wexler, J. "Continuity in Executive Staffing."

EDUCATION--SOUTHERN STATES--HISTORY

Bellows, B. "My Children, Gentlemen, Are My Own."
Berkeley, K. "Colored Ladies Also Contributed."
Blester, C. "The Perrys of Greenville."
Clinton, C. "Caught in the Web of the Big House."
Perdue, T. "Southern Indians and the Cult of True Womanhood."
Walsh, L. "The Experiences and Status of Women in the Chesa-
    peake, 1750-1775."

EDUCATION, HIGHER--UNITED STATES

Boggs, L. "Statement."
Chisholm, S. "Statement."
McBee, M. "The Values Development Dilemma."
Schneider, C. "Statement."

EDUCATION, HUMANISTIC

Howe, F. "Feminist Scholarship--The Extent of the Revolution."
Lerner, G. "The Challenges of Women's History."
Minnich, E. "A Feminist Critique of the Liberal Arts."

EDUCATIONAL EQUALIZATION

Bean, J. "The Development of Psychological Androgyny."
Bowman, B. "Sexism and Racism in Education."
Greenberg, S. "Preschool and the Politics of Sexism."
Guttentag, M. "The Social Psychology of Sex-Role Intervention."
Katz, L. "Teacher Education and Non-Sexist Early Childhood Education."
Pogrebin, L. "Non-Sexist Parenting at Home and at School."
Queen, R. "Towards Liberating Toys."
Rodriguez-Trias, H. "Problems and Priorities of Poor, Culturally Different Parents."
Serbin, L. "Teachers, Peers, and Play Preferences."

ELEANOR ROOSEVELT NATIONAL HISTORIC SITE (N.Y.)

Peterson, E. "Statement."

ELECTIONS--ROME

Taylor, L. "The Assemblies in Their Setting."
Taylor, L. "The Centuriate Assembly in the Light of New Discoveries."
Taylor, L. "Methods of Voting and Places of Assembly of Centuries and Tribes."
Taylor, L. "The Nature of the Assemblies."
Taylor, L. "Public Meetings in the Forum, on the Capitoline, and in the Circus Flaminius."
Taylor, L. "The Thirty-five Tribes and the Procedures in the Tribal Assemblies."

ELECTIONS--UNITED STATES

Aikens, J. "Working with the Federal Election Commission."
Schroeder, P. "Statement."

EMBASSY BUILDINGS--UNITED STATES--SECURITY MEASURES

Ferraro, G. "Statement."

EMIGRATION AND IMMIGRATION

Ferraro, G. "Statement."

ENERGY DEVELOPMENT

ENERGY INDUSTRIES

ENERGY POLICY

ENGLISH LANGUAGE--WRITING

ENGLISH LITERATURE--WOMEN AUTHORS

ENVIRONMENTAL PROTECTION--VERMONT

EQUAL PAY FOR EQUAL WORK--UNITED STATES

EQUAL PAY FOR EQUAL WORK--UNITED STATES (cont.)

EQUAL PAY FOR EQUAL WORK--UNITED STATES (cont.)
Taber, G. "Testimony."
Viviano, A. "Testimony."
Waelder, C. "Statement."
Wernick, E. "Statement."
Whitney, J. "Testimony."
Williams, M. "Testimony."
Witt, M. "Testimony."

EQUAL RIGHTS AMENDMENTS--UNITED STATES

Campanella, C. "Testimony."
Chayes, A. "Testimony."
Finn, J. "Testimony."
Freedman, A. "Testimony."
Ginsburg, R. "Realizing the Equality Principle."
Ginsburg, R. "Statement."
Greene, M. "Equality and Inviolability."
Height, D. "Testimony."
Hertz, J. "Testimony."
Humphrey, M. "Statement."
Jeffrey, M. "Testimony."
Johnson, S. "Testimony."
Levick, M. "Testimony."
Martin, J. "Testimony."
Shalala, D. "Testimony."
Sherburne, J. "Testimony."
Smeal, E. "Smeal Statement."
Tucker, M. "Testimony."
Wald, P. "Statement."
Wardle, L. "Testimony."
Wegner, J. "Testimony."
Willenz, J. "Testimony."
Zuckert, C. "Testimony."

ESTROGEN--THERAPEUTIC USE

Connell, E. "The Pill: Risks and Benefits."
Fasal, E. "Estrogen and Breast Cancer."
Jorgensen, V. "Adolescent Contraception."
Katzenellenbogen, B. "Cellular Actions of Estrogens and Oral
    Contraceptive Sex Steroid Hormones."

ETHYLENE OXIDE--UNITED STATES--SAFETY MEASURES

Snowe, O. "Statement."

ETIQUETTE

Martin, J. "Common Courtesy."

EXPORT CONTROLS

Byron, B. "Statement."

FAMILY--SOUTHERN STATES--HISTORY

Bellows, B. "My Children, Gentlemen, Are My Own."
Berkeley, K. "Colored Ladies Also Contributed."
Bleser, C. "The Perrys of Greenville."
Clinton, C. "Caught in the Web of the Big House."
Perdue, T. "Southern Indians and the Cult of True Womanhood."
Walsh, L. "The Experiences and Status of Women in the Chesa-
    peake, 1750-1775."

FAMILY--UNITED STATES

Battistella, A. "Statement."
Benton, M. "Statement."
Bernard, J. "Ground Rules for Marriage."
Bowman, H. "Statement."
Bridenthal, R. "The Family."
Brown, C. "Home Production for Use in a Market Economy."
Catt, C. "Address to the Seventh Congress of the International
    Woman Suffrage Alliance at Budapest, 15 June 1913."
Catt, C. "Mrs. Catt's International Address."
Conniff, M. "Statement."
Douvan, E. "Family Roles in a Twenty-Year Perspective."
Fleming, J. "Sex Differences in the Educational and Occupational
    Goals of Black College Students."
Gilligan, C. "Do Changes in Women's Rights Change Women's
    Moral Judgments?"
Gordon, L. "Why Nineteenth-Century Feminists Did Not Support
    'Birth Control' and Twentieth-Century Feminists Do."
Jones, T. "Statement."
Kramer, R. "Statement."
Lipman-Blumen, J. "Emerging Patterns of Female Leadership in
    Formal Organizations, or Must the Female Leader Go Formal?"
Lockwood, C. "Statement."
McCoy, C. "Statement."
Morfino, G. "Statement."
Praeger, S. "Shifting Perspectives on Marital Property Law."
Rivlin, A. "Statement."
Royle, D. "Statement."
Shaw, A. "Presidential Address at the 1905 Convention of the
    National American Woman Suffrage Association."

FAMILY--UNITED STATES (cont.)

Shaw, A. "Presidential Address at the 1906 Convention of the National American Woman Suffrage Association."

Stanton, E. "Fifteenth Amendment."

Thomas, M. "Present Tendencies in Women College and University Education."

Tovermale, T. "Statement."

FAMILY POLICY

Bergmann, B. "The Housewife and Social Security Reform."

Boggs, L. "Opening Statement."

Dennett, J. "Statement."

Elmer, E. "Statement."

Ferge, Z. "Explicit and Comprehensive Family Policy."

Fiedler, B. "Statement."

Fierst, E. "Discussion (of Supplemental OASI Benefits to Homemakers)."

Godley, A. "Statement."

Godley, A. "Statement."

Haynes, J. "Statement."

Holden, K. "Supplemental OASI Benefits to Homemakers Through Current Spouse Benefits."

Kuharski, M. "Statement."

Liljestrom, R. "Explicit and Comprehensive Family Policy."

McCord, R. "Statement."

Middletown-Jeter, V. "Statement."

Reno, V. "Discussion (of Earnings Sharing: Incremental and Fundamental Reform)."

Schaus, M. "Statement."

Smith, B. "Statement."

Smith, H. "Statement."

Stern, A. "Statement."

Vann, T. "Statement."

FAMILY SOCIAL WORK--UNITED STATES

Boggs, L. "Opening Statement."

Elmer, E. "Statement."

Haynes, J. "Statement."

Middletown-Jeter, V. "Statement."

Stern, A. "Statement."

FAMILY VIOLENCE--UNITED STATES

Aal, D. "Statement."

Crawford, S. "Statement."

Flynn, B. "Statement."

FAMILY VIOLENCE--UNITED STATES (cont.)
  Hansen, S. "Statement."
  Kelly-Dreiss, S. "Statement."
  Key, M. "Statement."
  Staples, E. "Statement."
  Whetsone, G. "Statement."

FEDERAL AID TO BIRTH CONTROL--UNITED STATES

  Babbott, J. "Statement."
  Brown, J. "Statement."
  Hammond, B. "Statement."
  Kasun, J. "Statement."
  Klaus, H. "Statement."
  Mann, D. "Statement."
  Marshner, C. "Statement."
  Maves, B. "Statement."
  Roylance, S. "Statement."
  Wattleton, F. "Statement."

FEDERAL AID TO CHILD WELFARE--UNITED STATES

  Kunin, M. "Statement."

FEDERAL AID TO EDUCATION--UNITED STATES

  Bellamy, C. "Statement."
  Boggs, L. "Statement."

FEDERAL AID TO THE ARTS--UNITED STATES

  Chisholm, S. "Statement."

FEDERAL AID TO TRANSPORTATION--NEW YORK (N.Y.)

  Bellamy, C. "Statement."

FEDERAL AID TO WOMEN-OWNED BUSINESS ENTERPRISES--UNITED
    STATES

  Andrulis, M. "Statement."
  Fitzpatrick, B. "Statement."
  Herre, S. "Statement."
  Hubbard, M. "Statement."
  Johnson, M. "Statement."

FEDERAL AID TO WOMEN-OWNED BUSINESS ENTERPRISES--UNITED
     STATES (cont.)
  Littlejohn, V. "Statement."
  Moss, T. "Statement."
  Shalala, D. "Statement."
  Snider, Y. "Statement."

FEDERAL-CITY RELATIONS--UNITED STATES

  Mikulski, B. "Statement."

FEDERAL RESERVE SYSTEM (U.S.)

  Hawkins, P. "Statement."

FEMALE OFFENDERS--UNITED STATES

  Chapman, J. "Testimony."
  Heffernan, E. "Testimony."
  Resnik, J. "Testimony."
  Schweber, C. "Testimony."
  Shaw, N. "Testimony."
  Taylor, P. "Testimony."

FEMINISM

  Anthony, S. "Guaranteed to Us and Our Daughters Forever."
  Allison, D. "Public Silence, Private Terror."
  Altman, M. "Everything They Always Wanted You to Know."
  Ampola, M. "Prenatal Diagnosis."
  Auerbach, N. "The Materfamilias."
  Axelsen, D. "Decisions About Handicapped Newborns."
  Bailey, P. "Thanks for the Gender Gap."
  Bankart, B. "From Our Work and Experience."
  Barazzone, E. "Women and the Scottish Enlightenment."
  Bell, S. "The DES Controversy."
  Bendix, H. "Rights of a Handicapped Neonate."
  Bernikow, L. "From Our Work and Experience."
  Bernstein, A. "Curriculum Reform, or What Do You Mean, 'Our
     College Should Have a Feminist Curriculum?'"
  Berrio, M. "Sex Differences in Choices of Toy and Modes of
     Play in Nursery School."
  Bonepath, E. "Evaluating Women's Studies."
  Briggs, S. "Images of Women and Jews in Nineteenth- and Twen-
     tieth-Century German Theology."
  Brown, K. "Why Women Need the War God."
  Buckley, M. "Women, Poverty, and Economic Justice."

FEMINISM (cont.)

FEMINISM (cont.)

Griffen, J. "A Cross-Cultural Investigation of Behavioral Changes at Menopause."

Griffin, G. "Still Crazy After All These Years."

Gubar, S. "Mother, Maiden, and the Marriage of Death."

Gutwirth, M. "The Education of Germaine de Stael, or Rousseau Betrayed."

Hackett, J. "In the Days of Jael."

Halley, J. "Harmonious Sisters, Voice and Verse."

Hamilton, M. "A History of Married Women's Rights."

Hammond, H. "Creating Feminist Works."

Hareven, T. "The Family and Gender Roles in Historical Perspective."

Harvey, B. "No More Nice Girls."

Herlands, R. "Biological Manipulations for Producing and Nurturing Mammalian Embryos."

Hilty, D. "From Our Work and Experience."

Hoagland, S. "On the Reeducation of Sophie."

Hoffman, L. "Childbearing and the Woman's Role."

Hollibaugh, A. "Desire for the Future."

Holtzman, J. "DES: Ten Points of Controversy."

Hooker, E. "History of a Weekend."

Hoskins, B. "Manipulative Reproductive Technologies."

Howe, F. "Breaking the Disciplines."

Hubbard, R. "The Case Against In Vitro Fertilization and Implantation."

Huber, J. "The Future of Parenthood."

Hunt, L. "Cygnets and Ducklings."

Hunt, M. "Political Oppression and Creative Survival."

Hunt, M. "A Political Perspective."

Johnson, R. "A Historical Addendum."

Kahn, D. "Interdisciplinary Studies and Women's Studies."

Kelly, J. "The Doubled Vision of Feminist Theory."

Kelly, J. "Early Feminist Theory and the Querelle Des Femmes."

Kenen, R. "A Look at Prenatal Diagnosis Within the Context of Changing Parental and Reproductive Norms."

Kessler, C. "Communities of Sisters."

King, N. "Making the World Live."

Kipp, R. "The Feminist Critique."

Kipp, R. "Have Women Always Been Unequal?"

Klay, R. "Analyzing Discrimination Against Women in the Labor Market."

Kreuger, R. "Loyalty and Betrayal."

Kruger, B. "No Progress in Pleasure."

Lane, A. "Keynote Address."

Lapham, E. V. "Living with an Impaired Neonate and Child."

Lee, V. "Lucille Clifton."

Locke, E. "Antenatal Diagnosis."

Logan, R. "Ectogenesis and Ideology."

Lorde, A. "Age, Race, Class, and Sex."

Lorde, A. "Learning from the 60s."

FEMINISM (cont.)

FEMINISM (cont.)

Webster, P. "The Forbidden."

Whelchel, M. "'Phantasia for Elvira Shatayev' as Revolutionary Feminist Poem."

Whitbeck, C. "The Neonate."

Whitbeck, C. "Response to Papers on Decisions About Handicapped Newborns."

Williams, D. "Women as Makers of Literature."

Williams, M. "The Structure of Knowledge."

Wilson, L. "My voice ... and Many Others."

Woods, B. "Historiogenic Art."

Young, M. "Women, Civilization, and the Indian Question."

Zavala, I. "Concluding Remarks."

FEMINISM--EUROPE

Bohachevsky-Chomiak, M. "Ukrainian Feminism in Interwar Poland."

Fischer, M. "Women in Romanian Politics."

Freeze, K. "Medical Education for Women in Austria."

Jancar, B. "Women in the Opposition in Poland and Czechoslovakia in the 1970s."

Kligman, G. "The Rites of Women."

Mabry, H. "The New Women's Movement and the Party and Trade Union Question."

Reed, M. "Peasant Women of Croatia in the Interwar Years."

Rosenberg, D. "The Emancipation of Women in Fact and Fiction."

Wolchik, S. "The Precommunist Legacy, Economic Development, Social Transformation, and Women's Roles in Eastern Europe."

Woodward, S. "The Rights of Women."

FEMINISM--HISTORY

Anthony, S. "Woman Wants Bread, Not the Ballot!"

Berry, M. "Deliberately Fraught with Difficulties."

Brown, O. "On Foreign Rule."

Ortiz, F. "Address to the First Feminist Congress in Mexico, 1916."

Stone, L. "Disappointment Is the Lot of Women."

Truth, S. "Ain't I a Woman?"

Truth, S. "Keeping the Thing Going While Things Are Stirring."

FEMINISM--MORAL AND ETHICAL ASPECTS

Harrison, B. "The Equal Rights Amendment."

Harrison, B. "The Power of Anger in the Work of Love."

Harrison, B. "Sexism and the Language of Christian Ethics."

FEMINISM--PHILOSOPHY

Allen, A. "Women and Their Privacy."
Donchin, A. "Concepts of Women in Psychoanalytic Theory."
Gould, C. "Private Rights and Public Virtues."
Harding, S. "Is Gender a Variable in Conceptions of Rationality?"
Hein, H. "Liberating Philosophy."
Holmes, H. "A Feminist Analysis of the Universal Declaration of Human Rights."
Jaggar, A. "Human Biology in Feminist Theory."
Kittay, E. "Pornography and the Erotics of Domination."
Nicholson, L. "Feminist Theory."
Perreault, G. "Contemporary Feminist Perspectives on Women and Higher Education."
Rothenberg, P. "The Political Nature of Relations Between the Sexes."
Ruether, R. "Sexism, Religion, and the Social and Spiritual Liberation of Women Today."
Smith, J. "Rights--Conflict, Pregnancy, and Abortion."
Steinbacher, R. "Sex Preselection."
Whitbeck, C. "A Different Reality."

FEMINISM--RELIGIOUS ASPECTS

Christ, C. "Why Women Need the Goddess."
Gearhart, S. "Womanpower."
Gimbutas, M. "Women and Culture in Goddess-Orientated Old Europe."
Heyward, C. "Being 'in Christ?'"
Heyward, C. "Compassion."
Heyward, C. "The Covenant."
Heyward, C. "The Enigmatic God."
Heyward, C. "Gay Pride Day."
Heyward, C. "God or Mammon?"
Heyward, C. "Judgment."
Heyward, C. "Liberating the Body."
Heyward, C. "Limits of Liberalism."
Heyward, C. "Living in the Struggle."
Heyward, C. "Must 'Jesus Christ' Be a Holy Terror?"
Heyward, C. "On Behalf of Women Priests."
Heyward, C. "On El Salvador."
Heyward, C. "Passion."
Heyward, C. "Redefining Power."
Heyward, C. "Sexual Fidelity."
Riddle, D. "Politics, Spirituality, and Models of Change."
Starrett, B. "The Metaphors of Power."

FEMINISM--SOUTHERN STATES

Anglin, M. "Redefining the Family and Women's Status Within the Family."
Flanders, J. "The Fallen Woman in Fiction."
Harper, A. "Human Sexuality."
Herman, D. "Does Equality Mean Sameness?"
Howett, C. "Careers in Landscape Architecture."
Langer, S. "Against the Grain."
Locke, M. "Sexism and Racism."
Muhlenfeld, E. "Of Paradigm and Paradox."
Ochshorn, J. "The Contest Between Androgyny and Patriarchy in Early Western Tradition."
Stimpson, C. "Women as Knowers."
Tedesco, M. "A Feminist Challenge to Darwinism."
Windram, I. "Sex Differences in the Brain."

FEMINISM--UNITED STATES

Benjamin, J. "The Bonds of Love."
Boyd-Franklin, N. "Black Family Life-Styles."
Breen, E. "Toward Freedom and Self-Determination."
Bridenthal, R. "The Family."
Bridenthal, R. "Notes Toward a Feminist Dialectic."
Brooks, E. "The Feminist Theology of the Black Baptist Church."
Brown, C. "Home Production for Use in a Market Economy."
Brown, O. "Address on Woman Suffrage."
Brown, O. "Christian Charity."
Brown, O. "Crime and the Remedy."
Brown, O. "Hand of Fellowship."
Brown, O. "On Margaret Fuller."
Brown, O. "The Opening Door."
Brown, O. "United States Citizenship."
Brown, O. "Where Is the Mistake?"
Brown, O. "Woman's Place in the Church."
Brown, O. "Woman's Suffrage."
Brown, O. "Women and Skepticism."
Brown, R. "Violence."
Bunch, C. "Not For Lesbians Only."
Burke, C. "Rethinking the Maternal."
Burke, Y. "Economic Strength Is What Counts."
Burnett, M. "Knots in the Family Tie."
Burstein, K. "Notes from a Political Career."
Carpenter, L. "God, But We're Getting Smart."
Chodorow, N. "Gender, Relation, and Difference in Psychoanalytic Perspective."
Clusen, R. "The League of Women Voters and Political Power."
Conway, M. "Women and Voluntary Political Activists."
Costain, A. "Lobbying for Equal Credit."
Daniels, A. "W.E.A.L."

FEMINISM--UNITED STATES (cont.)

Datan, N. "The Lost Cause."

Diamond, I. "Exploring the Relationships Between Female Candidacies and the Women's Movement."

Dill, B. "On the Hem of Life."

Dixon, M. "Chicanas and Mexicanas in a Transnational Working Class."

Duggan, L. "The Social Enforcement of Heterosexuality and Lesbian Resistance in the 1920s."

Dunlap, M. "Resistance to the Women's Movement in the United States."

Eastman, C. "Feminism."

Eastman, C. "Political Equality League."

Eastman, C. "The Three Essentials for Accident Prevention."

Eisenstein, Z. "Antifeminism and the New Right."

Farley, P. "Lesbianism and Social Function of Taboo."

Feit, R. "Organizing for Political Power."

Feral, J. "The Powers of Difference."

Fiedler, M. "The Congressional Ambitions of Female Political Elites."

Flax, J. "Mother-Daughter Relationships."

Gallop, J. "Psychoanalysis in France."

Gilkes, C. "From Slavery to Social Welfare."

Gilligan, C. "In a Different Voice."

Ginsberg, E. "Playwrights, Poets, and Novelists."

Ginsburg, R. "Women's Right to Full Participation in Shaping Society's Course."

Gordon, L. "Why Nineteenth-Century Feminists Did Not Support 'Birth Control' and Twentieth-Century Feminists Do."

Grossmann, A. "Crisis, Reaction, and Resistance."

Hartsock, N. "Feminism, Power, and Change."

Heilburn, C. "Androgyny and the Psychology of Sex Differences."

Higginbotham, E. "Laid Bare by the System."

Howe, F. "American Literature and Women's Lives."

Howe, F. "Breaking the Disciplines."

Howe, F. "Feminism and the Education of Women."

Howe, F. "Feminism and the Study of Literature."

Howe, F. "Feminism, Fiction, and the Classroom."

Howe, F. "Feminist Scholarship."

Howe, F. "The Future of Women's Colleges."

Howe, F. "Literacy and Literature."

Howe, F. "Myths of Coeducation."

Howe, F. "The Past Ten Years."

Howe, F. "The Power of Education."

Howe, F. "Sex-Role Stereotypes Start Early."

Howe, F. "Teaching the Modern Languages."

Howe, F. "Why Educate Women?"

Howe, F. "Women's Studies and Social Change."

Jacker, C. "Better Than a Shriveled Huck."

Janeway, E. "Women and the Uses of Power."

FEMINISM--UNITED STATES (cont.)

Jorge, A. "Issues of Race and Class in Women's Studies."
Lambert, J. "Becoming Human."
Lee, M. "Legitimate Theatre Is Illegitimate."
Liebschutz, S. "Republican Women and the Future of the Republican Party."
Lindsey, K. "Women & the Draft."
Lipman-Blumen, J. "A Crisis Perspective on Emerging Health Roles."
Lorde, A. "Poetry Is Not a Luxury."
Makward, C. "To Be or Not to Be ... A Feminist Speaker."
Mallan, L. "Women's Incomes as Workers and Dependents."
Malpede, K. "A Talk for the Conference on Feminism & Militarism."
McConnell-Ginet, S. "Difference and Language."
Messinger, R. "Women in Power and Politics."
Minnich, E. "Friends and Critics."
Omolade, B. "Black Women and Feminism."
Palmer, P. "White Women/Black Women."
Petchesky, R. "Reproduction and Class Divisions Among Women."
Phillips, R. "Women in Medicine."
Praeger, S. "Shifting Perspectives on Marital Property Law."
Quaglio, F. "Religion as an Instrument of Social Control."
Reid, I. "How Powerful Is Powerful?"
Robertson, A. "Continuing Education."
Robinson, L. "Women, Media, and the Dialectics of Resistance."
Rosenberg, J. "Feminism, the Family, and the New Right."
Saiving, V. "Androgynous Life."
Schor, N. "For a Restricted Thematics."
Schweber, C. "But Some Were Less Equal ... The Fight for Women Jurors."
Shanley, M. "Individualism, Marriage, and the Liberal State."
Smith, B. "Racism and Women's Studies."
Stadler, Q. "Visibility and Differences."
Stanton, D. "Language and Revolution."
Stitzel, J. "Challenging Curricular Assumptions."
Suchocki, M. "Openness and Mutuality in Process Thought and Feminist Action."
Taub, N. "Defining and Combating Sexual Harassment."
Valentine, B. "Women on Welfare."
Vellacott, J. "Women, Peace and Power."
Verheyden-Hilliard, M. "Education, Girls, and Power."
Walkowitz, J. "Male Vice and Female Virtue."
Warnock, D. "Patriarchy Is a Killer."
Washbourn, P. "The Dynamics of Female Experience."
Willis, E. "The Challenge of Profamily Politics."

FEMINISM--UNITED STATES--HISTORY

Anthony, S. "Constitutional Argument."

FEMINISM--UNITED STATES--HISTORY (cont.)

Anthony, S. "Homes of Single Women."

Anthony, S. "Response to the NAWSA Resolution Disavowing The Woman's Bible."

Anthony, S. "Suffrage and the Working Woman."

Catt, C. "Address to the Seventh Congress of the International Woman Suffrage Alliance at Budapest, 15 June 1913."

De Cleyre, V. "The Economic Tendency of Freethought."

Harman, L. "Some Problems of Social Freedom."

Howe, J. "Julia Ward Howe Addresses the Massachusetts Legislature."

Jacoby, R. "The Women's Trade Union League and American Feminism."

Kelly, G. "State Aid to Science."

Morgan, R. "International Feminism."

Morgan, R. "Lesbianism and Feminism."

Morgan, R. "The Proper Study of Womankind."

Shaw, A. "Presidential Address at the 1905 Convention of the National American Woman Suffrage Association."

Shaw, A. "Presidential Address at the 1906 Convention of the National American Woman Suffrage Association."

Stanton, E. "Address Delivered at Seneca Falls."

Stanton, E. "Address of Welcome to the International Council of Women."

Stanton, E. "Address to the Founding Convention of the National American Woman Suffrage Association."

Stanton, E. "Address to the Legislature of New York on Women's Rights."

Stanton, E. "Appeal for the Maine Law."

Stanton, E. "Fifteenth Amendment."

Stanton, E. "Home Life."

Stanton, E. "The Solitude of Self."

Stanton, E. "Speech at Lawrence, Kansas."

Stanton, E. "Speech to the Anniversary of the American Anti-Slavery Society."

Stanton, E. "Speech to the McFarland-Richardson Protest Meeting."

Thomas, M. "Present Tendencies in Women College and University Education."

FEMINISM AND ART

Alpers, S. "Art History and Its Exclusions."

Broude, N. "Degas's 'Misogyny.'"

Broude, N. "Miriam Schapiro and 'Femmage.'"

Comini, A. "Gender or Genius?"

Duncan, C. "Happy Mothers and Other New Ideas in Eighteenth Century French Art."

Duncan, C. "Virility and Domination in Early Twentieth-Century Vanguard Painting."

FEMINISM AND ART (cont.)
    Garrard, M. "Artesimsia and Susanna."
    Havelock, C. "Mourners on Greek Vases."
    Hofrichter, F. "Judith Leyster's Proposition."
    Kahr, M. "Delilah."
    Kampden, N. "Social Status and Gender in Roman Art."
    Luomala, N. "Matrilineal Reinterpretation of Some Egyptian
       Sacred Cows."
    Mainardi, P. "Quilts."
    Nochlin, L. "Lost and Found."
    Sherman, C. "Taking a Second Look."

FEMINISM AND MOTION PICTURES

    Mayne, J. "The Woman at the Keyhole."

FEMINISM AND THE ARTS

    Chinoy, H. "Suppressed Desires."
    Cook, B. "Women and Politics."
    Douglas, A. "Willa Cather."
    Hahn, E. "Salonists and Chronicles."
    Heilbrun, C. "Louisa May Alcott."
    Hollander, A. "Women and Fashion."
    Howard, M. "City of Words."
    Kendall, E. "Women and Dance."
    Pais, S. "Shapes of the Femine Experience in Art."
    Secor, C. "Gertrude Stein."
    Wall, C. "Poets and Versifiers, Singers and Signifiers."

FEMINIST THEATRE

    Flanagan, H. "Opening Address, Federal Theatre Production
       Conference, Poughkeepsie, July 1936."
    Stein, G. "From 'Plays' (Lectures in America)."

FEMINIST THERAPY

    Berman, J. "Ethical Feminist Perspectives of Dual Relationships
       with Clients."
    Brown, L. "Ethics and Business Practice in Feminist Therapy."
    Burch, B. "Another Perspective on Merger in Lesbian Relation-
       ships."
    Burtle, V. "Therapeutic Anger in Women."
    Butler, M. "Guidelines for Feminist Therapy."
    Clamar, A. "Stepmothering."
    Dehardt, D. "Can a Feminist Therapist Facilitate Clients'
       Heterosexual Relationships?"

Douglas, M. "The Role of Power in Feminist Therapy."
Faunce, P. "Teaching Feminist Therapies."
Fodor, I. "Assertiveness Training for the Eighties."
Hendricks, M. "Feminist Spirituality in Jewish and Christian Traditions."
Hendricks, M. "Feminist Therapy with Women and Couples Who Are Infertile."
Jeanette, D. "Feminism, the Future of?"
Lasky, E. "Psychotherapists' Ambivalence About Fees."
Lerman, H. "Some Barriers to the Development of a Feminist Theory of Personality."
Moss, L. "Feminist Body Psychotherapy."
Porter, N. "New Perspectives on Therapy Supervision."
Rave, E. "Pornography."
Resh, M. "Feminist Therapy with the Woman Over 50."
Robbins, J. "The Appointment Hassle."
Rosewater, L. "Feminist Interpretation of Traditional Testing."
Rosewater, L. "Schizophrenic, Borderline, or Battered?"
Seidler-Feller, D. "A Feminist Critique of Sex Therapy."
Siegel, R. "Beyond Homophobia."
Stere, L. "Feminist Assertiveness Training."
Walker, L. "Feminist Forensic Psychology."
Walker, L. "Feminist Therapy with Victim/Survivors of Interpersonal Violence."
Weiss, L. "Getting to 'No' and Beyond."

FEMINISTS--UNITED STATES

Anthony, S. "Constitutional Argument."
Anthony, S. "Homes of Single Women."
Anthony, S. "Response to the NAWSA Resolution Disavowing The Woman's Bible."
Anthony, S. "Suffrage and the Working Woman."
Stanton, E. "Address Delivered at Seneca Falls."
Stanton, E. "Address of Welcome to the International Council of Women."
Stanton, E. "Address to the Founding Convention of the National American Woman Suffrage Association."
Stanton, E. "Address to the Legislature of New York on Women's Rights."
Stanton, E. "Appeal for the Maine Law."
Stanton, E. "Home Life."
Stanton, E. "The Solitude of Self."
Stanton, E. "Speech at Lawrence, Kansas."
Stanton, E. "Speech to the Anniversary of the American Anti-Slavery Society."
Stanton, E. "Speech to the McFarland-Richardson Protest Meeting."

FEMININITY (PSYCHOLOGY)

   Mitchell, J.   "Femininity, Narrative and Psychoanalysis."
   Mitchell, J.   "Feminism and Femininity at the Turn of the Century."
   Mitchell, J.   "Feminism as a Political Movement."
   Mitchell, J.   "Psychoanalysis."
   Mitchell, J.   "The Question of Femininity and the Theory of Psychoanalysis."
   Mitchell, J.   "Romantic Love."
   Mitchell, J.   "What Is Feminism?"
   Mitchell, J.   "Women and Equality."

FENWICK, MILLICENT

   Fenwick, M.   "Statement."

FETAL ALCOHOL SYNDROME--UNITED STATES

   Luke, B.   "Statement."
   Randall, C.   "Testimony."

FINANCE, PUBLIC

   Spellman, G.   "Statement."

FIRE PREVENTION--UNITED STATES

   Collins, C.   "Statement."

FLOOD CONTROL

   Boggs, L.   "Statement."
   Fenwick, M.   "Statement."
   Oakar, M.   "Statement."
   Schroeder, P.   "Statement."

FOOD ADULTERATION

   Collins, C.   "Statement."

FOOD LAWS AND LEGISLATION--UNITED STATES

   Kunin, M.   "Statement."

FOOD RELIEF

    Kaptur, M. "Statement."
    Oakar, M. "Statement."

FOREIGN TRADE REGULATION

    Fiedler, B. "Statement."
    Kaptur, M. "Statement."
    Schroeder, P. "Statement."
    Smith, V. "Statement."
    Smith, V. "Statement."
    Snowe, O. "Statement."

FORENSIC GYNECOLOGY

    Bissette, B. "The North Carolina Rape Kit Program."
    Dorrill, M. "The Identification and Distribution of ABH and
        Lewis Substances in Seminal and Vaginal Secretions."
    Hulen, P. "Simultaneous Electrophoresis of Phosphogluecomutase
        (PGM) and Peptidase A (PepA)."

FOREST RESERVES

    Burton, S. "Statement."
    Fiedler, B. "Statement."

FOUR-DAY WEEK

    Ferraro, G. "Statement."
    Oakar, M. "Statement."
    Schroeder, P. "Statement." (2)

FREEDOM (THEOLOGY)--HISTORY OF DOCTRINES

    Douglass, J. "The Foundation and Significance of Christian
        Freedom."
    Douglass, J. "Freedom in God's Order."
    Douglass, J. "Freedom in Obedience."
    Douglass, J. "Women's Freedom in Church Order: Calvin in
        the Medieval and Renaissance Context."
    Douglass, J. "Women's Freedom in Church Order: Calvin in
        the Reformation Context."
    Douglass, J. "Women's Freedom in Church Order: Calvin's
        View."

FREEDOM OF SPEECH

Schroeder, P. "Statement."

GAS INDUSTRY

Byron, B. "Statement."
Kassebaun, N. "Statement."
Martin, L. "Statement."
Oakar, M. "Statement."

GOVERNMENT SALE OF REAL PROPERTY--UNITED STATES

Lloyd, M. "Statement."
Mikulski, B. "Statement."
Schneider, C. "Statement."

GOVERNMENT SECURITIES

Hawkins, P. "Statement."

GRAIN TRADE

Fenwick, M. "Statement."
Smith, V. "Statement."

HANDICAPPED CHILDREN--CARE AND TREATMENT--UNITED
STATES

Bertina, B. "Statement."
Latzko, T. "Statement."
Poyadue, F. "Statement."
Short, M. "Statement."
Turnbull, A. "Statement."
Vincent, L. "Statement."
Ziegler, M. "Statement."

HARBORS--UNITED STATES

Boggs, L. "Statement."
Mikulski, B. "Statement."

HAZARDOUS SUBSTANCES--TRANSPORTATION

Ferraro, G. "Statement."

HAZARDOUS WASTE SITES

Johnson, N. "Statement."
Lloyd, M. "Statement."

HECKLER, MARGARET M.

Heckler, M. "Statement." (2)

HISPANIC WOMEN

Correa, G. "Puerto Rican Women in Education and Potential Impact on Occupational Patterns."
Garcia, F. "The Cult of Virginity."
Gonzales, S. "Chicana Evolution."
Gonzales, S. "La Chicana."
Ivera, S. "The Need for an Anthropological and Cognitive Approach to the Education of Hispanic Women."
Jimenez-Vazquez, R. "Social Issues Confronting Hispanic-American Women."
Mulcahy, E. "Latinas in Educational Leadership."
Nieto, C. "Chicana Identity."
Shepro, T. "Impediments to Hispanic Women Organizing."

HOME LABOR

Behr, M. "Statement."
Clement, M. "Statement."
Kassenbaum, N. "Statement."
Kern, C. "Statement."
Pudvah, A. "Statement."

HOMELESSNESS

Bellamy, C. "Statement."

HOMOSEXUALITY--RELIGIOUS ASPECTS--CHRISTIANITY

Heyward, C. "Being 'in Christ.'"
Heyward, C. "Compassion."
Heyward, C. "The Covenant."
Heyward, C. "The Enigmatic God."
Heyward, C. "Gay Pride Day."
Heyward, C. "God or Mammon?"
Heyward, C. "Judgment."
Heyward, C. "Liberating the Body."

Heyward, C. "Limits of Liberalism."
Heyward, C. "Living in the Struggle."
Heyward, C. "Must 'Jesus Christ' Be a Holy Terror?"
Heyward, C. "On Behalf of Women Priests."
Heyward, C. "On El Salvador."
Heyward, C. "Passion."
Heyward, C. "Redefining Power."
Heyward, C. "Sexual Fidelity."

HORMONES, SEX--PHYSIOLOGICAL EFFECT

Connell, E. "The Pill."
Fasal, E. "Estrogen and Breast Cancer."
Jorgensen, V. "Adolescent Contraception."
Katzenellenbogen, B. "Cellular Actions of Estrogens and Oral Contraceptive Sex Steroid Hormones."

HOSPITALS

Boggs, L. "Statement." (2)
Hawkins, P. "Statement."
Holt, M. "Statement." (2)
Kraus, I. "Light and Help and Human Kindness."
Schroeder, P. "Statement."
Smith, V. "Statement."

HOUSING SUBSIDIES

Oakar, M. "Statement."

HUMANITIES--STUDY AND TEACHING

Craft, C. "Promoting the Humanities."
Minnich, E. "The Meaning of 'Human' in the Humanities."
Phillips, E. "The Prickly Art of Housekeeping."
Sacks, K. "Worlds in Collision or Ships Passing in the Night?"

INCOME TAX

Fenwick, M. "Statement."
Hawkins, P. "Statement." (3)
Martinez, V. "Proposed Sanctions Against Employers of Illegal Aliens."
Mikulski, B. "Statement." (2)
Smith, V. "Statement."

INDIANS OF NORTH AMERICA

INDUSTRY AND STATE

INFANTS--UNITED STATES--MORTALITY

INFLATION (FINANCE)

INLAND WATER TRANSPORTATION--UNITED STATES

INSURANCE, FLOOD--UNITED STATES

INSURANCE, GOVERNMENT EMPLOYEES' HEALTH

INSURANCE, UNEMPLOYMENT

> Chisholm, S. "Statement."
> Kaptur, M. "Statement."
> Oakar, M. "Statement."
> Schroeder, P. "Statement." (2)

INTEREST RATES

> Roukema, M. "Statement."

INTERGOVERNMENTAL FISCAL RELATIONS

> Lloyd, M. "Statement."

INTERNATIONAL BUSINESS ENTERPRISE--TAXATION

> Hawkins, P. "Statement."

INTERNATIONAL WOMEN'S YEAR, 1975

> Abzug, B. "Speech by Bella Abzug, Presiding Officer."
> Cahn, A. "The Economic Consequence of the Arms Race."
> Caldicott, H. "Nuclear War."
> Carpender, L. "Commissioner Liz Carpenter."
> Carter, J. "Speech by Judy Carter."
> Carter, R. "Speech by First Lady Rosalynn Carter."
> Costanza, M. "Speech by Honorable Margaret 'Midge' Costanza, Assistant to the President."
> Ford, B. "Speech by Betty Ford, National Commissioner and Former First Lady."
> Hecker, M. "Speech by Congresswoman Margaret M. Heckler."
> Johnson, L. "Introduction of Congresswoman Barbara Jordan by Lady Bird Johnson, Former First Lady."
> Jordan, B. "Keynote Speech by Congresswoman Barbara Jordan."
> Lall, B. "What Disarmament Policy for the United States?"
> Masters, B. "Speech by Billie Masters, Chair, National American Indian and Alaskan Native Women's Conference."
> Mead, M. "Speech by Honorable Margaret Mead."
> Mink, P. "Speech by Honorable Patsy Mink, Assistant Secretary of State (Former Congresswoman and Co-Sponsor PL94-167)."
> Parker, B. "Speech by Brenda Parker, President, Future Homemakers of America."
> Ruckelshaus, J. "Speech by Jill Ruckelshaus, Former Presiding Officer, National Commission."
> Scott, G. "Speech by Commissioner Gloria Scott."

INTERNATIONAL WOMEN'S YEAR, 1975 (cont.)
    Weddington, S. "World Conference on the U.N. Decade for Women Held in Copenhagen."
    Wyatt, A. "Speech by Commissioner Addie Wyatt."

INVESTMENTS, FOREIGN

    Schroeder, P. "Statement."

IONIZING RADIATION--PHYSIOLOGICAL EFFECT

    Lloyd, M. "Statement."

JAPANESE AMERICANS--CIVIL RIGHTS

    Burton, S. "Statement."

JUDGES--UNITED STATES

    Hawkins, P. "Statement." (2)
    Lloyd, M. "Statement." (2)
    O'Connor, S. "Statement."
    Smeal, E. "Statement."

JUVENILE DELINQUENCY

    Chisholm, S. "Statement."

JUVENILE JUSTICE, ADMINISTRATION--UNITED STATES

    Chisholm, S. "Statement."
    Fenwick, M. "Statement."

LABOR AND LABORING CLASSES--UNITED STATES

    Chisholm, S. "Statement."

LABOR PRODUCTIVITY

    Cunningham, M. "Productivity and the Corporate Culture."
    Whitman, M. "Black Hats, Economists and Societal Risk Assessment."

LANGUAGE POLICY--UNITED STATES

Fenwick, M. "Statement."

LATIN AMERICA

Long, C. "Latin America."

LATIN AMERICAN FICTION--WOMEN AUTHORS

Francescato, M. "Women in Latin America."
McCracken, E. "Manual Puig's Heartbreak Tango."
Patai, D. "Jorge Amado's Heroines and the Ideological Double
    Standard."

LAW ENFORCEMENT--UNITED STATES

Carter, M. "Myths and Realities."
Devlin, S. "Myths and Realities."
Drissell, K. "Career Conflicts and Solutions."
Hambrick, M. "The Realities of Women Correctional Officers in
    Male Correctional Institutions."
Kocher, J. "Career Conflicts and Solutions."
Lee, K. "Myths and Realities."
McChesney, K. "Myths and Realities."
McKenna, M. "The View from the White House."
Owens, M. "Career Conflicts and Solutions."
Pendergrass, V. "Stress in the Lives of Female Law Enforce-
    ment Officers."
Rawlings, E. "Myths and Realities."
Scrivner, E. "Acculturating Women into Law Enforcement Ca-
    reers."
Stillman, F. "Balancing Work, Family and Personal Lives."
Tischler, B. "Myths and Realities."

LAWYERS--UNITED STATES

Kennedy, F. "If You Want To Know Where the Apathy Is, You're
    Probably Sitting On It."
Kennedy, F. "Most People Are Not Taught to Understand That
    the Two O'Clock Orgasm Leads to the Three O'Clock Feeding."
Kennedy, F. "The Question Arises ... Whether All Lawyers
    Are the Same."
Kennedy, F. "Show the Power Structure That You're Prepared
    to Kick Your Mother and Father, and They'll Find You
    Relevant...."
Kennedy, F. "Silence Is Collaboration, and Rape Without Struggle
    Is No Rape, It's Just a Bad Screw."

LEADERSHIP

Burke, N. "Power and Power Plays."
Ferraro, G. "Women in Leadership Can Make a Difference."
Harris, P. "The Role of the American Intellectual Community in Redefining Our National Purpose."
Moe, A. "The Future Is Now For Business and Industry."
Taylor, A. "Women as Leaders."

LESBIANISM--UNITED STATES

Brown, R. "Violence."
Lorde, A. "Age, Race, Class, and Sex."
Lorde, A. "Learning from the 60s."
Lorde, A. "The Master's Tools Will Never Dismantle the Master's House."
Lorde, A. "The Transformation of Silence Into Language and Action."
Lorde, A. "The Use of Anger."
Lorde, A. "Uses of the Erotic."

LIABILITY FOR HAZARDOUS SUBSTANCES POLLUTION DAMAGES-- UNITED STATES

Johnson, N. "Statement."

LIABILITY FOR OIL POLLUTION DAMAGES--UNITED STATES

Dole, E. "Statement."

LIBERATION THEOLOGY

Heyward, C. "Being 'in Christ?'"
Heyward, C. "Compassion."
Heyward, C. "The Covenant."
Heyward, C. "The Enigmatic God."
Heyward, C. "Gay Pride Day."
Heyward, C. "God or Mammon?"
Heyward, C. "Judgement."
Heyward, C. "Liberating the Body."
Heyward, C. "Limits of Liberalism."
Heyward, C. "Living in the Struggle."
Heyward, C. "Must 'Jesus Christ' Be a Holy Terror?"
Heyward, C. "On Behalf of Women Priest."
Heyward, C. "On El Salvador."
Heyward, C. "Passion."
Heyward, C. "Redefining Power."
Heyward, C. "Sexual Fidelity."

LIBERTY OF THE PRESS

> Copley, H. "General Spirit of the People."
> Dyer, C. "The Costs of Freedom of the Press."

LITERATURE

> Ellis, K. "Paradise Lost."
> Hamilton, E. "Address to the Athenians."
> Hamilton, E. "Plato."
> Marshall, P. "Emerging Ones."
> Welty, E. "Finding a Voice."
> Welty, E. "Learning to See."
> Welty, E. "Listening."

LONG-TERM CARE OF THE SICK

> Boggs, L. "Statement."

LOTTERIES

> Holt, M. "Statement."

MACHINE-TOOL INDUSTRY

> Martin, L. "Statement."

MARINE TERMINALS

> Boggs, L. "Statement."

MARITIME LAW--UNITED STATES

> Boggs, L. "Statement." (3)
> Dole, E. "Statement."
> Schneider, C. "Statement."

MARRIED WOMEN--UNITED STATES

> Lloyd-Jones, E. "Education for Reentry into the Labor Force."
> Maccoby, E. "Effects Upon Children of Their Mothers' Outside Employment."
> Oettinger, K. "Maternal Employment and Children."

MASS MEDIA AND YOUTH--UNITED STATES

    Heckler, M. "Statement."
    Newman, S. "Statement."

MEAT INSPECTION

    Smith, V. "Statement." (2)

MEDICAL CARE, COST OF--UNITED STATES

    Heckler, M. "Statement."
    Kennelly, B. "Statement."
    Mikulski, B. "Statement." (2)

MEDICAL POLICY

    Ricardo-Campbell, R. "Major Issues in National Health Policy."

MEDICINE--RESEARCH GRANTS--UNITED STATES

    Boxer, B. "Statement."

MENSTRUATION DISORDERS

    Prior, J. "Hormonal Mechanism of Reproductive Function and
        Hypothalmic Adaptation to Endurance Training."
    Sanborn, C. "Etiology of Athletic Amenorrhea."

MENTAL HEALTH

    Carter, R. "As the Delegate from Georgia, Said...."
    Carter, R. "Statement."
    Carter, R. "Toward a More Caring Society."

MENTALLY HANDICAPPED--SERVICES FOR--UNITED STATES

    Heckler, M. "Statement."

MERCHANT SEAMEN--MEDICAL CARE--UNITED STATES

    Boggs, L. "Statement."

MIDWIVES--UNITED STATES

Lubic, R. "Testimony."
McCartney, M. "Testimony."
Mikulski, B. "Testimony."
Morris, L. "Testimony."
Norsigian, J. "Testimony."
Rooks, J. "Testimony."
Sizemore, S. "Testimony."
Tom, S. "Testimony."

MILITARY ASSISTANCE, AMERICAN

Mikulski, B. "Statement."
Mikulski, B. "Statement."
Oakar, M. "Statement."

MILITARY ORDER OF THE PURPLE HEART

Schneider, C. "Statement."

MILITARY SERVICE, COMPULSORY--UNITED STATES--DRAFT
    RESISTERS

Abzug, B. "Statement."
Goldsmith, J. "Statement."

MISSING CHILDREN

Hawkins, P. "Statement." (4)

MONETARY POLICY--UNITED STATES

McBee, M. "The Values Development Dilemma."

MURDER--UNITED STATES

Hawkins, P. "Statement."

NARCOTICS

Boggs, L. "Statement."
Falco, M. "Narcotics."
Hawkins, P. "Statement." (2)

NUCLEAR ARMS CONTROL--UNITED STATES

Boxer, B. "Statement."

NURSING

Aroskar, M. "Toward 1999."
Cleland, V. "Prospectives for Nursing."
Novello, D. "Prospectives for Nursing."

OBSTETRICS

Ampola, M. "Prenatal Diagnosis."
Axelsen, D. "Decisions About Handicapped Newborns."
Barnes, H. "Response (to the Depo-Provera Weapon)."
Berkman, J. "Historical Styles of Contraceptive Advocacy."
Bendix, H. "Rights of a Handicapped Neonate."
Brackbill, Y. "Drugs, Birth, and Ethics."
Carlton, W. "Perfectability and the Neonate."
Connors, D. "Response (to Unnatural Selection: on Choosing Children's Sex)."
Cook, K. "A Native American Response."
Corea, G. "The Depo-Provera Weapon."
Cowan, B. "Ethical Problems in Government-Funded Contraceptive Research."
Cuellar, R. "Response (to Woman-Controlled Birth Control)."
Culpepper, E. "Reflections."
Culpepper, E. "Sex Preselection."
Davis, A. "Diethylstilbestrol."
Edwards, M. "Neonatology."
Ekstrom, S. "A Report on Birth in Three Cultures."
Erhart, R. "DES and Drugs in Pregnancy."
Gaskin, I. "Community Alternatives to High Technology Birth."
Gray, M. "An Obstetrician's Perspective."
Herlands, R. "Biological Manipulations for Producing and Nurturing Mammalian Embryos."
Holtzman, J. "DES."
Hoskins, B. "Manipulative Reproductive Technologies."
Hubbard, R. "The Case Against In Vitro Fertilization and Implantation."
Kenen, R. "A Look at Prenatal Diagnosis Within the Context of Changing Parental and Reproductive Norms."
Korenbrot, C. "Value Conflicts in Biomedical Research into Future Contraceptives."
Lapham, E. "Living With an Impaired Neonate and Child."
Lashof, J. "Forces Impacting on the Policymaker."
Lebacqz, K. "The Ethicist in Policymaking."
Levine, C. "Depo-Provera."
Locke, E. "Antenatal Diagnosis."

OCCUPATIONAL TRAINING FOR WOMEN (cont.)

    Gascon, B. "Testimony."
    Hawkins, P. "Testimony."
    Johnson, N. "Statement."
    Joynes, M. "Testimony."
    Keller, M. "Testimony."
    Madison, A. "Testimony."

OIL AND GAS LEASES

    Boggs, L. "Statement."
    Boxer, B. "Statement." (2)
    Hawkins, P. "Statement."

OLD AGE ASSISTANCE

    Bader, J. "Statement."
    Fadeley, N. "Statement."
    Gleason, J. "Statement."
    Harris, E. "Statement."
    Laurence, I. "Statement."
    Lenhoff, N. "Statement."
    Linn, M. "Statement."
    Lifquist, E. "Statement."
    Meyer, E. "Statement."
    Moore, L. "Statement."
    Reisinger, M. "Statement."
    Russell-Young, N. "Statement."
    Snowe, O. "Statement."
    Tenant, L. "Statement."
    Thacker, P. "Statement."
    Turner, P. "Statement."

ORAL CONTRACEPTIVES

    Connell, E. "The Pill."
    Fasal, E. "Estrogen and Breast Cancer."
    Jorgensen, V. "Adolescent Contraception."
    Katzenellenbogen, B. "Cellular Actions of Estrogens and Oral
       Contraceptive Sex Steroid Hormones."

PEACE

    Balch, E. "Human Nature Seems to Me Like the Alps."
    Balch, E. "The Many-Sided Approach to World Organization."
    Balch, E. "Nobel Lecture."
    Balch, E. "The Self-Defeating Character of Coercion."

PEACE (cont.)

    Balch, E. "The Slow Growth Toward a World Community."
    Balch, E. "Temptations to Neo-Imperialism."
    Balch, E. "The Time to Make Peace."
    Balch, E. "Towards a Planetary Civilization."
    Balch, E. "The United Nations."
    Balch, E. "What It Means To Be An American."
    Caldicott, H. "A Commitment to Life."
    Caldicott, H. "Nuclear War."
    Caldicott, H. "We Are Curators of Life on Earth."
    Mullay, C. "Peace Forever--and Now."
    O'Hare, K. "Farewell Address of Kate Richards O'Hare."
    O'Hare, K. "Good Morning!"
    O'Hare, K. "Speech Delivered in Court by Kate Richards O'Hare Before Being Sentenced by Judge Wade."

PENSION TRUSTS

    Ferraro, G. "Statement."

PENSIONS, MILITARY--UNITED STATES

    Davis, S. "Statement."
    Cotton, K. "Statement."
    Grossman, C. "Statement."
    Quinlan, A. "Statement."
    Rodriguez, E. "Statement."
    Schroeder, P. "Statement." (3)

PETROLEUM--PRICES--UNITED STATES

    Heckler, M. "Statement."
    Kassebaum, N. "Statement."

PHARMACY

    Holtzman, E. "Statement."

PHILOSOPHY

    Hamilton, E. "Root of Freedom."
    Hamilton, E. "This I Believe."
    Le Doeuff, M. "Simone de Beauvoir and Existentialism."
    Roosevelt, E. "In Service of Truth."

POLITICAL ACTION COMMITTEES--UNITED STATES

Boxer, B. "Statement."
Ferraro, G. "Statement."

POLITICAL PARTIES--ROME

Taylor, L. "Caesar's Propaganda and the Gallic Succession."
Taylor, L. "The Campaign for Election and Legislation."
Taylor, L. "Catonism and Caesarism."
Taylor, L. "Cato's Leadership of the Optimates."
Taylor, L. "Cicero and Sallust on the Reform of the State."
Taylor, L. "The Criminal Courts and the Rise of a New Man."
Taylor, L. "Nobles, Clients, and Personal Armies."
Taylor, L. "Optimates and Populares Before Catiline's Conspiracy."
Taylor, L. "Personalities and Programs."
Taylor, L. "Politics and the Public Priesthoods."
Taylor, L. "Pompey's Sole Consulship."
Taylor, L. "Propaganda and Public Opinion from 58 to 53 B.C."
Taylor, L. "Religion and Divination in Politics."
Taylor, L. "The Removal of Cato."
Taylor, L. "The Role of the City Plebs and the Italians in the Voting."
Taylor, L. "The Union of Cato's Enemies."

POLITICAL SCIENCE

Ridings, D. "Advocating the People's Interest in Washington."
Rosoevelt, E. "Civil Liberties, the Individual and the Community."
Roosevelt, E. "The Meaning of Democracy."
Saldich, A. "Electronic Democracy."

PORNOGRAPHY

Barry, K. "Beyond Pornography."
Bart, P. "Dirty Books, Dirty Films, and Dirty Data."
Brady, K. "Statement."
Brown, S. "Testimony."
Bunch, C. "Lesbianism and Erotica in Pornographic America."
Burgess, A. "Testimony."
Dawson-Brown, C. "Testimony."
Diamond, I. "Pornography and Repression."
Dworkin, A. "Pornography and Grief."
Dworkin, A. "Testimony."
Gardner, T. "Racism in Pornography and the Women's Movement."
Goldsmith, J. "Testimony."

PORNOGRAPHY (cont.)
    Gosch, N. "Testimony."
    Heller, V. "Testimony."
    Leidholdt, D. "Testimony."
    Lorde, A. "Uses of the Erotic."
    Mackinnon, C. "Testimony."
    Marchiano, L. "Testimony."
    Russell, D. "Pornography and the Women's Liberation Movement."
    Sadler, A. "Statement."
    Seka. "Testimony."
    Smith, P. "Testimony."
    Specter, J. "Testimony."
    Vera, V. "Testimony."
    Yeamans, R. "A Political-Legal Analysis of Pornography."

POVERTY

    Baker, K. "Statement."
    Blum, B. "Statement."
    Ferraro, G. "Statement."
    Fiedler, B. "Statement."
    McAdoo, H. "Statement."
    Mobley, S. "Statement."
    Murphy, S. "Statement."
    Norton, E. "Statement."
    Shepard, A. "Statement."

POWER RESOURCES

    Boggs, L. "Statement."
    Fiedler, B. "Statement." (6)
    Hall, K. "Statement."
    Heckler, M. "Statement."
    Kaptur, M. "Statement."
    Meyer, J. "Statement."
    Schroeder, P. "Statement."
    Smith, V. "Statement." (2)

PRAYER IN THE PUBLIC SCHOOLS

    Roundtree, M. "Statement."

PREGNANCY, ADOLESCENT--UNITED STATES

    Baldwin, W. "Statement." (4)
    Bane, M. "Statement."
    Blanchard, M. "Testimony."

PREGNANCY, COMPLICATIONS OF

PREGNANCY, UNWANTED--UNITED STATES

PSYCHIATRIC ETHICS (cont.)

    Schiller, P. "Competence of Sex Therapists."

    Stuart, M. "Welfare of the Client."

PSYCHOANALYSIS

    Thompson, C. "Deviants Around 1912."

    Thompson, C. "Deviations and New Developments on the 1920's."

    Thompson, C. "The Ego and Character Structure."

    Thompson, C. "Evaluation of Freud's Biological Orientation."

    Thompson, C. "Freud's Cultural Orientation Compared with Modern Ideas of Culture."

    Thompson, C. "Recent Developments."

    Thompson, C. "Resistance and Transference."

    Thompson, C. "Therapy."

    Thompson, C. "Theories About Anxiety."

    Thompson, C. "Unconscious Processes and Repression."

PUBLIC LAND SALES

    Vucanovich, B. "Statement."

PUBLIC SERVICE EMPLOYMENT--UNITED STATES

    Bellamy, C. "Statement." (2)

    Martin, L. "Statement."

    Schroeder, P. "Statement."

PUBLIC SPEAKING

    Lomax-Cooke, C. "The Speaker and the Ghost."

PUBLIC WELFARE

    Bellamy, C. "Statement."

    Chisholm, S. "Statement."

    Kunin, M. "Statement."

    Schroeder, P. "Statement."

    Stevens, D. "Organizing for Welfare Rights."

QUAKERS--SERMONS

    Mott, L. "Abuses and Uses of the Bible."

    Mott, L. "The Argument That Women Do Not Want To Vote."

    Mott, L. "Discourse on Women."

QUAKERS--SERMONS (cont.)
   Mott, L.   "When the Heart Is Attuned to Prayer."
   Mott, L.   "Worship in Spirit and In Truth."

RADIO BROADCASTING TO CUBA (ORGANIZATION)

   Hawkins, P.   "Statement."

RAILROADS

   Dole, E.   "Statement." (3)

RAPE VICTIMS--UNITED STATES

   Bacon, S.   "H.R. 14666 The Privacy Protection for Rape Victims
      Act of 1976."
   Barr, Jr.   "Statement."
   Beaudry, J.   "Testimony."
   Frank, E.   "Statement."
   Guyker, E.   "Statement."
   Marks, L.   "Testimony."
   Webb, C.   "Statement."

REFORMATORIES FOR WOMEN

   Brenzel, B.   "Lancaster Industrial School for Girls."

REFUGEES

   Chisholm, S.   "Statement."
   Hawkins, P.   "Statement."
   Heckler, M.   "Statement."

RELIGION

   Cott, N.   "Young Women in the Second Great Awakening in New
      England."
   Hamilton, E.   "This I Believe."
   Harris, P.   "Religion and Politics."

RETIREMENT INCOME--UNITED STATES

   King, N.   "Statement."
   Lonsdale, E.   "Statement."

RETIREMENT INCOME--UNITED STATES (cont.)

Markson, E. "Statement."
Moss, A. "Statement."
Netherton, J. "Statement."
Sandage, S. "Statement."
Snowe, O. "Statement."

ROADS

Boxer, B. "Statement."
Ferraro, G. "Statement."
Martin, L. "Statement."
Oakar, M. "Statement."
Smith, V. "Statement."
Vucanovich, B. "Statement."

ROME--POLITICS AND GOVERNMENT

Taylor, L. "The Assemblies in Their Setting."
Taylor, L. "Caesar's Propaganda and the Gallic Succession."
Taylor, L. "The Campaign for Election and Legislation."
Taylor, L. "Catonism and Caesarism."
Taylor, L. "Cato's Leadership of the Optimates."
Taylor, L. "The Centuriate Assembly in the Light of New Discoveries."
Taylor, L. "Cicero and Sallust on the Reform of the State."
Taylor, L. "The Criminal Courts and the Rise of a New Man."
Taylor, L. "Methods of Voting and Places of Assembly of Centuries and Tribes."
Taylor, L. "The Nature of the Asemblies."
Taylor, L. "Nobles, Clients, and Personal Armies."
Taylor, L. "Optimates and Populares Before Catilines's Conspiracy."
Taylor, L. "Personalities and Programs."
Taylor, L. "Politics and the Public Priesthoods."
Taylor, L. "Pompey's Sole Consulship."
Taylor, L. "Propaganda and Public Opinion from 58 to 53 B.C."
Taylor, L. "Public Meetings in the Forum, On the Capitoline, and in the Circus Flaminius."
Taylor, L. "Religion and Divination in Politics."
Taylor, L. "The Removal of Cato."
Taylor, L. "The Role of the City Plebs and the Italians in the Voting."
Taylor, L. "The Thirty-Five Tribes and the Procedure in the Tribal Assemblies."
Taylor, L. "The Union of Cato's Enemies."

SALES PERSONNEL

> Greenberg, J. "A Profile of the Successful High-Tech Sales-
> person."

SANGER, MARGARET

> Conway, J. "Margaret Sanger and American Reform."
> Fee, E. "From Voluntary Motherhood to Planned Parenthood."
> Gordon, L. "From Voluntary Motherhood to Planned Parenthood."
> Harper, A. "From Voluntary Motherhood to Planned Parenthood."
> Harper, A. "Reproductive Freedom Today."

SAYERS, DOROTHY

> Auerbach, N. "Dorothy Sayers and the Amazons."

SCHOOL INTEGRATION--UNITED STATES

> Fiedler, B. "Statement."
> Oakar, M. "Statement."

SELF-EMPLOYED WOMEN--UNITED STATES

> Davison, D. "Statement."
> Hays, M. "Statement."
> Holmes, D. "Statement."
> Mater, C. "Statement."
> Muscato, P. "Statement."
> Rolls, K. "Statement."
> Seeman, M. "Statement."
> Taft, S. "Statement."
> Tate, J. "Statement."

SEPARATE MAINTENANCE--UNITED STATES

> Davis, S. "Statement."
> Cotton, K. "Statement."
> Grossman, C. "Statement."
> Quinlan, A. "Statement."
> Rodriguez, E. "Statement."
> Schroeder, P. "Statement."

SERMONS, AMERICAN--WOMEN AUTHORS

> Abernethy, A. "Unbinding for Life."

SERMONS, AMERICAN--WOMEN AUTHORS (cont.)
  Althouse, L. "Love's Winning Circle (Easter)."
  Bloomquist, K. "The Yes That Heals Our Paralysis."
  Bracken, J. "Advent III."
  Bracken, J. "Lent I."
  Bracken, J. "Pentecost VI."
  Carlson, C. "America--Finished or Unfinished."
  Carque, P. "The Wait of Pregnancy."
  Carroll, M. "A Homily for the Feast of Teresa of Avila."
  Couch, B. "Suffering and Hope."
  Crockett-Cannon, M. "What Do You Want Me To Do For You?"
  Crotwell, H. "Broken Community (The Seventh Sunday of East-
    er)."
  Cunneen, S. "Women."
  Clark, L. "The Day's Own Trouble."
  Daum, A. "'Sisterhood' Is Powerful."
  Davis, P. "The Best Is Yet To Be."
  Denham, P. "It's Hard to Sing the Song of Deborah."
  Foley, M. "A Homily for Midnight Mass (Christmas)."
  Fortune, M. "My God, My God, Why Have You Forsaken Me?"
  Frank, M. "How Can This Be?"
  Geller, L. "Can Isaac and Ishmael Be Reconciled?"
  Grindal, G. "Both Boxes."
  Gustafson, J. "Dry Bones and Rolled Stones."
  Hally, E. "Easter VI."
  Hally, E. "Lent III."
  Hally, E. "Pentecost XXVI."
  Hancock, E. "The Impatience of Job."
  Hardesty, N. "Just As I Am."
  Hellwig, M. "The Expectation and the Birth (The Fourth Sunday
    in Advent)."
  Heyward, C. "The Enigmatic God."
  Heyward, C. "Priesthood (The Ordination of Doug Clark)."
  Jones, E. C. "Lent V."
  Jones, E. C. "Pentecost XIV."
  Jones, E. "Sermon to the Seniors."
  Keller, R. "This Ministry."
  Klaaren, M. "Realism and Hope."
  Littleton, C. "Epiphany VIII."
  Littleton, C. "Lent IV."
  Littleton, C. "Pentecost VI."
  Mann, A. "Lazarus, Come Forth (Lent)."
  McGee, M. "In Celebration of Heroes and Nobodies."
  Mollenkott, V. "The Ephesians Vision."
  Nelson, C. "Job."
  Palmer, S. "The Wounded Healer."
  Pasternak, B. "Created in Her Image."
  Ransom, G. "Chafing Dish, Apron Strings."
  Rayburn, C. "Three Women from Moab."
  Roberts, N. "Last at the Cross."
  Ruether, R. "Woman as Oppressed."

SERMONS, AMERICAN--WOMEN AUTHORS (cont.)

  Ruether, R. "You Shall Call No Man Father."
  Russell, L. "The Impossible Possibility."
  Russell, V. "Giving Thanks or Making Do (Thanksgiving)."
  Sawatzky, S. "Sometimes There's God, So Quickly."
  Schaper, D. "The Movement of Suffering."
  Schaudt, Y. "Frontiers."
  Soelle, D. "The Children of Soweto."
  Steffey, S. "The Stuff That Covenant Is Made of."
  Stokes, J. "Jesus, Son of David, Have Mercy on Me."
  Taylor, B. "Pentecost II."
  Taylor, B. "Pentecost X."
  Taylor, B. "Pentecost XVIII."
  Tennis, D. "Suffering."
  Traxler, M. "Mary's Christmas Announces Freedom to Captives."
  Trebbi, D. "My Prayer 'Grows Up' As I Grow Older."
  Trible, P. "The Opportunity of Loneliness (The Ordination of Mary Beale)."
  Troxell, B. "The No Which Enables Our Yes."
  Way, P. "Fools, Clowns, and Temptations."
  Way, P. "You Are Not My God, Jehovah."
  Wedel, C. "The Story of the Transfiguration (Epiphany)."
  Werth, T. "Today Is All We Have."

SEX CRIMES--UNITED STATES

  Bako, Y. "Statement."
  Bendor, J. "Statement."
  Bissette, B. "The North Carolina Rape Kit Program."
  Boggs, L. "Statement."
  Burgess, A. "Statement."
  Burt, M. "Statement."
  Curtis, L. "Statement."
  Dorrill, M. "The Identification and Distribution of ABH and Lewis Substances in Seminal and Vaginal Secretions."
  Fields, M. "Statement."
  Flitcraft, A. "Statement."
  Hulen, P. "Simultaneous Electrophoresis of Phosphoglue-comutase (PGM) and Peptidase A (PepA)."
  Kutzke, E. "Statement."
  Largen, M. "Statement."
  McDonald, N. "Statement."
  Myers, T. "Statement."
  Sneed, M. "Statement."
  Sparks, C. "Statement."
  Steinmetz, S. "Statement."
  Swift, C. "Statement."
  Walker, L. "Statement."

SEX DETERMINATION, GENETIC

Ampola, M. "Prenatal Diagnosis."
Axelsen, D. "Decisions About Handicapped Newborns."
Bendix, H. "Rights of a Handicapped Neonante."
Carlton, W. "Perfectability and the Neonate."
Connor, D. "Response (to Unnatural Selection: On Choosing Children's Sex)."
Culpepper, E. "Reflections."
Culpepper, E. "Sex Preselection."
Davis, A. "Diethylstilbestrol."
Edwards, M. "Neonatology."
Erhart, R. "DES and Drugs in Pregnancy."
Herlands, R. "Biological Manipulations for Producing and Nurturing Mammalian Embryos."
Holtzman, J. "DES."
Hoskins, B. "Manipulative Reproductive Technologies."
Hubbard, R. "The Case Against In Vitro Fertilization and Implantations."
Kenen, R. "A Look at Prenatal Diagnosis Within the Context of Changing Parental and Reproductive Norms."
Lapham, E. "Living with an Impaired Neonate and Child."
Locke, E. "Antenatal Diagnosis."
Logan, R. "Ectogenesis and Ideology."
Major, G. "Prenatal Diagnosis."
Mayrand, T. "Response (to Ethics and Reproductive Technology)."
Menning, B. "In Defense of In Vitro Fertilization."
Nentwig, M. "Technical Aspects of Sex Preselection."
Peterson, S. "The Politics of Prenatal Diagnosis."
Powledge, T. "Unnatural Selection."
Raymond, J. "Sex Preselection: Introduction."
Raymond, J. "Sex Preselection: A Response."
Rozovsky, F. "The Legal Aspects of the DES Case."
Salladay, S. "Ethics and Reproductive Technology."
Steinbacher, R. "Futuristic Implications of Sex Preselection."
Tilley, B. "Assessment of Risks from DES."
Whitbeck, C. "The Neonate."
Whitbeck, C. "Response to Papers on Decisions About Handicapped Newborns."

SEX DIFFERENCES (PSYCHOLOGY)

Hamburg, B. "The Psychobiology of Sex Differences."
Korner, A. "Methodological Considerations in Studying Sex Differences in the Behavioral Functioning of Newborns."
Ward, I. "Sexual Behavior Differentiation."

SEX DISCRIMINATION--UNITED STATES

Acosta, K. "Testimony."
Bean, J. "The Development of Psychological Androgyny."
Belcher, L. "Testimony."
Bertrom, L. "Testimony."
Betz, C. "Testimony."
Bowman, B. "Sexism and Racism in Education."
Bradford, N. "Testimony."
Brookshier, K. "Testimony."
Carpio, P. "Testimony."
Casias, S. "Testimony."
Crandall, C. "Testimony."
Emerson, B. "Testimony."
Emery, J. "Testimony."
Escalante, A. "Testimony."
Etter, C. "Testimony."
Fenton, A. "Testimony."
Freeman, F. "Statement."
Fullington, S. "Testimony."
Greenberg, S. "Preschool and the Politics of Sexism."
Guttentag, M. "The Social Psychology of Sex-Role Intervention."
Hendee, L. "Testimony."
Johns, R. "Testimony."
Jordan, A. "Testimony."
Jordan, N. "Testimony."
Katz, L. "Teacher Education and Non-Sexist Early Childhood
    Education."
Kopec, J. "Testimony."
McClain, M. "Testimony."
McHenry, R. "Testimony."
Mentzler, N. "Testimony."
Noel, R. "Testimony."
Noel, R. "Welcoming Statement."
Pogrebin, L. "Non-Sexist Parenting at Home and at School."
Queen, R. "Towards Liberating Toys."
Radetsky, M. "Testimony."
Reed, K. "Testimony."
Rockwell, V. "Testimony."
Rodriguez-Trias, H. "Problems and Priorities of Poor, Culturally
    Different Parents."
Schomp, K. "Testimony."
Serbin, L. "Teachers, Peers, and Play Preferences."
Snyder, M. "Testimony."
Strandburg, M. "Testimony."
Sturgis, C. "Testimony."
Torres, T. "Testimony."
Valuck, D. "Testimony."
Vest, M. "Testimony."
Wheeler, D. "Testimony."
Widmann, N. "Testimony."

SEX DISCRIMINATION AGAINST WOMEN (cont.)

Reed, W. "Testimony."
Rosen, M. "Testimony."
Ross, O. "Testimony."
Roundtree, J. "Testimony."
Ryan, A. "Asian-American Women."
Sancier, B. "Beyond Advocacy."
Sapiro, V. "Women's Studies and Political Conflict."
Schaffer, J. "Testimony."
Schulenburg, J. "Clio's European Daughters."
Schwerin, S. "Testimony."
Sherif, C. "Bias in Psychology."
Smith, D. "A Sociology for Women."
Solomon, B. "Social Work Values and Skills to Empower Women."
Spancier, B. "Beyond Advocacy."
Stille, D. "Testimony." (2)
Stimpson, C. "The Power to Name."
Syler, M. "Testimony."
Taub, N. "Testimony."
Taylor, R. "Testimony."
Tessner, E. "Testimony."
Tuteur, M. "Testimony."
Weick, A. "Issues of Power in Social Work Practice."
Wetzel, J. "Redefining Concepts of Mental Health."
White, B. "Black Women."
Williams, O. "Welcoming Statements."
Wilson, S. "Testimony."
Winfield, A. "Testimony."
Woodman, N. "Social Work with Lesbian Couples."

SEX DISCRIMINATION AGAINST WOMEN--LAW AND LEGISLATION

Avner, J. "Statement."
Baer, P. "Statement."
Bell, C. "Statement."
Blank, H. "Statement."
Boggs, E. "Statement."
Burgess, G. "Statement."
Byrd, A. "Statement."
Chayes, A. "Testimony."
Cole, E. "Statement."
Crawford, S. "Statement."
Cross, N. "Statement."
Cruz, C. "Statement."
Curtis, C. "Statement."
Delk, Y. "Statement."
Denton, C. "Statement."
Easton, S. "Statement."
Ferraro, G. "Opening Statement."
Ferraro, G. "Statement." (2)

SEX DISCRIMINATION AGAINST WOMEN (cont.)
Taylor, A. "Statement."
Tice, P. "Statement."
Tucker, M. "Testimony."
Turner, P. "Statement."
Walsh, B. "Statement."
Wardle, L. "Testimony."
Wegner, J. "Testimony."
Wernick, E. "Statement."
Willenz, J. "Testimony."
Wolfe, J. "Statement."
Zuckert, C. "Testimony."

SEX DISCRIMINATION AGAINST WOMEN--UNITED STATES

Andrulis, M. "Testimony."
Anthony, S. "Woman Wants Bread, Not the Ballot!"
Baldwin, P. "Statement."
Beller, A. "Trends in Occupational Segregation by Sex and
    Race, 1960-1981."
Berger, B. "Occupational Segregation and the Earnings Gap."
Bergmann, B. "Statement."
Blau, F. "Concluding Remarks."
Blau, F. "Occupational Segregation and Labor Market Discrimina-
    tion."
Boggs, L. "Statement." (2)
Brothers, J. "Testimony."
Brown, O. "On Foreign Rule."
Byrd, A. "Statement."
Bystrom, M. "Statement."
Cain, P. "Commentary."
Candela, C. "Testimony."
Carlberg, G. "Statement."
Conable, C. "Testimony."
Davis, D. "Testimony."
Deaux, K. "Internal Barriers."
Deconcini, S. "Testimony."
Dewine, S. "Breakthrough."
Dorman, L. "Testimony."
Dixon, M. "Chicanas and Mexicanas in a Transnational Working
    Class."
Eidson, G. "Testimony."
England, P. "Occupational Segregation and the Earnings Gap."
Ferraro, G. "Statement."
Finn, J. "Statement."
Fitzpatrick, B. "Statement."
Fitzpatrick, M. "Effective Interpersonal Communication for Wom-
    en of the Corporation."
Fleming, J. "Statement."
Fleming, J. "Testimony."

SEX DISCRIMINATION AGAINST WOMEN--UNITED STATES (cont.)
    Verheyden-Hilliard, M. "Statement."
    Vermeulen, J. "Statement."
    Williams, K. "Statement."
    Wilpula, S. "Statement."
    Wolf, E. "Statement."
    Wolf, W. "Commentary."
    Wolf, W. "Commentary (on Sex Typing in Occupational Socialization)."
    Woods, R. "Statement."
    Wright, L. "Testimony."

SEX DISCRIMINATION IN EDUCATION--UNITED STATES

    Auchincloss, E. "Statement."
    Chase-Anderson, M. "Statement."
    Greenberger, M. "Statement."
    Howe, F. "American Literature and Women's Lives."
    Howe, F. "Breaking the Disciplines."
    Howe, F. "Feminism and the Education of Women."
    Howe, F. "Feminism and the Study of Literature."
    Howe, F. "Feminism, Fiction, and the Classroom."
    Howe, F. "Feminist Scholarship."
    Howe, F. "The Future of Women's Colleges."
    Howe, F. "Literacy and Literature."
    Howe, F. "Myths of Coeducation."
    Howe, F. "The Past Ten Years."
    Howe, F. "The Power of Education."
    Howe, F. "Sex-Role Stereotypes Start Early."
    Howe, F. "Teaching in the Modern Languages."
    Howe, F. "Why Educate Women?"
    Howe, F. "Why Educate Women? The Responses of Wellesley and Stanford."
    Howe, F. "Women's Studies and Social Change."
    Mayerson, A. "Statement."
    Simmons, A. "Statement."

SEX DISCRIMINATION IN EMPLOYMENT

    Alexander, F. "Statement."
    Alexander, L. "Statement."
    Barajas, G. "Statement."
    Beller, A. "Occupational Segregation and the Earnings Gap."
    Beller, A. "Trends in Occupational Segregation by Sex and Race, 1960-1981."
    Benson, S. "Women in Retail Sales Work."
    Berger, B. "Occupational Segregation and the Earnings Gap."
    Berry, M. "Statement."
    Blau, F. "Concluding Remarks."

SEX DISCRIMINATION IN EMPLOYMENT (cont.)

SEX DISCRIMINATION IN EMPLOYMENT (cont.)
    Stein, E. "Statement."
    Steinbacher, R. "Statement."
    Steinberg, R. "Comparable Worth Doctrine and Its Implementa-
        tion."
    Steinberg, R. "Statement." (2)
    Stelck, K. "Statement."
    Stone, E. "Statement."
    Strober, M. "Toward A General Theory of Occupational Sex
        Segregation."
    Thomas, P. "Statement."
    Tilly, L. "Paths of Proletarianization."
    Vermeulen, J. "Statement."
    Warren, A. "Statement."
    Wernick, E. "Statement." (2)
    Wertheimer, B. "Leadership Training for Union Women in the
        United States."
    Wolf, W. "Commentary."
    Wolf, W. "Commentary (on Sex Typing in Occupational Socializa-
        tion)."
    Woodruff, C. "Statement."
    Young, T. "Statement."

SEX DISCRIMINATION IN INSURANCE

    Davis, C. "Testimony."
    East, C. "Testimony."
    Lautzenheiser, B. "Testimony."
    Mikulski, B. "Testimony."
    Simmons, A. "Testimony."
    Steele, D. "Testimony."

SEX INSTRUCTION--UNITED STATES

    Driscoll, P. "Statement."
    Ellis, E. "Statement."
    Fernandez-Mattei, M. "Statement."
    Hardy, J. "Statement."
    Howard, M. "Statement."
    Jefferson, M. "Statement."
    Jones, J. "Statement."
    Lewis, J. "The Sixth Day."
    McGee, E. "Statement."
    Sanchez, P. "Statement."
    Sullivan, A. "Statement."
    Sullivan, M. "Statement."
    Wilson, M. "Statement."

SEX ROLES

Anthony, S. "Woman Wants Bread, Not the Ballot!"

Antler, J. "Was She a Good Mother?"

Bilinkoff, J. "The Holy Woman and the Urban Community in Sixteenth-Century Avila."

Bonner, D. "Women as Caregivers."

Brown, O. "On Foreign Rule."

Brumberg, J. "The Ethnological Mirror."

Dubois, E. "The Limitations of Sisterhood."

Ducrocq, F. "The London Biblewomen and Nurses Missions, 1857-1880."

Frenier, M. "The Effects of the Chinese Revolution on Women and Their Families."

Friedman, J. "Piety and Kin."

Gampel, G. "The Planter's Wife Revisited."

Gubar, S. "Mother, Maiden, and the Marriage of Death."

Gullett, G. "City Mothers, City Daughters, and the Dance Hall Girls."

Humez, J. "My Spirit Eye."

Lerner, E. "Jewish Involvement in the New York City Woman Suffrage Movement."

McGee, S. "Right-Wing Female Activists in Buenos Aires, 1900-1932."

Morantz, R. "Feminism, Professionalism, and Germs."

Sachs, B. "Changing Relationships Between Men and Women."

Shteir, A. "Linnaeus's Daughters."

Stone, L. "Disappointment Is the Lot of Women."

Truth, S. "Ain't I A Woman?"

Truth, S. "Keeping the Thing Going While Things Are Stirring."

Wilson, B. "Glimpses of Muslim Urban Women in Classical Islam."

Zappi, E. "If Eight Hours Seem Few to You."

SEX THERAPY

Johnson, V. "Welcome and Opening Remarks."

Kaplan, H. "Training of Sex Therapists."

Macklin, R. "Confidentiality in Sex Therapy."

Mudd, E. "The Historical Background of Ethical Considerations in Sex Research and Sex Therapy."

Sarrel, L. "Certification and Training of Sex Therapists."

Schiller, P. "Competence of Sex Therapists."

Stuart, M. "Welfare of the Client."

SEXISM

Bean, J. "The Development of Psychological Androgyny."

Bowman, B. "Sexism and Racism in Education."

Burlage, D. "Judaeo-Christian Influences on Female Sexuality."

SEXISM (cont.)

Daly, M. "Theology After the Demise of God the Father."
Greenberg, S. "Preschool and the Politics of Sexism."
Guttentag, M. "The Social Psychology of Sex-Role Intervention."
Hageman, A. "Women and Missions."
Harris, B. "Sexism and the Contemporary Church."
Hoover, T. "Black Women and the Churches."
Katz, L. "Teacher Education and Non-Sexist Early Childhood Education."
Morton, N. "Preaching the Word."
Neville, G. "Religious Socialization of Women Within U.S. Subcultures."
Pogrebin, L. "Non-Sexist Parenting at Home and at School."
Queen, R. "Towards Liberating Toys."
Rodriguez-Trias, H. "Problems and Priorities of Poor, Culturally Different Parents."
Russell, L. "Women and Ministry."
Serbin, L. "Teachers, Peers, and Play Preferences."
Shulman, G. "View from the Back of the Synagogue."
Stendahl, K. "Enrichment or Threat?"

SEXUAL DIVISION OF LABOR

Minge, W. "The Industrial Revolution and the European Family."
Mullings, L. "Uneven Development."
Safa, H. "Runaway Shops and Female Employment."
Tilly, L. "Paths of Proletarianization."
Weiner, A. "Forgotten Wealth."
Wong, A. "Planned Development, Social Stratification, and the Sexual Division of Labor in Singapore."

SEXUAL HARASSMENT OF WOMEN--UNITED STATES

Alley, M. "Statement."
Alley, M. "Testimony."
Armstrong, V. "Statement."
Baldwin, P. "Statement."
Byrd, A. "Statement."
Carlberg, G. "Statement."
Chandler, E. "Testimony."
Finn, J. "Statement."
Fleming, J. "Statement."
Goodin, J. "Statement."
Grossman, C. "Statement."
Hall, B. "Statement."
Height, D. "Statement."
Jacksteit, M. "Statement."
Johnson, M. "Statement."
Largen, M. "Statement."

SEXUAL HARASSMENT OF WOMEN--UNITED STATES (cont.)
Lenhoff, D. "Statement." (2)
Lewis, H. "Statement."
Madison, A. "Statement."
Mitgang, I. "Statement."
Nelms, D. "Statement."
Norton, E. "Statement." (3)
Nussbaum, K. "Statement."
Paschall, E. "Statement."
Poythress, M. "Statement."
Pressler, P. "Testimony."
Prokop, R. "Statement." (2)
Russo, N. "Statement."
Sandage, S. "Statement."
Sauvigne, K. "Statement."
Schlafly, P. "Statement."
Smeal, E. "Statement."
Smothers, L. "Statement."
Vermeulen, J. "Statement."
Waxman, M. "Statement."
Williams, D. "Statement."

SEXUALLY ABUSED CHILDREN--UNITED STATES

Frank, E. "Statement."
Webb, C. "Statement."

SHAKESPEARE, WILLIAM--STAGE HISTORY

Webster, M. "Shakespeare and the Modern Theatre."

SHIPBUILDING INDUSTRY

Smith, V. "Statement."

SMALL BUSINESS

Boxer, B. "Statement."

SOCIAL CASE WORK

Germain, C. "Casework and Science."
Hollis, F. "The Psychosocial Approach to the Practice of Case-
    work."
McBroom, E. "Socialization and Social Casework."
Perlman, H. "The Problem-Solving Model in Social Casework."

SOCIAL CASE WORK (cont.)

  Rapoport, L. "Crisis Intervention as a Mode of Brief Treatment."
  Simon, B. "Social Casework Theory."
  Smalley, R. "The Functional Approach to Casework Practice."

SOCIAL ETHICS

  Harrison, B. "The Equal Rights Amendment."
  Harrison, B. "The Power of Anger in the Work of Love."
  Harrison, B. "Sexism and the Language of Christian Ethics."

SOCIAL JUSTICE

  Ginsburg, R. "Realizing the Equality Principle."
  Greene, M. "Equality and Inviolability."

SOCIAL SECURITY--UNITED STATES

  Abramson, E. "Statement."
  Alden, L. "Statement."
  Bagnal, A. "Statement."
  Bazemore, A. "Statement."
  Bergmann, B. "The Housewife and Social Security Reform."
  Bergmann, B. "Testimony."
  Block, M. "Testimony."
  Bonder, E. "Testimony."
  Brown, H. "Statement."
  Brummond, N. "Statement."
  Buechler, J. "Statement."
  Burris, C. "Testimony."
  Campbell, J. "Testimony."
  Campbell, N. "Statement." (2)
  Campbell, N. "Testimony."
  Campbell, R. "Statement."
  Candela, C. "Statement."
  Candela, C. "Testimony."
  Cardin, S. "Testimony."
  Cauchear, M. "Statement."
  Collin, M. "Statement."
  Darner, K. "Statement."
  Davis, D. "Testimony."
  Dean, S. "Testimony."
  Donnelly, E. "Statement."
  Duskin, B. "Testimony."
  East, C. "Statement." (2)
  Eidson, G. "Testimony."
  Ellis, T. "Statement."
  Fenwick, M. "Statement."

SOCIAL SECURITY--UNITED STATES (cont.)

Ferraro, G. "Statement." (4)

Fierst, E. "Discussion (of Supplemental OASI Benefits to Homemakers)."

Fierst, E. "Statement." (3)

Fierst, E. "Testimony."

Fineshriber, P. "Testimony."

Finn, J. "Statement."

Flournoy, F. "Statement."

Forman, M. "Statement."

Foster, D. "Statement."

Fraser, A. "Statement."

French, J. "Testimony."

Gorie, M. "Statement."

Griffiths, M. "Testimony."

Hamlin, J. "Statement."

Heckler, M. "Statement."

Holden, K. "Supplemental OASI Benefits to Homemakers Through Current Spouse Benefits, A Homemaker Credit, and Child-Care Drop-Out Years."

Jeffrey, M. "Testimony."

Jones, M. "Statement."

Kaptur, M. "Statement."

Keys, M. "Statement." (2)

Keys, M. "Testimony."

King, N. "Statement."

Kobell, R. "Statement."

Kuhn, M. "Statement."

Lang, N. "Statement."

Lewis, R. "Statement."

Little, F. "Statement."

Lloyd, M. "Statement."

Madar, O. "Testimony."

Maher, M. "Statement."

Major, B. "Statement."

Marshall, M. "Statement."

McKenna, T. "Statement."

McSteen, M. "Statement."

Mikulski, B. "Statement." (2)

Mikulski, B. "Testimony."

Moen, C. "Testimony."

Nuland-Ames, L. "Statement."

Oakar, M. "Statement." (9)

O'Neill, A. "Statement."

Peak, J. "Statement."

Penfield, P. "Testimony."

Penman, R. "Testimony."

Podojil, T. "Statement."

Prior, M. "Statement."

Quinlan, A. "Statement."

Reed, C. "Testimony."

SOCIAL SECURITY--UNITED STATES (cont.)
    Renfro, S. "Statement."
    Reno, V. "Discussion (of Earnings Sharing: Incremental and
        Fundamental Reform)."
    Ricardo-Campbell, R. "Social Security."
    Ricardo-Campbell, R. "Statement."
    Richards, E. "Statement."
    Robb, L. "Testimony."
    Rutherford, T. "Statement."
    Sampey, E. "Statement."
    Schlafly, P. "Statement."
    Schneider, C. "Statement."
    Schneider, R. "Statement."
    Schmotzer, A. "Testimony."
    Schroeder, P. "Statement." (2)
    Schub, J. "Statement." (2)
    Shields, L. "Statement."
    Smeal, E. "Statement." (3)
    Smeal, E. "Testimony."
    Snowe, O. "Statement."
    Sweeney, E. "Statement."
    Todd, T. "Statement."
    Vadas, M. "Statement."
    Veve, K. "Statement."
    Wilson, (Mrs.) J. "Statement."

SOCIAL SERVICE

    Bowen, L. "Address at Juvenile Protective Association Dinner."
    Bowen, L. "Address on the Juvenile Protective Association of
        Chicago."
    Bowen, L. "Address to Woman's City Club."
    Bowen, L. "Annual Meeting of the M.P.A. 'Nobody Cared.'"
    Bowen, L. "Annual Meeting of United Charities."
    Bowen, L. "Before the Resolutions Committee of the Republican
        National Convention."
    Bowen, L. "Birth Control."
    Bowen, L. "Campaign Against Segregation."
    Bowen, L. "Campaign to Elect Mr. Robert Hall McCormick, Ald-
        erman."
    Bowen, L. "Can Children Afford It?"
    Bowen, L. "Child Labor Amendment."
    Bowen, L. "Christmas."
    Bowen, L. "Dedication of Boys' Club Building Hull-House."
    Bowen, L. "Dedication of Children's Building Mary Crane Nur-
        sery, Hull-House."
    Bowen, L. "Dedication of Elizabeth McCormick Open-Air School
        on Top of Hull-House Boys' Club Building."
    Bowen, L. "The Delinquent Children of Immigrant Parents."
    Bowen, L. "Dinner of Woman's Roosevelt Republican Club to

SOCIAL SERVICE (cont.)

Delegates of Illinois Republican Women's Clubs."

Bowen, L. "Egypt, Greece, and Turkey."

Bowen, L. "Eleventh Birthday of Hull-House Woman's Club."

Bowen, L. "Equal Suffrage." (2)

Bowen, L. "Equal Suffrage. What Has Been Done--What Ought To Be Done."

Bowen, L. "Famous Women's Luncheon Second Woman's World Fair."

Bowen, L. "Famous Women's Luncheon Women's World Fair."

Bowen, L. "Fortieth Anniversary of Hull-House."

Bowen, L. "Fortnightly Club Founders' Luncheon."

Bowen, L. "Greeting to Illinois Equal Suffrage Association from Woman's City Club."

Bowen, L. "The Home Woman's Need and Power."

Bowen, L. "Honoring Judge Merritt W. Pinckney."

Bowen, L. "How Will Women Use the Franchise?"

Bowen, L. "Impromptu Remarks at Meeting to Organize Friends of Juvenile Court Committee."

Bowen, L. "In Memoriam, Jane Addams."

Bowen, L. "Introducing Dr. William R. P. Emerson."

Bowen, L. "Introducing Hon. William Howard Taft."

Bowen, L. "Introducing Lady Astor."

Bowen, L. "Introducing Theodore Roosevelt."

Bowen, L. "Introducing Thomas Mott Osborne."

Bowen, L. "The Juvenile Court." (2)

Bowen, L. "Lessons from Other Lands for the Conduct of Life in Ours."

Bowen, L. "Mary Rozet Smith Memorial."

Bowen, L. "Mass Meeting."

Bowen, L. "Mass Meeting of Women Voters."

Bowen, L. "Mass Meeting, Woman's Roosevelt Republican Club."

Bowen, L. "Meeting on High Cost of Living."

Bowen, L. "A Memorial Day in the Country."

Bowen, L. "Mexico."

Bowen, L. "The Minimum Wage."

Bowen, L. "Money-Raising for Campaign."

Bowen, L. "National Urban League Annual Conference."

Bowen, L. "A Nature Talk."

Bowen, L. "The Need of Protective Work in Illinois."

Bowen, L. "The Need of Recreation."

Bowen, L. "Needed Legislation Suggested by Experiences in the Lower North District."

Bowen, L. "New Year's Talk."

Bowen, L. "On to the Polls!"

Bowen, L. "Opening of Hull-House Woman's Club."

Bowen, L. "Opening Remarks at the Speakers Institute."

Bowen, L. "Pan-American Congress of Women. Political Status of Women."

Bowen, L. "Pan-American Congress of Women. Prevention of Traffic in Women."

SOCIAL SERVICE (cont.)

Bowen, L. "Woman's City Club."

Bowen, L. "Woman's City Club Dinner."

Bowen, L. "Woman's Roosevelt Republican Club Banquet to Mr. and Mrs. Nicholas Longworth."

Bowen, L. "Woman's Roosevelt Republican Club Reception and Tea."

Bowen, L. "Woman's Roosevelt Republican Club Luncheon to Vice-President Dawes."

Bowen, L. "The Woman's World Fair."

Richmond, M. "Address to Students of the New York School of Philanthropy."

Richmond, M. "Adequate Relief."

Richmond, M. "Attitudes Toward Charitable Giving."

Richmond, M. "Book and Reading."

Richmond, M. "Charitable Co-Operation."

Richmond, M. "Charity and Homemaking."

Richmond, M. "The College and the Community."

Richmond, M. "The Concern of the Community With Marriage."

Richmond, M. "Criticism and Reform in Charity."

Richmond, M. "The Family and the Social Worker."

Richmond, M. "A Forward Look."

Richmond, M. "Friendly Visiting."

Richmond, M. "The Friendly Visitor."

Richmond, M. "How Social Workers Can Aid Housing Reform."

Richmond, M. "Industrial Conditions and the Charity Worker."

Richmond, M. "The Interrelation of Social Movements."

Richmond, M. "Lessons Learned in Baltimore."

Richmond, M. "The Long View."

Richmond, M. "Married Vagabonds."

Richmond, M. "Medical and Social Co-Operation."

Richmond, M. "The Need of a Training School in Applied Philanthropy."

Richmond, M. "Of the Art of Beginning in Social Work."

Richmond, M. "Our Relation to the Churches."

Richmond, M. "A Plea for Poetry."

Richmond, M. "The Profession and Practice of Begging."

Richmond, M. "The Relation of Output to Intake."

Richmond, M. "Report to the Mayor of Baltimore."

Richmond, M. "The Retail Method of Reform."

Richmond, M. "The Social Case Work Side of Probation and Parole."

Richmond, M. "The Social Case Worker in a Changing World."

Richmond, M. "The Social Case Worker's Task."

Richmond, M. "Some Next Steps in Social Treatment."

Richmond, M. "Some Relations of Family Case Work to Social Progress."

Richmond, M. "To the Volunteers of 1915."

Richmond, M. "The Training of Charity Workers."

Richmond, M. "War and Family Solidarity."

SOCIAL WORK WITH WOMEN--UNITED STATES

    Bako, Y. "Networking."
    Harm, M. "The Mission of the YWCA."
    Lawrence, G. "Funding."

SOCIALISTS

    Honeycutt, K. "Clara Zetkin."
    O'Hare, K. "Farewell Address of Kate Richards O'Hare."
    O'Hare, K. "Good Morning! Mr. American Citizen."
    O'Hare, K. "Speech Delivered in Court by Kate Richards O'Hare
      Before Being Sentenced by Judge Wade."

SOUTH AFRICA

    Bolton, F. "Treatment of Indians in South Africa."

SOUTHERN STATES--SOCIAL CONDITIONS

    Bellows, B. "My Children, Gentlemen, Are My Own."
    Berkeley, K. "Colored Ladies Also Contributed."
    Blester, C. "The Perrys of Greenville."
    Clinton, C. "Caught in the Web of the Big House."
    Perdue, T. "Southern Indians and the Cult of True Womanhood."
    Walsh, L. "The Experiences and Status of Women in the Chesa-
      peake, 1750-1775."

SOVIET UNION--STUDY AND TEACHING

    Oakar, M. "Statement."

SPACE INDUSTRIALIZATION

    Dole, E. "Statement."
    Smith, V. "Statement."

SPEED LIMITS--GOVERNMENT POLICY--UNITED STATES

    Vucanovich, B. "Statement."

SPORTS FRANCHISES--LOCATION

    Mikulski, B. "Statement."

STATE-LOCAL RELATIONS--UNITED STATES

Mikulski, B. "Statement."

STUDENT LOAN FUNDS--UNITED STATES

Chisholm, S. "Statement."
Schroeder, P. "Statement." (2)

SUICIDE--UNITED STATES--PREVENTION

Herbert, M. "Testimony."
Scherago, M. "Testimony."
Smith, J. "Testimony."

SUNSET REVIEWS OF GOVERNMENT PROGRAMS

Schroeder, P. "Statement."

SUPPLEMENTAL UNEMPLOYMENT BENEFITS--UNITED STATES

Kaptur, M. "Statement."

SURVIVOR'S BENEFITS--UNITED STATES

Bergmann, B. "The Housewife and Social Security Reform."
Cotton, K. "Statement."
Davis, S. "Statement."
Fierst, E. "Discussion (of Supplemental OASI Benefits to Home-
    makers)."
Grossman, C. "Statement."
Holden, K. "Supplemental OASI Benefits to Homemakers
    Through Current Spouse Benefits, A Homemaker's Credit,
    and Child-Care Drop-Out Years."
Quinlan, A. "Statement."
Reno, V. "Discussion (of Earnings Sharing: Incremental and
    Fundamental Reform)."
Rodriguez, E. "Statement."
Schlafly, P. "Statement."
Schroeder, P. "Statement." (2)
Taft, S. "Statement."

SYNTHETIC FUELS INDUSTRY

Heckler, M. "Statement."

SYNTHETIC FUELS INDUSTRY (cont.)

    Lloyd, M. "Statement."

    Schneider, C. "Statement."

TAXATION

    Smith, V. "Statement."

TECHNOLOGY--SOCIAL ASPECTS

    Huws, U. "Demystifying New Technology."

TECHNOLOGY TRANSFER

    Byron, B. "Statement."

TELEPHONE--UNITED UNITED--LONG DISTANCE--ACCESS
      CHARGES

    Smith, V. "Statement."

TENNESSEE VALLEY AUTHORITY

    Lloyd, M. "Statement."

TRADEMARKS--UNITED STATES--CRIMINAL PROVISIONS

    Hawkins, P. "Statement."

TRADE-UNIONS

    Dye, N. "Creating a Feminist Alliance."

    Dye, N. "Feminism or Unionism?"

    Jacoby, R. "The Women's Trade Union League and American
      Feminism."

    Kessler-Harris, A. "Where Are the Organized Women Workers."

TRAFFIC SAFETY--UNITED STATES

    Vucanovich, B. "Statement."

TRANSPORTATION

TRUCKS

TRUMAN, HARRY S

UNITED NATIONS

UNITED STATES--ADMINISTRATIVE AGENCIES

UNITED STATES--APPROPRIATIONS AND EXPENDITURES

UNITED STATES--APPROPRIATIONS AND EXPENDITURES (cont.)

Boxer, B. "Statement." (4)
Burton, S. "Statement."
Byron, B. "Statement." (2)
Collins, C. "Statement."
Dole, E. "Statement." (5)
Ferraro, G. "Statement."
Fiedler, B. "Statement." (5)
Hall, K. "Statement."
Heckler, M. "Statement." (5)
Holt, M. "Statement."
Johnson, N. "Statement."
Kaptur, M. "Statement."
Kennelly, B. "Statement." (2)
Mikulski, B. "Statement."
Oakar, M. "Statement." (3)
Schneider, C. "Statement." (2)
Schroeder, P. "Statement."
Smith, V. "Statement." (4)

UNITED STATES--ARMED FORCES--MEDICAL PERSONNEL--
MALPRACTICE

Schneider, C. "Statement."

UNITED STATES--ARMED FORCES--MILITARY CONSTRUCTION
OPERATIONS

Boxer, B. "Statement." (2)
Fiedler, B. "Statement."

UNITED STATES--CENSUS, 20TH, 1980

Chisholm, S. "Statement."

UNITED STATES--FOREIGN RELATIONS

Ahmad, S. "U.S.-Canada Relations."
Benson, L. "Antarctica."
Benson, L. "Munitions Sales to Saudi Arabia."
Benson, L. "Science and Technology: Their Interaction with
Foreign Policy."
Benson, L. "Science and Technology: U.S. Approach to the
UNCSTD."
Brunauder, E. "Statement."
Campbell, P. "Sub-Saharan Africa."
Carter, R. "Mrs. Carter Visits Thailand."

UNITED STATES--FOREIGN RELATIONS (cont.)
    Chang, M. "United States Relations with Taiwan."
    Colbert, E. "Poison Gas Use in Indochina."
    Coon, J. "South Asia--Old Problems, New Challenges."
    Coopersmith, E. "U.S. Contributions to the UNHCR."
    Derian, P. "Four Treaties Pertaining to Human Rights."
    Derian, P. "Human Rights and International Law."
    Derian, P. "Human Rights Conditions in Non-Communist Asia."
    Derian, P. "Human Rights in South Africa."
    Derian, P. "Missing and Disappeared Persons."
    Derian, P. "Review of Human Rights in Latin America."
    Derian, P. "Western Hemisphere."
    Fitch, (Mrs.) G. "Statement."
    Kassebaum, N. "Is the Proposed Anti-Apartheid Act of 1985 Sound Policy?"
    Kirkpatrick, J. "Beyond Sadat."
    Kirkpatrick, J. "Central America."
    Kirkpatrick, J. "Central America: Sandino Betrayed I."
    Kirkpatrick, J. "Central America: Sandino Betrayed II."
    Kirkpatrick, J. "Condemning Israel."
    Kirkpatrick, J. "Delitgitimizing Israel."
    Kirkpatrick, J. "Exacerbating Problems."
    Kirkpatrick, J. "Gaining Strength and Respect in the World."
    Kirkpatrick, J. "Golan Again."
    Kirkpatrick, J. "Human Rights and Wrong in the United Nations."
    Kirkpatrick, J. "Human Rights in Afghanistan."
    Kirkpatrick, J. "Human Rights in El Salvador."
    Kirkpatrick, J. "Human Rights in Nicaragua."
    Kirkpatrick, J. "Ideas and Institutions."
    Kirkpatrick, J. "International Conference on Assistance to Africa's Refugees."
    Kirkpatrick, J. "Israel as Scapegoat."
    Kirkpatrick, J. "Kirkpatrick's Remarks (U.N. on Israeli Raid)."
    Kirkpatrick, J. "Managing Freedom."
    Kirkpatrick, J. "A Miserable Resolution."
    Kirkpatrick, J. "The Peace Process Continued."
    Kirkpatrick, J. "Personal Virtues, Public Vices."
    Kirkpatrick, J. "The Problem of the United Nations."
    Kirkpatrick, J. "Problems of the Alliance."
    Kirkpatrick, J. "Promoting Free Elections."
    Kirkpatrick, J. "The Reagan Phenomenon and the Liberal Tradition."
    Kirkpatrick, J. "Reagan Policies and Black American Goals for Africa."
    Kirkpatrick, J. "The Regan Reassertion of Western Values."
    Kirkpatrick, J. "Redefining Asian-American Ties."
    Kirkpatrick, J. "Security Council Meets to Consider Israeli Raid."
    Kirkpatrick, J. "Southern Africa: Fair Play for Namibia."
    Kirkpatrick, J. "Southern Africa: Fair Play for South Africa."
    Kirkpatrick, J. "Southern Africa: Namibia, the United Nations, and the United States."

UNITED STATES. DEPARTMENT OF ENERGY

   Ferraro, G. "Statement."

UNITED STATES. DEPARTMENT OF HEALTH AND HUMAN SERV-
      ICES

   Hawkins, P. "Statement."
   Heckler, M. "Statement." (2)

UNITED STATES. DEPARTMENT OF JUSTICE--OFFICIALS AND
      EMPLOYEES

   Smeal, E. "Statement."

UNITED STATES. DEPARTMENT OF TRANSPORTATION

   Fiedler, B. "Statement."

UNITED STATES. LAW ENFORCEMENT ASSISTANCE ADMINISTRA-
      TION

   Chisholm, S. "Statement."

UNITED STATES. OFFICE OF SURFACE MINING RECLAMATION
      AND ENFORCEMENT

   Schroeder, P. "Statement."

UNITED STATES. SUPREME COURT--OFFICIALS AND EMPLOYEES

   O'Connor, S. "Statement."
   Smeal, E. "Statement."

UNITED STATES. WOMEN'S BUREAU

   Alexander, F. "Statement." (2)
   Boxer, B. "Statement."
   Cobb, G. "Statement."
   East, C. "Statement."
   Herman, A. "Statement."
   Mixer, M. "Statement."
   Stelck, K. "Statement."
   Thomas, P. "Statement."

UNITED STATES. WOMEN'S BUREAU (cont.)
Wernick, E. "Statement."
Woodruff, C. "Statement."

UNIVERSITIES AND COLLEGES--UNITED STATES

Chisholm, S. "Statement."
Ilchman, A. "The Public Purposes of Private Colleges."

URANIUM

Lloyd, M. "Statement."

VETERANS--DISEASES

Boxer, B. "Statement."
Fenwick, M. "Statement."
Hawkins, P. "Statement."

VICTIMS OF CRIMES

Bacon, S. "Statement."
Boyle, P. "Testimony."
Largen, M. "Testimony."
Lieberman, D. "Testimony."
Robinson, C. "Testimony."
Roundtree, D. "Testimony."

VOCATIONAL GUIDANCE FOR WOMEN--UNITED STATES

Campanella, C. "Testimony."
Jeffrey, M. "Testimony."
Johnson, S. "Testimony."
Keshena, R. "Relevancy of Tribal Interests and Tribal Diversity
    In Determining the Educational Needs of American Indians."
Kidwell, C. "The Status of American Indian Women in Higher
    Education."
Martin, J. "Testimony."
Medicine, B. "The Interaction of Culture and Sex Roles in the
    Schools."
Scheirbeck, H. "Current Educational Status of American Indian
    Girls."
Walker, T. "American Indian Children."
Whiteman, H. "Insignificance of Humanity, 'Man Is Tampering
    with the Moon and the Stars.'"
Williams, A. "Transition from the Reservation to an Urban

Setting and the Changing Roles of American Indian Women."
Wood, R. "Health Problems Facing American Indian Women."

VOLUNTARISM

Gates, M. "The Changing Role in Women in Voluntarism."

WAGES--WOMEN--UNITED STATES

Accord, L. "Statement."
Barajas, G. "Statement."
Beerhalter, B. "Statement."
Berglin, L. "Statement."
Berry, M. "Statement."
Boggs, L. "Statement." (2)
Boland, J. "Statement."
Boxer, B. "Statement."
Bradshaw, R. "Statement."
Brazile, D. "Statement."
Brown, Q. "Statement."
Bryant, C. "Statement."
Burton, D. "Statement."
Campbell, J. "Statement."
Cole, E. "Statement."
Cota, K. "Statement."
Denton, C. "Statement."
DeVries, C. "Statement."
Douglas, S. "Statement."
Edwards, L. "Statement."
Farris, B. "Statement."
Futrell, M. "Statement."
Goldsberry, B. "Statement."
Goldsmith, J. "Statement." (2)
Gray, M. "Statement."
Hartmann, H. "Statement."
Hendrixson, C. "Statement."
Hutchinson, B. "Statement." (2)
Jackson, J. "Statement."
Johnson, S. "Statement."
Jones, D. "Statement."
Kaptur, M. "Statement."
Keyes, M. "Statement."
Koole, F. "Statement." (2)
Lamp, V. "Statement."
Maddox, V. "Statement."
McFadden, O. "Statement." (2)
McGibbon, N. "Statement."
Mednick, M. "Women and the Psychology of Achievement."
Merry, M. "Statement."

WAGES--WOMEN--UNITED STATES
  Mikulski, B. "Statement."
  Miller, D. "Statement."
  Mondale, J. "Statement."
  Oakar, M. "Statement." (2)
  Overly, C. "Statement."
  Rachner, M. "Statement."
  Reder, N. "Statement." (2)
  Reid, M. "Statement."
  Rock, D. "Statement." (2)
  Rothchild, N. "Statement." (2)
  Schlafly, P. "Statement." (2)
  Schroeder, P. "Statement." (4)
  Snowe, O. "Statement." (2)
  Spigelmyer, S. "Statement."
  Stein, E. "Statement."
  Steinbacher, R. "Statement."
  Steinberg, R. "Statement."
  Ter Wisscha, G. "Statement."
  Waelder, C. "Statement."
  Wainwright, C. "Statement."
  Wallace, R. "Statement."
  Warren, A. "Statement."
  Young, T. "Statement."

WATER CONSERVATION

  Smith, V. "Statement."

WATER RESOURCES DEVELOPMENT--UNITED STATES

  Bentley, H. "Statement."
  Boggs, L. "Statement."
  Fenwick, M. "Statement."
  Fiedler, B. "Statement." (6)
  Hall, K. "Statement."
  Hawkins, P. "Statement."
  Heckler, M. "Statement."
  Kaptur, M. "Statement." (3)
  Meyer, J. "Statement."
  Oakar, M. "Statement."
  Roukema, M. "Statement."
  Schroeder, P. "Statement." (2)
  Smith, V. "Statement." (3)

WIFE ABUSE--UNITED STATES

  Aal, D. "Statement."

WIFE ABUSE--UNITED STATES (cont.)
Crawford, S. "Statement."
Flynn, B. "Statement."
Hansen, S. "Statement."
Kelly-Dreiss, S. "Statement."
Key, M. "Statement."
Staples, E. "Statement."
Whetsone, G. "Statement."

WILDERNESS AREAS

Burton, S. "Statement."
Hawkins, P. "Statement." (2)

WITNESSES--UNITED STATES--PROTECTION

Smith, V. "Statement."

WOMAN (CHRISTIAN THEOLOGY)

Brown, P. "My Ministry as a Parish Secretary."
Carter, N. "A Lay Theological Perspective."
Heyward, C. "Being 'in Christ?'"
Heyward, C. "Compassion."
Heyward, C. "The Covenant."
Heyward, C. "The Enigmatic God."
Heyward, C. "Gay Pride Day."
Heyward, C. "God or Mammon?"
Heyward, C. "Judgment."
Heyward, C. "Liberating the Body."
Heyward, C. "Limits of Liberalism."
Heyward, C. "Living in the Struggle."
Heyward, C. "Must 'Jesus Christ' Be a Holy Terror?"
Heyward, C. "On Behalf of Women Priests."
Heyward, C. "On El Salvador."
Heyward, C. "Passion."
Heyward, C. "Redefining Power."
Heyward, C. "Sexual Fidelity."
McEnamy, G. "Housewife, Mother, and Parish Volunteer."
Rouner, R. "Ministry and the Life of Faith."
Spinn;ey, E. "The Ministry of a Lay Associate."
Tieran, K. "Urban Team Ministry."

WOMAN'S PEACE PARTY

Addams, J. "Patriotism and Pacifists in War Time."

WOMEN (IN RELIGION, FOLKLORE, ETC.)

Christ, C. "Why Women Need the Goddess."
Gearhart, S. "Womanpower."
Gimbutas, M. "Women and Culture in Goddess-Oriented Old Europe."
Riddle, D. "Politics, Spirituality, and Models of Change."
Starrett, B. "The Metaphors of Power."

WOMEN (THEOLOGY)

Briggs, S. "Images of Women and Jews in Nineteenth- and Twentieth-Century German Theology."
Hackett, J. "In the Days of Jael."
Ruether, R. "Address at the Womanchurch Speakes Conference."

WOMEN--CONGRESSES

Mead, M. "A Comment on the Role of Women in Agriculture."

WOMEN--DEVELOPING COUNTRIES

Boulding, E. "Integration into What?"
Cain, M. "Java, Indonesia."
Carr, M. "Technologies Appropriate for Women."
Catalia, S. "Statement."
Dauber, R. "Applying Policy Analysis to Women and Technology."
Derryck, V. "Statement."
Elmendorf, M. "Changing Role of Maya Mothers and Daughters."
Enroe, C. "Women Textile Workers in the Militarization of Southeast Asia."
Fortmann, L. "The Plight of the Invisible Farmer."
Hemmings-Gapihan, G. "Baseline Study of Socio-Economic Evaluation of Tangaye Solar Site."
Hutar, P. "Statement."
Knowles, J. "Statement."
Lewis, B. "Women in Development Planning."
Lim, L. "Women's Work in Multinational Electronics Factories."
Mukhopadhyay, C. "Sati or Shakti."
Papanek, H. "The Differential Impact of Programs and Policies on Women in Development."
Pharr, S. "Tea and Power."
Reynolds, N. "Statement."
Sacks, K. "An Overview of Women and Power in Africa."
Seidman, A. "Women and the Development of 'Underdevelopment.'"
Smith, E. "Statement."

WOMEN--DEVELOPING COUNTRIES (cont.)

Srinivasan, M. "Impact of Selected Industrial Technologies on Women in Mexico."

Tinker, I. "New Technologies for Food-Related Activities."

Walsh, M. "Statement."

WOMEN--DISEASES--UNITED STATES

Alexander, C. "Women as Victims of Crime."

Anderson, S. "Statement."

Ashley, M. "Women, Alcohol, and the Risk of Disease."

Bell, C. "Panel Discussion of Societal Responsibilities as Seen by Women."

Bingham, E. "Conference Preview."

Braun, B. "Statement."

Brinton, L. "Etiologic Factors for Invasive and Noninvasive Cervical Abnormalities."

Clark, H. "Statement."

Culler, J. "Panel Discussion of Societal Responsibilities as Seen by Women."

Conibar, S. "Women as a High-Risk Population."

Detre, K. "Hypertension in Women--A Review."

Devesa, S. "Time Trends of Cancer Incidence and Mortality Among Women."

Dye, N. "Mary Breckinridge, the Frontier Nursing Service, and the Introduction of Nurse-Midwifery in the United States."

Ernster, V. "Risk Factors for Benign and Malignant Breast Disease."

Gold, E. "Epidemiology of Pituitary Adenomas."

Goldberg, E. "Health Effects of Becoming Widowed."

Goodwin, F. "Statement."

Hamlar, P. "Panel Discussion of Legal Requirements and Implications."

Hamon, E. "Statement."

Hardy, H. "Acceptance by Dr. Hardy (of the Second Award of the Society for Occupational and Environmental Health)."

Higgins, M. "Changing Patterns of Smoking and Risk of Disease."

Hong, H. "Statement."

Hricko, A. "Panel Discussion of Societal Responsibilities as Seen by Women."

Huebner, R. "Statement."

Hulka, B. "Estrogens and Endometrial Cancer."

Hunt, V. "Radiation Exposure and Protection."

Jacobsen, G. "Statement."

Kelsey, J. "Epidemiology of Osteoporosis."

Kelty, M. "Ethical Issues and Requirements for Sex Research with Humans."

Kilburn, K. "Women in the Textile Industry."

WOMEN--DISEASES--UNITED STATES (cont.)

Kline, J. "Environmental Exposures and Spontaneous Abortion."
Krekel, S. "Placement of Workers in High-Risk Areas."
Mararushka, J. "Workers' Compensation."
Mendez, D. "Statement."
Morantz, R. "Making Women Modern."
Murphy, A. "Statement."
Potter, J. "Statement."
Prieve, C. "Job Placement for Women in the Lead Trades."
Rouse, I. "Statement."
Scholten, C. "On the Importance of the Obstetrick Art."
Simmons, D. "Statement."
Smith, A. "Congenital Minamata Disease."
Taylor, P. "Placement of Workers in High-Risk Areas."
Trebilcock, A. "Panel Discussion of Legal Requirements and Implications."
Tyler, M. "Statement."
Waldron, I. "Employment and Women's Health."
Waskel, S. "Statement."
Wofford, S. "Health Problems in the Airline Industries."

WOMEN--ECONOMIC CONDITIONS

Buchanan, M. "Excerpted Testimony from the Southern California Hearings on the Feminization of Poverty."
Denny, A. "Excerpted Testimony from the Northern California Hearings on the Feminization of Poverty."

WOMEN--EDUCATION

Barazzone, E. "Women and the Scottish Enlightenment."
Bodek, E. "Salonieres and Bluestockings."
Bunting, M. "The University's Responsibility in Educating Women for Leadership."
Chancey, V. "Motivation of Women to Leadership."
Clapp, M. "Realistic Education for Women."
Cohen, S. "Feminism as a Sophisticated Concept."
Derryck, V. "Statement."
Dujon, D. "Overcoming Barriers to Education."
Gutwirth, M. "The Education of Germaine de Stael, or Rousseau Betrayed."
Helley, J. "Harmonious Sister, Voice and Verse."
Hunt, L. "Cygnets and Ducklings."
Hutar, P. "Statement."
Hymes, V. "The State Commission for Women."
Kessler, C. "Communities of Sisters."
Knowles, J. "Statement."
Kreuger, R. "Loyalty and Betrayal."
Lane, A. "Key Address."

WOMEN--EDUCATION (cont.)

    McLean, H. "Psychological Roles for Women Public Affairs."

    Michel, A. "Projected Future Employment and Leadership Needs and Areas."

    Reiss, M. "Rosa Mayreder (1858-1938) Pioneer of Austrian Feminism."

    Rendel, M. "Educating Women for Leadership."

    Rossi, A. "Social Trends and Women's Lives--1965-1985."

    Reynolds, N. "Statement."

    Rothenberg, P. "Feminist Issues and Feminist Attitudes."

    Smith, E. "Statement."

    Tree, M. "The Dimensions of Citizenship."

    Walsh, M. "Statement."

WOMEN--EDUCATION--EUROPE--HISTORY

    Davis, N. "Gender and Genre."

    Ferrante, J. "The Education of Women in the Middle Ages in Theory, Fact, and Fantasy."

    King, M. "Book-Lined Cells."

    Labalme, P. "Women's Roles in Early Modern Venice."

WOMEN--EDUCATION--UNITED STATES

    Bernard, J. "Ground Rules for Marriage."

    Chayes, A. "The Reward and Obstacles of Community Involvement."

    Cooke, F. "Fundamental Considerations Underlying the Curriculum of the Francis W. Parker School."

    Douvan, E. "Family Roles in a Twenty-Year Perspective."

    Dunkle, M. "Statement."

    Fleming, J. "Sex Differences in the Educational and Occupational Goals of Black College Students."

    Gilligan, C. "Do Changes in Women's Rights Change Women's Moral Judgments?"

    Howe, F. "American Literature and Women's Lives."

    Howe, F. "Breaking the Disciplines."

    Howe, F. "Feminism and the Education of Women."

    Howe, F. "Feminism and the Study of Literature."

    Howe, F. "Feminism, Fiction, and the Classroom."

    Howe, F. "Feminist Scholarship."

    Howe, F. "The Future of Women's Colleges."

    Howe, F. "Literacy and Literature."

    Howe, F. "Myths of Coeducation."

    Howe, F. "The Past Ten Years."

    Howe, F. "The Power of Education."

    Howe, F. "Sex-Role Stereotypes Start Early."

    Howe, F. "Teaching in the Modern Languages."

    Howe, F. "Why Educate Women?"

WOMEN--EDUCATION--UNITED STATES (cont.)

Howe, F. "Why Educate Women? The Responses of Wellesey and Stanford."

Howe, F. "Women's Studies and Social Change."

Jensen, P. "Statement."

Kostalos, M. "Statement."

Kirkcus, M. "The Status of East European Women in the Family."

Lamphere, L. "The Economic Struggles of Female Factory Workers."

Lee, S. "The Role of Learning in the Lives of Finnish and Other Ethnic Women and a Proposal for Self-Education."

Lowry, I. "Organizing Neighborhood Women for Political and Social Action."

Malcom, S. "Statement."

McCourt, K. "Irish, Italian, and Jewish Women at the Grassroots Level."

Minnich, E. "Friends and Critics."

Newell, B. "Impact for Change."

Noschese, C. "Ethnic Women and the Media."

Porter, E. "An Experiment in Part-Time Employment of Professionals in the Federal Government."

Scanlon, L. "Changing Needs of Ethnic Women in Higher Education."

Stein, B. "Statement."

Straus, E. "The Telephone and the Microphone."

Verheyden-Hilliard, M. "Achieving the Dreams Beyond Tradition."

Vetter, B. "Statement."

Williams, E. "Pushing Out the Walls."

Wilson, E. "Developing a Neighborhood-Based Health Facility."

Woehrer, C. "Family Roles and Identities of Scandinavian and German Women."

Wolfe, L. "Statement."

WOMEN--EDUCATION (HIGHER)--UNITED STATES

Bonder, G. "The Educational Process of Women's Studies in Argentina."

Chambers, M. "What Do You Wish to Accomplish?"

Comstock, A. "Inaugural Address."

Culley, M. "Anger and Authority in the Introductory Women's Studies Classroom."

Friedman, S. "Authority in the Feminist Classroom."

Miller, N. "Mastery, Identity and the Politics of Work."

Rich, A. "Taking Women Students Seriously."

WOMEN--EMPLOYMENT

Astin, H. "Patterns of Women's Occupations."

Bennett, S. "The Re-Entry Woman."

WOMEN--EMPLOYMENT (cont.)

Bergmann, B. "The United States of America."

Bird, C. "Two Paycheck Power."

Bonner, D. "Women as Caregivers."

Deaux, K. "Internal Barriers."

Dewine, S. "Breakthrough."

Ewell, Y. "Viable Alternative to Traditional Education for Minorities and Women."

Fitzpatrick, M. "Effective Interpersonal Communication for Women of the Corporation."

Gradford, J. "Caregivers' Wages."

Honig, E. "Burning Incense, Pledging Sisterhood."

Jones, T. "Sexual Harassment in the Organization."

Kamerman, S. "Work and Family in Industrialized Societies."

Kane, R. "The Occupational Choices of Young Women as Affected by Schools and Parents."

Lamphere, L. "Bringing the Family to Work."

Lapidus, G. "The Soviet Union."

Michel, H. "The Federal Government and the War on Youth Movement."

Minge, W. "The Industrial Revolution and the European Family."

Moe, A. "Women and Work."

Moore, K. "The Social and Economic Consequences of Teenage Childbearing."

Mullins, L. "Uneven Development."

Norwood, J. "The Facts of Life for a Teen-Aged Girl."

Papanek, H. "Low-Income Countries."

Perry, B. "Three Career Traps for Women."

Putnam, L. "Lady You're Trapped."

Reivitz, L. "Women's Achievements Towards Equality."

Safa, H. "Runaway Shops and Female Employment."

Seltzer, M. "Research Perspectives for Programming to Meet the Needs of Youth in Transition from School to Work."

Sexton, P. "Where Women Find Work."

Smith, P. "Networking."

Stead, B. "Why Does the Secretary Hate Me and Other Laments of the Professionally Educated Woman Employee."

Stead, B. "Women and Men in Management."

Taylor, B. "The Men Are as Bad as Their Master."

Tilly, L. "Paths of Proletarianization."

Verheyden-Hilliard, M. "Assisting the School-to-Work Transition for Young Women."

Weiner, A. "Forgotten Wealth."

Wernick, E. "The Concerns of the Labor Movement with Youth Programs for Women."

Wolf, M. "The People's Republic of China."

Ziadeh, M. "Woman and Work."

WOMEN--EMPLOYMENT--LAW AND LEGISLATION--UNITED STATES

Bell, C. "Implementing Safety and Health Regulations for Women

WOMEN--EMPLOYMENT--LAW AND LEGISLATION (cont.)
    in the Workplace."
  Bingham, E. "Should the Congress Enact S.2153 to Amend the
      Occupational Safety and Health Act?"
  Briscoe, A. "Statement."
  Bryd, A. "Statement."
  Canellos, G. "Testimony."
  Cooper, M. "Statement."
  Heagstedt, N. "Testimony."
  Heckler, M. "Testimony."
  Hernandez, A. "Statement."
  Holmes, J. "Statement."
  King-Reynolds, W. "Statement."
  MacLeod, J. "Testimony."
  Morisey, M. "Statement."
  Murray, L. "Statement."
  Piercy, D. "Statement."
  Porter, E. "Testimony."
  Sawhill, I. "Testimony."
  Schlafly, P. "Statement."
  Seaman, B. "Statement."
  Shoong, E. "Testimony."
  Smeal, E. "Statement."

WOMEN--EMPLOYMENT--UNITED STATES

  Abzug, B. "Statement."
  Alexander, F. "Statement."
  Alexander, L. "Statement." (2)
  Allen, C. "Statement."
  American, S. "Organization."
  Bailyn, L. "The Apprenticeship Model of Organizational Careers."
  Barrett, N. "Comment on 'New Evidence on the Dynamics of
      Female Labor Supply.'"
  Behr, M. "Statement."
  Bell, C. "Panel Discussion on Societal Responsibilities as Seen
      by Women."
  Bell, C. "Statement."
  Beller, A. "The Impact of Equal Employment Opportunity Laws
      on the Male-Female Earnings Differential."
  Beller, A. "Occupational Segregation and the Earnings Gap."
  Benson, S. "Women in Retail Sales Work."
  Berger, B. "Occupational Segregation and the Earnings Gap."
  Bergmann, B. "Statement." (2)
  Bernard, J. "Ground Rules for Marriage."
  Berry, M. "Statement."
  Bingham, E. "Conference Preview."
  Blank, H. "Statement."
  Blau, F. "The Impact of the Unemployment Rate on Labor Force
      Entries and Exits."

WOMEN--EMPLOYMENT--UNITED STATES (cont.)

Hardy, H. "Acceptance by Dr. Hardy."

Heckler, M. "Statement."

Herman, A. "Statement." (2)

Hock, C. "Residential Location and Transportation Analyses."

Honig, A. "Child Care Options and Decisions."

Howard, C. "Moving Into Senior Management."

Howe, S. "A Legislative Perspective."

Hilton, M. "Priorities as Viewed from a Federal Agency."

Hricko, A. "Panel Discussion on Societal Responsibilities as Seen by Women."

Hunt, V. "Radiation Exposure and Protection."

Johnson, G. "Statement."

Johnson, G. "Statement."

Johnson, M. "Statement."

Jones, B. "Introductory Remarks on Work and Family Roles."

Joyner, N. "Statement."

Kaplan, A. "Statement."

Kassebaum, N. "Statement." (2)

Kern, C. "Statement."

Kidder, A. "Transportation Problems of Low Income Women as Members of the Transportation Disadvantaged."

Kievit, M. "Statement."

Kilburn, K. "Women in the Textile Industry."

Klein, F. "The Transportation Implications of Women's Fear of Assault."

Klenke-Hamel, K. "Causal Determinants of Job Satisfaction in Dual Career Couples."

Kocher, J. "Career Conflicts and Solutions."

Kostalos, M. "Statement."

Krekel, S. "Placement of Workers in High-Risk Areas."

Krickus, M. "The Status of East European Women in the Family."

Lamphere, L. "The Economic Struggle of Female Factory Workers."

Lamphere, L. "On the Shop Floor."

Lee, K. "Myths and Realities."

Lee, S. "The Role of Learning in the Lives of Finnish and Other Ethnic Women and Proposal for Self-Education."

Liburdi, L. "Speech."

Lloyd-Jones, E. "Education for Reentry into the Labor Force."

Loden, M. "Networking."

Lopata, H. "Women's Travel Issues."

Lowry, I. "Organizing Neighborhood Women for Political and Social Action."

Lubetkin, R. "Statement."

Lyons, E. "Statement."

Maccoby, E. "Effects Upon Children of Their Mothers' Outside Employment."

Machung, A. "Work Processing."

Madden, J. "Comment on Occupational Segregation Among Women."

Madison, A. "Statement."

WOMEN--EMPLOYMENT--UNITED STATES (cont.)
   Makarushka, J. "Workers' Compensation."
   Malcom, S. "Statement."
   McChesney, K. "Myths and Realities."
   McCourt, K. "Irish, Italian, and Jewish Women at the Grassroots
      Level."
   McKenna, M. "The View from the White House."
   Mixer, M. "Statement."
   Murphree, M. "Brave New Office."
   Nieva, V. "The Feminization of the Labor Force."
   Noschese, C. "Ethnic Women and the Media."
   O'Farrell, B. "Women and Nontraditional Blue Collar Jobs in the
      1980s."
   O'Neill, J. "Comparable Worth as a Remedy for Sex Discrimina-
      tion."
   O'Neill, J. "Statement."
   Owens, M. "Career Conflicts and Solutions."
   Palmer, P. "Housework and Domestic Labor."
   Panzini, M. "Statement."
   Pendergrass, V. "Stress in the Lives of Female Law Enforcement
      Officials."
   Peters, L. "Statement."
   Pines, M. "Statement."
   Porter, S. "Statement."
   Prieve, C. "Job Placement of Women in the Lead Trades--A
      Workers' Position."
   Pudvah, A. "Statement."
   Rothchild, N. "Factual Overview."
   Quarm, D. "Sexual Inequality."
   Rawlings, E. "Myths and Realities."
   Robinson, J. "Statement."
   Rockefeller, S. "Statement."
   Ross, C. "Measuring the Distribution Impact of Transportation
      Service on Women."
   Sacks, K. "Computers, Ward Secretaries, and a Walkout in a
      Southern Hospital."
   Sacks, K. "Generations of Working-Class Families."
   Saenz, R. "Statement."
   Samora, B. "Statement."
   Sapienza, J. "Statement."
   Sawhill, I. "Comment on Male-Female Wage Differentials."
   Sawhill, I. "Conference Summary."
   Sawhill, I. "Statement."
   Scanlon, L. "Changing Needs of Ethnic Women in Higher Educa-
      tion."
   Schlafly, P. "Statement."
   Schroeder, P. "Statement." (2)
   Scrivner, E. "Acculturating Women into Law Enforcement Ca-
      reers."
   Sen, L. "Travel Patterns and Behavior of Women in Urban Areas."
   Shalala, D. "Speech."

WOMEN--EMPLOYMENT--UNITED STATES (cont.)

Shapiro-Perl, N. "Resistance Strategies."

Shed, S. "Statement."

Shaw, L. "Economic Consequences of Marital Disruption."

Smith, A. "Congenital Minamata Disease."

Snowe, O. "Statement." (2)

Sommers, T. "Statement."

Stein, E. "Statement."

Steinberg, R. "Comparable Worth Doctrine and Its Implementation."

Stelck, K. "Statement."

Stephenson, W. "Statement."

Stillman, F. "Balancing Work, Family and Personal Lives."

Strober, M. "Comment on An Evaluation of Sex Discrimination."

Strober, M. "Some Policy Research Issues Relating to Women's
Employment."

Taylor, P. "Placement of Workers in High-Risk Areas--A Legislative Viewpoint."

Tenopyr, M. "Implications of the Increasing Participation of
Women in the Work Force in the 1990's."

Thomas, M. "Statement."

Thomas, P. "Statement."

Tischler, B. "Myths and Realities."

Trebilcock, A. "Panel Discussion of Legal Requirements and Implications."

Turner, C. "Speech."

Vaughn, B. "Statement."

Verheyden-Hilliard, M. "Achieving the Dreams Beyond Tradition."

Verheyden-Hilliard, M. "Statement."

Vetter, B. "Statement."

Wallace, P. "Comment on Male-Female Wage Differentials."

Wallace, P. "Increased Labor Force Participation of Women and
Affirmative Action."

Weinberg, L. "Susie Weinberg."

Weiss, C. "Introductory Remarks on What Policymakers Need to
Know That Research Can Address."

Wernick, E. "Statement."

Wiener, M. "Statement."

Wilson, E. "Developing a Neighborhood-Based Health Facility."

Woehrer, C. "Family Roles and Identities of Scandinavian and
German Women."

Wofford, S. "Health Problems in the Airline Industries."

Woodruff, C. "Statement."

Young, J. "Statement."

Zavella, P. "Abnormal Intimacy."

Zemotal, L. "Travel Patterns of Women and Men Based on Stage
in Family Life Cycle."

WOMEN--EMPLOYMENT--UNITED STATES--HISTORY

Barry, L. "Report of the General Investigator, 1887."

WOMEN--EMPLOYMENT--UNITED STATES--HISTORY (cont.)

Barry, L. "Report of the General Investigator, 1889."
Hill, A. "Protection of Women Workers and the Courts."
Hunt, V. "A Brief History of Women Workers and Hazards in the Workplace."
Lemlich, C. "Address at Cooper Union in April, 1912."
Lemlich, C. "Senators Vs. Working Women."
O'Reilly, L. "Leonora O'Reilly's Congressional Statement."
Schepps, M. "Address at Cooper Union, April, 1912."
Schneiderman, R. "Senators Vs. Working Women."
Schneiderman, R. "Speech on Suffrage."
Scott, M. "Address at Cooper Union, April 1912."

WOMEN--EUROPE--HISTORY

Davis, N. "Gender and Genre."
Davis, N. "Women's History in Transition."
Falk, J. "The New Technology for Research in European Women's History."
Ferrante, J. "The Education of Women in the Middle Ages in Theory, Fact, and Fantasy."
King, M. "Book-Lined Cells."
Labalme, P. "Women's Roles in Early Modern Venice."

WOMEN--EUROPE, EASTERN

Bohachevsky-Chomiak, M. "Ukrainian Feminism in Interwar Poland."
Fischer, M. "Women in Romanian Politics."
Freeze, K. "Medical Education for Women in Austria."
Jancar, B. "Women in the Opposition in Poland and Czecho-slovakia in the 1970s."
Kligman, G. "The Rites of Women."
Reed, M. "Peasant Women of Croatia in the Interwar Years."
Rosenberg, D. "The Emancipation of Women in Fact and Fiction."
Wolchik, S. "The Precommunist Legacy, Economic Development, Social Transformation, and Women's Roles in Eastern Europe."
Woodward, S. "The Rights of Women."

WOMEN--FOLKLORE

Langlois, J. "Belle Gunness, The Lady Bluebeard."

WOMEN--GREECE

Humphreys, S. "Public and Private Interests in Classical Athens."

WOMEN--HEALTH AND HYGIENE--DEVELOPING COUNTRIES

Apodaca, P. "Migrant Workers."
Badran, M. "Contamination in Practice."
Blair, P. "The Women and Health Connection."
Cross, K. "Health Problems of Native Americans."
Elmendorf, M. "Women, Water, and Waste."
Gibbons, L. "The Challenge for Health Care Providers."
Jackson, E. "Two Projects in Rural North Carolina, U.S.A."
Jett-Ali, J. "Traditional Birth Attendants and the Need for
    Training."
Kramer, J. "Urban Indians, A Neglected Group."
Lear, J. "Women's Health Needs in the United States."
Lukas, T. "Integrating Women in Development."
Masson, V. "An Example of Holistic Care."
Salazar, S. "Recommendations Regarding Latina Women."

WOMEN--HEALTH AND HYGIENE--PHYSIOLOGY

Barnes, H. "Reproduction, Obstetric Care, and Infertility."
Blake, J. "Demographic Revolution and Family Evolution."
Block, J. "Psychological Development of Female Children and
    Adolescents."
Brown, M. "Black Women's Nutritional Problems."
Ferris, C. "The Women's Movement as Catalyst for Change in
    Obstetrical Care Service."
Hodgman, J. "Pregnancy Outcome, Neonatal Mortality."
Hoffman, L. "Social Change and Its Effects on Parents and
    Children."
Jackson, J. "Death Rate Trends of Black Females, United
    States, 1964-1978."
Maymi, C. "Women in the Labor Force."
Presser, H. "Working Women and Child Care."
Ramey, E. "The Natural Capacity for Health in Women."
Reid, P. "Socialization of Black Female Children."
Strober, M. "Market Work, Housework and Child Care."
Verbrugge, L. "Women's Social Roles and Health."

WOMEN--HEALTH AND HYGIENE--UNITED STATES

Anthony, S. "Guaranteed to Us and Our Daughters Forever."
Bellamy, C. "Keynote Address."
Dye, N. "Mary Breckinridge, the Frontier Nursing Service, and
    the Introduction of Nurse-Midwifery in the United States."
Ehrenreich, B. "Luncheon Address."
Gaynor, F. "Health Services Administration."
Goren, S. "Luncheon Address."
Hollinshead, M. "Health Professional Education."
Miles, P. "Opening Remarks."

WOMEN--HEALTH AND HYGIENE--UNITED STATES (cont.)
Morantz, R. "Making Women Modern."
Rodriguez-Trias, H. "Health Care Delivery."
Scholten, C. "On the Importance of the Obstetrick Art."
Waldron, I. "Employment and Women's Health."
Warden, G. "My Work and Welcome to It."
Young, M. "Women, Civilization, and the Indian Question."

WOMEN--HISTORY

Antler, J. "Was She a Good Mother?"
Berggren, A. "Education and Equality for Women."
Berggren, A. "Is the Question of Women a Political Question?"
Bilinkoff, J. "The Holy Woman and the Urban Community in
    Sixteenth-Century Avila."
Branca, P. "Image and Reality."
Brown, J. "Child Bearing, Child Rearing, Abortion, and Con-
    traception."
Brown, J. "Is the Question of Women a Political Question?"
Brumberg, J. "The Ethnological Mirror."
Bunting, M. "The University's Responsibility in Educating Women
    for Leadership."
Ceballos, J. "The Future of Women."
Chancey, V. "Motivation of Women to Leadership."
Cisler, C. "Child Bearing, Child Rearing, Abortion, and Con-
    traception."
Cisler, C. "Education and Equality for Women."
Cook, C. "Child Bearing, Child Rearing, Abortion, and Con-
    traception."
Cowan, R. "A Case Study of Technological and Social Change."
Decrow, K. "Is the Question of Women a Political Question?"
Dubois, E. "The Limitations of Sisterhood."
Ducrocq, F. "The London Biblewomen and Nurses Missions,
    1857-1880."
Fee, E. "The Sexual Politics of Victorian Social Anthropology."
Fisher, M. "The Future of Women in America."
Fisher, M. "Is the Question of Women a Political Question?"
Frenier, M. "The Effects of the Chinese Revolution on Women
    and Their Families."
Friedan, B. "Education and Equality for Women."
Friedan, B. "How Do Men Look at Women."
Friedan, B. "Is the Question of Women a Political Question?"
Friedman, J. "Piety and Kin."
Gampel, G. "The Planter's Wife Revisited."
Gordon, L. "Voluntary Motherhood."
Graham, P. "The Cult of True Womanhood."
Gullett, G. "City Mothers, City Daughters, and the Dance Hall
    Girls."
Handy, C. "The Black Woman in America."
Higgins, D. "Child Bearing, Child Rearing, Abortion, and Con-
    traception."

WOMEN--HISTORY--MIDDLE AGES, 500-1500

Bell, S. "Christine De Pizan (1364-1430)."
Willard, C. "A Fifteenth-Century View of Women's Role in Medieval Society."

WOMEN--HISTORY--GREAT BRITAIN

Davidoff, L. "Class and Gender in Victorian England."

WOMEN--INTELLECTUAL LIFE

Dye, N. "Clio's American Daughters."
Elshtain, J. "Methodological Sophistication and Conceptual Confusion."
Parsons, K. "Moral Revolution."
Schulenburg, J. "Clio's European Daughters."
Sherif, C. "Bias in Psychology."
Smith, D. "A Sociology for Women."
Stimpson, C. "The Power to Name."

WOMEN--JAPAN

Green, V. "A Japanese Experience."

WOMEN--LANGUAGES

Baumann, M. "Two Features of 'Women's Speech?'"
Dumas, B. "Male-Female Conversational Interaction Cues."
Hartford, B. "Phonological Differences in the English of Adolescent Chicanas and Chicanos."
Hartman, M. "A Descriptive Study of the Language of Men and Women Born in Maine Around 1900 as It Reflects the Lakoff Hypotheses in 'Language and Women's Place.'"
Nichols, P. "Black Women in the Rural South."
Redlinger, W. "Mothers' Speech to Children in Bilingual Mexican-American Homes."
Sole, Y. "Sociocultural and Sociopsychological Factors in Differential Language Retentiveness by Sex."
Swacker, M. "Women's Verbal Behavior at Learned and Professional Conferences."
Zimmerman, M. "Alignment Strategies in Verbal Accounts of Problematic Conduct."

WOMEN--LATIN AMERICA

Jacquette, J. "Legitimizing Political Women."

WOMEN--LATIN AMERICA (cont.)
Leacock, E. "Women, Development, and Anthropological Facts and Fictions."

WOMEN--LEGAL STATUS, LAWS, ETC.--UNITED STATES

Blank, H. "Statement."
Briscoe, A. "Statement."
Brubaker, C. "Statement."
Campbell, N. "Statement."
Compton, G. "Statement."
Dunkle, M. "Statement."
East, C. "Statement."
Ferraro, G. "Statement." (2)
Fiedler, B. "Statement."
Goldfarb, S. "Statement."
Greenburger, M. "Statement."
Hall, R. "Statement."
Hawkins, P. "Statement."
King-Reynolds, W. "Statement."
Kostalos, M. "Statement."
Malcom, S. "Statement."
Mallett, C. "Statement."
Mazo, J. "Statement."
McElderry, B. "Statement."
Mendelson, J. "Statement."
Moss, A. "Statement." (2)
Murphy, E. "Statement."
Murray, L. "Statement."
O'Connell, M. "Statement."
Palast, G. "Statement."
Rogin, C. "Statement."
Schlafly, P. "Statement."
Schroeder, P. "Statement."
Schub, J. "Statement."
Seaman, B. "Statement."
Smeal, E. "Statement."
Snowe, O. "Statement."
Sowards, J. "Statement."
Stuchiner, T. "Statement."
Theis, F. "Statement."
Tice, P. "Statement."
Vetter, B. "Statement."

WOMEN--LEGAL STATUS, LAWS, ETC. (CANON LAW)

Cardman, F. "Tradition, Hermeneutics and Ordination."
Foley, N. "Woman in Vatican Documents--1960 to the Present."
Meagher, K. "Women in Relation to Orders and Jurisdiction."

WOMEN--MENTAL HEALTH

    Blechman, E. "Behavior Therapies."
    Gilbert, L. "Feminist Therapy."
    Kravetz, D. "Consciousness-Raising and Self-Help."
    McMahon, S. "Women in Marital Transition."
    Sherman, J. "Therapist Attitudes and Sex-Role Stereotyping."
    Walker, L. "Battered Women."
    Weissman, M. "Depression."
    Wilkinson, D. "Minority Women."

WOMEN--PENSIONS--LAW AND LEGISLATION--UNITED STATES

    Brubaker, C. "Statement."
    Burgess, G. "Statement."
    Callahan, P. "Statement."
    Campbell, N. "Statement."
    Collin, C. "Statement."
    Compton, G. "Statement."
    East, C. "Statement."
    Ferraro, G. "Statement." (2)
    Fiedler, B. "Statement."
    Godbold, R. "Statement."
    Goldfarb, S. "Statement."
    Goode, M. "Statement."
    Gray, M. "Statement."
    Mallett, C. "Statement."
    Mazo, J. "Statement."
    Mendelson, J. "Statement."
    Moss, A. "Statement." (2)
    Murphy, E. "Statement."
    O'Connell, M. "Statement."
    Palast, G. "Statement." (2)
    Rogin, C. "Statement."
    Roukema, M. "Statement."
    Sandage, S. "Statement."
    Schneider, C. "Statement."
    Schroeder, P. "Statement."
    Schub, J. "Statement." (2)
    Snow, O. "Statement."
    Stuchiner, T. "Statement."
    Theis, F. "Statement."
    Tice, P. "Statement."
    Wyatt, A. "Statement."
    Yager, E. "Statement."

WOMEN--PSYCHOLOGY

    Barnes, H. "Reproduction, Obstetric Care, and Infertility."

WOMEN--PSYCHOLOGY (cont.)

Belle, D. "Mothers and Their Children."

Belovitch, T. "The Experience of Abortion."

Bem, S. "Beyond Androgyny."

Blake, J. "Demographic Revolution and Family Evolution."

Block, J. "Another Look at Sex Differentiation in the Socialization Behaviors of Mothers and Fathers."

Block, J. "Psychological Development of Female Children and Adolescents."

Brown, M. "Black Women's Nutritional Problems."

Ferris, C. "The Women's Movement as Catalyst for Change in Obstetrical Care Service."

Gullahorn, J. "Sex-Related Factors in Cognition and in Brain Lateralization."

Gump, J. "Reality and Myth."

Helson, R. "Creativity in Women."

Hodgman, J. "Pregnancy Outcome, Neonatal Mortality."

Hoffman, L. "Social Change and Its Effects on Parents and Children."

Jackson, J. "Death Rate Trends of Black Females, United States, 1964-1978."

Komarovsky, M. "Dilemmas of Masculinity in a Changing World."

Laws, J. "Work Motivation and Work Behavior of Women."

Lemkau, J. "Women and Employment."

Loewenstein, S. "Passion as a Mental Health Hazard."

Loewenstein, S. "Toward Choice and Differentiation in the Midlife Crisis of Women."

Maccoby, E. "Woman's Sociobiological Heritage."

Macklin, R. "Designated Discussion (Ethical Requirements for Sex Research in Humans)."

Maymi, C. "Women in the Labor Force."

Mednick, M. "The New Psychology of Women."

Parlee, M. "Psychological Aspects of Menstruation, Childbirth, and Menopause."

Presser, H. "Working Women and Child Care."

Ramey, E. "The Natural Capacity for Health in Women."

Reid, P. "Socialization of Black Female Children."

Rosenberg, R. "In Search of Woman's Nature, 1850-1920."

Russo, N. "Beyond Adolescence."

Spence, J. "Traits, Roles and the Concept of Androgyny."

Strober, M. "Market Work, Housework and Child Care."

Tyson, C. "Communicating With Self and Others."

Unger, R. "The Politics of Gender."

Verbrugge, L. "Women's Social Roles and Health."

Waber, D. "The Meaning of Sex-Related Variation in Maturation Rate."

Weissman, M. "The Treatment of Depressed Women."

WOMEN--RELIGIOUS LIFE

Hellwig, M. "Christian Women in a Troubled World."

WOMEN--RELIGIOUS LIFE (cont.)
   Pendergrass, V. "Stress in the Lives of Female Law Enforcement
      Officials."

WOMEN--RUSSIA

   Carden, P. "The Woman Student in Russia."
   Cox, R. "Marriage and the Family."
   Dunham, V. "The Changing Image of Women in Soviet Litera-
      ture."

WOMEN--SEXUAL BEHAVIOR

   Allison, D. "Public Silence, Private Terror."
   Altman, M. "Everything They Always Wanted You to Know."
   Bem, S. "Beyond Androgyny."
   Block, J. "Another Look at Sex Differentiation in the Socializa-
      tion Behaviors of Mothers and Fathers."
   Calderone, M. "Above and Beyond Politics."
   Dimen, M. "Politically Correct?"
   Echols, A. "The Taming of the Id."
   Espin, O. "Cultural and Historical Influences on Sexuality in
      Hispanic/Latin Women."
   Fuchs, J. "Female Eroticism in The Second Sex."
   Galler, R. "The Myth of the Perfect Body."
   Ginsberg, F. "The Body Politic."
   Gordon, B. "Variety."
   Gump, J. "Reality and Myth."
   Harvey, B. "No More Nice Girls."
   Helson, R. "Creativity in Women."
   Hollibaugh, A. "Desire for the Future."
   Kruger, B. "No Progress in Pleasure."
   Laws, J. "Work Motivation and Work Behavior of Women."
   Millett, K. "Beyond Politics?"
   Munter, C. "Fat and the Fantasy of Perfection."
   Nestle, J. "The Feminine Question."
   Parlee, M. "Psychological Aspects of Menstruation, Childbirth,
      and Menopause."
   Robinson, P. "The Historical Repression of Women's Sexuality."
   Rubin, G. "Thinking Sex."
   Russo, N. "Beyond Adolescence."
   Silverman, K. "Historie d'O."
   Spillers, H. "Interstices."
   Thompson, S. "Search for Tomorrow."
   Unger, R. "The Politics of Gender."
   Vance, C. "Pleasure and Danger."
   Webster, P. "The Forbidden."

WOMEN--SOCIAL CONDITIONS

Bem, S. "Beyond Androgyny."
Block, J. "Another Look at Sex Differentiation in the Socialization Behaviors of Mothers and Fathers."
Chaney, E. "Testimony."
Dye, N. "Clio's American Daughters."
Elshtain, J. "Methodological Sophistication and Conceptual Confusion."
Fraser, A. "Testimony."
Gump. J. "Reality and Myth."
Height, D. "Testimony."
Helson, R. "Creativity in Women."
Laws, J. "Work Motivation and Work Behavior of Women."
Leonard, K. "Women and Social Change in Modern India."
Michel, A. "Projected Future Employment and Leadership Needs and Areas."
Parlee, M. "Psychological Aspects of Menstruation, Childbirth, and Menopause."
Parson, K. "Moral Revolution."
Rendel, M. "Educating Women for Leadership."
Rich, A. "Notes Toward a Politics of Location."
Rossi, A. "Social Trends and Women's Lives--1965-1985."
Russo, N. "Beyond Adolescence."
Schulenburg, J. "Clio's European Daughters."
Sherif, C. "Bias in Psychology."
Smith, D. "A Sociology for Women."
Stimpson, C. "The Power to Name."
Turbitt, C. "Testimony."
Unger, R. "The Politics of Gender."
Willard, C. "A Fifteenth-Century View of Women's Role in Medieval Society."
Zavala, I. "Concluding Remarks."

WOMEN--SOCIAL REFORMERS--UNITED STATES

Addams, J. "The Subjective Necessity for Social Settlements."
Anthony, S. "Demand for Party Recognition."
Bethune, M. "A Century of Progress of Negro Women."
Catt, C. "Why Are Only Women Compelled to Prove Themselves?"
Dix, D. "On Behalf of the Insane Poor in Kentucky."
Eastman, C. "We Have the Vote, Now We Can Begin."
Eddy, M. "Christian Health."
Flynn, E. "The Truth About the Paterson Strike."
Foster, A. "It Is the Pulpit Who Casts Out 'Impure' Women."
Gilman, C. "The Humanness of Women."
Goldman, E. "Preparedness."
Grimke, A. "The North, Go On! Go On!"
Harper, F. "Liberty for Slaves."
Hutchinson, A. "The Examination of Mrs. Anne Hutchinson."

WOMEN--SOCIAL REFORMERS--UNITED STATES (cont.)

Kelley, F. "The Child, the State, and the Nation."

Laflesche, S. "The Plight of the Ponca Indians."

Lease, M. "The Red Dragon of Wall Street Vs. the Farmer."

Mott, L. "Why Should Not Woman Seek to Be a Reformer?"

Nation, C. "Prohibition of Abolition--What It Means."

O'Hare, K. "Farewell Address of a Socialist."

O'Reilly, L. "Women's Opportunities in the Civil Service."

Paul, A. "Forming the Woman's Party."

Rose, E. "The Necessity for the Utter Extinction of Slavery."

Sampson, D. "An Address on Life as a Female Revolutionary Soldier."

Sanger, M. "A Moral Necessity for Birth Control."

Schneiderman, R. "Under What Conditions Women Work."

Shaw, A. "The Heavenly Visitation."

Stanton, E. "The Case for Universal Suffrage."

Steward, M. "African Rights and Liberty."

Stone, L. "Nature and Revelation and Woman's Right to Vote."

Tarbel, I. "The History of the Standard Oil Company."

Terrell, M. "What It Means to Be Colored in the Capital of the United States."

Truth, S. "Ain't I a Woman?"

Truth, S. "Equal Rights for All."

Wald, L. "The Nurses' Settlement in New York."

Wells-Barnett, I. "Southern Horrors."

Willard, F. "Temperance and Home Protection."

Woodhull, V. "The Principles of Social Freedom."

Wright, F. "Of Free Enquiry."

WOMEN--SOUTHERN STATES--HISTORY

Friedman, J. "Women's History and the Revision of Southern History."

Harley, S. "Black Women in a Southern City."

Janiewski, D. "Sisters Under Their Skins."

Jones, A. "Southern Literary Women as Chronicles of Southern Life."

Scott, A. "Are We the Women Our Grandmothers Were."

Scott, A. "Education and the Contemporary Woman."

Scott, A. "Education of Women."

Scott, A. "Getting to Be a Notable Georgia Woman."

Scott, A. "Historians Construct the Southern Woman."

Scott, A. "Old Wives' Tales."

Scott, A. "Woman's Place Is in the History Books."

Scott, A. "Women's Perspective on the Patriarchy in the 1850s."

Scott, A. "Women's Voluntary Association in the Forming of American Society."

Swain, M. "The Public Role of Southern Women."

WOMEN--SOUTHERN STATES--SOCIAL CONDITIONS

Bellows, B. "My Children, Gentlemen, Are My Own."
Berkeley, K. "Colored Ladies Also Contributed."
Blester, C. "The Perrys of Greenville."
Clinton, C. "Caught in the Web of the Big House."
Perdue, T. "Southern Indians and the Cult of True Womanhood."
Walsh, L. "The Experiences and Status of Women in the Chesapeake, 1750-1775."

WOMEN--STUDY AND TEACHING (HIGHER)--UNITED STATES

Bergman, S. "Library Resources on Women."
Butler, J. "The Humanities."
Cott, N. "The Women's Studies Program."
Fritsche, J. "Moving Beyond the Curriculum."
Goldsmid, P. "In-House Resources."
Lynch, F. "A View from the Funding Agencies."
Maher, F. "Appropriate Teaching Methods for Integrating Women."
McIntosh, P. "Interactive Phases of Curricular Re-Vision."
Schmidt, R. "Women, Gender, and the Curriculum."
Schmitz, B. "From Issue to Action."
Schmitz, B. "Project on Women in the Curriculum."
Sims-Wood, J. "Resources in Black Women's Studies."
Spanier, B. "The Natural Sciences."
Spanier, B. "Toward a Balanced Curriculum."
Stimpson, C. "Where Does Integration Fit."
Tolpin, M. "Wheaton's Assessment Process."

WOMEN--SUFFRAGE--UNITED STATES

Brown, O. "Address on Woman Suffrage."
Brown, O. "Christian Charity."
Brown, O. "Crime and the Remedy."
Brown, O. "Hand of Fellowship."
Brown, O. "Margaret Fuller."
Brown, O. "The Opening Doors."
Brown, O. "United States Citizenship."
Brown, O. "Where Is the Mistake?"
Brown, O. "Woman's Place in the Church."
Brown, O. "Woman's Suffrage."
Brown, O. "Women and Skepticism."
Dubois, E. "The Radicalism of the Woman Suffrage Movement."

WOMEN--TAXATION

Blank, H. "Statement."

WOMEN--TAXATION (cont.)
  Brubaker, C. "Statement."
  Campbell, N. "Statement."
  Compton, G. "Statement."
  East, C. "Statement."
  Ferraro, G. "Statement."
  Fiedler, B. "Statement."
  Goldfarb, S. "Statement."
  Mallett, C. "Statement."
  Mazo, J. "Statement."
  Mendelson, J. "Statement."
  Moss, A. "Statement."
  Murphy, E. "Statement."
  O'Connell, M. "Statement."
  Palast, G. "Statement."
  Rogin, C. "Statement."
  Schroeder, P. "Statement."
  Schub, J. "Statement."
  Snowe, O. "Statement."
  Theis, F. "Statement."
  Tice, P. "Statement."

WOMEN--UNITED STATES

  Adlon, S. "Sex Differences in Adjustment to Widowhood."
  Albert, E. "The Unmothered Woman."
  Bane, M. "The American Divorce Rate."
  Bardwick, J. "The Seasons of a Woman's Life."
  Baum, J. "Coping Patterns in Widowhood."
  Bernard, J. "Ground Rules for Marriage."
  Candy, S. "Social Support for Women in Transition."
  Cole-Alexander, L. "Statement."
  Colten, M. "Heroin Addiction Among Women."
  Corcoran, M. "Sex-Based Wage Differentials."
  Diamond, I. "Women, Representation and Public Policy."
  Douvan, E. "Family Roles in a Twenty-Year Perspective."
  Douvan, E. "Toward A New Policy for the Family."
  Faver, C. "Generational and Life-Cycle Effects on Women's
      Achievement Orientation."
  Fethke, C. "Living Too Long, Dying Too Young, and Disability
      for the Homemaker."
  Fleming, J. "Sex Differences in the Educational and Occupational
      Goals of Black College Students."
  Forisha, B. "Assessing the Atmosphere."
  Gasper, J. "Statement."
  Giele, J. "Crossovers."
  Gilligan, C. "Do Changes in Women's Rights Change Woman's
      Moral Judgments?"
  Gilligan, C. "Restoring the Missing Text of Women's Development
      to Life Cycle Theories."

WOMEN--UNITED STATES
    Gordus, J. "Women in CETA."
    Hauserman, N. "The American Homemaker."
    Herrick, A. "Statement."
    Jensen, P. "Statement."
    Kane, M. "Statement of Pope John Paul II."
    Kohen, J. "Widowhood and Well-Being."
    Komarovsky, M. "Women's Roles."
    Lee, D. "To Be or Not to Be."
    Lutter, J. "The Minnesota Experience."
    Manis, J. "Transition to Work."
    Markus, H. "Work, Women and Well-Being."
    McGeorge, J. "Women and Policy Making in the Housing Area."
    Merriam, E. "Woman's Expectations."
    Mikus, K. "Psychological Correlates of Early Family Formation."
    Mueller, K. "Education."
    Parson, J. "The Effects of Teachers' Expectancies and Attribu-
        tion of Students' Expectancies for Success in Mathematics."
    Plunkett, M. "Meanings of Work for Mothers."
    Porter, S. "Representing the 80 Percent."
    Putney, G. "Children."
    Reynolds, N. "Statement."
    Rich, A. "Commencement Address at Smith College, 1979."
    Ruffin, J. "Address to the First National Conference of Colored
        Women."
    Schlafly, P. "Controversy over the Equal Rights Amendment."
    Scott, A. "Are We the Women Our Grandmothers Were?"
    Scott, A. "Education and the Contemporary Woman."
    Scott, A. "Education of Women."
    Scott, A. "Getting to Be a Notable Georgia Woman."
    Scott, A. "Historians Construct the Southern Woman."
    Scott, A. "Old Wives' Tales."
    Scott, A. "Woman's Place Is in the History Books."
    Scott, A. "Women's Perspective on the Patriarchy in the 1850s."
    Scott, A. "Women's Voluntary Association in the Forming of
        American Society."
    Scott, P. "Black Women and the Work Experience."
    Serlin, E. "Emptying the Nest."
    Stone, P. "Race, Sex, Age and Political Conservatism Among
        Partisan Elites."
    Tauber, I. "Dimensions of Living Space."
    Tamir, L. "Men at Middle Age."
    Thomas, M. "Address to the Students at the Opening of the
        Academic Year 1899-1900."
    Thompson, M. "Controversy Over the Equal Rights Amendment."
    Truth, S. "Address on Woman's Rights."
    Truth, S. "Speech at Akron Women's Rights Convention, 1851."
    Voydanoff, P. "Work-Family Life Cycle Among Women."
    Wiersma, J. "Women's Mid-Life Career Change."

WOMEN--UNITED STATES--ALCOHOL USE

Gomberg, E. "Risk Factors Related to Alcohol Problems Among Women."

Hill, S. "Introduction: The Biological Consequences."

Wilsnack, S. "Prevention and Education Research."

WOMEN--UNITED STATES--CIVIL RIGHTS

Auchincloss, E. "Statement."

Chase-Anderson, M. "Statement."

Greenberger, M. "Statement."

Mayerson, A. "Statement."

Simmons, A. "Statement."

WOMEN--UNITED STATES--CRIMES AGAINST

Brady, K. "Statement."

Brown, S. "Testimony."

Burgess, A. "Testimony."

Dawson-Brown, C. "Testimony."

Dworkin, A. "Testimony."

Goldsmith, J. "Testimony."

Gosch, N. "Testimony."

Heller, V. "Testimony."

Leidholdt, D. "Testimony."

MacKinnon, C. "Testimony."

Marchiano, L. "Testimony."

Sadler, A. "Statement."

Seka. "Testimony."

Smith, P. "Testimony."

Specter, J. "Testimony."

Vera, V. "Testimony."

WOMEN--UNITED STATES--ECONOMIC CONDITIONS

Brothers, J. "Testimony."

Candela, C. "Testimony."

Conable, C. "Testimony."

Davis, D. "Testimony."

Deconcini, S. "Testimony."

Dorman, L. "Testimony."

Eidson, G. "Testimony."

Fleming, J. "Testimony."

Friedan, B. "Testimony."

Gaines, R. "Testimony."

Herman, A. "Testimony."

Oakar, M. "Statement."

WOMEN--UNITED STATES--ECONOMIC CONDITIONS (cont.)
Oberstar, J. "Testimony."
Porcino, J. "Testimony."
Reuss, M. "Testimony."
Schlossberg, N. "Testimony."
Smeal, E. "Testimony."
Steiger, J. "Testimony."

WOMEN--UNITED STATES--FOLKLORE

Langlois, J. "Belle Gunness, The Lady Bluebeard."

WOMEN--UNITED STATES--HISTORY

Abrams, A. "Frozen Goddess."
Antler, J. "Was She a Good Mother?"
Bilinkoff, J. "The Holy Woman and the Urban Community in
    Sixteenth-Century Avila."
Bolin, W. "American Woman and the Twentieth-Century Work
    Force."
Bordin, R. "A Baptism of Power and Liberty."
Brumberg, J. "The Ethnological Mirror."
Chambers-Schiller, L. "The Single Women."
Corbett, K. "Louisa Catherine Adams."
Dubois, E. "The Limitations of Sisterhood."
Ducrocq, F. "The London Biblewomen and Nurses Missions,
    1857-1880."
Frenier, M. "The Effects of the Chinese Revolution on Women
    and Their Families."
Friedman, J. "Piety and Kin."
Gampel, G. "The Planter's Wife Revisited."
Gordon, L. "Co-Education on Two Campuses."
Grant, M. "Domestic Experience and Feminist Theory."
Green, N. "Female Education and School Competition."
Griffith, E. "Elizabeth Cady Stanton on Marriage and Divorce."
Gullett, G. "City Mothers, City Daughters, and the Dance Hall
    Girls."
Hartmann, S. "Women's Organizations During World War II."
Hersh, B. "The 'True Woman' and the 'New Woman' in Nine-
    teenth-Century America."
Higashi, S. "Cinderella Vs. Statistics."
Humez, J. "My Spirit Eye."
Kelley, M. "At War With Herself."
Lerner, E. "Jewish Involvement in the New York City Woman
    Suffrage Movement."
Lerner, G. "Black Women in the United States."
Lerner, G. "The Challenge of Women's History."
Lerner, G. "Community Work of Black Club Women."
Lerner, G. "Just a Housewife."

WOMEN--UNITED STATES--HISTORY (cont.)

Lerner, G. "Placing Women in History."

Lerner, G. "The Political Activities of Antislavery Women."

Mason, P. "From the Salutatory Oration, Delivered by Miss Priscilla Mason, May 15, 1793."

McGee, S. "Right-Wing Female Activists in Buenos Aires, 1900-1932."

Morantz, R. "Feminism, Professionalism, and Germs."

O'Brien, S. "Tomboyism and Adolescent Conflict."

Rogers, K. "Relicts of the New World."

Schissel, L. "Diaries of Frontier Women."

Scott, A. "Are We the Women Our Grandmothers Were?"

Scott, A. "Eduation and the Contemporary Woman."

Scott, A. "Education of Women."

Scott, A. "Getting to be a Notable Georgia Woman."

Scott, A. "Historians Construct the Southern Woman."

Scott, A. "Old Wives' Tales."

Scott, A. "Woman's Place Is in the History Books."

Scott, A. "Women's Perspective on the Patriarchy in the 1850s."

Scott, A. "Women's Voluntary Association in the Forming of American Society."

Shteir, A. "Linnaeus's Daughters."

Wallace, M. "From the Valedictory Oration, Delivered by Miss Molly Wallace, June 20, 1792."

Wilson, B. "Glimpses of Muslim Urban Women in Classical Islam."

Wilson, J. "Hidden Riches."

Zimmerman, J. "Daughters of Main Street."

WOMEN--UNITED STATES--HISTORY--CASE STUDIES

Anthony, S. "Address of Susan B. Anthony."

Catt, C. "Is Woman Suffrage Progressing?"

Dickinson, A. "Why Colored Men Should Enlist."

Flynn, E. "Statement at the Smith Act Trial."

Foster, A. "Remarks of Abbey Kelley, Before a Meeting of the Boston Female Anti-Slavery Society."

Friedan, B. "The Crisis in Women's Identity."

Gilman, C. "The Social Body and Soul."

Goldman, E. "Address to the Jury, July, 1917."

Grimke, A. "Speech in Pennsylvania Hall."

Howe, J. "Is Polite Society Polite?"

Jordan, B. "Who Then Shall Speak for the Common Good?"

Keller, H. "Strike Against War."

Kubler-Ross, E. "Death Does Not Exist."

Livermore, M. "What Shall We Do With Our Daughters?"

Lockwood, B. "The Political Rights of Women."

Luce, C. "Is the New Morality Destroying America?"

McPherson, A. "The Cat and the Canary."

Mott, L. "Discourse on Women."

Roosevelt, E. "Adoption of Declaration of Human Rights?"

WOMEN--UNITED STATES--HISTORY--CASE STUDIES (cont.)

Rose, E. "Speech of Mrs. E. L. Rose, May 1860."
Shaw, A. "The Fate of Republics."
Smith, M. "Declaration of Conscience I."
Smith, M. "Declaration of Conscience II."
Stanton, E. "Solitude of Self."
Stone, L. "Taxation Without Representation."
Truth, S. "Ain't I a Woman?"
Willard, F. "A White Life for Two."
Woodhull, V. "Constitutional Equality."
Wright, F. "Address, July 4, 1828."

WOMEN--UNITED STATES--HISTORY--SOURCES

Antony, S. "Guaranteed to Us and Our Daughters Forever."
Bellanca, D. "Sister Dorothy Jacobs Bellanca, Union Leader,
    Makes a Report: 1940."
Hargreaves, M. "Darkness Before the Dawn."
Hartmann, S. "Women in the Military Service."
Hinding, A. "An Abundance of Riches."
James, E. "Edith Bolling Wilson."
Levine, J. "An Appeal to Admit Women into the Hierarchy of
    Decision-Makers: 1972."
Martelet, P. "The Woman's Land Army, World War I."
Popkin, S. "Bat Mitzvah Address of a Young Aristocrat: 1977."
Purdy, V. "National Archives Resources for Research in The
    History of American Women."
Richman, J. "Women Wage-Workers."
Rose, E. "Addresses at Woman's Rights Convention in Syracuse,
    1852."
Rose, E. "Speech at 2nd National Woman's Rights Convention in
    Worcester, 1851."
Rose, E. "Speech on Slavery, Flushing, Long Island, August 4,
    1853."
Smith, E. "Mary McLeod Bethune and the National Youth Admin-
    istration."
Solomon, H. "Address to National Council of Jewish Women,
    Washington, 1902."
Straub, E. "Women in the Civilian Labor Force."
Truth, S. "And Ain't I a Woman?"
Ullman, (Mrs.) L. "The Ladies' Hebrew Benevolent Society,
    Anniston, Alabama."
Vaughan, M. "We Would Act as Well as Endure."
Wellman, J. "Women and Radical Reform in Antebellum Upstate
    New York."
Wolfe, A. "No Room at the Top."
Young, M. "Women, Civilization, and the Indian Question."

WOMEN--UNITED STATES--PENSIONS

Abramson, E. "Statement."
Alden, L. "Statement."
Arri, J. "Testimony."
Bagnal, A. "Statement."
Bazemore, A. "Statement."
Bergmann, B. "Testimony."
Block, M. "Testimony."
Bonder, E. "Testimony."
Brown, H. "Statement."
Brummond, N. "Statement."
Buechler, J. "Statement."
Burris, C. "Testimony."
Campbell, J. "Testimony."
Campbell, N. "Statement." (2)
Campbell, N. "Testimony."
Campbell, R. "Statement."
Candela, C. "Statement."
Cancela, C. "Testimony."
Cardin, S. "Testimony."
Cauchear, M. "Statement."
Collins, M. "Statement."
Damschroder, D. "Statement."
Darner, K. "Statement."
Davis, D. "Testimony."
Dean, S. "Testimony."
Donnelly, E. "Statement."
Duskin, B. "Testimony."
East, C. "Statement." (2)
Eidson, G. "Testimony."
Ellis, T. "Statement."
Falvey, M. "Testimony."
Fenwick, M. "Statement."
Ferraro, G. "Statement." (3)
Fierst, E. "Statement." (3)
Fierst, E. "Testimony."
Fineshriber, P. "Testimony."
Finn, J. "Statement."
Flournoy, F. "Statement."
Forman, M. "Statement."
Foster, D. "Statement."
Fraser, A. "Statement."
French, J. "Testimony."
Gordon, N. "Testimony."
Gorie, M. "Statement."
Griffiths, M. "Testimony."
Hamlin, J. "Statement."
Heckler, M. "Statement."
Holly, E. "Statement."
Jeffrey, M. "Testimony."

WOMEN--UNITED STATES--PENSIONS (cont.)
   Todd, T. "Statement."
   Vadas, M. "Statement."
   Veve, K. "Statement."
   Wilpula, S. "Statement."
   Wilson, (Mrs.) J. "Statement."
   Wolf, E. "Statement."
   Wright, L. "Testimony."

WOMEN--UNITED STATES--SEXUAL BEHAVIOR

   Dye, N. "Mary Breckinridge, the Frontier Nursing Service, and
      the Introduction of Nurse-Midwifery in the United States."
   Morantz, R. "Making Women Modern."
   Scholten, C. "On the Importance of the Obstetrick Art."
   Waldron, I. "Employment and Women's Health."

WOMEN--UNITED STATES--SOCIAL CONDITIONS

   Abrams, A. "Frozen Goddess."
   Abzug, B. "Making Change."
   Austin, S. "Plenary Session."
   Ballard, B. "Women and Fashion."
   Blanchard, E. "Observations on Social Work with American In-
      dian Women."
   Blume, S. "Motivation and the Alcoholic Woman."
   Bolin, W. "American Woman and the Twentieth-Century Work
      Force."
   Bordin, R. "A Baptism of Power and Liberty."
   Brandwein, R. "Toward Androgyny in Community and Organiza-
      tional Practice."
   Cappelli, D. "Vocational Rehabilitation."
   Chambers-Schiller, L. "The Single Woman."
   Cherry, V. "The Role of the Family in Teenage Pregnancy."
   Corbett, K. "Louisa Catherine Adams."
   Cummerton, J. "Homophobia and Social Work Practice with Les-
      bians."
   De Lange, J. "Depression in Women."
   Driscoll, G. "Women Without Men."
   Duffe, N. "Reaching the Middle Class Female."
   Farnham, M. "The Lost Sex."
   Fimbres, M. "The Chicana in Transition."
   Finkelstein, N. "Innovative Alcoholism Programs for Women."
   Gomberg, E. "Learned Helplessness, Depression, and Alcohol
      Problems of Women."
   Gordon, L. "Co-Education on Two Campuses."
   Grant, M. "Domestic Experience and Feminist Theory."
   Green, N. "Female Education and School Competition."
   Griffith, E. "Elizabeth Cady Stanton on Marriage and Divorce."

WOMEN--UNITED STATES--SOCIAL CONDITIONS (cont.)
Wilson, J. "Hidden Riches."
Woodman, N. "Social Work with Lesbian Couples."
Zimmerman, J. "Daughters of Main Street."

WOMEN AUTHORS

Marshall, P. "Emerging Ones."

WOMEN, FRENCH

Darrow, M. "French Noblewomen and the New Domesticity, 1750-1850."

WOMEN, JEWISH--UNITED STATES--HISTORY--SOURCES

Bellanca, D. "Sister Dorothy Jacobs Bellanca, Union Leader, Makes a Report: 1940."
Levine, J. "An Appeal to Admit Women into the Hierarchy of Decision-Makers: 1972."
Popkin, S. "Bat Mitzah Address of a Young Aristocrat: 1977."
Richman, J. "Women Wage-Workers."
Rose, E. "Addresses at Womans Rights Convention in Syracuse, 1852."
Rose, E. "Speech at 2nd National Woman's Rights Convention in Worcester, 1851."
Rose, E. "Speech on Slavery, Flushing, Long Island, August 4, 1953."
Solomon, H. "Address to National Council of Jewish Women, Washington, 1902."
Ullman, (Mrs.) L. "The Ladies' Hebrew Benevolent Society, Anniston, Alabama."
Wolfe, A. "No Room at the Top."

WOMEN, METHODIST--UNITED STATES

Barstow, A. "An Ambiguous Legacy."
Brannan, E. "A Partnership of Equality."
Brereton, V. "Preparing Women for the Lord's Work."
Brumberg, J. "The Case of Ann Hasseltine Judson."
Chai, A. "Korean Women in Hawaii, 1903-1945."
Crist, M. "Winifred L. Chappel."
Davis, M. "The Countess of Huntington."
Dodson, J. "Nineteen-Century A.M.E. Preaching Women."
Engelsman, J. "The Legacy of Georgia Harkness."
Everhart, J. "Maggie Newton Van Cott."
Frederickson, M. "Shaping a New Society."

WOMEN, METHODIST--UNITED STATES (cont.)
Gifford, C. "For God and Home and Native Land."
Gillespie, J. "The Sun in Their Domestic System."
Hardesty, N. "Minister as Prophet?"
Jacobs, S. "Three Afro-American Women."
Jeffrey, J. "Ministry Through Marriage."
Keller, R. "Creating a Sphere for Women."
Lee, S. "Evangelical Domesticity."
Motes, R. "The Pacific Northwest."
Nanez, C. "Hispanic Clergy Wives."
O'Donnell, S. "Distress from the Press."
Page, C. "Charlotte Manye Maxeke."
Scott, M. "Georgia Harkness."
Shadron, V. "The Laity Rights Movement, 1906-1918."
Sims, A. "Sisterhoods of Service."
Sklar, K. "The Last Fifteen Years."

WOMEN, POOR--HEALTH AND HYGIENE

Apodaca, P. "Migrant Workers."
Badran, M. "Contamination in Practice."
Blair, P. "The Women and Health Connection."
Cross, K. "Health Problems of Native Americans."
Elmendorf, M. "Women, Water, and Waste."
Gibbons, L. "The Challenge for Health Care Providers."
Jackson, E. "Two Projects in Rural North Carolina, U.S.A."
Jett-Ali, J. "Traditional Birth Attendants and the Need for
    Training."
Kramer, J. "Urban Indians, A Neglected Group."
Lear, J. "Women's Health Needs in the United States."
Lukas, T. "Integrating Women in Development."
Masson, V. "An Example of Holistic Care."
Salazar, S. "Recommendations Regarding Latina Women."

WOMEN, POOR--UNITED STATES

Alake, Z. "Personal Report to the Conference on Women and
    Poverty in Massachusetts."
Alexander, L. "Testimony."
Ambrogi, D. "Excerpted Testimony from the Northern California
    Hearings on the Feminization of Poverty."
Bauer, M. "Testimony."
Buchanan, M. "Excerpted Testimony from the Southern California
    Hearings on the Feminization of Poverty."
Darlington-Hope, M. "Women of Color and the Feminization of
    Poverty."
Dawson, K. "Excerpted Testimony from the Southern California
    Hearings on the Feminization of Poverty."
Denny, A. "Excerpted Testimony from the Northern California
    Hearings on the Feminization of Poverty."

WOMEN, POOR--UNITED STATES (cont.)

Edmonds, J. "Testimony."

Fire Thunder, C. "Excerpted Testimony from the Southern California Hearings on the Feminization of Poverty."

Fossedal, R. "Testimony."

Gascon, B. "Testimony."

Graham, M. "Personal Report to the Conference on Women and Poverty in Massachusetts."

Gwizdak, L. "Personal Report to the Conference on Women Poverty in Massachusetts."

Halverson, J. "Excerpted Testimony from the Southern California Hearings on the Feminization of Poverty."

Hawkins, P. "Testimony."

Joynes, M. "Testimony."

Keller, M. "Testimony."

Kragelund, L. "Personal Report to the Conference on Women and Poverty in Massachusetts."

Lee, S. "Personal Report to the Conference on Women and Poverty in Massachusetts."

Madison, A. "Testimony."

Monteiro, H. "The Hunger Emergency."

Norton, E. "Speech at the National Women's Political Caucus Conference, July, 1981."

O'Connor, R. "Excerpted Testimony from the Southern California Hearings on the Feminization of Poverty."

Praeger, R. "Personal Report to the Conference on Women and Poverty in Massachusetts."

Rivera, E. "Personal Reports to the Conference on Women and Poverty in Massachusetts."

Tillman-Blackston, J. "Excerpted Testimony from the Southern California Hearings on the Feminization of Poverty."

Winship, N. "Organizing Against Hunger."

WOMEN AND PEACE

Addams, J. "Account of Her Interview with the Foreign Ministers of Europe."

Addams, J. "Speech at Carnegie Hall, New York 9 July, 1915."

Carroll, B. "Feminist Politics and Peace."

Davis, N. "Men, Women and Violence."

Douvan, E. "Sex Differences in Aggression and Dominance."

King, C. "Opportunities Masquerade as Problems."

Near, H. "Speaking Out."

Nuss, S. "The Role of Women in Underdeveloped Countries."

Steinson, B. "The Woman's Peace Party."

Thorne, B. "Gender Imagery and Issues of War and Peace."

Tilly, L. "Women and Collective Action in Europe."

WOMEN AND RELIGION

WOMEN AND RELIGION (cont.)
    Starhawk. "Immanence."
    Stendahl, K. "Enrichment or Threat?"
    Umansky, E. "Reflections on the Creation of a Ritual Meal."
    Wakeman, M. "Affirming Diversity and Biblical Tradition."
    Weaver, F. "Cloister and Salon in Seventeenth Century Paris."
    Williams, D. "Women as Makers of Literature."
    Wilson, L. "My Voice ... and Many Others."

WOMEN AND SOCIALISM

    Eastman, C. "Feminism."
    Eastman, C. "Political Equality League."
    Eastman, C. "The Three Essentials for Accident Prevention."
    Leacock, E. "Women, Development, and Anthropological Facts
        and Fictions."

WOMEN AND SOCIALISM--EUROPE, EASTERN

    Bohachevsky-Chomiak, M. "Ukrainian Feminism in Interwar
        Poland."
    Fischer, M. "Women in Romanian Politics."
    Freeze, K. "Medical Education for Women in Austria."
    Jancar, B. "Women in the Opposition in Poland and Czechoslo-
        vakia in the 1970s."
    Kligman, G. "The Rites of Women."
    Reed, M. "Peasant Women of Croatia in the Interwar Years."
    Rosenberg, D. "The Emancipation of Women in Fact and Fiction."
    Wolchik, S. "The Precommunist Legacy, Economic Development,
        Social Transformation, and Women's Roles in Eastern Europe."
    Woodward, S. "The Rights of Women."

WOMEN AUTHORS--SOUTHERN STATES

    Friedman, J. "Women's History and the Revision of Southern
        History."
    Harley, S. "Black Women in a Southern City."
    Janiewski, D. "Sisters Under Their Skins."
    Jones, A. "Southern Literary Women as Chroniclers of Southern
        Life."
    Scott, A. "Historians Construct the Southern Woman."
    Swain, M. "The Public Role of Southern Women."

WOMEN AUTHORS, LATIN AMERICAN

    Francescato, M. "Women in Latin America."
    McCracken, E. "Manuel Puig's Heartbreak Tango."

WOMEN AUTHORS, LATIN AMERICAN (cont.)
  Patai, D. "Jorge Amado's Heroines and the Ideological Double
    Standard."

WOMEN CLERGY

  Bellinger, M. "Upright But Not Uptight."
  Booker, M. "A Prescription for Humility."
  Brown, N. "The Mind of the Insecure."
  Cannon, K. "On Remembering Who We Are."
  Delk, Y. "Singing the Lord's Song."
  Johnson, S. "God's Woman."
  Knight, C. "The Survival of the Unfit."
  Lewter-Simmons, M. "Our Spiritual Account."
  McGill-Jackson, D. "To Set at Liberty."
  Mills-Morton, C. "The Blessings and Burdens of the Divinely
    Chosen."
  Scott, P. "God Has a Master Plan for Your Life."
  Shamana, B. "Letting Go."
  Sinclair, L. "Can Your Bones Live?"
  Williams, S. "Studying War Some More."

WOMEN COLLEGE STUDENTS--U.S.

  Antler, J. "Culture, Service, and Work."
  Bennett, S. "Undergraduates and Their Teachers."
  Bielby, D. "Career Commitment of Female College Graduates."
  Brown, M. "Career Plans of College Women."
  Erkut, S. "Social Psychology Looks At But Does Not See the
    Undergraduate Woman."
  Fleming, J. "Sex Differences in the Impact of College Environ-
    ments on Black Students."
  Lockheed, M. "Sex Bias in Aptitude and Achievement Tests
    Used in Higher Education."
  Perun, P. "The Undergraduate Woman."

WOMEN COLLEGE TEACHERS--UNITED STATES

  Bonder, G. "The Educational Process of Women's Studies in
    Argentina."
  Culley, M. "Anger and Authority in the Introductory Women's
    Studies Classroom."
  Friedman, S. "Authority in the Feminist Classroom."
  Miller, N. "Mastery, Identity, and the Politics of Work."
  Rich, A. "Taking Women Students Seriously."

WOMEN ENGINEERS

Briscoe, A. "Scientific Sexism."

Brown, L. "Involvement of Students in Research Projects."

Burke, E. "Career Interruptions and Perceived Discrimination Among Women Students in Engineering and Science."

Cobb, J. "Planning Strategies for Women in Scientific Professions."

Davis, S. "Assertiveness."

Dresselhaus, M. "Responsibilities of Women Faculty in Engineering Schools."

Gonzalez, N. "Professional Women in Developing Nations."

Gough, P. "The Female Engineering Student."

Haraway, D. "Class, Race, Sex, Scientific Objects of Knowledge."

Hass, V. "Evolving Views of Women's Professional Roles."

Holmstrom, E. "The New Pioneers ... Women Engineering Students."

Hopkins, E. "Alternative Development of a Scientific Career."

Hornig, L. "Professional Women in Transition."

Hornig, L. "Response to the Social Scene."

Hubbard, R. "Should Professional Women Be Like Professional Men?"

Koop, M. "Response to the Social Scene."

Law, M. "The Problems Facing Women Scientists and Engineers in Academia."

McAfee, N. "You've Come a Long Way Baby."

O'Bannon, H. "The Social Scene."

Ott, M. "Attitudes and Experiences of Freshmen Engineers at Cornell."

Perrucci, C. "Central Issues Facing Women in the Science-Based Professions."

Rosenfeld, R. "Academic Career Mobility for Women and Men Psychologists."

Sloan, M. "Women in the Laboratory."

Theodore, A. "Response to the Social Scene."

Trescott, M. "Women Engineers in History."

Vetter, B. "Changing Patterns of Recruitment and Employment."

Widnall, S. "Response to the Social Scene."

WOMEN EXECUTIVES--UNITED STATES

Auerbach, S. "Personal Economics for Today's Woman."

Bartlett, L. "Coping with Illegal Sex Discrimination."

Bergen, P. "Blueprint for the Top Manager--Me."

Byrnes, E. "Dual Career Couples."

Coffey, M. "One Family's Decision."

Franklin, B. "Challenges for Women in Government Management."

Harragan, B. "Women and Men at Work."

Hershey, L. "Communicating and Managing the Media Challenge."

WOMEN EXECUTIVES--UNITED STATES (cont.)

WOMEN HEADS OF HOUSEHOLDS--UNITED STATES

WOMEN IN BUSINESS

WOMEN IN BUSINESS (cont.)
  Mater, C. "Statement."
  Moss, T. "Statement."
  Moss, T. "Testimony."
  Muscato, P. "Statement."
  Oesterle, P. "Working Couples and Child Care."
  Osterman, G. "Does Becoming a Parent Mean Falling Off the
      Fast Tract?"
  Rolls, K. "Statement."
  Rossman, M. "Statement."
  Schroeder, P. "Statement."
  Seeman, M. "Statement."
  Shalala, D. "Statement."
  Smith, D. "Personal Choices."
  Snider, Y. "Statement."
  Snowe, O. "Statement."
  Spellman, G. "Statement."
  Tate, J. "Statement."
  Williams, K. "Statement."
  Woods, R. "Statement."

WOMEN IN CHRISTIANITY

  Hellwig, M. "Christian Women in a Troubled World."

WOMEN IN CHRISTIANITY--HISTORY

  Douglass, J. "The Foundation and Significance of Christian
      Freedom."
  Douglass, J. "Freedom in God's Order."
  Douglass, J. "Freedom in Obedience."
  Douglass, J. "Women's Freedom in Church Order: Calvin in
      the Medieval and Renaissance Context."
  Douglass, J. "Women's Freedom in Church Order: Calvin in
      the Reformation Context."
  Douglass, J. "Women's Freedom in Church Order: Calvin's
      View."
  Gilkes, C. "Together and in Harness."
  McNamara, J. "Sexual Equality and the Cult of Virginity in
      Early Christian Thought."

WOMEN IN CHURCH WORK

  Barstow, A. "An Ambiguous Legacy."
  Branna, E. "A Partnership of Equality."
  Brown, P. "My Ministry as a Parish Secretary."
  Carter, N. "A Lay Theological Perspective."
  McEnamy, G. "Housewife, Mother, and Parish Volunteer."

WOMEN IN CHURCH WORK (cont.)
  Rounder, R. "Ministry and Life of Faith."
  Spinney, E. "The Ministry of a Lay Associate."
  Tieran, K. "Urban Team Ministry."

WOMEN IN CHURCH WORK--CATHOLIC CHURCH

  Cardman, F. "Tradition, Hermeneutics and Ordination."
  Foley, N. "Woman in Vatican Documents."
  Meagher, K. "Women in Relation to Orders and Jurisdictions."

WOMEN IN JOURNALISM--UNITED STATES

  Goldenberg, E. "An Overview of Access to the Media."
  Graber, D. "Agenda-Setting."
  Rice, P. "Women Out of the Myths and Into Focus."
  Robinson, G. "Women, Media Access and Social Control."
  Smith, M. "Access to the Media."

WOMEN IN LITERATURE

  Allen, P. "Answering the Deer."
  Burke, C. "The New Poetry and the New Woman."
  Deshazer, M. "My Scourge, My Sister."
  Diehl, J. "At Home With Loss."
  Dydo, U. "To Have the Winning Language."
  Francescato, M. "Women in Latin America."
  Friedman, S. "I Go Where I Love."
  Gilbert, S. "In Yeats's House."
  Gubar, S. "The Birth of the Artist as Heroine."
  Marcus, J. "Liberty, Sorority, Misogyny."
  Marshall, P. "Emerging Ones."
  McCracken, E. "Manuel Puig's Heartbreak Tango."
  Middlebrook, D. "I Tapped My Own Head."
  Miller, N. "Writing (from) the Feminine."
  Mitchell, J. "Femininity, Narrative and Psychoanalysis."
  Mitchell, J. "Feminism and Femininity at the Turn of the Century."
  Mitchell, J. "Feminism as a Political Movement."
  Mitchell, J. "Psychoanalysis."
  Mitchell, J. "The Question of Femininity and the Theory of Psychoanalysis."
  Mitchell, J. "Romantic Love."
  Mitchell, J. "What Is Feminism?"
  Mitchell, J. "Women and Equality."
  Mossberg, B. "Sylvia Plath's Baby Book."
  Ostriker, A. "The Thieves of Language."
  Patai, D. "Jorge Amado's Heroines and the Ideological Double Standard."

WOMEN IN LITERATURE (cont.)

Poovey, M. "Persuasion and the Promises of Love."

Rushing, A. "Lucille Clifton."

Willard, C. "A Fifteenth-Century View of Women's Role in Medieval Society."

Yalom, M. "Sylvia Plath, The Bell Jar, and Related Poems."

WOMEN IN MATHEMATICS

Casserly, P. "Factors Affecting Participation in Advanced Placement Programs in Mathematics, Chemistry, and Physics."

Ermarth, E. "Fictional Consensus and Female Casualties."

Fennema, E. "Sex-Related Differences in Mathematics Achievement."

Helson, R. "The Creative Woman Mathematician."

MacDonald, C. "An Experiment in Mathematics Education at the College Level."

Sells, L. "The Mathematics Filter and the Education of Women and Minorities."

WOMEN IN MEDICINE

Bellamy, C. "Keynote Address."

Dye, N. "Mary Breckinridge, the Frontier Nursing Service, and the Introduction of Nurse-Midwifery in the United States."

Ehrenreich, B. "Luncheon Address."

Gaynor, F. "Health Services Administration."

Goren, S. "Luncheon Address."

Hollinshead, M. "health Professional Education."

Marrett, C. "On the Evolution of Women's Medical Societies."

Morantz, R. "Making Women Modern."

Reverby, S. "Neither for the Drawing Room Nor for the Kitchen."

Miles, P. "Opening Remarks."

Scholten, C. "On the Importance of the Obstetrick Art."

Waldron, I. "Employment and Women's Health."

WOMEN IN MORMONISM

Anderson, L. "Mary Fielding Smith."

Arnold, M. "Pornography, Romance, and the Paradox of Freedom."

Arnold, M. "Reading and Loving Literature."

Avery, V. "Emma Smith."

Ballif, J. "Welcome."

Barlow, S. "A Response, and More Questions."

Bell, E. "All Write, All Write."

Brinton, S. "The Blessing of Music in the Home."

Cannon, E. "Daughters of God."

WOMEN IN MORMONISM (cont.)

Cannon, E. "Finding Our Peace on Earth."
Day, L. "Talents Bring Joy."
Eldredge, Y. "The Stewardship of Talents."
Eliason, C. "Making You and Your Child Successful."
Ford, K. "Gospel Principles and Women."
Harrison, B. "A Deliberate Choice."
Hawkins, P. "Choices in a Nation of Alternatives."
Hawley, C. "Fortifying Ourselves Against Evil."
Holland, P. "Pure Hearts and Pure Home."
Holland, P. "Women and the Priesthood."
Jacobsen, F. "Our Heritage."
Kapp, A. "Drifting, Dreaming, Directing."
Kimball, C. "Keys for a Woman's Progression."
Kimball, C. "The Rewards of Correct Choice."
Knowles, E. "The Scriptures."
Kump, E. "The Bread and Milk of Living."
Maxwell, C. "The Traditional Role of the Mormon Woman."
McKinlay, L. "To Love Our God."
Mouritsen, M. "Scholars of the Scriptures."
Mouritsen, M. "Welcome."
Ottley, J. "A Musical Stewardship."
Peterson, G. "Priesthood and Sisterhood."
Quick, T. "Personal Revelation."
Rasmus, C. "The Gift and Power of the Holy Ghost."
Rasmus, C. "Women in the Light of the Gospel."
Shumway, N. "Except You Become as Little Children."
Smith, B. "Blueprints for Living."
Smith, B. "Relief Society."
Smith, I. "A Woman's Role and Destiny."
Sorensen, E. "The Educated Woman Within Us."
Spafford, B. "The American Woman's Movement."
Staples, S. "Stress."
Sturlaugson, M. "Freedom to Become."
Thayne, E. "The Cat Fight and What Matters Most."
Thomas, S. "Women of Charity."
Winger, J. "Partners in Progress."
Young, D. "All Thy Children Shall Be Taught."

WOMEN IN POLITICS--EUROPEAN, EASTERN

Bohachevsky-Chomiak, M. "Ukrainian Feminism in Interwar Poland."
Fischer, M. "Women in Romanian Politics."
Freeze, K. "Medical Education for Women in Austria."
Jancar, B. "Women in the Opposition in Poland and Czecho-slovakia in the 1970s."
Kligman, G. "The Rites of Women."
Reed, M. "Peasant Women of Croatia in the Interwar Years."
Rosenberg, D. "The Emancipation of Women in Fact and Fiction."

WOMEN IN POLITICS--UNITED STATES (cont.)

Lipman-Blumen, J. "A Crisis Perspective on Emerging Health Roles."

Mallen, L. "Women's Incomes as Workers and Dependents."

O'Reilly, J. "Speech at the National Women's Political Caucus Conference, July, 1981."

Ortega, K. "Keynote Address at the Republic National Convention."

Reid, I. "How Powerful Is Powerful?"

Roosevelt, E. "Before the Democratic National Convention."

Roosevelt, E. "Communist Charges Against U.S. Territorial Policies."

Rothschild, J. "Technology, 'Women's Work' and the Social Control of Women."

Ruckelshaus, J. "Speech at the National Women's Political Caucus Conference, July, 1981."

Rupp, L. "The Women's Community in the National Woman's Party, 1945 to the 1960s."

Schroeder, P. "Great Expectations."

Schweber, C. "But Some Were Less Equal ... The Fight for Women Jurors."

Shanley, M. "Individualism, Marriage, and the Liberal State."

Steihm, J. "Women and Citizenship."

Steinem, G. "Speech at the National Women's Political Caucus Conference, July, 1981."

Stone, L. "Disappointment Is the Lot of Women."

Truth, S. "Ain't I a Woman?"

Truth, S. "And Ain't I a Woman?"

Truth, S. "Keeping the Thing Going While Things Are Stirring."

Vaughan, M. "We Would Act as Well as Endure."

Watts, M. "Biopolitics and Gender."

Young, M. "Women, Civilization, and the Indian Question."

WOMEN IN POPULAR CULTURE--UNITED STATES

Kane, M. "Statement to Pope John Paul II."

Rich, A. "Commencement Address at Smith College, 1979."

Ruffin, J. "Address to the First National Conference of Colored Women."

Schlafly, P. "Controversy Over the Equal Rights Amendment."

Thomas, M. "Address to the Students at the Opening of the Academic Year 1899-1900."

Thompson, M. "Controversy Over the Equal Rights Amendment."

Truth, S. "Address on Woman's Rights."

Truth, S. "Speech at Akron Women's Rights Convention, 1851."

WOMEN IN PUBLIC LIFE--SOUTHERN STATES

Friedman, J. "Women's History and the Revision of Southern History."

Harley, S. "Black Women in a Southern City."

Janiewski, D. "Sisters Under Their Skins."

Jones, A. "Southern Literary Women as Chroniclers of Southern Life."

Scott, A. "Historians Construct the Southern Woman."

Swain, M. "The Public Role of Southern Women."

WOMEN IN PUBLIC LIFE--UNITED STATES

Cotera, M. "Women in Power."

Deaux, K. "Internal Barriers."

Dewine, S. "Breakthrough."

Farenthold, F. "Women in Power."

Fitzpatrick, M. "Effective Interpersonal Communication for Women of the Corporation."

Griffiths, M. "Power--How to Get It and How To Use It."

Hubbard, L. "Lady School Managers."

Hughes, S. "Women in Power."

Jones, T. "Sexual Harassment in the Organization."

King, G. "Women Clerks."

Laise, C. "American Women and American Foreign Policy."

Putnam, L. "Lady You're Trapped."

Safa, H. "Runaway Shops and Female Employment."

Weiner, A. "Forgotten Wealth."

Wilson, L. "The Opposition of the Vigilance Association."

WOMEN IN RURAL DEVELOPMENT

Alabastro, E. "Women in the Food System."

Alabastro, E. "Report from the Phillipines."

Barnes, C. "Strengthening Voltaic Women's Roles in Development (Upper Volta)."

Bay, E. "Summary of Panel on Developing Country Women's Perceptions of Food/Nutrition Problems."

Boulding, E. "Integration Into What?"

Burke, M. "How Women Can Make a Difference."

Burke, M. "Session Summary."

Cain, M. "Java, Indonesia."

Calloway, D. "Food/Nutrition in the Third World."

Carr, M. "Technologies Appropriate for Women."

Cowan, A. "Session Summary."

Dauber, R. "Applying Policy Analysis to Women and Technology."

Dulansey, M. "Session Summary."

Elmendorf, M. "Changing Role of Maya Mothers and Daughters."

Ferguson, N. "Summary of Panel on Food/Nutrition Problems--

WOMEN IN RURAL DEVELOPMENT (cont.)
   Impact on Women and Women's Role in Interventions to Solve
   Them."
Finne, G. "What Can International Development Banks Do?"
Fortmann, L. "The Plight of the Invisible Farmer."
Hemmings-Gapihan, G. "Baseline Study for Socio-Economic Evalu-
   tion of Tangaye Solar Site."
Huggard, M. "Women as Agents of Change."
Lewis, M. "Costa Rica/Oregon Cooperative Nutrition Projects."
Lim, L. "Women's Work in Multinational Electronics Factories."
McGrath, M. "What Can Private Institutions, Particularly Coop-
   eratives Do?"
Minge, W. "The Industrial Revolution and the European Family."
Mullings, L. "Uneven Development."
North, J. "Women Participants in the Food Marketing System in
   West Africa."
Papanek, H. "The Differential Impact of Programs and Policies
   on Women in Development."
Sanica, S. "Report from Turkey."
Sanica, S. "Women in the Food System."
Seidman, A. "Women and the Development of 'Underdevelopment.'"
Srinivasan, M. "Impact of Selected Industrial Technologies on
   Women in Mexico."
Stewart, B. "Session Summary."
Tinker, I. "New Technologies for Food-Related Activities."
Turbitt, C. "Session Summary."
Whiting, M. "CARE/Kenya Water Development Program."

WOMEN IN SCIENCE--UNITED STATES

Aldrich, M. "Statement."
Bonosaro, C. "Affirmative Action and the Continuing Majority."
Briscoe, A. "Scientific Sexism."
Celender, I. "Careers in Industry for Scientifically Trained
   Women."
Cobb, J. "Filters for Women in Science."
Cobb, J. "Planning Strategies for Women in Scientific Profes-
   sions."
Cobb, J. "Statement."
Daniels, A. "Development of Feminist Networks in the Profes-
   sions."
Denmark, F. "Women in Psychology in the United States."
Dresselhaus, M. "Responsibilities of Women Faculty in Engineer-
   ing Schools."
Frieze, I. "Psychological Barriers for Women in Sciences."
George, Y. "Affirmative Action Programs That Work."
Gonzalez, N. "Professional Women in Developing Nations."
Hall, D. "Academics, Bluestockings, and Biologists."
Haraway, D. "Class, Race, Sex, Scientific Objects of Knowl-
   edge."

WOMEN IN SCIENCE--UNITED STATES (cont.)

Harrison, A. "Implications of Equality."
Hass, V. "Evolving Views of Women's Professional Roles."
Hewitt, G. "The Status of Women in Mathematics."
Hopkins, E. "Alternative Development of a Scientific Career."
Hopkins, E. "A Certain Restlessness."
Hornig, L. "Professional Women in Transition."
Hornig, L. "Scientific Sexism."
Howell, M. "The New Feminism and the Medical School Milieu."
Hubbard, R. "Feminism in Academia."
Hubbard, R. "Should Professional Women Be Like Professional Men?"
Humphreys, S. "Effectiveness of Science Career Conferences."
Jackson, S. "From Clerk-Typist to Research Physicist."
Kistiakowsky, V. "Women in Physics and Astronomy."
Kreinberg, N. "Equals."
Marinez, D. "Innovative Approaches."
Max, C. "Career Paths for Women in Physics."
Marriett, C. "Statement."
McAfee, N. "Women in Engineering Revisited."
McAfee, N. "You've Come a Long Way Baby."
Moulton, R. "Psychological Challenges Confronting Women in the Sciences."
O'Hern, E. "Women in the Biological Sciences."
Perrucci, C. "Central Issues Facing Women in the Science-Based Professions."
Pfafflin, S. "Equal Opportunity for Women in Science."
Pfafflin, S. "Statement."
Rosenstein, B. "Statement."
Ramaley, J. "Strategies for Change."
Rosenfeld, R. "Academic Career Mobility for Women and Men Psychologists."
Russell, D. "How a Scientist Who Happens to be Female Can Succeed in Academia."
Sandler, B. "Women in Academe."
Schwarzer, T. "The Changing Status of Women in the Geosciences."
Sells, L. "Leverage for Equal Opportunity Through Mastery of Mathematics."
Smith, E. "The Individual and the Institution."
Tate, C. "Statement."
Tobach, E. "An Agenda to Further Expand the Role of Women in Science and Technology."
Trecott, M. "Women Engineers in History."
Vetter, B. "Changing Patterns of Recruitment and Employment."
Vetter, B. "Labor Force Participation of Women Baccalaureates in Science."
Weaver, E. "Implications of Giving Woman a Greater Share of Academic Decision-Making."

WOMEN IN THE CATHOLIC CHURCH

WOMEN IN THE CIVIL SERVICE--UNITED STATES

WOMEN IN THE CIVIL SERVICE--UNITED STATES (cont.)
    Mikulski, B. "Statement."
    Miller, D. "Statement."
    Mondale, J. "Statement."
    Nelms, D. "Statement."
    Oakar, M. "Statement."
    Overly, C. "Statement."
    Prokop, R. "Statement." (2)
    Rachner, M. "Statement."
    Reder, N. "Statement."
    Reid, M. "Statement."
    Rock, D. "Statement." (2)
    Rothchild, N. "Statement." (2)
    Schlafly, P. "Statement." (2)
    Schroeder, P. "Statement." (2)
    Smothers, L. "Statement."
    Spigelmyer, S. "Statement."
    Stein, E. "Statement."
    Steinbacher, R. "Statement."
    Steinberg, R. "Statement."
    Ter Wisscha, G. "Statement."
    Venegas, H. "Greetings."
    Waelder, C. "Statement."
    Wainwright, C. "Statement."
    Wallace, R. "Statement."
    Warren, A. "Statement."
    Waxman, M. "Statement."
    Williams, D. "Statement."
    Witt, S. "Native Women in the World of Work."
    Young, T. "Statement."

WOMEN IN THE PRESS--UNITED STATES

    Goldenberg, E. "An Overview of Access to the Media."
    Graber, D. "Agenda-Setting."
    Rice, P. "Women Out of the Myths and Into Focus."
    Robinson, G. "Women, Media Access and Social Control."
    Smith, M. "Access to the Media."

WOMEN IN THE PROFESSIONS--UNITED STATES

    Breen, E. "Toward Freedom and Self-Determination."
    Burnett, M. "Knots in the Family Tie."
    Datan, N. "The Lost Cause."
    Dunlap, M. "Resistance to the Women's Movement in the United States."
    Ginsberg, R. "Women's Right to Full Participation in Shaping Society's Course."
    Phillips, R. "Women in Medicine."

WOMEN IN THE PROFESSIONS--UNITED STATES (cont.)
Robertson, A. "Continuing Education."
Stitzel, J. "Challenging Curricular Assumptions."
Verheyden-Hilliard, M. "Education, Girls, and Power."

WOMEN IN THE THEATRE

Ginsberg, E. "Playwrights, Poets, and Novelists."
Jacker, C. "Better Than A Shriveled Huck."
Lee, M. "Legitimate Theatre Is Illegitimate."

WOMEN IN THE TRADE-UNIONS

Bergmann, B. "The United States of America."
Lapidus, G. "The Soviet Union."
Papanek, H. "Low-Income Countries."
Wolf, M. "The People's Republic of China."

WOMEN JUDGES--UNITED STATES

Carbon, S. "Women on the State Bench."
Cook, B. "The Dual Role of Women Judges."
Cook, B. "Sex Discrimination in Politics and the All-Male Club."
Epstein, C. "The Role Strain of Balancing Political and Profes-
    sional Responsibilities with Family and Personal Responsibil-
    ities."
O'Connor, S. "Testimony of Sandra Day O'Connor."
Wikler, N. "Overcoming the Obstacles to Women in Judicial Edu-
    cation."

WOMEN LIBRARIANS--UNITED STATES

Cutler, M. "What a Woman Librarian Earns."
James, M. "Women and Their Future in Library Work."
Plummer, M. "The Training of Women as Librarians."
Sargent, M. "Women's Position in Library Science."
Thorne, W. "Librarianship as a Career for Women."

WOMEN PRISONERS--UNITED STATES

Chapman, J. "Testimony."
Heffernan, E. "Testimony."
Resnik, J. "Testimony."
Schweber, C. "Testimony."
Shaw, N. "Testimony."
Taylor, P. "Testimony."

WOMEN REFUGEES--UNITED STATES

Bryce, D. "Issues in Afro-Hispanic Development."
McGlauflin, D. "Mainstreaming Refugee Women's Economic Development."
Springer, E. "The Emergence of Immigrant Women Artists."

WOMEN SCHOLARS

Hammon, H. "Creating Feminist Works."
Merriam, E. "Creating Feminist Works."
Miller, N. "Creating Feminist Works."

WOMEN SCHOOL ADMINISTRATORS

Antonucci, T. "The Need for Female Role Models in Education."
Bogdan, J. "The Transition from Parenting to Working and Parenting."
Burstyn, J. "Historical Perspectives on Women in Educational Leadership."
Conoley, J. "The Psychology of Leadership."
Clement, J. "Sex Bias in School Administration."
Doughty, R. "The Black Female Administrator."
Gribskov, M. "Feminism and the Woman School Administrator."
Haines, P. "Coeducation and the Development of Leadership Skills in Women."
Johnson, M. "How Real Is Fear of Success."
Kohlstedt, S. "Single-Sex Education and Leadership."
Lightfoot, S. "Socialization and Education of Young Black Girls in School."
Schmuck, P. "Changing Women's Representation in School Management."
Winslow, M. "Leadership Training for Increased Effectiveness Among Women Educational Administrators."

WOMEN SCIENTISTS--UNITED STATES

Briscoe, A. "Scientific Sexism."
Briscoe, A. "Statement."
Cobb, J. "Planning Strategies for Women in Scientific Professions."
Dresselhaus, M. "Responsibilities of Women Faculty in Engineering Schools."
Dunkle, M. "Statement."
Gonzalez, N. "Professional Women in Developing Nations."
Haraway, D. "Class, Race, Sex, Scientific Objects of Knowledge."
Hass, V. "Evolving Views of Women's Professional Roles."
Hopkins, E. "Alternative Development of a Scientific Career."

WOMEN SCIENTISTS--UNITED STATES (cont.)

Hornig, L. "Professional Women in Transition."
Hubbard, R. "Should Professional Women Be Like Professional Men?"
King-Reynolds, W. "Statement."
Kostalos, M. "Statement."
Malcom, S. "Statement."
McAfee, N. "You've Come a Long Way Baby."
Murray, L. "Statement."
Perrucci, C. "Central Issues Facing Women in the Science-Based Professions."
Rosenfeld, R. "Academic Career Mobility for Women and Men Psychologists."
Seaman, B. "Statement."
Smeal, E. "Statement."
Trescott, M. "Women Engineers in History."
Vetter, B. "Changing Patterns of Recruitment and Employment."
Vetter, B. "Statement."

WOMEN SOCIAL REFORMERS--UNITED STATES

Addams, J. "Child Labor Legislation."
Addams, J. "The Public School and the Immigrant Child."
Addams, J. "Recreation as a Public Function in Urban Communities."
Addams, J. "The Subjective Necessity for Social Settlements."

WOMEN SOLDIERS

Abzug, B. "Statement."
Bloom, A. "Israel."
Brewer, M. "Statement."
Brown, N. "Statement."
Carpenter, M. "Statement."
Chayes, A. "Statement."
Chayes, A. "Testimony."
Clarke, M. "Statement."
Donnelly, E. "Statement."
Eidson, E. "Statement."
Ellis, T. "Statement."
Goldman, K. "Statement."
Goldsmith, J. "Statement."
Goldston, S. "Statement."
Goodman, J. "Testimony."
Griffiths-Boris, N. "Statement."
Hallaren, M. "Testimony."
Heckler, M. "Statement."
Hoisington, E. "Statement."
Holm, J. "Statement."

WOMEN SOLDIERS (cont.)

    Holm, J. "Testimony."
    Holt, M. "Statement."
    Jancar, B. "Yugoslavia."
    Kinzer, N. "Testimony."
    Lawlor, M. "Statement."
    Leeper, P. "Statement."
    McClendon, S. "Statement."
    McKee, F. "Statement."
    Parr, C. "Statement."
    Parr, C. "Testimony."
    Pierre, (Mrs.) H. "Statement."
    Richardson, S. "Statement."
    Schlafly, P. "Statement."
    Schnaier, J. "Statement."
    Segal, M. "The Argument for Female Combatants."
    Smith, R. "Statement." (2)
    Smith, R. "Statement."
    Starbuck, D. "Statement."
    Steele, D. "Statement."
    Steele, D. "Testimony."
    Strother, D. "Statement."
    Teague, K. "Statement."
    Thorman, R. "Statement."
    Underwood, L. "Statement."
    Van Devanter, L. "Statement."
    Van Devanter, L. "Testimony."
    Willard, V. "Statement."
    Willenz, J. "Statement."
    Willenz, J. "Testimony."
    Young, R. "Statement."

WOMEN TEACHERS--UNITED STATES--HISTORY

    Haley, M. "Why Teachers Should Organize."

WOMEN-OWNED BUSINESS ENTERPRISES

    Alford, B. "Statement."
    Andrulis, M. "Statement."
    Baird, S. "Statement."
    Bernhardt, M. "Statement."
    Bland, L. "Statement."
    Boggs, L. "Statement."
    Brunson, D. "Statement."
    Davidson, D. "Statement."
    Davis, S. "Statement."
    Fraser, L. "Statement."
    Hays, M. "Statement."

WOMEN-OWNED BUSINESS ENTERPRISES (cont.)

WOMEN'S AIR SERVICE PILOTS (U.S.)

WOMEN'S HEALTH SERVICES--UNITED STATES

WOMEN'S HEALTH SERVICES--UNITED STATES (cont.)

Luker, K. "Response (to Woman-Controlled Birth Control)."
Marrett, C. "On the Evolution of Women's Medical Societies."
Norsigian, J. "Response (to Woman-Controlled Birth Control)."
Punnett, L. "Women-Controlled Research."
Reverby, S. "Neither for the Drawing Room Nor for the Kitchen."
Rodriguez, H. "Concluding Remarks (on Depo-Provera and Sterilization Abuse)."
Ruzek, S. "Ethical Issues in Childbirth Technology."
Salk, H. "Response (to Benefits and Risks of Electronic Fetal Monitoring)."
Sewell, S. "Sterilization Abuse and Hispanic Women."
Shearer, B. "C/SEC."
Swallow, H. "Midwives in Many Settings."
Swenson, N. "Response (to an Obstetrician's Perspective)."
Wertz, D. "Man-Midwifery and the Rise of Technology."
Wolcott, I. "Response (to Forces Impacting on the Policymaker)."

WOMEN'S INTERNATIONAL LEAGUE FOR PEACE AND FREEDOM

Addams, J. "Patriotism and Pacifists in War Time."

WOMEN'S RIGHTS--UNITED STATES

Abzug, B. "Making Change."
Austin, M. "Recent Developments with Respect to Equal Opportunities in Revenue Sharing Programs."
Austin, S. "Plenary Session."
Bergmann, B. "The United States of America."
Blume, S. "Motivation and the Alcoholic Woman."
Bonsaro, C. "Women's Rights, ERA, and After."
Breen, E. "Toward Freedom and Self-Determination."
Brown, O. "Address on Woman Suffrage."
Brown, O. "Crime and the Remedy."
Brown, O. "Hand of Fellowship."
Brown, O. "On Margaret Fuller."
Brown, O. "The Opening Doors."
Brown, O. "United States Citizenship."
Brown, O. "Where Is the Mistake?"
Brown, O. "Woman's Place in the Church."
Brown, O. "Woman's Suffrage."
Brown, O. "Women and Skepticism."
Burke, Y. "Economic Strength Is What Counts."
Burnett, M. "Knots in the Family Tie."
Burstein, K. "Notes from a Political Career."
Cappelli, D. "Vocational Rehabilitation."
Carpenter, L. "God, But We're Getting Smart."
Catt, C. "Address to the Seventh Congress of the International Woman Suffrage Alliance at Budapest, 15 June 1913."

WOMEN'S RIGHTS--UNITED STATES (cont.)

Lapidus, G. "The Soviet Union."

Lee, M. "Legitimate Theatre Is Illegitimate."

Leone, R. "The Stigmatized Woman."

Lewis, B. "Sexism in Treatment."

Liebschutz, S. "Republican Women and the Future of the Republican Party."

Lipman-Blumen, J. "A Crisis Perspective on Emerging Health Roles."

Mainker, M. "Self-Power and Leadership."

Mallan, L. "Women's Incomes as Workers and Dependents."

Messinger, R. "Postintervention and Support Systems."

Norton, E. "Women in Crisis."

Oneglia, S. "Keynote Address."

Papanek, H. "Low-Income Countries."

Peacock, C. "Young Female Offenders in Massachusetts."

Phillips, R. "Women in Medicine."

Preciado De Burciaga, C. "Panel Discussion."

Reid, I. "How Powerful Is Powerful?"

Robe, L. "Pregnancy and Drinking."

Robertson, A. "Continuing Education."

Rodriguez-Mendoza, A. "Caucus Report of the Western Region."

Russianoff, P. "Learned Helplessness."

Saunders, M. "The Double Bind."

Schweber, C. "But Some Were Less Equal ... The Fight for Women Jurors."

Seizas, J. "Reaching the Middle Class Alcoholic."

Shanley, M. "Individualism, Marriage, and the Liberal State."

Shaw, A. "Presidential Address at the 1905 Convention of the National American Woman Suffrage Association."

Shaw, A. "Presidential Address at the 1906 Convention of the National American Woman Suffrage Association."

Snow, D. "Special Interest Report on Voting Rights."

Stanton, E. "Fifteenth-Amendment--Votes for Black Men Only?"

Stitzel, J. "Challenging Curricular Assumptions."

Taylor, B. "The Unique Employment Problems of Female Offenders Returning to the Community and Labor Market."

Tyler, J. "Panel Discussion."

Thomas, M. "Present Tendencies in Women College and University Education."

Verheyden-Hilliard, M. "Education, Girls, and Power."

Watts, M. "Biopolitics and Gender."

Weitzel, J. "The Sparse Ghetto."

Wolf, M. "The People's Republic of China."

WOMEN'S STUDIES

Bankart, B. "From Our Work and Experience."

Barazzone, E. "Women and the Scottish Enlightenment."

Bernikow, L. "From Our Work and Experience."

WOMEN'S STUDIES (cont.)

Bernstein, A. "Curriculum Reform, or What Do You Mean, 'Our College Should Have a Feminist Curriculum?'"

Berrio, M. "Sex Differences in Choices of Toy and Modes of Play in Nursery School."

Cadden, J. "Questions and Reflections on Science for Women."

Cohen, S. "Feminism as a Sophisticated Concept."

Dickie, J. "Women's Studies and the Re-vision of Liberal Education."

Distefano, A. "Feminist Counseling."

Du Bois, B. "Passionate Scholarship."

Dujon, D. "Bring It Back to the People You're Researching."

Fausto-Sterling, A. "The New Research on Women."

Friedensohn, D. "From Our Work and Experience."

Gillespie-Woltemade, N. "The Feminist Academy and Third World Women."

Goldsmid, P. "Curriculum Reform, or What Do You Mean, 'Our College Should Have a Feminist Curriculum?'"

Gouma-Peterson, T. "Three Decades of Reminiscences About Women in the Academy."

Griffin, G. "Still Crazy After All These Years."

Gutwirth, M. "The Education of Germaine de Stael, or Rousseau Betrayed."

Halley, J. "Harmonious Sisters, Voice and Verse."

Hammond, H. "Creating Feminist Works."

Hilty, D. "From Our Work and Experience."

Hooker, E. "History of a Weekend."

Howe, F. "Breaking the Disciplines."

Hunt, L. "Cygnets and Ducklings."

Jayaratne, T. "The Value of Quantitative Methodology for Feminist Research."

Kahn, D. "Interdisciplinary Studies and Women's Studies."

Kipp, R. "The Feminist Critique."

Kipp, R. "Have Women Always Been Unequal?"

Klay, R. "Analyzing Discrimination Against Women in the Labor Market."

Kessler, C. "Communities of Sisters."

Kreuger, R. "Loyalty and Betrayal."

Lane, A. "Keynote Address."

Lee, V. "Lucille Clifton."

Martin, E. "Role Conflicts for Women in Positions of Authority."

McGrath, E. "Government Publications for Women's Studies Research."

Merriam, E. "Creating Feminist Works."

Merrill, M. "Archives and Women's History Research."

Miller, N. "Creating Feminit Works."

Minnich, E. "Curriculum Reform, or What Do You Mean, 'Our College Should Have a Feminist Curriculum?'"

Minnich, E. "Friends and Critics."

Musil, C. "A Screen of Blooms."

Parr, J. "The Art of Quilting."

WOMEN'S STUDIES (cont.)

Parr, J. "Effects of Isolation on the Woman Artist."
Portis, K. "Closing Session."
Reinharz, S. "Experimental Analysis."
Reiss, M. "Rosa Mayreder."
Repetto, M. "The Development of Women's Liberation in Italy After World War II."
Reuben, E. "Toward a Feminist Transformation of the Academy."
Rich, A. "Keynote Address: Disobedience Is What NWSA Is Potentially About."
Richards, C. "The Emergence of Women in Twentieth-Century Chilean History and Literature."
Rogal, M. "Subject Access to Works on Women."
Rothenberg, P. "Feminist Issues and Feminist Attitudes."
Shaver, A. "Women in Epic."
Smith, B. "The Structure of Knowledge."
Spencer, D. "Theorising About Theorising."
Straumanis, J. "The Call for Feminist Theory."
Straumanis, J. "The Feminist Critique."
Straumanis, J. "Generic 'Man' and Mortal Woman."
Tiernan, K. "Closing Session."
Westkott, M. "Women's Studies as a Strategy for Change."
Whelchel, M. "'Phantasia for Elvira Shatayev' as Revolutionary Feminist Poem."
Williams, M. "The Structure of Knowledge."
Withorn, A. "Analysis and Action."
Woods, B. "Historiogenic Art."

WOMEN'S STUDIES--PHILOSOPHY

Bowles, G. "Is Women's Studies an Academic Discipline?"
Coyner, S. "Women's Studies as an Academic Discipline."
Rutenberg, T. "Learning Women's Studies."
Watkins, B. "Feminism."

WOMEN'S STUDIES--STUDY AND TEACHING

Howe, F. "Feminist Scholarship--The Extent of the Revolution."
Lerner, G. "The Challenges of Women's History."
Minnich, E. "A Feminist Critique of the Liberal Arts."

WOMEN'S STUDIES--UNITED STATES

Atwell, M. "Elsie Dinsmore Haunting the Minds of Millions of Women."
Bergman, S. "Library Resources on Women."
Bonder, G. "The Educational Process of Women's Studies In Argentina."

WOMEN'S STUDIES--UNITED STATES (cont.)

Kahne, H. "Women and Social Security."

Kellogg, S. "Aztec Women in the Sixteenth Century."

Kolmerton, C. "The Myth of Sexual Egalitarian Communities."

Longino, H. "Scientific Objectivity and Feminist Theorizing."

Lynch, F. "A View From the Funding Agencies."

Maher, F. "Appropriate Teaching Methods for Integrating Women."

Maslin, A. "A Typology of Motives and Attitudes Toward Women's Roles Among Black and White Older Undergraduate Women at an Urban University."

McIlwee, J. "Work Satisfaction Among Women in Non-Traditional Occupations."

McIntosh, P. "Interactive Phases of Curricular Re-Vision."

Miller, N. "Mastery, Identity and the Politics of Work."

Minnich, E. "The Meaning of 'Human' in the Humanities."

Olson, L. "Sex-Linked Values."

Petchesky, R. "Reproduction and Class Divisions Among Women."

Phillips, E. "The Prickly Art of Housekeeping."

Purdy, L. "Integrating Women's Studies Perspectives Into The Philosophy Curriculum."

Quaglio, F. "Religion as an Instrument of Social Control."

Rich, A. "Notes Toward a Politics of Location."

Rich, A. "Taking Women Students Seriously."

Robinson, L. "Women, Media, and the Dialectics of Resistance."

Rosenberg, J. "Feminism, the Family, and the New Right."

Russ, A. "Collegiate Women and Institutional Change, 1875-1920."

Russell, D. "Pornography and the Women's Liberation Movement."

Russell, D. "Mainstreaming Women's Studies Into Teacher Education."

Sacks, K. "Worlds in Collision or Ships Passing in the Night?"

Schmidt, R. "Women, Gender, and the Curriculum."

Schmitz, B. "From Issue to Action."

Schmitz, B. "Project on Women in the Curriculum."

Schramm, S. "Women's Studies."

Sims-Wood, J. "Resources in Black Women's Studies."

Slaughter, M. "Women and Socialism."

Spanier, B. "The Natural Sciences."

Spanier, B. "Toward a Balanced Curriculum."

Stimpson, C. "Scholarship About Women."

Stimpson, C. "Where Does Integration Fit."

Taub, N. "Defining and Combating Sexual Harassment."

Tolpin, M. "Wheaton's Assessment Process."

Triplette, M. "The Emerging Theory of Institutional Discrimination."

Valentine, B. "Women on Welfare."

Walkowitz, J. "Male Vice and Female Virtue."

Willis, E. "The Challenge of Profamily Politics."

Zavala, I. "Concluding Remarks."

WORKING CLASS WOMEN--SOUTHERN STATES

WORKING CLASS WOMEN--UNITED STATES

WORKING CLASS WOMEN--UNITED STATES (cont.)

Jones, M. "Speech at Meeting of Striking Coal Miners."

Jones, M. "Speech to Striking Coal Miners." (3)

Jones, M. "Testimony Before Committee on Rules, House of Representative, on H.J. Res. 201 Proving for a Joint Committee to Investigate Alleged Persecutions of Mexican Citizens by the Government of Mexico, Washington, D.C., June 14, 1910."

Jones, M. "Testimony Before House of Representatives Subcommittee of the Committee on Mines and Mining Investigating Conditions in the Coal Mines of Colorado, Washington, D.C., April 23, 1914."

Jones, M. "Testimony Before the Commission on Industrial Relations, Created by the Act of Congress, August 23, 1912, Washington, D.C., May 13, 14, 1915."

Jones, M. "Testimony of Mrs. Mary Jones."

Jones, M. "Thank God I Have Lived to be a Grandmother in Agitation!"

Jones, M. "This Is Not a Play, This Is a Fight!"

Jones, M. "To Be in Prison Is No Disgrace."

Jones, M. "A Tribute to Italian Miner."

Jones, M. "The Tyranny of Mexico."

Jones, M. "The Wail of Children."

Jones, M. "We Must Stand Together."

Jones, M. "Women Are Fighters."

Jones, M. "You Are Less Free Than the Negroes Were Before The Civil War!"

Jones, M. "You Can't Fool My Boys, Mr. Rockefeller."

Jones, M. "You Don't Need a Vote to Raise Hell!"

Jones, M. "You Ought to Be Out Raising Hell!"

Jones, M. "You Women Must Organize If You Want Your Men to Earn a Decent Living Wage."

YOUTH--EMPLOYMENT--UNITED STATES

Hawkins, P. "Statement."

Hecker, M. "Statement."

TITLE INDEX

"Abnormal Intimacy."   Zavella, P.
"Abortion as a Feminist Concern."   Smith, J. E.
"Above and Beyond Politics."   Calderone, M. S.
"An Abundance of Riches."   Hinding, A.
"Abuses and Uses of the Bible."   Mott, L.
"Academic Career Mobility for Women
    and Men."   Rosenfeld, R. A.
"Academics and Athletics."   Uehling, B. S.
"Academics, Bluestockings, and
    Biologists."   Hall, D. L.
"Acceptance by Dr. Hardy."   Hardy, H. L.
"Acceptance Speech."   Ferraro, G.
"Access to the Media."   Smith, M. Y.
"Account of Her Interview with the
    Foreign Ministers of Europe."   Addams, J.
"Acculturating Women Into Law En-
    forcement Careers."   Scrivner, E.
"Achieving the Dreams Beyond
    Tradition."   Verheyden-Hilliard, M.
"Address at Conference on Educational
    Programs for Veterans."   Roosevelt, E.
"Address at Cooper Union in April,
    1912."   Lemlich, C.
"Address at Cooper Union, April, 1912."   Schepps, M.
"Address at Cooper Union, April, 1912."   Scott, M.
"Address at Juvenile Protective Asso-
    ciation Dinner."   Bowen, L. D. K.
"Address at the Womanchurch Speakes
    Conference."   Ruether, R.
"Address Delivered at Seneca Falls."   Stanton, E. C.
"Address, July 4, 1828."   Wright, F.
"Address of Susan B. Anthony."   Anthony, S. B.
"Address of Welcome."   Hooker, E. H.
"Address of Welcome."   Sanger, M.
"Address of Welcome to the International
    Council of Women."   Stanton, E. C.
"An Address on Life as a Female Revo-
    lutionary Soldier."   Sampson, D.
"Address on the Juvenile Protective
    Association of Chicago."   Bowen, L. D. K.

529

"Denial of the Female." Setta, S.
"Depo-Provera." Levine, C.
"The Depo-Provera Weapon." Corea, G.
"Depression." Weissman, M. M.
"Depression in Women." De Lange, J. M.
"DES and Drugs in Pregnancy." Erhart, R.
"The DES Controversy." Bell, S. E.
"DES: Ten Points of Controversy." Holtzman, J. H.
"A Descriptive Study of the Language of Men and Women Born in Maine Around 1900 as It Reflects the Lakoff Hypotheses in Language and Women's Place." Hartman, M.
"Designated Discussion (Ethical Requirements for Sex Research in Humans)." MacKlin, R.
"Desire for the Future." Hollibaugh, A.
"Developing a Neighborhood-Based Health Facility." Wilson, E.
"Developing Meaningful Roles for Minority Women." Cabrera-Drinane, S.
"Development of Feminist Networks in the Professions." Daniels, A. K.
"The Development of Psychological Androgyny." Bean, J. P.
"The Development of Women's Liberation in Italy After World War II." Repetto, M.
"A Developmental Study of Sex Differences in Mathematics and Reading Avoidance." Douglas, J.
"Deviations and New Developments in 1920s." Thompson, C.
"Deviants Around 1912." Thompson, C.
"Dialogue With a Judge." Jones, M.
"Diaries of Frontier Women." Schissel, L.
"Diethylstilbestrol." Davis, A. J.
"Difference and Language." McConnel-Ginet, S.
"The Differential Impact of Programs and Policies on Women in Development." Papenek, H.
"A Different Reality." Whitbeck, C.
"Dilemmas of Masculinity in a Changing World." Komarovsky, M.
"The Dilemmas of Citizenship-- Demands of Political Leadership." Tree, M.
"Dimensions of Living Space." Taeuber, I. B.
"Dinner of Woman's Roosevelt Republican Club to Delegates of Illinois Republican Women's Clubs." Bowen, L. D. K.
"Dirty Books, Dirty Films, and Dirty Data." Bart, P. B.

"Disappointment Is the Lot of Women."	Stone, L.
"Discourse on Woman."	Mott, L. (2)
"Discussion (of Earnings Sharing)."	Reno, V. P.
"Discussion (of Supplemental OASI Benefits to Homemakers)."	Fierst, E. U.
"Distress from the Press."	O'Donnell, S. P.
"Do Changes In Women's Rights Change Women's Moral Judgments."	Gilligan, C.
"Do Not Keep Still."	Mott, L.
"Doctrine Concerning Death."	Mott, L.
"Does Becoming a Parent Mean Falling Off the Fast Track?"	Osterman, G. B.
"Does Equality Mean Sameness?"	Herman, D.
"The Domestic Drama of Louisa May Alcott."	Halttunen, K.
"Domestic Experience and Feminist Theory."	Grant, M. H.
"Don't Give the Master Class Any Weapon to Strike You With."	Jones, M.
"Dorothy Sayers and the Amazons."	Auerbach, N.
"The Double Bind."	Saunders, M.
"The Doubled Vision of Feminist Theory."	Kelly, J.
"Draupadi and the Dharma."	Falk, N. A.
"Drifting, Dreaming, Directing."	Kapp, A. G.
"Drugs, Birth, and Ethics."	Brackbill, Y.
"Dry Bones and Rolled Stones."	Gustafson, J. R.
"Dual Career Couples."	Byrnes, E.
"The Dual Role of Women Judges."	Cook, B. B.
"The Duty of Prayer and its Effects."	Mott, L.
"The Dynamics of Female Experience."	Washbourn, P.

"Early Feminist Theory and the Querelle Des Femmes, 1400-1789."	Kelly, J.
"Easter VI."	Hally, E.
"The Economic Case for Comparable Worth."	Bergmann, B. R.
"Economic Consequences of Marital Disruption."	Shaw, L. B.
"The Economic Consequences of the Arms Race."	Cahn, A. H.
"Economic Strength Is What Counts."	Burke, Y. B.
"The Economic Struggles of Female Factory Workers."	Lamphere, L.
"The Economic Tendency of Freethought."	De Cleyre, V.
"Ectogenesis and Ideology."	Logan, R. L.
"Edith Bolling Wilson."	James, E.
"The Educated Woman Within Us."	Sorensen, E. S.

"Family Roles and Identities of Scan-
dinavian and German Women." Woehrer, C.
"Family Roles in a Twenty-Year Per-
spective." Douvan, E.
"The Family: The View From a
Room of Her Own." Bridenthal, R.
"Famous Women's Luncheon Second
Woman's World Fair." Bowen, L. D. K.
"Famous Women's Luncheon Woman's
World Fair." Bowen, L. D. K.
"Farewell Address of a Socialist." O'Hare, K. R.
"Farewell Address of Kate Richards
O'Hare." O'Hare, K. R.
"The Fashionable Diseases." Wood, A. D.
"Fat and the Fantasy of Perfection." Munter, C.
"The Fate of Republics." Shaw, A. H.
"Federal Equitable Pay Practices Act." Long, C.
"The Federal Government and the
War on Youth Employment." Michel, H.
"Federal Support." Grygelko, M.
"Female Education and School Com-
petition." Green, N.
"The Female Engineering Student." Gough, P. W.
"Female Eroticism in The Second
Sex." Fuchs, J. P.
"The Feminine Question." Nestle, J.
"Femininity, Narrative and Psy-
choanalysis." Mitchell, J.
"Feminism." Watkins, B. J.
"Feminism." Eastman, C.
"Feminism and Feminity at the Turn
of the Century." Mitchell, J.
"Feminism and the Education of
Women." Howe, F.
"Feminism and the Study of Liter-
ature." Howe, F.
"Feminism and the Woman School
Administrator." Gribskov, M.
"Feminism as a Political Movement." Mitchell, J.
"Feminism as a Sophisticated Con-
cept." Cohen, S. H.
"Feminism, Fiction, and the Class-
room." Howe, F.
"Feminism in Academia." Hubbard, R.
"Feminism or Unionism?" Dye, N. S.
"Feminism, Power, and Change." Hartsock, N. C. M.
"Feminism, Professionalism, and
Germs." Morantz, R. M.
"Feminism, the Family, and the
New Right." Rosenberg, J.
"Feminism, The Future Of?" Jeanette, D.

"From Slavery to Social Welfare."   Gilkes, C. T.
"From the Salutatory Oration, Deli-
    vered by Miss Priscilla Mason,
    May 15, 1793."   Mason, P.
"From the Valedictory Oration,
    Delivered by Miss Molly Wallace,
    June 20, 1792."   Wallace, M.
"From Voluntary Motherhood to
    Planned Parenthood."   Fee, F.
"From Voluntary Motherhood to
    Planned Parenthood."   Gordon, L.
"From Voluntary Motherhood to
    Planned Parenthood."   Harper, A. L.
"Frontiers."   Schaudt, Y. V.
"Frozen Goddess."   Abrams, A. U.
"The Functional Approach to Case-
    work Practice."   Smalley, R. E.
"Fundamental Considerations Under-
    lying the Curriculum of the
    Francis W. Parker School."   Cooke, F. J.
"Funding."   Lawrence, G.
"Furrawn."   Nin, A.
"The Future Is Now for Business
    and Industry."   Moe, A. M.
"The Future of Parenthood."   Huber, J.
"The Future of Women."   Ceballos, J.
"The Future of Women."   Ruggen, B.
"The Future of Women."   Tobias, S.
"The Future of Women in America."   Fisher, M.
"The Future of Women's Colleges."   Howe, F.
"Futuristic Implications of Sex Pre-
    selection."   Steinbacher, R.

"Gaining Strength and Respect in
    the World."   Kirkpatrick, J. J.
"Gay Pride Day."   Heyward, C.
"Gender and Genre."   Davis, N. Z.
"Gender Gap '84--Women Reject
    Reagan."   Goldsmith, J.
"Gender Imagery and Issues of War
    and Peace."   Thorne, B.
"Gender or Genius?"   Comini, A.
"Gender, Relation, and Difference
    in Psychoanalytic Perspective."   Chodorow, N.
"General Spirit of the People."   Copley, H. K.
"Generational and Life-Cycle Effects
    on Women's Achievement Orienta-
    tion."   Faver, C. A.
"Generations of Working-Class Families."   Sacks, K. B.

"Generic 'Man' and Mortal Woman." Straumanis, J.
"'Gentle and Wavy and Graceful
   Huck'--An Androgynous Hero." Tenenbaum, B.
"Georgia Harkness." Scott, M. L.
"Gertrude Stein." Secor, C.
"Getting to Be a Notable Georgia
   Woman." Scott, A. F.
"Getting to 'No' and Beyond." Weiss, L.
"The Gift and Power of the Holy
   Ghost." Rasmus, C.
"Giving Thanks or Making Do." Russell, V.
"Glimpses of Muslim Urban Women
   in Classical Islam." Wilson, B. R.
"God, But We're Getting Smart." Carpenter, L.
"God Has a Master Plan for Your
   Life." Scott, P. R.
"God or Mammon?" Heyward, C.
"God's Woman." Johnson, S. D.
"Going to the Root of the Matter." Mott, L.
"Golan Again." Kirkpatrick, J. J.
"Good Morning!" O'Hare, K. R.
"Gospel Principles and Women." Ford, K.
"Government Publications for Women's
   Studies Research." McGrath, E.
"Governor's Message." Grasso, E. T.
"The Gradual Making of the Making
   of Americans." Stein, G.
"The Great Chain of Being and the
   Chain of Command." Scanzoni, L. D.
"Great Expectations." Schroeder, P.
"The Greater Freedom by Birth Con-
   trol." Dilla, H. A.
"Greeting to Illinois Equal Suffrage
   Association from Woman's City
   Club." Bowen, L. D. K.
"Greetings." Hilton, M. N.
"Greetings." Venegas, H.
"Ground Rules for Marriage." Bernard, J.
"Guaranteed to Us and Our Daughters
   Forever." Anthony, S. B.
"Guidelines for Feminist Therapy." Butler, M.

"H.R. 14666 The Privacy Protection
   for Rape Victims Act of 1976." Bacon, S.
"Hand of Fellowship." Brown, O.
"Happy Mothers and Other Ideas in
   Eighteenth-Century French Art." Duncan, C.
"Harmonious Sisters, Voice and Verse." Halley, J. E.
"Have Women Always Been Unequal?" Kipp, R. S.

"Jewish Involvement in the New York
    City Woman Suffrage Movement."   Lerner, E.
"Job Changing and Occupational Sex
    Segregation."   Rosenfeld, R. A.
"Job Placement of Women in the Lead
    Trades--A Workers' Position."   Prieve, C.
"Job: The Confessions of a Suffer-
    ing Person."   Nelson, C.
"Jorge Amado's Heroines and the
    Ideological Double Standard."   Patai, D.
"Judaeo-Christian Influences on
    Female Sexuality."   Burlage, D. D.
"Judgment."   Heyward, C.
"Judith Leyster's Proposition--
    Between Virtue and Vice."   Hofrichter, F.
"Julia Ware Howe Addresses the
    Massachusetts Legislature."   Howe, J. W.
"Jung After Feminism."   Goldenberg, N. R.
"Just a Housewife."   Lerner, G.
"Just As I Am."   Hardesty, N. A.
"The Juvenile Court."   Bowen, L. D. K. (2)

"Keep Yourselves From Idol."   Mott, L.
"Keeping the Thing Going While
    Things Are Stirring."   Truth, S. (2)
"Keynote."   Phelps, E. S.
"Keynote Address."   Bellamy, C.
"Keynote Address."   Lott, J. T.
"Keynote Address."   Oneglia, S. E.
"Keynote Address at the Republic
    National Convention."   Ortega, K. D.
"Keynote Address: Disobedience Is
    What NWSA Is Potentially About."   Rich, A.
"Keynote Address: Friends for
    Half a Century."   Lane, A. J.
"Keynote Speech by Congresswoman
    Barbara Jordan."   Jordan, B.
"Keys for a Woman's Progression."   Kimball, C. E.
"Kirkpatrick's Remarks (U.N. on
    Israeli Raid)."   Kirkpatrick, J. J.
"Knots in the Family Tie."   Burnett, M.
"Knowledge With Commitment."   Siegel, B. L.
"Korean Women in Hawaii, 1903-1945."   Chai, A.

"Labor Force Participation of Women
    Baccalaureates in Science."   Vetter, B. M.
"Laboring to Obtain the Divine
    Kingdom."   Mott, L.

"My Prayer 'Grows Up' As I Grow
    Older."   Trebbi, D.
"My Scourge, My Sister."   Deshazer, M.
"My Voice ... and Many Others."   Wilson, L.
"My Work and Welcome to It."   Warden, G. L.
"Mysticism and Feminism."   Smith, C.
"The Myth of Race."   Kopp, M. A.
"The Myth of Sexual Egalitarian Com-
    munities."   Kolmerton, C.
"The Myth of the Perfect Body."   Galler, R.
"The Mythology of Rape."   Halpern, S.
"Myths and Realities."   Carter, M.
"Myths and Realities."   Devlin, S.
"Myths and Realities."   Lee, K.
"Myths and Realities."   McChesney, K.
"Myths and Realities."   Rawlings, E.
"Myths and Realities."   Tischler, B.
"Myths of Coeducation."   Howe, F.

"Narcotics."   Falco, M.
"National Archives Resources for Re-
    search in the History of American
    Women."   Purdy, V. C.
"National Urban League Annual Con-
    ference."   Bowen, L. D. K.
"A Native American Response."   Cook, K.
"Native Women in the World of Work." Witt, S. H.
"The Natural Capacity for Health in
    Women."   Ramey, E. R.
"The Natural Instincts of Men Are For
    Peace."   Mott, L.
"The Natural Sciences."   Spanier, B.
"Nature and Revelation and Woman's
    Right to Vote."   Stone, L.
"The Nature of the Assemblies."   Taylor, L. R.
"A Nature Talk."   Bowen, L. D. K.
"The Necessity for the Utter Extinction
    of Slavery."   Rose, E.
"The Necessity of Our Cause."   Mott, L.
"The Need for an Anthropological and
    Cognitive Approach to the Educa-
    tion of Hispanic Women."   Ivera, S.
"The Need of a Training School in
    Applied Philanthropy."   Richmond, M. E.
"The Need for Female Role Models
    in Education."   Antonucci, T.
"The Need of Protective Work in
    Illinois."   Bowen, L. D. K.
"The Need of Recreation."   Bowen, L. D. K.

"President's Address--Juvenile Pro-
tection Association." (4) Bowen, L. D. K.
"President's Speech." Bowen, L. D. K.
"Prevention and Education Research." Wilsnack, S. C.
"The Prickly Art of Housekeeping." Phillips, E.
"Priesthood (The Ordination of Doug
Clark)." Heyward, C.
"Priesthood and Sisterhood." Peterson, G. B.
"Primary Campaign." Bowen, L. D. K.
"The Primary Elections Campaign." Bowen, L. D. K.
"The Principles of Social Freedom." Woodhull, V.
"The Principles of the Co-Equality
of Woman With Man." Mott, L.
"Priorities as Viewed from a Federal
Agency." Hilton, M.
"Private Rights and Public Virtues." Gould, C. C.
"The Problem of the Delinquent
Girl." Young, V. C.
"The Problem of the United Nations." Kirkpatrick, J. J.
"The Problem-Solving Model in Social
Casework." Perlman, H. H.
"Problems and Priorities of Poor,
Culturally Different Parents." Rodriguez-Trias, H.
"The Problems Facing Women Scien-
tists and Engineers in Academia
--A Review." Law, M. E.
"Problems in Pension Systems as
Specifically Related to Women
Retirees." Litwak, E.
"Problems of Older Women." Bellamy, C.
"Problems of the Alliance." Kirkpatrick, J. J.
"Proceed from the Dream." Nin, A.
"Productivity and the Corporate
Culture." Cunningham, M. E.
"The Profession and Practice of
Begging." Richmond, M. E.
"Professional Schools and Their Im-
pact on Black Women." Shaw, E.
"Professional Women in Developing
Nations." Gonzalez, N. L.
"Professional Women in Transition." Hornig, L. S.
"A Profile of the Successful High-
Tech Salesperson." Greenberg, J.
"Progress of the Religious World." Mott, L.
"Progress Toward Completion of
Human Rights Covenants." Roosevelt, E.
"Prohibition or Abolition--What It
Means." Nation, C.
"Project on Women in the Curriculum." Schmitz, B.
"Projected Future Employment and
Leadership Needs and Areas." Michel, A.

"Promoting Free Elections." Kirkpatrick, J. J.
"Promoting the Humanities." Craft, C. R.
"Propaganda and Public Opinion from
  58 to 53 B.C." Taylor, L. R.
"A Proper Perspective." Conway, J. K.
"The Proper Study of Womankind." Morgan, R.
"Proposed Sanctions Against Em-
  ployers of Illegal Aliens." Martinez, V. S.
"Prospectives for Nursing: Forces
  for Forecasting." Novello, D. J.
"Prospectives for Nursing: Old
  Dreams, New Visions." Cleland, V.
"Prospects for Pay Equity in a
  Changing Economy." Cain, P. S.
"Prostitution and Sexual Violence." James, J.
"Protection of Women Workers and
  the Courts." Hill, A. C.
"Protest Against Endorsement of
  Certain Candidates." Bowen, L. D. K.
"Protest Against Endorsement of
  Governor Len Small." Bowen, L. D. K.
"Psychoanalysis." Mitchell, J.
"Psychoanalysis in France." Gallop, J.
"The Psychobiology of Sex Differ-
  ences." Hamburg, B. A.
"Psychological Aspects of Menstru-
  ation, Childbirth, and Meno-
  pause." Parlee, M. B.
"Psychological Barriers for Women
  in Sciences." Frieze, I. H.
"Psychological Challenges Confronting
  Women in the Sciences." Moulton, R.
"Psychological Correlates of Early
  Family Formation." Mikus, K. C.
"Psychological Development of Female
  Children and Adolescents." Block, J. H.
"Psychological Differences Between
  Men and Women." Feldman, M.
"Psychological Effects of Segregation." Chambers, B.
"Psychological Roles for Women in
  Public Affairs." McLean, H. V.
"The Psychology of Leadership." Conoley, J. C.
"The Psychosocial Approach to the
  Practice of Casework." Hollis, F.
"Psychotherapists' Ambivalence About
  Fees." Lasky, E.
"Puberty to Menopause." Smith-Rosenberg, C.
"Public and Private Interests in
  Classical Athens." Humphreys, S. C.
"Public Meetings in the Forum, on
  the Capitoline, and in the Cir-
  cus Flaminius." Taylor, L. R.

"The Public Purposes of Private Colleges."   Ilchman, A. S.
"The Public Role of Southern Women."   Swain, M. H.
"The Public School and the Immigrant Child."   Addams, J.
"Public Silence, Private Terror."   Allison, D.
"Puerto Rican Women in Education and Potential Impact on Occupational Patterns."   Correa, G.
"Pure Hearts and Pure Homes."   Holland, P. T.
"Pushing Out the Walls."   Williams, E. T.

"Quarterly Meetings, No Ordinary Occasions."   Mott, L.
"Quest for Dignity."   Aptheker, B.
"The Question Arises ... Whether All Lawyers Are the Same."   Kennedy, F.
"The Question of Femininity and the Theory of Psychoanalysis."   Mitchell, J.
"Questions and Reflections on Science for Women."   Cadden, J.
"Quilts."   Mainardi, P.

"Race, Sex, Age and Political Conservatism Among Partisan Elites."   Stone, P. T.
"Racism and the Bonding of Women."   Phelps, J.
"Racism and Women's Studies."   Smith, B.
"Racism in Pornography and the Women's Movement."   Gardner, T. A.
"Radiation Exposure and Protection."   Hunt, V.
"The Radicalism of the Woman Suffrage Movement."   Dubois, E.
"Ramakrsna Paramahamsa."   Sharma, A.
"Reaching the Middle Class Alcoholic."   Seizas, J.
"Reaching the Middle Class Female."   Duffe, N. N.
"Reading and Loving Literature."   Arnold, M.
"The Reagan Phenomenon and the Liberal Tradition."   Kirkpatrick, J. J.
"Reagan Policies and Black American Goals for Africa."   Kirkpatrick, J. J.
"The Reagan Reassertion of Western Values."   Kirkpatrick, J. J.
"Realism and Hope."   Klaaren, M. D.
"Realistic Assessment of the Needs of Older Women."   Safford, F.
"Realistic Education for Women."   Clapp, M.
"The Realities of Women Correctional

"Statement."	Baldwin, P.
"Statement."	Baldwin, W. (3)
"Statement."	Bane, M. J.
"Statement."	Barajas, G.
"Statement."	Barnes, H. B.
"Statement."	Barr, J.
"Statement."	Battistella, A.
"Statement."	Bayne, S.
"Statement."	Bazemore, A.
"Statement."	Beerhalter, B.
"Statement."	Behr, M. R.
"Statement."	Bell, C. S.
"Statement."	Bell, C.
"Statement."	Bellamy, C. (8)
"Statement."	Bendor, J.
"Statement."	Benesch, J. S.
"Statement."	Bentley, H. D.
"Statement."	Benton, M.
"Statement."	Beresford, T.
"Statement."	Berger, B.
"Statement."	Berglin, L.
"Statement."	Bernhardt, M.
"Statement."	Bergmann, B. R. (2)
"Statement."	Berry, M. F. (4)
"Statement."	Bertin, B.
"Statement."	Berube, S. C.
"Statement."	Bland, L. L.
"Statement."	Blank, H. (4)
"Statement."	Blum, B. B. (2)
"Statement."	Boggs, E. M.
"Statement."	Boggs, Lindy (33)
"Statement."	Boland, J.
"Statement."	Bolton, F. P.
"Statement."	Bowman, H.
"Statement."	Boxer, B. (22)
"Statement."	Bradshaw, G. M.
"Statement."	Bradshaw, R.
"Statement."	Brady, K.
"Statement."	Braun, B.
"Statement."	Brazile, D.
"Statement."	Breen, A.
"Statement."	Brewer, M. A.
"Statement."	Bricker-Jenkins, M.
"Statement."	Briscoe, A. M.
"Statement."	Brookins, L.
"Statement."	Brown, A. V.
"Statement."	Brown, C. G. (2)
"Statement."	Brown, H. S.
"Statement."	Brown, J.
"Statement."	Brown, N. E.
"Statement."	Brown, Q.

"Statement."	Brubaker, C. C.
"Statement."	Brummond, N.
"Statement."	Brunauer, E. C.
"Statement."	Brunson, D. E.
"Statement."	Bryant, B. E.
"Statement."	Bryant, C.
"Statement."	Bryant, D.
"Statement."	Buechler, J.
"Statement."	Burgess, A.
"Statement."	Burgess, G. (2)
"Statement."	Burt, M. R. (2)
"Statement."	Burton, D.
"Statement."	Burton, S. (6)
"Statement."	Byrd, A. (3)
"Statement."	Byron, B. (6)
"Statement."	Bystrom, M. J.
"Statement."	Callahan, P.
"Statement."	Campbell, J. L.
"Statement."	Campbell, N. D. (3)
"Statement."	Campbell, R.
"Statement."	Candela, C.
"Statement."	Carlberg, G. J. M.
"Statement."	Carpenter, L.
"Statement."	Carpenter, M. K.
"Statement."	Carter, R.
"Statement."	Catania, S.
"Statement."	Cauchear, M.
"Statement."	Chapple, J. F.
"Statement."	Chase-Anderson, M.
"Statement."	Chavez, L. (2)
"Statement."	Chayes, A. H. (2)
"Statement."	Chisholm, S. (13)
"Statement."	Clark, H. S.
"Statement."	Clarke, M. E.
"Statement."	Clauss, C.
"Statement."	Clement, M.
"Statement."	Cobb, G. P.
"Statement."	Cobb, J.
"Statement."	Cocciolone, D.
"Statement."	Cole, E. (2)
"Statement."	Cole-Alexander, L.
"Statement."	Collins, C. (7)
"Statement."	Collins, J.
"Statement."	Collin, M. J.
"Statement."	Compton, G.
"Statement."	Conniff, M.
"Statement."	Conway, J.
"Statement."	Cooper, D. L.
"Statement."	Cooper, M. A.
"Statement."	Cooper, M.
"Statement."	Cota, K.

"Statement."	Cotner, S.
"Statement."	Cotton, K.
"Statement."	Crawford, S. (3)
"Statement."	Cross, N. J.
"Statement."	Cruz, C.
"Statement."	Curtis, C.
"Statement."	Curtis, L.
"Statement."	Damschroder, D.
"Statement."	Darner, K.
"Statement."	Davidson, D.
"Statement."	Davis, A. J.
"Statement."	Davis, C. K.
"Statement."	Davis, J. G.
"Statement."	Davis, K.
"Statement."	Davis, S. A.
"Statement."	Davis, S.
"Statement."	Decter, M.
"Statement."	Delaney, G.
"Statement."	Delk, Y.
"Statement."	Denecke, A.
"Statement."	De Neely, Y. A.
"Statement."	Dennett, J.
"Statement."	Denton, C. (2)
"Statement."	Derrig, N. L.
"Statement."	Derryck, V. L.
"Statement."	Devanesan, M.
"Statement."	DeVries, C.
"Statement."	Dolch, D.
"Statement."	Dole, E. H. (19)
"Statement."	Donnelly, E. (2)
"Statement."	Douglas, S.
"Statement."	Doyle, J.
"Statement."	Driscoll, P.
"Statement."	Dryfoos, J. G. (2)
"Statement."	Dunkle, M. (2)
"Statement."	East, C. (4)
"Statement."	Easton, S.
"Statement."	Ebeling, E.
"Statement."	Edwards, J.
"Statement."	Edwards, L.
"Statement."	Eidson, E.
"Statement."	Ellis, E. O.
"Statement."	Ellis, T. (2)
"Statement."	Elmer, E.
"Statement."	Fadeley, N.
"Statement."	Farris, B.
"Statement."	Feiger, L. D.
"Statement."	Feistritzer, E. C.
"Statement."	Fenwick, M. (10)
"Statement."	Fernandez-Mattei, M.
"Statement."	Ferraro, G. A. (23)

"Statement."	Ferrell, D.
"Statement."	Fiedler, B. (21)
"Statement."	Fields, M.
"Statement."	Fierst, E. U. (3)
"Statement."	Finn, J. (2)
"Statement."	Fitch, (Mrs.) G. A.
"Statement."	Fitzpatrick, B. (2)
"Statement."	Fleming, J. P. (2)
"Statement."	Flitcraft, A.
"Statement."	Flournoy, F.
"Statement."	Flower, R.
"Statement."	Flynn, B.
"Statement."	Forman, M.
"Statement."	Forrest, J. D. (2)
"Statement."	Foster, D. M.
"Statement."	Frank, E.
"Statement."	Fraser, A.
"Statement."	Fraser, L. O.
"Statement."	Freeman, F. M. (2)
"Statement."	Friedan, B.
"Statement."	Futrell, M. H. (2)
"Statement."	Galler, J.
"Statement."	Gardner, E.
"Statement."	Gasper, J. A. (2)
"Statement."	Gaston, C.
"Statement."	Gavett, P.
"Statement."	Gentry, C. M.
"Statement."	Gerster, C.
"Statement."	Gilbert, M.
"Statement."	Ginsburg, R. B.
"Statement."	Gleason, J.
"Statement."	Godbold, R.
"Statement."	Godley, A.
"Statement."	Godley, A. L.
"Statement."	Goldfarb, S. P.
"Statement."	Goldman, K.
"Statement."	Goldsberry, B.
"Statement."	Goldsmith, J. (5)
"Statement."	Goldstein, N.
"Statement."	Goldston, S. M.
"Statement."	Goode, M. P.
"Statement."	Goodin, J. M. (2)
"Statement."	Goodwin, F. L.
"Statement."	Gordon, N.
"Statement."	Gorie, M.
"Statement."	Gould, S. K.
"Statement."	Grant, E.
"Statement."	Gray, K. O.
"Statement."	Gray, M. W. (3)
"Statement."	Gray, N.
"Statement."	Gray, W.

"Statement."	Greenberger, M. D. (4)
"Statement."	Griffiths-Boris, N. J.
"Statement."	Grossman, C. B. (2)
"Statement."	Grune, J. A.
"Statement."	Gueron, J. M.
"Statement."	Gurieva, D. M.
"Statement."	Guyker, E.
"Statement."	Hall, B. J.
"Statement."	Hall, J. H.
"Statement."	Hall, K. (2)
"Statement."	Hall, R. M.
"Statement."	Hamlin, J.
"Statement."	Hammond, B.
"Statement."	Hamon, E.
"Statement."	Hansen, S.
"Statement."	Hardy, D. R. (2)
"Statement."	Hardy, J. (2)
"Statement."	Harmon, E. D.
"Statement."	Harris, E.
"Statement."	Hart, B. J.
"Statement."	Hartmann, H. I. (2)
"Statement."	Hatwood-Futrell, M.
"Statement."	Hawkins, P. (30)
"Statement."	Hays, M.
"Statement."	Haynes, J.
"Statement."	Haywood, D. P.
"Statement."	Heckler, M. M. (24)
"Statement."	Height, D. I. (2)
"Statement."	Henderson, D.
"Statement."	Hendrixson, C.
"Statement."	Herman, A. M. (2)
"Statement."	Hernandez, A.
"Statement."	Herre, S. R. (2)
"Statement."	Herrick, A.
"Statement."	Higgs, C.
"Statement."	Hill, F.
"Statement."	Hirano, I.
"Statement."	Hobb, O. C.
"Statement."	Hoisington, E.
"Statement."	Holly, E. L.
"Statement."	Holm, J. M.
"Statement."	Holmes, D.
"Statement."	Holmes, J. A. (2)
"Statement."	Holt, M. S. (5)
"Statement."	Holtzman, E. (2)
"Statement."	Hong, H.
"Statement."	Howard, M. (2)
"Statement."	Howe, C.
"Statement."	Hsu, L.
"Statement."	Hubbard, M. F.
"Statement."	Huebner, R.

"Statement."	Humphrey, M.
"Statement."	Hunter, S.
"Statement."	Hutar, P.
"Statement."	Hutchinson, B. B. (3)
"Statement."	Hutchinson, C.
"Statement."	Jackson, J.
"Statement."	Jacksteit, M.
"Statement."	Jacobsen, G.
"Statement."	Jefferson, M. F. (3)
"Statement."	Jenks, M.
"Statement."	Jensen, P. A. (2)
"Statement."	Johnson, B.
"Statement."	Johnson, B. S.
"Statement."	Johnson, D.
"Statement."	Johnson, G. B.
"Statement."	Johnson, G.
"Statement."	Johnson, G.
"Statement."	Johnson, M. (2)
"Statement."	Johnson, M.
"Statement."	Johnson, N. (5)
"Statement."	Johnson, S.
"Statement."	Johnson, S.
"Statement."	Jones, D.
"Statement."	Jones, J. E. B. (2)
"Statement."	Jones, L. R. W.
"Statement."	Jones, M. B.
"Statement."	Jones, T.
"Statement."	Jordan, R.
"Statement."	Joyer, P.
"Statement."	Joyner, N. D.
"Statement."	Kaplan, A.
"Statement."	Kaptur, M. (12)
"Statement."	Karowe, M.
"Statement."	Kassebaum, N. L. (11)
"Statement."	Kasun, J. R.
"Statement."	Kay, H. H.
"Statement."	Keeley, K. S.
"Statement."	Kelly, P.
"Statement."	Kelly-Dreiss, S.
"Statement."	Kennelly, B. B. (6)
"Statement."	Kern, C. S.
"Statement."	Key, M. L.
"Statement."	Keys, M. (3)
"Statement."	Kievit, M.
"Statement."	King, N. R. (2)
"Statement."	King-Reynolds, W. A.
"Statement."	Klaus, H.
"Statement."	Klein, A.
"Statement."	Klein, J. D.
"Statement."	Knowles, J.
"Statement."	Kobell, R. E.

"Statement."	Markson, E. W.
"Statement."	Marrett, C.
"Statement."	Marshall, M. A.
"Statement."	Marshner, C.
"Statement."	Martin, L. (8)
"Statement."	Martinez, V. S.
"Statement."	Massinga, R. W. (2)
"Statement."	Mater, C.
"Statement."	Matulis, S.
"Statement."	Maves, B.
"Statement."	Mayerson, A. B. (2)
"Statement."	Mazo, J. F.
"Statement."	McAdoo, H. (2)
"Statement."	McClendon, S.
"Statement."	McCord, R.
"Statement."	McCoy, C.
"Statement."	McDonald, N.
"Statement."	McElderry, B.
"Statement."	McFadden, O. (2)
"Statement."	McGee, E. A.
"Statement."	McGibbon, N.
"Statement."	McIntosh, S.
"Statement."	McKee, F. E.
"Statement."	McKenna, T.
"Statement."	McSteen, M.
"Statement."	Mecklenburg, M.
"Statement."	Meehan, M.
"Statement."	Mendelson, J. S. R. (2)
"Statement."	Mendez, D.
"Statement."	Menken, J.
"Statement."	Mercer, E.
"Statement."	Merry, M.
"Statement."	Metress, E.
"Statement."	Meyer, E.
"Statement."	Meyer, J.
"Statement."	Meyer, R.
"Statement."	Middletown-Jeter, V.
"Statement."	Mikulski, B. A. (17)
"Statement."	Miller, D.
"Statement."	Milstein, B.
"Statement."	Mitgang, I. (2)
"Statement."	Mixer, M. H.
"Statement."	Mobley, S.
"Statement."	Mondale, J.
"Statement."	Monsman, D.
"Statement."	Montgomery, B. J.
"Statement."	Moore, E. (2)
"Statement."	Moore, K.
"Statement."	Moore, L.
"Statement."	Morfino, G.
"Statement."	Morisey, M.

"Statement."   Porter, S. V. (2)
"Statement."   Portnoy, M.
"Statement."   Potter, J.
"Statement."   Poyadue, F. M.
"Statement."   Poythress, M.
"Statement."   Pratt, P.
"Statement."   Presser, H. B.
"Statement."   Preston, J. E.
"Statement."   Prior, M.
"Statement."   Prokop, R. T. (2)
"Statement."   Pudvah, A. L.
"Statement."   Purcell, M.
"Statement."   Quinlan, A. (2)
"Statement."   Quinn, M. J.
"Statement."   Rachner, M. J.
"Statement."   Rankin, J.
"Statement."   Reach, B.
"Statement."   Reder, N. (2)
"Statement."   Reid, M.
"Statement."   Reinecker, J.
"Statement."   Reisinger, M.
"Statement."   Renfro, S. T.
"Statement."   Reuss, P.
"Statement."   Reynolds, N. C. (2)
"Statement."   Ricardo-Campbell, R.
"Statement."   Richardson, S. K.
"Statement."   Rich, D.
"Statement."   Richards, E.
"Statement."   Rivlin, A. M.
"Statement."   Robinson, J.
"Statement."   Rocha, B.
"Statement."   Rock, D. (2)
"Statement."   Rockefeller, S. P.
"Statement."   Rodriguez, E.
"Statement."   Rogers, E. N. (2)
"Statement."   Rogin, C. M.
"Statement."   Rolls, K.
"Statement."   Rosenstein, B.
"Statement."   Rosoff, J. I.
"Statement."   Ross, J. A. B. (2)
"Statement."   Rossman, M.
"Statement."   Rothchild, N. (2)
"Statement."   Roukema, M. S. (6)
"Statement."   Roundtree, M.
"Statement."   Rouse, I. M.
"Statement."   Roylance, S.
"Statement."   Royle, D.
"Statement."   Ruether, R. R.
"Statement."   Russell, B. L.
"Statement."   Russell-Young, N.
"Statement."   Russo, N. F.

"Statement."	Rutherford, T.
"Statement."	Sadler, A.
"Statement."	Saenz, R.
"Statement."	Salmon, R. W.
"Statement."	Samora, B.
"Statement."	Sampey, E.
"Statement."	Sanchez, P.
"Statement."	Sandage, S. (3)
"Statement."	Sapienza, J.
"Statement."	Sauvigne, K.
"Statement."	Sawhill, I.
"Statement."	Schain, J.
"Statement."	Schaus, M.
"Statement."	Schlafly, P. (6)
"Statement."	Schnaier, J. A.
"Statement."	Schneider, C. (14)
"Statement."	Schneider, R.
"Statement."	Schramm, P. C.
"Statement."	Schroeder, P. (41)
"Statement."	Schubb, J. (5)
"Statement."	Schultz, P.
"Statement."	Seaman, B. (2)
"Statement."	Seeman, M.
"Statement."	Seltzer, M. M.
"Statement."	Shalala, D. E.
"Statement."	Shed, S. K.
"Statement."	Shepard, A.
"Statement."	Shields, L.
"Statement."	Shipp, D.
"Statement."	Short, M. K.
"Statement."	Simmons, A.
"Statement."	Simmons, A. T. L.
"Statement."	Simmons, D. A.
"Statement."	Smeal, E. C. (8)
"Statement."	Smith, B.
"Statement."	Smith, E. F.
"Statement."	Smith, H.
"Statement."	Smith, R. (2)
"Statement."	Smith, V. (22)
"Statement."	Smithson, E.
"Statement."	Smothers, L. (2)
"Statement."	Sneed, M.
"Statement."	Snider, Y. B.
"Statement."	Snowe, O. J. (15)
"Statement."	Snyder, D.
"Statement."	Sommers, T.
"Statement."	Sowards, J.
"Statement."	Spaeth, D.
"Statement."	Sparks, C.
"Statement."	Spear, R.
"Statement."	Spellman, G. N. (3)

"Statement." Vann, T.
"Statement." Vaughn, B.
"Statement." Veve, K.
"Statement." Verdesi, E.
"Statement." Verheyden-Hilliard, M.
"Statement." Vermeulen, J.
"Statement." Vetter, B. M.
"Statement." Vincent, L. J.
"Statement." Vucanovich, B. F. (6)
"Statement." Waelder, C. (2)
"Statement." Wainwright, C.
"Statement." Waite, L.
"Statement." Wald, P. M.
"Statement." Walker, L. (2)
"Statement." Wallace, J.
"Statement." Wallace, R.
"Statement." Wallerstein, J. S.
"Statement." Walling, R.
"Statement." Walsh, B.
"Statement." Walsh, M. L.
"Statement." Warren, A.
"Statement." Waskel, S.
"Statement." Waters, M.
"Statement." Wattleton, F. (2)
"Statement." Waxman, M.
"Statement." Webb, C. C.
"Statement." Weddinton, S.
"Statement." Weitz, J.
"Statement." Wells-Schooley, J.
"Statement." Wernick, E. (2)
"Statement." Wertz, T.
"Statement." Whetsone, G.
"Statement." White, D.
"Statement." White, R.
"Statement." Widdecombe, J.
"Statement." Wiener, M.
"Statement." Wilkins, J.
"Statement." Willard, V. J.
"Statement." Willenz, J. A.
"Statement." Willhoite, B.
"Statement." Williams, C. M.
"Statement." Williams, D. R.
"Statement." Williams, K. H.
"Statement." Wilcox, L. A.
"Statement." Wilpula, S.
"Statement." Wilson, (Mrs.) J. M.
"Statement." Wilson, K.
"Statement." Wilson, M.
"Statement." Wisman, R.
"Statement." Wolf, E.
"Statement." Wolfe, J.

"Temptations to Neo-Imperialism."	Balch, E. G.
"Ten Years of Work."	Bowen, L. D. K.
"Testimony."	Acosta, K.
"Testimony."	Albert, M.
"Testimony."	Alexander, L. C.
"Testimony."	Alley, M. L.
"Testimony."	Andrulis, M.
"Testimony."	Arri, J. K.
"Testimony."	Baldwin, W. H. (2)
"Testimony."	Beaudry, J.
"Testimony."	Bauer, M.
"Testimony."	Belcher, L.
"Testimony."	Bere, P.
"Testimony."	Bertrom, L.
"Testimony."	Betz, C. Y.
"Testimony."	Betz, H. M.
"Testimony."	Beller, A.
"Testimony."	Bergmann, B. (2)
"Testimony."	Bird, C. M.
"Testimony."	Blanchard, M. L.
"Testimony."	Blaunstein, P.
"Testimony."	Block, M.
"Testimony."	Blockwick, J.
"Testimony."	Bloomrosen, M.
"Testimony."	Blum, B. B.
"Testimony."	Blume, S.
"Testimony."	Bonder, E.
"Testimony."	Boyle, P.
"Testimony."	Bradford, N.
"Testimony."	Brookshier, K.
"Testimony."	Brothers, J.
"Testimony."	Brown, J.
"Testimony."	Brown, S.
"Testimony."	Bucknell, S.
"Testimony."	Burgess, A.
"Testimony."	Burris, C. (2)
"Testimony."	Burt, M. R.
"Testimony."	Campbell, J. L.
"Testimony."	Campbell, N. D.
"Testimony."	Campanella, C.
"Testimony."	Candela, C. (2)
"Testimony."	Canellos, G.
"Testimony."	Cardin, S.
"Testimony."	Carpio, P.
"Testimony."	Casias, S.
"Testimony."	Cassedy, E.
"Testimony."	Connell, E. G.
"Testimony."	Cerda, G.
"Testimony."	Chandler, E. L.
"Testimony."	Chaney, E.
"Testimony."	Chapman, J. R.

"Testimony."	Jordan, A.
"Testimony."	Jordan, N.
"Testimony."	Joseph, R. A.
"Testimony."	Joynes, M.
"Testimony."	Keller, C.
"Testimony."	Keller, M.
"Testimony."	Kelley, M.
"Testimony."	Kelly, C.
"Testimony."	Keys, M. (2)
"Testimony."	Kilbreth, M. G.
"Testimony."	Kinzer, N. S.
"Testimony."	Kopec, J.
"Testimony."	Krieter, N.
"Testimony."	Ladky, A.
"Testimony."	Lanam, L. L.
"Testimony."	Lansburgh, (Mrs.) M.
"Testimony."	Largen, M. A.
"Testimony."	Laurie, L. T.
"Testimony."	Lautzenheiser, B. J.
"Testimony."	Lehnhard, M. N.
"Testimony."	Leidholdt, D.
"Testimony."	Lenhoff, D. R.
"Testimony."	Levick, M.
"Testimony."	Lichtman, J. L.
"Testimony."	Lieberman, D.
"Testimony."	Liss, L.
"Testimony."	Lo Sasso, R.
"Testimony."	Lubic, R. W.
"Testimony."	Mabry, R.
"Testimony."	MacKinnon, C. A.
"Testimony."	MacLeod, J. S.
"Testimony."	Madar, O.
"Testimony."	Madden, J. F.
"Testimony."	Madison, A.
"Testimony."	Majcher, J.
"Testimony."	Mann, D.
"Testimony."	Marchiano, L. L.
"Testimony."	Marks, L.
"Testimony."	Martin, J. M.
"Testimony."	Mayer, L.
"Testimony."	McCabe, C.
"Testimony."	McCartney, M.
"Testimony."	McClain, M. A.
"Testimony."	McClean, G. P.
"Testimony."	McConnell, N. F.
"Testimony."	McGoldrick, R. C. (4)
"Testimony."	McHenry, R.
"Testimony."	Mecklenburg, M. (3)
"Testimony."	Mears, J.
"Testimony."	Mentzer, N.
"Testimony."	Merrill, B.

"Testimony."	Meyer, K. A.
"Testimony."	Mikulski, B. A. (3)
"Testimony."	Miller, T.
"Testimony."	Moen, C. A.
"Testimony."	Moffat, (Mrs.) D.
"Testimony."	Mooney, C.
"Testimony."	Moore, K. A.
"Testimony."	Moore, M.
"Testimony."	Morris, L. H.
"Testimony."	Moses, M. L.
"Testimony."	Moss, T.
"Testimony."	Mulhauer, K.
"Testimony."	Myers, M.
"Testimony."	Nelms, D.
"Testimony."	Noble, S.
"Testimony."	Noel, R.
"Testimony."	Norsigian, J.
"Testimony."	Nortell, E. T.
"Testimony."	Norton, M. T. (3)
"Testimony."	Oakar, M. R.
"Testimony."	Oberstar, J.
"Testimony."	Orijel, J.
"Testimony."	Palast, G.
"Testimony."	Palmer, E. (2)
"Testimony."	Palmer, P.
"Testimony."	Parr, C. C.
"Testimony."	Penfield, P.
"Testimony."	Penman, R.
"Testimony."	Perlman, N.
"Testimony."	Pilpel, H. F.
"Testimony."	Podojil, T.
"Testimony."	Porcino, J.
"Testimony."	Porter, E. A.
"Testimony."	Pressar, A.
"Testimony."	Pressler, P.
"Testimony."	Pryor, V.
"Testimony."	Radetsky, M.
"Testimony."	Randall, C.
"Testimony."	Reed, C. (2)
"Testimony."	Reed, K.
"Testimony."	Reed, W.
"Testimony."	Regan, A. S. (4)
"Testimony."	Remick, H.
"Testimony."	Resnik, J.
"Testimony."	Reuss, M.
"Testimony."	Rini, M.
"Testimony."	Robb, L. J. (2)
"Testimony."	Robinson, C.
"Testimony."	Rockwell, V.
"Testimony."	Rooks, J.
"Testimony."	Rosen, M.

"Testimony."	Ross, O. G.
"Testimony."	Roundtree, D.
"Testimony."	Roundtree, J.
"Testimony."	Russell, S.
"Testimony."	Ryden, H.
"Testimony."	Sanger, M. H. (5)
"Testimony."	Sawhill, I. V.
"Testimony."	Schaffer, J.
"Testimony."	Scherago, M.
"Testimony."	Schlossberg, N. K.
"Testimony."	Schmotzer, A.
"Testimony."	Schoenrich, E.
"Testimony."	Schomp, K.
"Testimony."	Schweber, C.
"Testimony."	Schwerin, S.
"Testimony."	Seka.
"Testimony."	Shalala, D. E.
"Testimony."	Shaw, N. S.
"Testimony."	Sherburne, J. C.
"Testimony."	Shipp, D. A.
"Testimony."	Shoong, E.
"Testimony."	Shriver, E. K.
"Testimony."	Simmons, A. T. L.
"Testimony."	Sizemore, S. J.
"Testimony."	Smeal, E. C. (2)
"Testimony."	Smith, J. E.
"Testimony."	Smith, J.
"Testimony."	Smith, P.
"Testimony."	Snyder, M.
"Testimony."	Solyom, (Mrs.) H. L.
"Testimony."	Specter, J.
"Testimony."	Steele, D. A.
"Testimony."	Steiger, J.
"Testimony."	Steorts, N. H. (2)
"Testimony."	Stevens, C.
"Testimony."	Stille, D. (2)
"Testimony."	Stone, H. M.
"Testimony."	Stone, V.
"Testimony."	Strandburg, M.
"Testimony."	Sturgis, C.
"Testimony."	Syler, Rm.
"Testimony."	Taber, G.
"Testimony."	Taub, N.
"Testimony."	Taylor, P. P.
"Testimony."	Taylor, R.
"Testimony."	Tessner, E.
"Testimony."	Tom, S.
"Testimony."	Torres, T.
"Testimony."	Trauner, J. B.
"Testimony."	Trent, K.
"Testimony."	Tucker, M. S.

"United States Relations With Taiwan." Chang, M. H.
"Unity of Spirit in the Bond of
    Peace." Mott, L.
"Universal Validity of Man's Right
    to Self-Determination." Roosevelt, E.
"The University's Responsibility in
    Educating Women for Leadership." Bunting, M. I.
"The Unmothered Woman." Albert, E. M.
"Unnatural Selection." Powledge, T. M.
"The Unpublished Diaries of Mary
    Morangne Davis." Craven, D. M.
"The Unveiling of Woman." Nin, A.
"Unwritten History." Mangan, M.
"Upright But Not Uptight." Bellinger, M. A.
"Urban Indians, A Neglected Group." Kramer, J. M.
"Urban Team Ministry." Tieran, K.
"Urging Election of Mr. Alexander
    A. McCormick as President of
    Board of Cook County Com-
    missioners." Bowen, L. D. K.
"The Uses of Anger." Lorde, A.
"Uses of the Erotic." Lorde, A. (2)

"The Vaginal Occlusive Pessary." Stone, H. M.
"Value Conflicts in Biomedical Re-
    search Into Future Contracep-
    tives." Korenbrot, C.
"The Value of Quantitative Methodol-
    ogy for Feminist Research." Jayaratne, T.
"The Values Development Dilemma." McBee, M. L.
"Variety." Gordon, B.
"Viable Alternatives to Traditional
    Education for Minorities and
    Women." Ewell, Y.
"View from the Back of the Syna-
    gogue." Shulman, G. B.
"A View From the Funding Agencies." Lynch, F.
"The View From the White House." McKenna, M.
"Violence." Brown, R. M.
"Virility and Domination in Early
    Twentieth-Century Vanguard
    Painting." Duncan, C.
"Visibility and Difference." Stadler, Q. P.
"A Visit in Constantinople." Bowen, L. D. K.
"Vocational Rehabilitation." Capelli, D.
"Vocational Training, the Labor Mar-
    ket, and the Unions." Cook, A. H.
"Voluntary Motherhood." Gordon, L.